NICK HOLT has published a num
film, and other aspects of popular cu
association football or soccer.

The Mammoth Book of

THE WORLD CUP

NICK HOLT

ROBINSON

RUNNING PRESS
PHILADELPHIA · LONDON

Constable & Robinson Ltd
55–56 Russell Square
London WC1B 4HP
www.constablerobinson.com

First published in the UK by Robinson,
an imprint of Constable & Robinson Ltd, 2014

UK ISBN: 978-1-47211-046-6 (paperback)
UK ISBN: 978-1-47211-051-0 (ebook)

1 3 5 7 9 10 8 6 4 2

First published in the United States in 2014 by Running Press Book Publishers,
A Member of the Perseus Books Group

US ISBN: 978-0-7624-5224-8
US Library of Congress Control Number: 2013953114

9 8 7 6 5 4 3 2 1
Digit on the right indicates the number of this printing

Running Press Book Publishers
2300 Chestnut Street
Philadelphia, PA 19103-4371

Visit us on the web!
www.runningpress.com

Printed and bound by CPI Group (UK) Ltd, Croydon, CR0 4YY

CONTENTS

AUTHOR'S NOTE

There have been a lot of books published about football in recent years – that man Hornby is to blame, the success of *Fever Pitch* prompted a generation of intelligent football fans and observers to air their views on the game's socio-political significance. Articulate and well-conceived theories expounded how the game taught us about the nature of history's conflicts; how football is a mirror for the economic corruption that blights the western political arena; how a nation's way of playing the game represents a profound statement about its people; how a passion for football can lift underpaid, socially marginalised people out of a spiral of neglect and poverty. Mostly claptrap, but interesting and well written.

What takes place on the field is, however, my primary motivation. The politics and the scandals and the off-field shenanigans in Colombian jewellery shops provide the sequins and baubles, but the football is the party dress, be it the beige of 1962 and 2010 or the Vivienne Westwood-like extravagance of 1958 or 1970. A naff analogy, possibly, but this is the sporting event that is invariably hailed in the modern era as *The Greatest Show on Earth* – yes, the capacity of the football authorities and the compliant media to over-hype the game has reached epic proportions. The 2010 World Cup was like watching a Cecil B. DeMille movie; huge budgets, no expense spared on costume and make-up, eye-catching lead players. But like DeMille's movies the end product was stale and uninspiring. It's to be hoped the 2014 tournament will restore one's faith.

Analysing football is a little like being a film critic – sorry to push the cinema theme but stay with me, I'm on a roll. The best team doesn't always win the World Cup, just as the best directors don't always make the best movies – winning the World Cup is often about coming to the boil at the right time, finding the right man to play the starring role (Paolo Rossi in 1982) or having the best ensemble cast (Spain in 2010). Like a film critic, a football writer reserves the right to disagree with the generally held opinion. James Cameron hasn't made a good film since 1992 (*Titanic* and *Avatar* were appalling abuses of enormous amounts of money); England's World Cup achievements under Sven-Göran Eriksson were actually quite impressive, not a national disgrace; Johnny Depp is a terrible actor (a Cristiano Ronaldo step-over without the rest of Ronaldo); the modern Spanish side are not the "best ever", they're just better than the mediocre competition, over-rated by a handful of pretentious purists. Read on – I'll prove it. (Of course I won't, but I will attempt to justify it – except the Johnny Depp bit; I actually rather like him and probably won't mention him again.)

There are technical observations to be made and facts to be adhered to. Germany won 1–0, blah blah blah, the referee missed a clear handball, blah blah blah. But behind the facts there are stories; mysterious sins of omission, injuries to key players, coaching *volte faces*, they all contribute to the ongoing saga. Why did Brazil not contribute in 1966, despite winning the two previous tournaments and the next one? Why did Alf Ramsey take off Bobby Charlton in 1970? Why did Johann Cruyff not go to the 1978 World Cup? Why did one of Germany's greatest players never play in the World Cup? They are all questions that affected the destiny of the trophy. There are titbits, too; I love a titbit; small facts or incidents that didn't change the course of anything much, but give one a little frisson of excitement on discovery. The rubbing of the hands with glee when we discover that Wayne Rooney's grandmother played in the first ladies' match at Anfield or Andrei Shevchenko was born in a Soviet Gulag to a dissident journalist. Both of these are untrue, by the way, but there are dozens like them, no less startling, that *are* true.

Football fans like their stats, so there are lots of tables, some with obvious stuff, some with more quirky observations. The need for "Best ofs" and "Teams of" are satisfied, to spark the popular pre-match pub game of "Right, what's your best-ever Holland team . . ." No? Never played that? Oh dear, I appear to have misjudged my audience . . .

There are accounts of epic games and mini biographies of favourite World Cup heroes. And not just the Finals and the great players, but games that you probably didn't bother watching at 4 o'clock on a Sunday afternoon in 1986, and balding playmakers from unfashionable German clubs in the 1990s. The great players didn't always shine in the World Cup – George Best and Alfredo Di Stéfano never even made it to the Finals, while the modern Messi(ah) has been a shadow of his Barca self playing for Argentina.

Here we go then – a chronological (why any other way?) history of the world's second greatest sporting event. Only second? Unless you slept through last year's Olympics you couldn't make an opposing case. That's not disrespectful to football, just the bigger picture.

Thanks to everyone who contributed to the extensive bibliography, to David for the copyedit, and to Duncan, Becca and everyone at Constable & Robinson for allowing me to indulge myself. And thanks to my adorable wife Nicole for pretending to be vaguely interested when I shared yet another meaningless titbit of World Cup trivia.

Naming

In the text, footballers' surnames are used for the most part, as is the convention and unless a first name is required to distinguish between, say, two Charltons or van der Kerkhofs. The principal exception to this rule are the Brazilians who have that engaging habit of adopting a "football name" to be known by. Part of the reason is the repetition of names, and the complexity and length of some of the family names; the other part is explained only by the suggestion that it is just a very Brazilian thing to do. Read Alex Bellos' book if you want a more detailed explanation, otherwise just accept it and love them for it. One thing I did learn is that Ronaldinho means "Little Ronaldo" and was first used so he wasn't confused with the existing Ronaldo. Bless.

The Portuguese have adopted the same methodology, but less consistently, and – don't ask me why – somehow, especially in recent years when footballers have social media to feed, it smacks more of affectation. Turkey also used to list players by their first names, and occasionally still do.

BIBLIOGRAPHY

Here is a list of my source books; rather than just list them I have given some indication as to whether they are worth follow-up reading or of merely academic interest to the researcher / addict like me. If a book isn't here, it doesn't mean I didn't read it, it just means it added less to my notes.

Ball, Phil, *Morbo: The Story of Spanish Football* (WSC – When Saturday Comes – Publications, 2001 & various revisions)
This is a really excellent history of the Spanish game at club and international level, with interesting cultural and historical background. I have the 2003 edition, but the new one has a happier ending!

Foot, John, *Calcio: A History of Italian Football* (4th Estate, 2006)
Superb history of Italian football, but the international section is limited as the book concentrates largely on the domestic game.

Freddi, Cris, *Complete Book of the World Cup* (HarperCollins, 2006 edition)
Until now the best history of the World Cup on the market with exemplary stats and a host of fabulous *where are they now*-type fillers. A mini masterpiece that has been wrongly ignored when discussing great football books simply because it doesn't have a straight narrative format.

Galeano, Eduardo, *Football in Sun and Shadow* (4th Estate, 1997)
A venerable journalist and novelist in his country (Uruguay),

Galeano gives us his own take on the beautiful game. Often more concerned with wordplay and poetry than fact, this is a whimsical experience, but a pleasurable one. Mark Fried's translation is entertaining if a little too fanciful for my taste.

Glanville, Brian, *The Story of the World Cup* (Faber, 2010 edition)
  For Club and Country (Guardian Books, 2008)
Brian Glanville was once the man for football on Fleet Street and his word still carries much weight. Much of his analysis feels a bit dated now, and some find his writing style ponderous, but his *Story of the World Cup* is still an important and authoritative history from a journalist who was around for every post-war competition. *For Club and Country* is an anthology of Glanville's obituaries for the *Guardian*; a dip-in book, with occasional gems.

Goldblatt, David, *The Ball is Round: A Global History of Football* (Penguin Viking, 2006)
Goldblatt undertakes an immense (c900pp) and scholarly history of the game from its roots to modern times. There are lengthy notes at the end and the way the book is edited gives it the feel of a text book, which I suspect is the fault of the publisher not the author. For the committed.

Hayes, Dean, *England – The Football Facts* (Michael O'Mara, 2006)
Good layout, good presentation, but the two halves of the book duplicate each other to an extent, and the book could have used more context for the stats and more detail.

Hamilton, Ian (editor), *The Faber Book of Soccer* (Faber and Faber, 1992)
A bit disappointing, given the breadth of the subject and quality of publisher.

Hesse-Lichtenberger, Ulrich, *Tor! The Story of German Football* (WSC publication, 2002 edition)
Read this wonderfully humorous and engaging history of the game from a German perspective, and learn to respect and understand the national team. Brilliant book.

Hunt, Chris, *World Cup Stories* (Interact/BBC 2006)
This takes an interesting approach to an illustrated book, using photos and memorabilia alongside memories from former stars and participants. Unfortunately the revelations of the participants are not always as interesting as they might be.

Imlach, Gary, *My Father and Other Working Class Football Heroes* (Yellow Jersey, 2005)
The book looks at the lot of the professional footballer before the abolition of the maximum wage as Gary looks at that era of football history through the experiences of his father, Stewart, a Scottish international winger. A worthy project and an interesting period piece.

Kuper, Simon, *Football Against the Enemy* (Orion, 1994)
   Soccernomics (with Stefan Szymanski, HarperCollins, 2009)
   The Football Men (Simon & Schuster, 2011)
Simon Kuper is undoubtedly a great journalist with access to great sources, but he sometimes strains to make his point. *Football Against the Enemy* is the best of the three, *Soccernomics* is a good idea that begins to feel a bit limited after a hundred pages and *The Football Men* is a series of interviews, many of them with modern footballers who all too often do not have that much to say.

Ludden, John (editor), *Fields of Fire – The Greatest Football Matches Ever* (Mainstream, 2001)
A good anthology of match reports from fans of the various games, which could have been improved by the inclusion of some stats and introductory context to each article.

McColl, Graham, *'78 – How a Nation Lost the World Cup* (Headline, 2006)
An interesting and not overly long-winded account of Scotland's hubristic and ill-fated 1978 World Cup campaign.

Mortimer, Gavin, *A History of Football in 100 Objects* (Serpent's Tail, 2012)
Quirky approach, but the format too often forces the content into a box it doesn't naturally fit.

Pawson, Tony (editor), *The* Observer *on Soccer* (Unwin Hyman, 1989)
Some great content, as there should be from the archives of a quality newspaper. A different design approach would have served the idea better.

Pougatch, Mark, *Three Lions versus the World* (Mainstream, 2010)
The FiveLive sports' presenter is really well connected and his wide access lends some interesting revelations, and Pougatch's personal observations give some nice colour. Analysis of the team's foibles and limitations, and more statistics would have improved the book.

Seddon, Peter, *The World Cup's Strangest Moments* (Robson, 2005)
Not a continuous narrative but a series of articles about contro-versial or odd matches and incidents in the competition's history. It has a rather *gasp! shock! horror!* tabloid feel.

Spurling, Jon, *Death or Glory – The Dark History of the World Cup* (Vision Sports, 2010)
Spurling's book tries to convince us that dark deeds and political shame lie beneath the surface of every World Cup, and that much of what we watch is sanitised and covered by a patina of respect-ability. But we knew that already, surely.

Wilson, Jonathan, *Inverting the Pyramid* (Orion, 2008)
 The Anatomy of England (Orion, 2010)
These are both interesting books. *Inverting the Pyramid* is a detailed and informative history of tactics, and *The Anatomy of England* traces England's fortunes through detailed analysis of ten games. My only issue with either is that the author takes his subject a little too seriously – football is a game, whatever Bill Shankly may have claimed to the contrary.

Winner, David, *Brilliant Orange* (Bloomsbury, 2000 and 2010 editions)
The subtitle is the neurotic genius of Dutch football, and Winner's book is a fascinating attempt to explain why the Dutch are so

different and so perverse in their use and misuse of an abundance of talent. And David Winner can write.

The Football Yearbook
I am a sad, sad man and I have these going back to the 1980s when they were *The Rothmans Football Yearbook*. Since the title became the *Sky Sports' Football Yearbook*, the content has been tailored to suit Sky's marketing needs and stylistic demands, and for the most part this is not a good thing, but it remains the go-to source book for stats and facts, and errors are relatively infrequent.

I have also read a large number of biographies and autobiographies over the years which have influenced this book, and used innumerable websites, including the much-maligned, but now much-improved Wikipedia. (Authors seldom admit to consulting Wikipedia, but don't believe those who say they don't.)

A BRIEF(-ISH) GUIDE
TO TERMS AND TACTICS

This isn't a history of football, so I won't go into great detail about the game's origins, but it is necessary to understand the changes in the way coaches and teams have approached the game over the years.

The first proper formation to evolve from the game's early days of kick-and-rush was the 2–3–5 (see Figure 1; annotation of football formations dispenses with the need to include the goalkeeper, so there is no need to write 1–2–3–5). The two defenders playing in front of the goalkeeper were called full-backs, but weren't wide players in the modern sense, but old-fashioned win-the-ball-and-clear-it types. In front of them was the centre-half, who combined tackling with distribution in a pivotal role, while the two half-backs either side of him shared defensive and attacking duties. Up front the centre-forward – usually the blood-and-thunder type – would be flanked by two wingers, whose job was to get to the byline and deliver crosses; cutting in and shooting was very rare, the only time the winger came infield was when the ball was crossed from the opposite flank. In between the wingers and the centre-forward were inside-forwards, often the cannier players who created space and fed passes through for the wingers to collect.

Goalkeeper

Right full-back   Left full-back

Right-half   Centre-half   Left-half

Right-wing   Inside-right   Centre-forward   Inside-left   Left-wing

Figure 1: 2–3–5 formation

This method of setting out a team remained the norm until the 1920s, when innovative coaches such as Herbert Chapman at Huddersfield (later Arsenal) started to tweak the system to gain an advantage. Tweaks were frowned upon by the authorities – there was a clear English notion of how to play the game, and innovation and divergence were treated with suspicion. Playing a swift passing game like most Scottish teams (as opposed to the English preference for a dribble-based cavalry charge) was one thing, but withdrawing one's centre-half to play as an extra defender – why, sir, that's not the game!

Chapman developed a system where the centre-half filled in between the full-backs and the inside-forwards dropped a little deeper to link play between the defence and forwards. It is referred to by football historians as WM (see Figure 2); 3–2–2–3 if you will. Even with this system most English sides still relied on pace and power to get results; the wiles of the inside-forwards were relevant only to offer passes for swift wingers to provide ammunition for battering-ram strikers.

Goalkeeper

Right full-back   Centre-half   Left full-back

Right-half   Left-half

Inside-right   Inside-left

Right-wing   Centre-forward   Inside-left

Figure 2: 3–2–2–3 formation

Elsewhere the game moved on; in the 1930s central European sides developed a game based on movement off the ball and bewildering, intricate passing, especially in the Central European countries, where Austria pioneered the style under their thoughtful coach Hugo Meisl. English coaches didn't even discuss movement off the ball. In South America the accent was on individual skill rather than a rigid system. Crowds would applaud a trick or shimmy as loudly as a goal, and the game was about getting the ball to these explosive talents so they could show off their repertoire.

The traditional formation held sway through to the Second World War; the Italians won two World Cups playing a hybrid of 2–3–5 and the withdrawn centre-half, and even Meisl's team played their whirligig football within the constraints of a strict 2–3–5 – Meisl was a traditionalist as well as a purist.

Once the withdrawn central defender became the norm, the transition to formations still familiar to modern audiences was less a case of sudden innovation than a gradual shifting of responsibilities within the formation. The Hungarians of the 1950s are often credited with "inventing" a new formation, but it was a variation on a theme rather than a massive divergence from the norm. Gustáv Sebes, the Hungarian coach, recognised that his two principal half-backs, Bozsik and Zakariás, offered very different qualities. Bozsik was a major creative force and Zakariás a hard-working ball-winner. It made perfect sense to use the left-sided Zakariás in a more defensive capacity and let Bozsik play a little further upfield where his passing could hurt the opposition. He also had a centre-forward, Nándor Hidegkuti, whose gifts were dribbling and passing, not barging the goalkeeper or thumping headers. Withdrawing Hidegkuti to a deeper role left his prolific inside-forwards Puskás and Kocsis, both expert finishers, to thrust forward, and also left the opposing centre-half with a dilemma over whether to follow Hidegkuti or stay put and let the maestro do as he pleased. The system worked to devastating effect (twice) against England immediately prior to the 1954 World Cup and banished any assumptions of British superiority that may have lingered amongst officials and press. To all intents and purposes Hungary were playing a fluid 4–2–4 (or maybe 3–2–3–2) long before this annotation was ever used in a match programme (see Figure 3).

Goalkeeper

Right full-back   Centre-half   Left full-back

Right-half   Left-half

Right-wing   Centre-forward   Left-wing

Inside-right   Inside-left

Figure 3: 3–2–3–2 formation

Brazil in 1958 played a similarly creative variation on the same theme – though that particular front five was so outrageously talented they seemed to be everywhere at once. But Zagallo, for example, was no orthodox winger in the English style, but a complete hard-working midfield player, as adept at tracking back and helping the defence as he was at providing searching balls for Pelé and Vavá to attack. Brazil on paper lined up 2–3–5, but the captain Bellini was an out-and-out defender, and the left-half Orlando rarely wandered too far into the last third. Didi, ostensibly the right inside-forward would sit back to dictate play, with right-half Zito in tow as a minder. This allowed Pelé to play as a free second striker alongside Vavá. Left-winger Zagallo would regularly sit tight when Garrincha had the ball, where a European winger would instinctively head into the penalty area (see Figure 4).

Goalkeeper

Right full-back   Centre-half   Left-half   Left full-back

Right-half   Inside-right

Right-wing   Centre-forward   Inside-left   Left-wing

Figure 4: 4–2–4 formation

By the 1960s all international sides played four at the back; Bobby Moore wore No.6, the left-half jersey, but he was no one's idea of a midfield player, just a defender with excellent passing and vision. Bobby Charlton wore No.9, but he didn't spearhead the attack, he filled the gap between midfield and attack, lurking behind the strikers to unleash his explosive shooting. Once he discarded the old-fashioned wingers, Alf Ramsey played a 4–1–2–1–2 system that left opposing sides with a problem; the full-backs had no one to mark, and many 1960s full-backs weren't given to exploiting that opportunity by offering themselves as an attacking option. England were able to dominate the midfield, starve the opposition forwards of the ball, and give Charlton and company plenty of ammunition to hurt the opposition (see Figure 5).

Goalkeeper

Right full-back   Centre-half   Centre-half   Left full-back

Defensive Midfield

Right Midfield   Left Midfield

Playmaker

Forward   Forward

Figure 5: 4–1–2–1–2 formation

The Italians had developed a new method, the *catenaccio*, whereby one central defender would sit deeper than the other as a last resort, a sweeper. The system allowed for one defensive and one athletic attacking full-back; on the defensive side the winger would also be slightly withdrawn into midfield in a position that became known as the *tornata*. This system, especially successful at Internazionale of Milan in the early 1960s under their coach Helenio Herrera, was eventually found out. When under pressure the defensive midfielder tended to withdraw alongside the "stopper" centre-half and form a defensive back five in a very narrow 5–3–2. Intended to stifle opponents, the formation, the apogee of defensive systems, ended up stifling Italian football (see Figure 6).

Goalkeeper

Sweeper

Right-back   Centre-half   Defensive Midfield   Left-back

Right Midfield   Playmaker   Left Midfield

Forward   Forward

Figure 6: 5–3–2 formation

As football moved into the 1970s most sides were employing a variation on a theme. Four defenders, with the middle two playing either side by side or as a more sophisticated pairing with a sweeper (deep-lying) defender behind a stopper who would mark the centre-forward; four in midfield, two of them nominally wide players, one a holding player and the other a creative playmaker; two up front, one a goalscorer, the other more creative, or, in Northern Europe, a target man. The regional variations that had always stood were still relevant; the British and northern Europeans favoured a game based on pace and power and getting the ball forward early; the central and southern European countries were more technical, retaining possession and launching fast attacks when the opportunity presented itself; the South Americans relied more on individual artistry and freedom of expression – but unlike the pre-war years it was backed up by uncompromising defending (see Figure 7).

Goalkeeper

Right full-back   Centre-half   Centre-half   Left full-back

Right-wing   Defensive Midfield   Playmaker   Left-wing

Forward   Forward

Figure 7: 4–4–2 formation

The next forty years have been about tweaks and layers of sophistication. The Dutch developed a fluidity of movement and position that their superb technique allowed. The Germans added a level of stamina and athleticism no one had seen before. The Soviets, especially under the Dynamo Kyiv manager Valeri Lobanovsky, introduced a pressing system. Pressing was a tactical device that used fitness and teamwork to allow the team to play higher up the pitch and reduce the space in which the opposition could play. It was the first system in which the development of a workable offside trap was an absolute necessity, as it left space behind the pressing team's defence. Liverpool in the seventies and eighties allied British strength and aggression to European possession and movement, but – alarmingly – British national managers failed to do the same. Argentina used three central defenders for the first time, with wide midfield players as auxiliary full-backs, and soon everyone copied them, until it was discovered that using an old-fashioned winger destroyed the system and forced it back into the shell of 5–3–2. Some English sides reverted to launching the ball forward to turn the defence around – with great success (Watford, Wimbledon) at home, but continental teams dropped deep and gleefully accepted the wasted possession when British sides tried to translate it to international level (see Figure 8).

Goalkeeper

Centre-half   Sweeper   Centre-half

Right wing back   Midfield   Midfield   Left wing back

Playmaker

Forward   Forward

Figure 8: 3–5–2 formation

The favoured formation of the better sides as I write is four at the back, three in midfield – either two deeper plus a playmaker (Martínez and Schweinsteiger behind Thomas Müller for Bayern Munich) or one holding player plus a runner and a playmaker (Makélélé-Vieira-Zidane for France in 2006) – and two wide attacking players flanking a mobile centre-forward (see Figures 9 and 10).

Goalkeeper
Right back   Centre-half   Centre-half   Left-back
Midfield   Midfield
Ring-wing   Playmaker   Left-wing
Striker
Figure 9: 4–2–3–1 formation

Goalkeeper
Right full-back   Centre-half   Centre-half   Left-back
Right Wing   Midfield Runner   Defensive Midfield   Left-wing
Playmaker
Striker
Figure 10: 4–4–1–1 formation

All through the last decades of the twentieth century the game underwent steady shifts. This was down to one principal factor: speed. The speed at which the world moves, speed of foot and the speed at which the game is played. Nutrition, conditioning, managing injury, psychology – all the scientific advances made in the world were affecting football, too. Coaches became analysts as well as scientists, aided by first television and later computers. Set pieces became more important – it was no longer just about letting your best striker of a ball have a pot-shot, but about positioning players cleverly to anticipate where the ball ended up if it was parried or cleared. Footballers have to think – not something with which they have traditionally been associated – as well as act on instinct. No longer is it acceptable for a defender to simply defend and clear the ball (if he does, he's probably British), no longer are there work-shy goal-hangers whose sole purpose is to put the ball in the net and no longer are there wide players who hog the touchline and wait for the ball so they can skin their full-back. The defender must be able to control the ball and find a colleague, the striker must offer movement and create space for advancing midfield players and the winger must track back and help the full-back.

Modern football is played at such a hectic pace and in such confined space (every team uses pressing now, it is a standard rather than a tactic) that it is no longer about a rigid formation, but about creating space and time within the maelstrom of a match. Touch is assumed (except in Britain), power and fitness are a given. The four things that set teams apart now all begin with P.

- Possession is nine-tenths of the law (or something like that) – keep the ball, the opposition can do nothing.
- Pressing means, if you do lose the ball, you can win it back (and possession is nine-tenths of the law).
- Positioning means you are in the right place to receive the ball and, if it is lost, the right place to defend (press) and win it back (possession being nine-tenths of the law).
- Pace is the wildcard. There is very little any team can do about pace if deployed intelligently.

Will it all change again in the next few years? Will some clever coach find a way to counter Spain's immaculate retention of the ball, like Di Matteo and Heynckes did when they respectively frustrated and overpowered the much-vaunted Barcelona team? Yes, it will change, it always does, and like all the other times we won't really notice what changed until a few years down the line.

THE ORGANISATION OF FOOTBALL

This is a guide to some of the organisations mentioned in the book, with a (very) potted history where relevant.

FIFA

Fédération Internationale de Football Association

FIFA is the game's primary international governing body, formed in 1904 and headquartered in Zurich, Switzerland. It has 209 national associations affiliated.

"*I share the tendency of fans to attribute most of what is good about the game to the people who play it, and most of what is bad to those who govern it.*" So wrote Ulrich Hesse-Lichtenberger in his book *Tor!* (a history of German football aimed at non-Germans). It is a generalisation – footballers have proved themselves greedy and unworthy of the adulation heaped upon them and the game's administrators have made good decisions as well as bad – but it is a sentiment most writers share, and with good reason. Decisions made for the benefit of politicians, sponsors and TV channels are rarely good news for the ordinary fan, and FIFA are enslaved to these money-wielders. They have proved themselves incompetent, pusillanimous and greedy, and senior officials, including former President João Havelange, have been found guilty of corruption. They are presided over by an incumbent President whose inane contributions to crucial debates within the game would be crass coming from a teenager, never mind the leader of a wealthy and influential body. Apart from that they're fine.

FIFA Presidents:
Robert Guérin (France), 1904–06
Daniel Woolfall (England), 1906–18 (his death)
Jules Rimet (France), 1921–54
Rodolphe Seeldrayers (Belgium), 1954–55 (his death)
Arthur Drewry (England), 1955–61 (his death)
Stanley Rous (England), 1961–74
João Havelange (Brazil), 1974–98
Sepp Blatter (Switzerland), 1998–incumbent

UEFA

The Union of European Football Associations

UEFA is the most wealthy, and remains marginally the most influential, of the continental agencies within FIFA. UEFA was set up in 1954 with twenty-five members, a number that has expanded considerably since the break-up of the Soviet Union and Yugoslavia.

UEFA has had only six Presidents: Ebbe Schwartz (Denmark, 1954–62), Gustav Wiederkehr (Switzerland, 1962–72), Artemio Franchi (1973–83), Jacques George (1984–90), Lennart Johansson (Sweden, 1990–2007), Michel Platini (2007–incumbent). Both Wiederkehr and Franchi died in office, Franchi following a motor accident. Johansson's tenure was noted for the hard-nosed commercialisation of European football, including the expansion of the European Cup into the modern Champions League format, increasing revenue and opportunity for the larger clubs and creating the gulf that exists today between the haves and have-nots.

It took UEFA a while to organise a European Championship and it started as an itsy-bitsy sort of competition, not really warming up fully until the Finals expanded to eight teams in 1980 and then sixteen for the 1996 event in England. The 2016 Finals in France have gone over the top in the onwards and upwards search for revenue and will see twenty-four sides challenging for the trophy, almost half of UEFA's fifty-four-strong membership.

European Championship Finals

1960   10 July, Parc des Princes, Paris, France
USSR   (0) (1) 2   **Yugoslavia**   (1) (1) 1
Metreveli, Ponedelnik   Galic

1964   21 June, Santiago Bernabéu, Madrid, Spain
Spain   (1) 2   **USSR**   (1) 1
Pereda, Marcelino   Khusainov

1968   8 June, Stadio Olimpico, Rome, Italy
Italy   (0) (1) 1   **Yugoslavia**   (1) (1) 1
Domeghini   Dzajic
Replay: 10 June, Stadio Olimpico, Rome, Italy
Italy   (2) 2   **Yugoslavia**   (0) 0
Riva, Anastasi

1972   18 June, Heysel Stadium, Brussels, Belgium
West Germany   (1) 3   **USSR**   (0) 0
Müller 2, Wimmer

1976   20 June, Crvena Zvezda (Red Star) Stadium, Belgrade, Yugoslavia
Czechoslovakia   (2) (2) 2   **West Germany**(1) (2) 2
Svehlík, Dobias   Müller★, Hölzenbein
Czechs won 5–3 on penalties

1980   22 June, Stadio Olimpico, Rome, Italy
West Germany   (1) 2   **Belgium**   (0) 1
Hrubesch 2   Vandereycken (p)†

1984   27 June, Parc des Princes, Paris, France
France   (0) 2   **Spain**   (0) 0
Platini, Bellone

1988   25 June, Olympic Stadium, Munich, Germany
Holland   (1) 2   **USSR**   (0) 0
Gullit, van Basten

1992   26 June, Ullevi, Gothenburg
Denmark   (1) 2   **Germany**   (0) 0
Jensen, Vilfort

★ In scoring in this match Gerd Müller became the first player to score in two European Championship Finals, a record unmatched until Fernando Torres scored in 2008 and 2012. Müller was also, in 1974, the first man to score in a European Championship Final and a World Cup Final, a record that remains unique.
† Indicates scoring from a penalty – annotation will be used without explanation henceforward.

1996   30 June, Wembley Stadium, London, England
Germany   (0) (1) 2   **Czech Republic**   (0) (1) 1
Bierhoff 2   Berger (p)

2000   2 July, Feyenoord Stadium, Rotterdam, Holland
France   (0) (1) 2   **Italy**   (0) (1) 1
Wiltord, Trezeguet   Delvecchio

2004   4 July, Stadium of Light, Lisbon, Portugal
Greece   (0) 1   **Portugal**   (0) 0
Charisteas

2008   29 June, Ernst Happel Stadium, Vienna, Austria
Spain   (1) 1   **Germany**   (0) 0
Torres

2012   1 July, Olympic Stadium, Kyiv, Ukraine
Spain*   (2) 4   **Italy**   (0) 0
Silva, Alba, Torres, Mata

CONCACAF

The Confederation of North, Central American and Caribbean Football Association

CONCACAF was formed in 1961 by the merger of the organisation that governed North American football, and the CCCF, which organised (I use the word loosely) football in Central America and the Caribbean. Ramón Coll Jaumet of Costa Rica oversaw the merger, and handed over the reins to Joaquín Soria Terrazas of Mexico in 1969. In 1990 Terrazas was succeeded by Jack Warner of Trinidad and Tobago. This fine, upstanding pillar of society, a government minister in Trinidad until 2013, was president for twenty-one years until he agreed to stand down and withdraw from football amid allegations of corruption. Who knows if they will stick, football is such a murky business, but at least Warner is off the world stage, hopefully for good. His accuser and former ally Chuck Blazer, the General Secretary of CONCACAF, was suspended in May 2013 and is under investigation by the FBI.

---

* Spain were the first team to retain the trophy, generally regarded as the hardest international competition to win outside the World Cup.

The new President of CONCACAF is Jeffrey Webb, a lawyer from the Cayman Islands. And we all know the Cayman Islands would have no truck with shady financial deals.

The CONCACAF Gold Cup began in 1991, and has been held twelve times; Mexico have won six, United States five (including the most recent in July 2013), with Canada the surprise winners in 2000.

CONMEBOL

Confederación Sudamericana de Fútbol

Formed in 1916 and now based in Luque, Paraguay, home of the President since 1986, Nicolás Léoz, Conmebol is the representative body of the South American countries, excepting the knot of countries lying on the continent's north-eastern coast – these nations are part of CONCACAF. This leaves Conmebol with only ten member countries, of which Venezuela is the only one never to have appeared in a World Cup Finals tournament. (At time of writing they have a slim chance of qualifying for 2014.) The ten countries habitually play out a round-robin tournament for World Cup qualification. They also compete (with two invited guest teams from North America) for the Copa América, a tournament held at inconsistent intervals – currently it seems to have settled on every four years, the year following a World Cup. Conmebol sides suffer from having their squads spread far and wide, with many key players employed by the big European clubs, making release, especially for friendlies, an irksome process.

Uruguay are the most frequent winners of the Copa América – perhaps a surprise to most European fans, who would most likely assume Brazil or Argentina.

Winners of the **Copa América** (and its forerunners)

1916 Uruguay	1939 Peru	1975 Peru (2)
1917 Uruguay (2nd win)	1941 Argentina (6)	1979 Paraguay (2)
1919 Brazil	1942 Uruguay (8)	1983 Uruguay (12)
1920 Uruguay (3)	1945 Argentina (7)	1987 Uruguay (13)
1921 Argentina	1946 Argentina (8)	1989 Brazil (4)
1922 Brazil (2)	1947 Argentina (9)	1991 Argentina (13)

1923 Uruguay (4)	1949 Brazil (3)	1993* Argentina (14)
1924 Uruguay (5)	1953 Paraguay	1995 Uruguay (14)
1925 Argentina (2)	1955 Argentina (10)	1997 Brazil (5)
1926 Uruguay (6)	1956 Uruguay (9)	1999 Brazil (6)
1927 Argentina (3)	1957 Argentina (11)	2001 Colombia
1929 Argentina (4)	1959 Argentina (12)	2004 Brazil (7)
1935 Uruguay (7)	1959 Uruguay (10)	2007 Brazil (8)
1937 Argentina (5)	1963 Bolivia	2011 Uruguay (15)
	1967 Uruguay (11)	

CAF

The Confederation of African Football

The African federation is located in Cairo and oversees African football and the African Cup of Nations. It is a vast, unwieldy beast, which has to cope with myriad different cultures and attitudes, not to mention constant civil wars and border disputes of extreme brutality. There have been two Egyptian Presidents, two from Sudan and one from Ethiopia; the current incumbent, installed in 1988, is Issa Hayatou of Cameroon.

Hayatou was instrumental in the suspension of Togo for two African Cup of Nations tournaments after they withdrew from the 2010 Finals. They withdrew after an armed attack on their convoy on the way to the Finals saw two of their support staff killed. Clearly a man of compassion, Mr Hayatou.

Africa Cup of Nations Winners

1957 Egypt	1988 Cameroon (2)
1959 Egypt (2†)	1990 Algeria
1962 Ethiopia	1992 Ivory Coast
1963 Ghana	1994 Nigeria (2)
1965 Ghana (2)	1996 South Africa
1968 Congo-Kinshasa	1998 Egypt (4)
1970 Sudan	2000 Cameroon (3)

* From 1993 selected nations from other regions were invited to join the tournament; invitees have included Costa Rica, Honduras, USA, Japan and, in every competition since 1993, Mexico, who have twice been runners-up. In 2011 Spain were invited but withdrew (as did Japan), while Canada rejected her only invitation in 2001.
† Competing as a United Arab Republic

1972 Congo
1974 Zaire (2*)
1976 Morocco
1978 Ghana (3)
1980 Nigeria
1982 Ghana (4)
1984 Cameroon
1986 Egypt (3)

2002 Cameroon (4)
2004 Tunisia
2006 Egypt (5)
2008 Egypt (6)
2010 Egypt (7)
2012 Zambia
2013 Nigeria (3)

AFC

Asian Football Confederation

The Asian Football Confederation also includes Australia since 2006 – why they don't just combine Asia and Oceania, Lord only knows. Countries that have land within Asia and Europe are all UEFA affiliated, as is Israel, for obvious political reasons.

The AFC President from 2002 to 2011, Mohamed bin Hammam, was banned from football for life after allegations of corruption were investigated, but a court later overturned this ban, and bin Hammam is seeking to be reinstated as President. He was the President when the ridiculous decision to hold the Finals in Qatar was ratified, amid widespread accusations of bribery and vote-buying.

Are you getting any sense of pattern in these summaries of the various organisations running the game? A faint whiff in the nostrils, perhaps . . .?

Asian Cup Winners

1956 South Korea
1960 South Korea (2)
1964 Israel
1968 Iran
1972 Iran (2)

1976 Iran (3)
1980 Kuwait
1984 Saudi Arabia
1988 Saudi Arabia (2)
1992 Japan

1996 Saudi Arabia (3)
2000 Japan (2)
2004 Japan (3)
2007 Iraq[†]
2011 Japan (4)

* (2) because Zaire and Congo-Kinshasa (1968) are the same country, which is now known as the Democratic Republic of Congo.
† Barely covered in the West, Iraq's recovery from the 2001 invasion and subsequent occupation to win this tournament was one of the game's most impressive feats in recent years, and testimony to people's resilience and determination to get on with positive stuff even amid such an appalling upheaval. Iraq has subsequently been suspended twice by FIFA after excessive political involvement in the administration of the game.

FA

Football Association

These are the guys responsible for running the English game. Convinced for years they were the only ones who knew the real meaning of football, having founded the game, they fell further and further behind their peers in Europe and South America in their understanding of tactics and sports science, and they are still struggling desperately to catch up.

If you need to know why England have found it so hard to maintain a place at football's top table, look no further than the guys pulling the handle on the fruit machine of club football – the FA and their rivals running the Premier League (and I use the word rivals deliberately, any pretence at cooperation is utterly misleading).

The FA was formed in 1863 and initially did wonderful work organising the game and initiating the professional league, most notably under the stewardship of Charles Alcock, Secretary from 1870 to 1895. Alcock organised the first match between England and Scotland, set up the FA Cup and also organised the first Test match at cricket between England and Australia – not a bad CV!

For the next ninety-four years Alcock had only four successors: Frederick Wall, Stanley Rous (later President of FIFA), Denis Follows and Ted Croker. Croker endured a particularly tormented tenure as Secretary, dealing with the worst of the hooligan era that embraced the disasters at Heysel and Hillsborough. His replacement, Graham Kelly, was the first to carry the title of Chief Executive – an attempt to make an old-fashioned, slow-moving organisation sound more businesslike – and he had nine years in office before resigning amid allegations (unproven and debatable) of corruption. His successor was Adam Crozier, who left to go and upset postal workers (i.e. run Royal Mail), followed by the hapless Mark Palios, Brian Barwick, Ian Watmore (remember him? no? me neither) and the current incumbent, Alex Horne.

The CEO reports to a board headed by a Chairman. The recent appointment of Greg Dyke, former head of the BBC, holds some hope for an era of decent communication and clarity – Dyke's time at the BBC was viewed as largely positive until he fell on his sword in the wake of the Hutton inquiry, the usual scapegoat for the righteous indignation of the newspaper owners in their lifelong vendetta against the BBC. The last FA Chairman to talk sense and breathe fresh air into the organisation was Lord Triesman, a former Labour MP, but he was stitched up by the *Mail on Sunday* and forced to resign. The press, eh? They moan about the running of the game, and, as soon as they get someone in charge who seems equipped and prepared to tackle the problems, they can't wait to bring them down.

SFA

Scottish Football Association

The Scottish Football Association, a group of small-minded people who, Nero-like, have sat and watched while their towers tumble around them. This has resulted in a league with the potency of the Latvian second division and a national side sandwiched between the Cape Verde Islands and Panama at No.50 in the FIFA rankings – and those dizzy heights attained with a victory over Croatia that saw them rise twenty-four places to sprint away from football superpowers such as Togo and Jordan.

EARLY DAYS

1.1 WORLD CUP 1930

When FIFA first convened in 1904, their charter reserved the right to host a full-scale international tournament. At first there seemed no need; the Olympic Games served as a perfectly good means of sorting the men from the boys. It was the success of these Olympic Games that soon prompted FIFA to see the opportunities presented by hosting their own tournament. The 1928 Olympic final, won by Uruguay, was watched by more than 40,000 people, with over six times that number applying for tickets. Football was easily the biggest event at these Amsterdam Olympics, representing, as it did, the only opportunity for global bragging rights in the world's most popular sport.

Jules Rimet was the President of FIFA in 1929, but it was his countryman Henri Delaunay (the Secretary of the organisation) who proposed a resolution to host a world tournament in 1930. Twenty-five of the thirty member countries voted in favour. Another, Sweden, performed a remarkable *volte face*; they voted against and then promptly offered themselves as inaugural hosts. That honour was reserved for Olympic champions Uruguay, who offered up Montevideo as the host city in Olympic manner, and promised a shiny new stadium to showcase the big games. Most of the big economies had suffered in the Wall Street Crash, but the downturn was still to hit Uruguay in the same way – it would do so, with great severity, the following decade. Montevideo was a thriving, bustling port city boasting some of the most adventurous new architecture on the continent and Uruguay had a President keen to publicise the nation's resources and pride. Elsewhere in South America, Generals were replacing Presidents

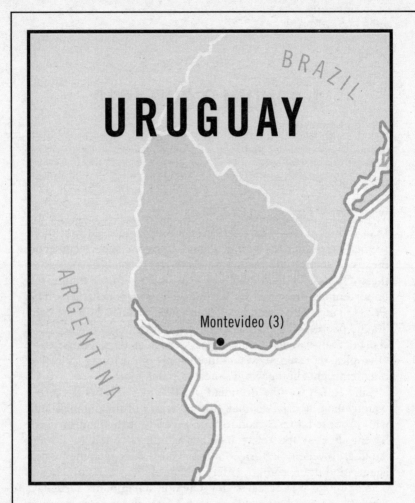

URUGUAY

BRAZIL

ARGENTINA

Montevideo (3)

1930
URUGUAY
The first tournament was more like an Olympic competition, with all the matches held in one city, Montevideo.

Three grounds were used:

Estádio Centenário
The Centenário was built for the 1930 World Cup, and held 90,000 spectators for Uruguay's match against Yugoslavia. The stadium still stands in the Parque Batlle area of the city. The Centenário is unusual in that it is owned by the municipal government, and clubs wishing to use it (which the biggest Montevideo clubs do often – Peñarol, especially) pay rent to the city.

Estádio Gran Parque
This stadium still stands, holding 27,000 people, having been refurbished a number of times since opening in 1900. It is the home of Nacional, one of Uruguay's premier clubs, although it often relocates to the Centenário for big continental fixtures.

Estádio Pocitos
Pocitos was a tiny suburban stadium used as an emergency third ground for the 1930 tournament while the Centenário was hastily finished. It was the home of Peñarol, but was demolished at the end of the decade as the club was playing the majority of its matches in the Centenário and the space occupied by the Pocitos was needed for housing as the city expanded.

and the military fist was closing around the people, just as it would across Europe in the ensuing years.

Uruguay loved its football, and a series of popular club tours by major European clubs had whetted the Uruguayan appetite for seeing opponents from Europe; this new tournament provided a good opportunity. Disappointingly for the hosts, many of the top European sides failed to show; Hungary, Austria, Spain and Italy all stayed at home, while a squabble over definitions of amateurism had led England and Scotland to resign their brief four-year tenure as FIFA members in 1928. Even had they travelled, England and Austria, the best European sides, would have struggled against the best of the South Americans on foreign soil. The Copa América (initially called the South American Championships) had been in place since 1910, and the South American sides were used to competing for a trophy over an intensive period, as Uruguay's success at the last two Olympics had shown. Four European sides – France, Belgium, Romania and Yugoslavia – crossed the Atlantic to appear, the first three of them on the same boat, which also collected the Brazilian squad in passing. Peter Seddon (*The World Cup's Strangest Moments*) describes the decision to give Uruguay the tournament as "FIFA's first major cock-up" but that's Eurocentric nonsense. Have a go at Mexico in 1986 and Russia in 2018, fine, but this was an appropriate and correct choice of venue.

Two different companies worked feverishly from February to make the Estádio Centenário fit for purpose. The name was easy, as 1930 was also the first centenary of the establishment of the constitution of Uruguay after the Treaty of Montevideo established independence from the Brazilian Empire two years earlier. The initial schedule was hastily rearranged when it became obvious the Centenário couldn't host the opening game. Instead of the hosts, the honour of playing the first match fell to France and Mexico, and the venue wasn't the glitzy new stadium but the tiny Pocitos stadium of Peñarol in the suburbs. The ground was originally the home of the Uruguay Railway Cricket Club, founded for its many expat British employees. The new stadium was still being finished by the time Uruguay played their first match of the competition, but in 1930 health and safety inspectors did not wield the power they do today. The stadium still exists in roughly the same format, with a slightly reduced 65,000 capacity, and Uruguay remain a tough side to beat on their home turf, even if they are not the force of old.

GROUP 1

France Laurent 19, Langiller 40, Maschinot 42, 87	(3) 4	**Mexico** Carreño 70	(0) 1	13 July, Pocitos; 4,444
Argentina Monti 81	(0) 1	**France**	(0) 0	15 July, Parque Central; 23,409
Chile Vidal 4, 86, own goal 51	(1) 3	**Mexico**	(0) 0	16 July, Parque Central; 9,249
Chile Subiabre 65	(0) 1	**France**	(0) 0	19 July, Centenário; 42,100
Argentina Stábile 8, 17, 80, Zumelzu 10, 55, Varallo 53	(3) 6	**Mexico** M Rosas 37 (p), 72 (p), Gayón 78	(1) 3	19 July, Centenário; 42,100*
Argentina Stábile 12, 14, M Evaristo 51	(2) 3	**Chile** Arellano 15	(1) 1	22 July, Centenário; 41,459

1. **Argentina 6pts (10–4); 2. Chile 4pts (5–3); 3. France 2pts (4–3); 4. Mexico 0pts (4–13)**

This first game was hardly a glamorous fixture. France, also-rans in Europe, were in South America on sufferance largely because the tournament was a Frenchman's brainchild. Mexico were poor, an occasional side who lost 7–1 to Spain (no great shakes) at the previous Olympic Games. France won, easily, despite losing their goalkeeper to injury in the first half (no substitutes, remember). The honour of scoring the first ever World Cup goal fell to Lucien Laurent, an inside-forward.

Laurent was less fortunate in the next match against Argentina – he spent most of the game limping after a diabolical challenge from Argentinian hard man Luis Monti. The rough and ready organisation dictated that France play again two days after the Mexican match – why Argentina couldn't face the fourth team in the group, Chile, is anyone's guess. France, with their excellent goalkeeper Alex Thépot of Red Star FC (Paris, not Belgrade, they're a French third division club these days) in good form, held

---

* These games were played one after another as a double header, hence the same attendance; the figures quoted are FIFA's official attendance figures and are highly debatable, like most things coming out of that organisation.

out for eighty minutes. Monti scored the winner from a free-kick, but Argentina would need to improve to match Uruguay – their forwards were overly fond of displaying their extravagant skills and less fond of giving the ball to a better-placed colleague to score. The game ended in farce as the Brazilian referee blew for full time six minutes prematurely and took ten minutes explaining his error to the dejected French and celebrating Argentinians.

France also lost to Chile, despite Thépot saving a penalty, and went out. Lucien Laurent appeared on French TV during the 1998 World Cup, describing his experiences enthusiastically and – predictably, but not without reason – criticising the mercenary attitude and disrespectful behaviour of modern players. Laurent had taken weeks off from his job in a car factory to travel to Uruguay, receiving only basic expenses from the French FA. Later he spent three years in a German prisoner-of-war camp and they took away his France shirt from 1930. Unlike most of us, he has earned the right to say *"j'accuse"* to the pampered Premiership millionaires.

After their ordinary showing in the first match, Argentina gave their supposed second string a chance against Mexico – one change was enforced by their captain Nolo Ferreira sitting a law exam on the day of the match! Imagine John Terry flying home to sit a law exam ... One of the beneficiaries of the changes was an inside-forward called Guillermo Stábile, who made his debut for the national team and set an unusual record by scoring a hat-trick in his first international and also his first World Cup match. Stábile kept his place for the tougher fixture against Chile and added two more goals in a 3–1 victory.

GROUP 4

USA McGhee 41, Florie 44, Patenaude 88	(2) 3	**Belgium**	(0) 0	13 July, Parque Central; 18,436
USA Patenaude 10, 15, 50*	(2) 3	**Paraguay**	(0) 0	17 July, Parque Central; 18,306
Paraguay Vargas Peña	(1) 1	**Belgium**	(0) 0	20 July, Centenário; 9,000

1. USA 4pts (6–0); 2. Paraguay 2pts (1–3); 3. Belgium 0pts (0–4)

* Patenaude's hat-trick was disputed in different sources and only officially ratified by FIFA in 2006.

Argentina's semi-final opponents would be the USA, who had won through Group 4 with relative ease, beating Belgium and Paraguay without conceding. The USA were strong and quick and made light of their international experience. The win over Paraguay, recent conquerors of Uruguay in the Copa América, was excellent and saw the World Cup's first hat-trick, by Bert Patenaude, all created by the dangerous Bart McGhee. Patenaude scored in the match against Belgium as well, and remains a famous figure in US soccer, even though he only played one further international after the competition, against Brazil in a post-World Cup tour. Patenaude played his club football for the splendidly named Fall River Marksmen, a Massachusetts club in the first American Soccer League, which ran successfully throughout the 1920s until financial failure in the wake of the Wall Street Crash.

GROUP 2

Yugoslavia	(2) 2	**Brazil**	(0) 1	14 July, Parque Central; 24,059
Tirnanic 21, Bek 31		Preguinho 62		
Yugoslavia	(0) 4	**Bolivia**	(0) 0	17 July, Parque Central; 18,306
Bek 60, 67, Marjanovic 65, Vujadinovic 85				
Brazil	(1) 4	**Bolivia**	(0) 0	20 July, Centenário; 25,466
Moderato 27, 73, Preguinho 57, 83*				

1. Yugoslavia 4pts (6–1); 2. Brazil 2pts (5–2); 3. Bolivia 0pts (0–8)

Paraguay weren't the only South American side to come a cropper in the early stages. Brazil, even with an almost completely new side, were still expected to get the better of Yugoslavia, but they paid the price for a poor first half and lost 2–1. The undoubted star was the Yugoslav goalkeeper Jaksic, who stayed calm and strong during a second half onslaught by the Brazilians. The young Yugoslav team were far too good for Bolivia – as would any respectable pub team have been – winning 4–0. Pictures show one of the Bolivian side sporting a natty beret

---

* Brazilian captain and centre-forward Preguinho of Fluminense was one of the first superstars of Brazilian football. He was a brilliant multi-disciplined sportsman, excelling at basketball and water polo as well as football; he once swam for the Fluminense club in the state championships then promptly took a taxi to play in a football match.

thirty-odd years before Che Guevara made them *de rigeur* amongst the continent's trendies. Yugoslavia's 4–0 win rendered Brazil's win over Bolivia irrelevant.

GROUP 3

Romania	(1) 3	**Peru**	(0) 1	14 July, Pocitos; 300
Desu 1, Stanciu 74, Kovacs 85		Souza Ferreira 60		
Uruguay	(0) 1	**Peru**	(0) 0	18 July, Centenário; 57,735
Castro				
Uruguay	(4) 4	**Romania**	(0) 0	21 July, Centenário; 70,022
Dorado 7, Scarone 16, Anselmo 31, Cea 35				

1. Uruguay 4pts (5–0); 2. Romania 2pts (3–5); 3. Peru 0pts (1–4)

Yugoslavia's reward for their good work was a semi-final against hosts Uruguay. Drawn in an easy group with Romania and Peru, Uruguay had to delay their first appearance until the main stadium was ready, leaving Peru and Romania to open the group with a violent match in front of a pathetic crowd at Pocitos. Uruguay made their delayed first appearance at the Centenário on 18 July, and produced a stumbling performance against unfancied Peru, missing a hatful of chances and finding twenty-year-old Pardón in the Peruvian goal in excellent form. Three days later, nerves settled, they produced a much better performance to brush aside Romania. Coach Alberto Suppici restored the experienced Héctor Scarone to the starting line-up and the added guile made life easier for the forwards, who shared the goals in a 4–0 win as Uruguay dominated the first half then took the foot off the pedal and saved themselves for harder tasks ahead.

SEMI-FINALS

Argentina	(1) 6	**USA**	(0) 1	26 July, Centenário; 72,886
Monti 20, Scopelli 56, Stábile 69, 87, Peucelle 80, 85		Brown 89		
Uruguay	(3) 6	**Yugoslavia**	(1) 1	27 July, Centenário; 79,867
Cea 18, 67, 72, Anselmo 20, 31, Iriarte 61		Vujadinovic 4		

In the first semi-final the USA started well against Argentina, creating a couple of good chances, but soon the superior skill of the Argentinians took effect, as did Monti's own brand of physical endeavour; USA centre-half Ralph Tracy suffered a knee injury that meant he missed the second half. After reaching the interval only a goal to the good, through Monti, Argentina overran the under-manned Americans in the second half, running in a further five goals, with two more for Stábile. The USA deserved their late consolation.

In one of those frequent statistical quirks the game throws up, the other semi-final ended with the same scoreline. Yugoslavia scored first – the first goal that Uruguay's tough back line conceded – but the goal spurred on Uruguay and they were the stronger side throughout. Some sources claim a second goal for Yugoslavia at 2–1 down should not have been disallowed, but Uruguay were very convincing in the second half and ran out easy winners. The strolling inside-forward Pedro Cea scored a hat-trick and the asthmatic centre-forward Anselmo twice – although the latter suffered a flare-up in his condition that meant he lost his place for the final.

Yugoslavia were far from disgraced, and their young (twenty-four-year-old) captain Milutin Ivković, was one of the stars of the tournament, along with the lively centre-forward Ivan Bek (later capped by France where he played club football). Ivković was intelligent and politically active, and it would cost him his life during the Second World War when he was executed by the Nazis as a Communist agitator.

WORLD CUP FINAL No.1
30 July 1930, Centenário; 68,346

Uruguay	**(1) 4**	Dorado 12, Cea 57, Iriarte 68, Castro 89
Argentina	**(2) 2**	Peucelle 20, Stábile 37

Referee: **John Langenus** (Belgium)
Coaches: **Francisco Olazar** (Argentina) & **Alberto Suppici** (Uruguay)

Uruguay (2–3–5): Enrique Ballestrero (Rampla Juniors); José Nasazzi (Bella Vista), Ernesto Mascheroni (Olimpia); José Andrade (Nacional), Lorenzo Fernández (Peñarol), Álvaro Gestido (Peñarol); Pablo Dorado (Bella Vista), Héctor Scarone (Nacional), Héctor Castro (Nacional), Pedro Cea (Nacional), Santos Iriarte (Racing Club, Montevideo)
Argentina (2–3–5): Juan Botasso (Argentino de Quilmes); José Della Torre (Racing Club, BA), Fernando Paternóster (Racing Club, BA); Pedro Suárez (Boca Juniors), Luis Monti (San Lorenzo), Juan Evaristo (Sportivo Barracas); Mario Evaristo (Boca Juniors)*, Nolo Ferreira (Estudiantes), Guillermo Stábile (Huracán), Francisco Varallo (Gimnasia), Carlos Peucelle (Sportivo BA)

* Mario and Juan Evaristo became the first brothers to play in a World Cup Final.

This match may not have had much impact in Europe, but the atmosphere during the build-up in Montevideo and Buenos Aires was near rabid. Thousands were left disappointed on the docks at Buenos Aires when boats of all shapes and sizes set sail down the coast in the fog carrying excited Argentinians to the game. There are stories of government officials commandeering sailing vessels and commercial boats to carry them – early warning that a down-side of a World Cup is the sight of politicians with negligible knowledge of the game doing their "I'm a genuine fan" face while snacking on corporate canapés in a box.

In keeping with the gangster age, there were death threats issued before the match; Luis Monti was told by Buenos Aires mobsters that unpleasant things might happen to his family if Argentina lost. He was told similar things by Uruguayan gang-sters if he masterminded a victory over their team – Argentina's most effective player needed more than a little persuading to take the field. He wasn't the only one; the Belgian referee insisted on protection for himself and his family, and a boat ready and wait-ing to take him back to Europe as soon as the game was over. Langenus had another minor crisis before the game – both sides wanted to provide the match ball. The Belgian used the "little grey cells" so beloved of his famous fictional countryman Hercule Poirot and decreed that a different ball be used for each half.

Finishing touches had been applied to the stadium and it was a magnificent edifice to grace a fabulously passionate occasion. The authorities made the sensible decision to reduce the capacity for the final (hence the lower attendance than for the semis) to enable the stadium to be policed more effectively given all the warning signs of trouble.

This was the final everyone wanted; a final between two teams and two nations with a rivalry so intense it spilled way beyond the pitch. Uruguay taking on their bigger neighbours was Scotland versus England, New Zealand versus Australia, Hungary versus the Soviet Union in the fifties, it was David against Goliath, the oppressed against the evil empire.

Both sides had cause to be optimistic. Argentina had the more skilful players, great dribblers and artists, and they also had Monti, who not only struck fear into opposing attackers but was also one of the best passers of the ball in the game. Uruguay had their teamwork and their pride, their fierce will-to-win, and their memory of beating the same opponents in the Olympic Final in 1928. There is a word, *garra*, that is meant to encapsulate the Uruguayan pride in their footballing prowess. It has been over-used and ascribed too much mystique, but it's a good word – aggression, pride and guts all rolled into one with a smidgen of nationalism thrown in. Uruguay also had a superb back line, marshalled by the durable Nasazzi, and an excellent defensive half-back line in front; the only conspicuous weakness was in goal, where they missed Andrés Mazali, left out of the squad after a night on the tiles and an "assignation" in defiance of his manager. Ballestrero was okay, but Mazali was the best in the world.

They would need their *garra*, would Uruguay. They scored first; Castro, back in for the unfortunate Anselmo, set up Dorado for a cross shot past the exposed Botasso. Dorado was by pref-erence a left-winger, but Suppici picked him on the right after a hesitant performance by the regular Urdinarán in the first group game. Despite the early goal Uruguay failed to settle and estab-lish the neat interpassing for which they were known, and which had destroyed Yugoslavia in the semi-final. They gave Argentina too much space and Peucelle and Ferreira started to run at them. When Ferreira slipped a pass between Nasazzi and Gestido for the winger, Peucelle cut back outside Gestido and beat Ballestrero at his near post – he should have stopped it. A rare error from Nasazzi gave Argentina a second when the Uruguay skipper allowed a long ball from Monti to drop behind him – Stábile was lurking and scored. Half-time came with Argentina leading 2–1.

The second half could not have been a starker contrast. Andrade sat a little deeper and the other two half-backs moved further forward, Fernandez to deny Monti the room to spray his long passes. The forwards started threading those little passes between them, and the momentum of the game changed. Uruguay looked more determined and more purposeful, self-belief had been restored. Before the hour, Cea equalised after Scarone clev-erly helped on a free-kick. Ten minutes later Iriarte was put in after a strong run by Mascheroni from the left-back position; Botasso should have done better with the winger's scuffed strike.

Argentina rallied and Stábile came close, but a late, slightly fortuitous, header from Castro sealed the result. An Italian journalist described the teams as "ants" (Uruguay) and "cicadas" (Argentina) – colour and music succumbing to endeavour and spirit. Quaint and a little over-simplified, but essentially accurate.

The anticipated trouble came after the match, mostly in Buenos Aires, where nationalist mobs stoned the Uruguayan consulate and gangs roamed the streets burning anything they didn't like. Apparently this new trophy was important.

> *On the fields of Buenos Aires and Montevideo a style was born. A home-grown way of playing football, like the home-grown way of dancing which was being invented in the milonga clubs. Dancers drew filigrees on a single floor tile, and football players created their own language in that tiny space where they chose to retain and possess the ball rather than kick it, as if their feet were hands braiding the leather.*
>
> Eduardo Galeano: *Football in Sun and Shadow, 1997*

World Cup Heroes No.1

José Leandro Andrade (1901–57)

Uruguay

During the 1924 Olympic Football tournament, won by Uruguay, one player stood out among the general excellence of the Uruguayan side; half-back José Andrade, one of the few black men holding down a place in a South American national side.

Andrade was tall, rangy and powerful (think Patrick Vieira) and could break down opposition moves and launch attacks with equal aplomb. With the uncompromising José Nasazzi behind him, Andrade enjoyed licence to roam forward – his game was about striding runs rather than sprayed passes – and cause havoc in the opposition half.

Andrade started with the smaller Montevideo club before spells with Nacional (where he played for most of his peak years) and Peñarol. He won four Uruguayan championships with Nacional. At international level he broke into the side and made his mark at the Paris Olympics; stories exist of Andrade roaming the fashionably seedy streets of Pigalle after the tournament dressed in top hat and silks, enjoying the respect accorded to the Negro Merveille, as the French press dubbed him (it stuck).

Andrade won another Olympic medal in 1928, three Copa América championships and the 1930 World Cup – a fine return for only thirty-four caps. Never much of a goalscorer (one for Uruguay) he was more of an enabler for the talented Uruguayan front line, especially his club colleague at Nacional, the prolific inside-forward Héctor Scarone.

Andrade was a guest of the Uruguayan authorities at the 1950 World Cup Final, where his nephew, Victor Rodriguez, played in the winning side. A plaque was created in his honour at the Estadio Nacional. After that he fell off the radar until a German journalist tracked him down living in poverty in Montevideo; he died of tuberculosis a year later, an unfitting end for a national hero, the first great black international player.

1930 Team of the Tournament: 2–3–5

Thépot (France)

Nasazzi (Uruguay)   Ivkovic (Yugoslavia)

Andrade (Uruguay)   Monti (Argentina)   Tracy (USA)

Peucelle (Argentina)   Ferreira (Argentina)   Stábile (Argentina)   Cea (Uruguay)   Iriarte (Uruguay)

Leading scorers: Stábile (8); Cea (5); Patenaude (4)

The official team (chosen retrospectively) was: Ballestrero (Uruguay); Nasazzi (Uruguay), Ivkovic (Yugoslavia); Gestido (Uruguay), Monti (Argentina), Andrade (Uruguay); Cea (Uruguay), Stábile (Argentina), Scarone (Uruguay), Castro (Uruguay), Patenaude (USA).

1.2 FOOTBALL AT THE OLYMPICS

The Olympics was for a time the unofficial world championship of football, but the World Cup changed all that. By the time football resumed after the war, professionalism was so well established that the amateur game had become a sideshow and the Olympic football tournament followed suit – a display of shamateurism by the Eastern bloc countries used to boost their self-esteem and provide propaganda; their displays during the same period in the World Cup expose the truth beneath the sheen. The exception was the 1952 Hungarian side, which featured all the big names that helped them reach the final of the World Cup two years later. Hungary twice won the Olympic tournament in the 1960s, but made less impact on the World Cup, a terrific win over Brazil in 1966 aside.

From 1974, professionals were allowed to compete, but the stronger nations were not allowed to pick players who had already played in a World Cup; in 1984 the tournament adopted the current method of making the Olympics an Under-23 tournament, although the inclusion of three over-age stars renders this nonsensical. Either make it a proper youth tournament or forget it – Olympic boxing doesn't suffer from excluding all the big names, on the contrary, it is a far more edifying spectacle than the over-hyped professional bills.

A strong feeling remains that football, such a global money-spinner already and so in thrall to the suits and sunglasses fraternity, has no place in the Olympic Games at all – not that the Olympics is a bastion of honesty and fair play, but because it is an opportunity for sportspeople who get less everyday acclaim (and less money) to shine. It is also the competition that provides those athletes with an opportunity to achieve the Holy Grail of their sport; no one remembers the winners of the world championships in athletics, swimming, cycling, rowing or badminton. The same (very valid) objection is raised to the presence of tennis and golf at the games.

The 2012 London Games was a case in point. It was largely agreed the Games were a triumph; well organised with good facilities, good competition and lots of lovely medals for the home team. But the football? Who cared? Certainly not the public, who stayed away from all but the Team GB matches. The men's tournament was a non-event, and the sight of Luis Suárez at an event that celebrates the inclusiveness and Corinthian ideals of sport stuck in the craw. At least it produced a surprise winner in Mexico, and two African sides (Nigeria and Cameroon) have lifted the Olympic trophy, so perhaps the nature of the competition levels out the standard and provides an opportunity for teams other than the usual suspects to win. But Mexico won't win the World Cup anytime soon, and nor will an African side, so the tournament is nowhere near the pinnacle of the sport, which is the intention of the Olympic Games.

At this point I should defend the presence of women's football at the Games; the women's game is starved of publicity in the main, and, if it became the primary focus for those who want to watch Olympic football, it would do the women's game much good. And they play the game, in the main, in a far better spirit than their male counterparts.

The tournaments and winners:

Paris 1900 – Upton Park FC, representing the UK, in what was a demonstration sport later upgraded in status.

St Louis 1904 – Galt FC for Canada; this now-defunct Canadian side played only two matches, beating two US collegiate teams.

London 1908 & **Stockholm 1912** – Great Britain, who beat Denmark in the final on both occasions. The team captain was

Vivian Woodward, England's first great centre-forward and scorer of twenty-nine goals in twenty-three full internationals.

Antwerp 1920 – Belgium. The final was a stormy affair, with the English referee, John Lewis, accused of partisanship by the Czechs, who walked off the field when Lewis dismissed Karel Steiner, with the score at 2–0 to Belgium – the Czechs having protested about both goals. Belgian soldiers promptly led a pitch invasion to ensure the game could not restart, but the Czechs' protests were ignored and they were ejected from the tournament and given no medals.

Paris 1924 and **Amsterdam 1928** – Uruguay won both these unofficial world championships, beating Switzerland in 1924 and Argentina in 1928. In 1924 the Uruguayans had to battle through a tough semi against Holland, who protested furiously about the late penalty that clinched the game. The 1924 Uruguay side featured Nasazzi, Andrade, Scarone and Cea of the 1930 World Cup Final winning team, while Fernandez and Gestido from that team also played in the 1928 Olympic Final.

Los Angeles 1932 – No football, please, we're American . . .

Berlin 1936 – Italy. Germany were expected to do well under Hitler's gaze, but they lost 2–0 to Norway in the quarter-final in what is believed to have been the only match Hitler actually attended in person. The final was played out between two other states in the grip of fascism as Italy beat the last knockings of the Austrian Wunderteam 2–1. Both goals were scored by Annibale Frossi, later a notable coach. GB's participation ended with a 5–4 defeat by Poland; two of England's goals were scored by Bernard Joy, who also won a full cap that year, the last amateur to do so.

London 1948 – Sweden. A fast and efficient Sweden team beat Yugoslavia 3–1 in the final. The key to the side was the talented trio of Gunnar Nordahl, Gunnar Gren and Nils Liedholm – all were bought by AC Milan the following year, and all were still around for the 1958 World Cup Final, albeit a tad heavier in the legs. GB's amateur side did well to make the semi-finals.

Helsinki 1952 – Hungary. The Magyars were the best team in Europe and won easily under the pretence that their big names were amateurs playing for the army team – one suspects Puskás, Grosics, Bozsik and the like did relatively few kitchen chores or forty-mile slogs with full pack.

Melbourne 1956 – The Soviet Union beat Yugoslavia, runners-up for the third successive games, in the final at the end of a drab tournament. It was the only major international medal won by the great Soviet goalkeeper Lev Yashin.

1960–1980 (Rome, Tokyo, Mexico City, Munich, Montreal, Moscow). For these two decades the teams from behind the Iron Curtain dominated. After Yugoslavia finally won the thing in 1960 (beating Denmark), every finalist was part of the Soviet bloc. Hungary won in 1964 and again in 1968, Poland in 1972 (with much of the team that would eliminate England from the 1974 World Cup qualifying group and go on to reach the semi-finals), East Germany in 1976 and Czechoslovakia in 1980.

Los Angeles 1984 – France. The gold medal finally left Eastern Europe when France beat a youthful Brazilian side that included future World Cup captain Dunga.

Seoul 1988 – Soviet Union. An altogether more impressive Soviet win, with a young side that included Dmitri Kharin (later of Chelsea) in goal; they came from behind to beat a Brazil team that included Taffarel, Jorginho, Bebeto and Romário, all World Cup winners six years later.

Barcelona 1992 – Spain won on their own patch, beating Poland 3–2 with a last-minute winner from Kiko. A side that included Abelardo, Guardiola and Luis Enrique suggested Spain were a coming force – in the end it was the next generation of youngsters who delivered, not this class.

Atlanta 1996 – Nigeria. Nigeria became the first African winners in the most exciting of the modern tournaments. In the semi-final they beat Brazil in a minor classic after Kanu equalised in the dying seconds of ordinary time to make it 3–3 and scored a decisive Golden Goal four minutes later. In the final they left it until the last minute again, Emmanuel Amunike's goal seeing off Argentina 3–2. The squad included Kanu, Amokachi, Okocha, Taribo West and Babayaro, all of whom would become familiar to Premier League audiences in years to come.

Sydney 2000 – Cameroon. Favourites Brazil, who included the prodigy Ronaldinho in their squad, again succumbed to a Golden Goal from an African side, this time nine-man Cameroon at the quarter-final stage. In the final Cameroon went 2–0 down to Spain but fought back to draw 2–2 and win on penalties as Spain imploded, finishing the game with nine men.

Athens 2004 – Argentina. An all-South American final was settled by a goal from Carlos Tévez, the tournament's dominant player and not yet the tool of marketing men and trouble magnet of later years.

Beijing 2008 – Argentina. Argentina won again, beating Nigeria 1–0 in the final with a goal from Angel Di Maria, now of Real Madrid. Hardly surprising given their squad also included the divine Messi, with Riquelme and Mascherano as over-age players.

London 2012 – Mexico. After much agonising, GB put together a squad in the face of objections from the FAs other than England; in the event the squad was English and Welsh, with Ryan Giggs made captain, a well-deserved accolade towards the end of a career that had embraced much frustration at international level. They went out (on penalties, of course!) to South Korea. In the final a brace from Oribe Peralta surprised a Brazilian side including Hulk, Neymar, Oscar and Thiago Silva.

1.3 WORLD CUP 1934

The 1934 tournament, like most events in Europe in the 1930s, had an uncomfortable backdrop, with the competition held in Italy, a country run by a fascist dictator. Before we get too carried away with all the "shadows over Europe" stuff, let's also remember that the average football fan didn't give two hoots about the political climate, just as the modern football fan's primary concerns on a Saturday afternoon aren't potential conflagration in the Middle East or nuclear posturing by North Korea. Characters like Mussolini and Hitler thrived in the first place because of the indifference of the bulk of the population to the bigger picture.

Italy was a divided country (still is), the prosperous north in sharp contrast with the agricultural peasant south, and most of the games were played in the north, with just a couple in Naples. While it would be an exaggeration to suggest war was "in the air" by 1934, there was an ominous shift in mood in Europe discernible to the well-read or interested. Tough financial times demand scapegoats, and foreigners and immigrants and minorities were the obvious target – aren't they always? Already, dissident voices in Europe's fascist states and the Soviet Union were being quietly removed from whatever office or position they held. It would be years before western Europe cottoned on to the Nazis' game; many in Britain positively approved of Hitler, including numerous members of the aristocracy and elements in the government.

Not that Mussolini was yet in Hitler's pocket; he had come to power almost a decade earlier, and provided a model for the

1934
ITALY

Eight cities and eight stadia were used to stage the 1930 tournament in Italy.

Rome: Stadio Nazionale del PNF
The stadium that hosted the 1934 final was built seven years previously as a showpiece for the Italian fascist party. Roma and Lazio both used the ground before transferring to the more modern Stadio Olimpico in 1953, when the SNPNF was demolished and replaced with a multi-sports facility, the Stadio Flaminio, home of the Italian rugby union side from 2000–2011.

Milan: Stadio San Siro
Now officially called the Stadio Giuseppe Meazza, after one of the stars of the 1934 tournament, the San Siro is home to both the great Milan clubs, AC Milan and Internazionale. It holds just over 80,000, having peaked at 100,000 in the mid-fifties.

Naples: Stadio Giorgio Ascarelli
This 40,000 capacity stadium was destroyed during the Second World War. It was the home of Napoli until the club moved to the Arturo Collana and later, in 1959, to the club's current home, the Stadio San Paolo.

Florence: Stadio Giovanni Berta (*aka Comunale*)
The Comunale is still the home of Fiorentina, the city's principal club, although it now carries the official name of the Stadio Artemio Franchi. It once held nearly 60,000, but the current all-seater capacity is 47,290.

Genoa: Stadio Luigi Ferraris
Home at the time to Genoa, the Luigi Ferraris now also plays home to Sampdoria, which has superseded Genoa as the city's most successful club. It held around 30,000 for the 1934 World Cup and now holds 37,000 – the record attendance coming from the post-war years when a reported 60,000 squeezed inside (which is slightly scary as this is not a big ground).

Bologna: Stadio Littoriale
This was a host stadium in two World Cups, and also saw San Marino score against England inside a minute in 1993. The stadium, home to Bologna, holds just over 38,000 and was opened in 1927; it now goes by the name of the Stadio Renato Dall'Ara.

Turin: Stadio Benito Mussolini
It was inevitable that one of the stadia at this tournament would carry Mussolini's name. This particular ground would play host to Torino and Juventus up to 1989–90 when the teams moved to a new stadium (Stadio delle Alpi) built for the 1990 World Cup. In 2006 Torino subsequently moved back into the old stadium, now called the Stadio Olimpico Torino (it was redesigned for the 2006 winter Olympics held in the city). The ground now holds slightly less than 30,000.

Trieste: Stadio Littorio
A new stadium, opened in 1932, the Littorio hosted only one match in the 1934 tournament. It was much the smallest of the grounds used, with a capacity of only 8,000. Trieste had been a top-flight side pre-war, but the club has declined since relegation in the fifties, and the city is now better known as a centre for rugby union.

Munich putsch that brought the German Chancellor to power. The Italian leader regarded Hitler's victory as a triumph for fascism, but there was little personal regard between the two – a meeting shortly after the end of the 1934 World Cup went very badly. For now, 1934, and this World Cup, Mussolini wore the long trousers, and this was a chance for him to show the world that Italian culture and manhood was once again pre-eminent.

Fascism aside, Italy was a sensible choice of host. They had a good team and a number of decent, modern stadia, including the 1927 Stadio Nazionale PNF (National Fascist Party), a 50,000 capacity purpose-built national stadium. Other than Rome and Naples, six Italian cities hosted matches during the tournament: Milan, Trieste, Genoa, Florence, Bologna and Turin. Apart from the Stadio Giorgio Ascarelli in Naples, which was flattened during the Second World War, all the stadia (or the sites on which they stood) are still in use, with obvious refurbishments. The PNF was demolished in 1953 when work started on the new Olympic stadium, and was replaced with the Stadio Flaminio, which became Italy's premier rugby union venue when they joined the Six Nations in 2000.

For the first time there was a qualifying tournament, but it was more a winnowing exercise than a serious test for the major players; even Italy, the hosts, were asked to play an eliminator, but Greece were still footballing novices and easily dispatched. There was another change to the format used in 1930, as groups were dispensed with, and the competition was conducted as a straight knockout, with eight seeded teams kept apart in the first round. In every round the matches kicked off simultaneously in different cities – not sure the world's TV channels would approve of that in the modern era . . .

The tournament would feature a larger proportion of the top sides than in 1930, although, sadly, Uruguay could not be persuaded to make the trip to defend their title, perhaps because they knew their team was on the wane, but more likely in pique at the absence of the best European sides in 1930. The British sides all stayed away – the associations were run by prickly and pompous officials who didn't like anyone else running the party. The eight seeded teams included the favourites, Italy and Austria. Austria had been one of the best teams around for the last few

years and had beaten Italy only months before. Under their
revered coach Hugo Meisl, they had adopted the "Scottish
method" of slick, quick interchanging passes rather than long
balls out to the wingers. It was a method favoured by most Central
European sides, and Austria's "Wunderteam" had perfected it.
Their fear was that the team was slightly past its best. The other
seeds were Czechoslovakia and Hungary, who also favoured the
passing game, Argentina, Germany (for no obvious reason),
Brazil and Holland (also for no obvious reason).

There was a bizarre preamble to the tournament three days
before the opening match when FIFA arranged a play-off for the
last place in the Finals to be staged at the Nazionale del PNF – a
surprising choice of venue as the participants were Mexico and
the United States. Mexico were peeved, and had every right to be,
as the USA entry was late and Mexico believed they had already
qualified by beating Cuba. The USA won 4–2, all four goals
scored by Aldo Donelli under the gaze of Mussolini. *Il Duce*
would have been pleased – an American proving the prowess of
Italian bloodstock.

FIRST ROUND (both games 27 May)

Germany	(1) 5	**Belgium**	(2) 2	Comunale, Florence; 8,000
Kobierski 28, Siffling 47,		Voorhoof 32, 44		
Conen 67, 70, 86				
Sweden	(1) 3	**Argentina**	(1) 2	Littoriale, Bologna; 19,000
Jonasson 9, 67, Kroon 80		Belis 3, Galateo 50		

SECOND ROUND (31 May)

Germany	(0) 2	**Sweden**	(0) 1	San Siro, Milan; 16,000

In modern times it's a surprise if the business end of the tournament doesn't feature the Germans, but in 1934 little was
expected of them. The Italian press described them as no-hopers
and they came into the tournament with very little form – including two recent defeats by 5–0 and 6–0 to neighbouring Austria –
and a ton of political pressure.

Germany's best club side Schalke 04 were excellent, a club
version of the Austrian Wunderteam, even aping the Austrians'
intricate passing in a style the German press labelled the spinning

top. Unfortunately for the national team, head coach Otto Nerz was an admirer of the fast-paced and aggressive English style, and was suspicious of the Schalke artistry. He deployed his (and their) best player, the Polish-born Fritz Szepan, in a defensive centre-half position, rather than as a ball-playing inside-forward, and he ignored another talented forward Ernst Kuzorra altogether. Despite these tactical shortcomings the Germans had enough attacking clout to recover from a first-half runaround against Belgium and win 5–2. They then outmuscled Sweden 2–1 in a dull affair, Hohmann scoring twice while Sweden's physio attended to two of his players after a clash of heads. Hohmann himself was injured in the game and missed the semi-final against Czechoslovakia.

Sweden reached the second round as an unseeded team, knocking out the finalists from four years earlier, Argentina. The South Americans were in the midst of a domestic row over professionalism and sent over an amateur team. They scored two spectacular goals, one an outstanding individual effort by Galateo, but were woeful at the back and conceded three to an average Swedish outfit. The match heralded a period of international isolation for Argentina, at least so far as playing outside South America went – it was the 1958 tournament before they entered a team again.

FIRST ROUND (both games 27 May)

Czechoslovakia	(0) 2	**Romania**	(1) 1	Littorio, Trieste; 8,000
Puc 48, Nejedly 65		Dobay 11		
Switzerland	(2) 3	**Holland**	(1) 2	San Siro, Milan; 35,000
Kileholz 6, 43,		Smit 29, Vente 69		
Abegglen 66				

SECOND ROUND (31 May)

Czechoslovakia	(1) 3	**Switzerland**	(1) 2	Benito Mussolini, Turin; 9,000
Svoboda 23, Sobotka 49,		Kielholz 18, Jäggi 80		
Nejedly 83				

Germany's semi-final opponents were Czechoslovakia. They were fortunate to win their first game against Romania, who led 1–0 at half-time but succumbed to goals from left-winger Antonin Puc and a disputed winner from playmaker Nejedly, scored while Romania had an injured player writhing in agony. With Svoboda replacing Silny for the next game, Czechoslovakia fielded an XI made up entirely of players from the two dominant Prague clubs, Slavia Prague and Sparta Prague. They were only just good enough against an improving Swiss team. The Swiss had beaten Holland 3–2 in their first match, an attacking encounter with chances galore. Against the Czechs, it was their opponents who got the odd goal in five. Switzerland took the lead and then found enough spirit for an eightieth-minute equaliser after Czechoslovakia came back. Three minutes later Nejedly found the net again and it was over.

FIRST ROUND (both games 27 May)

Austria	(1) (1) 3	**France**	(1) (1) 2	Benito Mussolini, Turin; 15,000	
Sindelar 44, Schall 93,		Nicolas 18,			
Bican 109		Verriest 115 (p)			
Hungary	(2) 4	**Egypt**	(2) 2	Giorgio Ascarelli, Naples; 8,000	
Teleki 11, Toldi 31, 61,		Fawzi 39, 43			
Vincze 54					

SECOND ROUND (31 May)

Austria	(1) 2	**Hungary**	(0) 1	Littoriale, Bologna; 14,000
Horvath 5, Zischek 51		Sárosi 62 (p)		

The first World Cup match to need extra-time featured one of the favourites, Austria. France, with Alex Thépot still in goal (and now captain), caused Das Wunderteam much anxiety, taking the lead after eighteen minutes and holding out with ten able men for all the second half after goalscorer Jean Nicolas took a bash to the head. Austria equalised just before time through Matthias Sindelar (more of him anon) and took control in extra-time – but France had gone out with credit again. Which is more than can be said for Hungary, who exchanged more blows than passes in their second-round match against Austria. The two countries, once part of a great empire, were clearly not so friendly now. Hungary had let a two-goal lead slip against Egypt, the first African side to compete in the finals, before winning 4–2, and they showed the same frailty here, conceding after five minutes and having a man sent off just after reducing Austria's lead. Austria were through to a semi-final against Italy but looked less than imperious.

FIRST ROUND (both games 27 May)

Spain   (3) 3   **Brazil**   (0) 1   Luigi Ferraris, Genoa; 30,000
Iraragorri 17 (p),   Leônidas 52
Lángara 23, 28
Italy   (3) 7   **USA**   (0) 1   Nazionale PNF, Rome; 25,000
Schiavio 18, 29, 64,   Donelli 57
Orsi 20, 69, Ferrari 63,
Meazza 90

SECOND ROUND (both games 31 May)

Italy   (1) (1) 1   **Spain**   (1) (1) 1   Comunale, Florence; 40,000
Ferrari 45   Regueiro 31
Replay:
Italy   (1) 1   **Spain**   (0) 0   Comunale, Florence; 40,000
Meazza 11

Italy themselves had arrived by a fortuitous route. In the first
round the USA got their come-uppance for their cheeky gate-
crashing trick; Donelli scored again but the Italians scored
seven in reply. I say Italians – they fielded five players who were
born in South America, four previously capped by Argentina
and one by Brazil. Raimundo Orsi, an Argentinian winger, got
two of Italy's goals against the USA, while the experienced
Bologna striker Angelo Schiavio scored a hat-trick. The five
imports included the monstrous Luis Monti, already a World
Cup winner and back once more to terrorise opponents, this
time with the might of a fascist state behind him. This flagrant
use of *oriundi* (immigrants, loosely) was a deliberate policy of
the Italian manager Vittorio Pozzo. One can hardly blame
Pozzo for using any means at his disposal to win (and he did
just that) – the political pressure on him to succeed was
immense. Brian Glanville argues strongly that Pozzo was not a
fascist – and there is evidence, cited in John Foot's *Calcio*, that
he aided the anti-fascist resistance during the war. A number of
former supporters of Mussolini turned against the fascists
when they allied with Hitler, and Pozzo served Mussolini's
regime willingly enough and instructed his team to make the
traditional fascist salute during the national anthem. Support
need not always be enthusiastic and vocal; it can be enough to
accept the yoke.

The second-round match against Spain needed a replay to
decide it. Both teams knew the other had a penchant for

rough-housing and both decided they would get their retaliation in first. A weak referee allowed a free-for-all, and the game ended 1–1, but at cost to both sides. It was Spain who suffered most, losing their brilliant and courageous goalkeeper Zamora for the replay after being targeted by the Italians.

Italy made changes for the hastily arranged replay, and an even weaker referee meant another bruising encounter. Italy's outstanding player, the inside-forward Giuseppe Meazza of Milan, scored the only goal from a corner. It was unedifying stuff.

South American interest ended in the first round. Brazil were a collection of talented individuals rather than a team and it showed against Spain, whose best player and captain Ricardo Zamora saved a penalty in their comfortable 3–1 win. The match saw the World Cup debut of Leônidas, an exciting Brazilian forward and their only black player in 1934. Short for a forward, but supple and fast, he showed glimpses of what was to come four years later.

SEMI-FINALS

Italy Guaita 20	**(1) 1**	**Austria**	**(0) 0**	3 June, San Siro, Milan; 45,000
Czechoslovakia Nejedly 21, 69, 80	**(1) 3**	**Germany** Noack 59	**(0) 1**	3 June, Naz PNF, Rome; 13,000

THIRD-PLACE MATCH[*]

Germany Lehner 1, 43, Conen 29	**(3) 3**	**Austria** Horvath 30, Sesta 55	**(1) 2**	7 June, Naples; 7,000

Legend has it that Mussolini issued an edict to the Italian team that they must "*win or die*". The story has no provenance, and if

---

[*] This was the first time this meaningless fixture had taken place. Forcing beaten semi-finalists to drag themselves out once again has always seemed like a peculiar form of torture to me, and most teams nowadays devalue the event further by giving a game to squad players who haven't featured in the tournament, affording it the intensity of a friendly match. The match had begun in farce when both sides declined to use a change strip and the game started with two teams in white shirts and black shorts. This first game was a familiar rivalry that was about to turn that bit more sour.

it was said it was probably half in jest; Il Duce was not a man without colour or humour. Luis Monti jested later in life that if he had won the 1930 World Cup the Uruguayans would have had him killed, and if he hadn't won the 1934 World Cup the Italians would have done the same. Whatever the reason there was desperation about Italy in the semi-final game that bordered on psychotic.

The Austrian game was built on possession and neat, intricate passing. The fulcrum was a deep-lying centre-forward (long before Hungary's Hidegkuti "invented" the position) called Matthias Sindelar. Seemingly insubstantial in build, Sindelar was known as *Der Papierene* (*The Paper Man*) by elements of the press, but he was sinewy and deceptively strong, and a good finisher as well as creator. Italy's strategy for nullifying Austria was simple – Sindelar was "Montied", the bruising presence of the former Argentinian centre-half totally negating the Austrian playmaker. It worked. The Italians scored the game's solitary goal after twenty minutes when the other Argentinian winger, Enrique Guaita, netted amid a goalmouth scramble during which the referee ignored the Italians' deliberate baulking of the goalkeeper. Austria hit the woodwork and had a couple of half-chances but Monti and Co kept them largely at arm's length. Austrian striker Bican's claim that the referee for the semi-final headed his pass to an Italian player should be taken with a pinch of salt. For all their thuggery and the compliance of the officials, Italy deserve much credit for their stamina and resolve; this was their third match in five days and the three and a half hours against Spain had been gruelling, physical encounters.

In the other semi-final the possession game held sway as Czechoslovakia beat Germany 3–1. Oldřich Nejedly opened the scoring, but Germany equalised after a rare goalkeeping error from Czech captain Plánicka. Nejedly, a match-winning inside-forward like Sindelar, had no Monti marking him and was in irresistible form, completing his hat-trick with a brace of firm headers. German goalkeeper Willi Kress carried the can for the result at home, but the better side won the day. They came within ten minutes of doing so again a week later.

WORLD CUP FINAL No.2
10 June 1934, Nazionale del PNF, Rome; 50,000

Italy	(0) (1) 2	Orsi 81, Schiavio 95
Czechoslovakia	(0) (1) 1	Puc 71

Referee: **Ivan Eklind** (Sweden)
Coaches: **Vittorio Pozzo** (Italy) & **Karel Petru** (Czechoslovakia)

Italy (2–3–5): Gianpiero Combi (Juventus); Eraldo Monzeglio (Bologna), Luigi Allemandi (Inter*); Attilio Ferraris (Roma), Luis Monti (Juventus), Luigi Bertolini (Juventus); Enrique Guaita (Roma), Giuseppe Meazza (Inter), Angelo Schiavio (Bologna), Giovanni Ferrari (Juventus), Raimundo Orsi (Juventus)

Czechoslovakia (2–3–2–3): Frantisek Plánicka (Slavia Prague); Ladislav Zenísek (Slavia), Josef Ctyroky (Sparta Prague); Josef Kostálek (Sparta), Stefan Cambal (Slavia), Rudolf Krcil (Slavia); Frantisek Svoboda (Slavia), Oldřich Nejedly (Sparta); Frank Junek (Slavia), Jiri Sobotka (Slavia), Antonín Puc (Slavia)

If Italy were favourites in the final, then it wasn't by much. After a sluggish start Czechoslovakia had warmed to their task, and in Nejedly had a creative and potent player at the peak of his game. Karel Petru, the coach, had the guts to drop all-time leading scorer Josef Silny after the first game and the team, made up entirely of players from two Prague clubs, responded positively. Silny, who played his club football for Nimes in France, was never picked again. The stars of the side were Nejedly, Plánicka, the captain – this was the only final with two goalkeeper-captains – and the goalscoring left-winger Puc, but they were solid throughout with a great mutual understanding.

Pozzo had also dropped an experienced player, Virginio Rosetta, the captain for the first match against the USA. Like Silny, he too had played his last international match. Pozzo liked defenders and half-backs that just defended; he had Monti to distribute the ball from the back, two fast wingers in the *oriundi* Guaita and Orsi, and a centre-forward in Schiavio who was not averse to getting in where it hurts and dishing out a bit of rough stuff. Inter's Giuseppe Meazza provided any tricks that were

* At the time Internazionale's official name was AS Ambrosiana-Inter. At the insistence of their new President in 1929, the club changed its name to AS Ambrosiana, after the patron Saint of Milan. Two years later, after various protests from fans, the new compromise name was reached. The modern name of FC Internazionale Milano has been used since the Second World War. To supporters and pundits, the team has always been Inter.

required, but this side was not about the beautiful game, just winning.

Both sides had bags of experience – there were only five players under twenty-five on the pitch – and the game was cagey, no one prepared to take a chance and make a critical risk. Italy relied on long balls into the penalty area, but Plánicka ate those up, and for all their neatness the Czechs were struggling to get a sight of the target.

The first goal came when the match seemed to be drifting inevitably towards extra-time. Antonin Puc stole in from the left wing to take a clever pass inside his full-back and beat a badly positioned goalkeeper from a tricky angle. Reports state Puc was off the field for treatment only a minute or two before he scored; perhaps the rest did him good. Czechoslovakia should have won after that but they missed two or three chances, the best when Sobotka hit the post after a mazy run. Nejedly, not as effective as against Germany, escaped Monti for once and hit a drive that skimmed the bar. They proved costly errors when Orsi, quiet for most of the game, shimmied inside and curled a shot beyond Plánicka. Italy had equalised against the run of play.

Now it was the Czechs who looked short of ideas, and the game was settled five minutes into extra-time. Cris Freddi claims it was a gambit of Pozzo's to switch Schiavio and Guaita, but I would suggest it was just a coincidence that it was Guaita in a central position who found his centre-forward to his right with a simple pass. Schiavio's finish was firm and final.

Il Duce had the result he wanted and he beamed broadly as he handed the trophy to Combi. Pozzo was a hero to those who cared about such things, but not all of Italy bought into football as a symbol of fascist pride, and there were empty seats even for the final. The tournament itself was well organised, and suggestions of pressured officials have never been proved nor convincingly denied. And Italian football does have some serious form in that regard. The football was largely uninspired, and too many matches were settled by one team proving they were more macho than the other. Italy's defence was the key – they shut out both Spain and Austria while no other side kept a clean sheet.

The two sides that might have matched them physically, Uruguay and England, weren't there. Later in the year England took on the world champions in a game that was dubbed The Battle of Highbury, when hostilities broke out after a nasty tackle on Monti that left the destroyer a limping passenger on the right wing – now that does have a hint of irony. England were three-up after twelve minutes but were left hanging on after Meazza scored twice in the second half. A number of England players needed treatment as Monti's colleagues exacted revenge for his incapacity. Nothing was conclusively proved, although the English press thought otherwise.

World Cup Heroes No.2

Luisito Monti (1901–83)

Argentina & Italy

Luis Monti made his debut for Argentina in 1924 after a successful couple of seasons with the San Lorenzo club. He waited three more years for his next game, but rapidly became a fixture in the Argentina side, and by the time of the 1930 World Cup he was the pivot of the team, a combined ball-winner and playmaker in the centre of the pitch.

Monti was born and bred within the large Italian community in Buenos Aires and he was an obvious target for the wealthy Italian clubs; a move to Juventus in 1931 was hardly surprising, especially as he had been vilified by the Argentinian press after their failure to win the 1930 World Cup Final.

Monti was an immediate success as Juventus won the *Scudetto* (Italian league title) in his first season. The move had mutual benefits, too, as the game in Italy was physically more demanding and the club took steps to address Monti's weight and made him a slimmer, fitter player. Vittorio Pozzo had no hesitation in introducing him to the national side and he was a major factor in their 1934 victory, especially

---

against Austria when he negated Sindelar; that he was treated leniently by referees in the tournament seems to be accepted, but football was a far rougher game in the 1930s.

To describe Monti as a hero, given his disruptive role and menacing demeanour, is stretching a point, but he was a colossal figure in the first two tournaments, and he remains the only player to appear in two World Cup Finals for different teams, a record that will remain unchallenged unless there is a bizarre change in FIFA's thinking.

Monti went into management on his retirement – he briefly managed Juve during the war – but he enjoyed little success and dropped out of football altogether.

1934 Team of the Tournament: 2–3–5

Plánicka (Czechoslovakia)

Monzeglio (Italy)   Allemandi (Italy)

Szepan (Germany)   Monti (Italy)   Bertolini (Italy)

Orsi (Italy)   Meazza (Italy)   Schiavio (Ita)   Nejedly (Czechoslovakia)   Puc* (Czechoslovakia)

Leading scorers: Nejedly (5); Conen & Schiavio (4)

The official team (chosen retrospectively): Zamora (Spain); Monzeglio (Italy), Quincoces (Spain); Monti (Italy), Ferraris (Italy), Cilauren (Spain); Orsi (Italy), Meazza (Italy), Sindelar (Austria), Nejedly (Czechoslovakia), Guaita (Italy)

* Puc remains Czechoslovakia's all-time leading scorer with thirty-four goals in sixty games; Nejedly and Silny lie joint-third. Jan Koller and Milan Baros have both scored more for the Czech Republic, but both played over ninety games.

1.4 ORIUNDI

Until the last forty years, FIFA's rules about playing for one's country were pretty lax. This presented an exceptional opportunity for the Mediterranean countries (largely Italy and Spain, but also Portugal) to exploit their large expat communities in South America and poach some of the talented players from that continent. In 1934 Italy proved particularly adept, their winning team in the final using not only Luis Monti but also two Argentinian wingers; earlier in the tournament a former Brazilian international, Guarisi (known by a shortening of his first name as Filó in Brazil), had played for them at inside-forward.

This practice continued right through the post-war years; Alfredo Di Stéfano, the great Argentinian, came to play with Real Madrid and helped them dominate the early years of the European Cup, winning caps for the Spanish international team. Omar Sivori, another Argentinian, was a maverick presence for Italy at the start of the 1960s. The great Ferenc Puskás, after eighty-five caps for Hungary, played four times for Spain in his mid-thirties as he sought sanctuary there after the Russian occupation of his home country. His countryman László Kubala went one better; born in Hungary but brought up in Czechoslovakia, he appeared first for his country of upbringing, then for Hungary and lastly for Spain after the same self-imposed exile as Puskás.

The *oriundi* were invariably viewed as traitors by the nation they "deserted": it was a no-win situation, as their adopted country usually viewed them with suspicion as well. After the debacle of their exit from the 1962 World Cup, the Italian press rounded on the supposed meagre contribution of the imported players in their team. FIFA changed the rules soon after, and the *oriundi* en masse (forgive the mixture of languages) were a thing of the past. The biggest loser was José Altafini; he appeared in the 1958 World Cup for Brazil as Mazzola and in the 1962 tournament for Italy, but now he was an international pariah at twenty-four years old.

Even after FIFA insisted that players make a definitive choice before committing to a full international game, there have been players who have chosen to play for an adopted country rather than their country of birth; the Italian World Cup winner Mauro Camoranesi, the Brazilian-born Portuguese star Deco, any number of Anglo-Irish stars (Townsend, Aldridge, Cascarino, McAteer). Even in recent years Thiago Motta won two caps for Brazil before settling in Italy, renouncing Brazilian citizenship and becoming an Italian international.

This is just a selection of players who have switched allegiance and doesn't include the countless players who have emigrated to Europe in their formative years and played for their adopted countries, especially those of African or Caribbean origin – Eusébio, John Barnes, Patrick Vieira, Clarence Seedorf to name but a handful. This diaspora has worked both ways in recent years, many Caribbean teams adding pros from the English leagues to their ranks through West Indian heritage. The 2010 World Cup saw the appearance of two brothers on the same pitch playing for different countries when Jérome Boateng of Germany came up against his elder brother Kevin-Prince Boateng who had opted to play for his ancestral home, Ghana. Kevin had played for Germany at every junior level up to U-21 but this is permissible under FIFA rules – the final choice need only be made at full international level. A common practice in modern times is to offer a player with potential a cap while very young to solidify their commitment to their chosen country – England capped Wilfred Zaha (born in Côte d'Ivoire) in 2012, before he played in the Premier League for just this reason.

This is not a phenomenon unique to football. In Rugby Union the Italians beg, steal and borrow players from other nations, while the All Blacks have always been quick to nationalise any promising player from the neighbouring Pacific islands. England's cricket team in recent years has rarely been without a South

African-born player. African athletes, especially distance runners, often run for European countries, such is the strength in depth in Kenya and Ethiopia and the North African countries. The European basketball leagues are littered with not-quite-good-enough NBA Stars. Even in individual sports, players shift from one nationality to another; Martina Navratilova and Monica Seles both adopted US citizenship, British sporting heroes Greg Rusedski and Lennox Lewis are both Canadian (as is footballer Owen Hargreaves), and Rory McIlroy appears very confused as to whether he is British or Irish.

Sport is competitive. Teams or countries will use every advantage possible to put out the best side they can, and, if players, overlooked in one country, use expediency to create an opportunity elsewhere, should we hold that against them?

1.5 WORLD CUP 1938

If the England v Italy game immediately after the 1934 tournament was symbolic of where football power lay, then the last
significant match before the next competition was a symbol of an
altogether different and more menacing power play. The match
was played between Germany and Austria as a last hurrah for the
Austrian national side before they were absorbed into a Federal
Germany in the Anschluss of 1938.

After their humiliating defeat to Norway at the 1936 Olympic
Games in Berlin, Otto Nerz had a change of heart and started
picking the best of the Schalke players and giving them some
licence to play in the style they favoured. An 8–0 hammering of
Denmark in 1937, with Szepan pulling the strings and the sinuous Otto Siffling flitting between defenders and scoring four
goals, is regarded as a landmark for German football, the moment
they consider themselves as catching up with the rest of Europe,
and defining that irresistible combination of athletic power and
efficiency with intelligence, control and technique that has served
them well ever since. Nerz gave way to his natural successor,
once his protégé, Sepp Herberger shortly before the World Cup
began.

Germany and Austria should both have been a major force
at this World Cup. Both sides had qualified for the Finals tournament, but the Austrians were made to forfeit their place and
represent the Reich instead. After the Anschluss, the Nazi
regime dictated that the Germans and the Austrians would
pool their resources and produce an indomitable combined XI
– they even went so far as to dictate the team had to have five

of one nation and six of the other. Hitler was born in Austria, after all. All well and good on paper, but the two sides hated each other.

The largely Viennese Austrian team was emblematic of the café culture of the city; sophisticated and artistic and with low regard for the "prosaic" Germans. The Wunderteam of the early thirties had disintegrated, but Austria had a few stars left, chiefly Matthias Sindelar, a deep-lying centre-forward of slender stature but enormous poise and ability. His legs were so thin they looked like they could snap at any moment, so he was called *Der Papierene* (*The Paper Man* – or *The Wafer* as David Goldblatt more poetically translates it). In the farewell match for the Wunderteam, Sindelar masterminded a 2–0 victory for Austria in a game that many accounts claim was intended to be an "honourable" draw; his reported extravagant celebration in front of Nazi dignitaries would not have gone down well. Sindelar declined to play for the combined XI in the World Cup the following year. It would be pleasing but incorrect to report things ended well for Sindelar. The following year this gifted player was found dead in an apartment with his recently acquired girlfriend. Suggestions of Nazi skulduggery are inevitable but have never been corroborated.

England were offered the vacant place in the tournament left by the Austrians' default, but declined; at least they sent observers to watch this tournament, unlike in 1930 and 1934. The rest of the European-dominated list of finalists arrived by means of a short qualifying tournament – except Romania, Brazil, Cuba and the Dutch East Indies (roughly equivalent to modern day Indonesia), whose prospective opponents all withdrew. None of the British teams entered, but Ireland (newly inaugurated as an independent state in 1937 and not yet a Republic) gave it a go, only to lose to Norway over two legs. Hungary, who were one of the better European teams, beat Greece, who weren't, 11–1; Greece earned the fixture by beating Palestine, the only time a team bearing that name has entered the competition.

Argentina, beginning their splendid (?) isolation, withdrew in favour of Brazil, while Uruguay were just too skint to send a team.

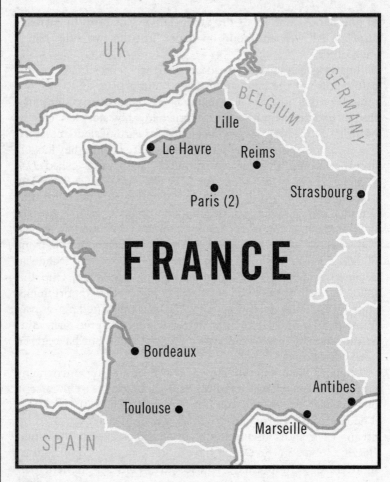

1938
FRANCE

Ten venues in nine cities were used for the 1938 tournament; Lyon was unlucky, it was selected as a host city, but Australia's withdrawal meant that the only game due to be played there was called off.

Paris: Parc des Princes

The Parc des Princes was opened in 1897 as a velodrome, and was the traditional finishing point for the Tour de France from 1903 until the 1960s. In 1972 a new Parc was constructed without the cycle track and has played host to Paris St Germain and the national French team, as well as the French rugby union team.

Paris: Stade Olympique de Colombes (or Stade Olympique Yves-Manoir)
The stadium used for the 1938 final was built for the 1924 Olympic Games and held 45,000 people. It has expanded and contracted in the years, but was marginalized by the appearance of the refurbished Parc des Princes in 1972. Racing Club Paris still uses the ground, as does Racing Métro 92 (rugby union).

Marseille: Stade Vélodrome
The biggest sporting venue in the south of France was built especially for the 1938 finals on the site of the old velodrome (but you guessed that, right?). It became the home of OM (Olympique de Marseille) and remains its home.

Bordeaux: Parc Lescure
Parc Lescure was, and remains, the home of FC Girondins de Bordeaux, and holds just under 35,000 people. Its new name is Stade Chaban-Delmas, named for a chap who served as Mayor of Bordeaux for forty-eight years – most people still refer to it as Lescure.

Lille: Stade Victor Boucquey
This 15,000 capacity ground was knocked down in 1975. It was the home of Lille and the club's forerunners Olimpique Lillois.

Toulouse: Stade Municipal de Toulouse
This famous old stadium was opened for the 1938 World Cup and remains the home of Toulouse FC and occasionally for Heineken Cup matches, the powerful rugby union club based in the city. The capacity is 35,472.

Strasbourg: Stade de la Meinau
La Meinau, as it is popularly known, is the municipal stadium of Strasbourg and serves as the home for RC Strasbourg, once a top-flight club, but, after going into liquidation, now fighting its way back up the divisions à la Rangers.

Reims: Vélodrome Municipal
This small stadium (21,600), now called the Stade Auguste Delaune, is home to Stade de Reims, a famous old club which reached the European Cup Final twice in the 1950s.

Antibes: Stade du Fort Carré
Antibes is a small town on the Cote d'Azur between Nice and Cannes, and its tiny 7,000 stadium hosted one game (Sweden versus Cuba) in the 1938 finals.

Le Havre: Stade Cavée Verte
Another small stadium that holds just over 16,000. Now known as the Stade Jules Deschaseaux, the ground was replaced in 2012 by the Stade Océane as the home of second tier club Le Havre AC.

The Dutch East Indies would probably have lost to Japan, had Japan not had the small matter of a war with China to attend to.

Paris was the home of the World Cup, brainchild of a Frenchman, but it was a city (and continent) in turmoil in 1938. Hitler was running roughshod over the wishes of anyone who disagreed with Nazi policy in his own country, while the rest of Western Europe was deluding itself into believing he wasn't that bad, or, worse, installing a government with similar leanings, like in Spain. In the East Stalin was too busy imposing his own form of dictatorship on the Soviet bloc to oppose Herr Hitler.

FIRST ROUND

Switzerland Abeggien 43	(1) (1) 1	**Germany** Gauchel 29	(1) (1) 1	4 June, Parc des Princes; 27,152
Switzerland Walaschek 42, Bickel 64, Abeggien 75, 79	(1) 4	**Germany** Hahnemann 8, own goal 22	(2) 2	9 June, Parc des Princes; 20,025
Hungary Kohut 12, Toldi 16, Sárosi 25, 88, Zsengellér 30, 67	(4) 6	**Dutch E. Indies** (0) 0		5 June, Rheims; 9,091

SECOND ROUND

Hungary Sárosi 42, Zsengellér 89	(1) 2	**Switzerland** (0) 0	12 June, Lille; 14,800

Germany's footballing stock had dipped alarmingly in the months leading up to the tournament, and the hostility that greeted them in Paris, where the locals tore down their swastikas and threw bottles at the team bus, came as a shock to the travelling Germans whose heads were full of Nazi propaganda. Their form was dodgy, their only recent victory a narrow one over Luxembourg, and in Switzerland they faced a team who had beaten them (and England) recently, and who had the support of just about everyone else at the tournament, especially when, unlike a compliant England team earlier that year, they refused to give the Nazi salute. The Swiss, under an astute coach Karl Rappan (an Austrian, ironically), employed their central defender in a deep-lying position akin to a modern sweeper in a formation the European press called the Swiss Bolt.

It took them a replay, and they went behind in both matches (2–0 in the second), but the Swiss won through 4–2 with two goals from Trello Abegglen*. Abegglen was the brother of Max Abegglen, who had retired the previous year with 34 goals to his name (Trello scored 29) – a record for a Swiss international until Alexander Frei topped it in 2008. Trello died aged only thirty-five in a train accident in 1944. Switzerland, with one of their best ever sides, were unlucky in 1938, having to play Hungary, one of the tournament's best sides, only three days after the replay against Germany. The Germans were goose-stepping home two weeks earlier than they hoped; the meshing of the German and Austrian sides had proved far less than the sum of its parts – Cris Freddi, for once, gets it wrong in his excellent book in suggesting Sepp Herberger was keen to use the Austrian players.

After their thrashing of Greece in qualifying, the Hungarians were handed equally untesting opposition in the first round, and racked up another six against the Dutch East Indies without ever getting out of second gear. The Dutch East Indies team were a scratch XI and pretty clueless – none of them played international football again. Hungary proved too strong for a tired Swiss side, and their skilful centre-forward György Sárosi looked the equal of any forward in the tournament.

FIRST ROUND

Cuba		(1) (2) 3	**Romania**	(1) (2) 3	5 June, Toulouse; 6,707	
Socorro 44, 103,			Bindea 37, Barátky 88,			
Magriña 69			Dobay 105			
Cuba		(0) 2	**Romania**	(1) 1	9 June, Toulouse; 7,536	
Socorro 51, Fernández 57			Dobay 35			

SECOND ROUND

Sweden	(4) 8	**Cuba**	(0) 0	12 June, Antibes; 6,846	
H Andersson 9, 81, 89,					
Wetterström 22, 37, 44,					
Keller 80, Nyberg 84					

* Abegglen played for Sochaux in France, and one of his countrymen played for Le Havre. Kohut, the Hungarian forward, played for Marseille; these three were the only squad members from 1938 not playing club football in the country they represented. How things change.

Cuba, and especially their buccaneering goalkeeper Benito Carvajales, were one of the few positives from this most oppressive World Cup. They arrived in confident voice and backed it up with victory over Romania in a first-round replay. The first game started as expected, with Romania taking charge and opening the scoring, but Cuba's fast and tricky forwards were causing problems and they equalised, then took the lead. Romania's late equaliser took the game to extra-time, and they had to come from behind again when Héctor Socorro scored his second goal.

The second game followed a similar pattern, with Romania comfortable at 1–0 at half-time, but nervy when Socorro equalised soon into the second half, and beaten when Fernández added another. Most accounts report the second goal as highly debatable but Cuba earned their place in the second round. After a good game in the first match, Carvajales was left out of the replay in favour of Juan Ayra (described as "a remarkable acrobat", which in fact he was). Far from being resentful, Carvajales predicted (correctly) that his understudy would have a fine match and Cuba would win.

Cuba's second-round opponents, Sweden, had a bye as a result of a draw caused by Austria's absence. Carvajales probably wished Ayra had kept his place as the Cuban defence was overwhelmed and Sweden ran in eight goals with three apiece for Gustav Wetterström and Harry Andersson (on his debut), the first time two players had scored a hat-trick in the same finals match.

FIRST ROUND

Italy	(1) (1) 2	Norway	(0) (1) 1	5 June, Marseille; 18,826
Ferraris 2, Piola 94		Brustad 83		
France	(2) 3	Belgium	(1) 1	5 June, Colombes; 30,454
Veinante 1, Nicolas 10, 69		Isemborghs 19		

SECOND ROUND

| Italy | (1) 3 | France | (1) 1 | 12 June, Colombes; 58,455 |
| Colaussi 10, Piola 52, 72 | | Heisserer 11 | | |

Germany weren't the only unpopular side in France in 1938. In Marseille there was a massive demonstration waiting to greet the Italian team on their arrival, with a near riot ensuing when riot police with batons waded in. In the stadium – the famous Stade Vélodrome – when the Italians went to make their fascist salute to the four corners of the ground the anthem was drowned out by the derision of the French.

The game itself hardly went to plan for Italy, either, as they were outplayed by Norway for much of the game after scoring an early goal. An equaliser from left-winger Arne Brustad (Norway's first genuine top-class footballer) took the game to extra-time; Norway nearly finished the job inside ninety minutes only for Aldo Olivieri (from the unfashionable Lucchese club in Tuscany, now in the fourth tier of Italian football) to intervene with an outstanding save. In extra-time a mistake from Olivieri's opposite number Henry Johansen allowed Silvio Piola to score what proved to be the winner and Italy scraped through to face the hosts France and another wave of hostility in the second round.

France kicked off their campaign at the Yves du Manoir Stadium in Colombes, built for the 1924 Olympic Games and renamed after a tragic French sporting hero, rugby player Yves du Manoir, who died in 1928 in a plane crash aged only twenty-four. Their opponents were Belgium, under English coach Jack Butler. Butler masterminded Belgium's win over England in 1936, but that was a weak England side and Belgium were no match for France here, going down 3–1 with Jean Nicolas, unluckily injured in 1934, involved in all three goals. The French team also included Oscar Heisserer from Racing Strasbourg, who would later turn down repeated attempts by the Germans to recruit him first to the SS and then to the German national team. He survived, unlike many others, and was rewarded with the captaincy of the national side. His story is in stark contrast to another French international captain, Alex Villaplane from the 1930 World Cup team, who was executed for collaborating with the Nazis during the war.

The game was a disappointing sign-off for Raymond Braine, the best Belgian player of his generation. Braine had missed the 1930 tournament because the Belgian FA disapproved of players owning cafés, and Braine refused to give up his secondary occupation. Instead he took his talents to Czechoslovakia where he made a fearsome inside-forward pairing with Nejedly. Braine was offered Czech citizenship but he declined and was back at his first club, Beerschot, and back in the Belgian team by the time the 1938 tournament started.

The Colombes stadium was only half-full for the game against Belgium – it was packed for the Italy game. Both sides preferred to play in blue, but something had to give and it was the Italians who were told to change. The order came from Rome that the change strip would not be the usual white but fascist black. The gesture did not go unnoticed by crowd or press.

After ten minutes the groans could be heard in Montmartre when Di Lorto made a total hash of a tame shot from Colaussi. Goalkeeper and ball both ended up in the back of the net; ball propelled by goalkeeper, goalkeeper via a collision with the post. The groans turned to cheers when Heisserer equalised a minute later, but the French were fire-fighting and surviving, not dominating.

Pozzo, still manager of Italy, had tweaked his side, omitting the ponderous Monzeglio, no longer the player he was in 1934, for the younger Foni. It was Piola who made the difference in the second half, scoring with a header from the debutant Biavati's cross and lashing in a third at the near post. Italy went through, and with something to spare.

FIRST ROUND

Czechoslovakia	**(0) (0) 3 Holland**	**(0) (0) 0** 5 June, Le Havre; 10,550
Kostálek 93, Zeman 111, Nejedly 118		
Brazil	**(3) (4) 6 Poland**	**(1) (4) 5** 5 June, Strasbourg; 13,452
Leônidas 18, 95, 104, Romeu 25, Perácio 44, 71	Scherfke 23 (p), Wilimowski 53, 60, 89, 118	

SECOND ROUND

Brazil	**(1) (1) 1 Czechoslovakia (0) (1) 1** 12 June, Bordeaux; 22,021	
Leônidas 30	Nejedly 65 (p)	
Brazil	**(0) 2 Czechoslovakia (1) 1** 14 June, Bordeaux; 18,141	
Leônidas 57, Roberto 62	Kopecky 25	

Brazil, the sole South American representatives, brought a squad of mainly new faces to the 1938 Finals. One a little more familiar was the raw centre-forward of 1934, Leônidas. Strangely he hadn't played for the national team in the interim, but here he seemed a more potent player. To the pace and shooting power he had added awareness and positioning – and he had better colleagues, at least up front. Some reports claim the striker played in his bare feet in the opening game. The truth is less interesting; he felt his boots were sticking in the mud and removed them briefly before the referee told him to put them back on.

Brazil opened against Poland in what was undoubtedly the tournament's most fun fixture. A match played on a quagmire in Strasbourg saw eleven goals shared between the sides. A few were good goals, a few more were the result of defending that would give Alan Hansen a heart attack on *Match of the Day*. Brazil led 3–1 at half-time and should have gone on to win easily, but their midfield players stood off Poland striker Ernest Wilimowski and he helped himself to a second-half hat-trick, including an equaliser in the dying moments to make it 4–4* – at times there were two, three or even four Polish attackers bearing down on the Brazilian goal, with Domingos the only defender attempting to stop them. Leônidas scored twice more to complete his own hat-trick in extra-time to make the game safe before Wilimowski became the first player to score four in a match in the Finals. He remains the only man to do so and end up on the losing side.

Wilimowski scored another fine hat-trick the following year as Poland beat Hungary 4–2 in a friendly match. A month later the Germans invaded and there was no more football. Wilimowski was of German extraction, and during the war he played a few internationals for the country that had occupied his birthplace. Whether he was coerced or went along merrily is unclear, but Wilimowski was brought up in Silesia speaking German – not all the Poles were as anti-German as we might imagine. Assertions in some sources that he had six toes on his right foot cannot be verified.

---

* The Brazilian goalkeeper Algisto Lorenzato went by an adopted name in traditional Brazilian footballer style. The name he chose was Batatais – which is Portuguese for potatoes. (Thanks to Cris Freddi for this splendid piece of translation.) He was dropped after letting in five and his replacement, Walter, was the only other player who retained his place after the fisticuffs in Bordeaux.

Brazil's second-round game took place in a swanky new stadium in Bordeaux. Their opponents, Czechoslovakia, should have been a good side, as they still had many of the ingredients that made them such tricky opponents in 1934. Somehow they never quite gelled; it took three goals in extra-time to see off a weakened Dutch team reduced to ten men. Brazil, quite rightly, identified Nejedly as the Czech's main threat, but there was nothing right about the way they dealt with him. Zezé was sent off early for a wild lunge but the tackles kept flying in and the bruised and battered Czechs responded – Riha and Machado followed Zezé before half-time for scrapping. Nejedly's penalty equalised Leônidas' first-half strike, but soon after the playmaker was off with a broken leg and goalkeeper Plánicka finished the game with a fractured arm. Neither made the replay two days later.

The second match went off calmly as both sides made wholesale changes, mostly enforced on the Czechs' part – the Brazilians appeared belatedly contrite about their conduct in the first game. Leônidas stayed and equalised Kopecky's first-half opener; Roberto headed the winner five minutes later. Brazil were through, but faced their third match in five days against the holders in Marseille.

SEMI-FINALS

Italy	(0) 2	**Brazil**	(0) 1	16 June, Marseille; 33,000
Colaussi 55, Meazza 60 (p)		Romeu 87		
Hungary	(3) 5	**Sweden**	(1) 1	16 June, Pc des Princes; 20,155
Own goal 19, Titkos 37,		Nyberg 1		
Zsengellér 39, 85, Sárosi 66				

THIRD-PLACE MATCH

Brazil	(1) 4	**Sweden**	(2) 2	19 June, Bordeaux; 12,500
Romeu 44, Leônidas		Jonasson 28, Nyberg 38		
63, 74, Peracio 80				

Sweden had reached the semi-finals almost by default – a bye then a gimme against Cuba – and were still an unknown quantity. Hungary also had an easy first-round tie but then looked mightily impressive against a good Swiss team and started here as clear favourites. It was justified. After Sweden took a first-minute lead, the Hungarians refused to panic, carried on with their measured, fluid passing and tore the Swedish defence apart. Sárosi and Gyula Zsengellér were great rivals in domestic football, the spearheads of Ferencváros and Ujpest respectively, but here they dovetailed well, Sárosi dropping deep to launch Zsengellér and his own club colleague Géza Toldi. The 1950s is hailed as the Golden Age of Hungarian football, and rightly so, but this earlier lot were far from ordinary.

Brazil, despite the bruising encounter with Czechoslovakia, were the crowd favourites in Marseille simply because their opponents were Italy. But they were without Leônidas, who was simply too knackered to play after his exertions in the earlier rounds – suggestions that he was saved for the final are way off mark; Brazil would have taken no chances against opponents of this calibre. What was unfortunate was the fact that Brazil's most natural substitute, Niginho, was being harried by the Italian authorities; he had dual citizenship and had broken a contract with Lazio to return to Brazil, thus avoiding military service. Brazil had to compromise and use Romeu, an inside-forward, in the centre.

However loathed they were in France, the Italians were good. Meazza was experienced and in his prime, and had an instinctive link with the other inside-forward, his Inter club colleague Giovanni Ferrari. Silvio Piola was visibly growing in confidence and potency, and the new wingers were providing plenty of ammunition. At the back Olivieri was a safe pair of hands and, in the twenty-two-year-old Rava, Pozzo had discovered a more than adequate replacement for the discarded Monzeglio.

Italy controlled the game, untroubled at the back in Leônidas' absence and patient up front. The goals came in the second half, first from Colaussi and then a coolly taken penalty from Meazza after Domingos dragged down Piola. Piola was a spiky, physical presence and he troubled all the defences he faced in this tournament. He scored thirty goals in thirty-four games for his country, and would surely have scored more but for the war. His last cap came against England in 1952, aged thirty-nine. It is Piola's record as a serial goalscorer in *Serie A* that stands out; he is the league's most prolific scorer, with 290 goals for Pro Vercelli, Lazio, Torino, Juventus and lastly Novara – for all but Torino and Juve, he remains the club's highest scorer.

World Cup Heroes No.3
Leônidas da Silva (1913–2004)
Brazil

Leônidas was fit again for the third-place match and showed what might have been with another two goals as Brazil fought back from 2–0 down to beat Sweden 4–2.

Leônidas made his name in Brazil as a youngster playing for the unfashionable Bonsucesso team on the outskirts of Rio. He received an international call-up before he was twenty and scored twice against Uruguay, earning a handsome move to Peñarol. He flitted between clubs in those early days before settling at Flamengo for a six-year stint.

During this time he lit up the 1938 World Cup, and finished as the competition's top scorer with seven goals in four matches (eight in five if you add in the game from 1934). In 1942 he moved to São Paulo and was still there when he retired in 1950. He worked as a radio commentator in his middle years, but struggled with Alzheimer's before he finally died in 2004, aged ninety.

Pre-war football footage is very rare, so we only have newspaper reports on which to judge Leônidas as a player, and these were notoriously colourful in the pre-war years. Leônidas doesn't appear to have been especially skilful – he left that to the more dilettante inside-forwards – but he was much the most purposeful and direct of the Brazilian forwards. Small for a striker, he compensated for lack of height with agility and speed, and was a notable chaser of lost causes, harrying defenders into mistakes. Some accounts claim he invented the bicycle kick – Leônidas himself among them – but the overhead kick was known for many years as a *chilena* in South America, which would back up claims that it was a manoeuvre pioneered in Chile. Whether he was the first or not, Leônidas' ability to conjure attempts at goal from unpromising positions was a feature of his game.

Leônidas may not be as big a name as many of the Brazilian stars who came after him, but as the first Brazilian player to earn international acclaim and shine at a World Cup he was a torch-bearer for the likes of Didi, Pelé and Garrincha and deserves his place here.

WORLD CUP FINAL No.3
19 June 1938, Yves du Manoir, Colombes; 45,124

| Italy | (3) 4 | Colaussi 6, 35, Piola 16, 82 |
| Hungary | (1) 2 | Titkos 8, Sárosi 70 |

Referee: **Georges Capdeville** (France)
Coaches: **Vittorio Pozzo** (Italy) & **Károly Dietz** (Hungary)

Italy (2–3–5): Aldo Olivieri (Lucchese); Alfredo Foni (Juventus), Pietro Rava (Juventus); Pietro Serantoni (Roma), Michele Andreolo (Bologna), Ugo Locatelli (Inter); Amedeo Biavati (Bologna), Giuseppe Meazza (Inter), Silvio Piola (Lazio), Giovanni Ferrari (Inter), Gino Colaussi (Triestina)
Hungary (2–3–5): Antal Szabó (MTK); Sándor Biró (MTK), Gyula Polgár (Ferencváros); Antal Szalay (Ujpest), György Szücs (Ujpest), Gyula Lázár (Ferencváros); Ferenc Sas (MTK), Jenó Vincze (Ujpest), György Sárosi (Ferencváros), Gyula Zsengellér (Ujpest), Pál Titkos (MTK)

Italy were clear favourites. Four years previously they had beaten Czechoslovakia, exponents of the Central European school of possession football, and now they faced another in Hungary. Italy's tactic was the same as in 1934: throw a wall in front of the Hungarians and invite them to pick their way through, put a man-marker (Andreolo) on the opposition's best player (Sárosi) and get the ball to their wingers on the counter and have them exploit the space left by an old-fashioned midfield.

It worked. Twice in the first half counter-attacks down the right and a cross found the opposite winger, Colaussi, in absurd amounts of space to score at leisure. A neat triangular move allowed Piola the opportunity to belt another, and a half-time lead of 3–1 made the game nearly safe. Like all Central European teams, Hungary played at a prosaic pace; they liked to stroll in midfield and play short, measured passes, gaining ground in small increments – think Spain in 2010 in slo-mo. Italy, fit, fast and committed, refused them the time they craved and Hungary had no Plan B.

There was the briefest of hiccoughs in the second half when Sárosi lost his marker for once and tapped in a cross, but Italy never lost control and Piola restored their two-goal cushion towards the end. The crowd were unhappy, but any football follower among them knew deep down the best team had won the match and the tournament. There could be no grumbling about the twelfth man in the refereeing jersey this time. After their faltering start against Norway, Italy had improved with every game – a trait that has followed them down the years – and by the last two rounds were head and shoulders above any other team, not just in organisation but in pace, decision-making and fitness.

Mussolini and the Italian press crowed about the prime breeding stock that was Italian manhood, and the rise of fascism continued unabated. They would get their come-uppance, but not on the football field and at a more appalling cost than anyone could conceive – certainly not the British Prime Minister, who returned from Munich and a meeting with Hitler later that year clutching a symbolic straw that would taint his reputation forever. A very real and very cruel test of manhood was coming.

World Cup Heroes No.4

Giuseppe Meazza (1910–79)

Italy

Probably the best pre-war footballer and a true jazz-age gent. Born in Milan in 1910, Meazza was rejected (too small, how often have we heard that?) by Milan and ended up across the city at Inter where he quickly established himself, winning his first *Serie A* title and first cap in 1930. He scored twice for Italy on his debut against Switzerland and followed up with a hat-trick against Hungary later in the year.

Initially an out-and-out centre-forward, Meazza was skilful and strong and surprisingly adept in the air for a man of only about five foot seven. He was *Serie A* top scorer in that title-winning year and continued to hit the net regularly even after he converted to inside-forward. The prime mover behind the conversion was international manager Vittorio Pozzo, who wanted to accommodate both Meazza and the bustling Schiavio in his 1934 World Cup squad; it was Meazza, the more adaptable and skilful player and better passer of the ball who moved back a shade and allowed Schiavio to get in where it hurts and mix it up with the full-backs. Meazza would later form a similar combination with Piola, setting up goals for the centre-forward and using the latter's strength and hold-up play to move forward and take chances himself.

In 1940 Meazza did the unthinkable and moved from Inter to AC Milan. Even more surprisingly the Inter fans forgave him, perhaps swayed by stories that circulated that he cried in the dressing room after scoring for Milan against their rivals. When the famous San Siro stadium, home to both clubs, was renamed in 1980, it was Meazza's name that was used, although most fans carried on calling it the San Siro and still do.

There is a lot of myth and legend surrounding Meazza's private life, but he was certainly a playboy, and certainly beloved of the ladies, with his smooth, hawkish, unmistakably Italian features and slicked-back hair. Accounts exist of him receiving the 1938 World Cup from Mussolini as if he had just been for a stroll around a piazza and a coffee with his girlfriend, not played a full ninety minutes in a World Cup Final.

Meazza was a notoriously poor timekeeper and often appeared at the last minute for league matches, and he was too impatient for detailed tactical briefings; Pozzo compensated by briefing the other players instead, instructing them how to play around Meazza's gifts and try to read his passes. *"Having him on the team was like starting the game 1–0 up,"* said Pozzo of his star.

Giuseppe Meazza scored over 250 goals for Inter and thirty-three for Italy in fifty-three matches, a record that stood until surpassed by Gigi Riva. Riva's record of thirty-five still stands, a much lower figure than the record for most other major football nations – Italy have always made keeping them out rather than sticking them in their priority. Meazza was the first dual World Cup winner, and remained the only one until Brazil won in 1962 with most of the team that won in 1958.

1938 Team of the Tournament: 2–3–5

Olivieri (Italy)
Domingos (Brazil)   Rava (Ita)
Szalay (Hungary)   Andreolo (Italy)   Martim Silveira (Brazil)
Abegglen (Switzerland)   Sárosi (Hungary)   Leônidas (Brazil)   Meazza (Italy)   Colaussi (Italy)

Leading scorers: Leônidas (7); Zsengellér, Sárosi, Piola (5)

Official team (chosen retrospectively): Plánicka (Czechoslovakia); Domingos (Brazil), Rava (Italy), Foni (Italy); Andreolo (Italy), Locatelli (Italy); Zsengellér (Hungary), Sárosi (Hungary), Leônidas (Brazil), Piola (Italy), Colaussi (Italy)

POST-WAR

2.1 WORLD CUP 1950

Brazil was awarded the 1942 World Cup, but the event never happened, so it seemed only right they got the tournament in 1950, the first renewal after the war ended. Europe was still in the throes of reconstruction and repatriation and was ill-equipped to host such an extravaganza, though London had managed to produce an Olympic Games on a shoestring budget in 1948. Jules Rimet had been President of FIFA for twenty-five years (the anniversary was actually in 1956) and it was decided the trophy would carry his name to honour that landmark.

Qualifying

The organisation was a bit rough and ready and there was the usual rash of pre-tournament withdrawals. Argentina couldn't be bothered, nor could Peru or Ecuador, so four South American teams qualified alongside Brazil without kicking a ball in anger. The same happened to India, but they in turn withdrew for a variety of reasons – a story circulated that it was because they were told they would have to wear boots to compete and were accustomed to playing barefoot. Indian sources have claimed FIFA reneged on a deal to cover all their expenses.

In the European qualification games two places were left open for British teams, based on results in the annual Home International series. England made a firm commitment but Scotland announced they would be unlikely to travel as runners-up of the local competition. Scotland started by hammering Northern Ireland 8–2; a striker with East Fife called Henry Miller

1950
BRAZIL

Six cities shared responsibility for hosting the tournament in this vast country.

Rio de Janeiro: Estádio do Maracanã
One of the most famous of all football stadiums, the Maracanã hosted the memorable 1950 final into which almost 200,000 people (officially – there were probably almost a quarter of a million) crammed to watch Uruguay beat Brazil.

São Paulo: Estádio do Pacaembu
Officially (since 1958) the Estádio Municipal Paulo Machado de Carvalho (which is a bit of a mouthful even if you speak Portuguese), the Pacaembu was built in 1940. Current capacity is around 40,000, although 70,000 squeezed in for a match in the 1950s. It it is the home of the Corinthians.

Belo Horizonte: Estádio Sete de Setembro
The name comes from Brazil's day of independence (7 September), and was the name of the now defunct club which played in Belo Horizonte, north and inland of Rio de Janeiro. Now officially the Raimundo Sampaio, the ground is still referred to colloquially as Independençia. It is the home ground of both América and Atlético Mineiro.

Curitiba: Estádio Durival Britto
This stadium is known to all as the Vila Capanema, holds 20,000 and was built in 1947 as one of the venues for the forthcoming World Cup.

Porto Alegre: Estádio dos Eucaliptos
Opened in 1931 in the southernmost of the venues used for the 1938 finals with a capacity of 20,000, Estádio dos Eucaliptos was closed in 1969 when it was superseded by the much bigger (56,000) Estádio Beira-Rio. Both grounds served as the home of SC Internacional, the city's premier team.

Recife: Estádio Ilha do Retiro
Recife is in Pernambuco, much further up the coast from the other host cities in 1938. The Estádio Ilha do Retiro holds around 35,000 and was used for only one world cup match (Chile versus the USA) in 1950.

Morris helped himself to a hat-trick and was never picked again – nice strike rate. Jackie Milburn netted a hat-trick as England won well in Cardiff and Manchester United's Jack Rowley grabbed four as poor Northern Ireland were trounced again, 9–2 this time. It came down to the decider at Hampden; Scotland hit the bar, Chelsea's Roy Bentley hit the back of the net. Scotland were true to their word and turned down their place in the Finals, despite pleas from the players, a gesture of utterly futile pride that typified the Scottish FA, an organisation that makes even their English counterparts look a bastion of common sense.

None of the countries behind the Iron Curtain entered, not even the losing finalists from 1934 and 1938, Czechoslovakia and Hungary. Germany were disbarred, but Italy gained a place as the holders. Italy had much more sympathy than in the 1930s, having been rocked by an awful tragedy the previous year.

The Torino team was returning from a friendly match in Lisbon when their Italian Airlines plane hit some bad weather and crashed into a shrine on the side of a mountain near their home city. The entire team was wiped out. Torino were by some distance the best side in Italy at the time and were cruising to a fifth consecutive league title. The tragedy didn't decimate the national squad, but it made a dent and it did enormous damage to the psyche of Italian football. Torino were forced to use their youth team to complete their fixtures; as a mark of respect all their opponents did the same and the fifth *scudetto* was secured. Scant consolation for family and friends and club, but a rare gesture of solidarity in a league synonymous with corruption and animosity.

When Turkey joined Scotland and withdrew after qualifying, FIFA looked around for replacements and invited Portugal and France, beaten in qualifying by Spain and Yugoslavia respectively. Portugal declined but France accepted and the draw was made. India then chimed in with their objections and France looked at the schedule and changed their mind. They had a point – there was no attempt made to coordinate the matches to limit teams' travel across such a vast country.

Finals

FIFA were left with a lopsided draw, as France were drawn in the one group that had three teams rather than four. In a moment of obstinacy they decided to leave things as they were, with two groups of four, one of three and one containing only two sides. Go figure.

Brazil were many people's favourites. They had just won the Copa América and handed out some heavy beatings in the process. They put nine past Ecuador, ten past Bolivia, seven past Peru and five past a good Uruguay team. Their forward line was dazzling, their only problem being which ones to leave out. The "dream team" favoured by most pundits was the trio of Zizinho, Ademir and Jair.

Yugoslavia were as good as anyone in Europe, but found themselves in Brazil's group; England and Spain would fight out the other four-team group, and surely even a weakened Italy would see off Sweden and Paraguay. Uruguay got a very long straw, with only a weak Bolivia team to beat – their biggest problem would be raising the intensity for the second phase, for here FIFA had made a change.

The winners of the four groups were not being asked to play semi-finals but to form another round-robin group to decide the tournament winner. FIFA had gone from one extreme to another – the lottery of knockout rounds to no final at all. It had the potential to be a damp squib of a tournament.

The hosts opened up on 24 June at the Maracanã in Rio in front of over 80,000 fervent fans. The Maracanã was built with government money for just this occasion and was an awesome edifice, the work of four major architects. Like the Centenário in Montevideo in 1930, it was barely finished in time, but it was worth the weight, a steel and concrete tribute to the modern Brazil. The nationalist dictatorship of Gestulio Vargas may have fallen when he stepped down at the end of the Second World War, but he would have applauded the creation of this stadium, as fine an example of the new industrial Brazil he started to build, a symbol of Brazilian pride, not Portuguese- or Italian-influenced, but Brazilian.

GROUP 1

Brazil Ademir 31, 79, Jair 65, Baltazar 71	**(1) 4**	**Mexico**	**(0) 0**	24 June, Maracanã; 81, 649
Yugoslavia Mitic 59, Tomašević 70, Ognjanov 84	**(0) 3**	**Switzerland**	**(0) 0**	25 June, Belo Horizonte; 7,336
Yugoslavia Vidal 4, 86, own goal 51	**(2) 4**	**Mexico** Ortiz 87 (p)	**(0) 1**	28 June, Pôrto Alegre; 11, 078
Brazil Alfredo 3, Baltazar 32	**(2) 2**	**Switzerland** Fatton 17, 88	**(1) 2**	28 June, São Paulo; 42,032
Brazil Ademir 3, Zizinho 69	**(1) 2**	**Yugoslavia**	**(0) 0**	1 July, Maracanã; 142,429
Switzerland Bader 12, Antenen 44	**(2) 2**	**Mexico** Casarin 75	**(0) 1**	2 July, Pôrto Alegre; 3,580

1. Brazil 5pts (8–2); 2. Yugoslavia 4pts (7–3); 3. Switzerland 3pts (4–6); 4. Mexico 0pts (2–10)

A twenty-one-gun salute greeted the players from Brazil and Mexico, and 5,000 pigeons were released into the air. When the smoke and the plaster dislodged from the newly built stands had drifted away, the players started the game on a pitch covered in guano. Reports suggest the Brazilians hit the woodwork maybe five or six times, but they also hit the net four times, despite the heroics of Antonio Carbajal in goal for Mexico for the first time. More of him anon. The Brazilians switched positions frequently, still trying to find the perfect formula in which to mix all that talent.

Brazil made changes for the second game, played in São Paulo more through political expediency than any sensible reason. Zizinho was still unfit and they left out Jair and Bigode, and nearly paid the price. Switzerland were well organised but decidedly ordinary, and should have been brushed aside. Instead, the Brazilians showed their defensive frailty, Jacques (Jacky) Fatton frequently "doing" Augusto for pace and twice equalising for the Europeans, the second in the eighty-eighth minute when it was too late for Brazil to up a gear and win the game. Coach Flávio Costa was nearly lynched – the hosts would have to up their game.

And how. Yugoslavia had breezed past Switzerland and Mexico and now needed only a draw to top the group and eliminate the hosts. Given what happened in the country in the 1990s, it seems remarkable that this disparate and hostile ethnic group could be turned into a potent unit, but they were a really good side here, hard at the back where their young (Croatian) full-back Ivica Horvat was dominant, aggressive in midfield and skil-ful up top.

In the decider, in a rocking Maracanã restored to near capac-ity after safety concerns were alleviated, the Brazilians got an early break when Rajko Mitic, one of six Red Star Belgrade players in the side, cut his head on a crudely finished girder and had to have treatment. (Obviously the safety precautions didn't extend to looking after the opposition players.) Momentarily thrown, Yugoslavia conceded early to an Ademir header. Back to a full complement, they pressed Brazil all the way; the Dream Team were excellent, but so too were Mitic, the Cajkovski brothers and Tomasevic. Zizinho had a goal chalked off by the Welsh referee, but not before Zeljko Cajkovski missed a gilt-edged chance at the other end. Brazilian 'keeper Barbosa made a good stop from Mitic, but it was all over when Zizinho repeated his earlier dribble and scored a second. It was tight, but Brazil did enough and knocked out one of the other strong teams.

GROUP 2

England Mortensen 39, Mannion 51	(1) 2	**Chile**	(0) 0	25 June, Maracanã; 29,703
Spain Igoa 80, Basora 82, Zarra 85	(0) 3	**USA** Pariani 17	(1) 1	25 June, Curitiba; 9,511
Spain Basora 17, Zarra 30	(2) 2	**Chile**	(0) 0	29 June, Maracanã; 19,790
Spain Zarra 48	(0) 1	**England**	(0) 0	2 July, Maracanã; 74, 462
Chile Robledo 16, Cremaschi 32, 61, 82, Prieto 54	(2) 5	**USA** Wallace 47, Maca 48 (p)	(0) 2	2 July, Recife; 8,501

1. Spain 6pts (6–1); 2. England 2pts (2–2); 3. Chile 2pts (5–6); 4. USA 2pts (4–8)

An upset was narrowly avoided in the top group but not in the second. It nearly came in the first round of matches; the USA were beating Spain with ten minutes to go before a flurry of goals gave the Spaniards a 3–1 win. In the other game England produced a competent display to see off Chile 2–0, Mortensen heading Mullen's cross back past the goalkeeper and Mannion hitting a daisy-cutter from fifteen yards after Finney teed him up.

England brought a squad to this tournament that was neither young nor experienced. Only Billy Wright, Tom Finney and Stanley Matthews had more than twenty caps, yet the youngest players were a couple of twenty-four-year-olds. It was a legacy of the war, which had deprived a good crop of players of some of their best years. Matthews arrived late so he missed the game against Chile, but it was assumed he would replace Mullen for the second match – he was England's most likely match-winner. Arthur Drewry, the one selector who travelled with the team, decided otherwise and stuck with the team that beat Chile. This was a huge part of England's problem; the team was selected by committee, with the post of manager, held by Walter Winterbottom, little more than a chaperone and dispenser of tactical advice. Even that was pretty redundant, English sides knew only one way to play. The system meant selection was inconsistent, biased towards establishment men and wholly conservative. The press consoled themselves with the thought that maybe Matthews was being held back for the tough final game against Spain that would decide the group.

WORLD CUP SHOCKS No.1
29 June 1950, Independencia Stadium, Belo Horizonte, Brazil; 10,151

England	(0) 0	
USA	(1) 1	Gaetjens

Referee: **Generoso Dattilo** (Italy)
Coaches: **Walter Winterbottom** (England) & **Bill Jeffrey** (USA)

England (WM): Bert Williams (Wolverhampton Wanderers); Alf Ramsey (Tottenham Hotspur), Laurie Hughes (Liverpool), John Aston (Manchester United); Billy Wright (Wolves), Jimmy Dickinson (Portsmouth); Wilf Mannion (Middlesbrough), Roy Bentley (Chelsea); Tom Finney (Preston North End), Stan Mortensen (Blackpool), Jimmy Mullen (Wolves).
United States (3–2–5): Frank Borghi (St Louis); Harry Keough (St Louis), Charlie Colombo (St Louis), Joe Maca (Brooklyn); Ed McIlvenny (Philadelphia), Walter Bahr (Philadelphia); Frank Wallace (St Louis), Gion Pariani (St Louis), Joe Gaetjens (Brookhattan), John Souza (Ponta Delgada), Ed Souza (Ponta Delgada).

This was the most extraordinary result in the brief history of the World Cup to date, and remains one of the more inconceivable results that has rocked the Finals. This was England, inventors of the game, so confident in their supremacy they hadn't bothered to even enter the competition before the war. (Maybe they should have – they had a much better side relative to the competition than they did in the 1950s.) Even with the problematic heat and all the travelling, they were one of the clear favourites for the tournament.

Cris Freddi suggests the result wasn't as seismic as the reaction would suggest, but he's being wise after the event. The USA had played well against Spain – but then Spain weren't regarded as any good, either. The USA had only narrowly lost to an FA XI, but that XI was a much weaker side, featuring only Matthews of the World Cup side (and a young Nat Lofthouse, who scored for fun on the tour). In qualifying, the USA had been trounced twice by Mexico, who proved the whipping boys in the first group; make no mistake, this was a massive shock, the modern equivalent would be China beating France or something similar.

Most sources, even US ones, cite their team as giving a backs-to-the-wall performance. Not that there were many US sources; only one reporter, from St Louis – who provided five of the starting line-up – attended the game. His name, in wonderfully 1950s Chandleresque film-noir style, was Dent McSkimming, and he reported back the exciting news with great pride. It was met, as most soccer news still is in the USA, with massive indifference.

What has been misrepresented is Gaetjens' goal, a clever header from a mishit shot, and certainly not the "in off his ear" fluke Alf Ramsey claimed it to be. The experience in Brazil confirmed Ramsey's view of South America as an uncivilised place and put in place some of the festering resentment that came out as England manager. Most of the other England players dismissed the result as "one of those days", which is probably a fair assessment. Tom Finney claims it was the most awful game of his long and distinguished career, ninety minutes of monumental frustration.

The Americans played well and deserve enormous credit. They worked hard and kept their discipline – the ostensible 3–2–5 formation became nearer to 5–4–1 as they were pressed back in the second half, but McIlvenny and Bahr were excellent, the former a Scot who had played a bit of lower-division football (how he must have loved beating England!). The goalkeeper Borghi had played a bit of pro baseball so presumably had a safe pair of hands – he played really well and deserved the odd piece of good fortune. And for all their heroics the Americans had a fair slice of luck, too – this is not apologist stuff, just accurate; if one team has around twenty attempts on goal (with finishers of the quality of Mortensen and Finney in the side) and the other has three or four, which is expected to win? The chances were fluffed – Roy Bentley was the chief culprit and his claims to have hit the bar three times aren't borne out by other reports.

You often read reports after FA Cup giant-killing games about a postman or a welder scoring the winner; Gaetjens, a Haitian awaiting US citizenship, washed dishes in a New York diner. He went back to Haiti and disappeared a few years later, presumed a victim of Papa Doc Duvalier's murderous Tontons Macoute.

Even in 1950, England's reputation abroad was not what we wanted to believe it was; the Brazilian crowd waved white hand-kerchiefs in a farewell taunt to the homeward-bound losers. It says much for English attitudes that Drewry and Winterbottom took the team straight home rather than stay and watch the denouement of the tournament.

> *If ever there was a time when English football should have sat down and taken a long, hard look at itself, it was in the aftermath of the 1950 World Cup . . . We stood still, our insular attitude rein-forced by the notion we had invented the game.*
>
> Stanley Matthews in his autobiography
> *The Way It Was* (2001)

For 1950 you could equally read qualifying in 1974, failure in 1982 and embarrassment in 2010. English football dances to the ringing of the cash register not the waltz, the samba, the flamenco or the tango. In a musical game, England are Status Quo.

England, to their credit, didn't moan about their defeat – stiff upper lip and all that. They did moan a bit more when they lost their next match, to Spain. Jackie Milburn, in alongside Eddie Baily of Spurs for Bentley and Mannion, was denied a perfectly decent headed goal and there was plenty of time-wasting and theatrics after Spain took the lead early in the second half. The goal was scored by Zarra (Telmo Montoya) of Atletico Bilbao, who scored twenty in twenty for Spain and is a legend of Basque football. Ramallets, the Spanish goalkeeper who made his debut at the tournament, was the next in a line of great Spanish 'keepers starting with Zamora – he was their first choice for the rest of the 1950s.

Chile put things in perspective when they beat the USA 5–2 in a dead rubber. Their opening goal was scored by George Robledo of Newcastle United, son of a Chilean father and English mother. When Newcastle signed him from Barnsley in 1949, he refused to sign unless his brother, Ted, a left-half, was part of the deal. He followed Ted back to Chile to play for Colo Colo in 1953. While at Newcastle, Robledo became the first South American to play (1951) and score (1952) in an FA Cup Final as the Magpies won the trophy in successive seasons. Robledo was the only player at this World Cup not playing domestic football in the country he represented.

England Squad 1950:
GK: Bert Williams (Wolverhampton Wanderers, 30 years old, 7 caps), Ted Ditchburn (Tottenham Hotspur, 28, 2)
DEF: John Aston (Manchester United, 28, 14), Bill Eckersley (Blackburn Rovers, 24, 0), Laurie Hughes (Liverpool, 26, 0), Alf Ramsey (Tottenham, 30, 5), Laurie Scott (Arsenal, 33, 17), Jim Taylor* (Fulham, 32, 0), Billy Wright (Wolves, 26, 29)
MID & WIDE: Eddie Baily (Tottenham, 24, 0), Henry Cockburn (Man Utd, 28, 10), Jimmy Dickinson (Portsmouth, 25, 7), Bill Nicholson* (Tottenham, 31, 0), Willie

* It is unthinkable now that England would take players to a major tournament without first giving them experience in at least a friendly match. In this squad there are two players over thirty who are yet to be capped. The squad is far from young but still not experienced at this level – only Wright has more caps than his age. Taylor and Nicholson (nowhere near as good a player as a manager) won two and one caps respectively (not in this

Watson* (Sunderland, 30, 2), Tom Finney (Preston North End, 28, 25), Stanley Matthews (Blackpool, 35, 30), Jimmy Mullen (Wolves, 27, 4)

FWD: Roy Bentley (Chelsea, 26, 4), Wilf Mannion (Middlesbrough, 32, 19), Jackie Milburn (Newcastle United, 26, 7), Stan Mortensen (Blackpool, 29, 18)

USA Squad 1950:
GK: Frank Borghi (St Louis Simpkins-Ford), Gino Gardassanic (Chicago Slovaks)
DEF: Robert Annis (St Louis SF), Geoff Coombes (Chicago Vikings), Harry Keough (St Louis McMahon), Joe Maca (Brooklyn Hispano)
MID & WIDE: Walter Bahr (Philadelphia Nationals), Charlie Colombo (St Louis SF), Ed McIlvenny (Philadelphia Nationals), Benny McLaughlin (Philadelphia Nationals)[†], Ed Souza (Ponta Delgada), Frank Wallace (St Louis SF), Adam Wolanin (Chicago Eagles)
FWD: Robert Craddock (Pittsburgh Harmarville), Nicky DiOrio (Pittsburgh Harmarville), Joe Gaetjens (Brookhattan), Frank Moniz (Ponta Delgada), Gino Pariani (St Louis SF), John Souza (Ponta Delgada)

tournament) and were clearly not there to play as first choice, so why bother? The answer lies in the innate conservatism of the England selection panel.
* Willie Watson was one of that rare breed, a dual international at cricket and football. He was an elegant wing-half who made a handful of appearances as a teenager for Huddersfield before the war, but enjoyed most success with Sunderland post-war, where he made over 200 appearances, despite having intense commitments as a county and Test cricketer. He played most of his cricket for Yorkshire, with a late spell as captain of Leicestershire (the same route Ray Illingworth would later take). Watson played in twenty-three Tests but never really held down a regular place in a strong team. His finest moment came in 1953 when an unbeaten century was instrumental in saving an Ashes Test at Lord's – he was still dropped for the next game!
† McLaughlin, a tricky winger for the USA and one of their better players, was selected in the final squad but was unable to get time off work and did not travel.

GROUP 3

Sweden	(2) 3	**Italy**	(1) 2	25 June, São Paulo; 56,502
Jeppson 25, 69,		Carapellese 7,		
Sune Andersson 33		Muccinelli 75		
Sweden	(2) 2	**Paraguay**	(1) 2	29 June, Curitiba; 7,903
Sundkvist 17,		López 34,		
Palmér 25		López Fretes 74		
Italy	(1) 2	**Paraguay**	(0) 0	29 June, Maracanã; 19,790
Carapellese 12,				
Pandolfini 62				

1. Sweden 3pts (5–4); 2. Italy 2pts (4–3); 3. Paraguay 1pt (2–4)

The third group comprised three teams and looked close on paper. Paraguay were a quick, inventive side but had no experience of this kind of opposition. Italy were still recovering from the Torino disaster, and sent an inexperienced squad with only eighty-five caps between twenty-two players. Sweden were shorn of three of their best players, the trio of Gren, Nordahl and Liedholm who were barred from playing by the Swedish FA for accepting professional contracts in Italy. The Swedes were managed by George Raynor, a plain-talking Englishman who had put too many noses out of joint to succeed in his own country. Raynor's own nose was for spotting talent and clever tactics.

Raynor's skill was put to the test in the first match as a rebuilt Italy took an early lead. Raynor opted for fast, nimble forwards to pick their way through the Italian defence, and it worked. Hasse Jeppson scored twice and centre-half Sune Andersson scored with a drive that beat an unsighted goalkeeper. Both scorers were among a host of Swedish players who were picked up by Italian clubs over the next two years; Jeppson had a good season at Atlanta and moved to Napoli for a huge fee (which he justified with a good scoring record over four seasons), while Andersson went to Roma along with Stig Sundkvist. The most successful from this team was the young inside-left Lennart Skoglund, who played for Inter from 1950 to 1959, winning two *Serie A* titles.

In the second game Sweden took a two-goal lead through Sundkvist and Karl-Erik Palmér and looked in total control. They relaxed and let Paraguay back into the game and Sweden were thankful a late effort from Attilio López was disallowed. Paraguay were well beaten by Italy (who were already out) in the last match in the group and so missed a good opportunity to progress. The Italians' best player Gino Cappello was banned for life (and forgiven after serving twelve months) for punching a referee in 1952. Cappello is an iconic figure at Bologna where he played for a decade after the war.

GROUP 4

Uruguay	(4) 8	**Bolivia**	(0) 0		2 July, Belo Horizonte; 5,204

Míguez 13, 40, 51, Vidal 18,
Schiaffino 17, 53, Pérez 83,
Ghiggia 87

The final group was a bit of a farce. A team really ought to have been moved from one of the first two groups to add some competition for Uruguay, because Bolivia were a really weak team. Uruguay looked good in slaughtering them, but the Dog & Duck Second XI would have looked handy against Bolivia. Peter Seddon states in his book that playing just this one game gave Uruguay a huge advantage going into the final phase (or Final Pool, as FIFA liked to call it), but I would demur. Good teams tend to ease into tournaments and often need two or three games to get into their stride; Brazil had three to decide upon their best forward line – no one proved anything against Bolivia.

FINAL POOL

Brazil	(3) 7	**Sweden**	(0) 1		9 July, Maracanã; 138,886
Ademir 17, 36, 52, 58,		Andersson 67 (p)			
Chico 39, 88, Maneca 85					
Spain	(2) 2	**Uruguay**	(1) 2		9 July, São Paulo; 44,802
Basora 37, 39		Ghiggia 29, Varela 73			
Brazil	(3) 6	**Spain**	(0) 1		13 July, Maracanã; 152,772
Own goal 15, Jair 21,		Ioga 71			
Chico 31, 55, Ademir 57,					
Zizinho 67					
Sweden	(2) 2	**Uruguay**	(1) 3		13 July, São Paulo; 7.987
Palmér 5, Sundkvist 40		Ghiggia 39, Míguez 77, 85			
Spain	(0) 1	**Sweden**	(2) 3		16 July, São Paulo; 11,227
Zarra 82		Sundkvist 15, Mellberg* 34,			
		Palmér 79			

* Bror Mellberg was the great-uncle of modern Swedish star Olof Mellberg; he joined Italian club Genoa after the tournament before moving to France, where he spent the remainder of his club career. Mellberg returned to the Swedish squad for the 1958 Finals when the ban on players who played abroad was lifted.

The organisers got away with it in the Final Pool. A format that could have ended as a real anti-climax produced a final, and a spectacular one at that. Perhaps they guessed that making Brazil v Uruguay the last scheduled match would produce a decider, perhaps they just got lucky.

Uruguay's lack of preparation against decent opposition nearly cost them straight away, as they encountered problems against Spain. They coped well with the aerial threat of Zarra, but ignored the potent Barcelona winger Estanislau Basora, who stole in twice past Tejera to put Spain ahead. Uruguay dominated the second half, but found the net only once, through their captain Obdulio Varela. It was a rough game – most involving this Spain team were – and a draw was about right. Uruguay would be without their in-form goalkeeper Máspoli for the next match.

The game played the same day in the Maracanã wasn't anywhere near as evenly matched as Brazil simply tore Sweden apart. Sweden weren't awful – they had good, experienced players at the back, including their captain Erik Nilsson, who played in the last World Cup before the war. He was one of two, the other being Swiss captain Fred Bickel. Both players would have won about a gazillion caps but for the war – as it was, Bickel ended his international career in 1954 with seventy-one and Nilsson played until 1952 and won fifty-seven. They were both significant servants to their only clubs, Nilsson for Malmö and Bickel for Grasshoppers of Zurich.

Brazil's attacking players were in scintillating form, the trio of Ademir, Zizinho and Jair exchanging the ball at mesmerising speed. Of the three Ademir was the out-and-out goalscorer (he finished with thirty-two in thirty-nine internationals), and he scored four in this match.

The first was avoidable – Svensson shouldn't have been beaten at his near post with a low, scuffed strike – but the second was magnificent as the big striker played a wonderful one-two and pushed the ball past the onrushing Svensson with consummate timing. Chico wandered in from the left-wing to thrash high past the exposed goalkeeper for a three-goal half-time lead and the game was over as a contest. The second half was more like an exhibition match as Brazil strolled around with the ball showing off their party tricks. Sweden's only consolation was a penalty for a foul committed by Bigode a good foot or two outside the area – one of the earliest theatrical dives I can remember seeing on video.

The Swedish defenders look amateurish by today's standards, defending in static ranks and allowing players to run between them, but that was the game in 1950. A defender marked his opposite man and if that man's movement took him away then gaps would appear, and the Brazilians were fleet enough of foot and mind to fill the gaps effectively. There was no high defensive line and no sort of pressure in the midfield on ball players like Zizinho and Jair.

Spain should have been a much tougher proposition but Brazil were on a roll by now, and their big strong defenders weren't intimidated by Spain's macho men. The first goal again owed something to fortune; Ademir's shot was hit at a good height for Ramallets until it took a huge looping deflection and flopped into the other side of the goal. There was nothing friendly about Jair's thumping effort for the second, although the way Spain backed off as he ran from the halfway line was pretty hospitable. Chico was proving a lively presence on the left wing and he added two more goals to the pair he scored against Sweden, before Zizinho did well to set up a tap-in for Ademir and then jinked through to score himself. Igoa's adept finish came with the game lost and Brazil on cruise control.

Uruguay needed to beat Sweden to stay in the tournament and add meaning to the final match. Conceding after four minutes was presumably not part of the plan, but the control and finish from Palmér was excellent. Slowly Varela and Rodriguez Andrade, nephew of the great Jose Andrade, took control of the midfield and gave the forwards more space. Ghiggia, who was proving Uruguay's most effective player, equalised with an excellent run and a dipping shot. Sweden were ahead again two minutes later when Anibal Paz, deputising for Máspoli, obligingly dropped a cross at Sundkvist's feet.

The second half of this match was perhaps the moment when Uruguay's easier schedule did count in their favour. Sweden tired and Uruguay just kept coming at them with their neat little inter-locking moves and occasional burst of speed from Ghiggia and the inside-forwards. Neither of the two goals from Omar Míguez that earned them the vital win was noteworthy, both coming from goalmouth scrambles, one of them when Svensson cancelled out that gaffe by Paz by dropping a similar cross for Míguez to ram home.

Sweden's consolation was third place as they comfortably beat a chastened Spain; they had shown great resolve throughout the tournament and demonstrated what a sound coach English football was missing in George Raynor.

> *Only three people have silenced the Maracanã with just one movement: Frank Sinatra, The Pope, and me.*
>
> Alcides Ghiggia, years after scoring the winning goal in the 1950 World Cup Final

WORLD CUP FINAL No.4
16 July 1950, Maracanã, Rio de Janeiro; 205,000*

Brazil	(0) 1	Friaça 47
Uruguay	(0) 2	Schiaffino 66, Ghiggia 79

Referee: **George Reader** (England)
Coaches: **Flávio Costa** (Brazil) & **Juan López** (Uruguay)

Brazil (2–3–5): Moacyr Barbosa (Vasco de Gama); Augusto *da Costa* (Cpt; Vasco de Gama), Juvenal Amarijo (Flamengo); José Carlos Bauer (São Paulo), Danilo Alvim (Vasco de Gama), *João Ferreira, known as* Bigode (Flamengo); Albino Friaça (São Paulo), *Thomaz Soares da Silva, known as* Zizinho (Bangu), Ademir *Menezes* (Vasco de Gama), Jair Rosa Pinto (Palmeiras), *Francisco Aramburu, known as* Chico (Vasco de Gama)
Uruguay (W-M): Roque Máspoli (Peñarol); Matías González (Cerro), Obdulio Varela (Cpt; Peñarol), Eusebio Tejera (Nacional); Schubert Gambetta (Nacional), Victor Rodríguez Andrade (Central); Julio Pérez (Nacional), Juan Alberto Schiaffino (Peñarol); Alcides Ghiggia (Peñarol), Oscar Míguez (Peñarol), Rubén Morán (Cerro)

Before you start emailing my publisher, yes, I do realise it is technically incorrect to refer to this match as a World Cup Final. But in every other sense it was the final of this tournament. It was

---

* This record attendance for a football match is unlikely ever to be surpassed in an age of heightened health and safety and all-seater stadia. The four highest attendances for World Cup games were for Brazil's games against Uruguay, Spain, Yugoslavia and Sweden in this tournament.

the last game and the winner would be awarded the trophy; the only difference from any other last game was that a draw would see Brazil crowned champions – let us be thankful the competition wasn't decided in such an anti-climactic manner.

The entire city of Rio was at fever pitch before the tournament. There was an assumption among press and officials that Brazil would win. Stories abound of presentations to the President being arranged and commemorative coins being hammered out before a ball had been kicked in anger. Thousands crammed into the Maracanã; the official paying figure was just over 170,000 but contemporary photographs suggest more than that packed into this glorious edifice – the noise was deafening.

It's hard to overstate the importance of football in Brazil, although Alex Bellos, in *Futebol: The Brazilian Way of Life*, tries hard. Bellos claims that twentieth-century Brazilian history is divided into World Cups – a glance at a couple of chapter headings in Brazilian histories is enough to suggest that is a bit over the top. But they are passionate about it, and it is a symbol of national identity and pride, just as Rugby Union is in New Zealand or weightlifting in Turkey. It can be divisive at times – look at the furore over the expenditure on the 2014 tournament, and the accompanying protests – but it is also a great unifier. In 1950 all Brazil was behind the team – but woe betide them if they failed to deliver.

It was inconceivable that Brazil would play for the draw. They had a decent goalkeeper and a couple of rugged tacklers, but their defence was no better than average. Their attackers, on the other hand, were sublime. The right-half, Bauer, was a skilful player as well as a good tackler, and he was the principal feeder to the inside-forwards, Jair and Zizinho. Jair was a powerful runner who liked exchanging quick passes with his colleagues; he would often be the one to inject some urgency into the languid passing moves of the Brazilians; Zizinho was all close control and tricks and flicks, able to go past defenders at close quarters and fire off a shot with no backlift. Both sported the clichéd colonial look of swept-back hair and pencil moustache, as did many of the other South American footballers of the day. Ademir had a large, jutting jaw that made him look fierce, and he was a pretty fearless sort, good in the air and not afraid to give the goalkeeper a hard time under crosses. But it was his finishing that set him apart in this tournament; he adopted a shoot-on-sight policy and was a clean, accurate striker of the ball, usually choosing to hit low and make the goalkeeper scramble. Put through on goal in a couple of games, he seemed to have remarkable composure and time to pick his spot.

The wingers outside them were not the influence they were in later Brazilian teams but they were energetic and had an eye for goal. The best wide player on the pitch, Ghiggia, was playing for the opposition. He was Uruguay's form player and had scored in all three of their games so far. In contrast to Brazil, their defence was their strength; Máspoli was the tournament's best goalkeeper, Tejera was a limpet-like marker, Varela was dominant and composed and the half-backs Gambetta and Andrade could tackle. Gambetta did not look like an athlete; slightly tubby and prematurely lined, he looked like someone's dad who had sneaked onto the pitch for a dare. The prompter in chief was Juan Alberto Schiaffino, a stick-thin sliver of a man who glided through the midfield with the ball glued to his feet. The other inside-forward Pérez was a worker, another who added grit to the Uruguayans when they were defending.

And did they have some defending to do. The Brazilians came at them in waves, urged on by the vast crowd. Uruguay defended in numbers; Varela truly did play as a centre-half, rarely venturing forward in the way he liked, while the two half-backs sat tight on Zizinho and Jair. Brazil had chances – reports claim thirty shots on goal, but many of these were over-ambitious – but few were clear cut. Ademir might have twice done better in the first half but shot straight and hard at Máspoli and didn't get enough power on a rare clean header after escaping Tejera's clutches for once. Half-time arrived with no score – Uruguay at least knew they weren't going to be steamrollered like Sweden and Spain.

Only two minutes into the second half Ademir feinted to turn but released the ball instead to Friaca, cutting in from the right wing. The São Paulo winger chose a fine moment to score his first international goal, scudding the ball into the far corner when

Máspoli seemed to expect a drive for the near post. The decibel level in the stadium soared, if that were possible, and you could sense the dissipation of tension as if a valve were released. Everything was going to be fine.

That illusion lasted almost twenty minutes. Uruguay hadn't read the script; having conceded, they were supposed to bow before the invincible champions. Instead, they upped their game. Varela, an awesome professional and terrific leader, started to step out from the back and Andrade started to press forward behind Schiaffino allowing the playmaker to go walkabout a little more. Uruguay had worked out that Ghiggia had the beating of stocky Bigode, and that he wasn't frightened of the clattering the Brazilian had handed out to previous opponents. Schiaffino concentrated on feeding the ball to the right instead of to the debutant (in a World Cup Final!) Morán on the left, and Ghiggia did his thing. Three or four times he teased and tormented Bigode before sprinting past on the outside; finally Schiaffino timed his run into the box to get on the end of the cross and the ball flew high and handsome past Barbosa.

The Brazilians later stated that the stunned reaction of the Maracanã crowd did them more damage than the goal. The doubts of the audience transferred to the pitch and the game was up for grabs. Brazil were just getting back into it when Ghiggia got past Bigode again, this time played in by Pérez. Brazil had done nothing to compensate for the gaping hole on their left side and no one stepped across to cover Bigode, so Ghiggia just kept on going. Instead of crossing as he done three or four times already, he hit a low shot to the unguarded near post, almost passing the ball into the goal. There were ten minutes left and Brazil needed a goal. They made some half chances and Máspoli made one last good sprawling save from a Jair shot, but Brazil had lost the belief and lost the crowd, and they lost the game. The Maracanã (and the nation) was heartbroken. They would need to wait sixty-four years for another shot at redemption on their own turf.

Reports state that Jules Rimet, the guest of honour, had a speech in his pocket congratulating Brazil on their victory; let's hope the FIFA President was able to extemporise. It was the end for most of this generation of Brazilian stars; only Bauer of the starting XI in the Maracanã made the squad for the next tournament. One other thing would never be the same again; Brazil dropped the white shirts with a blue neckline, believing them cursed after this defeat. They went instead for yellow.

> *"We won because we won, no more . . . if we had played a hundred times we would have won only that one."*
>
> Uruguay captain and leader, Obdulio Varela,
> reflects later on the match

In an unsavoury coda to the defeat, the Brazilian press focused on the "poor contribution" of the black players in the team – goalkeeper Barbosa, one of the best in the world, was picked out for particularly harsh treatment. It was a hangover from colonial days that took a while longer to tackle – only with the establishment of Pelé and his golden generation of black players did a truer sense of acceptance arrive.

World Cup Heroes No.5
Alcides Ghiggia (1920–)
Uruguay

Ghiggia, with his distinctive sunken cheeks and round shoulders, is one of the forgotten greats of the World Cup. He only won twelve caps, four of them in this tournament, but he was Uruguay's key weapon in the attacking third. Whippet thin and whippet quick, Ghiggia had an astonishing change of pace from a hunched run with the ball to a sudden sprint past a defender.

He played for Peñarol alongside Schiaffino, hence their fabulous understanding, and won the league title in 1949 and 1951. Part of the reason he won so few caps was a ban for attacking a referee – a slightly out of character act for a quiet, if determined, man. The other reason was a move to Italy – perhaps prompted by the ban – to start an eight-year

spell with AS Roma. The Uruguay World Cup squad of
1954 featured only players still resident in Uruguay. Like
many others, Ghiggia took citizenship of his adopted country and became one of the *oriundi* while at Roma, winning
five caps for Italy.

Ghiggia is the oldest surviving World Cup winner and it
is hoped that he will appear at the Maracanã again in 2014,
having survived a head-on collision with a lorry in 2012
(aged eighty-six) – that's a tough old boy.

1950 Team of the Tournament: 2–3–5

Máspoli (Uruguay)

Tejera (Uruguay)   Nilsson (Sweden)

Bauer (Brazil)   Varela (Uruguay)   Rodríguez Andrade (Uruguay)

Ghiggia (Uruguay) Zizinho (Brazil) Ademir (Brazil) Schiaffino (Uruguay) Basora (Spain)

Leading scorers: Ademir (8); Míguez (5); Basora, Zarra, Chico, Ghiggia (4)

Official Team of the Tournament: Máspoli (Uruguay); Parra (Spain), Nilsson (Sweden);
Rodríguez Andrade (Uruguay), Bauer (Brazil), Varela (Uruguay); Ghiggia (Uruguay), Zizinho
(Brazil), Ademir (Brazil), Schiaffino (Uruguay), Jair (Brazil).

Heaven Eleven Features

Just for fun (and because we can), I have selected, along with a
panel of global football experts, some all-time sides to contest a
Fantasy World Cup (post-war players only). Seven of the eight
winners get a team – Uruguay get help from the other South
Americans apart from Brazil and Argentina, as their recent
history has been less glorious. Holland also get an entry as the
only team to lose three finals, and to have underachieved with
such consistency.

The rest of Europe is divided into five teams: Scandinavia,
Central Europe, Eastern Europe, former Soviet Union and a
Mediterranean team, with some help from North Africa. There is
also a British Isles team and a Rest of the World team.

I've stuck to post-war players – so hard to compare otherwise.

Heaven Eleven No.1

Uruguay & South America (Bolivia, Chile, Colombia, Ecuador, Paraguay, Peru, Venezuela)

Coach:
Juan López: coach of the Uruguay side that won in 1950 and beat England in 1954

Goalkeepers:
René Higuita (Col): just for a giggle, I am aware he wasn't actually that good
José Luis Chilavert (Par): you never know when a game might go to penalties . . .
Roque Máspoli (Uru): a top goalkeeper, best in his day along with Grosics of Hungary

Defenders:
Iván Cordóba (Col): hold down a centre-back spot at Inter for a decade and you ain't a mug
Carlos Gamarra (Par): played the 2002 World Cup without conceding a foul and outstanding at the Olympics two years later
Hector Chumpitaz (Per): put in a couple of almost Beckenbauer-like performances in 1970
Elías Figueroa (Chi): classy, played mostly in Uruguay and Brazil so missed a lot of caps
Obdulio Varela (Uru): the captain and tank in the 1950 winning team, a veritable one-man army, could play at centre-back or as a holding player
Maxi Pereira (Uru): exciting wing-back, a real star of 2010
José Santamaria (Uru): pedestrian for Portugal in the early 1960s but in his youth for Uruguay he was an imposing presence
José Navarro (Chi): captain of the 1962 team, unavailable for the semi-final when Garrincha roasted his replacement

Midfield & Wide:

Freddy Rincón (Col): more urgent and effective than his countryman Valderrama and less likely to be left a passenger against high-tempo opposition

Teófilo Cubillas (Per): Peru's greatest, and one of South America's greatest; fantastic passing ability and a rocket shot

Eliado Rojas (Chi): the tough guy in midfield in Chile's 1962 team; here for balance, because he could pass better than most enforcers

Enzo Francescoli (Uru): Zidane's favourite player, he was a solitary beacon in a grim era for Uruguay

Juan Schiaffino (Uru): the twig-like inside-forward who inspired his side in the 1950 and 1954 World Cups

Alcides Ghiggia (Uru): blisteringly quick right-winger – his career for Uruguay was curtailed when he defected to Italy

Juan José Muñante (Per): another speedster, part of the Peru team that destroyed Scotland in 1978 – inconsistent but lethal

Arsenio Erico (Par): Paraguay's best creative player, he played in the 1930s and 1940s and became the Argentinian league's highest ever goalscorer during his years with Independiente

Strikers:

Victor Ugarte (Bol): Bolivia's solitary world-class player in an era where they struggled in the main; scored twice against Brazil to clinch their shock 1963 Copa América win

Iván Zamorano (Chi): successful in Spain and Italy, and a consistent and passionate performer for his country

Marcelo Salas (Chi): just sneaked in ahead of Carlos Caszely on his World Cup record – I wanted Caszely in because he was one of the few public figures to openly oppose Pinochet's government, but I couldn't really justify it!

Diego Forlán (Uru): one of the great workhorses and hold-up players of the modern game; one of the few players from whom Alex Ferguson didn't get the best

Omissions: Carlos Caszely (Chi, see above); **Carlos Valderrama** (Col, see above); **Hugo Sotil** (Per, another top attacking player in the 1970s team); **Luis Suárez** (Uru – he and

I wouldn't get on); **Óscar Míguez** (Uru) – the punchy, direct goalscorer in the great 1950s Uruguay side

Strengths: Excellent central defenders, good creative midfield players
Weaknesses: Lack of outstanding full-backs, lack of power up front

Likely first XI:

Máspoli
Santamaria Figueroa Cordóba Pereira
Rojas
Cubillas Schiaffino
Ghiggia Francescoli
Zamorano

2.2 WORLD CUP 1954

This was a good one. Brutal, occasionally, one famous game in particular, but a good tournament with some terrific football, a ton of goals and an unexpected outcome. Switzerland had eight years to prepare, having been the only country to put their name forward in 1946; it made sense, they had suffered less depredations during the war than most European countries. If there was any resentment, it was that they had done rather well out of their neutrality.

Switzerland had good stadiums, all holding more than 50,000, in Basle, Berne and Lausanne, while smaller grounds in Zurich, Lugano and Geneva would be used in support. The final was earmarked for the 50,000 Wankdorf Stadium in Berne. No tittering at the back, please. One can assume everything ran on time – they're good at timekeeping, the Swiss. Actually they are, it's a national stereotype for a reason.

Qualifying

Qualification went pretty much to plan. The only minor shock in Europe was the elimination of 1950 semi-finalists Sweden by Belgium, but Sweden were being stubborn about not picking their Italian-based professional stars and were hugely weakened by their absence. Once again the British Home Internationals served as a qualifying group with two places up for grabs; this time Scotland didn't get sniffy about qualifying in second place. Maybe the trip to Switzerland was more appealing than crossing the Atlantic by boat. England won all three matches easily, but a better assessment of their standing came in two friendlies against Hungary.

The Soviet bloc countries were still reclusive; East Germany's membership of FIFA was not yet ratified, Poland withdrew and the Soviets declined to enter. Few in the West had any notion of the horrors Stalin's government were perpetrating on their own people and it was another decade before they were admitted and apologised for by the new administration. Soviet domestic football was strong, as evidenced by the impressive post-war goodwill tour by Dynamo Moscow. There were technical and conditioning innovations taking place behind the iron curtain that would impact heavily in the 1960s – and I don't just mean the systematic doping that tainted so many athletes, especially in East Germany.

Hungary, rightly, were the pre-tournament favourites. They had inflicted some heavy defeats on some of the best sides around; home and away wins, 5–0 and 5–1, against Czechoslovakia, a hammering of Italy, and, most relevant, the humbling of England at Wembley in November 1953. England had never lost at home to a non-British side, and yet here they were, floundering against a Hungarian side superior in every department of the game. Technically adept and with a superb goalkeeper and tough defence, the *Magical Magyars* (as the press dubbed them) looked simply unstoppable, averaging four goals a game with a range of passing and movement no one had seen before. If they had a weakness, it was lack of strength in depth, but their first team included seven world-class players and four good ones. A chance for revenge in May, a month before the World Cup started, ended in even deeper humiliation as Hungary ran away with the game in Budapest; 7–1 remains a record defeat for England, and, inept as England can be at times, it is a record that looks likely to stand for a long time.

Seven world-class players? Yup. The goalkeeper Grosics, fullback Buzánszky, the brilliant half-back József Bozsik, the deep-lying pass-master Nándor Hidegkuti, the left-winger Czibor and the goalscoring inside-forwards Puskás and Kocsis. This was the most talented side put on to a football field to date.

The South American challenge would come from holders Uruguay and a rebuilt Brazil, while Mexico and South Korea

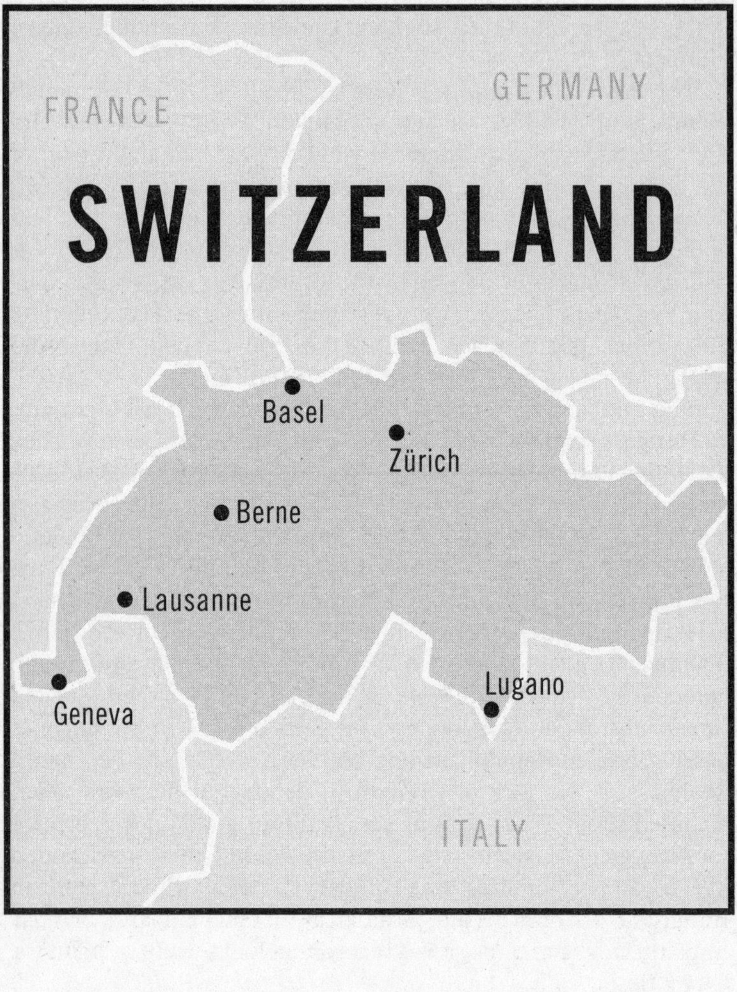
FRANCE
GERMANY
SWITZERLAND
Basel
Zürich
Berne
Lausanne
Geneva
Lugano
ITALY

1954
SWITZERLAND

Berne: Wankdorf Stadium
The stadium chosen for the final was opened in 1927, and capacity had gradually increased from the original 22,000 to 64,000 for the finals tournament. The Wankdorf (which has been making supposedly grown-up Englishmen titter for decades) is named for the district of Berne in which it is situated and is home to the Young Boys club.

Basel: St Jakob Stadium
The home of FC Basel was demolished in 1998 and replaced with the custom-built St Jakob-Park. The ground hosted six games at the 1954 finals, and anyone lucky enough to have watched them all would have seen a remarkable forty-four goals. A record 58,000 attended West Germany's victory over Austria.

Geneva: Charmilles Stadium
Replaced with the Stade de Genève in 2002, the Charmilles held around 20,000 and was the home of Servette Geneva.

Lausanne: Stade Olympique de la Pontaise
Reduced now from its original near-50,000 capacity to 15,850 seats, La Pontaise remains on the same site as when it opened in 1904, and is the home of FC Lausanne.

Zürich: Hardturm Stadium
The Hardturm, home of the Grasshoppers club, claimed 35,000 people watched the third place match at the 1954 World Cup Finals, but this is questionable. The ground was closed in 2007 and the club temporarily shared its grounds with hated rivals FC Zürich.

Lugano: Cornaredo Stadium
The Cornaredo hosted only one game in the 1954 finals – that between Italy and Belgium. That 26,000 people attended, as FIFA claim, is unlikely; the stadium now has a capacity of just over 15,000 and is home to AC Lugano.

represented the northern half of America and Asia. The luckiest qualifier was Turkey, whose name came out of a hat after a decider against Spain ended 2–2; under current rules Spain would have qualified comfortably on goal difference.

Finals

The rules were stupid – of course they were – with each group featuring two seeded teams who only played the two non-seeded teams. WHY? In addition, the seeding was wrong-headed and inaccurate; there were no FIFA rankings in those days. Not that FIFA rankings count for much, really (see the Terms and Tactics chapter).

The top group was a case in point. A few weeks before the World Cup, Yugoslavia beat France 3–1, yet here they were unseeded, which meant they had to play Brazil as well as the French. In Group 2, similarly, Turkey were seeded at the expense of Germany, who were a decent team albeit one with no great recent form. In the last group, England and Italy were seeded and the hosts, oddly, were not, which seemed a bit harsh (and would never happen now where the hosts are always in the top pool of seeded teams and always seem to get a kind draw).

Once the groups were sorted, there was some further FIFA nonsense to deal with; in their infinite wisdom, they decided the four group winners would play each other in the last eight, with the two winners contesting a semi-final, while the group runners-up would do likewise – some reward for winning the group!

GROUP 1

Brazil Baltazar 24, Didi 30, Pinga 34, 43, Julinho 69	(4) 5	**Mexico**	(0) 0	16 June, Geneva; 13,000
Yugoslavia Milutinovic 15	(1) 1	**France**	(0) 0	16 June, Lausanne; 16,000
France Vincent 19, own goal 46, Kopa 89 (p)	(1) 3	**Mexico** Lamadrid 54, Balcázar 85	(0) 2	19 June, Geneva; 19,000
Brazil Didi 69	(0) (1) 1	**Yugoslavia** Zebec 48	(0) (1) 1	19 June, Lausanne 25,000

Yugoslavia kicked off against France knowing they most likely needed a win; France would surely beat Mexico, the group whipping boys, and Yugoslavia, while a decent side, entertained little expectation of beating Brazil. A fourteenth-minute goal decided the game – Yugoslavia's main gripe would have been not adding to that goal, for they certainly created chances. They seemed to like 1–0 – they won all four of their qualifying matches by the same score. France were an improving team, but they would have to wait another four years to reach the latter stages for the first time. In the other opener Brazil saw off Mexico comfortably enough and could have scored more than five. An international audience was treated to a first view of Didi's trademark free-kicks as he dinked one into the corner for Brazil's second.

Mexico were more competitive against France and did really well to come back from 2–0 down to level with five minutes to go. A late penalty for handball was tough on them; it was coolly converted by French playmaker twenty-two-year-old Raymond Kopaszewski. France had to rely on Brazil beating Yugoslavia for a crack at a play-off.

Yugoslavia were an experienced side, with much the same team that played in 1950 and gave a good account of themselves against Brazil. They did the same here, and enjoyed the better of the first half. Brazil made the error of trying to use Baltazar's strength in the air, but he was well marshalled by Horvat, and it was only when Brazil started to play through Didi and the right winger Julinho that they made progress. It was Yugoslavia who took the lead when Zebec, equally comfortable anywhere across the front line, advanced from a deep central position, went past a feeble tackle and shot a hummer across the goalkeeper into the left-hand side of the goal.

Brazil were starting to play, though, and should have had a penalty when Baltazar was taken out as he was about to shoot with the 'keeper grounded – nothing doing, said the splendidly named referee Charlie Faultless. Minutes later, Yugoslavia had a double escape when Julinho's angled drive was blocked on the line and a viciously struck follow-up was saved superbly by Beara. But the goal was coming, and it was a terrific strike, Didi teeing off with scant room at the edge of the penalty area and driving in off the crossbar. Brazil pushed on and dominated the first period of extra-time (another weird FIFA ruling . . .) and Julinho was unlucky to see a shot rebound off the bar. In the second period Yugoslavia steadied the ship, despite an injury to Cajkovski, and it was Castilho's turn to save his side with a fine point-blank stop from Zebec.

GROUP 2

Hungary	(4) 9	**South Korea** (0) 0	17 June, Zurich; 13,000

Puskás 11, 89, Lantos 17,
Kocsis 24, 35, 49, Czibor 58,
Palotás 77, 84

West Germany (1) 4		**Turkey** (1) 1	17 June, Berne; 28,000

Schäfer 12, Klodt 50,   Suat 3
O Walter 60, Morlock 84

West Germany (1) 3		**Hungary** (3) 8	20 June, Basle; 53,000

Pfaff 25, Rahn 78,   Kocsis 3, 21, 69, 79,
Herrmann 84   Puskás 17, Hidegkuti 52, 55,
    Tóth 75

Turkey	(4) 7	**South Korea** (0) 0	20 June, Geneva; 2,000

Suat 10, 28, Lefter 24,
Burhan 36, 64, 70, Erol 76

Play-off

West Germany (3) 7		**Turkey** (1) 2	23 June, Zurich; 17,000

O Walter 7, Schäfer 12, 79,   Mustafa 17, Lefter* 82
Morlock 31, 62, 77,
F Walter 63

Sepp Herberger had managed to hang onto his job after the debacle of the 1938 World Cup by expediently shifting the blame onto the Austrian contingent within his side, claiming they lacked stomach for the contest – the accusation was probably true, in part, as some of the Austrians were less than passionate about fighting Hitler's propaganda war on the field. He survived the war and was teaching coaching in Cologne. When the new West German football federation reappointed a national coach in 1949, Herberger lobbied furiously and got the job.

---

* Lefter Küçükandonyadis, a tricky and mobile inside-left, was Turkey's best footballer in the 1950s and early '60s. He played more than 500 games for Fenerbahçe, where he is revered, and scored over 300 goals; he scored twenty-two more in fifty internationals, a record overtaken only this century, by Hakan Sükür.

West Germany missed the 1950 World Cup – they were still in the political naughty corner following reparations at the end of the Second World War – but played their first international under the new federation in 1950, against Switzerland, who were more forgiving than most European nations – presumably because they were one of the few that hadn't been invaded. On a foul evening 115,000 people turned out – the Germans needed something to soothe the wounds to their national psyche.

The portents for the 1954 World Cup were not good; West Germany lost badly to France in 1952 and made heavy weather of an easy qualifying group that contained Norway and the briefly convened republic of Sarland, managed by Herberger's fellow-German Helmut Schön – more of him anon. Herberger relied heavily on a declining Kaiserslautern side and was getting stick for it in the press. Things didn't get any easier when the draw was made for the Finals and West Germany found themselves in with Hungary, regarded as comfortably the best team in Europe, and Turkey, an emerging side who had beaten them two years previously. Under the ridiculous system FIFA adopted, West Germany were denied a crack at a laughably bad South Korea side.

As it transpired Turkey didn't present much of a threat, despite taking the lead after three minutes. Once the Germans got going their superior organisation and fitness carried the day easily. West Germany won 4–1, while Hungary racked up nine in their opener against South Korea; it could have been more but the Hungarians eased off in the second half and seemed unwilling to completely humiliate their exhausted opponents.

West Germany got trounced 8–3 by Hungary when Herberger cautiously rested half his team for the inevitable (and absurd) play-off against Turkey. Some writers find this explanation awkward, but why else would Herberger leave out Morlock, Ottmar Walter, Schäfer and his best goalkeeper, the experienced Turek? Hungary kept their big stars in, but replaced Palotás with the more flexible Hidegkuti, and their movement bewildered the Germans even after the great Ferenc Puskás limped off in the second half.

The play-off proved to be the match that instilled some self-belief in the German side, who were pilloried at home for their performance against Hungary. West Germany had three top-notch performers; centre-half Jupp Posipal, and the two inside-forwards, Max Morlock and the veteran Fritz Walter. The barrel-shaped winger Helmut Rahn was a bit of a wild card, but had played well against Hungary and kept his place.

Second time around, Turkey were beaten even more emphatically; Morlock scored a hat-trick, and the second half became a bit of a stroll. West Germany were starting to look like a team again, with the return of Fritz Walter adding stability and experience to a previously haphazard system with no self-belief. Walter's craft and the high work-rate of right-half Horst Eckel allowed Morlock to play more as an out-and-out attacker, which suited this quick and elusive player. West Germany went through alongside Hungary, who looked every bit the tournament favourites.

GROUP 3

Uruguay	(0) 2	**Czechoslovakia**	(0) 0	16 June, Berne; 20,000
Míguez 71, Schiaffino 84				
Austria	(1) 1	**Scotland**	(0) 0	16 June, Zurich; 25,000
Probst 32				
Uruguay	(2) 7	**Scotland**	(0) 0	19 June, Basle; 34,000
Borges 17, 48, 58,				
Míguez 31, 81,				
Abbadíe 55, 87				
Austria	(4) 5	**Czechoslovakia**	(0) 0	19 June, Zurich; 26,000
Stojaspal 2, 65,				
Probst 4, 21, 25				

Group 3 looked more straightforward, as the seeded teams, Uruguay and Austria, seemed a lot better than Czechoslovakia and Scotland, both at low ebb.

So it proved, but Scotland gave Austria a bit of a fight in the opening game – literally in Allan Brown's case, he and the Austrian captain Ernst Ocwirk were lucky not to be sent off for fighting. Austria scored somewhat against the run of play when Alfred Körner, one of two winger-brothers in the Austrian side, hit a hard, low cross which Probst controlled and put away neatly at the near post. Late in the game Willie Ormond (a future Scotland manager) hit a low drive that forced a sprawling save from Schmied, but generally Scotland didn't pose enough problems for their opponents in the second half – which begs the question why their most potent forward, Lawrie Reilly, was left out; his club colleague Bobby Johnstone was named in the squad but withdrew with an injury. Scotland manager Andy Beattie resigned after the match, fed up with a selection policy that left him with limited options.

Uruguay started hesitantly against Czechoslovakia, who defended in numbers and had goalkeeper Theo Reimann in terrific form. Schiaffino, just signed by Milan for a world record figure of £72,000, was closely marked and few chances were created. Míguez, who had a shot stopped by Reimann's face (ouch! – those old leather balls were heavy), finally broke the deadlock and there was time for Schiaffino to show what the fuss was about with a super free-kick.

The second round of games re-established the pecking order in no uncertain terms. Austria beat their Czech neighbours 5–0, with a hat-trick for Ernst Probst inside twenty-five minutes as the Austrians ran up a four-goal cushion against some shoddy marking. Stojaspal added a fifth, his second, minutes after being carried off in apparent agony.

Uruguay turned on the style against Scotland, especially in the second half. They had the core of the victorious side from 1950 still – Máspoli, Andrade, Varela, Schiaffino – but fielded two new exciting wingers in Julio César Abbadíe and Carlos Borges. Borges was a real flyer, and was simply too quick for Aird and Cunningham at the back for Scotland, helping himself to a hat-trick as Schiaffino's movement and passing pulled the Scottish marking all over the place. Uruguay weren't flattered by their win, and it was a record defeat for Scotland that they should have heeded – they were yards behind their opponents in fitness, tactics and technique. Scotland, who had viewed the World Cup as pretty pointless until this tournament, left Switzerland in the same state – pointless; and not so pretty.

Scotland Squad 1954:
GK: Fred Martin (Aberdeen, 25 years old, 2 caps)
DEF: Willie Cunningham (Preston North, 29, 3), Jock Aird (28, 2), Bobby Evans (Glasgow Celtic, 26, 17)

MID & WIDE: Tommy Docherty* (Preston, 25, 5), Jimmy Davidson (Partick Thistle, 28, 2), Doug Cowie (Dundee, 28, 6)
FWD: Allan Brown (Blackpool, 27, 11), Willie Fernie (Celtic, 25, 1), George Hamilton (Aberdeen, 36, 5), John Mackenzie (Partick, 28, 4), Neil Mochan (Celtic, 27, 1), Willie Ormond (Hibernian, 27, 3)

Named but left at home as cover:

John Anderson (Leicester City, GK); Alex Wilson (Portsmouth, DEF); Jimmy Binning (Queen of the South, DEF); David Mathers (Partick, MF); Bobby Combe (Hibernian, MF); Jackie Henderson (Portsmouth, FWD); Ernie Copland (Raith Rovers, FWD); Ian McMillan (Airdrie, FWD)

GROUP 4

England Broadis 25, 62 Lofthouse 37, 91	(2) (3) 4	**Belgium** Anoul 4, 74, Coppens 77, own goal 93	(1) (3) 4	17 June, Basle; 24,000
Switzerland Ballaman 18,	(1) 2	**Italy** Hügi 78	(1) 1	17 June, Lausanne; 43,000
England Mullen 44, Wilshaw 70	(1) 2	**Switzerland** (0) 0		20 June, Berne; 43,500
Italy Pandolfini 41 (p), Galli 48, Frignani 58, Lorenzi 78	(1) 4	**Belgium** Anoul 81	(0) 1	20 June, Lugano; 26,000

Play-off

Switzerland (1) 4 Hugi 14, 85, Ballaman 48, Fatton 89		**Italy** Nesti 67	(0) 1	23 June, Basle; 30,000

England and Italy were seeded in the last group, but it looked the toughest of all, with no whipping boys. Both the opening games showed how open it was.

Switzerland provided the first minor shock by beating Italy 2–1. The game was fractious – the referee was escorted off by police after disallowing an Italian "goal" for offside – but the Swiss defence held firm. Italy were heavily reliant, at least creatively, on Giampiero Boniperti, but the Juventus playmaker, so

---

* Yes, him, the motor-mouth future manager of Chelsea and Manchester United. Docherty was one of the few who recognised just how inadequate the Scots' preparation and performance was in this tournament.

adored and so potent in *Serie A*, was never the same influence for Italy. The Swiss were defensive and limited, but well organised by their coach Karl Rappan, and dangerous on the break. Fatton was still there from 1950, and Hügi, the new centre-forward from Basle, looked a robust handful.

England usually had no problem beating Belgium, but in their opening game in Basle some jittery defending gave the Belgians a sniff; Anoul opened the scoring after England failed to clear the ball effectively. England bounced back and, prompted by the evergreen thirty-nine-year-old Matthews, they equalised when Broadis just beat the goalkeeper to the maestro's through ball. Nat Lofthouse headed in a Tom Finney cross before half-time – a sane man would have volleyed the ball not headed it at knee height – and Broadis rammed home a third just past the hour. The game looked safe but unfortunately goalkeeper Gil Merrick didn't, and centre-half Syd Owen was carrying an injury. Belgium came back and scored a neat second, then Coppens left Owen in his wake as he scored an equaliser. It was the first time England had played extra-time in an international, but they took to it well and went back ahead when Lofthouse slammed home a cross from Broadis. Belgium's final leveller was a freak, the ball looping over Merrick off Dickinson's head as he was put under pressure trying to deal with a deep cross from the right-wing. Four-all; breathless stuff, but not the defensive improvement England sought after their nightmare evening in Budapest.

That came in the next game when dependable Billy Wright moved to centre-half and Bill McGarry came in at right-half. Both Matthews and Lofthouse picked up knocks in the first game, so in came Jimmy Mullen and Dennis Wilshaw, both colleagues of Wright at Wolves; Tommy Taylor moved to his more natural position at centre-forward, a more skilful and fluent player than Lofthouse, but not so quick or powerful. The game was played in the impressive Wankdorf Stadium in Berne. The old stadium was knocked down and this new 64,000-capacity ground built in plenty of time for the start of the tournament – no half-finished stands or botched jobs for the Swiss. England did not expect to be intimidated – the Swiss fans were not known for fervency or intimidation.

Switzerland were pliant opposition, offering little in attack, and
Wright hoovered up any threat that materialised as if he had
played centre-half all his life. Mullen came up with a good run
and finish just as England were getting edgy, and Wilshaw netted
a second after a fine slaloming run. England breathed a collective
sigh of relief; they were in the next round and avoided the ignominy of 1950. With Italy beating Belgium easily, England's next
challenge lay in the fact that they won the group and ended up in
the tough winners' half of the draw.

Switzerland and Italy had to play off for the last spot in the
quarter-final line-up and it was the Swiss who came out on top.
The win was never as comfortable as 4–1 suggests and Lorenzi
– who had chased the referee across the pitch after the first game
between the two – had an effort cleared off the line at 1–0 to
Switzerland. Welshman Mervyn Griffiths was a better official and
this match never got out of hand.

QUARTER-FINALS (all 26 June)

Uruguay	**(2) 4**	**England** (1) 2	Basle; 28,000
Borges 5, Varela 38,		Lofthouse 15, Finney 65	
Schiaffino 47, Ambrois 79			
Austria	**(5) 7**	**Switzerland** (4) 5	Lausanne; 32,000
Wagner 25, 28, 54,		Ballaman 16, 36,	
A Körner 26, 34,		Hügi 17, 19, 60	
Ocwirk 32, Probst 77			
West Germany (1) 2		**Yugoslavia** (0) 0	Geneva; 17,000
Own goal 9, Rahn 86			

This World Cup saw an average of more than five goals per
game. Later, in *The Winning Formula*, Charles Hughes ascribed
the downturn in that statistic through the next two decades as an
indication that standards of football were in decline. But then
pretty much everything he set down in his FA manual was bunk,
so we shouldn't get over-excited. The four quarter-finals produced
twenty-five goals and bags of excitement, but some of the defending was amateur hour, and none of the games was a feast of pure
football. Only one has passed into legend and that for very different reasons.

Let's start with the lowest scoring, West Germany against
Yugoslavia. Yugoslavia were a good side technically, but here they
looked toothless. They enjoyed plenty of possession, especially in

the first half, but couldn't convert it. Milutinovic, a promising right-winger, speedy and direct, missed a good chance when through, and Kohlmeyer headed off the line when Turek punched clear and was left stranded when the ball was promptly knocked back towards the goal. Turek was an experienced shot-stopper but a bit of a lemon on crosses.

West Germany's goals bookmarked the match. In the tenth minute Horvat, under pressure from Schäfer, headed past his own goalkeeper, who was in no man's land. Four minutes from time Rahn let a crossfield pass bounce before hitting it hard across Beara and in off the far post. The chunky winger gave Crnkovic a torrid time, just pushing the ball past and charging through him; this last time the full-back stood off, expecting the charge and gave Rahn room for a sweet strike.

Now the highest-scoring game. There was nothing in the group matches to suggest Austria versus Switzerland would produce twelve goals, so maybe it was the searing heat that was responsible for some school playground defending. The game was played at a very gentle pace (understandably in 40-degree temperatures), and the closing down was non-existent, allowing a succession of shots to fly goalwards from the edge of the penalty area. It was one of those days when they all seemed to find the back of the net. Ballaman's opener for Switzerland was a good strike and Hügi added two more in two minutes, first when he was allowed to walk through the middle of the defence and then when he slammed Vonlanthen's cutback in off the bar. Austria replicated Switzerland's three in four minutes when Wagner, Alfred Körner and Wagner again all shot home – Parlier should have stopped both Wagner's goals but Körner's was the best of the day, struck from the left-hand corner of the penalty area with the outside of his left foot and in off the far post. Perfect. Now Austria were in the ascendant and took the lead five minutes later with a clinical strike from Ocwirk, and added to it when Parlier spilled the ball at Alfred Körner's feet – although there was more than a suspicion he was fouled by the Austrian winger.

The Swiss hit back almost immediately with a close-range finish from Ballaman, and that was it for first-half goals, but only because Robert Körner, Alfred's brother and opposite wing, missed a penalty. Wagner and Hügi completed their hat-tricks in the second half before Probst gave Austria some daylight, dinking the ball over the 'keeper after running through the inside-left channel. For running read trotting, as the game was at walking pace by now; the Swiss had no energy to muster another fight-back and the twists and scoring were over. A freak game, explained largely by freak conditions and some poor goalkeeping. The Swiss were out, but hadn't disgraced themselves in their home tournament. Austria would now face their old nemesis, West Germany, in the semi-final.

England got a tough draw in the quarter-finals against the holders. Uruguay looked strong in their second match and would surely test England's porous defence and nervy goalkeeper. England made two changes, restoring the fit-again pair of Matthews and Lofthouse at the expense of Mullen and Tommy Taylor; Wilshaw kept his place at inside-left. Uruguay fielded their best eleven but were hampered by an early injury to Abbadíe.

Abbadíe contributed to the opening goal before his injury. Borges attacked from the left and his cross was only half-cleared to the opposite wing; whether Abbadíe meant to return the ball to Borges rather than shoot is questionable but the no.11 gleefully hooked it home. England's reply was a good spell of attacking with Matthews to the fore and a terrific equaliser. Wilshaw ran square across the eighteen-yard line looking for a shooting angle; when one didn't appear he cleverly reversed the ball into space where Lofthouse spun off his marker and scored with his left.

A well-balanced game swung Uruguay's way when Varela, stepping out from the back in a way Wright never did, hit an accurate drive from the edge of the penalty area; Merrick moved late and not far enough. Within a minute Varela was hobbling, reduced to a defensive role as Andrade took his place in the middle. England failed to take advantage, their backs unwilling to advance and make the extra fit man count, and the Uruguayans dropped deeper and deeper and relied on the pace of Borges to counter. Another disastrous piece of goalkeeping effectively settled the game, when Merrick dived too early for Schiaffino's half-hit shot and watched it roll into the corner. Schiaffino was superb, withdrawing almost to a half-back role but still able to relieve any pressure with little surging runs and accurate passing.

England continued to compete, Matthews and Finney especially, and they scored a scrappy goal when Lofthouse's shot deflected off Máspoli's knee to the prone Finney, who stabbed it home. Hope stirred, but England looked the more tired of the two teams, Uruguay's walking wounded notwithstanding, and Ambrois added a fourth when the England defence was slow to close him down and Merrick stayed on his line too long. The goalkeeper had a bad game, and was – predictably, even in the 1950s – slaughtered by the press at home; it was his last international cap. A quarter-final exit was about right for England – they weren't terrible, they just lost to a better, more tactically aware team. Uruguay looked like contenders, if they could patch up their half-fit captain.

This game, along with England's group games, was broadcast live on British TV, the first World Cup transmissions to go out live in the UK. Football coverage began in the 1930s, and in 1938 the FA Cup Final and an England v Scotland international were both broadcast live. The BBC had gradually extended coverage after the war, but it was another ten years before their extended highlights programme *Match of the Day* aired for the first time.

England Squad 1954:
GK: Gil Merrick (Birmingham City, 32 years old, 20 caps), Ted Burgin (Sheffield United, 28, 0)
DEF: Roger Byrne (Manchester United, 25, 3), Ken Green (Birmingham, 30, 0), Syd Owen (Luton Town, 32, 2), Ron Staniforth (Huddersfield Town, 30, 3), Billy Wright (Wolverhampton Wanderers, 30, 58)
MID & WIDE: Ivor Broadis (Newcastle United, 31, 11), Jimmy Dickinson (Portsmouth, 29, 35), Bill McGarry (Huddersfield, 27, 0), Albert Quixall (Sheffield Wednesday, 20, 3), Tom Finney (Preston North End, 32, 51), Stanley Matthews (Blackpool, 39, 36), Jimmy Mullen (Wolves, 31, 11)
FWD: Nat Lofthouse (Bolton Wanderers, 28, 19), Tommy Taylor (Man Utd, 22, 3), Denis Wilshaw (Wolves, 28, 1)

Named as reserves but did not travel*: Ken Armstrong (MF, Chelsea, 30, 0); Allenby Chilton (DEF, Man Utd, 35, 2); Johnny Haynes (MF, Fulham 19, 0); Harry Hooper (FWD, West Ham United, 21, 0), Bedford Jezzard (MF, Fulham, 26, 1)

WORLD CUP CLASSIC No.1
27 June 1954, Wankdorf Stadium, Berne, Switzerland; 40,000

Hungary	(2) 4	Hidegkuti 4, Kocsis 7, 88, Lantos 81 (p)
Brazil	(1) 2	D Santos 18 (p), Julinho 66

Referee: **Arthur Ellis**† (England)
Coaches: **Gusztáv Sebes** (Hungary) & *Alfredo Moreira, known as* **Zézé** (Brazil)

Hungary (2–3–3–2): Gyula Grosics (Honved); Jenö Buzánszky (Dorogi Bányász), Mihály Lantos (MTK); József Bozsik (Cpt, Honved), Gyula Lóránt (Honved), József Zakariás (MTK); József Tóth (Csepeli), Nándor Hidegkuti (MTK), Mihály Tóth (Ujpest Dozsa); Sandor Kocsis (Honved), Zoltán Czibor (Honved)
Brazil (3–2–5): Carlos Castilho (Fluminense); Djalma Santos (Portuguesa), João Carlos Pinheiro (Fluminense), Nílton Santos (Botafogo); José Carlos Bauer (Cpt, São Paulo), *Antenot Lucas, known as* Brandãozinho (Portuguesa); *Júlio Botelho, known as* Julinho (Portuguesa), *Waldir Perreira, known as* Didi (Fluminense), Humberto *Tozzi* (Palmeiras), *Aloísio da Luz, known as* Indio (Flamengo), *Mauro Raphael, known as* Maurinho (São Paulo)

Watch the highlights of this on YouTube and you wonder what all the fuss was about. Some super football, a dodgy decision, a spectacular goal – good game, thanks very much. The full game was a different story.

The opening was good – especially for Hungary. The Brazilian stopper Pinheiro was strong in the tackle and effective, but, being a Brazilian footballer, he also liked to show off his little bag of tricks. Tricky, yes; but shrewd, no – that little dribble in your penalty area in a World Cup quarter-final was not your best

---

* Why bother? (The reason was money, actually.) Of these makeweights, only Haynes wasn't. He would have been worth a gamble at nineteen, even though he was a disappointment when he finally did play in the World Cup. The other four won five caps between them (Hooper never played for the senior team) – makeweights indeed.
† Ellis lost control of this game in the second half, but referees in those days weren't given the extensive training they are now and didn't get the back-up of the football authorities – witness FIFA's pusillanimous decision not to punish either team or any of the players involved in this match. Ellis later found fame as the portly arbiter on TV's *It's A Knockout*.

moment. Hidegkuti robbed him and hit a piledriver that Castilho saved brilliantly; as Tóth ran in to follow up, the ball ran loose to Hidegkuti again and this time he made no mistake, thrashing high and hard into the goal. The second goal came three minutes later courtesy of a deep cross, some non-existent marking and a typically emphatic header from Kocsis.

Brazil decided it was time to up the ante, and the tackling became fiercer. Djalma Santos was in the thick of the action, clearing off the line, flooring Czibor with a broadside tackle and converting a penalty after Indio was brought down clumsily from behind. Hungary's two-goal lead was restored with another penalty award as Kocsis received Czibor's cross and tried to turn his man. There was only the minimum contact from the defender but Arthur Ellis pointed to the spot. Lantos converted as brutally as Santos before him – unusual in those days to see two full-backs taking the penalties.

The tackling got uglier. Bozsik and József Tóth both had to leave the field with injuries, and on his return Bozsik decided to dish some out with a retaliatory crunch on his opposite number Bauer. Julinho pulled one back for Brazil with a delicious strike, hit with his right foot at a sharp angle across Grosics, who was beaten for sheer pace. Five minutes later Bozsik put in another thunderous tackle and, when Nílton Santos reacted, both were escorted off by referee Ellis like a pair of naughty schoolboys. Humberto followed a few minutes later for an assault on Kocsis, and Hidegkuti and Djalma Santos were fortunate not to join the other three – Santos chased Czibor halfway up the pitch after the Hungarian winger made some derogatory remark. When the game ended the trouble didn't. There was a fracas in the tunnel that left Pinheiro with a head wound and further fighting in the Hungarian dressing room left Tóth needing stitches.

All the blood and thunder made the game a bit messy and spoiled what was potentially a superb match between two technically gifted teams. FIFA left it to the individual countries' authorities to deal with the culprits; irrelevant for Brazil and one could hardly blame Hungary for playing Bozsik in the next game given such a reprieve. In fairness his conduct was out of character.

In an uncomfortable coda to the match, Brazil's populist, but increasingly unpopular President, Getulio Vargas, committed suicide (he shot himself in August that year) in the Presidential Palace; Vargas was under heavy pressure from the military to resign and opted for a melodramatic way out.

SEMI-FINAL

West Germany (1) 6	Austria (0) 1	30 June, Basle; 57,000
Schäfer 31, Morlock 47,	Probst 52	
F Walter 62 (p), 88 (p),		
O Walter 62, 89		

THIRD-PLACE MATCH

Austria (1) 3	Uruguay (1) 1	3 July, Zurich, 32,000
Stojaspal 15 (p),	Hohberg 21	
own goal 59, Ocwirk 78		

The Austrians were one of the few teams in the competition still playing in what was effectively a pre-war style – two full-backs, a defensively minded centre-half flanked by two half-backs and five forwards. They played patient possession football, advancing with a succession of short passes, orchestrated by their centre-half Ernst Ocwirk, who captained the Rest of the World side in a celebratory friendly the previous year. It was all very pretty – and all very slow. That was their undoing.

West Germany simply had too much pace and power in the semi-final, playing at a tempo the Austrians couldn't match. And Germany were not only tactically superior, they also showed no little creativity, contrary to some reports. Fritz Walter, quiet so far in this tournament, came out of his shell and strolled elegantly through the game, and his brother Ottmar completely dominated Ocwirk in the air. Rahn and Morlock gave the chain-smoking, elegant full-back Ernst Happel an afternoon to forget. Happel, a fine player who would take Ocwirk's place in the middle a couple of years down the line, found even greater fame as a coach, winning the European Cup twice (the first man to do so) with Feyenoord and Hamburg, and taking Holland to the 1978 World Cup Final.

The first half was tight, but Schäfer opened the scoring when Walter squared the ball across a static defence that stood and watched as the Cologne winger touched in from six yards out. Early in the second period Morlock added another, heading in a corner; Walter's flat, hard delivery from set pieces caused Austria myriad problems. Turek handed the Austrians a lifeline, palming a shot back into Probst's path, but West Germany added three in ten minutes to settle the game around the hour mark. Happel and the Austrian goalkeeper gave away two penalties (both would have been red-carded for professional fouls under modern rules), which Fritz Walter put away without any fuss, and brother Ottmar scored – from another Fritz corner – with a clever flick header. In the final moments Ottmar Walter netted his second when Walter Zeman, Austria's goalkeeper, went walkabout and Schäfer crossed for Ottmar to get ahead of two defenders and head into an empty net. All very impressive from West Germany, but Hungary would surely not be so accommodating. It was the last time Austria made serious inroads into the competition until the 1980s.

WORLD CUP CLASSIC No.2
30 June 1954, Semi-final, Olympique Stadium, known as La Pontaise, Lausanne, Switzerland; 45,000

Hungary	(1) (2)	4	Czibor 12, Hidegkuti 47, Kocsis 109, 116
Uruguay	(0) (2)	2	Hohberg 76, 87

Referee: **Mervyn Griffiths** (Wales)
Coaches: **Gusztáv Sebes** (Hungary) & **Juan López** (Uruguay)

Hungary (2–3–3–2): Gyula Grosics (Honved); Jenö Buzánszky (Dorogi Bányász), Mihály Lantos (MTK); József Bozsik (Cpt, Honved), Gyula Lóránt (Honved), József Zakariás (MTK); László Budai (Honved), Nándor Hidegkuti (MTK), Zoltán Czibor (Honved); Sandor Kocsis (Honved), Péter Palotás (MTK)
Uruguay (3–3–4): Roque Máspoli (Peñarol); José Santamaria (Nacional), Néstor Carballo (Nacional), William Martínez* (Cpt, Rampla Juniors); Victor Rodriguez Andrade (Peñarol), Javier Ambrois (Nacional), Luis Cruz (Nacional); Rafael Souto (Nacional), Juan Alberto Schiaffino (Peñarol), Juan Hohberg (Peñarol), Carlos Borges (Peñarol)

The best game thus far in the World Cup, and still one of the very best. Hungary picked Bozsik despite his indiscretions against

---

* One Uruguayan source suggests Martinez was made captain to avoid discord between the Peñarol and Nacional players; the two Montevideo clubs were bitter rivals.

Brazil, but Puskás was still unfit. Back came Honved winger
László Budai, who was selected for the first game, and Palotás
returned as a more conventional centre-forward allowing
Hidegkuti to stay deep. Varela was still hobbling and was replaced
by Carballo, while Hohberg, Argentinian-born but living in
Uruguay, came in for Míguez. Both wingers were a doubt –
Abbadíe didn't make it, but a ninety per cent fit Borges was
patched up and sent out. Varela never played for Uruguay again
– he was thirty-six – but he remains one of their greats. Later that
year Peñarol announced a shirt sponsorship deal – the first
recorded. Legend has it that ten players wore the new shirt, Varela
being the exception: *"They used to drag us blacks around by rings
in our noses. Those days are gone."* The story is from Galeano, so
assume some poetic licence.

Hungary sensed Uruguay were vulnerable and went for the
jugular. They had picked an attacking line-up and used it to the
full. Palotás shot straight at the 'keeper early on when well placed,
and shots were raining in even before Hungary took the lead. The
goal was simple; a dinked ball from Hidegkuti was headed on
smartly by Kocsis and Czibor hit a bobbling shot across Máspoli,
which the goalkeeper ought really to have stopped.

Hungary continued to dominate possession but there were
warning signs. Three times in the first half Uruguay played
through the middle and found gaps between the Hungarian full-
backs that Lóránt couldn't get back to plug. The big centre-half
was a favourite of the team manager Sebes (who was also the
Minister for Sport). In 1949 Lóránt was detained after trying to
flee the newly Communist Hungary, but he was rescued by Sebes
who had a role for him in his vision for the team. The centre-half
was showing his years here, and looked the one cumbersome
element in such a fluent line-up. Fortunately for Hungary, Grosics
was alert and effective as a sweeper behind his defenders, twice
coming out of his area to intercept through balls – something that
most 1950s goalkeepers didn't tend to do.

The game was being played in the right spirit and not a repeat
of the Brazil match, nor Uruguay's game against England, which
got rough in the last quarter. The odd heavy challenge was
dismissed with a handshake and forgotten – the appointment of

Mervyn Griffiths as referee was presumably not just a happy coincidence; he had a reputation as a strict official.

Having wrested some control back before half-time, Uruguay lost it immediately after the break. Budai, a tricky customer, bent a hanging cross around Martínez that cleared Máspoli. The ball appeared to be drifting safe until Hidegkuti dived bravely, risking smacking his head on a boot or the post, and sneaked it in the corner. Uruguay were struggling, their wingers making no headway and their midfield outplayed by the masterful Bozsik and rapid passing of the opposition.

But Uruguay were nothing if not determined and they showed that *garra*, that refusal to bow, so in evidence in the Maracanã four years earlier. With fifteen minutes to go Hohberg picked up a clearance on the halfway line and fed Ambrois who put the ball into Schiaffino's path. A few urgent strides and the playmaker pushed the ball into the path of Hohberg, who had run on into the space behind Lóránt. The striker's finish was cucumber cool, passing the ball past Grosics into the corner.

The game was end to end; Czibor dispossessed a defender (manhandled might be a more apt description), rounded the goalkeeper and thought he had scored, only for the covering full-back to clear off the line. Uruguay hit the bar following a corner and then Borges saw a cross-shot past the stranded Grosics cleared by Lantos. The equaliser came the same way as Uruguay's first; Schiaffino put on a spurt past his man in midfield and then stretched to toe-poke the ball through to Hohberg; the first shot was well blocked by Grosics, but the tall striker composed himself and drove in the rebound.

Heartened, Uruguay had the better of the opening exchanges in extra-time. Hohberg might have carved his name in history, first miscuing when through, then hitting the base of the post with a twenty-yard piledriver; Grosics reacted well to clear the danger from the rebound when a defender put it back into trouble. In the end it was the aerial power of Kocsis that settled it. Budai was sent away down the right and another excellent cross was met by the immortal head and buried. He repeated the dose a few minutes later from a fine deep cross from Bozsik and that was that. Uruguay went out with great honour; Hungary would play in the final against a team they had already beaten 8–3.

Had Varela been fit, who knows what the outcome might have been? Uruguay were missing the fleet-footed Abbadíe and their regular centre-forward, although Hohberg did ever so well as a replacement that to use the absence of Míguez as any sort of excuse would be flabby reasoning. And Hungary were without one of the greatest goalscorers in the history of the game. The fitness of Ferenc Puskás would be the main talking point of the next few days. The pointless third-place match, which saw Austria beat a drained Uruguay 3–1, certainly wasn't.

World Cup Heroes No.6

Juan Alberto Schiaffino (1925–2002)

Uruguay & Italy

The great conjuror played his last game for Uruguay in this semi-final. His move to Milan was already assured (and included a personal payment of at least £20,000 – Schiaffino was an astute businessman with no need of an agent to fight his corner); within six months he was wearing an Italian shirt just like his countryman Alcides Ghiggia.

Schiaffino was the first great post-war playmaker. Brazil had their artists and Hungary had their inventive centre-forward Hidegkuti, but Schiaffino was a more modern player than even these pioneers. He was slender and looked a bit weedy, but it was a deception; he could ride tackles as well as anyone when he had to. It wasn't usually necessary, his positioning was so good he always seemed to have an extra few seconds on the ball than most. His combination with Varela linked defence to attack in a completely seamless way, and such was Schiaffino's positional nous that if his captain rampaged forward he would often step in behind to guard against a counter-attack should Varela be dispossessed. Against England he played much of the second half as an auxiliary half-back, breaking up England attacks by reading the game and intercepting and retaining possession.

In the semi-final against Hungary he did the opposite and played further forward than usual to compensate for the absence of Óscar Míguez. He was the complete player.

At Milan he joined a strong entourage of Swedish players and formed an outstanding inside-forward pairing with Nils Liedholm. Schiaffino won three *Serie A* titles and scored the opening goal of the 1958 European Cup Final, which the *Rossoneri* lost narrowly to Real Madrid, 3–2 in extra-time. He won four further international caps for Italy – odd it was no more; Italy were a poor side and he was just about the world's best footballer in the mid-fifties. One of those games was in a bloody encounter against Northern Ireland in Belfast when Schiaffino uncharacteristically lost his rag (along with the rest of the Italians) and nearly broke Wilbur Cush's leg.

In the 1970s he briefly managed both the national team and Peñarol, the Montevideo club with whom he started his career and spent eleven years, winning four league titles. None of that would compare with scoring against Brazil in the 1950 World Cup Final as his team came from behind to be crowned world champions.

WORLD CUP FINAL No.5
4 July 1954, Wankdorf Stadium, Berne, Switzerland; 62,472

West Germany	**(2) 3**	Morlock 10, Rahn 19, 85
Hungary	**(2) 2**	Puskás 6, Czibor 8

Referee: **Bill Ling** (England)
Coaches: **Gusztáv Sebes** (Hungary) & **Sepp Herberger** (West Germany)

West Germany (3–3–4): Toni Turek (Fortuna Dusseldorf); Josef Posipal (Hamburg), Werner Liebrich (Kaiserslautern), Werner Kohlmeyer (Kaiserslautern); Horst Eckel (Kaiserslautern), Fritz Walter (Cpt, Kaiserslautern), Karl Mai (Fürth); Helmut Rahn (Rot-Weiss Essen), Max Morlock (Nuremberg) Ottmar Walter (Kaiserslautern), Hans Schäfer (Cologne)
Hungary (2–3–3–2): Gyula Grosics (Honved); Jenö Buzánszky (Dorogi Bányász), Mihály Lantos (MTK); József Bozsik (Honved), Gyula Lóránt (Honved), József Zakariás (MTK); Zoltán Czibor (Honved), Nándor Hidegkuti (MTK), Mihály Tóth (Ujpest Dozsa); Sandor Kocsis (Honved), Ferenc Puskás (Cpt, Honved)

Had the semi-final not been so good, this match would have been written up as a classic itself. Again the Hungarians threw away a two-goal lead, but again they faced opponents with great resolve and willpower that compensated for having less talent than Hungary. And if Hungary had seven world-class players, West Germany had a solid team with no weak links. The young right-half Eckel looked a player, and Rahn was showing more consistency to go with his undoubted natural ability. They had discovered a new centre-half in Liebrich – he had done so well against Yugoslavia in Posipal's absence that the more experienced man dropped back to full-back to accommodate Liebrich. It was Liebrich who had inflicted the injury to Puskás in the first meeting between the two sides. The German press insisted it was a disgraceful challenge, but they were out of love with their team in the tournament's early stages and a couple of the Hungarians later said the tackle was nothing out of the norm and certainly not the sinister plot Puskás claimed just after the competition.

The best of the action came in the first twenty minutes. Germany began brightly and created the first chance, but Morlock headed over from a good position. Hungary's first significant attack produced the opener. Bozsik put Kocsis in space; the striker's instant shot was stopped by Turek but fell fortuitously to Puskás, who steadied and shot home. Injury? What injury? The second goal, two minutes later, was a disaster for Kohlmeyer as the big full-back sold Turek short and Czibor pinched the ball and scored easily.

Germany hit back almost straight away, which was surely crucial for their self-belief. *Tor!* credits Max Morlock with the call to arms after the second Hungarian goal saw one or two heads drop – Fritz Walter, the captain, later admitted he couldn't see the team winning at that point. Hans Schäfer drove a hard cross into the business area and both Zakarias and Morlock stretched out a leg; Zakarias missed and Morlock made just enough contact to deflect the ball past Grosics. Then, with only nineteen minutes on the clock, the game was all-square again. One of Walter's teasing corners was missed by everyone in the middle, but not by Rahn who gleefully half-volleyed the ball home.

Hungary recovered well, and most of the game's momentum was towards the German goal, although it was never the siege some reports suggest. Puskás dribbled through but was stopped by a superb challenge from Liebrich; Kocsis stung Turek's palms; Hidegkuti dummied a cross when he was well placed to just leather it. The worst culprit, though, was Tóth. In acres of space on the corner of the six-yard box he elected to cut back inside Turek and shoot with his left foot, leaving Kohlmeyer time to get back and clear off the line. The winner came from nothing. Schäfer challenged Grosics for a long cross and the goalkeeper's punch came out to Rahn. The winger, an invaluable outlet for West Germany all afternoon, cut back inside onto his left foot and curled a shot past a flat-footed defence.

Puskás was denied a late equaliser by a linesman's flag; video evidence shows him putting the ball in the net a long way ahead of the defender. Right at the death Turek palmed away a fierce shot from Czibor. This was The Miracle of Berne, the day that Germany forged a reputation as a team that never knew it was beaten. It is a reputation that England and Holland, among many, have never come to terms with. The German radio commentator was Herbert Zimmerman, a restrained reporter not given to hyperbole. Zimmerman's reaction as Rahn scored the winner is as etched in German folklore as Kenneth Wolstenholme's *"They think it's all over"* is in England.

> *"Rahn schiesst . . . Tor! Tor! Tor! Tor! . . . Tor für Deutschland! . . . Drei zu zwei führt Deutschland. Halten Sie mich für verrückt, halten Sie mich für ubergeschnappt!"* (Rahn shoots – Goal! Goal! Goal! . . . Goal for Germany! 3–2 to Germany – call me a madman, call me crazy!)

Hungary are treated sympathetically by football writers – the best side never to win the World Cup etc – but they could and should have won this game. Some writers say Puskás shouldn't have played, but he was a proven performer; he scored, nearly saved the game and was still running until the end of the match. The German man-marking worked well on the gifted Hungarian forwards – for once a defender (Eckel) followed Hidegkuti wherever he went and denied him the space to cause his customary havoc.

The Magical Magyars were never the same after this. After the 1956 uprising was brutally quashed by the Soviets three of the big names upped sticks and left for Spain – Puskás for Real Madrid, Kocsis and Czibor for Barcelona. Bozsik stayed and captained the side in the next World Cup. He remains the only Hungarian to win 100 caps (a record that will doubtless fall in the modern era with so many more games scheduled) and was the great prompter and the backbone of the side. Grosics, Budai and Hidegkuti were still around in 1958, although the No.9 was well past his sell-by date. He was a pioneer, a centre-forward who wasn't, ambling around behind the forwards, his bald head ever prominent, and available for the ball, always looking for an opening. Grosics, too, was different – a goalkeeper who played as a sweeper if needed, and who started attacks with fantastic distribution from the hand.

Kocsis was the leading scorer in 1954 – though who knows how many Puskás would have racked up had he remained fit throughout. Kocsis was tidy enough with the ball at his feet, yet in the air he was phenomenal. He was nowhere near six feet, but was adept at dropping off his man or attacking the ball ahead of the defender. And he could head the ball harder than many players could shoot, with neck muscles like a rhino.

Puskás was just a dream. Short, stocky, rather unathletic looking, one-footed, he looked like a park player. But the one foot was lethal, he just never seemed to miss chances, and the stocky build contained explosive power that meant he was fast where he needed to be, over the first ten yards. The ball was glued to his feet – he would show it to the defender and then drag it back as they lunged and accelerate away. Puskás won two European Cups with Madrid and scored four goals in their epic 7–3 win over Eintracht Frankfurt in the 1960 final; undoubtedly an all-time great.

Hungary were beaten by a team of great resolve and some significant talent. West Germany was a country still coming to terms with the shame of the Nazi years, and this team gave the country a sense of pride that didn't smack of anything more sinister. They were led by a canny manager and a modest, self-effacing captain. They didn't play with any of the horrible swagger of German sides in the eighties and nineties; they just had big balls.

World Cup Heroes No.7

Fritz Walter (1920–2002)

West Germany

The story goes that Fritz Walter, having been called to military service in the final years of the Second World War, along with many other notable athletes, was waiting in a camp to be taken back to the Soviet labour camps. The prognosis for those taken back across the Russian border was not good – only one in ten returned to Germany.

A game of football was played between the Ukrainian and Hungarian guards, and it was one of the Hungarians who spotted Walter when he returned the ball after it went out of play. Walter had been the star man in the games played in his prisoner-of-war camp. The Hungarians persuaded the Soviets that Walter was Austrian, not German, and should be sent back to the West. How ironic (yes, genuinely) that they saved the man who helped deny them their greatest footballing moment.

Walter was capped during the war, and was one of the big names on the resumption of domestic football. His club Kaiserslautern became the team to beat in the new German league, winning the title in 1951 and 1953. The 1953–54 season went less well and Herberger, the German coach, was under pressure to place less reliance on their players.

Herberger stuck to his guns, and West Germany grew in stature throughout the tournament; the coach cleverly roomed Walter with the irrepressible, beer-loving Rahn, who wouldn't allow the captain's introspection to get the better of him.

By 1956 Walter was in international retirement and playing out his career at Kaiserslautern. The new generation of German stars weren't really following up on the 1954 success, and three months before the 1958 tournament Herberger persuaded Walter to come out of retirement and galvanise the squad. West Germany reached the semi-final and satisfied expectations in the press, and Walter retired again. He resisted an attempt to lure him into the 1962 squad – he was forty years old and hadn't played in two years. That was Herberger's way, to keep the faith in the talismanic players.

Walter is a figure of mythic status at Kaiserslautern, his only club, where he played nearly 450 games and scored nearly 400 goals. Their stadium was renamed Fritz Walter Stadion in 2002 on his death, and his house is open to the public as a museum.

1954 Team of the Tournament: 3–3–4

Grosics (Hungary)
Buzanszky (Hungary)   Varela (Uruguay)   Posipal (West Germany)
Bozsik (Hungary)   F Walter (West Germany)   Didi (Brazil)
Rahn (West Germany)   Kocsis (Hungary)   Schiaffino (Uruguay)   Matthews (Eng)

Leading scorers: Kocsis (11); Hügi*, Probst, Morlock (6)

Official Team of the Tournament: Grosics (Hungary); D Santos (Brazil), Ocwirk (Austria), Santamaria (Uruguay); Bozsik (Hungary), F Walter (West Germany), Hidegkuti (Hungary); Rahn (West Germany), Kocsis (Hungary), Puskás (Hungary) Czibor (Hungary).

Heaven Eleven No.2

Central Europe (Austria, Czech Republic, Hungary, Slovakia, Switzerland)

Coach:
Ernst Happel (Aut): nearly got in as a player; won the European Cup with Feyenoord and Hamburg, and won the league title in four different countries

---

* Mention of Josef Hügi's name at FC Basel will have fans in raptures. He is the club's all-time leading goalscorer with 244 league goals in a fourteen-year span starting as an eighteen-year-old in 1948. Big and direct and with a sweet left foot, Hügi netted twenty-two goals in thirty-four games for Switzerland.

Goalkeepers:
Gyula Grosics (Hun): one of the best.
Friedrich Koncilia (Aut): Austria's most-capped 'keeper –
severely under-rated
Petr Cech (Cze): one of the modern greats, now with added
skullcap (shouldn't jest, he showed great guts coming back from
that injury – even if not quite as peerless subsequently)

Defenders:
Jenö Buzánszky (Hun): the best defender in the great Hungary
team
Sándor Mátrai (Hun): centre-back in 1958, 1962 and 1966 –
good in all of them
Gerhard Hanappi (Aut): top all-round player, picked here as
a ball-playing defender
Ján Popluhár (Slo): excellent central defender in the 1962
Czechoslovakia side – born in Slovakia
Ladislav Novák (Cze): captain of the 1962 side and a rugged
left-back
Marek Jankulovski (Cze): superb attacking left-back in the
terrific (if unfulfilled) Czech side in the early 2000s
Tomás Ujfalusi (Cze): distinctive caveman appearance but
nothing brutal about his quick, decisive tackling – can also play
right-back
Kálmán Mészöly (Hun): really good attacking centre-back,
can play equally comfortably as a deep midfielder

Midfield & Wide:
József Bozsik (Hun): captain and prompter of the Magical
Magyars
Zoltán Czibor (Hun): one of the Famous Five of the Hungarian
side in the 1950s
Ferenc Bene (Hun): fast, direct, skilful winger with a great
scoring record, a true star in 1966
Nandor Hidegkuti (Hun): the original deep-lying centre-
forward, playing in what is now termed "the hole"
Herbert Prohaska (Aut): deep-lying midfielder, would be
perfect as a holding player in the modern game

Jacky Fatton (Swi): quick, tiny but energetic goalscoring winger in the 1950s

Josef Masopust (Cze): fulcrum of the side that reached the 1962 World Cup Final

Pavel Nedvěd (Cze): terrific player with flair and energy, best of the modern generation in the region

Strikers:

Ferenc Puskás (Hun): one of the best goalscorers ever

Flórián Albert (Hun): genius who orchestrated a good run in the 1966 tournament when Hungary knocked out favourites Brazil

Hans Krankl (Aut): Austrian legend, scored "those" goals (see 1978)

Alexander Frei (Swi): Good, mobile striker who got better as he got older – retired in early 2013 after problems with injury

Omissions: The Czech wingers **Zdeněk Nehoda (Cze)** & **Marián Masny** and midfielders **Antonin Panenka** and (Arsenal's) **Tomas Rosicky** all probably merit a place ahead of Prohaska and Fatton, who are in for national balance, as is Frei ahead of Hungary's **Sándor Kocsis**, **Tibor Nyliasi** and another Austrian, **Toni Polster**. **Ivo Viktor**, the Czech goalkeeper, was tough to leave out.

Strengths: Awesome creativity in midfield and a finisher par excellence

Weaknesses: Lack of robust defenders

Likely first XI:

Cech
Buzánszky Popluhár Mátrai Jankulowski
Bozsik Nedvěd Masopust
Hidegkuti Albert
Puskás

2.3 THE BEST SIDE NEVER TO WIN THE WORLD CUP

This unwanted mantle has been draped around the shoulders of various sides throughout the history of the tournament.

Austria, 1930s
Das Wunderteam were the best team of the late 1920s, and had they bothered to travel to the inaugural World Cup in 1930 they would have stood as the European side most capable of challenging Uruguay and Argentina. They didn't, and by the time the competition came to Europe in 1934 they were past their best, and never hit the same heights.

Hungary, 1950s
They were fantastic (see the section on the 1954 Final), full of world-class attacking players. They butchered weak sides (and some decent ones) and refused to concede ground even to strong opponents, opting for a policy of all-out attack. They could respond to a bit of argy-bargy, too, as the Brazilians found in Berne. They were far from flawless at the back, with a tendency to open up when teams counter-attacked at speed. Great team, should have won in '54.

Holland, 1970s
The team that played Total Football. They were rock solid in defence – just look at the games they won 1–0 and 2–0 – creative in midfield and could score goals. And they had Cruyff, just as

Hungary had Puskás, the best forward of his generation. Their weakness was a tendency to sit on narrow leads and a tendency to overplay – plus the age-old Dutch problem of internecine squabbling and unseemly rows over money. Should have won in 1974.

France, 1980s
They had an outstanding midfield quartet, with a supreme playmaker in Platini and a reliable defence. They lacked a seriously good international striker, despite the occasional flash from the injury-prone Dominique Rocheteau, and never found a top goalkeeper. At the 1984 European Championships they were sublime, and Platini was in such sensational form that he was midfield maestro and goalscorer all rolled into one.

Brazil, 1982
They were full of exciting midfield talents, just like France (who beat them in 1986), but they too lacked a genuinely great striker – unlucky for a Brazilian side. Their defence was no better than competent, and the full-backs too often went missing when attacks broke down.

Holland, 1980s
Like France in 1984, they peaked for a European Championships rather than a World Cup, winning the 1988 tournament in sensational style with a team built around the "holy Trinity" of Rijkaard, Gullit and van Basten. Two years later they went out in tetchy fashion to West Germany.

Portugal's Golden Generation
They flattered to deceive. For all the gifted players they possessed, they never brought their "A" game to a major tournament. Good goalkeeper, wonderful midfield, decent finishers, no bottle.

The best? Hungary, just, from the Cruyff Holland team, with Platini's France third.

BRAZIIIIIIL!

3.1 WORLD CUP 1958

Sweden seemed a good selection as hosts; good infrastructure, good stadia, nice, friendly people. Argentina, Chile and Mexico all put their names forward – by no coincidence they would be the next three non-European hosts.

Qualifying

Sixteen teams again, with four groups then straight to knock out, and the groups would be all-play-all, none of that easy passage for seeded teams nonsense. This was the classic, simple formula that would serve the next four tournaments well. Europe got a generous eleven places, including the hosts and holders, Sweden and West Germany; South America was given three places and North America one, with a single place shared between Asia and Africa – and it only earned them the right to enter a play-off with yet another European side. This last one was an emergency ruling that no team could qualify without playing a match, and, when Turkey and Sudan declined to play Israel, the ruling came into force.

Wales, granted a reprieve after being eliminated by Czechoslovakia, duly won home and away and packed their bags for Sweden. With Northern Ireland also springing a surprise by beating a woeful Italy side, England cruising through their group and Scotland also winning through, it was a first (and last) full house for the home nations. Scotland owed much to their diminutive centre-forward Jackie Mudie, who scored five goals including a vital hat-trick at home against Spain.

SWEDEN

NORWAY

FINLAND

ESTONIA

LATVIA

LITHUANIA

Jernvallen

Tunavallen   Arosvallen

Solna
(Stockholm)

Eyravallen

Norrköping

Rimnersvallen

Gothenburg   Ryavallen

Helsingborg

Örjans Vall

Malmö

1958
SWEDEN

Sweden used twelve stadia in twelve cities for the World Cup in 1958.

Solna (Stockholm): Råsunda Stadium
The Råsunda was the traditional home of Sweden's national side until 2012 when the purpose-built Friends Arena (65,000) replaced it. Just over 50,000 attended the 1958 World Cup Final in the Råsunda; the stadium later (1995) hosted the Women's World Cup Final. Solna is a city to the north of the Swedish capital Stockholm, and is part of the Stockholm municipality.

Gothenburg: Ullevi Stadium
The Ullevi was a 53,500 capacity (now 43,000) stadium built especially for the 1958 finals. The Ullevi has no club attachment, but hosts occasional big matches and lots of open-air concerts and events.

Malmö: Malmö Stadion
Another stadium built for the finals, with a 30,000 capacity, was in Malmö at the southern tip of the country. The ground was shared by Malmö FF (the team with which European football fans will be familiar) and IFK Malmö.

Norrköping: Idrottsparken
Idrottsparken or Nya Parken opened in 1904 and still stands today, albeit with extensive refurbishments. The stadium now holds around 17,000 and is home to three clubs, including IFK Norrköping.

The other eight stadia were located in various smaller cities around the country:

- **Örjans Vall, Halmstad:** 15,000 capacity.
- **Olympia** in **Helsingborg:** 14,500; opened in 1898, it is the oldest of the grounds used.
- **Ryavallen, Borås:** 15,000 capacity; home of IFK Elfsborg and replaced by the Borås Arena in 2004; England played one match here in the 1958 finals.
- **Jernvallen, Sandviken:** claimed 20,000 attended one World Cup match (highly unlikely), but now has a capacity of 7,000.
- **Arosvallen, Våsterås.**

Three stadia hosted just one game each:

- **Tunavallen, Eskilstuna**
- **Rimnersvallen, Uddevalla:** built on a hill, so according to some accounts a few thousand people just camped higher up the hill and watched Brazil play Austria from that vantage point!
- **Eyravallen, Örebro.**

England's centre-forward did even better, scoring successive hat-tricks in emphatic wins over Denmark and Ireland. Tragically, by the time of the Finals, Tommy Taylor was dead, killed in the Munich air disaster that also claimed the lives of England players Roger Byrne and Duncan Edwards. Edwards, in particular, was being talked about as a cornerstone of the team for the next decade; powerful and strong in the tackle, he could use the ball too, as a ball-carrying half-back, and was a goal threat with his shooting from distance – the first and last complete English holding midfielder. Prior to that, Brazil, England and the Soviet Union were the pressmen's pick, but England's form after the devastating plane crash was understandably patchy.

Elsewhere the usual suspects won through, except for Uruguay, in some decline and surprisingly knocked out by Paraguay. Mexico won the North American place yet again – they might as well just have been given a Finals' spot, so weak was the competition. The only other debutant finalists were the Soviet Union, who deigned to come and play with the capitalists.

In preparation for the games Sweden built two new stands in their main international stadium in Stockholm, and constructed two brand-new grounds in the cities of Gothenburg and Malmö. The rest of the games would be played in existing club stadia around the country.

West Germany, for all their poor recent form, were expected to qualify comfortably from the first group. Czechoslovakia had rebuilt a modest side, while Argentina were still finding their feet after a long period in self-imposed international exile, and had, as before the war, lost key players to the Italian leagues. Northern Ireland were newbies and had qualified in odd circumstances.

The final match of their group had left Italy needing a point in Belfast. The original game was beset with problems, as foul weather prevented both the original Swiss referee and his English replacement getting to the game on time. The Irish offered a local substitute but Italy declined and FIFA – correctly, for once – declared the game a friendly and ordered a rematch. Some friendly; a partisan crowd and a spiteful Italian performance almost led to a riot, and there were fears for the safety of the Italians for the rescheduled game the following month. It was an

anti-climax; the Italians surrendered meekly. Northern Ireland
won 2–1 and played in the World Cup Finals for the first time.

Finals

GROUP 1

West Germany	**(2) 3**	**Argentina** (1) 1	8 June, Malmö; 31,156
Rahn 32, 79, Seeler 42		Corbatta 3	
Northern Ireland	**(1) 1**	**Czechoslovakia (0) 0**	8 June, Halmstad; 10,647
Cush 21			
Argentina	**(1) 3**	**Northern Ireland (1) 1**	11 June, Halmstad; 14,174
Corbatta 37 (p), Menendez 56, Avio 60		McParland 4	
Czechoslovakia	**(2) 2**	**West Germany (0) 2**	11 June, Hälsingborg; 25,000
Dvorák 24 (p), Zikán 42		Schäfer 60, Rahn 71	
Northern Ireland	**(1) 2**	**West Germany (1) 2**	15 June, Malmö; 21,990
McParland 18, 60		Rahn 20, Seeler 78	
Czechoslovakia	**(3) 6**	**Argentina** (0) 1	15 June, Malmö; 16,148
Dvorák 8, Zikán 17, 39, Feureisl 68, Hovorka 81, 89		Corbatta 64 (p)	

1. West Germany 4pts (7–5); 2. Northern Ireland (4–5) & Czechoslovakia 3pts (8–4);
4. Argentina 2pts (5–10)

Play-off

Northern Ireland	(1) (1) 2 **Czechoslovakia** (1) (1) 1	17 June, Malmö; 6,196
McParland 44, 97	Zikán 18	

West Germany recalled the elegant Fritz Walter, now thirty-
seven, so concerned were they about the lack of a playmaker, but
it was another recalled player, the revitalised Helmut Rahn, who
was to the fore as they beat Argentina after conceding early. Later
the same day in Halmstad, Northern Ireland upset the apple cart
by beating Czechoslovakia 1–0. Perhaps it shouldn't be written as
such a surprise; Northern Ireland had a top-notch goalkeeper in
Harry Gregg, who had just survived the Munich air crash with
Manchester United. A workmanlike defence sat behind the
masterful Danny Blanchflower, ably assisted by Jimmy McIlroy
and Willy Cush in a strong midfield. The wingers were Billy
Bingham of Sunderland and Peter McParland of Aston Villa,
both highly rated top division players. It was the diminutive but
combative Cush who scored the only goal of the first game.

The surprises in the group continued when Argentina beat
the Irish in their best display of the tournament, full of

flamboyance and party tricks, and the Czechs held the Germans. Northern Ireland failed to play at sufficient tempo to trouble Argentina, but Czechoslovakia watched and learned and crushed the South Americans 6–1 in their last match. They had spotted a vulnerability to pace in the Argentinian defence, and fed their speedy wingers Zikán and Hovorka all afternoon – both scored twice. Northern Ireland played with much more gusto and passion against West Germany; McParland twice gave them the lead (and nearly sneaked a winner at the death) before first Rahn and then the young centre-forward Uwe Seeler (only twenty-one, but already thin on top, the German Bobby Charlton in appearance as well as playing style) equalised, Seeler with a rasper that left the hobbling Gregg floundering. Northern Ireland withstood a ton of pressure and Harry Gregg was heroic, despite playing virtually the entire match on one leg. Gregg had exhibited a different and more telling brand of heroism when he braved the flames of the Munich air crash to drag colleagues clear of the wreckage.

These results condemned the Irish to a play-off against Czechoslovakia (no goal difference was applied), and another two goals from McParland finished the job. It was a real backs-to-the-wall performance, the paper-thin Irish squad was already depleted by injury and they suffered two more here, with Cush and Peacock limping through extra-time. Czechoslovakia were obliging opponents, very patient and pretty but lacking punch up front. Peter McParland, scorer of an FA Cup Final winner for Aston Villa a year earlier, hadn't scored for Northern Ireland for two years until the Argentina game, but he scored his fourth of the competition during a goalmouth scramble and his fifth with a deft volley from a Blanchflower cross. He finished as fourth highest scorer in the tournament, just behind Rahn and Pelé – elevated company.

This was a fantastic achievement by Northern Ireland, not because they were a weak side but because everything was stacked against them with the bad run of injuries. The Irish never stopped playing for each other and never felt sorry for themselves; on two out of the three occasions they have qualified for the Finals, they have acquitted themselves magnificently.

GROUP 2

France Fontaine 24, 30, 68, Piantoni 51, Wisnieski 62, Kopa 70, Vincent 84	**(2) 7**	**Paraguay** Amarilla 20, 43 (p), Romero 50	**(2) 3**	8 June, Norrköping; 16,518
Scotland Murray 47	**(0) 1**	**Yugoslavia** Petakovic 6	**(1) 1**	8 June, Västerås; 9,591
Paraguay Agüero 3, Ré 44, Parodi 74	**(2) 3**	**Scotland** Mudie 32, Collins 76	**(1) 2**	11 June, Norrkööping; 11,665
Yugoslavia Petakovic 16, Veselinovic 63, 87	**(1) 3**	**France** Fontaine 4, 85	**(1) 2**	11 June, Västerås; 12,217
Yugoslavia Ognjanovic 12, Veselinovic 28, Rajkov 73	**(2) 3**	**Paraguay** Parodi 20, Agüero 51, Romero 80	**(1) 3**	15 June, Eskilstuna; 13,103
France Kopa 22, Fontaine 45	**(2) 2**	**Scotland** Baird 65	**(0) 1**	15 June, Örebro; 13,554

1. France 4pts (11–7); 2. Yugoslavia 4pts (7–6); 3. Paraguay 3pts (9–12); 4. Scotland 1pt (4–6)

The second group looked by far the weakest. Yugoslavia were a good side – they had beaten the reshaped England side 5–0. France had scored freely but against untested opposition; Paraguay were an unknown quantity, though their 5–0 win over Uruguay in qualification demanded respect. Scotland were given little or no chance, their squad bereft of world-class players.

The Scots did really well in their first game to hold Yugoslavia. The Yugoslavs were rich in talent but they did precious little with an abundance of possession here after taking the lead early, and the Scots' policy of pumping crosses at a flaky goalkeeper proved effective when Jimmy Murray eventually beat Beara to one of them.

France had some silky ball players, especially Raymond Kopa (he had pruned the Polish surname Kopaszewski) of Real Madrid, their one expat; he had five of his former colleagues from the strong Stade de Reims squad alongside him, including the veteran centre-half Bob Jonquet. Jonquet was no stopper, but a quick and mobile athlete, adept at setting up attacks. What he was less good at was defending, so France adopted a policy of all-out attack. Another Reims player, René Bliard, was injured, so the French played his club colleague Just Fontaine further forward.

With the wisdom of hindsight, it was a wise move by the coaching team.

Paraguay scored first with a hammer of a free-kick from the dangerous left-winger Florencio Amarilla – he had hit a hat-trick in that famous win over Uruguay, and he scored Paraguay's second with a penalty that nearly broke the net. In between, Just Fontaine had sprinted through the centre of the defence to score twice – on the first occasion the ball nearly reached the six-yard box before the goalkeeper thought to come out! Paraguay took the lead again through Romero, who held off a challenge in the penalty area and drove in low through a crowd. Almost immediately Piantoni scored with a deft curler from the left-hand edge of the area, and France moved up a gear. Wisnieski scored from Kopa's free-kick – the Madrid star was dictating the game now – and Piantoni unselfishly set up Fontaine for his hat-trick. Fontaine turned provider for number six, running clear again and crossing for Kopa to score (deliberately) with his knee; Kopa made a tap-in for Jean Vincent to complete the scoring.

Paraguay scored three again in their next match, but Scotland were never going to muster seven in reply, especially as Paraguay replaced their goalkeeper after the first horror show. An ageing, small side was barged and bullied by the South Americans and goalkeeper Tommy Younger brought the curtain down on his career (a bit like Merrick for England in 1954) with a stinker of a performance. He dropped a corner at Parodi's feet for the third and it was a bridge too far for Scotland, despite a heroic performance from Bobby Collins, who pulled one back with a thumper. Scotland deserved what they got; their selection was mystifying. Tommy Docherty wrote later that he was asked to watch Paraguay against France and reported on their intimidating size and style, yet both he and Dave Mackay, Scotland's two toughest players, were left out. Here begins a theme of the book for the next thirty years.

Fontaine was still firing in France's second game, converting a left-wing cross while the Yugoslav defence stood and watched. He added a late second, outpacing the defence in what was becoming a familiar style. Unfortunately for France, there was some defending to do in between and they were characteristically negligent in that regard. Petakovic diverted Milutinovic's shot during a goal-mouth melee and Veselinovic scored twice from crosses that bypassed a clutch of Frenchmen on their way to him.

Scotland played better in their last match (Mackay was picked; horse, stable door ...) but full-back John Hewie missed a penalty just after Kopa opened the scoring, and they couldn't cope with Fontaine's greyhound speed. He added the second just before half-time and Baird's second-half goal was merely consolation for an improved performance. The win meant France topped the group, as Paraguay confirmed three was their favourite number against Yugoslavia. Had Yugoslavia not also scored three, Paraguay would have qualified. They provided huge entertainment – and some huge bruises – on their debut, but their defending just wasn't up to scratch.

Scotland Squad 1958:

GK: Tommy Younger (Liverpool, 28 years old, 22 caps), Bill Brown (Dundee, 26, 0)

DEF: Eric Caldow (Glasgow Rangers, 24, 10), Doug Cowie (Dundee, 32, 18), Tommy Docherty (Preston North End, 29, 22), Bobby Evans (Glasgow Celtic, 30, 34), John Hewie (Charlton Athletic, 30, 12), Harry Haddock (Clyde, 32, 6), Ian McColl (Rangers, 31, 14), Alex Parker (Everton, 22, 14)

MID & WIDE: Sammy Baird (Rangers, 28, 6), Bobby Collins (Celtic, 27, 19), Dave Mackay (Heart of Midlothian, 23, 1), Archie Robertson (Clyde, 28, 4), Stewart Imlach* (Nottingham Forest, 26, 2), Graham Leggat (Aberdeen, 23, 5), Alex Scott (Rangers, 20, 5)

FWD: John Coyle (Clyde, 25, 0), Willie Fernie (Celtic, 29, 11), Jackie Mudie (Blackpool, 28, 14), Jimmy Murray (Hearts, 25, 3), Eddie Turnbull (Hibernian, 35, 5)

* Stewart Imlach was the subject of a book by his son Gary that won the William Hill Sports Prize in 2005. Entitled *My Father and Other Working-Class Football Heroes*, it serves as a useful counterpoint to the Hollywood lifestyles of the pampered modern stars. A worthy rather than thrilling book, it highlighted the fact that the Scottish FA only handed caps to players who played in Home Internationals prior to the 1970s, so players like Imlach, who played four times, twice in this tournament (ineffectually), never officially received a cap. The ruling was typically nonsensical, the reluctance to rectify the situation characteristically stubborn.

GROUP 3

Sweden	(1) 3	**Mexico**	(0) 0	8 June, Stockholm; 34,107
Simonsson 16, 64,				
Liedholm 57 (p)				
Hungary	(1) 1	**Wales**	(1) 1	8 June, Sandviken; 15,343
Bozsik 4		J Charles 26		
Mexico	(0) 1	**Wales**	(1) 1	11 June, Stockholm; 15,150
Belmonte 89		Allchurch 32		
Sweden	(1) 2	**Hungary**	(0) 1	12 June, Stockholm; 38,850
Hamrin 34, 55		Tichy 76		
Sweden	(0) 0	**Wales**	(0) 0	15 June, Stockholm; 30,287
Hungary	(1) 4	**Mexico**	(0) 0	15 June, Sandviken; 13,310
Tichy 19, 46, Sándor 54,				
Bencsics 60				

1. Sweden 5pts (5–1); 2. Hungary (6–3) & Wales (2–2) 3pts; 4. Mexico 1pt (1–8)

The hosts were given a gentle opener, perhaps in deference to their years; the team had an average age of thirty, over thirty-one if you take out the stylish winger Hamrin and the new young striker Agne Simonsson. The two biggest names, Nils Liedholm of Milan and Gunnar Gren, now back in Sweden with Örgryte, were thirty-five and thirty-seven respectively. The Swedish FA had finally accepted the need to pick the Italian-based professional stars a couple of years earlier; presumably the thought of embarrassing themselves at their own World Cup served as suitable motivation. So Hamrin, Liedholm, Gustavsson and Skoglund were all available. Mexico had a few moments, but Sweden slowed the game down and took control in the second half. Skoglund and Hamrin tormented the Mexican defence and created all three goals, two of them coolly finished by Simonsson.

Wales had endured a fretful time prior to the tournament. Their best player, John Charles, played for Juventus in Italy, where he was known as *Il Gigante Buono* (Gentle Giant) for his courteous demeanour and clean playing style. Juve, perhaps in a little fit of pique at Italy's failure to qualify, sought to deny Charles the right to play in the tournament and the will-he-won't-he saga went on for a week or two before it was confirmed Charles would definitely play in Sweden. Charles' brother, Mel, was a decent centre-half, while the other attacking Welsh star was Ivor Allchurch of Swansea – and he also had a brother, Len, in the squad.

John Charles was fantastic in the air, and he scored Wales' equaliser against Hungary in their first game. Hungary were a fading team, with few of the superstars left from 1954; here they resorted to the sort of spoiling that marred their game against Brazil four years earlier, Sipos clattering Charles on numerous occasions – enough, certainly, to attract censure even from the forgiving referees in the 1950s. One of the stars of old, Bozsik, by now an MP in the Hungarian Parliament, rolled back the years with a super dribble and floated chip for the opening goal.

Wales were disappointing against Mexico; they seemed unsure what tactics to use, whether to use Charles' aerial dominance or get the wingers behind the defence. They should have learned from Sweden that Mexico were vulnerable down the flanks but Colin Webster and Cliff Jones, the latter about to join Tottenham from Swansea and become part of their famous double-winning team, didn't see enough of the ball and didn't go and look for it.

The group was proving a godsend for Sweden, who were able to win their second game without being overtaxed by Hungary. Hungary claimed a shot from Tichy crossed the line after bouncing down off the bar at 1–0 down, but it didn't, and Grosics was the busier goalkeeper. Hamrin shot home in the first half after two defenders failed to clear, and got a second when Mátrai's challenge ballooned the ball off his shin and over the stranded Grosics. Tichy (who really wasn't) hit another blockbuster in the second period and this time it was under the bar. By then Sweden had offered them a reprieve when Liedholm steered a woeful penalty two feet wide of the post.

The Swedes left a few of the old guard out for the game against Wales, and a stalemate ensued, although again the opposition goalkeeper was the busier, Jack Kelsey making a couple of fine saves. Hungary's comfortable win over Mexico meant they faced Wales again for a place in the quarter-finals, as goal difference meant diddly-squat in this tournament.

Hard to find much sympathy for Hungary, given their tactic in the play-off match seemed to involve kicking John Charles even harder. For almost an hour it seemed it might work as Tichy's goal separated the sides. When Charles flicked a pass to Ivor Allchurch on the left-hand edge of the penalty area, there seemed little or no danger. Allchurch watched the ball drop and swung, and the perfect volley arced across and past Gyula Grosics. Twenty minutes later Terry Medwin pinched the ball off Sárosi and ran clear to score; in the dying minutes Sipos finally got the sending off various Hungarians had merited over the two matches. Wales were through, courtesy of team spirit, some dogged defending and a good goalkeeper, but Charles would play no further part, victim of three hours of Hungarian spite.

It was a sad end for the Magical Magyars; the revolution and counter-revolution of 1956 had torn the team apart, despite a heart-warming tour organised by the players themselves the same year in defiance of the authorities. Imre Nagy, the free Hungarian leader, was executed during this tournament and black flags and protest banners were seen at their games.

GROUP 4

England	(0) 2	**USSR**	(1) 2	8 June, Gothenburg; 49,348
Kevan 66, Finney 85 (p)		Simonian 13, A Ivanov 56		
Brazil	(1) 3	**Austria**	(0) 0	8 June, Uddevalla; 17,778
Mazzola* 37, 85, N Santos 50				
Brazil	(0) 0	**England**	(0) 0	11 June, Gothenburg; 40,895
USSR	(1) 2	**Austria**	(0) 0	11 June, Borås; 21, 239
A Ivanov 15, V Ivanov 62				
Austria	(1) 2	**England**	(0) 2	15 June, Borås; 15,872
Koller 15, Körner 71		Haynes 56, Kevan 74		
Brazil	(1) 2	**USSR**	(0) 0	15 June, Gothenburg; 50,928
Vavá 3, 77				

1. Brazil 5pts (5–0); 2. England (4–4) & USSR (4–4) 3pts; 4. Austria 1pt (2–7)

Play-off				
USSR	(0) 1	**England**	(0) 0	17 June, Gothenburg; 23,182
Ilyin 69				

* Mazzola's grown-up name was José Altafini, and that was the name he adopted when he moved to Milan from Palmeiras later in the summer. He won just eight caps for Brazil (he was only twenty in July that year) and only six more for Italy, as the rules were tightened during his time in *Serie A*. He scored over 120 goals for Milan and nearly 100 more in spells with Napoli and Juventus, leaving him on 216, the same as the great Giuseppe Meazza. (The pre-war star Piola, Francesco Totti and Sweden's Gunnar Nordahl are the three most prolific goalscorers in the Italian top flight.) He named himself after one of the great players lost in the 1949 Torino air crash, Valentino Mazzola.

The bottom group was a tough draw for England. Deprived of three top players, they needed a break with the draw and didn't get one. Brazil were jam-packed with exciting attackers and the Soviets were a powerful and athletic side. Austria looked like they might offer a crumb of comfort, as they were a shadow of their former selves.

Brazil predictably steamrollered Austria; the nineteen-year-old Mazzola scored twice, the first a fabulous first-time hit from Didi's pinpoint cross. England and the USSR were engaged in a far less one-sided affair in Gothenburg. England goalkeeper Colin McDonald gifted the Soviets the opener, palming a cross into Simonian's path and the Soviet skipper returned it with interest. England huffed and puffed but Kessarev and Voinov were getting away with some strong-arm stuff on Tom Finney and England's options looked limited with the rather static Derek Kevan at centre-forward. When Alekasandr Ivanov broke clear and added a second ten minutes into the second half it looked all over.

Lev Yashin, the legendary Soviet goalkeeper, proved even the greats have off moments when he couldn't deal with a long free-kick and the ball found the back of the net off Kevan's head without the West Brom striker knowing too much about it. Another Kevan goal was disallowed for a foul on Yashin by Bobby Robson; plenty of worse challenges went unpunished, so a rather flaky penalty converted by Finney was just about fair. Yashin threw a rather undignified little wobbly after the penalty award – not the great man's best moment.

The USSR, like Brazil before them, kept a clean sheet against Austria, but only because Hans Buzek missed a penalty at 1–0. Valentin Ivanov's goal settled the game. There were two Ivanovs involved here. Valentin of Torpedo Moscow arrived with a reputation; he played two World Cups and ended his international scorer as the USSR's highest scorer to date – only Blokhin and Protasov subsequently passed his tally. He was married to an Olympic gymnast and his son became a referee. Aleksandr Ivanov was no relation; he played for Zenit St Petersburg, which was not then a fashionable club, and had not won a full cap before the World Cup, making his debut against England, aged thirty. This Soviet squad was largely Russian, with a handful of Ukrainians from Dynamo Kyiv, and a Latvian, Leonid Ostrovsky, who didn't get on the pitch (for now).

Against Brazil, England opted wisely for caution. They sacrificed a half-back to bolster the defence and played Wright almost as a sweeper to counter the runs of Mazzola. It worked, but Mazzola was wasteful, too, hitting a post when he should have scored and shooting when colleagues were better placed. England offered little at the other end. It was the first 0–0 in World Cup Finals history.

England expected to beat Austria and hoped Brazil would do them a favour and beat the Soviets. Brazil did their bit, with help from a couple of team changes. Vicente Feola, the coach, was miffed with Mazzola after his selfish showing against England, and replaced him with seventeen-year-old Edson do Nascimento. He wanted more thrust on the flanks and brought back the maverick Botafogo winger Manuel dos Santos. Some suggest player power was at work, and the senior players demanded the inclusion of the two newcomers, but there is no consistency to these claims, so I shall give the coach the benefit of the doubt. Dos Santos was better known to football followers as Garrincha and the relatively unknown do Nascimento preferred to be called Pelé. Nice reserves, Vicente. Feola kept faith with the battering-ram centre-forward Vavá, brought in against England but well handled by a defence who played against big lads every week. Garrincha had already skinned Kuznetsov and hammered a shot against the post before Vavá scored in the third minute, thumping home a beautifully threaded through ball from Orlando. The second goal came late, with Vavá prodding home after the ball broke to him in the area after a move broke down. The Soviets worked hard, as always, and chased, but much of the time they were chasing a ball that had already moved on.

So England qualified for the second phase . . . no, hang on, they didn't, because they failed to finish the job and beat Austria. With Finney injured and unlikely to play in the tournament again, the press clamoured for the inclusion of young Bobby Charlton, a survivor of the Munich air crash and the rising star of the Busby Babes, as Matt Busby's young Manchester United team was dubbed. Instead, the committee had included Alan

A'Court of Liverpool, an inferior player in every aspect of the game. He contributed little against Brazil but was picked again to play Austria. England dominated the game, but Austria scored two excellent goals, twice taking the lead. England's full-backs, Howe and Banks, were steady, and Wright had improved as a player since switching to centre-half and was still in good fettle at thirty-four. The half-backs were a problem, England just couldn't find the right combination; having picked two defensively minded players in Clamp and Slater to combat Brazil, they stuck with them here and found themselves short of creativity, with Haynes struggling to impose his skills at this level. England equalised in the second half when Szanwald spilled a shot (hit with all the pace of a measured back-pass) at the feet of Haynes, but went behind again soon after when McDonald was unsighted and couldn't reach Körner's scuffed shot. Kevan scored the second when found in space by Haynes. It was the big striker's second goal, but he was easy to mark and Lofthouse, even at thirty-three, would surely have caused more problems for international defences. Walter Winterbottom had a theory that continental defences and goalkeepers were vulnerable to the ball to the back post; it may have been true of some, but Hanappi and co looked comfortable enough here. Lofthouse was a cleverer, more experienced player, or maybe England could have gambled and taken the uncapped Brian Clough – anything to offer an alternative to the one-dimensional football the team offered in Sweden.

After a disappointing performance, England changed things around for the USSR match, but the changes weren't the ones the pundits wanted. A'Court stayed but Douglas and Bobby Robson (who had done little wrong) made way for Peter Brabrook and Peter Broadbent – surely not a game to be introducing two new caps? Clamp, who had a poor tournament, was replaced by Blackburn's Ronnie Clayton, an equally defensive player, and he did no better.

In the event the two new caps did well, and Haynes played better. Broadbent was a good player (George Best was a big admirer) and Brabrook, big and strong for a winger, played with youthful freedom. He had England's best chances, hitting the

post twice after forcing his way through, and finding the net with
a fine solo effort, only for play to be called back as he had handled
the bobbling ball during a long run on goal. Unfortunately, he
missed his best chance when Broadbent's pass found him
unmarked six yards out – it was easier to score than do what he
did and scoop the ball into Yashin's hands. The Soviets made
chances too, and their own right-winger, Ivanov, caused problems all afternoon. The USSR's goal was avoidable. They won
possession from a rank bad goal-kick and the ball came back with
interest, finding Ilyin unmarked amid regrouping defenders, and
he shot home via the base of the post. The margin of victory was
very fine – a post's width – but England had underachieved again.
Later that year they annihilated the Soviets at Wembley, with
Haynes, no longer fettered by the expectation of a World Cup,
scoring a brilliant hat-trick and the recalled Lofthouse leading the
line. It was Tom Finney's last game and Lofthouse played only
one more – both scored thirty goals for England, the same mark
as Alan Shearer.

England Squad 1958:
GK: Colin McDonald (Burnley, 27 years old, 1 cap), Eddie
Hopkinson (Bolton Wanderers, 22, 6), Alan Hodgkinson
(Sheffield United, 21, 4)
DEF: Tommy Banks (Bolton, 28, 1), Eddie Clamp
(Wolverhampton Wanderers, 23, 1), Ronnie Clayton (Blackburn
Rovers, 23, 20), Don Howe (West Bromwich Albion, 22, 7),
Maurice Norman (Tottenham Hotspur, 24, 0), Peter Sillett
(Chelsea, 25, 3), Billy Wright* (Wolves, 34, 92)
MID & WIDE: Peter Broadbent (Wolves, 25, 0), Johnny Haynes
(Fulham, 23, 20), Bobby Robson (West Brom, 25, 2), Maurice
Setters (West Brom, 21, 0), Bill Slater (Wolves, 31, 6), Alan
A'Court (Liverpool, 23, 1), Peter Brabrook (Chelsea, 20, 0),

* The games at the World Cup took Wright to ninety-six caps; he added
three more in the autumn and became the first England player to pass 100
in a friendly against Italy before signing off on a tour of the Americas in
May 1959 with 105. The next 100-club men were Charlton, a fixture in
the side the season after the World Cup, and Wright's successor as the
central defender and hub of the team, Bobby Moore.

Bryan Douglas (Blackburn, 24, 7), Tom Finney (Preston North End, 36, 73)
FWD: Bobby Charlton (Manchester United, 20, 3), Derek Kevan (West Brom, 23, 7), Bobby Smith (Tottenham, 25, 0)

QUARTER-FINALS (all 19 June)

France	(1) 4	**Northern Ireland** (0) 0		Norrköping; 11,800
Wisnieski 44, Fontaine 56, 64, Piantoni 68				
Sweden	(0) 2	**USSR**	(0) 0	Stockholm; 31,900
Hamrin 49, Simonsson 88				
Brazil	(0) 1	**Wales**	(0) 0	Gothenburg; 25,923
Pelé				
West Germany	(1) 1	**Yugoslavia** (0) 0		Malmö; 20,055
Rahn				

Three sides in the quarter-finals had sandwiched an extra play-off game in between the groups and the knockout rounds, which meant they were playing for the third time in four days. It showed – they all lost.

Wales struggled manfully against Brazil without their best player, and Arsenal 'keeper Kelsey had another blinder. Suggestions that Brazil were lucky are ill-judged. They made all the play and had a goal disallowed – a brilliant overhead kick by Mazzola, back in for Vavá, rested after picking up a minor injury against the USSR. Pelé's goal came after he cleverly took down a cross and forced the ball home through a despairing tackle. Wales didn't disgrace themselves on their only appearance in the Finals, but it was a campaign strait-jacketed by caution and over-reliance on one player, and they were, in truth, lucky to be there at all, having had a reprieve in qualifying and a second bite in their group without winning a game.

A third game in four days against France proved a bridge too far for a side with an injured goalkeeper. Harry Gregg's understudy, Portsmouth's Norman Uprichard, had broken his hand and no replacements were allowed back then, so Gregg limped through the match; the twenty-third player in the squad to accommodate a third goalkeeper was some way off. Northern Ireland defended stoutly for forty-four minutes but once France got their noses in front the game was a procession and the 4–0 scoreline could have been worse.

The USSR paid the price for their efforts against England. Their energy levels deserted them against Sweden, and Gren and Liedholm were allowed to dictate the pace and pattern of the game. Hamrin, becoming one of the tournament's big stars, had too much wit for Kuznetsov, although his goal had an element of luck. He tried to slip the ball inside the covering defender to Simonsson, but the ball looped up off the defender's foot. Hamrin had simply to incline his head to send it bouncing past a goal-keeper already committed to the save. Simonsson added a late second after Hamrin set him up. The USSR had only one clear-cut chance, when Gustavsson headed a shot off the line after a corner fell kindly for Salnikov.

West Germany remained in low gear for their quarter-final, but their solid defence quashed any resistance from a timid Yugoslavia side who did little to justify some pre-tournament predictions that they would be there at the business end. Rahn's early goal was enough to see West Germany through to meet the hosts after a pretty dire match. Yugoslavia were disappointing; much was expected after their thrashing of England in Belgrade.

Wales Squad 1958:
GK: Jack Kelsey (Arsenal, 28 years old, 20 caps), Ken Jones (Cardiff City, 22, 0) Graham Vearncombe (Cardiff, 24, 1)
DEF: Stuart Williams (West Bromwich Albion, 27, 11), Mel Hopkins (Tottenham Hotspur, 23, 13), Derrick Sullivan (Cardiff, 23, 9), Mel Charles (Swansea Town, 23, 14), Trevor Edwards (Charlton Athletic, 21, 2), Colin Baker (Cardiff, 23, 0), Vic Crowe (Aston Villa, 26, 0)
MID & WIDE: Dave Bowen (Cpt, Arsenal, 30, 11), Ron Hewitt (Cardiff City, 29, 2), Colin Webster (Manchester United, 25, 1), John Elsworthy (Ipswich Town, 26, 0), Ivor Allchurch (Swansea, 28, 30), Terry Medwin (Tottenham, 25, 14), Len Allchurch (Swansea, 24, 6), Cliff Jones (Swansea, 23, 17)
FWD: John Charles (Juventus, 26, 25), Ken Leek (Leicester City, 22, 0), Roy Vernon (Blackburn Rovers, 21, 7), George Baker (Plymouth Argyle, 24, 0)

Northern Ireland Squad 1958:

GK: Harry Gregg (Manchester United, 28 years old, 10 caps), Norman Uprichard (Portsmouth, 30, 15)

DEF: Willie Cunningham (Leicester City, 28, 16), Alf McMichael (Newcastle United, 30, 29), Dick Keith (Newcastle, 25, 3), Bertie Peacock (Glasgow Celtic, 29, 15), Tommy Casey (Newcastle, 28, 8)

MID & WIDE: Danny Blanchflower (Tottenham Hotspur, 32, 30), Jimmy McIlroy (Burnley, 26, 26), Sammy McCrory (Southend United, 33, 1), Billy Bingham (Sunderland, 26, 28), Peter McParland (Aston Villa, 24, 14), Jackie Scott (Grimsby Town, 24, 0)

FWD: Wilbur Cush (Leeds United, 29, 11), Billy Simpson (Glasgow Rangers, 28, 0), Derek Dougan (Portsmouth, 20, 0), Fay Coyle (Nottingham Forest, 25, 0)

Picked but did not travel:

Roy Rea (GK, Glenavon, 23, 0), Len Graham (DEF, Doncaster Rovers, 23, 13), Tommy Hamill (MF, Linfield, 24, 0), Sammy Chapman (MF, Mansfield Town, 20, 0), Bobby Trainor (MF, Coleraine, 24, 0)

SEMI-FINAL

Sweden	**(1) 3**	**West Germany**	**(1) 1**	24 June, Gothenburg; 49,471
Skoglund 33, Gren 80, Hamrin 87		Schäfer 25		

THIRD-PLACE FINAL

France	**(3) 6**	**West Germany**	**(1) 3**	28 June, Gothenburg; 32,483
Fontaine 15, 37, 77, 89, Kopa 27 (p), Douis 50		Cieslarczyk 17, Rahn 52, Schäfer 83		

Their semi-final is a game that rankled with German supporters for the next generation. Much more than the final against England in 1966, it stands as a game that they feel was stacked against them from the off. West Germany started as slight favourites, their team quicker and more solid than Sweden, who relied on slowing the pace of the game and maximising the craft and guile of their ageing stars. The Germans enjoyed the better chances in the first half, with Uwe Seeler prominent. Seeler had the beating of the Swedish defenders on either side. First he sprinted past Axbom to drive a stinging shot against Svensson's palms, then he went past Bergmark on the other side and cut back a looping cross to the edge of the penalty area; Schäfer met it with a beautifully clean half-volley, which rocketed into the top corner. Svensson barely moved. There was a handball in the move that led to Sweden's opener, but it received more protests in the press box than on the pitch.

The real controversy came in the second half when Hamrin – a little wind-up merchant as well as a fine player – reacted to a late tackle by Juskowiak. The pair tangled but it was the German who was singled out by the Hungarian referee and sent from the field. Moments later Fritz Walter was rendered a limping passenger for much of the second half after a reckless challenge from Parling – no punishment, hence the Germans' ire. The match was tetchy without ever becoming out-and-out violent.

A wonderful strike from Gunnar Gren gave Sweden the lead with ten minutes remaining, hammering a punched clearance by Herkenrath back into the top corner. With West Germany pressing for an equaliser, Hamrin slalomed through the German defence and cheekily chipped the ball home for a third. The hosts were in the final, but would their stylish wingers be enough against the flair of Brazil? It was unlikely to be 0–0 . . .

WORLD CUP CLASSIC No.3
24 June 1958, Råsunda, Stockholm; 27,100

Brazil   (2) 5   Vavá 2, Didi 39, Pelé 52, 64, 75
France   (1) 2   Fontaine 9, Piantoni 82

Referee: **Mervyn Griffiths** (Wales)
Coaches: **Vicente Feola** (Brazil) – France had a coaching team

Brazil (3–4–3): Gylmar (Dos Santos Neves) (Corinthians); Nilton De Sordi (São Paulo), Hilderaldo Bellini (Cpt, Vasco de Gama), Nílton Santos (Botafogo); *José Ely de Miranda, known as* Zito (Santos), *Waldir Pereira, known as* Didi (Botafogo), Orlando *de Carvalho* (Vasco de Gama), Mário Zagallo (Flamengo); *Manuel dos Santos, known as* Garrincha (Botafogo), *Edvaldo Neto, known* as Vavá (Vasco de Gama), *Edson do Nascimento, known as* Pelé (Santos)
France (3–3–4): Claude Abbes (St Étienne); Raymond Kaelbel (Monaco), Bob Jonquet (Cpt, Reims), André Lerond (Lyon); Armande Penverne (Reims), Raymond Kopa (Real Madrid), Jean-Jacques Marcel (Marseille); Maryan Wisnieski (Lens), Just Fontaine, Roger Piantoni, Jean Vincent (all Reims)

The scoreline isn't a true reflection of a game that was far from one-sided and swung on an injury to French captain Jonquet after a late, heavy tackle from the muscular Vavá. Even with Jonquet France would have struggled to keep Brazil out; with him limping on the wing they were completely at sea defensively – and with goalkeeper Abbes not having his best day, Brazilian goals were inevitable.

They had scored one before the injury when Jonquet had an aberrant moment and passed the ball straight to Garrincha – as Cris Freddi deliciously put it, like *"throwing a grenade at a trampoline"*. Jonquet chased the little winger and made a good tackle but the ball broke to Didi and the midfielder deftly picked out Vavá, standing where Jonquet should have been; the big man just whacked it and Abbes stood no chance.

France came back strongly and Fontaine's pace was unsettling the Brazilian defence. He had three decent chances in the first fifteen minutes, once when put through by a clever kick and once from a first-time pass from Wisnieski. He missed those, but in between played a wonderful one-two-three with Kopa, scuttled past Gylmar and shot high and decisively past the last man. It was a finish worthy of Jimmy Greaves or Thierry Henry at their absolute best.

Didi, such a clever player, was the first to exploit Jonquet's absence, shooting home after thirty-nine minutes when he drifted into the box while the French backs were watching the Brazilian strikers.

The second half was more like the one-sided affair later reports had us believe; the stuffing went out of the French when their goalkeeper dropped a harmless cross at Pelé's feet; the youngster couldn't miss – Harry Redknapp's proverbial missus would have put it away. Pelé added a fourth for Brazil when Vavá made a complete marmalade of a pass, the ball rebounding to Pelé who showed him how it should be done. Pelé's best was his third, cushioning the ball on his thigh before striking it early when the defender and the goalkeeper thought he would try to beat his man. It was an early sign that the great man had instinctive football intelligence to complement his ability; it can't have hurt that he had such hard-working, crafty players as Didi and Zagallo around him. There was time for the French to score another classy goal, when Piantoni nutmegged a defender, ran on and hit a terrific shot from the edge of the penalty area.

Brazil had won well, but there were enough questions – and France were the first opponents to ask any – about the Brazilian defence that the final wasn't a foregone conclusion, for all the inventiveness and technique of their forwards.

Pelé became the youngest player to score a hat-trick in the World Cup Finals, eclipsing Edmund Conen of Germany in 1934. The record has lasted – all five of the youngest players to score a hat-trick played in tournaments no later than 1962. Five days later he became the youngest player to play in the final, another record that still stands.

France – and Fontaine – were among the goals yet again against West Germany in the third-place match. West Germany left out a few of their semi-final team, including the injured Fritz Walter, who had played his final match. Helmut Rahn played and signed off his own personal World Cup history with another great goal, ending a weaving run by thrashing the ball past Abbes, who could only twitch like a marionette as the ball passed him by a few inches.

But this was Fontaine's game, the German reserves simply had no answer to his pace and the accuracy of Kopa's through balls. The striker finished with thirteen goals in the tournament, a record that will take some beating, even in the modern competition in which a team plays seven games – Fontaine played only six.

World Cup Heroes No.8

Just Fontaine (1933–)

France

In modern times France has fielded teams replete with players of various ethnicities, but in the 1950s it was much more unusual for European sides to have players from former colonies, first or second generation. In 1958 France had two, Celestin Oliver, an Algerian, and Just Fontaine, born in Marrakech, Morocco to a French father and Spanish mother, and brought up in Casablanca.

Fontaine was an inside-forward in the successful Stade de Reims side in the 1950s; he missed the 1956 European Cup Final but was in the side that lost 2–0 to Real Madrid in 1959, and he scored ten goals en route. Lightning fast and a composed finisher, Fontaine thrived on through balls down the centre of a defence where he was adept at finding space between the full-backs and the centre-half. He was particularly expert at rounding the goalkeeper while retaining full control of the ball – as evidenced by his fabulous goal against Brazil in the semi-final. He made his debut for France in 1953 (scoring a hat-trick against Luxembourg), but never cemented a regular place in the French side until the tournament in Sweden.

Although Fontaine's great moment was the 1958 World Cup, his scoring record beyond that marks him as a special finisher; thirty goals in twenty-one internationals leaves him with seventeen in fifteen even without the extraordinary scoring streak he enjoyed in Sweden.

The ease with which players such as Fontaine, Pelé, Di Stéfano and, later, Greaves found these channels led more and more sides to use one of their half-backs as not just a deep-lying midfielder but a permanent second centre-back. Is it pushing it a bit to include Fontaine alongside these greats? He retired at twenty-eight after two serious leg injuries – without these he might have achieved much more, and in his one chance to shine on the international stage, he looked world class.

World Cup Heroes No.9

Helmut Rahn (1929–2003)

West Germany

One of the great characters of post-war football. Rahn played his best football for his home-town club, Rot-Weiss Essen (Red & White Essen). He earned a call-up while with the unfashionable Ruhr team but found himself unpopular with the German fans in a team held in contempt by their own press. All that changed a year later.

Rahn wasn't even picked in the provisional twenty-two for the World Cup, and only got the nod when Herberger heard he was in special form on Essen's tour of South America. Rahn flew home immediately to join up with the squad and was appointed room-mate to the introspective Fritz Walter. Introspection around Rahn was a challenge; he was a good-natured, light-hearted "hail fellow, well met" type, fond of a smoke and a beer (or two, or ten, or more . . .)

Rahn played well in the otherwise calamitous group match against Hungary and never looked back, scoring twice against the same opponents in the final and doing much to salve the wounds of a conscience-stricken nation.

Four years later Herberger was on the phone again, imploring Rahn, who was drinking heavily and overweight, to get his act together and help out. Rahn responded, and got better and better through the 1958 tournament, dragging West Germany through the quarter-final against Yugoslavia. Only in the semi-final when Sweden doubled up on him, using the abrasive Parling to help the left-back, did Rahn not impress. He finished with ten goals in two World Cup tournaments, most of them at important times in crucial matches – but none more so than the two in The Miracle of Berne.

Rahn left Essen in 1959 and was never the same. A season at Cologne and then three in Enschede in Holland ended with him in prison after causing a motor accident while under the influence – a horrible downside of his over-fondness for beer. He was brought back to play for Meidericher (in Duisburg) in the newly formed Bundesliga in 1963, but the first impression he made wasn't a good one – sent off for headbutting an opponent.

In 2004, a year after his death, a statue of Rahn was erected in Helmut Rahn Square, just down the road from the stadium in Essen – a fitting tribute, but it's missing a foaming tankard.

WORLD CUP FINAL No.6
29 June 1958, Rasunda, Stockholm; 49,737

Brazil   (2) 5   Vavá 9, 32, Pelé 55, 90, Zagallo 68
Sweden   (1) 2   Liedholm 4, Simonsson 79

Referee: **Maurice Guigue** (France)
Coaches: **Vicente Feola** (Brazil) & **George Raynor** (Sweden)

Brazil (3–4–3): Gylmar (Corinthians); Djalma Santos (Portuguesa), Hilderaldo Bellini (Cpt, Vasco de Gama), Nílton Santos (Botafogo); Zito (Santos), Didi (Botafogo), Orlando (Vasco de Gama), Mário Zagallo (Flamengo); Garrincha (Botafogo), Vavá (Vasco de Gama), Pelé (Santos)
Sweden (3–2–2–3): Kalle Svensson (Helsingborg); Orvar Bergmark (Örebro), Bengt Gustavsson (Atalanta), Sven Axbom (Norrköping); Reino Börjesson (Norrby), Sigge Parling (Djurgården); Gunnar Gren (Örgryte), Nils Liedholm (Cpt, AC Milan); Kurt Hamrin (Padova), Agne Simonsson (Örgryte), Lennart Skoglund (Inter Milan)

The game was an interesting clash of the European and South American football culture. Sweden were a good side full of technically accomplished players. They had vast experience in defence and midfield and two dangerous wingers in the deceptively languid Hamrin and inconsistent but rapid Skoglund (pronounced Shka-lund). For all their talent Sweden were an old-fashioned side, playing a standard European formation with an excellent centre-half (Gustavsson) between the full-backs and two tough-tackling half-backs prepared to drop in and help – Parling was the Rottweiler, Borjesson the more cultured of the two. All the attacking play stemmed from the veterans Gren and Liedholm at inside-forward. Both could pass and shoot exceptionally well, but opponents could hope to run past them with some ease when in possession. The Germans' attempt to do this was baulked by the injury to Walter and by George Raynor's clever deployment of Gren in a deeper role to combat Walter and Schäfer; but Uwe Seeler had shown how vulnerable the defence was against pace and energy.

Brazil were using a more fluid, modern system. Orlando, ostensibly a half-back, rarely ventured beyond the defence but would set up play with sensible, economical distribution; Zito would roam the area in front of the defence and break up the opposition's attacks. Didi, the playmaker, and Zagallo, a defensively minded left-winger, would bolster the midfield, while Garrincha, the other winger, had licence to play more offensively as Zito would cover his forays. Vavá was an old-fashioned brute-force centre-forward, but alongside him Pelé would come off the defenders to receive the ball and run at them or play in the wingers; he was proving a real handful to pick up for the more conventional sides.

Raynor wanted a good start and the first goal in the hope it would bruise the Brazilians' morale, which he perceived to be fragile. He got the former, but was misguided in believing the latter; all Liedholm's opener did was galvanise Brazil and remind them the opposition were not to be taken lightly. It was a good goal, too – two neat sidesteps to take out the retreating defenders and an accurate shot past Gylmar's right hand into the corner.

The first two Brazilian goals were a carbon copy of each other; Garrincha down the right, too quick for Axbom – hard, low cross – goal for Vavá, sliding in. Half-time came with Brazil 2–1 ahead and completely dominant – a vicious strike from Pelé that streaked across Svensson and hit the post nearly made it 3–1. Didi seemed to be everywhere, slowing down the pace when receiving the ball deep to look for options, then quickening it where the Swedes didn't like it in their own half. Whenever the ball went wide towards the Swedish wingers, Zito and Zagallo were in position to help Djalma Santos (recalled to negate Skoglund) and his namesake Nílton Santos. When Nílton Santos burst forward to help launch attacks, the disappointing Hamrin was nowhere to be seen.

The seventeen-year-old Pelé needed only ten minutes of the second half to get his goal and it was a masterpiece of technique and inventiveness. Nílton Santos hit a long cross into the penalty area where Pele was waiting. He had a lot to do. He chested the ball down to eliminate the defender behind him, then nipped it over the covering man, Gustavsson, the best centre-half in the tournament. There was still another man trying to get across so Pelé hit the ball first time past Svensson, low into the corner. A moment of unadulterated genius – the game's greatest player had announced himself on the biggest stage of all.

With just over twenty minutes to go, Zagallo ended the game as a contest. Sweden dithered as they tried to clear and Zagallo dispossessed the last man and shot past Svensson – unfussy and effective, like everything the under-rated winger did. Brazil took their foot off the pedal and Gren carved open the defence with a slide-rule through ball; Simonsson, who ran his heart out for ninety minutes to help his older colleagues, converted coolly. There was still time for the boy wonder to have the last word. Pelé started the move with a cheeky back-heel to Zagallo; Zagallo simply bided his time while his colleague sauntered into the box, then floated up an enticing cross. Pelé got there first – in mid-air he had the presence of mind to realise the cross was high and that too much power on the ball would take it over the bar. He simply let the ball hit the side of his temple, cushioning it past the already committed goalkeeper.

The old order was blown away – Sweden had a great tournament and it was a fitting last hurrah for their veterans, stupidly ignored for so long by their own FA. But it was Brazil and their adventurous new flexible football that now held sway – a new blueprint had been drawn up, and it was down to European coaches to try to catch up.

Sweden's coach, George Raynor, flexible and innovative and in demand all over the world, returned to England and dropped hints about being available if required. The FA had its ostrich head so firmly planted in the sand it was oblivious to the notion, and they were stuck with the willing and worthy, but regressive, Winterbottom for another four years.

World Cup Heroes No.10

Didi, born Waldyr Pereira (1928–2001)

Brazil

Didi went to play for Real Madrid in Spain a year after winning the World Cup with Brazil. He was a replacement for Raymond Kopa, the French international who was returning to his beloved Reims. Kopa was forced to play on the wing at Madrid, and Didi, too, was used badly and out of position, amid suggestions that Di Stéfano, the Argentinian-born star, and the Hungarian Puskás were not too happy about sharing the limelight with the Brazilian newcomer.

So Didi returned to Botafogo in Brazil, and continued to do his thing and inspire the Brazilian team to another World Cup win in 1962. It was Spain's loss, he was a fantastic player and a superb team man.

Didi first played for Brazil in 1952 and was part of the side that let themselves down in Berne against Hungary, although his role was mainly that of bemused and slightly ineffectual bystander, one tit-for-tat foul on Bozsik apart.

In 1958 he was the fulcrum of a young team; adept at finding space he was always available to receive the ball and play in the exciting array of young stars around him. He was the one Brazilian who slowed the game, preferring a little time to practise his art – "She's the one who runs," he once stated, pointing at the ball. Didi's set pieces were always dangerous – he had a trademark free-kick that he struck with the outside of his foot that was known as the "dead leaf" because it swirled and dipped unpredictably, fooling many a decent goalkeeper. He was a regular rather than prolific goalscorer by the standards of the day, but, with the likes of Vavá and Pelé in the side, that was hardly a problem.

By 1962 he was one of the team's wise old men, forming a canny left-sided axis with another 1958 veteran, Mario Zagallo. He called time on his playing career after the tournament and concentrated on coaching; he would return to the World Cup arena eight years later as the coach of the best team Peru have ever had.

1958 Team of the Tournament: 3–3–4

Kelsey (Wales)

Voinov (USSR)   Gustavsson (Sweden)   Nílton Santos (Brazil)

Kopa (France)   Didi (Brazil)   Liedholm (Sweden)

Garrincha (Brazil)   Fontaine (France)   Pelé (Brazil)   Hamrin (Sweden)

The unofficial team of the tournament had Harry Gregg in goal – understandable, a nod given for guts as well as performance, but Kelsey was flawless and superb. It also had Bergmark (an odd inclusion, he was exposed in the final); Bellini, the Brazilian captain, was in at centre-half and the workmanlike German half-back Szymaniak was included. The official team also had Skoglund rather than Hamrin. They left out Gustavsson, Liedholm and, extraordinarily,

Fontaine. Apparently votes were counted for each position and Fontaine's were split between inside-right and inside-left. He played as France's centre-forward. Doh!

There was no Player of the Tournament – it would (certainly should) have been Didi.

The FIFA All-Star team, selected later, was as follows: Gregg (Northern Ireland); D Santos (Brazil), Bellini (Brazil), N Santos (Brazil); Kopa (France), Blanchflower (Northern Ireland), Gren (Sweden), Didi (Brazil); Garrincha (Brazil), Pelé (Brazil), Fontaine (France).

Leading scorers: Fontaine (13); Pelé & Rahn (6); Vavá & McParland (5)

Heaven Eleven No.3

Scandinavia (Denmark, Finland, Iceland, Norway, Sweden)

Coach:
George Raynor – the English coach was the only one to take a Scandinavian team to a World Cup Final

Goalkeepers:
Peter Schmeichel (Den): big hands, big talent
Thomas Ravelli (Swe): played until he was about a hundred and twelve years old – seemed to, anyway
Antti Niemi (Fin): really good in the Premier League for Southampton – it was like London buses for Finland, two world-class 'keepers at once after a long wait

Defenders:
Gudni Bergsson (Ice): the Ice-man was a late developer but was one of the most under-rated Premiership players at Bolton in his thirties
Sami Hyypiä (Fin): tall, commanding and never replaced at Liverpool
Björn Nordqvist (Swe): the mainstay of Sweden in the 1970s.
Thorbjørn Svenssen (Nor): was a rock for Norway before they were a competitive side
Morten Olsen (Den): cool as cucumber, the *eminence grise* of the first competitive Danish side
Henning Berg (Nor): equally at home at right-back or in the middle, won Premiership titles with Blackburn and Manchester United

Olof Mellberg (Swe): great centre-half – Martin O'Neill played him at full-back to accommodate Zat Knight – that fact alone bars O'Neill from being considered a top manager

Julle Gustavsson (Swe): centre-half in the 1958 World Cup Final team, no shame in being exposed by that Brazil team

Midfield & Wide:

Jari Litmanen (Fin): Finland's best-ever outfield player by an embarrassingly large distance

Michael Laudrup (Den): ditto for Denmark

Martin Jorgensen (Den): clever and nimble wide player, outlet for Laudrup's passes

Henning Jensen (Den): playmaker in a bad Denmark side – won the league at Borussia Mönchengladbach, Real Madrid and Ajax, no mean feat

Gunnar Gren (Swe): part of the Gre-No-Li triumvirate that served Sweden and (especially) AC Milan so well in the 1950s.

Nils Liedholm (Swe): he was the Li part

Kurt Hamrin (Swe): quick-footed winger in the Sweden team in the late 1950s and early 1960s – a good finisher

Strikers:

Zlatan Ibrahimovic (Swe): the great enigma – if only he lived up to his own billing of himself

Preben Elkjaer (Den): he galloped rather than ran; big, leggy rangy striker, a real handful

Brian Laudrup (Den): not even the best player in his family, but worth a place here

Gunnar Nordahl (Swe): "No" (see above)

Henrik Larsson (Swe): great movement, superb finisher, and quite a nice chap

Omissions: Ole Gunnar Solskjaer & Tore André Flo of recent Norwegian vintage deserve mention, as does long-serving Danish defender **Thomas Helveg**. Niemi was a six of one half a dozen of the other pick ahead of **Jussi Jaaskelainen**; **Roland Nilsson** and **Patrik Andersson** were both excellent defenders for Sweden, while the massive **Kennet Andersson** was a powerhouse forward for a few years just before Larsson. Whisper it quietly to Crystal Palace fans but **Thomas Brolin** was once a damn fine player too.

Strengths: Plenty of talent and determination; great playmakers in Laudrup and Litmanen
Weaknesses: Inclined to be a bit predictable and a bit slow at the back

Likely first XI:

Schmeichel
Berg   Olsen   Gustavsson   Hyypiä
Liedholm   Gren
Hamrin   Litmanen   M Laudrup
Larsson

3.2 AGE

When does a player cease to be promising and become an established star? And when does an experienced international suddenly become a veteran? Age is odd. It is there, a stark fact, a statistic – so and so has been alive for x many years, months and days. But it is also a perception. When I was a kid a twenty-eight-year-old footballer seemed vastly experienced, a role model for adulthood, far more interesting than Dad or Uncle John-Joe-Jack. Now that I'm a middle-aged man, a player of thirty-three seems young, a guy just entering his best years, when you know stuff but also acknowledge there's lots of stuff you don't know – an awareness that passes you by in those earlier years of absolute conviction.

The simple answer: in football terms players age at very different rates. Some play their best football in their instinctive, youthful years – Michael Owen exploded onto the international scene, enjoyed a few years as a potent striker and then let injuries and a changing game leave him behind because he didn't learn to grow into a new role or new systems. Others need time to mature and find their best role; Teddy Sheringham was regarded as just another big lad up front and far from international class until Terry Venables saw his potential as a striker partner for Alan Shearer. Sheringham was deployed just behind Shearer where his football intelligence and use of the ball were an advantage and his lack of pace or fancy footwork not an issue – Sheringham was still getting in the England squad at thirty-six, while Owen retired in 2013 three years shy of that mark.

Some of the truly great players have adapted their game to suit their advancing years. Pelé started off as an out-and-out attacker for Brazil, but by 1970 he was playing in a leisurely free role behind the forwards. Franz Beckenbauer was an energetic attacking midfield player at the 1966 World Cup, but lifted the trophy eight years later as a ball-playing central defender. Occasionally it backfires – Lothar Matthäus did the same, largely because he wanted to be as revered as Beckenbauer, but unfortunately he was never in the same class as a defender. Ryan Giggs, once an exhilarating winger, now plays as a crafty, old-fashioned inside-forward when his hamstrings allow. Giggs has just signed a further one-year deal with Manchester United that means he will almost certainly play in the Premiership at the age of forty; he made his debut at seventeen in 1991.

Pelé set a few World Cup records when he played for Brazil aged seventeen in 1958. He was the youngest scorer in the competition's history, at 17 years and 239 days, against Wales, and the youngest to score a hat-trick (that'll be a tough one to beat) five days later against France. He was the youngest player to appear until Norman Whiteside turned out for Northern Ireland against Yugoslavia in 1982, aged seventeen years and forty-one days. Injuries finished Whiteside's international career at twenty-four.

The oldest player (and oldest scorer) accolade is held by the inestimable Roger Milla of Cameroon. In 1994 Milla's penultimate game at the World Cup was played alongside Rigobert Song; Song was a week shy of his eighteenth birthday, twenty-four years younger than the wiggle-hipped wonder.

The next four on the oldies list are goalkeepers and include England's Peter Shilton, who played (and captained, the oldest to do so) when just coming up to his forty-first birthday. He is just below another evergreen 'keeper, Northern Ireland's Pat Jennings. Tottenham sold Jennings to their great rivals in 1977, when he was thirty-two, believing he was past his best. Arsenal got eight years out of him; Spurs waited an age for an adequate replacement. England can boast the oldest debutant – David James was thirty-nine when he made his first Finals appearance in 2010, having been an unused squad member in 2002 and 2006. Just below Shilts is Italy's Dino Zoff, the oldest player to win the World Cup, captain of the Italian side that won in 1982. Like

Milla, he had a team-mate who probably called him Uncle Dino
– Giuseppe Bergomi was only eighteen.

The vast majority of World Cup squads have an average age
between twenty-six and twenty-nine. No surprise there, the opti-
mum age for a player, allowing for all the exceptions noted above,
is late twenties. Hence the observation that the German squad in
2010, which averaged only twenty-five, would be ripe for success
in 2014 – only Arne Friedrich has subsequently packed in, and
the only other over-thirty in the first team, Miroslav Klose, looks
like he may play for ever.

Examine the winning teams and no clear pattern emerges. The
team with the lowest average age of its ten starting outfield players in the final was Argentina in 1978 (it surprised me, too); the
oldest was the 1962 Brazilian side – eight of the same eleven as
the 1958 team, which was the second youngest to date. Here's the
order, youngest first, for those who like that sort of thing:
Argentina '78; Brazil '58; Italy '38; Brazil '70; Uruguay '50 &
Argentina '86; England '66; Italy '82; Brazil 2002; West Germany
'74; Uruguay '30 & Spain 2010; West Germany '54; West
Germany '90; France '98; Brazil '94; Italy '34; Italy 2006; Brazil
'62.

There may be no message to be gleaned here; if there is, it is
that over-reliance on youth or on old heads probably won't pay
off, and a team that balances both or has a group of players in
their prime who grew up together will probably prevail. It's
common football knowledge that Italian sides like to have a weight
of experience (the 1982 side was vastly experienced, but had an
eighteen-year-old), and equally common knowledge that the
South American sides are more likely to throw in a talented teenager. Lies, damned lies and statistics. Ghana will probably win
with a squad of twenty-three-year-olds.

3.3 WORLD CUP 1962

After the extravagant football of the World Cups of the 1950s, we were due a dismal tournament and Chile duly delivered. Apathy from the home crowds towards anyone other than the home team, combined with the unwillingness of European supporters to travel to a volatile country, meant crowds were small and quiet away from the main stadium in Santiago. European attitudes towards Chile as a venue proved a source of no little animosity during this tournament. FIFA mandated a South American country to host the competition as far back as 1954, but everyone assumed it would be Argentina, who had a far superior infrastructure in place and more than enough large stadia. But Carlos Dittborn, the President of the Chilean Federation, worked tirelessly to ensure Chile's voice was heard, using the relative political stability and tolerance of the country compared to other South American nations – and of course he was speaking of the military influence in Argentina, where the President was deposed by the army in 1955. Dittborn's campaign worked, and Chile won the bid by thirty-two votes to eleven against a complacent Argentina.

At first glance it seems a shocking choice of host, with too few venues, too few spectators and poor organisation. But there were mitigating circumstances – a massive earthquake that claimed 50,000 casualties shook the seaboard of the entire country (which is nearly all seaboard . . .). The government was old-school and conservative and was heavily criticised for its unsympathetic response to the disaster. Jorge Alessandri had won an election victory in 1958 against General Ibañez del Campo, the ageing

1962
CHILE

With the problems the country faced after the catastrophic earthquake prior to the tournament, Chile could offer only four stadia for the 1962 finals, so the games were carefully spread out to prevent the pitches becoming over-used – easier in a dry country like Chile than would have been the case in Europe.

Santiago: Estádio Nacional
Started in 1937, the main stadium in the capital Santiago was extensively refurbished to host the 1962 final and fortunately escaped any significant damage in the earthquake. It had a capacity of 66,660, now reduced to 47,000 and is the home of Universidad de Chile as well as the national team.

Viña del Mar: Estádio Sausalito
The 18,000 capacity stadium at Viña del Mar was damaged but repairable, and was ready in time for the finals. It still stands and is home to the local top-flight club, Everton.

Rancagua: Braden Copper Company Stadium
The stadium in Rancagua was owned by an American company which ran the local copper mine; the Braden Company rented it to the organizers for the finals tournament. The stadium, still in use, is the home of the splendidly named local team O'Higgins FC. Rancagua played host to England's 1962 campaign.

Arica: Estádio Carlos Dittborn
Arica is the northernmost city in Chile, right on the north-eastern tip. The stadium was hurriedly renovated after the earthquake with a capacity of almost 18,000 and had the honour of hosting Chile's quarterfinal win against the Soviet Union.

"benevolent dictator" of Chilean politics. The social reforms of Salvador Allende and subsequent coup and persecution under General Pinochet's rule was a decade away, but the factors that saw Allende come to power were evident; widespread poverty, rank inequality and social deprivation. Chile wasn't an especially wealthy country, and most of the money was in mining, not an industry noted for wide-scale distribution of largesse amongst its workforce in the post-war years. The response to the disaster was slow, and the aid agencies that offer invaluable support in such times of crisis in modern times were only in their formative years and not geared up for missions on this scale. The earthquake set the preparations for the tournament back significantly – what was intended as an eight-venue competition became four, and two of these cities needed significant outside help in order to be ready – the stadium at Rancagua, one of the four eventually used, was "borrowed" from its owners, an American copper mining company. Tragically Dittborn never saw the fulfilment of his dream, as he died from a huge heart attack a few weeks before the start of the tournament.

Qualifying

The qualification was weighted towards the stronger sides yet again. Chile and Brazil were already in, and another three South American sides would join them. Eight teams from Europe also qualified automatically. That makes thirteen – keep up at the back. The North American (CONCACAF) challenger would have to beat another South American side to earn a place, while the two best African and Asian sides would also have to get through a play-off, against two European sides. A tough proposition for sides who played few competitive fixtures against European or South American opposition.

With Venezuela not bothered and Paraguay sent direct to a play-off against the CONCACAF winners, three South American sides qualified after winning just a home-and-away tie. Argentina thumped Ecuador, while Uruguay and Colombia scraped past Bolivia and Peru respectively.

South Korea and Morocco, the Asian and African winners, fell to Spain and Yugoslavia – seriously, what chance did they have? Morocco acquitted themselves really well against a Spain side that included the great Di Stéfano – the closest he ever got to a World Cup Finals.

European qualification was at least a little more demanding, except for Spain and Yugoslavia, who had to win only one two-leg tie to reach their play-off and an almost certain qualifying spot. Wales and Poland were the sides they beat.

The 1958 finalists didn't make it. Sweden were always facing problems once their ageing stars from 1958 retired, but they were still in the box seat before the last game, needing only a draw against an ordinary Switzerland side. They thought they had it with an equaliser with ten minutes left but a late Swiss goal forced a replay, which Switzerland won 2–1 after trailing at half-time. France, the losing semi-finalists from 1958, also fell by the wayside, surprisingly losing a play-off to Bulgaria, who reached the Finals for the first time. Had either of these groups been decided on goal difference, Sweden and France would have advanced.

The other play-off involved Scotland, who finished level on points with Czechoslovakia despite a 4–0 hammering in Prague. Two Denis Law goals won them the return match 3–2 and the replay was equally close, going to extra-time before the Czechs wore down the Scots to win 4–2. Scotland had some quality (Law, Ian St John, Paddy Crerand, Jim Baxter) but also some gaps, and the better side qualified.

West Germany, Holland, England, Italy and the Soviet Union all qualified easily; England, the Soviets and West Germany looked the strongest European contenders, although Italy had bolstered their team with more *oriundi*, including the clever Argentinian Omar Sivori. Spain did much the same, naming Di Stéfano (now thirty-five) and Puskás (a year older) in their squad. Di Stéfano never got on the pitch – it was all a bit of a mystery and it was later reported he was injured – so why take a half-fit thirty-five-year-old to sit on the bench?

Finals

The clear favourites were Brazil; if they had won in 1958 in
Europe, who could stop them in South America? This was a new
Brazil, with a new capital (Brasilia was officially opened the day
after the 1958 World Cup Final) and a new government headed
by the left-wing former Minister of Labour Goulart. But it was
virtually the same team – Brazil had much the same squad as in
1958, although one or two had been in and out of the team in the
meantime. Most of them were now past thirty, Pelé being an
obvious exception, but in terms of ability they were streets ahead
of the competition.

There was a minor change in format – no play-offs, but goal
average was to separate teams who finished level on points. Goal
average was the precursor of goal difference and was the ratio of
goals scored to goals conceded. So twelve scored and eight
conceded gave a goal average of 1.5 whereas twenty scored and
fifteen conceded gave a goal average of only 1.33. Under the later
system, goal difference, 20–15 would have topped 12–8 – it was
introduced to encourage teams to attack and score more.

GROUP 1

Uruguay	(0) 2	**Colombia**	(1) 1	30 May, Arica; 7,908
Cubilla 57, Sasia 73		Zuluaga 18 (p)		
USSR	(0) 2	**Yugoslavia**	(0) 0	31 May, Arica; 9,622
V Ivanov 53, Ponedelnik 85				
Yugoslavia	(2) 3	**Uruguay**	(1) 1	2 June, Arica; 8,829
Skoblar 26 (p), Galic 30,		Cabrera 19		
Jerkovic 49				
Colombia	(1) 4	**USSR**	(3) 4	3 June, Arica; 8,040
Aceros 22, Coll 68,		V Ivanov 5, 13,		
Rada 70, Klinger 76		Chislenko 11, Ponedelnik 57		
USSR	(1) 2	**Uruguay**	(0) 1	6 June, Arica; 9,973
Mamykin 38, V Ivanov 89		Sasia 53		
Yugoslavia	(2) 5	**Colombia**	(0) 0	7 June, Arica; 7,167
Galic 20, 51, Jerkovic 25, 88,				
Melic 82				

**1. USSR 5pts (8–5); 2. Yugoslavia 4pts (8–3); 3. Uruguay 2pts (4–6); 4. Colombia 1pt
(5–11)**

The top group featured the strongest two East European sides,
Yugoslavia and the Soviet Union, and probably the two weakest

South American sides, Uruguay, in a bit of a trough and lacking real quality, and Colombia.

Two years previously the USSR and Yugoslavia had met in the first European Nations' Cup Final. This new competition was ignored by England and the other home nations (how typical), and also by Italy and West Germany. The USSR won the final, but it took a winner in extra-time after Yugoslavia scored first, all of which suggests there was little between the teams.

The gulf seemed wider here. An early flurry from Yugoslavia saw the gifted but infuriating Sekularac bring a superb save out of Yashin, but once the Soviets scored early in the second half the Yugoslavs lost their composure. Jerkovic should have been sent off for manhandling the referee, and Mujic broke Dubinsky's leg with a shocker that should have also seen red. The tone was set for the tournament; bad tackling, lack of discipline, poor refereeing.

The first goal came from a free-kick won by Ponedelnik; he took it himself and crashed a thunderbolt against the bar from nearly thirty yards. Valentin Ivanov beat everyone to the rebound and nodded the ball over the line. Ponedelnik scored the late second himself, playing a fine one-two with Voronin and beating Soskic with an angled shot.

Contemporary commentary refers casually to the Soviet side as Russians – the two were commonly presumed to be the same thing, Russia being the dominant state in the union. Their team for this first match included only seven actual Russians; Viktor Kanevsky was from Lyiv in the Ukraine, Metreveli and Meskhi were Georgian and left-back Ostrovsky was a Latvian Jew, the first Latvian to represent the Soviet Union. They were a physically strong team and not without skill. The captain, Igor Netto, was a quality midfield general; he had played only one match in the previous World Cup, when only half-fit, and was anxious to make amends here. Metreveli was a tricky customer and Ponedelnik was an unstoppable bruiser of a centre-forward, always pointing straight at goal and hard to knock off the ball. Had Eduard Streltsov (see *Best Players Never to Play in the World Cup*) been available, this Soviet squad would have been a genuine threat to Brazil.

Yugoslavia seemed always to offer the same mix of talent and self-destruction, and in this tournament the uneasy mix of Serbs, Croatians and Bosnians fell short in familiar manner. They were a young squad – only two players over thirty – and suffered from the lack of a genuine leader. Dragoslav Sekularac was one of the great under-achievers, hugely talented but a fair weather player and petulant to a fault – he served an eighteen-month ban after striking a referee later that year.

Uruguay, who won their first match against Colombia (another rough affair), started well against Yugoslavia, and Sasía had already missed one glorious chance before Cabrera headed them into the lead. Yugoslavia responded better than against the Soviets, and Sekularac and Galic began to dictate the game. Skoblar converted a penalty after a blatant foul on Jerkovic, whose snap volley caught out Sosa two minutes later – the Uruguayan 'keeper managed only a feeble half-save and Galic poked home the loose ball. A third goal – a brave header from the rangy Jerkovic after Galic ran his man ragged on the right – settled it, but Uruguay kept pressing and hit the post. Sasía was a bit over-eager; the Uruguayan striker's late challenge on Soskic provoked a fracas in the Yugoslav penalty area that saw Cabrera and Popovic (one from each side) dismissed. Galba, the Czech referee, did well to restore order, so, of course, FIFA didn't use him again.

Colombia picked up their only point against the USSR. It was a bizarre game. With an hour gone the Soviets were coasting, 4–1 ahead after an opening blitz that saw Ivanov (twice) and Chislenko give them a 3–0 lead inside fifteen minutes. The Colombian goalkeeper Sánchez did not cover himself in glory. Over-confident, the USSR sat back, and Colombia, skilful and willing if not especially quick, hit back. Coll hit a woeful corner to the near post, but the Soviet right-back wandered off the post and the ball bobbled and rolled almost apologetically over the line. Flustered, the Soviet defence failed to clear a cross three minutes later and Rada put it away after a few seconds of penalty-area pinball. Another five minutes and Yashin, of all people, failed to get down properly to a through ball and Klinger broke his challenge and scored the equaliser. Twenty mad minutes and the

USSR went from cruise control to damage limitation, holding on for a draw.

Colombia's quality was put in perspective by Yugoslavia, who ran in five without reply, two each for Galic and Jerkovic, who was looking one of the tournament's top strikers. The USSR needed to beat Uruguay to top the group, and they did, just, with a late goal from Valentin Ivanov.

GROUP 2

Chile L Sánchez 44, 54, Ramírez 51	**(1) 3**	**Switzerland** Wüthrich	**(1) 1**	30 May, Santiago; 65,006
Italy	**(0) 0**	**West Germany**	**(0) 0**	31 May, Santiago; 65,440★
Chile Ramírez 74, Toro 88	**(0) 2**	**Italy**	**(0) 0**	2 June, Santiago; 66,057
West Germany Brülls 44, Seeler 60	**(1) 2**	**Switzerland** Schneiter 76	**(0) 1**	3 June, Santiago; 64,922★
West Germany Szymaniak 22 (p), Seeler 82	**(1) 2**	**Chile**	**(0) 0**	6 June, Santiago; 67,224
Italy Mora 2, Bulgarelli 65, 67	**(1) 3**	**Switzerland**	**(0) 0**	7 June, Santiago; 59,828★

1. West Germany 5pts (4–1); 2. Chile 4pts (5–3); 3. Italy 3pts (3–2); 4. Switzerland 0pts (2–8)

The Germans were a strong and physical side, with Karl-Heinz Schnellinger added to an already muscular defence. Their 0–0 draw with Italy in the opening game set the tone for their campaign; two weak defences stifling two attacks short on creativity. The second game was equally poor, West Germany making heavy weather of seeing off a Switzerland side reduced to ten men for the second half. A win against Chile meant the Germans would win the group, and it came courtesy of a referee (Bobby Davidson of Scotland) brave enough to give a penalty against the hosts – it was a clear barge, Davidson was absolutely correct – and a diving header from Seeler. Germany's tactics were of note – Herberger played a cannily defensive game, using the pace and power

★ These are official figures and are manufactured. Reports suggest only the Chile matches saw the stadium full; the other games attracted less than half the figures suggested here – Italy against Switzerland probably no more than 15,000.

and fitness traditionally associated with German sides to contain and counter.

With all three sides beating Switzerland, the second spot in the group would go to the winners of Chile v Italy, in the second pair of matches. The game was introduced on the BBC's highlights programme by David Coleman as *"The most stupid, appalling, disgusting and disgraceful exhibition of football, possibly in the history of the game."* It was a typically pompous British response, especially when a dreadful refereeing performance by Ken Aston was a factor in the mayhem, but it may be accurate.

The run-up to the game was a controversy in itself. Two Italian journalists had run a couple of lifestyle pieces suggesting Santiago was little more than a crime-and-prostitution-infested slum. The two culprits promptly scarpered and left the team to try to repair the diplomatic damage. They failed, approaching this game as if the only response to assumed hostility from the opposition was to get one's retaliation in first. Both sides were at it; spitting, shirt-pulling, sly little digs off the ball. Ken Aston – by all accounts a decent ref at home, and the man who would oversee the introduction of yellow and red cards – just couldn't get a handle on it. In England, sir, one simply kicks one's opponent in a decent and honourable manner, sir! Aston had stood by in Chile's first match against Switzerland and let them get away with some intimidatory tackling and a lot of complaining – presumably they liked what they saw because he was drafted in here as a late change to the schedule with no explanation offered. He sent off Ferrini for retaliation after seven minutes, despite ignoring worse offences in the opening exchanges, and then stood helpless as the police had to clear the pitch when Ferrini refused to go and half the Italian retinue crowded onto the playing area. A running feud between David and Leonel Sánchez ended with David following his compatriot down the tunnel – apparently a left hook by Sánchez in front of the referee didn't merit the same treatment. At least two other Chilean players threw punches without punishment. The Italians were far from guiltless in the affair, but it's no wonder they accused Aston of being dodgy, he was anything but even-handed – although the explanation probably lies in lack of competence. It was Aston's last World Cup match in charge.

Oh, and Chile scored two late goals to win the game and go through.

GROUP 3

Brazil	(0) 2	**Mexico**	(0) 0	30 May, Viña del Mar; 10,484
Zagallo 56, Pelé 72				
Czechoslovakia	(0) 1	**Spain**	(0) 0	31 May, Viña del Mar; 12,700
Stibrányi 79				
Brazil	(0) 0	**Czechoslovakia**	(0) 0	2 June, Viña del Mar; 14,903
Mexico	(0) 0	**Spain**	(0) 1	3 June, Viña del Mar; 11,875
		Peiro 89		
Brazil	(0) 2	**Spain**	(1) 1	6 June, Viña del Mar; 18,715
Amarildo 72, 85		Adelardo 35		
Mexico	(2) 3	**Czechoslovakia**	(1) 1	7 June, Viña del Mar 59,828
Díaz 13, Del Aguila 30,		Masek 1		
H Hernández 88 (p)				

1. Brazil 5pts (4–1); 2. Czechoslovakia 3pts (2–3); 3. Mexico 2pts (3–4); 4. Spain 2pts (2–3)

The favourites found themselves in a cosy group. Brazil opened up against Mexico but found opening up Mexico tougher than expected. Two bursts from Pelé settled the game. First he attacked down the inside-right channel, lost the ball, got it back from Didi and dinked a nice cross for Zagallo to dive in and head past Carbajal. The Mexican goalkeeper was making a bit of history – he was the first player to appear in four World Cup Finals – and he wasn't done yet.

Czechoslovakia made a good start against Spain, winning with a late goal from Stibrányi. They were a good technical side with a good defence who knew their limitations. Less reliant on the Prague teams than of old, they included a number of Slovaks in the squad, including Popluhár, a solid centre-half, Scherer, the centre-forward, and Jozef Adamec, a free-scoring inside-forward. Adamec was one of a number of players with the army team Dukla Prague but he returned to Slovakia at the end of his national service. Most of the play came through the left-half Josef Masopust, a ball-carrier with good positional sense and defensive nous.

The Czech defence neutered Brazil in the next game, but in the main it was because Pelé suffered a groin strain in the first half and spent the rest of the game a passenger. The Czechs were courteous opponents and never went in to hurt the young genius, and the match petered out in a rather gentlemanly stalemate very much out of kilter with this tournament.

Mexico played well against Spain but again failed to score and lost by the odd goal, scored agonisingly late. The veteran Puskás wasn't making the impact Spain had hoped and the former Uruguay international José Santamaría, another of the Real Madrid *oriundi*, looked well past his best. Spain's best player was the left-winger Francisco Gento, another Madrid star. His shot was only half stopped by the excellent Carbajal and Peiró put in the rebound.

Gento made inroads against Brazil as well; he was extra quick and had the beating of Djalma Santos, who was no spring chicken. Shortly after Adelardo gave Spain the lead with a good early strike from a through ball, Gento outpaced the Brazilian defence and sent over a hanging cross that was volleyed narrowly over by the Atlético Madrid youngster. Brazil seemed unsure of themselves without the injured Pelé. Garrincha was in his shell and Vavá seemed to have lost some of the oomph he had in 1958. In the second half Spain had claims for a penalty when Enrique Collar was sent tumbling on the edge of the penalty area, and a smart overhead kick from Peiró was ruled out for no apparent reason by the Chilean referee.

Brazil needed something or they were going out, assuming Czechoslovakia beat Mexico. Something came from Amarildo, Pelé's replacement; first he converted a low cross from the left by his Botafogo team-mate Zagallo, nipping between two static defenders. Then Garrincha rediscovered his mojo, sprinted down the right and sent over a hanging cross, which was met by Amarildo at the far post for the winning header.

The following day Czechoslovakia blew their chance to top the group and suffered a surprise defeat to Mexico, despite taking the lead after only fifteen seconds – the fastest goal in the Finals until 2002. Their response was terrific, the lively forward line repeatedly picking their way through a defence that looked far less secure than against Brazil. The win, Mexico's first in their fifth appearance in the Finals, was a splendid birthday treat for captain Carbajal.

GROUP 4

Argentina Facundo 4	(1) 1	**Bulgaria**	(0) 0	30 May, Rancagua; 7,134
Hungary Tichy 16, Albert 70	(1) 2	**England** Flowers 58 (p)	(0) 1	31 May, Rancagua; 7,938
England Flowers 17 (p), Charlton 42, Greaves 65	(2) 3	**Argentina** Sanfilippo 78	(0) 1	2 June, Rancagua; 9,794
Hungary Albert 1, 6, 54, Tichy 8, 70, Solymosi 12	(4) 6	**Bulgaria** Sokolov 64	(1) 1	3 June, Rancagua; 7,442
Argentina	(0) 0	**Hungary**	(0) 0	6 June, Rancagua; 7,945
England	(0) 0	**Bulgaria**	(0) 0	7 June, Rancagua; 5,700

1. Hungary 5pts (8–2); 2. England 3pts (4–3); 3. Argentina 3pts (2–3); 4. Bulgaria 1pt (1–7)

England's group produced little football worth watching, and the little that emerged was played by the Hungarians. Argentina, under Juan Carlos Lorenzo, were ugly and defensive, England lacked creativity and Bulgaria just weren't very good.

England were completely outplayed in their first game – in fairness Hungary looked a tasty side, their centre-forward Flórián Albert was the best striker in the tournament. Alongside him the giant Tichy caused problems with his power and shooting, while England struggled to make anything happen in the final third, with Haynes suppressed by the close marking of Rákosi. The England backs' tendency to go to ground when tackling left them very exposed on a wet surface, and Hungary exploited it. Tichy was allowed to run with the ball from the centre circle, shaped to shoot with his right to wrong-foot Bobby Moore, then switched to his left to unleash an unstoppable drive. England's equaliser came from a corner, when Sárosi saved Greaves' shot on the line – all very well except Sárosi wasn't the goalkeeper, he (Grosics) was on the ground after a borderline legal challenge from Hitchens. England looked more solid at the back in the second half until Flowers slipped in the mud and Albert sprinted past him, went round

Springett and squeezed the ball in at the near post past the covering full-back.

Hungary (and Albert) were even more impressive in their second game, annihilating Bulgaria. The Ferencváros centre-forward was already one of the most talked-about players in the tournament, especially now Pelé was out through injury. Albert scored twice inside six minutes (Hungary were four-up after twelve) and completed a hat-trick in the second half; none were outstanding goals but all were taken with efficiency and coolness. With the impressive Tichy alongside and a competent defence, Hungary looked the most likely threat to Brazilian pre-eminence. The margin of victory did not flatter Hungary, who were better than Bulgaria in every area of the pitch.

The previous day in the Rancagua Stadium, England had partially redeemed themselves after their poor showing against Hungary by beating Argentina. It was another rough game, but England refused to be intimidated and managed to play some decent football in between the kicking. Bobby Charlton had a good game, playing as a conventional outside-left, and the gamble on picking debutant Alan Peacock of Middlesbrough up front paid off as he proved more effective than Hitchens in the first game. For the second game running England were awarded a penalty after a man handled on the line – an automatic red card for this came much later. Ron Flowers was a penalty taker of some repute and scored both.

I shall draw a polite veil over the final two games in the group. Both finished 0–0; both were unwatchable.

QUARTER-FINALS (all 10 June)

Yugoslavia	(0) 1	**West Germany**	(0) 0	Nacional, Santiago; 63,324
Radakovic				
Chile	(2) 2	**USSR**	(1) 1	Carlos Dittborn, Arica; 17,268
L Sánchez 10, Rojas 28		Chislenko 26		
Brazil	(1) 3	**England**	(1) 1	El Tranque, Viña del Mar; 17,736
Garrincha 31, 59, Vavá 53		Hitchens 38		
Czechoslovakia	(1) 1	**Hungary**	(0) 0	Braden, Rancagua; 11,690
Scherer				

For the third time West Germany would play Yugoslavia in the quarter-final, confident of victory having seen off the same opponents at the same stage in the previous two tournaments. It was a cagey game, West Germany negative again and Yugoslavia nervous of their unsuccessful history against these opponents. Szymaniak, the German enforcer (not that the others were anything other than rugged in the tackle), controlled Sekularac, and the German attackers created little other than the occasional run from Seeler. The No.9 hit the post, but clear chances were rare. The winner came late, when the Yugoslavia captain Galik, who was having an outstanding tournament, got behind the German defence and cut the ball back for Radakovic to hit home. Third time lucky for Yugoslavia and a disappointing German campaign was over; like England they paid for a lack of creative spark. It was Sepp Herberger's last World Cup match in charge of the national team he served so admirably. His successor was Helmut Schön, born in Dresden but now living in the West. In 1953 West Germany played the region of Saarland in a World Cup qualifier; in 1956 the former German territory rejoined West Germany and Schön joined Herberger's staff. He now faced the task of replacing and matching his mentor.

The favourites were still in. England had a good side and played reasonably well in this World Cup, but against Brazil their shortcomings were plain to see. England's full-backs were excellent. Ray Wilson, then with Huddersfield Town, had settled in to the left-back position, while Jimmy Armfield was probably the world's best right-back. Up front Charlton and Greaves were high quality, but they didn't get enough bullets to fire. The midfield pairing of Bobby Moore and Johnny Haynes wasn't as good as it looked on paper. Moore was soon to find his best position at the back, and Haynes, for all his consistency and talent, struggled to make an impact at this highest level – a footballing Graeme Hick, if you will. Like Tom Finney, he was an England legend who never put his best foot forward in the World Cup.

The game was reasonably well balanced in the first half, but worryingly for England the maverick winger Garrincha appeared to be "in the mood" and was giving Ray Wilson a torrid time, and the full-back was getting little or no help from Bobby

Charlton, never the greatest defender. England should have switched Charlton with the more defensively adept Bryan Douglas, but that sort of flexibility wasn't in their armoury. Garrincha looked the most likely player on the field to score, but no one thought it would be with his head; Maurice Norman was slow to react to Garrincha's run and he powered Zagallo's corner home. To their credit England didn't buckle and equalised from another set play when a header by Greaves looped tantalisingly over Gylmar and came back off the bar into Hitchens' path. Either side of half-time England enjoyed their best spell. If Garrincha was tormenting Wilson, then Brazil's own left-back, the veteran Nílton Santos, was having trouble against Douglas and the aggressive overlapping of Armfield. The pair created chances for Haynes and Greaves, but neither was clear cut and both went begging.

Free-kicks were causing problems for goalkeepers in this tournament. The balls were lighter than those used in Europe and were swerving late in the thin air – not so markedly as eight years later in Mexico but enough to make the 'keepers uneasy. I'm telegraphing the next bit, aren't I? Yup, the England goalkeeper made a hash of a Brazilian free-kick, forty years before David Seaman had his fateful encounter with Ronaldinho. Garrincha's shot was low and hard and may have moved a fraction but it was straight at Ron Springett. The ball didn't merely bounce off the England goalkeeper, he actually clawed it up into the path of Vavá; the big centre-forward barely had to move a muscle to score. Vavá had a nothing game; Norman and Flowers were unfussed by his aggression and elbows, but he made his one contribution here and it was vital. Garrincha added a third a few minutes later with a cute curling shot, and Brazil had enough of a cushion to be able to sit back and play keep-ball.

Jimmy Greaves didn't have a great time in either of the World Cup tournaments he played in; his misery was compounded here when he took it on himself to snare a rogue pooch that wandered onto the pitch. The little four-legged midfielder had shown a clean pair of heels to Bobby Moore and even side-stepped Garrincha, but Greavesie got down on all fours, won the ensuing wrestle and coaxed the intruder into the arms of a security guard.

No prizes for guessing what the Tottenham star was wiping on his shirt shortly afterwards . . .

England came home, not in disgrace, but with a feeling they had missed out. They were missing a couple of good players; Greaves' strike partner at Spurs, Bobby Smith, future manager Bobby Robson and the commanding Sheffield Wednesday centre-half Peter Swan, who travelled but went down with dysentery. All were good players but not world-beaters; Swan was highly rated by his peers but fell from grace (and went to jail) when he was mixed up in a match-fixing scandal later that year.

The game against Brazil was Johnny Haynes' last appearance for England. The Fulham playmaker at his best was one of the finest England have had, assured with his passing, able to read the game well and give himself time to pick a colleague or attempt a shot. He delivered a superlative performance only the year before this World Cup as England destroyed Scotland 9–3, and the same season saw him become English football's first £100-a-week player when the archaic maximum wage was abolished after an intense campaign whipped up by Jimmy Hill, a colleague of Haynes at Fulham. Haynes crashed his sports car not long after the end of this tournament, and the new England manager harboured a suspicion that he never properly recovered – not that Ramsey ever needed much excuse to ignore a creative player.

The hosts also made the semi-final. Davidson, the referee who brooked little of their nonsense in their previous game, was ignored (obviously, this was a FIFA competition and we can't have the hosts going out too early, can we?). The USSR matched the Chileans physically, but they couldn't break down a massed defence once Chile got their noses in front for a second time. They took the lead in the tenth minute when a free-kick from the left-hand edge of the penalty area was thrashed in at Yashin's near post – it was an extraordinary decision from such an experienced goalkeeper not to build a wall. The USSR responded well and when Ponedelnik's shot was palmed out to Meskhi, the Georgian's mishit shot was turned in by the other winger, Chislenko.

Chile scored again within a minute, Rojas hitting a fine, low shot into the corner when he was left far too much space in midfield. The USSR pressed hard but lacked the spark needed to penetrate a well-drilled, massed defence – surely the absent Streltsov would have made the difference. Chile and their raucous supporters had a semi-final against Brazil to look forward to, but they were one of the weakest sides to go that deep into a World Cup tournament.

Another of the fancied sides went out when Czechoslovakia beat Hungary. The Czechs were doing the World Cup the Italian way, improving slowly and making unspectacular progress while other sides grabbed the headlines. Like Chile they defended in numbers and thwarted the Hungarians, but they needed an element of luck when Tichy nearly broke the bar with a rocket of a free-kick (after a run-up to rival that of Michael Holding) that left Schrojf a spectator. The ball bounced down on the line, but not over it, despite Hungarian protests to the contrary. The Czech goalkeeper was the man-of-the-match, making a series of saves, none better than a flying stop to keep out a Rákosi piledriver aimed at the top corner. The Czechs could barely make it out of their own half, but when they did Josef Masopust was invariably their outlet, and it was his urgent burst forward and clever through ball that set up Adolf Scherer to drive past Grosics for the only goal of the game. Not for the first or last time, the romantics weren't the victors.

England Squad 1962:
GK: Ron Springett (Sheffield Wednesday, 26 years old, 21 caps), Alan Hodgkinson (Sheffield United, 25, 5)
DEF: Jimmy Armfield (Blackpool, 26, 25), Don Howe (West Bromwich Albion, 26, 23), Bobby Moore (West Ham United, 21, 1), Maurice Norman (Tottenham Hotspur, 28, 1), Peter Swan (Sheffield Wed, 25, 19), Ray Wilson (Huddersfield Town, 27, 11)
MID & WIDE: Jimmy Adamson (Burnley, 33, 0), Stan Anderson[*] (Sunderland, 29, 2), George Eastham (Arsenal, 26, 0), Ron Flowers (Wolverhampton Wanderers, 27, 32), Johnny

[*] An unused squad member, Sunderland captain Anderson made his debut just before the tournament. A year later he moved to Newcastle after 400 games for Sunderland and later captained Middlesbrough for a season, becoming the only man to skipper all three big north-east sides.

Haynes (Fulham, 27, 52), Bobby Robson (West Brom, 29, 20), Bobby Charlton (Manchester United, 24, 35), John Connelly (Burnley, 23, 8), Bryan Douglas (Blackburn Rovers, 28, 29)
FWD: Jimmy Greaves (Tottenham, 22, 18), Gerry Hitchens (Inter Milan, 27, 5), Roger Hunt (Liverpool, 23, 1), Derek Kevan (West Brom, 27, 14), Alan Peacock (Middlesbrough, 24, 0)

In 1960 one of the England squad, George Eastham, became involved in a dispute with his club, Newcastle United. Eastham asked for a transfer but Newcastle denied the request whilst retaining his registration, even though the terms of his contract had been fulfilled. This retain-and-transfer system was the norm at the time, putting all the power in the hands of the clubs. Eastham responded by refusing to play, and, although the matter was resolved when Arsenal paid a fee for the talented midfielder later that year, Eastham, with the help of the PFA, pursued Newcastle legally for wages owed. He lost the claim for compensation, but, crucially, the court decreed, in 1963, that the retain-and-transfer system was unfair. Players now had more bargaining power with their employers and a transfer tribunal was set up to settle disputes over the price of out-of-contract players wishing to move to a new club.

In 1995 the courts went a step further when Jean-Marc Bosman, a journeyman Belgian pro, took his club to court for refusing to agree a fee for him when he requested a move at the end of his contract. The European Court of Justice (I can hear the baying of the *Daily Mail* editorial writers from here ...) determined that this was restraint of trade and that once a player had fulfilled the terms of a contract he was free to move without the club being able to demand any sort of fee. Exceptions were made for young players to prevent larger clubs poaching talent from smaller teams (and that's worked, hasn't it ...?)

The Eastham case was a necessary landmark – just read Gary Imlach's book for the detail of the iniquity of football contracts in the 1950s. The Bosman ruling makes sense, although it has undoubtedly affected the ability of lesser clubs to earn revenue through transfers. Unfortunately the whole opening up of the transfer system has led to the proliferation of football agents. An agent acts for a footballer and undertakes all negotiations on his part, whether contractual, with the player's club, or secondary deals involving sponsorship or media work. They are a poison – and this with a mumbled apology to the tiny majority of sensible, ethical agents. They whisper in players' ears and unsettle them even when they are doing well at a club. They take a hard-working, talented player from a difficult background like Carlos Tévez and turn him into a posturing, arrogant, distracted young man with no appreciation of where he has come from. They tell Scott Sinclair that Swansea are too small for him, even though he made it into the England side while he was there, and that he would be much better off sitting on the bench at Manchester City and watching his career go down the toilet. Why? Because they get a cut. Every time a player moves, or does a hilarious pizza advert, or signs a deal to wear luminous boots, they get money. And that's what the game is all about, is it not?

I feel better now. Shall we move on to the semis?

SEMI-FINAL

Czechoslovakia   (0) **3** **Yugoslavia** (0) **1**   13 June, El Tranque, Viña del Mar; 5,890
Kadraba 48,
Scherer 80, 84 (p)   Jerkovic 68

THIRD-PLACE MATCH

Chile   (0) **1**   **Yugoslavia** (0) **0**   16 June, Nacional, Santiago; 66,697
Rojas

The semi-finals were weak. A great team enjoying an Indian summer, a weak host nation there by the grace of God and some weak officials, a defensive but prosaic European side and a talented but sloppy Yugoslavia. If Brazil could have hand-picked the winners of the other three quarter-finals they would have opted for these three to ease their passage to victory.

In Viña del Mar the Czechs set out to do to Yugoslavia what they had done to Hungary; slow the game down, take the sting out of more talented opposition and catch them on the counter-attack. They nearly paid the price for sitting back in a bright start by Yugoslavia. Schrojf got down well to save Popovic's thumper, and then Galic should have done better from Jerkovic's knock-down, shooting wide across the goal with only the 'keeper to beat from six yards. Another chance for the same player went begging when he stretched for another Jerkovic header and put the ball over the bar. Czechoslovakia started to string a few passes together, with most of the play going through Masopust as usual.

The first goal came at the start of the second half, when Yugoslav defender Popovic lost the ball to the left of the goal-line as he tried to usher it out. When the cross came over, Kadraba's hard hit shot rebounded back in his direction and the Czech scored with a clever diving header. Yugoslavia kept coming, and Skoblar hit the bar with a fine header. The equaliser was in stark contrast with most of Yugoslavia's intricate football. A hopeful punt forward caught the otherwise excellent Schrojf in no man's land and Jerkovic just had to get his head to it to score – no challenge there for a man who looks a head taller than any other player in the tournament in the videos – his stats list him as six foot one, but that is surely an underestimation.

It was overconfidence that cost Yugoslavia; having equalised, they knew they could win the game and continued to press. Jerkovic just failed to put away a chance after a powerful run from Galic and the disappointing Sekularac forced a save from Schrojf. When another attack broke down, a through ball from the Czech captain Ladislav Novák found Kadraba in acres of space. As the only defender in the same post code came across to challenge, Kadraba slid the ball sideways to Scherer, who poked it past the 'keeper and watched it dribble slowly over the line. Three minutes later a brainless handball by Markovic, under no pressure, handed the Czechs a penalty that Scherer put away to seal the tie and a second final appearance for Czechoslovakia. Soskic watched the spot-kick go past him rather like the last boy to be picked in the playground who is forced to play in goal against his will.

WORLD CUP CLASSIC No.4
13 June 1962, Nacional, Santiago; 76,594

Brazil	**(2) 4**	Garrincha 9, 32, Vavá 49, 78
Chile	**(1) 2**	Toro 42, L Sánchez 62 (p)

Referee: **Arturo Yamasaki** (Peru)
Coaches: **Aymoré Moreira** (Brazil) & **Fernando Riera** (Chile)

Brazil (4–3–3): Gylmar (Santos); Djalma Santos (Palmeiras), Mauro Ramos (Cpt, Santos), Zózimo *Calazäes* (Bangu), Nílton Santos (Botafogo); *José Ely de Miranda, known as* Zito (Santos), *Waldir Pereira, known as* Didi (Botafogo), Mário Zagallo (Botafogo); *Manuel dos Santos, known as* Garrincha (Botafogo), *Edvaldo Neto, known as* Vavá (Palmeiras), Amarildo *da Silveira* (Botafogo)
Chile (4–2–4): Misael Escuti (Colo-Colo); Luis Eyzaguirre (Universidad de Chile⋆), Carlos Contreras (Univ de Chile), Raúl Sánchez (Santiago Wanderers), Manuel Rodriguez (Unión Española); Eladio Rojas (Everton†), Jorge Toro (Colo-Colo); Jaime Ramírez (Univ de Chile), Honorino Landa (Unión Española), Armando Tobar (Univ Católica), Leonel Sánchez‡ (Univ de Chile)

The atmosphere for the semi-final in Viña del Mar was muted; the Nacional stadium on the same day was rocking. Packed to capacity with fans as demented and passionate for their own team as they were disinterested and apathetic towards others, the stadium was a cauldron. Many opponents would have quailed but this was a been-there-done-that Brazil team – eight of them had already experienced a World Cup Final.

Chile had nowhere near the talent at the disposal of the Brazilians, but they had home advantage, a handful of decent players and some considerate officiating in their favour. Their main threat was down the left, where the powerful left-half Rojas and the busy winger Leonel Sánchez could cause problems. In different times Sánchez would have sat out the rest of the tournament after his less than angelic performance against Italy. The captain, Toro, could play, and he packed a fearsome shot if given too much room – he was captain because Sergio Navarro, who led the team for the first four matches, was left out of the starting line-up.

Brazil soon settled and began to dictate the flow of the game – which was heading mainly in the direction of the Chilean goal. Zagallo hit a long driven cross into the penalty area and Amarildo

⋆ Universidad de Chile – nicknamed the Blue Ballet – were the dominant team in Chile at the time, and arguably the best in South America. They had eight players in the Chile squad, including Carlos Campos, who formed a deadly partnership with Sanchez at club level but was only used in the third place game in the finals.
† No, silly, not that one. This team was formed in 1909 after a tour of South America by the Liverpudlian version.
‡ Chile's most-capped player, with eighty-four, and leading goalscorer on his retirement, with twenty-three (since passed by Caszely, Zamorano and Salas).

attempted an outrageous overhead kick; he miscued and the ball rebounded off a defender to Garrincha on the edge of the penalty area – who was most definitely in the mood after the England match. One step to the left and a searing hit into the top corner – 1–0 to Brazil. Garrincha's next touch of the ball saw him go the other way past his full-back, whose despairing grasp at his shirt would have brought a penalty had Brazil's opponents not been Chile. Rojas showed his drive and spirit with a powerful shot that rebounded off the inside of a post, but Chile forays into the Brazilian penalty box were rare.

Chile got another break when what looked a perfectly legitimate goal from Vavá after an interchange with Amarildo was disallowed by the referee with no recourse to his linesman. Even the referee couldn't help with Brazil's second goal, when Garrincha scored from a corner with a header as uncompromising as the one he scored against England; he was short but he could leap and the timing of his run for both goals was perfect – quick enough to reach the ball but late enough to give the marker no time to react.

Toro sent a free-kick fizzing past the post – Brazil knew about his shooting but didn't heed the warning and gave away another free-kick in the same area a few minutes later. This time Toro put the kick inside the post rather than past it – Gylmar got nowhere near it, the kick had pace and movement. Chile went in to half-time with a glimmer of hope.

It lasted less than four minutes; Garrincha tossed a corner into the middle of the area, Vavá flung himself at the ball and Escuti could only palm it past the defender on the line. Chile didn't give up. They kept working and getting stuck in – not always legally – and when Leonel Sánchez made a clever run across the line, his opposite wing Ramírez slipped a little pass down the side of the full-back. Sánchez hit it first time and the ball caught Zózimo's outstretched arm. Sánchez converted the penalty. The referee was badly positioned but gave it anyway – he probably feared for his life, the Chilean crowd was kicking up a crescendo.

By now Chile were doubling up on Garrincha, Rojas going in hard two or three times and the notoriously unpredictable

Brazilian was clearly getting riled. Brazil's defence was looking a little rattled as well, and their fourth goal came at a good time for them. A patient build-up left Zagallo in space and he put in another of his wicked, dipping crosses. Vavá read it best and squeezed himself between two defenders to head past Escuti from close range.

There was still time for some uglies. Chile knew they were on their way out but declined to go quietly. Landa was dismissed for a crude tackle on Zito, and Garrincha followed when he reacted angrily to yet another challenge from behind by Rojas. Rojas crumpled on the floor in agony but seemed in remarkably good shape moments later after Garrincha left the arena. Garrincha, the tournament's brightest star, left to a volley of abuse and spittle from Sánchez – vile and spiteful to the end – and a volley of missiles from the crowd. Brazil would have to play Czechoslovakia without their two best players, Pelé and Garrincha.

Or would they? A couple of days of frenzied negotiations and diplomatic intervention saw Garrincha's sending off rescinded and he was cleared to play in the final. It seems an extraordinary decision now, especially as Garrincha was clearly culpable, no matter that Rojas made a meal of the reaction. To their credit the Czechs didn't complain.

WORLD CUP FINAL No.7
17 June 1962, Nacional, Santiago; 68,679

| Brazil | (1) 3 | Amarildo 16, Zito 69, Vavá 78 |
| Czechoslovakia | (1) 1 | Masopust 14 |

Referee: **Nikolai Latyshev** (USSR)
Coaches: **Aymoré Moreira** (Brazil) & **Rudolf Vytlačil** (Czechoslovakia)

Brazil (4–3–3): Gylmar (Santos); Djalma Santos (Palmeiras), Mauro Ramos (Cpt, Santos), Zózimo (Bangu), Nílton Santos (Botafogo); Zito (Santos), Didi (Botafogo), Mário Zagallo (Botafogo); Garrincha (Botafogo), Vavá (Palmeiras), Amarildo (Botafogo)
Czechoslovakia (3–2–2–3): Viliam Schrojf (Slovan Bratislava); Jiří Tichy (Inter Bratislava), Svato Pluskal (Dukla Prague), Ján Popluhár (Slovan Bratislava), Ladislav Novák (Cpt, Dukla Prague); Andrej Kvasňák (Sparta Prague), Josef Masopust (Dukla Prague); Tomás Pospichál (Banik Ostrava), Josef Kadraba (Kladno), Adolf Scherer (Inter Bratislava), Josef Jelinek (Dukla Prague)

Like Oliver Kahn many years later, Czechoslovakia's brilliant goalkeeper left it to the final to have his one flawed game. Born in

Prague but brought up in Slovakia, Schrojf was a member of the Czech squad in 1954 and 1958, but it was not until 1962, by which time he was the established no.1, that he made an appearance in the Finals. Excellent in the groups, he saved his best for the knockout rounds, with a quite outstanding performance against Hungary and another top-notch showing against Yugoslavia. There was nothing flashy, he was just a good reliable goalkeeper who bucked the trend of the age and came to catch crosses.

Shame, then, that he blew it in the final. Schrojf was at fault for two of the Brazilian goals, leaving space for Amarildo to shoot home at the near post in the first half and then making a mess of a cross for Vavá to score. Not that he alone was to blame, especially for the first goal; Kvasnák and Pluskal were beaten too easily by Amarildo on a run that should have seen him ushered away from goal.

Amarildo was making things happen for Brazil, with Garrincha strangely quiet. Perhaps the Czechs' understandable nervousness about the winger's presence left space elsewhere. The young striker nearly got on the end of a cross from Garrincha that Schrojf punched away, and then some clever play set up Zagallo for a cross that Vavá headed straight at the goalkeeper. The goal came soon after, but at the other end. Some patient build-up play found Pospichal coming in off the right wing; he spotted a lung-bursting run from Masopust and timed the pass perfectly for the left-half, usually the creator not the finisher, to drive under Gylmar's body.

Fortunately for Brazil, Amarildo's first goal came two minutes later, so there was no time for them to feel unsettled; this was a much more disciplined defence than Sweden's four years earlier, and they could not have been so sure of scoring. Schrojf was unfazed – he did well with a Zagallo free-kick when the Brazilian midfielder cheekily tried to beat him at the same near post, then he dived to stop a thunderbolt from Garrincha.

The Czechs did better in the second half, with both wingers playing a little deeper to deny Garrincha and Zagallo space, and giving them room to run at the ageing Brazilian full-backs. But there was little they could do against brilliance. Zozimo broke up a Czech attack with a fine tackle and Zito carried the ball into the opposition defence before releasing Amarildo on the left. The youngster was wide of the goal but had the presence of mind to cut back onto his right foot and curl a delightful cross past Schrojf to where Zito had continued his run. The right-half hadn't scored for four years but he couldn't miss, he was virtually on the goal line.

Now the Czechs' rigidity and lack of creativity began to tell. They could make little inroad into the Brazilian defence – although one penalty appeal had some merit – and were increasingly vulnerable on the counter-attack. The crucial third goal was a disaster for the unfortunate Schrojf. He came out of his goal to make a routine catch from an up-and-under by Djalma Santos and caught the full glare of the sun. The ball brushed his fingertips and dropped at the feet of the lurking Vavá, who wasn't the type to miss an open goal.

The best team won, not with the flair of four years previously, but with conviction nonetheless – and at least we were spared the sight of Chile putting the boot in and berating the officials in the final.

World Cup Heroes No.11
Garrincha, born Manuel Francisco dos Santos
(1933–83)
Brazil

Garrincha was born into poverty, like so many black Brazilians. He overcame a severe polio attack as a child that left him with an imbalance in his legs and a curious bow-legged gait. Unlike Pelé, he didn't hang around after his career and reach ambassadorial status for his country and the game of football.

Garrincha had a terrible concentration span – other players in the Brazil squads in 1962 and 1966 claim he would play table tennis while the coach gave his tactical talk. A psychiatrist with the 1958 squad adjudged him not worthy of a place in the side as he had the mental capacity of a child. (The man proved as useful in his advice to a football team as Eileen Drewery, of whom more anon.) The notion of the innocent abroad is belied by his womanising and drinking, both pursued wilfully and at times with no regard for the consequences to him and others. He was reputed to not know until the day of the game who his team were playing that day; not sure I believe that, but he certainly treated every opponent with the same lack of respect, waltzing around quality international full-backs and then going back and beating them again, just for a giggle. He gave England's Ray Wilson a horrible time in the 1962 quarter-final – the same Wilson who looked solid as a rock in the 1966 event.

Garrincha had electrifying acceleration from his low centre of gravity (similar to Maradona), and he was equally happy going round the outside and banging over a cross (usually flat and hard), or cutting across the front line and hitting a shot with his left. If Garrincha went walkabout, so be it, the hard-working right-half Zito would cover and do his defensive work for him – not Garrincha's strong point, he wasn't the complete player like Pelé.

It took some persuading by friends and colleagues for him to join a professional football club, but when he ran rings around Brazilian international full-back Nílton Santos in a trial for Botafogo his career path was decided. He scored a hat-trick on his debut for the first team in 1953 but was considered unready for the national team for the 1954 World Cup.

In 1958 he was brought into the team for the third match of the World Cup after a faltering start by the team, and he and Pelé gave the team the balance it lacked. But it was in 1962, in Pelé's absence, that Garrincha's extraordinary gifts came to the fore. He imposed his power and pace and dribbling on the games against England and Chile, providing inspiration and scoring goals when it mattered most.

Garrincha played all his club football of significance for Botafogo, resisting numerous lucrative offers to play in Europe. When he left Botafogo in 1965 his career declined quickly; in the 1966 World Cup he was a shadow of the player of 1962, and lost his remarkable record of never having played on a losing Brazilian team when they were knocked out. With him and Pelé both in the side, Brazil never lost.

By this time his chaotic private life was in the press as much as his football. He had left his wife (and eight children) for a cabaret singer, Elza Soares, also a divorcee, and they never found approval in a deeply Catholic country. Soares left him when he beat her in an alcohol-induced rage, and Garrincha died a lonely, alcoholic mess in January 1983, a sad (but maybe inevitable, given his personality?) end for a brilliant footballer.

1962 Team of the Tournament: 4–2–4

Schrojf (Czechoslovakia)
Armfield (England)   Mészöly (Hungary)   Popluhár (Czechoslovakia)   Eyzaguirre (Chile)
Masopust (Czechoslovakia)   Rojas (Chile)
Garrincha (Brazil)   Jerkovic (Yugoslavia)   Albert (Hungary)   Zagallo (Brazil)

Leading scorers: Albert, Ivanov, Garrincha, Sánchez, Jerkovic, Vavá (all scored 4)

All-Star XI, selected retrospectively: Schrojf (Czechoslovakia); D Santos (Brazil), Maldini (Italy), Voronin (USSR), Schnellinger (West Germany); Zito (Brazil), Masopust (Czechoslovakia), Zagallo (Brazil); Garrincha (Brazil), Vavá (Brazil), Sánchez (Chile). They got this hopelessly wrong – the inclusion of Sánchez is nonsense, his behaviour was a disgrace.

Heaven Eleven No.4

Eastern Europe (former Yugoslavia – principally Croatia and Serbia, but also Montenegro, Bosnia & Herzegovina, Macedonia and Slovenia, plus Poland, Romania & Bulgaria)

Coach:
Dimitar Penev – masterminded Bulgaria's best-ever World Cup and nurtured a generation of excellent players at CSKA

Sofia. He was a good centre-back in his time. Good luck knitting this lot into a team, feller

Goalkeepers:
Borislav Mihailov (Bul): expert at dealing with those hairy moments . . .
Bogdan Stelea (Rom): consistent and reliable 'keeper
Vladi Beara (Yug, Cro): acrobatic shot-stopper from the 1950s

Defenders:
Dan Petrescu (Rom): Super-Dan, excellent attacking full-back
Toni Szymanowski (Pol): solid right-back in the Polish heyday
Robert Jarni (Cro): attacking wing-back in the '98 Croatia side
Miodrag Belodedici (Rom): exceptionally quick and decisive centre-back
Slaven Bilic (Cro): really sound defender, read the game so well
Nemanja Vidic (Ser): hard as nails modern stopper
Fahrudin Jusufi (Yug, Ser): top left-back from 1962 Yugoslavia side
Wladyslaw Zmuda (Pol): ball-playing sweeper in 1970s Polish side

Midfield & Wide:
Gheorghe Hagi (Rom): gorgeous left foot attached to a pocket genius
Marius Lăcătus (Rom): dangerous winger, could shred a full-back on his day
Dorinel Munteanu (Rom): someone has to do the work, useful emergency defender
Dejan Savicevic (Yug, Mont): another enigma, just hope he isn't sulking
Dragan Dzajic (Yug, Ser): fast and powerful left-winger from Yugoslavia's heyday

Milan Galic (Yug, Ser): hard-working box-to-box midfielder before they were fashionable, sort of a Slavic Alan Ball

Grzegorz Lato (Pol): great goalscorer from wide, searing pace, always produced at the top level

Kazi Deyna (Pol): calm, good leader, lets others do the damage

Zbigniew Boniek (Pol): gifted attacking midfielder, if he had been five years younger, who knows . . .?

Strikers:

Dimitar Berbatov (Bul): looks lazy, isn't, forget the United experience, just didn't fit the system

Hristo Stoichkov (Bul): fruit nut loop, but awesome player and dead ball striker

Wlodi Lubanski (Pol): first great post-war Polish attacker, really good grafting front man

Omissions: There are a lot of talented players from this region. Here are a few who have been left out: **Hristo Bonev** (Bulgarian forward); **Zlatko Zahovic** (temperamental Slovenian playmaker when they qualified for the Euros); **Sinisa Mihajlovic** (good player, but not such a nice boy); **Robert Prosinecki** (elegant playmaker for Yugoslavia and later Croatia); **Savo Milosevic** (hopeless at Villa, fab everywhere else); **Branko Oblak** (first really good Slovenian to play for Yugoslavia); **Ivica Horvat** (centre-back in the Yugoslavia side of the early 1960s); **Davor Suker** (goal-poacher for Croatia, great left foot, bit of a passenger unless scoring); **Andrzej Szarmach** & **Robert Gadocha** (excellent centre-forward and winger in the great Poland side); **Predrag Mijatovic** (Yugoslav playmaker from Montenegro); **Gica Popescu** (Romanian sweeper); **Ilie Dumitrescu** (the new Pelé – at least he thought so); **Nicolae Dobrin** (Romanian playmaker in the late '60s and early '70s); **Robert Prosinecki** (Croatian playmaker, gifted but inconsistent); **Dragoslav Sekularac** and **Safet Susic** (two top Yugoslav midfielders, one Macedonian, the other Bosnian, and those countries' best players).

Strengths: vast amounts of talent, lots of goalscoring potential from midfield

Weaknesses: temperament – it has always found out Yugoslavia and Serbia, and the others have often fallen just short. Full-backs a bit weaker than most

Likely first XI:

Mihailov

Petrescu Bilic Vidic Jarni

Deyna

Boniek   Hagi

Lato   Stoichkov

Lubanski

(Blimey, that's a good team, you wouldn't want to catch them in the mood . . .)

3.4 INDISCIPLINE

The rules of football have changed a lot since the World Cup began, and the referee's job has changed with it. A lot is made of the modern professional's lack of respect for the referee. It's nothing new – old World Cup footage shows teams surrounding the referee and voicing protests well back in the supposed Corinthian age.

What has changed is permissible foul play. The 1950s and 1960s matches were replete with tackles from behind, high tackles, fist fights and general skulduggery of all kinds. Pelé was heard to call for greater protection for skilful players as early as 1966, when he was literally kicked out of the tournament. Referees were sanctioned to send players off in those eras, they just appeared very reluctant to do so – hardly surprising when you see the reaction of the Italians to having a player dismissed in the notorious Battle of Santiago in 1962.

While the increased numbers of cards has offered protection for skilful players and seen the end of the "hackers", it has also seen a number of sendings-off for ludicrous offences, and it has engendered the iniquitous habit of players waving imaginary cards at the referee to propose the censure of an opponent. Now *that* should be an automatic red.

Foul play has been addressed; what is still left for FIFA to do is get a grip on the cheats and moaners who pollute the game in the twenty-first century, and to find a better way of punishing minor offences, maybe a sin-bin like rugby or a three-tiered card system. Forget the nonsense about slowing the game down – modern technology is fast enough to deal with monitoring a sin-bin. And enough time is already wasted watching coiffured posers rolling around pretending to be injured to get an opponent in trouble.

There have been 159 sendings-off (henceforth to be referred to as red cards, irrespective of whether the actual card system was in place) in the World Cup Finals, and the progressive statistics show how referees (and by definition FIFA's) tolerance for foul play has changed:

Uruguay 1930 – 1
Italy 1934 – 1
France 1938 – 4
Brazil 1950 – 0
Switzerland 1954 – 3
Sweden 1958 – 3
Chile 1962 – 6
England 1966 – 5
Mexico 1970 – 0
West Germany 1974 – 5
Argentina 1978 – 3
Spain 1982 – 5
Mexico 1986 – 8
Italy 1990 – 16
United States 1994 – 15
France 1998 – 22
Japan & South Korea 2002 – 17
Germany 2006 – 28
South Africa 2010 – 17

The spike in 1990 was after a FIFA clamp-down on the professional foul, including deliberate handball to prevent a goal. The jump from fifteen to twenty-two in 1998 is explained by the addition of another eight teams to the Finals roster.

The South American countries don't come out well in these statistics; Uruguay have notched up eight red cards, Argentina ten and – surprisingly top of the list – Brazil eleven. England are way down the list on three, below the USA and Australia. And one of England's three was for the equivalent of flicking an elastic band at teacher. (*See 1986 ...*)

Three sides, Argentina in 1990 and France and Cameroon in 1998, received three reds in a tournament – oddly, both Argentina and France reached the final.

Four players have been given their marching orders in the final.

Two players have been red-carded twice – Zinedine Zidane (a stain on his career that he can't wipe out, great player or not) and Rigobert Song (more forgivable, he was just a clumsy so-and-so).

The record for most yellow cards in the Finals goes to Cafu, not a dirty player, just one who played a lot of Finals' matches.

The Dirtiest Matches in World Cup Finals

10. **Germany 2 Cameroon 0, group match, 2002**
     Statistically, this was the dirtiest World Cup Finals game ever, with sixteen bookings from the Spanish referee. There was some stiff tackling, from an uneasy German team in the first half and a panicky Cameroonian side in the second, but it didn't get out of hand and the number of cautions is more down to some prickly refereeing. Two players got two each of the yellow cards and took the walk of shame. Germany's Carsten Ramelow earned two yellows in three minutes at the end of the first half, and Patrick Suffo lasted just twenty-three minutes after coming on as a substitute in the second half. Brainless and ill-disciplined, but never a dark game.

9. **South Africa 1 Denmark 1, group match, 1998**
     Three red cards, but, again, never what might be termed a violent match. Referee Rendon of Colombia was harshly ridiculed by the press, but all three red cards were justifiable under FIFA's own guidelines. FIFA, of course, defended their man to the hilt – like bananas they did, they sent him home after this. Peter Schmeichel was among those cautioned, apparently for undermining the referee's authority – that naughty Mr Ferguson, passing on bad habits . . .

8. **Argentina 0 West Germany 1, Final, 1990**
     A terrible final and a terrible performance by Argentina. The Germans man-marked Maradona and there wasn't the

back-up of 1986; Argentina fell back on their usual Plan B, which was to kick anyone in sight and had two players rightly red-carded. The referee was criticised, but it's tough to ref a game when no one is trying to play football. Two ugly sides, one ugly match.

7. **Portugal 3 Brazil 1, group match, 1966**

The game was a match-up supposedly of the two most exciting sides in the tournament, but, where Hungary had beaten Brazil with scintillating football, Portugal beat them by stamping their authority – very literally – on Pelé. Perhaps they were embarrassed by the manner of their victory here, because they were good as gold in their next two games, standing off England with almost excessive politeness in the semi-final.

6. **Spain 1 Holland 0, Final, 2010**

Popular opinion had it that if you got in Spain's face they would quail, so Holland did just that, and how. Tackle after tackle thundered in, and the Spanish didn't just stand by passively either. (And, like Barcelona, they exacerbated matters with a little roll-around or two.) Holland were convinced the referees were all pro-Spanish, but they gave Howard Webb no choice but to hand out cards like confetti; the Englishman was criticised for missing De Jong's waist-high assault, but there was so much happening it was impossible to catch everything; he did a pretty good job.

5. **Czechoslovakia 1 Brazil 1, quarter-final, 1938**

Luis Monti had handed out some rough stuff in 1930 and 1934, but this was the first full-on pitched battle in the World Cup. The Czech playmaker Nejedly had his leg broken and their goalkeeper played on with a fractured arm. A replay passed off without incident but the Czechs were missing a number of senior players, all *hors de combat* after this encounter.

4. **England 1 Argentina 0 & West Germany 4 v Uruguay 0, quarter-finals, 1966**

I cover these in detail in the 1966 entry; South American skulduggery against European strength. There was some strong-arm "get your retaliation in first" tackling from

England and Germany, but the response was unwarranted and unspeakable – and some of the revisionist accounts that would have the games seen as brave new world pioneers baulked by a conservative colonial conspiracy are, frankly, hogwash.

3. Hungary 4 Brazil 2, quarter-final, 1954

Two of the best footballing sides on the planet – ever – and they decide to kick lumps out of each other. A shocking penalty decision from Arthur Ellis seemed to fuel a sense of injustice in Brazil and the tackles flew in; Hungary had talent but also some big aggressive defenders who were happy to respond in kind – although it was odd to see suave talents like Bozsik and Didi going at it hammer and tongs. Three sent off, lots of bruises; there were fears for Hungary's semi-final against the abrasive Uruguayans, but it passed off peacefully enough.

2. Portugal 1 Holland 0, second round match, 2006

Just unpleasant. Another example of Holland losing their rag, although with more justification this time; Portugal were a provocative team full of sly shirt-pullers and divers. There were sixteen cards and could have been more – no blame attached to the Russian referee who did his best to keep control in the face of some disgraceful behaviour. All the red cards were merited, even the mild-mannered van Bronckhorst got his marching orders in injury-time. The match-up in the centre of midfield between the sneaky little play-actor Deco and the dead-eyed Dutch enforcer van Bommel was spawned in some unspeakable footballing hell.

1. Chile 2 Italy 0, group match, 1962

The Battle of Santiago. A true bloodbath (see 1962 entry). Absolutely the most violent game in international football history, two teams with a preconceived plan to hurt and incapacitate as many of the opposition as possible. A truly bilious affair marked by offensive machismo and posturing and palpable racial hatred. Ghastly.

BACK HOME

4.1 WORLD CUP 1966

Not that England fans cared much, but the fare that was offered up before the memorable final in 1966 wasn't always the best. It was a dirty tournament and one spoiled by the wave of negative tactics that had global football in its grip at the time. The stronger sides were flawed or more about perspiration than inspiration, and the hard men that prevailed in the 1960s and into the '70s football spoiled many of the games with their unlovely brand of defending.

England had known they were hosting the event since 1960, and the country was ripe for such a jamboree. The first four years of the decade had seen relative prosperity and growth. The shadows of the Second World War started to recede and rationing and National Service were abolished. Two years previously thirteen years of Conservative dominance in Westminster had ended when the Labour Party gained power with a tiny majority; in March, three months before the World Cup, Prime Minister Harold Wilson surprised the new Leader of the Opposition, Edward Heath, and won a much larger majority in a snap election. Britain was embracing a little of the new liberalism – The Beatles were no longer long-haired layabouts to many, but a prime British export of which the country could be proud. Even footballers were seen sporting long hair, as George Best led the vanguard of Beatnik mavericks that gave a drab game some colour throughout the next decade. Not that the England manager would countenance any such nonsense.

Alf Ramsey wasn't appointed immediately after England's exit from the 1962 World Cup as some sources lazily claim – he was

ENGLAND

Seven English cities hosted the 1966 World Cup and eight stadia were used. This was a well-attended competition, setting new records, partly due to a high interest among a dense population, but also because the country was one of the few that could offer eight stadia with a capacity in excess of 40,000.

London: Wembley Stadium
The famous old stadium, opened in 1923 for the FA Cup Final, had a capacity of 100,000. The Twin Towers saw their last game in 2000, with the new

Wembley opening three years later. The stadium was originally built as part of the 1924 British Empire Exhibition.

London: White City
This old ramshackle stadium was built for the 1908 Olympics. It held over 75,000 people, but it was an odd choice ahead of White Hart Lane or Highbury and hosted only a low-key fixture between Uruguay and France. By the time it was demolished in 1985 White City was little more than a dog track (not that there's anything wrong with that). Ironically, White City got its one game because the Wembley authorities refused to cancel their own greyhound racing fixture for the World Cup – not sure that would happen now.

Birmingham: Villa Park
Aston Villa's 55,000 home shared a group with Hillsborough. The stadium remains on the same site it occupied on opening in 1897 with a reduced capacity of 42,700.

Sheffield: Hillsborough
The home of Sheffield Wednesday and holding 42,730, Hillsborough Stadium will sadly be associated forever with the 1989 disaster, which saw ninety-six fans crushed to death. It still stands, holding slightly fewer people, all seated; in 1966 it hosted the quarterfinal between West Germany and Uruguay.

Manchester: Old Trafford
Manchester United's Theatre of Dreams, as it is preposterously labelled these days, held around 45,000 compared to the current 75,700, which makes it one of the few stadia to have a larger capacity as an all-seater than it did when it sported terraces. Old Trafford shared Group 3 with Goodison Park, but the Liverpool venue got all the Brazil games.

Liverpool: Goodison Park
Chosen in preference to Anfield, Everton's 40,000-plus ground hosted all the Brazil games as well as Portugal's extraordinary game against North Korea and a semi-final. The local crowd cheering on the Koreans in that classic game was one of the features of the tournament.

Middlesbrough: Ayresome Park
Replaced by the Riverside Stadium in 1995, the old (1904) ground was chosen ahead of St James's Park Newcastle as a World Cup venue. The games in the North-East were the least well-attended.

Sunderland: Roker Park
Another defunct north-east ground, Roker Park has been replaced by the Stadium of Light, opened in 1998. The ground, famous for the 'Roker Roar', boasted a record attendance of 75,000, but only about a third of that number came to watch the World Cup games (even the quarterfinal between the Soviet Union and an attractive Hungary side). It was one of the earliest instances of the working-classes being priced out of attendance at an English football match.

offered the job after only Burnley's Jimmy Adamson turned it down – but in October that year it was announced he would take control of the team at the end of the current season. He had enjoyed great success with his Ipswich Town team, taking them from the Third Division South to the 1962 league title in the space of six years. Ramsey was a manager who believed in developing a style and system and picking players to fit the system; it worked a treat at Ipswich where a team of far from stellar players stuck to Ramsey's game plan and caught the opposition on the hop. With Ramsey distracted by the England appointment – he was involved in the games that took place between the announcement of his appointment and its enactment – the same group of Ipswich players finished seventeenth the following season and were relegated the year after he left.

Convinced he was ahead of the game tactically and looking forward to the prospect of harnessing better players to his system, Ramsey boldly predicted England would win the 1966 World Cup. Most pundits sneered, but Ramsey knew he had a high-quality squad if he could only get more out of them and devise a system that played to their strengths and didn't leave them languishing in the wake of more tactically astute opponents.

Success wasn't immediate, and come 1966 Ramsey was still tinkering with his line-up. He had the basic shape in place. The defence was established; the excellent 1962 left-back Ray Wilson was still there, but his compadre in Chile was now a back-up player, with Fulham's George Cohen established as a regular at right-back – he got his chance after a serious groin injury to Jimmy Armfield, and the former captain picked up another injury on the eve of the tournament, securing Cohen's place. In late 1965 Ramsey stumbled across an important piece of the jigsaw when he picked the thirty-year-old Leeds centre-half Jack Charlton, brother of Manchester United's Bobby. Another Bobby – Moore – was first choice at the heart of the defence, where his passing ability and anticipation was vital to retention of the ball. Jimmy Greaves was another survivor from 1962, and his preferred partner up front now seemed to be the prolific Liverpool striker Roger Hunt. Charlton (Bobby) attacked from the left side, but he played a freer, more central role now, with licence to look for space from which to unleash his explosive shooting. Inside him Nobby Stiles was a typical Ramsey selection. Stiles was a player of his time, limited, even awkward, on the ball but an uncompromising tackler and man-marker.

Two slots were definitely still up for grabs going into the tournament. One of them would probably go to the feisty young Blackpool player Alan Ball, who Ramsey introduced to the side a year earlier. Ball combined energy and desire with decent ball skills and a good team ethic – all attributes Ramsey admired. Many pundits still thought him a little young and callow for a major tournament. The biggest conundrum was whether to play a winger. Ramsey was no fan of the old-fashioned wide player, who he (rightly) believed to be an anachronism, especially as England hadn't found one of genuine international quality since Matthews and Finney retired. There were three in the squad: John Connelly of Manchester United, Terry Paine of Southampton and the untested Ian Callaghan of Liverpool (one cap against Finland during the pre-tournament tour of Scandinavia).

It was a squad good enough to be one of the favourites for the tournament – they had suffered few defeats in the last two years and learned from all of them – but not good enough to be an obvious winner.

Qualifying

And what of the opposition? There would be sixteen teams again, in the same format as the last two tournaments: four groups of four then the last eight to play a knockout. All the African teams withdrew in protest at the decision to award only one place to Africa and Asia combined – this would be the last tournament where these continents didn't get at least one automatic place. The withdrawals left the qualification for this place as a farce, even more so when the final Asian group was reduced to two because South Africa were banned from international competition and South Korea refused to play when the games were moved from Japan to Cambodia, where the former monarch, now Presidential-style Head of State, Norodom Sihanouk was sympathetic to the Communist Democratic People's Republic of Korea.

This left two teams to play a two-leg match (both in Phnom Penh) for a World Cup place. The Koreans easily beat Australia to qualify for the first time.

Nine European teams joined England in the Finals, while three other South American sides joined holders Brazil. The last place was allocated to CONCACAF, the usual freebie for Mexico who breezed through without losing a game.

In South America the old order was observed, with Uruguay and Argentina qualifying easily and Chile joining them after beating Ecuador in a play-off. All four South American sides looked tough opponents without appearing irresistible, but the presence of Pelé put Brazil amongst the favourites, along with Argentina, who had just beaten the Brazilians 3–0.

The other home nations were very keen to get to the Finals and spoil the party for the English, but none quite made it. Wales found themselves in a tough group with the Soviet Union; they did manage to beat the Soviets in Cardiff but it was a dead rubber as Wales could no longer qualify. The Republic of Ireland had it easier, with only a poor Spain team in their group after Syria withdrew in solidarity with the African nations. The Irish won in Dublin but were well beaten in the return and beaten again in a decider in Paris.

Northern Ireland blew it. This should have been the tournament where the brilliant new star George Best paraded his talents, and a kind draw that saw them grouped with Switzerland, Holland and Albania gave them a genuine chance. All the games between the three better teams were tight; Northern Ireland traded home wins with Switzerland and took three points off the Dutch after a disciplined defensive performance in Rotterdam. The Swiss also took three points off Holland, leaving Northern Ireland to match them and force a play-off by beating the group fall-guys, Albania, in Tirana. Johnny Crossan's hat-trick had helped them see off Albania 4–1 in Belfast, and this return fixture should have been a banker – no one in the group had annihilated Albania, but they had lost every game. Except this one, of course. You know the script – Northern Ireland took the lead and everything seemed rosy until a rare Albania attack brought an equaliser thirteen minutes from time. There is no guarantee Northern Ireland would have beaten Switzerland in the play-off, but surely Best – so rarely at his most potent for his country – would have raised his game for such a monumental fixture.

It was a similar story for Scotland. In a tricky group with Italy and improving Poland, they let themselves down by conceding twice at the end of a home fixture they largely dominated against the Poles. Partial redemption came with a fine win over Italy at Hampden Park. Faced with the predictable wall of blue shirts – Italy needed only a draw to qualify – Scotland were frustrated until two minutes from time when Rangers' John Greig advanced from right-back, played a one-two with Jim Baxter and slotted home past a limping goalkeeper with his wrong foot. Scotland needed a win in Naples, Italy, to go through or a draw to force a play-off despite a vastly inferior goal difference. The Scots were missing the injured Billy McNeill, while Denis Law and Jim Baxter were not released by their clubs, but they might not have helped. Scotland got hammered – the game was a horror story for Burnley goalkeeper Adam Blacklaw – and were left to rue the careless two minutes against Poland.

Elsewhere, West Germany, Hungary and France all qualified comfortably – France coasted past a fading Yugoslavia team – while Bulgaria forced a play-off against Belgium, which they won, to general surprise. Both goals were scored by Georgi Asparuhov (in Bulgarian names ending "hov" the "h" is hard), the Levski Sofia striker. Asparuhov was outstanding for Levski in the European Cup, where they were only narrowly beaten by Benfica. Benfica had a decent striker, too, called Eusébio da Silva Ferreira (I do love a tenuous link), and his goals helped Portugal qualify for the Finals for the first time in a group that included 1962 runners-up Czechoslovakia. Eusébio scored the winner in Prague in a 1–0 win, the key result in a group that also included Romania. Portugal's only defeat, in Bucharest, came after they had already qualified; Eusébio scored seven of the team's nine goals. The debutants came to England as many pundits' nod and a wink tip for success.

Finals

The four groups were located geographically. England would play all their matches at Wembley – it was hoped (assumed?) they would win their group and stay there. The second group would play in Sheffield (at Hillsborough) and Birmingham (Villa Park); the third would stay in the north-west, playing at either Old Trafford or Goodison Park in Liverpool, while the final group would be in the north-east, at Middlesbrough's Ayresome Park or Sunderland's Roker Park. Neither of the north-east grounds is in use today, nor is the second London venue, White City, which hosted only the Uruguay v France game. The stadia all had decent capacity and were filled for most of the games, the provincial cities embracing the non-England matches with great enthusiasm and supporting their adopted favourites.

The otherwise seamless organisation of the contest suffered one major hiccough before the start. In March the actual Jules Rimet Trophy was borrowed, after much diplomacy and deliberation, as a showpiece for a Stanley Gibbons stamp exhibition – only for it to be nicked on 20 March, a Sunday. A ransom of £15,000 was demanded, and a pay-off arranged. A go-between was arrested but he refused to give details of his employer. A week later (by which time there were some seriously loose bowels at the FA) David Corbett was walking his dog in South London, when the dog, curious as dogs tend to be, sniffed around a carrier bag tucked under a bush. Guess what the bag contained? Pickles the dog was on the front pages of all the newspapers – the first hero of the World Cup. Mr Corbett pocketed a bigger bonus than any of England's winning team. The suits at the FA breathed a collective sigh of relief and got on with the task of making money, taking credit for any success and abnegating responsibility for any of the ills that beset the game.

Talking of ills that beset the game, this was the first World Cup where the host country took maximum opportunity to reap economic benefit from having the tournament on home soil. It was small beer to the modern marketing grab-all, but there were mugs, key-rings, shirts, coins, stamps and all sorts of other paraphernalia. For the first time there was a World Cup mascot – a lion called World Cup Willie, the first in a shameful line of cringe-inducing anthropomorphised animals that have polluted the planet.

The favourites in the four groups were England, Argentina, Brazil and Italy – but rarely do all the favourites win the groups in a World Cup and this was no exception.

GROUP 1

England	**(0) 0**	**Uruguay**	**(0) 0**	11 July, Wembley; 87,148
France	**(0) 1**	**Mexico**	**(0) 1**	13 July, Wembley; 69,237
Hausser 61		Borja 48		
Uruguay	**(2) 2**	**France**	**(1) 1**	15 July, White City; 45,662
Rocha 27, Cortés 32		de Bourgoing 16 (p)		
England	**(1) 2**	**Mexico**	**(0) 0**	16 July, Wembley; 92,570
R Charlton 36, Hunt 76				
Mexico	**(0) 0**	**Uruguay**	**(0) 0**	19 July, Wembley; 61,112
England	**(1) 2**	**France**	**(0) 0**	20 July, Wembley; 98,270
Hunt 36, 76				

1. England 5pts (4–0); 2. Uruguay 4pts (2–1); 3. Mexico 2pts (1–3); 4. France 1pt (2–5)

The jamboree opened on 11 July with the hosts playing against potentially the toughest opponents in their group, Uruguay. For tough, read uncompromising. No, make that plain dirty. England were no shrinking violets – any side that picked a player like Stiles was clearly happy to mix it – but this was something else. Shirt-pulling, high tackles, spitting, pinching – the South American sides (and a few Italian ones) in the 1960s took football's dark arts to a new level. This isn't high-handed European taking the colonial line, they were ugly sides full of ugly characters with chips the size of baked potatoes on their shoulders. Uruguay and Argentina had talent, but they seemed happier negating (i.e. kicking) the opposition than using their creative players. Opening games at World Cup tournaments have a habit of being stinkers – this was probably the worst of the lot.

The other opener saw France and Mexico play out a rather more interesting draw. The young Mexican striker Enrique Borja had a goal (debatably) disallowed in the first half and scored a rather fortunate one at the start of the second. His air shot at Padilla's centre rebounded rather fortuitously to him off a defender and he forced the ball in via Aubour's legs. Borja continued to torment the French defence, but France managed an equaliser against the run of play when Hausser caught Chaires in possession and ran away to score with a smart low drive that went in off the post. Borja should have won the game when he missed from close in after clever movement earned him space for a free header, and Hausser could have had a second at the other end when he sent a dipping volley just over. Mexico looked the more skilful side, but a draw was just about fair.

Mexico were really disappointing against England, resorting to a massed defence instead of using Borja's aerial threat and their quick wide players. England left out the ineffectual Connelly and tried Paine on the right (he proved just as ineffectual), replacing Ball, surprisingly, with Martin Peters of West Ham, another young midfield player who made his debut shortly before the Finals. The game was one-way traffic, and England needed to be patient. Moore went close with a header, and Hunt had the ball in the net only for the goal to be chalked off because Peters strayed offside. England's first goal of the tournament was a bit special when it came. Bobby Charlton picked up the ball in space inside his own half and accelerated towards the Mexican defence. No challenge came – surely they had been warned about Charlton's shooting – so the England man just belted a twenty-five-yarder into the far corner with his weaker (!?!) right foot.

Mexico's response was limp. England created few clear-cut openings and the game was fizzling out before another surge from Charlton put Greaves in. The Tottenham striker's far from lethal shot was only half-stopped by Calderón, who had already provided a couple of Chaplinesque moments, and Hunt tapped in.

For their second game against Uruguay France dropped their most talked-about player prior to the tournament, the Argentinian-born Nestor Combin. Combin played in Italy (after a successful few years at Lyon), and two years later he was in the Milan squad that played Estudiantes in the Intercontinental Club Cup. Argentina was in the control of a military junta – not for the first or last time – and, shortly after a match in which he had his nose broken and was knocked unconscious, Combin was arrested by the Argentinians for desertion (essentially avoiding military service). It took a few days for the French diplomats to have him released. His replacement for the Uruguay match in '66 was Héctor de Bourgoing, born in Posadas, Argentina, and with five caps for his native country to his name.

France opened the scoring when their hasty young right-winger Yves Herbet was body-checked by Manicera. The penalty award was iffy; the offence was just outside the area, whatever ITV commentator Hugh Johns claimed, but it was a cynical tackle that merited punishment. De Bourgoing scored the penalty. Uruguay, compelled to play some football, showed they could and scored twice before half-time, first when Rocha shot through a crowd after some patient approach play, and then when a bout of head tennis ended with a fierce angled volley from Cortés. The French never really looked like getting back into it.

The Mexicans were more enterprising again in their last match – they had seemed resigned to their fate against England – but they still couldn't find the net against that obdurate Uruguayan defence. Another 0–0 draw for Uruguay and a place in the last eight. Mexico recalled their veteran goalkeeper Carbajal to make an appearance in his fifth and final World Cup Finals tournament – and he finally kept a clean sheet, bless 'im.

England needed to beat France to win the group. Ramsey tried his third winger, Callaghan, but kept faith with the rest of the team that beat Mexico. They weren't great, but then neither were France – although at least they ventured into England's half occa-sionally. England put the ball in the net five times, but three of them were ruled out for offside and even Hunt's opener probably should have been ruled out. He was lurking when Jack Charlton headed a cross against the base of the post and had a simple tap-in. Hunt made it 2–0 fifteen minutes before the end when he met Callaghan's cross with a firm header. Aubour should have done better than palm it into the net – in fairness the Lyon goal-keeper had already made a couple of excellent saves to keep his side alive. Unconvincing from England but the right result, Herbin's early header was France's only clear chance. The same player spent the rest of the game limping after a stiff challenge from Stiles, and, when the same player dropped Jacky Simon with a crunching late tackle, England must have feared the worst. In World Cup tournaments fortune favours the home team, not the brave, and Stiles was allowed to stay on by the Peruvian referee. Stiles provided the game's superior slapstick moment when an attempted twenty-yarder ended up as a pass to Callaghan some ten yards from the corner flag – the Liverpool man was so surprised to get the ball he made a complete pig's ear of his cross.

It was France's last appearance in the Finals for twelve years, so none of this squad would make another appearance. One of them did enjoy a particularly proud World Cup moment – Jean Djorkaeff, the right-back, watched his son, Youri, pick up a winners' medal in 1998.

Job done for England, but at the cost of an injury to Jimmy Greaves, who would miss the quarter-final with a gashed leg and had played his last World Cup Finals match. Greaves was a brilliant, predatory striker with a great scoring ratio wherever he played (including forty-four in fifty-seven internationals), but he never quite found his best form in a major tournament. At least the defence was working – they hadn't really looked like conceding a goal yet, and Gordon Banks had little chance to display his ability.

GROUP 2

West Germany Held 16, Haller 21, 77 (p), Beckenbauer 40, 62	**(3) 5**	**Switzerland** (0) 0		12 July, Sheffield; 36,127
Argentina Artime 65, 76	**(0) 2**	**Spain** (0) 1 Pirri 71		13 July, Birmingham; 42,738
Spain Sanchis 57, Amancio 75	**(0) 2**	**Switzerland** (1) 1 Quentin 31		15 July, Sheffield; 32, 028
Argentina	**(0) 0**	**West Germany** (0) 0		16 July, Birmingham; 46,587
Argentina Artime 52, Onega 79	**(0) 2**	**Switzerland** (0) 0		19 July, Sheffield; 32,127
West Germany Emmerich 39, Seeler 84	**(1) 2**	**Spain** (1) 1 Fusté 23		20 July, Birmingham; 45,187

1. **West Germany 5pts** (7–1); 2. **Argentina 5pts** (4–1); 3. **Spain 2pts** (4–5); 4. **Switzerland 0pts** (1–9)

West Germany were a side supposedly in transition, with Herberger's successor, Helmut Schön, trying to instil fresh blood amongst a few tried and trusted stars like Seeler and the goalkeeper Tilkowski – and Seeler was not yet thirty, despite looking about fifty and seeming to have been around for decades. Only six of their squad had played in a World Cup Finals tournament before. German domestic football had undergone a shake-up since the last World Cup, with the antediluvian dinosaurs in charge of their game finally realising that a professional league was the only way to keep up with the rest of Europe and prevent a haemorrhaging of talent to Italy. The first three winners might surprise the modern reader: Köln (Cologne), Werder Bremen and TSV München 1860 (Munich). Bayern Munich had not yet emerged as Germany's dominant club; they had won only one league title, and that as far back as 1932.

West Germany had a minor stumble on the way to the Finals. A home draw against Sweden in qualifying left them vulnerable, and Schön took a gamble playing the uncapped Bayern Munich star Beckenbauer in the return in Stockholm. West Germany came from 1–0 down to win and the victory gave them some confidence as well as a superstar in the making.

They made a good start at Hillsborough, thrashing Switzerland 5–0. Beckenbauer and Haller were imperious in midfield and Seeler gave the Swiss defence a right old runa-round. The young Cologne midfielder Wolfgang Overath looked a player, too, spraying passes with his cultured left foot. Siggi Held's brilliant weaving run brought the first goal; he crossed for Seeler, Elsener made a good save and Held tucked in the loose ball. Helmut Haller scored the second after a long, surging run: blonde, arrogant (Cris Freddi: *"full of talent as well as himself"*) and a notorious diver and actor, Haller was the Aryan dream that non-Germans loved to hate. He scored the fifth here, too, from the penalty spot after Seeler was brought down. With typical disregard for the acceptable conduct of the time he checked his run-up while taking the penalty and poked the call casually into the corner – cheeky from most players, contemp-tuous from this one. The third was scored by young Beckenbauer. This wasn't the strolling *libero* (sweeper) of later years but a quick, urgent, complete midfield player. He had already broken clear of the defence once (Elsener saved his shot well) and now he received the ball after good work by Haller, played a superbly precise one-two with Seeler and slotted the ball under the advancing goalkeeper. The goal wasn't greeted with the nonchalant shrug of his later years, but a beam of joy from a young player enjoying his outing on the big stage. He added another in the second half – the Swiss just couldn't contain his runs – picking up a through ball, skipping past the last man and finishing with aplomb. West Germany were outstanding – the Swiss defence not so much.

The following day at Villa Park we saw the best of Argentina, but with enough dark shading to suggest there was trouble brewing. Their coach was still Juan Carlos Lorenzo, who had sent them out with such malevolent intent in 1962 – in the meantime he had produced two ugly, cynical teams at Lazio and Roma. Argentina had bags of ability and it shone as they dominated the early stages, with Onega of River Plate to the fore. Stocky, with powerful, muscular legs and great balance, Onega was a classic Argentinian *trequartista* (literally trick-artist, an attacking player allowed a free role to use his ability to beat players and create openings), prompting and charging from a deep-lying position – a forerunner of Maradona, Ortega and Tévez. Behind Onega the captain Rattin was a massive presence, both physically and psychologically, a towering, glowering giant with a demeanour that told opponents this was not their lucky day. Up front was Luis Artime, a pure finisher with excellent movement and first touch and a hammer of a left foot. The attacking left-back Marzolini was a class act, too, strong in the tackle and a genuine threat coming forward. Spain had good players as well, and won the European Championships two years earlier with this squad, but most of them were the wrong side of thirty; their inspiration was the Internazionale playmaker Luis Suárez (*no, no, no, not that one, he wasn't born yet!*), and he nearly opened the scoring with a delicious swerver with the outside of his right foot as Spain came back into the game.

There were chances galore but the first goal came past the hour, when González wriggled free on the right and crossed (mishit shot?) for the lurking Artime to help himself. Artime's second, the winner, was spectacular; Onega's pass was slightly behind him but his first touch deflected it forwards where he could hit it with his left foot one stride later – the shot flew past an astonished Iribar. The Basque goalkeeper was starting a good international career, the latest in a long line of terrific Spanish goalies. Spain's equaliser, sandwiched between Artime's goals, was a messy affair. A cross from Suárez was headed up into the air and a clash between Spanish debutant Pirri and Roma in the Argentina goal saw the ball land in the net.

West Germany's second game was against Argentina and suddenly they looked less indomitable. This World Cup saw an uneasy match of South American skulduggery and European machismo, with the referees and officials generally leaning towards the Europeans. The north European game has always found old-fashioned fouling more acceptable than the underhand stuff. It was Argentina who had a man dismissed – Albrecht, rightly, for a horrible assault on Weber – but a couple of Germans could easily have followed for bone-jarring tackles. Both sides knew a draw would probably help them through so chances were few and far between. FIFA issued a warning after the match – but only to Argentina, fuelling the sense of injustice that Lorenzo exploited to fire up his players.

Spain beat Switzerland – they were still amateurs and looked a level below the other sides in the group – with two second-half goals after the Swiss took the lead with a nicely worked number. Manuel Sanchis dribbled half the length of the field past some feeble resistance before toe-poking the ball over Elsener as he came out, then Gento rolled back the years with a blistering run down the left and a fine cross that Amancio met with a bullet of a diving header. Really, really good goal. The Swiss went home with *nul points*, losing their (very boring) last match 2–0 to Argentina.

In their final match West Germany gave away the lead against a depleted Spain (no Suárez, del Sol or Gento, three of their most experienced players) before re-asserting themselves. The first German goal was a super finish from the recalled left-winger Emmerich, in for Haller, who had a niggle. Emmerich was a spit for Helmut Rahn physically but a shadow of him as a player, all bulk and bluster and rarely much end product (this goal, thrashing the ball high and hard from an unfeasible angle, a definite exception). A draw was enough for West Germany but a late winner from Seeler, tucking home Held's cross, put them through as group winners and avoided an early match-up with England.

They might well have won at that stage; they certainly started the tournament better than England.

GROUP 3

Brazil Pelé 13, Garrincha 63	(1) 2	**Bulgaria**	(0) 0	12 July, Liverpool; 47,308	
Portugal José Augusto 2, 65, Torres 88	(1) 3	**Hungary** Bene 60	(0) 1	13 July, Manchester; 29,886	
Portugal Own goal 7, Eusébio 38, Torres 82	(2) 3	**Bulgaria**	(0) 0	16 July, Manchester; 25,438	
Portugal Simões 15, Eusébio 24, 85	(2) 3	**Brazil** Rildo 71	(0) 1	19 July, Liverpool; 58,479	
Hungary Own goal 42, Mészöly 44, Bene 53	(2) 3	**Bulgaria** Asparuhov 15	(1) 1	20 July, Manchester; 24,129	

1. **Portugal 6pts (9–2); 2. Hungary 4pts (7–5); 3. Brazil 2pts (4–6); 4. Bulgaria 0pts (1–8)**

Like Group 2, this foursome appeared to be a case of two from three, presumably Brazil plus either Hungary or Portugal – most pundits favoured Portugal, the normally perspicacious Hugh McIlvaney described Hungary as *"wan, unworthy successors"* to the great 1950s team. All three sides were packed with attacking talent.

The first game went to form, with Brazil beating an overawed Bulgaria side – though not so overawed that they refrained from kicking Pelé out of the next match. The maestro opened the scoring, belting a free-kick through the wall and past a surprised goalkeeper. Garrincha despatched another free-kick, but he didn't look the same player as four years earlier.

Portugal met Hungary the next day. Hungary had built another tidy side after the break-up of their great 1940s team. The genius playmaker Flórián Albert was back, as was another who impressed as a youngster in 1962, centre-half Kálmán Mészöly (who I shall mention as little as possible – these stress marks are a nightmare to type). They had also unearthed a tricky and mobile player in Ferenc Bene of Ujpest Dózsa, converted from inside-forward to goalscoring winger. Portugal were a team of two halves; a defence built around Sporting of Lisbon, and an attack consisting entirely of Benfica players – like Benfica, the team was better going forward than in retreat. The undoubted star was the Mozambique-born Eusébio.

For all the wonderful players on both sides, the game was decided by some crappy goalkeeping. Szentmihályi, the Hungarian goalkeeper, was injured in the warm-up but had to play through the pain as the line-ups had already been declared – I'm against meaningless substitutions, and would ban them in the last five minutes or injury-time, but this was plainly unfair. After only two minutes he stood like a statue on his line as José Alberto charged in and headed home a distinctly soft opener. The next hour was end-to-end, with Albert pulling the strings for Hungary and Eusébio always threatening on the break. If Albert had brought his best finishing with him to go with his wonderful approach play, Hungary would have been out of sight, but five times he got a sight of goal and five times failed to score, hitting the bar with one header. Mészöly (he just had to get involved, didn't he?) was even worse with his one chance, blazing over with the goalkeeper grounded.

Still, anything Szentmihályi (who made one superb save from Eusébio) could do, Carvalho could match, and he completely bottled a challenge with the onrushing Albert, scooping the ball to Bene, who gratefully accepted the gift. Szentmihályi wasn't done yet, though, and Portugal were back in the lead five minutes later when the hapless minder let a woeful cross from Torres (six foot four centre-forward on the right wing?) bounce up at a perfect height for José Augusto to head his second. He can never have scored an easier brace.

Hungary missed their last chance for a point when Farkas couldn't put away an inch-perfect through ball from Albert, and Szentmihályi had the last word, running around under a Eusébio cross like a headless chicken, getting nowhere near it and watching helplessly as Torres calmly headed home at the back post. Hungary's veteran defender Sándor Matrai threw himself to the ground in frustration after Portugal's second goal – now he just turned his back on his goalkeeper and walked silently away.

The game had lit up the tournament, and there was better to come a mere two days later.

WORLD CUP CLASSIC No.4
15 July 1966, Goodison Park, Liverpool; 51,387

Brazil	**(1) 1**	Tostäo 15
Hungary	**(1) 3**	Bene 3, Farkas 64, Mészöly 72 (p)

Referee: **Ken Dagnall** (England)
Coaches: **Vicente Feola** (Brazil) & **Lajos Baróti** (Hungary)

Brazil (4–2–4): Gylmar (Santos); Djalma Santos (Palmeiras), Hilderaldo Bellini (Cpt, São Paulo), Paulo Henrique *de Oliveira* (Flamengo), Altair *Gomes de Figueiredo* (Fluminense); *Antônio* Lima (Santos), Gérson *de Oliveira; Manuel dos Santos, known as* Garrincha (Botafogo), Alcindo *de Freitas* (Grêmio), *Eduardo Gonçalvez, known as* Tostäo (Cruzeiro), *Jair Ventura, known as* Jairzinho (Botafogo)
Hungary (1–4–2–3): József Gelei (Tàtabánya Bányász); Sandor Matrai (Ferencváros); Benõ Káposzta (Ujpest Dózsa), Kálmán Mészöly (Vasas), Ferenc Sipos (Cpt, Honved), Gusztáv Szepesi (Tàtabánya Bányász); Imre Mathesz (Vasas), Gyula Rákosi (Ferencváros); Ferenc Bene (Ujpest Dózsa), Flórián Albert (Ferencvàros), János Farkas (Vasas)

The Brazilians were as badly prepared for this tournament as they were well prepared for the previous two. In Sweden and Chile they had undergone intensive training camps and altitude work, preparing a well-knit, comfortable squad. This time they thought, *"Hey, we're Brazil, let's just bring all the good old boys back and we'll breeze this – we have Pelé after all!"* Well they didn't have Pelé for this game, the Bulgarians saw to that, and they hadn't brought Amarildo either. And the good old boys meant the back five had an average age of thirty-two, including a twenty-three-year-old (who wasn't old, just not very good). They brought in the talented midfield playmaker Gérson for the more defensive Denilson and gave Pelé's place to Alcindo – the leading scorer of all time for his club Grêmio, but a bit-part player at this level.

Hungary were distressed at losing to Portugal and knew this was their last chance to seal a place in the next round. Hardly surprisingly, they brought in a new goalkeeper – I know I've been harsh on Szentmihályi, especially as he was carrying a knock in the first game, but it was as calamitous a goalkeeping perform-ance as the Finals have seen. His replacement, Gelei, came from the unfashionable suburban Tatabánya club, as did Szepesi, drafted in to replace Sóvári. Hungary's formation was novel, with Matrai, now thirty-three and short of pace, lying really deep and allowing the full-backs to operate as wing-backs, a term that is often assumed to be a more modern one but which is heard clearly on the TV commentary. A midfield two was augmented both by these overlapping wide players and the deep-lying centre-forward and playmaker Flórián Albert, in a variant on the role perfected by his predecessor Hidegkuti. Ahead of them were two strikers who attacked from wide positions, leaving the opposition centre-backs no one to mark. Against Brazil this was deadly, as the attacking players received the ball with space to run at the oldsters – Bellini and co just couldn't deal with it.

The proof came in the third minute. Matrai broke up a Brazilian attack, Sipos brought the ball out and fed Bene, running through the inside-right channel. The winger turned Altair inside, then went back outside and left him on the floor; Bellini tried to cover but Bene just cut inside him and fired low past Gylmar with his left foot. An exhilarating counter-attack that set the tone for what was to come.

No Brazil side is without talent and they came back. Lima enjoyed trying his luck from distance and he stung the goalkeeper's fingers in the first minute with a forty-yarder. After fifteen minutes he had another go and blasted a free-kick into a wall and the ball fell at the feet of Tostão who hit an instant shot high past Gelei. This was it, surely Brazil would show their true colours and dictate the game. Er, no. Gérson's radar was off, Lima was more brawn than brains, and, with no Pelé to drop deep and help, no one was making things happen.

The Hungarians were fantastic, their passing and movement precise and varied. The Goodison Park crowd, which started the game very much behind Brazil, was roaring its appreciation of the second generation of Magical Magyars – far from wan or unworthy. (I have read a suggestion that the Everton fans in the crowd reacted to the Liverpool supporters cheering for Brazil by rooting for the opposition – it makes sense in the nonsensical world of football tribalism.) One move saw the front players move the ball between them without touching the ground before Bene sent in a header that lacked the power to trouble Gylmar. Another saw Farkas force a tougher save from the Brazilian goalkeeper with a fierce low drive after Albert played him in. Brazil were reduced to occasional raids, like when Sipos did brilliantly to hook the ball off the line after Gelei aped his predecessor trying to collect a cross from Alcindo after a quick throw from Jairzinho let him in. Jairzinho was Brazil's principal threat and he began to wander infield looking for the ball when he realised Szepesi had Garrincha comfortably under control on the opposite side.

Brazil started the second half better, with Jairzinho playing through the middle and causing problems, once giving Sipos and Matrai a yard start and outsprinting them only to shoot into the side netting. Hungary reverted to a back four and pushed Mészöly further forward to use his height, yet it was Bene on the right who posed the bigger problems for Brazil. Every time Albert received the ball he looked for the ball inside Paulo Henrique for Bene. First the winger crossed for Farkas to volley hastily when he had time to bring the ball down – Rákosi told him so in no uncertain terms. Next Bene beat his man and fired in a drive when a cross was the better option. Hungary kept coming and it was third time lucky when Albert put Bene away again with a sublime first-time pass. The winger looked up this time and hit a flat cross at Farkas. No complaints from his colleagues on this occasion as Farkas took the ball first time and smashed it past Gylmar, a goal fit for any game and hugely appropriate as the decisive moment in this one.

Brazil were truly on the rack now and Hungary didn't make the mistake of sitting back. Szepesi dispossessed Garrincha and strode away with the ball. Albert ran up to him and demanded it, turned, sprinted between two retreating Brazilians and fed Bene. The winger beat Altair (twice) and was brought down when Henrique realised he couldn't stop him either. Kálmán Mészöly (%&^!!@&&) banged away the penalty. Hungary weren't done. Bene, struggling with cramp, headed over after Rákosi teased the defence, and Albert sprinted past four weary defenders to set up Farkas for a fourth only for the referee to chalk it off – a risible decision that marred an otherwise good performance by the Englishman. Brazil had one last chance, when Alcindo met Jairzinho's free-kick on the half-volley, but Gelei earned his corn with a fantastic reflex save.

Very rarely have a Brazilian team looked so ragged in a World Cup match. Hungary were more skilful, more tactically astute and more determined – Mészöly finished the match with his arm in a sling rather than leave the field. In Albert they had a player capable of lifting his game to the very highest level, and he surpassed even that here, producing one of the very best individual performances in World Cup history.

Brazil were in trouble but both teams could still feasibly go through. It was the reigning champions' first defeat since the infamous Battle of Berne in 1954, when they fell to the same opponents.

By the end of the following day Brazil knew they would probably need a handsome win over Portugal in their last match, as the Portuguese blew away Bulgaria with a minimum of fuss. Bulgaria, like Switzerland, looked out of their depth. Eusébio scored Portugal's second goal to open his account for the tournament, while the tall but not unskilful Torres looked the perfect foil for the African-born star's quick feet and powerful shooting.

Brazil made nine changes for the game – an absurd overreaction to a defeat at the hands of an inspired team. One of the more justifiable was the return of Pelé, even if only half-fit. Less justifiable was the Portuguese decision to kick him out of the match.

Portugal were already in the lead. Eusébio, coming in off the left, had tested Manga three times already; his testing cross was punched away by the goalkeeper but straight onto the head of Simões, who looked mightily surprised to score. The second goal was as basic as they come; Coluna pumped a long free-kick at Torres and the giant headed it across goal for Eusébio to finish off past a flat-footed Manga. Way too easy.

Already in deep trouble, Brazil's day got much worse when Pelé was hacked mercilessly by Morais on the edge of the Portuguese area. Made of stern stuff, Pelé rode the tackle only to be chopped down even harder by the same player. Referee George McCabe deemed a wag of the finger sufficient for a tackle that would have the player in a police interview room in later years. Disgraceful from the Portuguese defender – pathetic from the English referee. Pelé spent the rest of the game limping forlornly on the left wing.

Rildo gave Brazil hope with a drilled shot but it was shortlived. Manga saved well from a Eusébio piledriver, but, when the

resultant corner came back to the striker in a near-identical position, he simply hit the second shot even harder. Had Manga been
able to get in the way he would probably just have ended up in the
back of the net with the ball.

Hungary joined Portugal in the next round with a routine win
over Bulgaria. They looked tired after their efforts against Brazil,
and conceded early when Asparuhov ran on to a through ball;
Gelei came out suicidally far and left the Bulgarian an age to find
the net past a retreating defender. Five years later Asparuhov and
his colleague Nikola Kotkov (who made his first appearance in
the tournament in this match) were killed when their car spun out
of control. The striker was a legend at Levski Sofia, where he
earned cult status for turning down a lucrative move to Milan,
and was still a regular in the Bulgarian side when the accident cut
him off. Hungary needed a bit of help with the equaliser; Rákosi
crossed while on the ground after a tackle, Davidov, the covering
defender, hit his clearance at Vutsov, his colleague, and the ball
ricocheted back onto Davidov and into the net. Laughably bad.
That was three minutes before half-time and Hungary were
ahead before the break, Mészöly chesting down Bene's corner
and blasting into the goal – poor marking again, though. Bene
added a third with a good glancing header from Rákosi's corner,
and that was that. The holders were out.

GROUP 4

USSR Malofeyev 30, 88, Banishevsky 31	(2) 3	**North Korea**	(0) 0	12 July, Middlesbrough; 23,006
Italy Mazzola 9, Barison 88	(1) 2	**Chile**	(0) 0	13 July, Sunderland; 27,199
Chile Marcos 27 (p)	(1) 1	**North Korea** Park Seung-jin 88	(0) 1	15 July, Middlesbrough; 13,792
USSR Chislenko 57	(0) 1	**Italy**	(0) 0	16 July, Sunderland; 27,793
USSR Porkujan 29, 87	(1) 2	**Chile** Marcos 33	(1) 1	17 July, Middlesbrough; 16,027

The final group looked a doddle for Italy and the USSR, with
Chile, the weakest of the South American sides, and North Korea,
the joke team, for company. England didn't really get the
Democratic People's Republic of Korea – they called them plain

old North Korea, for a start, although it is true to say there is nothing democratic about that country's government.

When they qualified, the Suits in Whitehall went into hugger-mugger with the Suits at the FA. The Whitehall Suits didn't want the Koreans in England at all – they were dirty, filthy Communists – but the FA Suits were concerned they would be censured by the FIFA Suits. A compromise was reached: no one used the North Korean flag or played the North Korean anthem, and the team were banished to the north-east, where they were, of course, immediately adopted by the locals as their favourites – the Suits forgot to tell the commoners the North Koreans were BAD PEOPLE.

"That must be the strangest team sheet ever to appear on television," mused commentator Hugh Johns at the start of the opening game in the group between the Koreans and the USSR. Why, Hugh? Do they not have TV in the Far East, or do they think *"Why don't we call our kids Bobby or Geoff or Flórián or Franz instead of Yung and Seung and Lee?"* I know it was a long time ago, but our attitude to overseas cultures was appalling – with no one more culpable than the xenophobic England manager.

The Soviets steamed through North Korea – they were twice their size – and should have added to the three they did score. The nineteen-year-old goalkeeper Lee Chan-myung did well, and the Koreans never stopped running – they had been in a fitness camp for two years, supposedly, determined not to suffer the ignominy of South Korea in 1954. Malofeyev, later a celebrated coach in Russia, scored twice and the poodle-haired striker Banishevsky headed in a free-kick. Malofeyev's second, late goal was tasty, taking a chip from Sabo in his stride and half-volleying past Lee as the ball dropped.

The assumed order was still in place after two more games; first Italy beat Chile with some ease – Chile were surprisingly supine, a far cry from the blood and gore of the 1962 horror show between the two. Two days later at Ayresome Park, with the crowd behind their every move, North Korea forced a draw with Chile after conceding a first-half penalty. Chile tried to brutalise their slender opponents, but the Koreans kept coming, and got their deserts two minutes from time when a header dropped to

Park Seung-jin (excellent throughout the tournament), who returned it with interest into the corner. Great stuff, with more to come.

The USSR beat Italy the following day, and were well worth their win in a cagey game between two sides who assumed they would qualify. The chunky winger Igor Chislenko scored the goal that settled it after fifty-seven minutes, cutting inside the great Italian wing-back Facchetti and firing home into the far corner – the fearsome shooting was a feature of this World Cup. Lev Yashin, who had never lived up to his reputation in a Finals tournament, had a fine game, saving twice in the closing minutes.

The USSR put out a few reserves in their last game and still beat Chile. The reserve striker, Valeriy Porkujan, had enjoyed a good season with Odessa and just signed for Dynamo Kyiv. He took his chance here on his debut and scored both goals, cementing his place for the knockout rounds. The USSR duly won the group and went through with North Korea. No, no, of course, I mean Italy . . . don't I? No, actually, I don't, because the previous day had seen the biggest shock thus far in any World Cup Finals match.

WORLD CUP SHOCKS No.2

19 July 1966, Ayresome Park, Middlesbrough; 17,829

Italy	**(0) 0**	
North Korea	**(1) 1**	Park Doo-ik 42

Referee: **Pierre Schwinte** (France)
Coaches: **Edmondo Fabbri** (Italy) & **Mung Rye-hyun** (North Korea)

Italy (4–3–3): Enrico Albertosi (Fiorentina); Spartaco Landini (Inter Milan), Aristide Guarneri (Inter), Francesco Janich (Bologna), Giacinto Facchetti (Inter); Romano Fogli (Bologna), Giacomo Bulgarelli (Cpt, Bologna), Gianni Rivera (AC Milan); Marino Perani (Bologna), Sandro Mazzola (Inter), Paolo Barison (Roma)
North Korea (4–4–2): Lee Chan-myung; Ha Jung-won, Oh Yoon-kyung, Shin Yung-kyoo, Lim Zoong-sun; Im Seung-hwi, Han Bong-jin, Park Seung-jin (Cpt), Kim Bong-hwan; Park Doo-ik, Yang Sung-kook

A victory for hard work over complacency. The Italians made unnecessary changes and played badly. The Koreans worked their socks off, fought for every ball and used their extra man intelligently after Bulgarelli went off injured – a victim of his own reckless tackle.

Italy had their chances; Perani in particular could have had a hat-trick in the first half. The Italian No.17 saw his volley saved brilliantly by Lee, poked the ball past the post when Barison's cross found him six yards out and then missed a one-on-one with the 'keeper.

A free-kick was tossed around the box for a moment or two then cleared, but a Korean defender sent a powerful header back towards the Italian area. A defender misread the bounce and the ball broke for Park Doo-ik, who drove it unerringly past Albertosi.

Italy tried to get back into the game in the second half, and the recalled Rivera nearly found a way through with a blockbuster, but Lee was equal to it – and brave moments later when Rivera nearly latched onto a deflection. There were chances at the other end, too – Korea broke at pace and very directly and could have scored two or three more with more judicious use of the final ball. Italy's night was summed up when a cross from the right found Barison and Perani unmarked on the far post; they got in each other's way and the last chance went begging.

The 1960s was the decade Italy established their reputation for defensive play, as sides sought to hold a line and counter-attack down the flanks. Inter under Helenio Herreira won success with the system but no friends, and it became the prevailing style as Italian club chairmen demanded success. The *catenaccio* defence (sounds like a chess game opening) negated the skills of players like Rivera and Mazzola, as the football culture became risk averse and cynical. Italy, and their coach, Edmondo Fabbri, paid the price for their negativity at this World Cup, losing lazily to the Soviet Union and comically to North Korea. They returned home to the ritual bombardment with ripe foodstuffs (if they were lucky) – the four Bologna players were booed by their own fans at the start of the following season.

The Italians were ridiculed in newspapers across Europe and beyond; unsurprisingly I can find no record of how the result was received in North Korea, although it's safe to say that it stood as proof of the glorious power of the people and a beacon in their fight against encroaching capitalism. Yeah, yeah, yeah – left-wing, right-wing, a cross is still a cross.

232   *Back Home*

QUARTER-FINALS (all 23 July)

England   (0) 1   **Argentina** (0) 0   Wembley; 90,584
Hurst 77
West Germany   (1) 4   **Uruguay**   (0) 0   Sheffield; 40,007
Haller 11, 84,
Beckenbauer 70, Seeler 77
USSR   (1) 2   **Hungary**   (0) 1   Sunderland; 22,103
Chislenko 5, Porkujan 48   Bene 58

WORLD CUP CLASSIC No.5
23 July 1966, Goodison Park, Liverpool; 40,248

Portugal   (2) 5   Eusébio 26, 43 (p), 57, 60 (p), José Augusto 80
North Korea   (3) 3   Park Seung-jin 1, Lee Dong-woon 20, Yang Sung-kook 24

Referee: **Menachem Ashkenazi (Isr)**
Coaches: **Manuel Afonso / Otto Glória** (Portugal) & **Mung Rye-hyun** (North Korea)

Portugal (4–2–4): José Pereira (Belenenses); João Morais (Sporting), Vicente da Fonseca (Belenenses), Alexandre Baptista (Sporting), Hilário da Conceição (Sporting); Jaime Graça (Vitória Setúbal), Mário Coluna (Cpt, Benfica); José Augusto de Almeida (Benfica), Eusébio Ferreira (Benfica), José Torres (Benfica), António Simões (Benfica)
North Korea (4–4–2): Lee Chan-myung; Ha Jung-won, Oh Yoon-kyung, Shin Yung-kyoo, Lim Zoong-sun; Im Seung-hwi, Han Bong-jin, Park Seung-jin (Cpt), Lee Dong-woon; Park Doo-ik, Yang Sung-kook

Not actually a classic in terms of the football played – some of the defending was too risible for that – but a nailed-on classic if you want thrills, spills, shocks, shades of genius and a preposterous scoreline.

Portugal probably afforded themselves a little chuckle when North Korea beat Italy and secured second place in Group 4. Some later accounts assume they were complacent at the start of the quarter-final, but it is hard to believe they would have underestimated opponents who had just beaten one of the favourites. The truth lies more in the fact that Portugal didn't expect the Koreans to come out quite so hard and fast, and the adrenaline created by that first goal led to a sustained assault that only petered out when Portugal got Eusébio into the game and made the Koreans go backwards. That and the fact that the Portuguese defence was a bit crap. Their selection was along the lines of the 1970 Brazilians: *"We'll have him, and him, and him ... he's good, oh and him ... and oh, yes, we'd better have a defender or two – pick those Sporting chaps or they may get upset that we've picked the entire Benfica forward line ..."*

Park Seung-jin had shown he packed a punch against Chile, but that was nothing compared to the spectacular hit he unleashed in the first minute here as the ball rolled across the face of the penalty area.

The second goal, which sent the Goodison Park crowd into raptures after twenty minutes, was a mini-masterpiece. A Portuguese attack foundered and Lee Dong-woon picked the ball up in midfield, fed Park and went for the return. Lee picked out another good ball to Hang Bong-jin, and his long deep cross cleared the flailing Pereira and sailed all the way to the other winger, Yang Sung-kook, who returned it to the middle. Lee's energy had carried him into the box and he was first to the ball – 2–0.

Five minutes later it was dreamland for North Korea, as another move found Park lurking on the edge of the area with room to fire in a shot. The ball hit a defender but again it was a Korean who anticipated better, and Yang had time to measure his shot and ram it in the corner for a third.

Sounds like one-way traffic but it wasn't. Eusébio had gone close twice and José Augusto brought a fine, leaping save out of Lee Chan-myung. David Coleman was of the opinion that Korea erred in continuing to attack, as do most hindsight sources; Cris Freddi, by contrast, deems this a patronising explanation. They are both right, in a way. It is patronising, but it was also a valid observation. The Koreans were well coached – they held a disciplined line for all of the Italy game and for most of this – but they only knew one way to play. Kept in isolation in their training camp, they had no exposure to the cynical attitudes of the European teams – sitting back was alien to them. And might well have proved equally fatal against Eusébio.

Portugal desperately needed respite, their defence was creaking and groaning like an over-laden pirate ship. It came out of nowhere and at a good time, only three minutes after Korea's third goal. A pushed pass from José Augusto looked unthreatening until two defenders left it to each other and Eusébio nipped between them and toe-poked it past the goalkeeper. I say toe-poked, Eusébio could toe-poke harder than most players could hit the ball on the full – it flew past Lee's shoulder.

The attacks came in waves and two minutes from half-time Torres burst between two defenders and was hauled down from behind for a blatant penalty. Eusébio, the biggest boy in the playground who took all the free-kicks and penalties, banged it home. The equaliser came just before the hour; it was a replica of the first Portuguese goal, only on the right-hand side and it was a pass from Simões that the great one scooped into the goal past Lee.

There was only team winning this now and Portugal were ahead on the hour. This one really was all about Eusébio. He received wide right surrounded by defenders but backed his pace and power to get past, sprinting down the line past one and beating another as he cut into the area. The last man, Lim Zoong-sun, came crashing through him – another penalty. Eusébio had a little sit down on the pretext his knee was sore – it certainly didn't stop him taking the spot-kick. That was the end of the genuine excitement, although there was time for one more when Eusébio's corner was headed back by Torres and finished off by an unmarked José Augusto.

It was a fun game, played in an excellent spirit – for which Portugal deserve credit, they just kept playing instead of getting tetchy (compare and contrast with 2002 and their game against South Korea), and there was none of the rough stuff that characterised their performance against Brazil. Eusébio was Man of the Match, the other lot had eleven heroes who made those who billed them as the tournament's joke team look a little foolish.

Next to nothing was seen of the North Koreans until Daniel Gordon's 2002 documentary (see *World Cup Movies*); the squad returned to the secrecy of the bosom of that odd nation. If they were from any other country, then offers would have poured in for the excellent Park Seung-jin, the wrigglesome forward Park Doo-ik, and the splendidly agile (if diminutive) goalkeeper Lee Chan-myung. Their next appearance in the Finals was in 2010 and their reunion with Portugal was altogether less glorious.

The only all-European quarter-final saw the artistes of Hungary take on the juggernaut of the Soviet Union. The USSR did what was expected and marked the Hungarian ball-players Albert and Bene tightly, relying on their fitness to get their defence forward when they were in possession. They were helped by Gelei – swap the teams' goalkeepers and Hungary might have gone all the way in this tournament – who clutched a shot from Porkujan to his chest then let it squirm from his grasp so Chislenko could jab it into the net.

From there on the Hungarians strained and stretched to get back in the game but created little as the Soviets thundered into tackles and cramped the room in the middle of the field the Hungarians needed to express themselves – it was a surprisingly modern, if overly functional style. Most pundits thought the USSR too limited at the beginning of the tournament, but this was a competition of limited teams, and they looked mightily powerful.

The man-to-man marking worked a treat, as the outstanding captain Albert Shesternev put the shackles on the Hungarian genius Flórián Albert, and put in some powerhouse tackles.

Hollow-cheeked, handsome and personable, married to a notable figure skater, Shesternev was the darling of the Soviet bureaucracy; loyal to the state and hardly ever injured, he went on to make ninety appearances for the USSR, sixty-two of them as captain, a record until the Ukrainian Blokhin became the first to pass 100. One or two reports suggest the Soviets kicked Hungary off their game, but in comparison to some games in this tournament this was above-the-line stuff; the USSR were just a big, intimidating side.

The game looked safe when Porkujan was left unmarked at the far post and headed home early in the second half, but Hungary scored a good goal when Mészöly put Bene in on the right and the winger kept up his record of scoring in every match. Briefly Hungary stirred, but Albert still couldn't get in the game and the revival petered out after Yashin saved a rasping free-kick from Sipos.

The English commentators still referred to the Soviet team as "Russians", as was the norm in the 1960s. Just as in 1962, not all of them were Russian: one of their best players, Dynamo Kyiv's Josip Sabo, was born József Szabo in Hungary – he would later coach both Kyiv and the Ukrainian national team after the break-up of the Soviet Union. Left-winger Porkujan was one of four Ukrainians in the squad, centre-forward Banishevsky was an Azerbaijani and there were two Georgians, Metreveli and Khurtsilava, both with the strong Dynamo Tbilisi team, and both of whom won more than forty caps for the USSR. Malofeyev, the clever inside-forward, was born in Russia but played over 300 games for Dynamo Minsk in Belarus and later coached the team to their only Soviet title in 1982. More of him later.

The two Europe v South America ties saw West Germany play Uruguay at Hillsborough while England and Argentina met at Wembley. Both games were billed as muscle against malevolence and both games lived up to the billing.

Opinions diverge wildly as to where the blame lies for the violent nature of both these encounters. Better refereeing would have helped, as would better direction from FIFA to clamp down on foul play, but this was nearly two decades away. Much was made in the South American press that West Germany got an English referee and England got a German referee, but if Uruguay or Argentina had a problem with this they were allowed to raise an objection before the game, and neither did. There was certainly a divergence in interpretation of foul play between the two continents; perhaps in Europe it was right that European rules apply. In Europe hard tackling was the norm – the tackle from behind was not yet outlawed and if the tackler played the ball first any consequent damage was deemed accidental. Players like Stiles and Schnellinger exploited this rule to intimidate opponents by following through with hard, ostensibly fair tackles. In South America this was deemed foul play. But in South America shirt-pulling and jabbing and pinching were all part and parcel of the marker's job, so the likes of Albrecht and Troche thought nothing of a bit of hair-pulling or gouging, whereas European players objected to this kind of stuff as unsporting. The same culture clash – exacerbated by these two games – manifested itself in a series of Intercontinental Club Cup matches during the next decade. The two-leg contest between the champion clubs of Europe and South America, especially when the latter came from

Argentina, was constantly marred by outbursts of violence and fighting.

There was no middle ground. Throw in European distrust of the New World and a wedge of reciprocal anti-colonial resentment, and there was a ready-made recipe for animosity.

Both games saw excessively hard tackling from the European side; England totted up almost twice as many fouls as Argentina, same for West Germany against Uruguay. That this was a deliberate policy from both sides to show they were not intimidated by their opponents' tough reputations was undoubtedly the case. So the South American sides had some cause for grievance. What was not forgivable was the intensity of the reaction and the complete lack of regard for the match officials of both South American sides. This is the dark side of the South American game, and in Uruguay for twenty years it became the nature of their game, the passion and pride spilling over into near-psychotic anger. Conclusion? England and West Germany were not blameless, but the two South American sides were beyond the pale.

At Hillsborough the tone was set early. As the Uruguayans probed the defence, in their first foray forward, a couple of bone-jarring tackles came their way. The ball came out to Cortes who beat Tilkowski all ends up only for the ball to rebound to the goalkeeper from a post. Schulz was shielding Tilkowski in the time-honoured fashion, so Silva tried to kick him out of the way. With both Germans on the ground Silva thought it would be a good idea to try to kick the ball out of Tilkowski's hands, inevitably kicking the 'keeper instead.

This was before referee Jim Finney gave the Uruguayans cause for complaint by failing to spot Schnellinger's handball on the line to stop a certain goal from Rocha's header. Their sense of grievance was exacerbated by West Germany's opening goal – nothing untoward, just a big slice of luck as Haller deflected Held's miscued shot past Mazurkiewicz. The rest of the first half passed relatively peaceably, with both sides restricted mainly to long shots, which two useful goalkeepers gobbled up – the best was Beckenbauer's thirty-five-yard free-kick, which Mazurkiewicz tipped brilliantly round the post.

It all kicked off – literally – five minutes into the second half when Troche, the Uruguayan captain, was sent off for kicking Emmerich off the ball. When Seeler offered an opinion Troche slapped him around the face and at one point it looked as though he might give Jim Finney a slice as the referee ushered him from the field. Troche wasn't picked for the national team again. Five minutes later Silva added to his first half mischief with a scythe at Haller that left the German sprawling on the ground and was sent after his captain to use the bathing facilities ahead of schedule. Now Haller was a diver and a play-actor, and may well not have been as badly hurt as he purported to be – and frankly, had I been a professional player, I might have given the arrogant so-and-so a bit of a kicking, too, but just accept the red card, don't hang around arguing the toss when you've just hacked the man's legs from under him. Silva didn't see things that way and was eventually escorted from the field by the police with half the Uruguayan coaching staff in baying attendance.

With nine men they were stuffed, and good riddance. West Germany added three more; Beckenbauer with a replica of his one-two-round-the-keeper against Switzerland, Seeler with a right-footed howitzer and Haller passing into an unguarded net after an error by an exhausted Manicera, who used up all his energy chasing the referee. Comic relief amidst all the *sturm und drang* was provided by a tubby middle-aged bloke with a flag wearing lederhosen who staged a one-man pitch invasion after the third goal. There simply are no circumstances in which lederhosen look cool.

Meanwhile, at Wembley in front of 90,000+ England and Argentina were fighting a more even battle. Ramsey finally dispensed with wingers altogether – none of the three used had impressed – and brought back feisty Alan Ball, which was guaranteed to raise the temperature (and the volume, if you happened to possess the hearing of a dog). Greaves's leg was still sore, so Ramsey introduced Geoff Hurst of West Ham, better in the air and more robust, though not as skilful or quick as Greaves.

Argentina were a good side, perfectly capable of beating England, and it was odd that they chose to play the way they did – odd unless you know a little of the history of their coach, Juan

Carlos Lorenzo. Lorenzo thrived on a feeling of "us against the world", creating a siege mentality within his teams. It was intended to bond teams – Sam Allardyce uses the same motivational tool in a more positive way – and make them more determined; Lorenzo's sides were invariably defensive, both tactically and psychologically, and paranoid. Argentina decided the only way to beat England was by intimidation, and from the start the kicking and spitting off the ball got underway. England, also wound up by the suspicious Alf Ramsey, responded with some aggressive tackling. Kreitlein, the German referee, was harsh on the skulduggery, less so on the tackling; this in turn prompted the Argentinian captain, Rattín, to conduct a running battle with the officials, questioning every decision, remonstrating when a colleague was cautioned and spitting at Kreitlein's feet. When Kreitlein went to caution Artime, Rattín insisted on offering his opinion, and Kreitlein had had enough, sending the Argentinian captain off, having already booked him for a foul. Rattín's claim that he was asking for an interpreter is hollow, and later claims that Kreitlein sent him off for "looking at me oddly" are internet-fostered codswallop. Rattín was sent off for persistent foul play and dissent. The rest of the team threatened to follow, prompted by Albrecht, only just back from suspension after being dismissed against West Germany. It took nearly ten minutes for the pitch to be cleared of all the hangers-on from the Argentinian camp who wished to put in their bit.

The game itself was pale. England did most of the attacking, even against eleven men, but Argentina defended with discipline and had a couple of chances. They knew England played without conventional wingers and defended narrow, concentrating play into the middle third of the field – when England remembered to use all the huge Wembley pitch, they had more joy. The goal came from the left wing, when Wilson found Peters in acres of space and he picked out his West Ham colleague with a pin-point cross – Hurst's glancing header was just as precise. Argentina appealed for offside – of course they did – but it wasn't.

England kept their heads during all the fuss and bother, and played a sensible and patient game – although a lack of imagination was exposed. Alan Ball was outstanding, riding tackles and driving through the Argentinian midfield without letting his fiery temper loose. The only one who fanned the flames was Alf Ramsey, with his borderline racist post-match comments about playing "animals". Then remarks weren't forgotten by the Argentinian press, and an ongoing football feud was born.

One footnote. Argentinian pressmen were at great pains to point out what a decent, softly spoken chap Rattín was – the same chap who years later stood for office for a right-wing party with a leader accused of torture and extortion. May be nothing in it.

SEMI-FINALS

West Germany (1) 2		**USSR**	**(0) 1**	25 July, Liverpool; 38,273
Haller 43,		Porkujan 87		
Beckenbauer 68				
England	**(1) 2**	**Portugal**	**(0) 1**	26 July, Wembley; 94,493
R Charlton 30, 79		Eusébio 82 (p)		

THIRD-PLACE MATCH

Portugal	**(1) 2**	**USSR**	**(1) 1**	28 July, Wembley, 87,696
Eusébio 13 (p),		Malofeyev 44		
Torres 87				

The Goodison Park semi-final was not one for the squeamish, as West Germany and the Soviet Union squared off. Even without the history between the countries there would have been no prisoners, both sides were full of big, strong players who liked to impose themselves on their opponents.

The game turned on an incident in the first half. Schnellinger went through Chislenko, as was his wont, leaving the winger writhing on the floor as the German defender ran on and sent in Haller to ram home. A moment later a nondescript retaliatory tackle by Chislenko on Held brought a red card from the Italian referee. That was harsh on the Soviets but the better team won, Beckenbauer's second-half goal settling the result before Porkujan's late consolation. The Soviets played better in the second half when down to ten men – and missing one of their best, at that – but West Germany did enough. Don't they always?

Portugal knew they would have to defend better and start better against England than they did against North Korea, and they made two changes at the back, leaving out the guys who kicked Pelé out of the game. Neither side favoured man-marking, so Eusébio and Bobby Charlton were left to free range, but England played Moore a little deeper to allow cover if the Portuguese genius beat his man. The tactics worked: Portugal created little in the first half and England went in one-up after a route-one opener. A long ball from Ray Wilson found Hunt, whose first heavy touch fortuitously took the ball past his marker. Pereira cleared the immediate threat but only found Charlton, who passed the ball nonchalantly back into the net.

The second goal was the near-perfect expression of the same tactic, with no element of luck. Portugal were defending too deep, so Cohen played a long, raking ball into the area. Hurst outmuscled José Carlos with some ease – he was a big, powerful lad – and laid the ball back for Charlton to smash it past Pereira. Cris Freddi suggests (heresy, he admits) the shot took a deflection. Not heresy, Cris, just irrelevant – no one was stopping that rocket.

A rare error from Gordon Banks gave Portugal a glimmer. Banks came for a deep cross and missed it, Torres headed goalwards and Jack Charlton handled on the line. No prizes for guessing who took the penalty. Banks made amends by tipping a late effort from Coluna over the bar.

The apologists don't give England enough credit for this win. They grew into this tournament (as winners often do) and looked a good side here, especially the well-organised, compact defence who coped comfortably with a hugely talented forward line. Portugal resorted to deep crosses aimed at Torres – even as good a header of the ball as Jack Charlton had problems with the human telegraph pole.

Portugal seemed happy with third place – they won the meaningless play-off against the USSR; their biggest disappointment was not pressing on following this tournament and continuing to improve. The result was a slide back among the also-rans in the next decade. The England players, if later accounts and interviews are to be believed, were just happy to play opponents who weren't poking fingers in their eyes or gobbing at them.

World Cup Heroes No.12

Eusébio da Silva Ferreira (1942–)

Portugal

José Carlos Bauer (see Brazil 1950 & 1954; his father was Swiss) went on to be a coach and scout and spotted a youngster playing in Mozambique in the late 1950s. Impressed, he recommended this young Eusébio to both São Paulo and his old friend Béla Guttmann at Benfica; it was Guttmann who trusted Bauer and Eusébio went to Portugal.

The young African star made an almost immediate impact at Benfica – in the summer of 1961 Guttmann brought the youngster off the bench in a summer tournament match against Santos and he scored a second half hat-trick. He was capped for the first time later that year. It was an inauspicious debut as Portugal lost 4–2 to Luxembourg, the first game won by the Duchy in a World Cup qualifier. Ady Schmidt's hat-trick earned the headlines that day, but the Portuguese debutant would soon be the name on everyone's lips.

In 1962 Eusébio scored twice as Benfica won the European Cup for the first time, beating the mighty Real Madrid 5–3. He would play in three more Finals, including the 1968 encounter against Manchester United, but wouldn't win again. Always a generous player to opponents, Eusébio memorably applauded an Alex Stepney save in the dying moments of ordinary time in that terrific match against United.

He ended a twelve-year international career in 1973 as Portugal's all-time top scorer and with most appearances. Both records have now gone and the top scorer is Pauleta, which feels terribly wrong somehow (see World Cup 2006).

I have read one or two mystifying accounts suggesting Eusébio wasn't all he was cracked up to be. It was Portugal who weren't all they were cracked up to be, never able to find a defence to match their scintillating forward line. Eusébio scored nine goals in six matches in the only major tournament in which he played. 'Nuff said.

He was quick (really quick), powerful, had a hammer of a right foot and an okay left, he could head and was a master dead-ball kicker. Apart from that, nah, not much cop.

And unlike so many others he hasn't spent his years since he retired talking crap and rattling on about how much better it was in his day.

WORLD CUP FINAL No.8
30 July 1966, Wembley Stadium; 93,802
England (1) (2) 4   Hurst 19, 100, 119, Peters 78
West Germany (1) (2) 2 Haller 13, Weber 89

Referee: **Gottfried Dienst** (Switzerland)
Coaches: **Alf Ramsey** (England) & **Helmut Schön** (West Germany)

England (4–3–1–2): Gordon Banks (Leicester City); George Cohen (Fulham), Jack Charlton (Leeds United), Bobby Moore (West Ham United), Ray Wilson (Everton); Alan Ball (Blackpool), Nobby Stiles (Manchester United), Martin Peters (West Ham); Bobby Charlton (Man Utd); Roger Hunt (Liverpool), Geoff Hurst (West Ham)
West Germany (4–3–3): Hans Tilkowski (Borussia Dortmund); Horst Höttges (Werder Bremen), Karl-Heinz Schnellinger (AC Milan), Willi Schulz (Hamburg), Wolfgang Weber (Cologne); Franz Beckenbauer (Bayern Munich), Helmut Haller (Bologna), Wolfgang Overath (Cologne); Siggi Held (Borussia Dortmund), Uwe Seeler (Hamburg), Lothar Emmerich (Borussia Dortmund)

Much has been written about the game, and it has been replayed endlessly on TV, so most football enthusiasts, even those too young to remember the match (this author included, just) have watched it. Remarkable then that the apologists for English football make such a meal of Hurst's "illegal" goal; to present the result as a grave injustice is nonsense. No, the ball didn't cross the line; that is incontestable, except by the deluded. But the same people who argue that Argentina would have beaten England in 1986 even without Maradona's cheating – they are right, by the way – do not present the same argument for this game. England's superiority may not have been as marked as Argentina's in that later game, but it was noticeable, and in Charlton they had a player whose presence instilled fear and caution in the West Germany side; it severely inhibited them as an attacking force.

West Germany's team picked itself after the opening games; a tight defence with Beckenbauer playing just in front, Overath and Haller providing the ammunition, Held and Emmerich out wide and Uwe Seeler, Germany's best player for a few years now, leading the line. There was talk of England bringing back Jimmy Greaves, but he was barely fit and had been out of form in the group matches, so Ramsey stuck with his replacement, Geoff Hurst, who was no slouch, as his quarter-final performance had shown.

West Germany made the better start; the wet surface aided their slick passing and had they had better wide players than Held and the lumbering Emmerich they would have caused England more problems. The first goal came from a rare misunderstanding between Gordon Banks and one of his full-backs, Ray Wilson, and was scraped in by Helmut Haller. The goal seemed to galvanise England. Bobby Charlton began to push his marker, Franz Beckenbauer, further back, and the youngsters Ball and Peters scurried busily in the space left behind. Bobby Moore began to venture further forward, and it was his quickly taken free-kick after a foul by Overath that produced an equaliser, Hurst eluding his marker and burying a powerful header.

England looked in control now, without ever threatening to over-run the disciplined German defence. Their build-up was patient – none of the helter-skelter stuff so often criticised by England teams at previous tournaments – but the final ball or cross was thwarted by a thumping tackle from Hottges or Schnellinger or Weber, or a neat interception by Schultz or Beckenbauer, showing already the defensive nous that would make him the leader of Germany's greatest generation of players. England just about deserved the next goal – but it was a scrappy affair, Peters ramming home after a Hurst shot was blocked. The late equaliser by Weber was equally unmemorable; a poke over a despairing Banks after some penalty-box-ping-pong. The teams were well matched, and the game was still in the balance.

Alf Ramsey had his finest moment, as he stood ramrod-straight and stared down his crestfallen team, exhorting them to go and win again a match they had won once. The manner of the winning goal was unfortunate, but England dominated extra-time, the energy of Ball and Stiles and the cool distribution of Moore and Peters pushing the Germans deeper into their own half. Stiles overhit a pass to Ball, but the little feller chased it down and belted it back into the middle. Hurst beat his marker to the ball and hammered it – no luck about the strike, it was clean and hard – against the underside of the bar. The referee prevaricated and bottled it; the linesman, Tofik Bakhramov, made the wrong call; England won the World Cup. England's fourth was a classic break as a tired West Germany chased the game, a sumptuous pass from Moore setting Hurst clear to make his own personal mark on World Cup history.

The English penchant for self-flagellation has marked the third goal as a roaring controversy. It is not a view shared by the German players – all but the goalkeeper Tilkowski acknowledge the best side on the day and in the competition won the tournament. England were favourites and, a statistic few writers note, had never lost an international match to Germany or West Germany. England were not the best team to win a World Cup, but they weren't the worst either; they had four world-class players and the rest were all top international standard, with the exception of Jack Charlton and Stiles, and these two performed very specific functions within the framework of the side. England were beaten only rarely in the late sixties, and only by good sides – they were the second-best team at the next World Cup in Mexico behind one of the best Brazilian sides to take the field, so to suggest they only won the cup because of a slice of luck and home advantage is twaddle.

I still don't know if the shot was in or not. I have to say that I was standing in a poor position for that shot, exactly head-on instead of diagonal with the goal. I wouldn't have allowed the goal if Bakhramov hadn't pointed to the middle with his flag.

Gottfried Dienst, Final referee,
in an interview many years later

England Squad 1966:

GK: Gordon Banks (Leicester City, 29 years old, 27 caps) Ron Springett (Sheffield Wednesday, 30, 33), Peter Bonetti (Chelsea, 24, 1)

DEF: Jimmy Armfield (Blackpool, 30, 43), Gerry Byrne (Liverpool, 27, 2), Jack Charlton (Leeds United, 31, 16), George Cohen (Fulham, 26, 24), Norman Hunter (Leeds, 22, 4), Bobby Moore (West Ham United, 25, 41), Ray Wilson (Everton, 31, 45)

MID & WIDE: Alan Ball (Blackpool, 21, 10), Ian Callaghan (Liverpool, 21, 1), John Connelly (Manchester United, 27, 19), George Eastham (Arsenal, 29, 19), Ron Flowers (Wolverhampton Wanderers, 31, 49), Terry Paine (Southampton, 27, 18), Martin Peters (West Ham, 22, 3), Nobby Stiles (Man Utd, 24, 14)

FWD: Bobby Charlton (Man Utd, 28, 68), Jimmy Greaves (Tottenham Hotspur, 26, 51), Roger Hunt (Liverpool, 27, 13), Geoff Hurst (West Ham, 24, 4)

World Cup Heroes No.13

Geoff Hurst (1941–)

England

The first World Cup I remember was the 1970 tournament. I recall thinking England were invincible – we had the two Bobbies, Gordon Banks, my hero Peter Osgood and, of course, Geoff Hurst. Hurst had scored a hat-trick in the 1966 Final, I read all about it, so he had to the best, didn't he?

No, actually, in 1966 he was very much the third-choice striker behind the prolific Jimmy Greaves and Roger Hunt. The West Ham man, then twenty-four, had only been handed an England debut in the spring – he had four caps, while Hunt had thirteen and Greaves over fifty. Weirdly they were the only three out-and-out strikers in the squad, so, when Greaves picked up an injury, Hurst was in. His goal against Argentina and another bustling performance against Portugal, setting up Bobby Charlton's second goal, cemented his place in the final, even when Greaves was declared fit.

Hurst was back at the World Cup in Mexico in 1970, and added another splendid hard-working shift to his CV. He scored in the first game, worked his butt off against Brazil, was rested for the third group match and played wonderfully well in the fateful encounter with West Germany in León. Hurst was probably at his peak then – his career tailed off a little after that World Cup, both at domestic and international level.

Hurst only came through as a player in his early twenties, after he stopped flirting with a first class cricket career (a couple of seasons with Essex Second XI and one, slightly embarrassing, first team game against Lancashire, the county where he was born). He was part of the "School of Science" West Ham side coached by future England boss Ron Greenwood. West Ham had an excellent youth system and a cavalier way of playing that endeared them to neutrals, but the notion that the World Cup-winning side was "built" around the West Ham trio of Moore, Hurst and Peters is nonsense – the last two only established themselves during the tournament. All of Hurst's England caps came during his thirteen years at West Ham, which also brought him an FA Cup and a European Cup Winners' Cup medal – you didn't stay at West Ham to fill the trophy cupboard, they were an entertaining dilettante side, not serial winners.

Hurst had no particular attribute that made him stand out; he was quick enough without being express, strong and good in the air without being a battering ram, dexterous enough without being gifted. He was a good, unselfish team player, which endeared him to Ramsey, and was a conspicuous trier, which endeared him to fans.

Hurst spent a few years as a coach, assisting his former mentor Ron Greenwood, with England and taking over at Chelsea in 1979. He wasn't an especially good manager and started up an insurance business instead, at which he proved more successful. Hurst became Sir Geoffrey in 1998, for no apparent reason other than something he achieved thirty-two years previously. But then, if pressed, I would admit to believing the entire honours system is a combination of fatuous PR stunt and maintenance of the established order. And yes, I would back my convictions, so no thank you, Prime Minister, kind of you to ask . . .

So, Sir Geoff. Not a folk hero but part of a hard-working, successful unit. Not a great footballer, but a very good one, and one with a unique place in football history, even if one of them shouldn't have counted.

1966 Team of the Tournament: 4–2–4

Lee Chan-myung (North Korea)
Schnellinger (West Germany)   Shesternev (USSR)   Moore (England)   Marzolini (Argentina)
Beckenbauer (West Germany)   Ball (England)
Bene (Hungary)   Albert (Hungary)   Eusébio (Portugal)   R Charlton (England)

Leading scorers: Eusébio (9); Haller (6); Bene, Beckenbauer, Porkujan, Hurst (4)

The official All Star XI selected by FIFA was: Banks (England); Cohen (England), Moore (England), Vicente (Portugal), Marzolini (Argentina); Beckenbauer (West Germany), Coluna (Portugal), R Charlton (England); Albert (Hungary), Seeler (West Germany), Eusébio (Portugal) – not too much difference, and I only left out Banks because I intended to include him in 1970 (and the Korean 'keeper was utterly heroic).

Heaven Eleven No.5

England

Coach:
Bob Paisley – well why not? He's the only English coach to win the European Cup. Ramsey had severe tactical limitations, Bobby Robson was indecisive, Hoddle was . . . well, see 1998, and Venables, the best coach the FA actually employed, was just a little too much of a geezer

Here we go then. Cue hate mail from the Steven Gerrard fans.

Goalkeepers:
David Seaman: fabulous
Peter Shilton: better
Gordon Banks: best

Defenders:
Bobby Moore: stupendous player
Billy Wright: played his best stuff as a defender in his thirties
Terry Butcher: the best stopper we've had, just pips Adams and Terry
Rio Ferdinand: cover for Moore – not everyone's cup of tea, but a brilliant player on his game
Jimmy Armfield: best right-back in the world for a couple of years
Ashley Cole: England's best player for a decade
Stuart Pearce: much more than the sum of his parts, a laudable self-made player

Midfield & Wide:
Duncan Edwards: if only . . .
Alan Ball: the fourth world-class player in the '66 side
Bobby Charlton: class, his shooting was worth the admission alone
Stanley Matthews: amazing player
Tom Finney: almost as amazing as Stan
David Beckham: best dead-ball kicker we've had, tireless, committed
Bryan Robson: enormous lungs and heart, just the best box-to-box player England have had – deserved better support
Frank Lampard: wonderful goalscorer from deep; super-reliable
Paul Gascoigne: best English player in my adult viewing era
Paul Scholes: see Lampard above

Strikers:
Gary Lineker: if he got past you, you didn't catch him, and he usually scored
Jimmy Greaves: skilful, neat, lovely finisher
Alan Shearer: just in case we need a battering ram, even though I'm not a big fan at international level

Omissions: Both **George Cohen** and **Ray Wilson** were fine full-backs, as was **Roger Byrne** (killed at Munich with Edwards) and **Terry Cooper** and **Gary Neville** (such a smart player). **Johnny Haynes:** beautiful passer, but found wanting at very top on occasions. **Gerrard** is a good player, just hasn't delivered at crucial times, **Hoddle** even more so. One I wanted to include was **Alan Hudson** – two caps? TWO CAPS? Ramsey and Revie deserve jail for that. **Michael Owen** was terrific in his pomp but similar in position and style to Lineker and Greaves, while Shearer was just that bit more potent at his best than **Nat Lofthouse** or **Geoff Hurst**. **Wayne Rooney**? You're having a laugh, aren't you?

Strengths: Excellent defence, good goalscorers
Weaknesses: Tactical deficiencies need addressing, bit lacking in genius in midfield unless Gascoigne is sober

Likely first XI:

Banks
Armfield   Butcher   Moore   Cole
Edwards
Matthews   Robson   Gascoigne   Charlton
Lineker

4.2 WINGERS

A word about wingers. Ramsey became disillusioned with them during this World Cup, and they were a breed who were beginning to be treated with a deal of suspicion.

In the pre-war years wingers had been an integral part of football tactics, especially in the British Isles. Get the ball to the wide man, let him have a little dribble, sling over a cross and the big lad in the middle can kill a few more brain cells nutting a heavy piece of leather. Wingers only scored when their opposite number was the one crossing – they were encouraged to join in and attack the ball beyond the centre-forward.

During the 1920s and 1930s some more innovative coaches would have their winger cut in and try a shot – Cliff Bastin of Arsenal frequently caught defences on the hop by doing this. By the 1950s the best wingers were a more sophisticated breed. Czibor of Hungary could play equally well at inside-forward and would occasionally swap positions with Puskás to fool the defenders. Both Matthews and Finney for England were as adept at slipping clever passes inside to free their forwards as they were at going around their man on the outside; Finney frequently played in the middle, such was the quality of his finishing. The Brazilian Zagallo played deeper than most wingers, augmenting the midfield while his opposite wing, Garrincha, went walkabout. Zagallo perfected the deep, accurate cross from in front of the full-back, obviating the need for pointless dribbling. A precursor of the Beckham-style wide player, if you will.

By the 1960s wingers needed to defend. The widespread use of the defensive *catenaccio* system by Italian and South American teams meant a plethora of attacking full-backs (some of them as fast and skilful as a winger, like Facchetti of Italy) who needed to be watched when the opposition had the ball. No longer could you just let the full-back go and rely on the half-back and full-back to deal with the problem. Players with drive and work rate were needed, and Alf Ramsey, for one, found using men like Alan Ball and Martin Peters, all-round players, more satisfactory than a beat-'em-and-cross-it winger. His tactic was enforced partly by an absence of genuinely talented wide players and partly by an innate suspicion of players with flair. Had he had any one of a number of Scottish wingers at his disposal things may have been different; in an era where England had a dearth, Scotland had Jimmy Johnstone, Charlie Cooke and Eddie Gray.

By the next decade the working winger was a part of most teams, especially in Europe. Steve Coppell was the personification of the wide player in England; hard-working, quick, intelligent and able to defend as well as pass and cross. Other countries boasted similar hybrids. The Pole Grzegorz Lato, ostensibly a winger, was his side's biggest goal threat attacking from a wide position and using his extreme pace (think Cristiano Ronaldo or Bale). The Germans Littbarski and Graboswki, both clever players, combined old-fashioned wing play with link play in an inside-forward position (think Ginola or Waddle). In 1982 the Italians had Bruno Conti, who would play on both wings as a solitary wide player – whichever side he chose the ever-willing striker Graziani would move out to the opposite side. Neither Brazil nor Poland nor West Germany in the latter stages could cope with the movement and flexibility. There were no longer pure wingers, they were too much of a luxury. After Conti, no side fielded a proper winger in a World Cup Final until France started the 2006 Final with Ribéry and Malouda as the wide players in a five-man midfield. The modern system favoured by the big sides demands wide attacking players, but they are the outer prongs in a 4–3–3, and expected to offer an extra dimension than the old-fashioned run-and-cross brigade.

4.3 WORLD CUP 1970

Mexico was awarded the 1970 World Cup in 1964 when the only rivals for the honour, Argentina, pulled out after a doing a deal that saw them granted the 1978 tournament in a similarly uncontested manner. Mexico offered up only five grounds for the tournament, allowing them time to make each as suitable as possible. The principal ground, the magnificent, raucous Azteca Stadium, was already in progress for the 1968 Olympic Games – a convenient economy for the Mexicans. The large Estadio Jalisco in Guadalajara was updated and another near-50,000-capacity ground was built in Puebla (Estadio Cuauhtémoc). The smaller, high-altitude ground at Tolucs would share group duties with Puebla, while the final group would take place in the Estadio Nou Camp in Leon, the most northerly city used.

The division of places, finally, was more equable, as each of Africa, Asia and North America were awarded a place, with Mexico effectively taking one South American place and Europe losing one spot.

Qualifying

Qualification threw up a shock or two. Brazil – forced to undergo the indignity of qualifying for the first time in twelve years – found it remarkably easy. Played six, won six, twenty-three goals scored, two conceded. The centre-forward, Tostão, scored ten of the goals, including two hat-tricks. He was quick and mobile as well as good in the air and strong, but he had just come back from an operation on a detached retina and no one knew whether he

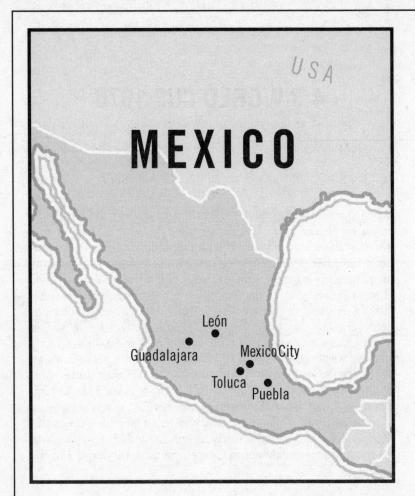

1970
MEXICO

Mexico offered up five large stadia, all in the heavily populated central part of the country.

Mexico City: Estádio Azteca
This huge edifice was begun in 1961 and finished five years later as part of Mexico's plans for the 1968 Olympic Games. It has held innumerable major sporting contests and 107,412 people watched the 1970 World Cup Final inside this overheated cauldron.

Guadalajara: Estádio Jalisco
Another impressive stadium with capacity for over 50,000 spectators, the Jalisco was England's home for the group stages in 1970 and hosted Brazil's semi-final against Uruguay. The city's major club, Guadalajara, left the stadium in 2010 for the newly constructed Omnipan.

Léon: Estádio Nou Camp
Like the Azteca this stadium was built for the Olympic Games and opened in 1967; this was a smaller ground, holding around 24,000.

Puebla: Estádio Cuauhtémoc
Sitting right next door to the city's baseball stadium, the Cuauhtémoc was also built for the Olympics and opened in early 1968. This stadium held 35,000 spectators but wasn't full for its three 1970 group matches.

Toluca: Estádio Luis Dosal
Older than the other stadia used, the Luis Dosal was opened in 1954 and held around 27,000 people. Now known as the Estadio Nemesio Diaz, the ground is known to all and sundry as *La Bombonera*.

would be quite the same player. It should be said that the opposition in the group was less than taxing. The manager who revived the squad's fortunes, a former journalist João Saldanho, was replaced just before the tournament after one more fiery outburst; his successor Mario Zagallo, was looking to be the first man to play in and manage a World Cup-winning team.

Unlike Brazil, Argentina had not such an easy ride, coming up against a tidy Bolivia and the best group of players Peru has ever produced. The first five games in the group were all won by the home team, and Argentina needed a win against Peru in their final match; 2–1 down, they equalised in the eighty-ninth minute, and a scandalous ten minutes of further time was played while they pressed in vain for a winner. It wasn't the last Argentina–Peru match with a bit of an odour to it. On this occasion it was Peru who took their place in the Finals, while Argentina retreated to rebuild their squad. The coach Pedernera, one of the greats of Argentinian football during their years of isolation either side of the Second World War, was sacked with the unenviable record of overseeing the only unsuccessful qualification campaign in Argentinian football history – although another great player, Maradona, almost managed it with a far better squad. England must have been relieved; had they played Argentina in Mexico there would have been scars. Uruguay clinched the last place without conceding a goal to Chile (in a trough) or Ecuador (still finding their way). They only scored five, mind, but that was the Uruguay way in the sixties and seventies. Defend, kick, see what happens.

The fun and games (far from it, actually) took place in the CONCACAF qualification. Four groups produced four semi-finalists; Haiti would play the United States (not such a mismatch as it might appear now), while neighbours El Salvador and Honduras contested the other.

Trouble was brewing between the two; the larger but less populous country, Honduras, had drafted punitive legislation to seize back land from Salvadoran immigrants who propped up the smaller, non-corporate agricultural system in the country's rural areas. Two years later, with the legislation still souring relations between the nations, the countries met in a World Cup qualifier. There was fighting in Tegucigalpa after the first leg (won by

Honduras) and more after the second match a week later in San Salvador. Eleven days later a decisive play-off in Mexico City was won by El Salvador with two late goals deep into extra-time. Whether football passions fanned the flames, who knows, but El Salvador broke off all diplomatic relations with her neighbour immediately, and less than three weeks later troops were massing on the border between the countries. The war lasted only days and a peace was brokered by the Organization of American States, a loose pan-American alliance intended to keep the peace in the region.

El Salvador still had a match to negotiate, and they needed another play-off to see off Haiti, a goal by Juan Ramón Martinez settling the decider in Kingston, Jamaica.

African and Asian qualification passed off relatively peacefully, although the heroes of 1966, North Korea, withdrew in objection to the presence of Israel in their qualifying group – the Israelis played in various qualifying groups to avoid the other Middle Eastern nations before settling in, sensibly, as part of the European zone. The Israelis had their first decent side, and their two best players, Mordechai Spiegler and Giora Spiegel, scored the goals that took them past Australia in the final eliminator. Spiegler, the captain, remains Israel's leading goalscorer. Morocco just pipped Nigeria in a final group of three to clinch the African spot.

In Europe it was largely as you were. Scotland put in some creditable performances, but defeats in their last two away games, one a humdinger in Hamburg, meant they lost out to West Germany. Wales were in a tough threesome with Italy – European Champions in 1968 – and East Germany; nul points for a weak Wales team. Both Wales and East Germany were savaged by Italy's star striker, the fast, aggressive Luigi "Gigi" Riva, who scored seven times in the four games. Northern Ireland also had a tough gig and were unable to get past the Soviet Union, especially with George Best missing for the crucial away tie.

In the other three-team group France blew their chance with a home defeat to Norway, allowing Sweden unencumbered passage. The goal by Odd Iversen gave Norway their best competitive win to date. The Swedes' centre-forward Ove Kindvall netted six times in the three matches he played and came to the Finals high on confidence after scoring the winner for Feyenoord against Celtic in the European Cup Final. Bulgaria came through a tough group that included Poland and Holland by winning their home games and getting a point in Amsterdam courtesy of Hristo Bonev's goal. Both Holland and Poland were entering a decade of unprecedented success, but this qualification came too soon.

In the European Group 1 the favourites Portugal managed to finish last in the group. Portugal relied on a generation of fading stars, and they weren't up to the challenge. The key results came in the spring of 1969 when Romania fought hard for a point in Athens and won in Switzerland; when they beat Portugal later that year they were as good as through. Hungary were another team whose fading stars couldn't earn them a place after they finished level on points with Czechoslovakia (and would have won through if goal average or difference had counted). The play-off in Marseilles swung on a disputed penalty at the end of the first half for Czechoslovakia; a flurry of second-half goals saw the Czechs go through comfortably – the fourth team from the Communist East to qualify.

Yugoslavia, the European Championship finalists from 1968, were expected to be the fifth, but they had to get through easily the toughest group, which included Spain, Belgium, improving fast, and Finland. Finland, like Norway, took a good scalp with a 2–0 home win over Spain, and, while Spain took points off Yugoslavia, Belgium won all their home games and did well to draw in Madrid. An early goal from Johann Devrindt set the stage for a Spanish siege, but it only yielded a solitary goal in reply. Devrindt then scored twice in the return to put Belgium in the box seat. Yugoslavia's 4–0 defeat of Belgium came too late as placings in the group were already decided and the Belgians put in an appearance at the Finals for the first time since 1954. The Belgium team was built around the Anderlecht side that dominated their domestic football at the time – in a 1964 international against Holland the entire Belgian side was made up of Anderlecht players after the coach brought on their goalkeeper as a substitute. The World Cup squad had eight from Anderlecht and seven from their closest rivals Standard Liège. They were regarded as the tournament's dark horses by many pundits.

Finals

In the heat of Mexico, Brazil were the favourites for the 1970 World Cup, although many European journalists, including some who should have known better, thought they lacked the heart for the campaign. Memories were still strong of an all-European semi-final line-up in 1966, and the best of the competition would come from the European sides. Since winning the trophy four years previously England had been beaten only four times; by Brazil, Scotland (famously in 1967), West Germany (for the first time in the history of matches between the two) and Yugoslavia, in the 1968 European Championship semi-final. Add West Germany and European Champions Italy for the main threats to a gifted but defensively suspect Brazil.

I mentioned heat. It was a major factor. This was the first World Cup where games were scheduled for the convenience of TV channels rather than players or live spectators. It is a common problem now, and coaches take precautions to deal with it, but in 1970 nutritional science was more basic, and slow-release salt tablets were all players had to combat midday heat in the high thirties. It nullified some major performers, and led to numerous cases of serious dehydration and sunstroke – there were reports of players losing half a stone during a game.

The format was the same as in 1966, but this time two substitutes were allowed per game

GROUP 1

Mexico	**(0) 0**	**USSR**	**(0) 0**	31 May, Azteca St; 107,160
Belgium	**(1) 3**	**El Salvador** (0) 0		3 June, Azteca St; 92,205
Van Moer 8, 55, Lambert 79 (p)				
USSR	**(1) 4**	**Belgium**	**(0) 1**	6 June, Azteca St; 95,261
Byshovets 14, 63, Asatiani 57, Khmelnitsky 75		Lambert 86		
Mexico	**(1) 4**	**El Salvador** (0) 0		7 June, Azteca St; 103,058
Valdivia 44, 47, Fragoso 58, Basaguren 81				
USSR	**(0) 2**	**El Salvador** (0) 0		10 June, Azteca St; 25,000
Byshovets 51, 73				
Mexico	**(1) 1**	**Belgium**	**(0) 0**	11 June, Azteca St; 108,192
Peña 15 (p)				

1. **USSR** 5pts (6–1); 2. **Mexico** 5pts (5–0); 3. **Belgium** 2pts (4–5); 4. **El Salvador** 0pts (0–9)

The opener in the top group, the last opening game for a while to feature the host country rather than the holders, was the usual stinker, Mexico and the USSR cancelling each other out. The German referee was hard on some of the Soviet tackling, but equally censorious of some of the play-acting by the Mexicans, which augured well after the excesses of 1966. In the other opening game – three days later, oddly – Belgium easily beat El Salvador, who looked way out of their depth.

El Salvador were better against Mexico, but were undone by an odd goal. Referee Kandil (woeful throughout the match) clearly awarded a free-kick to El Salvador on the right touchline and the players started moving back towards the Mexican half. When the ball was knocked back onto the field, the Mexican left-back Mario Pérez cheekily took the kick and played the ball up the line to Padilla. Instead of bringing play back and telling Pérez to stop playing silly buggers, the referee just waved his arms pathetically and allowed Padilla to cross the ball into the middle, where Valdivia scored after Borja missed the ball completely. Play to the whistle, fine, but there was nothing ambiguous about the initial decision, it was El Salvador's free-kick. The second half was a rout as El Salvador lost the plot, but the game turned on that incident as they looked comfortable for the first half and Mexico were short of creativity. In the other match the USSR surprised many by completely outplaying Belgium. Belgium suffered more than most in the heat, certainly more than the super-fit Soviets, and their touted forward line just didn't deliver, especially their respected playmaker Van Himst; he, and his team, fared better in the European Championships two years later, finishing third. Early on, Semmeling's header was cleared off the line and Van Moer drove the follow-up against the bar, but that was it for Belgium. The Soviets took over the game, with Shesternev imperious at the back and Byshovets and Muntian running the Belgian defence ragged.

Byshovets scored twice, with a low daisy-cutter into the corner and an unsaveable left-footer thrashed into the top corner after Shesternev broke up a Belgian attack and released him down the right – a brilliant goal. Asatiani cut in from the left, turned his marker and slotted the ball across the face of the goal and in off the post for the second and Khmelnitsky completed the scoring with a clever diving header after feeding Evryuzhikin and moving for the return. Now the USSR looked the dark horses while Belgium had to beat Mexico. It was never going to happen, and an awful game was settled when the Argentinian referee gave a penalty even though Jeck clearly hooked the ball away from Valdivia. Perhaps he was confused and thought Fragoso was refereeing the game – the Mexican No.21 did a complete mime show to help him along, whistle to the mouth, point to the spot, loud applause when Señor Coerezza gets it right. The Mexicans were through but this was the worst team to contest the last eight in a World Cup Finals tournament. Byshovets added a couple more as the Soviets cruised past El Salvador; the Ukrainian was looking one of the best forwards in the tournament and his Dynamo Kyiv colleague Muntian one of the better creative players. Unfortunately for both, the Uruguayans had noticed.

GROUP 2

Uruguay	(1) 2	**Israel**	(0) 0	2 June, Puebla; 20,654
Maneiro 22, Mújica 51				
Italy	(1) 1	**Sweden**	(0) 0	3 June, Toluca; 13,433
Domenghini 10				
Italy	(0) 0	**Uruguay**	(0) 0	6 June, Puebla; 29,968
Israel	(0) 1	**Sweden**	(0) 1	7 June, Toluca; 9,624
Spiegler 57		Turesson 54		
Sweden	(0) 1	**Uruguay**	(0) 0	10 June, Puebla; 18,163
Grahn				
Israel	(0) 0	**Italy**	(0) 0	11 June, Toluca; 9,860

1. Italy 4pts (1–0); 2. Uruguay 3pts (2–1); 3. Sweden 3pts (2–2); 4. Israel 2pts (1–3)

A group containing Italy and Uruguay, past masters of doing just enough, was never going to be exciting. The other teams, functional, hardworking, uninspired Sweden and the debutants Israel, were hardly likely to bring us an attacking fiesta either. No blame attached to Israel – they did well, drawing twice, once with Sweden when Spiegler scored a long-range belter, and once with a comatose Italy, who had already qualified for the last eight. Italy and Uruguay drew 0–0 – colour me stunned! – and Domenghini's early goal got Italy past Sweden, who never looked likely to breach the *Azzurri* wall. Sweden scored a late winner to beat Uruguay, but they needed to win by two.

The great debate in the Italian media was which of the two great playmakers to include. Coach Valcareggi was inclined towards Inter's Sandro Mazzola, a more all-round, disciplined player than his rival, the silky, creative Gianni Rivera of Milan. Up front Riva's partner was the inexperienced Robert Boninsegna of Internazionale, winning only his second cap in the first game against Sweden. It paid off as Boninsegna's fitness and work-rate benefited Riva, who struggled to put in the miles in the heat and was able to better conserve his energy with the unselfish Boninsegna in the side.

Uruguay's coach, Juan Eduardo Hohberg, who played in the 1954 World Cup, would have liked a choice of playmaker – his own, Pedro Rocha, was in the squad but injured and never got on the pitch. This only served to cement the tactics the Uruguayans would have adopted anyway; sit deep, kick the ball or any player who gets near the penalty area and counter-attack with caution. Six goals, six games – goals aren't everything but this was cautious fare.

GROUP 3

England Hurst	**(0) 1**	**Romania**	**(0) 0**	2 June, Guadalajara; 50,560
Brazil Rivelino 24, Pelé 59, Jairzinho 64, 82	**(1) 4**	**Czechoslovakia** Petrás 12	**(1) 1**	3 June, Guadalajara; 52,897
Romania Neagu 53, Dumitrache 78 (p)	**(0) 2**	**Czechoslovakia** Petrás 3	**(1) 1**	6 June, Guadalajara; 56,818
Brazil Jairzinho 62	**(0) 1**	**England**	**(0) 0**	7 June, Guadalajara; 79,950
Brazil Pelé 19, 66, Jairzinho 21	**(2) 3**	**Romania** Dumitrache 33, Dembrowski 82	**(1) 2**	10 June, Guadalajara; 50,804
England Clarke 48 (p)	**(0) 1**	**Czechoslovakia**	**(0) 0**	11 June, Guadalajara; 49,292

1. **Brazil 6pts (8–3)**; 2. **England 4pts (2–1)**; 3. **Romania 2pts (4–5)**; 4. **Czechoslovakia 0pts (2–7)**

England knew they would be facing Brazil a full twelve months before the tournament, even before they played them in a very competitive friendly in Rio in the summer of '69 (*how very Bryan Adams*). That summer tour was a sensible attempt by England to get used to South American playing conditions and they added a couple more games in the lead-up to the actual tournament. They probably wished they had avoided going to Colombia.

It was while staying in the Colombian capital, Bogotá, that England encountered the most bizarre pre-tournament experience, an incident that made David Beckham's metatarsal look like . . . well, a toe injury. Staying in a nice hotel in the middle of the city, Bobby Moore and his friend Alan Mullery were wandering aimlessly around the shops in the foyer. They sauntered out of the Fuego Verde jewellery shop back into the lobby, and were mightily surprised when the shop owner followed them, demanding an explanation as to the whereabouts of a missing bracelet. The police were called, there was a furore, and Alf Ramsey had to be called to try to smooth things over. Initially it seemed the incident was forgotten, and England's mini tour continued – successfully – with victories over Colombia and Ecuador.

It was when England returned to Bogotá on their way to Mexico that the second, more serious wave of trouble started. Police burst into the England meeting room and arrested Moore – it became apparent that a witness had come forward claiming he saw Moore take the bracelet. It was a popular scam in Colombia; accuse a tourist of a crime and then extort money as the only means of making the problem go away. Moore was held for four days, although he was allowed to train while in captivity. In the end the judiciary found no case to answer, but only after intense diplomatic pressure and after the Colombian press turned against the prosecution, affected partly, it is claimed, by Moore's charming demeanour and great dignity.

It was all a bit surreal, with the most unlikely "criminal" at the heart of it. Lesser men may have buckled, if that was part of the intention – CIA involvement is one particularly paranoid suggestion, but isn't it always? Not Moore, he returned to the camp and what could have been an unsettling situation was turned into a means of celebration.

At home there had been one or two calls for Moore, whose domestic form had dipped, to be left out, mainly from Leeds manager Don Revie – a man as paranoid and labyrinthine in his reasoning as the CIA. Revie's suggested replacement, Norman Hunter, was a shadow of Moore, a destructive player with none of the ease on the ball and unhurried distribution required at the top level. Apart from Moore, Alf Ramsey had changed his back four; Jack Charlton was in the squad at thirty-five, but as back-up to the Everton captain Brian Labone, while the new full-backs were Keith Newton and Terry Cooper, both high-quality players. Alan Mullery, a much better footballer, was fulfilling the Stiles role as the marking midfielder; he had done his job a little over-zealously against Yugoslavia in the European Championships, and was the first England player to be sent off in an international. Mullery amusingly reports that, although he escaped the expected censure from Ramsey – he was always loyal to his charges – he certainly got it in the ear from his wife and mother!

The five attacking players were largely the same, with Roger Hunt replaced by the more mobile Manchester City striker Francis Lee. Lee's club colleague Colin Bell, renowned for his stamina and power, was a more than handy midfield substitute.

The group was played at the lowest elevation of any of the cities used, but the heat was stifling and took its toll before England's first game, when Romania's young midfield star Nicolae Dobrin succumbed to heatstroke and was flown home. Without him Romania resorted to cynical, defensive tactics, in spite of their star forward Florea Dumitrache's boast that he would score twice. Alan Ball's provocative and graphic reminder of that boast after England won the game 1–0 was unnecessary, but you could see his point after some horrible tackling went unpunished – shades of 1966 that happily did not manifest again in the competition. Hurst scored the goal just after the hour when he took down a cross from Ball expertly, turned his man and scuffed a shot past the sprawling Adamache. England would have to play Brazil without right-back Keith Newton after a shocking tackle from Mocanu – a straight red in any era, it was legalised GBH.

If there were doubts about the Brazilian defence, they resurfaced in the opening fifteen minutes against Czechoslovakia when twice Ladislav Petrás exposed their lack of concentration. First he burst past Brito and then skipped another challenge as he was allowed to run along the goal-line, cut back and send a shot whistling over the bar. With ten minutes gone he caught Clodoaldo in possession and beat Brito again, this time finishing better with a clip past Felix. Petrás's second match was going better than his first, which ended prematurely when he was sent off. Later in the half Carlos Alberto played a suicidal pass inside, which Fran Vesely seized on – the Czech striker delayed his shot and could only chip over the bar.

Brazil were level by then, a Rivelino free-kick bending viciously past the wall while never getting above knee high. Unstoppable. Pre-tournament predictions that the ball would fly in the rarefied air were being borne out. One of the tournament's defining moments came just before half-time when Pelé spotted Viktor off his line and tried a shot from inside his own half. It scraped past the post to the obvious relief of the backpedalling Czech custodian. As Cris Freddi points out, it has been done since (take a bow, David), but Pelé was the first with the audacity to try. And this was no mug goalkeeper (I would have fancied scoring past Félix, the Brazil goalkeeper), Ivo Viktor was acknowledged as his country's best until Petr Cech came along, and he had already made one brilliant save from Tostão.

Czechoslovakia kept trying, but chasing guys with this level of technique and ball retention was a task and a half in that heat. Petrás created a good chance for Vesely just after half-time but he couldn't finish and soon the one-way traffic towards the Czech goal resumed. Chances went begging and Gérson hit the base of the post with a left-foot shot. The same left foot spotted a late run from Pelé with a superb lob, the master controlled it on his chest and volleyed past Viktor. Olé. Even in the lead Brazil made basic errors – Adamec's short corner caught them napping and the experienced Kvasnák should have done better than hook over the bar from five yards out. It was their last sniff, as Brazil increased their lead with their next attack, Jairzinho running clear and lifting the ball over Viktor before smashing joyously home. Jairzinho had played a little deeper in the second half, to get more of the ball and run at tiring defenders, and now he caught the Czechs out by getting beyond the forwards. He added another late on when he rode a couple of tackles and fired across the goalkeeper. Jairzinho never seemed to have the ball completely under control, and he tended to go through rather than round defenders, but he took as much stopping as his predecessor – Brazil were no longer missing Garrincha.

It was the Czechs in this group who suffered most from the heat. They lost their next match to Romania after taking the lead again through Petrás, and lost a poor game to England 1–0 with a debatable penalty converted by Allan Clarke on his international debut. He was ever a cheeky one. England had expended a lot of energy against Brazil, and supine opposition like the already eliminated Czechs suited them fine, and meant they could rest Ball, Hurst and Lee and rely on the defence. Which is what happened, so a bit harsh to carp. But it was an awful game. The day before saw another sumptuous attacking performance by Brazil as well as another shaky defensive one. Dumitrache got his goal for Romania (he also scored a penalty against Czechoslovakia) when the Brazilian defence let him wander through. He later missed a sitter that would have made it 3–3 and went home with few believing he was as good as he said he was. Pelé belted in a free-kick and Paulo César, in for Rivelino, made a second for Jairzinho before Dumitrache pegged one back. Pelé added a second, but the Brazilian reserve defenders looked even less assured than the first team and Romania gave them some nervy moments, pulling one back through Dembrowski's header.

Oh, missed a game. Silly me. It was a classic.

WORLD CUP CLASSIC No.6
7 June 1970, Jalisco Stadium, Guadalajara; 70,950

Brazil	(0) 1	Jairzinho 62
England	(0) 0	

Referee: **Avraham Klein** (Israel)
Coaches: **Mário Zagallo** (Brazil) & **Alf Ramsey** (England)

Brazil (4–4–1–1): Félix *Miélli Venerando* (Fluminense); Carlos Alberto *Torres* (Cpt, Santos), Everaldo *Marques* (Grêmio), Wilson Piazza (Cruzeiro), Hercules Brito (Flamengo); *Jair Ventura, known as* Jairzinho (Botafogo), Clodoaldo *Tavares* (Santos), Gérson *de Oliveira*, Roberto Rivelino (Corinthians); *Edson do Nascimento, known as* Pelé (Santos); *Eduardo Gonçalves,* known as Tostão (Cruzeiro). **Subs:** Roberto *Miranda* (Botafogo) 68m, for Tostão

England (4–3–1–2): Gordon Banks (Stoke City); Tommy Wright (Everton), Brian Labone (Everton), Bobby Moore (Cpt, West Ham United), Terry Cooper (Leeds United); Alan Ball (Everton), Alan Mullery (Tottenham Hotspur), Martin Peters (Tottenham); Bobby Charlton (Manchester Utd); Francis Lee (Manchester City), Geoff Hurst (West Ham). **Subs:** Jeff Astle (West Bromwich Albion) 64m, for Lee; Colin Bell (Man City) 64m, for Charlton **Cautioned:** Lee (Eng) 30m

Possibly England's finest performance in a World Cup Finals match, including the year they won. The discipline was tremendous; solid lines, no diving in to tackle like the Czechs and Romanians, good composure. At the heart of it was Moore at the back and Mullery just in front of the defence. Time after time Brazilian attacks broke down as one of these two tackled or intercepted; one last-ditch tackle to dispossess Jairzinho by Moore was uncanny in its precision. Labone stuck diligently to Tostão, and Ball scampered around the midfield with his usual extraordinary energy.

Brazil were, quite simply, brilliant. Much better than against Czechoslovakia or Romania, their concentration honed by the knowledge that this was a key game, and winning it meant almost certainly avoiding the dangerous West Germans in León. When Brazil broke through the defence, it wasn't because of errors or poor positioning, but through individual skill, or mesmerising passing. The goal came from a piece of persistence from Tostão, refusing to concede possession and bustling his way through to get in a cross. Pelé controlled it and, under challenge from Cooper, immediately slipped it to Jairzinho, who made no mistake from six yards.

The goal came just past the hour, after a sustained period of Brazilian pressure that drained the England midfield. Banks made one superb stop from a Rivelino thunderbolt and did ever so well to clear outside his area as Jairzinho ran through. Neither save was his best. That came in the first half when a Jairzinho cross found Pelé and the master's downward header was scooped over the bar by the England No.1. It was a thumping header and the ball was virtually past Banks when he got his palm to it – incredible agility and strength.

Even when they went behind England responded with great courage. Ramsey made a planned substitution, and Bobby Charlton – Sir Bob was thirty-two now and struggling to last ninety minutes in the conditions – gave way to Bell, while Jeff Astle came on for Lee. Astle was a successful goalscorer for West Bromwich Albion, but his touch was not good enough for this level – Clarke or Chelsea's Peter Osgood would have been a better bet but neither was on the bench here.

England varied their attack, mixing the patient approach they had favoured so far with longer balls so Hurst and Astle could test the suspect goalkeeper; Astle should have gone for goal from one long cross from Mullery rather than head back towards Ball. He missed England's best chance a few minutes later, ramming the ball wide when it broke to him off Everaldo's shin – more comedy defending from Brazil. Late on Bobby Moore created another opening with a deep cross, which reached Alan Ball via a Brazilian hand – Ball sent the ball whizzing back in but it clipped the top of the bar.

Defeat with glory and not out of the competition; England could reflect on the fact that they had not been completely outclassed by Brazil and had the players to ask questions of their far-from-perfect defence and amateurish goalkeeper. There was confidence within the squad – with justification – that no one in the tournament held any fear for them and they would be playing Brazil again two weeks later.

Pelé swapping shirts with the peerless Moore at the end of the game remains an indelible image, one of the most famous football pictures. Two great players acknowledging mutual respect: Pelé was the greatest player the game has known, Moore had just given the greatest defensive performance in history. Pelé later admitted that England were the only side in the tournament who held any terrors for Brazil.

GROUP 4

Peru	(0) 3	**Bulgaria**	(1) 2	2 June, León; 13,765
Gallardo 51, Chumpitaz 56, Cubillas 74		Dermendijev 13, Bonev 49		
West Germany	(0) 2	**Morocco**	(1) 1	3 June, León; 12,942
Seeler 56, Müller 78		Houmane 22		
Peru	(0) 3	**Morocco**	(0) 0	6 June, León; 13,537
Cubillas 65, 76, Challe 70				
West Germany	(2) 5	**Bulgaria**	(1) 2	7 June, León, 12,710
Libuda 19, Müller 27, 52 (p), 88, Seeler 69		Nikodimov 12, Kolev 89		

West Germany	(3) 3	**Peru**	(1) 1	10 June, León; 17.875	
Müller 19, 27, 38		Cubillas 44			
Bulgaria	(1) 1	**Morocco**	(0) 1	11 June, León 12,299	
Zhechev 39		Ghazouani 59			

West Germany had the easiest group of the favourites. Morocco gave them a scare by taking a first-half lead, but the Germans dug in and scored twice in the second half. The winner came from the new centre-forward Gerd Müller, a team-mate of Beckenbauer at Bayern Munich, whose rivalry with Borussia Mönchengladbach would dominate the Bundesliga for the next decade and provide West Germany with the bulk of their side. The other came from Uwe Seeler, who scored in his fourth World Cup (as did Pelé, setting a record they still share). Seeler, now a veteran in years as well as appearance, had lost a yard and Schön cannily moved him back into midfield where his strength and experience would count.

Peru kicked off the group with a cracker against Bulgaria. Two days before Peru had been rocked by a massive earthquake that caused huge landslides and eventually claimed more than 20,000 lives. The players were told to stay and play to give the people something to cheer. They did just that, recovering from a rocky start to win well.

Both Bulgarian goals came from free-kicks, the first a well-rehearsed set piece that played in Dermendjiev and the second a vicious swerver from Bonev that slipped through Rubiños' hands. Peru had played well, their passing neat and clever – a younger, smaller version of Brazil – but they overplayed in the final third and were suspect in defence where the captain Héctor Chumpitaz looked a much better player with the ball at his own feet than his opponents'. Within eight minutes of Bulgaria's second, Peru were level, showing commendable spirit and no little skill. First Gallardo crashed a shot in from a tight angle after Leon held off a stiff challenge, then young substitute Hugo Sotil was brought down on the edge of the area. The Peruvians lined up at the end of the Bulgarian wall – an unfamiliar tactic in 1970 – and Chumpitaz crashed his free-kick straight through them and into the corner.

Bulgaria were wilting and Peru kept coming, looking for a winner. When it came it was special. Teófilo Cubillas was only twenty-one and already a world-class player with superb close control and a powerful shot. He received the ball in a crowd of players from Ramon Mifflin, waited, played a one-two with the advancing Mifflin, then veered to the right, taking out two retreating defenders; another touch took him past the last man and he fired a low, hard shot past Simeonov. Cubillas added two more in the next match as Peru strolled past Morocco – they should have won by a hatful, not 3–0.

The rather lumpen German performance against Morocco prompted Schön to drop the experienced Held and Haller, and pick Löhr of Cologne alongside Müller. He also introduced the winger Reinhard Libuda of Schalke, a renowned speed merchant. The latter change was crucial; in the next match Libuda ran Bulgaria ragged as West Germany again recovered from conceding an early goal to win 5–2, with a hat-trick from Müller. Bulgaria wilted again in the second half – they, like Belgium, did not acclimatise well. Peru, too, were Müllered, two tap-ins and a header sealing a first-half hat-trick for the predatory striker. West Germany won the group, avoided Brazil and got instead … England, the old enemy, the nemesis.

QUARTER-FINALS (all 14 June)

Uruguay	(0) (0) 1	**USSR**	(0) (0) 0	Azteca, Mexico City; 96,085*	
Espárrago 118					
Italy	(1) 4	**Mexico**	(1) 1	Dosal, Toluca; 26,851	
Own goal 25,		González			
Riva 63, 76, Rivera 70					
Brazil	(2) 4	**Peru**	(1) 2	Jalisco, Guadalajara; 54,233	
Rivelino 11, Tostão 15, 52,		Gallardo 27,			
Jairzinho 75		Cubillas 68			

The main stadium in Mexico City had the misfortune to host Uruguay against the USSR, which didn't have the feel of a classic and wasn't. Nearly two hours of repetitive fouling and nine men behind the ball mercifully ended by Espárrago's late, disputed goal. Evidence proved the referee was right and the Soviets paid for their caution. It was hoped Uruguay wouldn't be able to repeat the success of their defensive tactics in the next round against Brazil; they kicked Muntian and Byshovets out of the

---

* Yeah, right; lucky if there was half that number.

game – not that the USSR were above putting in the odd hair-raising tackle. Uruguay were a tough side, but they never got out of control as they had in 1966 and their defence was mightily impressive, marshalled by their unheralded captain Luis Ubiña and shielded by the tenacious marker Montero, father of Paolo Montero, a quality international centre-half of the next generation.

Brazil 4 Peru 2 sounds like it might have been a ripper, and in fairness to Peru they were good enough going forward to test Brazil at the back. But their own defending was execrable and they could have conceded ten. Pelé had already hit the post when Rivelino opened the scoring from Tostão's lay-off – Tostão was gifted the ball by a nonsensical attempt to chest the ball down by Peruvian right-back Campos. Rivelino made a tricky finish look simple with a ground shot of pinpoint accuracy. The second goal was a disaster for Peru – you just didn't give this Brazilian team a two-goal start. A short corner routine between Tostão and Rivelino left the centre-forward free on the left-hand side; seeing the full-back leave the post to come and tackle him, and the goalkeeper in a nothing position, Tostão simply whacked the ball between the defenders and the post – schoolboy stuff.

The Brazilians were playing at walking place, conserving energy – Pelé had barely broken sweat in the tournament except against England. Maybe they got complacent, because Peru's first goal came out of the blue. A long ball from Chumpitaz found Gallardo charging down the left. Carlos Alberto put in a feeble challenge that the winger rode, and Felix made a complete hash of the shot from an impossible angle, all but throwing it over his shoulder into the goal. Risible defending. There was time before the break for more comedy goalkeeping from Rubiños in the Peru goal; he flapped like a seal at a tame shot from Pelé, watched it bounce out of his hands onto the post and then nearly carried it over the line as he dived, panic-stricken, on the rebound. He did better with a low save from Rivelino, and recovered in time to grab the rebound as a defender almost kneed it over the line.

At the start of the second half Brazilian forwards (and the odd defender) were queuing up to get on the scoresheet. Pelé was allowed to wander between two defenders to take a pass from Jairzinho and cross – the ball was going nowhere until a retreating defender deflected it to Tostão, who had an open goal. He nearly missed.

Cubillas pulled one back again with a thumping volley after the ball rebounded to him as Sotil was tackled, but Brazil looked like they could score if they needed to, and they did, six minutes later, when Jairzinho latched on to Rivelino's pitching wedge through ball and rounded the 'keeper. Brazil's possession and tricks and skill levels were outstanding, but really, Peru's defending would have shamed a pub team. They had the consolation of winning the fair play award for not receiving any cautions or red cards.

There was optimism in Mexico that their team could reach the semi-final, particularly as Italy had been uninspired thus far. The hosts played their quarter-final at the extreme altitude of Toluca, but it didn't help them. Denied the 100,000+ support that a game in Mexico City would have given them, they surrendered tamely to Italy, despite taking the lead with a well-worked early goal. Italy were level after twenty-five minutes when Domenghini's show was deflected past Calderon, who was slow to react to the change of direction, and slow again in the second half when a precise but underhit shot from Gigi Riva went across him into the corner. Italy were much improved in the second half when Gianni Rivera replaced Sandro Mazzola – the substitution was billed as a compromise by coach Valcareggi to pacify advocates of both players. Surely a coach wouldn't position his best players on such a flimsy basis? In this game it just seemed logical to have the more attacking player on the field – it paid off as Rivera and Riva pulled the Mexican defence all over the place. Rivera finished off a period of sustained pressure with a well-placed shot, and Riva banged the final nail in the fourth corner when he was given two bites after being put clear, and tucked away the second opportunity. Easy, and much more impressive from the reigning European Champions. The remaining quarter-final was far from easy, especially if you were an England fan.

WORLD CUP CLASSIC No.7
14 June 1970, Guanajuato, Léon; 23,357

West Germany (0) (2) 3   Beckenbauer 67, Seeler 82, Müller 109
England (1) (2) 2   Mullery 32, Peters 50

Referee: **Angel Norberto Coerezza** (Argentina)
Coaches: **Helmut Schön** (West Germany) & **Alf Ramsey** (England)

West Germany (4–3–3): Sepp Maier (Bayern Munich); Berti Vogts (Borussia Mönchengladbach), Klaus Fichtel (Schalke 04), Karl-Heinz Schnellinger (AC Milan), Horst Höttges (Werder Bremen); Franz Beckenbauer (Bayern Munich), Uwe Seeler (Cpt, Hamburg), Wolfgang Overath (Cologne); Reinhard Libuda (Schalke 04), Gerd Müller (Bayern Munich), Hannes Löhr (Cologne). **Subs:** Willi Schulz (Hamburg) for Höttges, 45m; Jürgen Grabowski (Eintracht Frankfurt) for Libuda, 57m
England (4–3–1–2): Peter Bonetti (Chelsea); Keith Newton (Everton), Brian Labone (Everton), Bobby Moore (Cpt, West Ham United), Terry Cooper (Leeds United); Alan Ball (Everton), Alan Mullery (Tottenham Hotspur), Martin Peters (Tottenham); Bobby Charlton (Manchester United); Francis Lee (Manchester City), Geoff Hurst (West Ham). **Subs:** Colin Bell (Man City) for Charlton, 70m; Norman Hunter (Leeds) for Peters, 81m
Cautioned: Lee (Eng) 10m; Müller (WGer) 18m

"Back home, they'll be watching and waiting and cheering every move." So went the England team's pre-tournament sing-a-long, a monster No.1 chart hit.

They were certainly cheering the first part of this match; for an hour West Germany probably wished they had drawn Brazil. England were outstanding, the Germans muted. In midfield Ball and Mullery dominated in the centre, making Seeler look his age for the first time, meantime Francis Lee was dragging German defenders all over the pitch while they frantically looked around to see where the dreaded Hurst was lurking.

The first goal was a cracker, Mullery, Lee and Newton interchanging beautifully before Mullery finished the move at the near post – his only England goal. The second was a typical Martin Peters effort, finding space at the far post to force home another right-wing cross from Newton.

Franz Beckenbauer had a muted first hour. He had painful memories of the 1966 Final to contend with, when his shadowing of Bobby Charlton neutered his attacking instincts. Here the roles were reversed, as Ramsey instructed Charlton to cleverly return the favour – it had unnerved Beckenbauer and the two cancelled each other out again.

Ramsey's critics point to his poor substitutions, but West Germany scored while Charlton was still on the field. The introduction of Grabowski for Libuda had an instant effect. The winger, not as quick as Libuda but a clever dribbler who liked to show his opponent the ball, was the sort of player Cooper hated, and the England full-back, who had covered a lot of ground, was forced to sit back and watch his man. England dropped deeper and the penalty area was crowded when Beckenbauer, free for once, tried a shot. There was no alarm as Francis Lee got in a good block, and Beckenbauer's strike at the rebound with his weaker foot was far from clean. Bonetti was partly unsighted by the extra defenders; he went down late and the ball crept under him.

England responded by replacing Charlton with Bell – a pre-planned substitution that made perfect sense; preserve the older man's legs for a tough game three days later. And Colin Bell was ideal for these circumstances, a fit, strong ball-carrier. Soon after West Germany scored he produced a lung-bursting run and cross for Hurst to narrowly miss with a diving header.

The substitution of Peters with Norman Hunter after eighty minutes made no sense at all; Peters wasn't near his best, but it left England with precious little fire-power should extra-time beckon. Hunter, nicknamed "Bites-Yer-Legs", was a footsoldier, offering defensive cover but scant creativity. Much more practical would have been Wright, a more defensively minded full-back, for the exhausted Cooper.

A minute later West Germany equalised; opinions differ on whether Seeler meant to loop a backward header over Bonetti (who was blameless whether the goal was inspired or flukey), or whether he was merely flicking the ball on for Müller and got lucky.

England looked very tired and demoralised in extra-time; Ramsey's exhortations didn't have the same effect as in 1966. Müller latched on to a Löhr knock-down to volley athletically past Bonetti – who wouldn't be the first goalkeeper to be surprised by the power the striker could generate with both feet off the ground. The cross came from Grabowski, who was walking around a knackered Cooper. Even after this heartbreaking setback, England mustered what they thought was an equaliser of their own, but Hurst's conversion of Lee's cross was disallowed by referee Coerezza for no obvious reason. Maybe he thought it was balancing the global karma for '66, both for West Germany and his Argentinian countrymen. Or maybe he was just a dismal referee.

The press largely got the game wrong – surprise, surprise. No, England shouldn't have played wingers; Ramsey had a tried and trusted system that worked well for the country's best players – no point picking a winger if none was worth his place. No, England shouldn't have played Alex Stepney, Bonetti was a better goalkeeper. The Chelsea goalkeeper was only playing because Gordon Banks had gone down with an upset stomach. (I give only these incidental parentheses to the conspiracy theories that talk of Banks being poisoned.) He carried the can (along with Ramsey) in the media and with the fans for this defeat, but that's an absurd over-simplification. Brian Labone was at least as culpable for the last goal, and Ramsey missed an opportunity to give Bonetti a run-out in one of the two pre-tournament friendlies in South America. Bonetti had only six caps in four years, all of them ending in England victories. And no, England shouldn't have kept Charlton on – imagine if they had won in extra-time and the playmaker had been unfit for the semi-final. If Ramsey made a mistake it was in filling his squad with perspiration not inspiration. Mullery, Stiles, Hunter and Hughes were all hardworking players with a similar style and this left him short of attacking options on the bench other than out-and-out forwards.

The legacy of the game was huge. England were shell-shocked (Ramsey: "*It was unreal, like a freak of nature.*") and would suffer a hangover from this match whenever they played Germany for the next forty years (and counting), one extraordinary night in Munich apart. It was twelve years before they appeared in a World Cup Finals tournament again, and only for a brief period in the 1990s have they shed the risk-averse tactics espoused by Ramsey and his successors.

In Germany the game was a great escape; a courageous comeback with a stroke of good fortune. Beckenbauer later acknowledged that the team had as good as given up on the game before his speculative strike, so comprehensively were they outplayed for the first hour. Little did they know they had another epic to come.

No one should be surprised that West Germany came back from the dead to win this game, they make a habit of it. Twelve times in World Cup Finals encounters the Germans have conceded a lead and still won the game – not including the semi-final against France in 1982 when they were 3–1 down in extra-time and still won the tie on penalties. Even when the cause is seemingly lost the Germans keep playing and maintain their discipline and at least a show of self-belief. The same drive and refusal to bow is what led them to three successive World Cup Finals between 1982 and 1990 with the most ordinary teams. The extraordinary 5–1 defeat by England in 2001 remains the only time in living memory that a German side has truly wilted in the face of the opposition – that it remains one of only two defeats in qualifying matches is a truer reflection of their irresistibility.

It seems unfair to pick out Germany as the "comeback kings" when Brazil have overturned a deficit on fourteen occasions, but it is a different story with Brazil. Like Germany, Brazil have a swagger and a presumption of victory, but it is coupled with an inclination to take inferior opponents lightly, which often results in concession of the first goal – like the Australian cricket team in their turn-of-the-century heyday, they were only vulnerable when they assumed they would win. Brazilian teams have (almost) always been more talented than their opponents and so able to move up a gear when required; that has not always been the case with Germany, who have had to rely on drive and willpower to combat more creative opponents.

The closest another side has come to enjoying a similar repu-tation to Germany for resolve and fortitude when down was Uruguay in their early days, resorting to their mythical *garra* to spur them on. Alas it is something England have sorely lacked in World Cup competition; only twice have they overturned a defi-cit, once in the 1966 Final and again in 1990 when they went 2–1 down to Cameroon in the quarter-final before Gary Lineker intervened. England have only twice been beaten after taking the lead; British, French, Italian sides seem to feed off the confidence engendered by scoring first. The Germans seem to thrive on the challenge of not doing so.

England Squad 1970:
GK: Gordon Banks (Leicester City, 32 years old, 59 caps), Peter Bonetti (Chelsea, 28, 6), Alex Stepney (Manchester United, 27, 1)
DEF: Jack Charlton (Leeds United, 35, 34), Terry Cooper (Leeds, 25, 8), Norman Hunter (Leeds, 26, 13), Brian Labone (Everton, 30, 23), Bobby Moore (West Ham United, 29, 80), Keith Newton (Blackburn Rovers, 28, 24), Tommy Wright (Everton, 25, 9)
MID & WIDE: Alan Ball (Blackpool, 25, 41), Colin Bell (Manchester City, 24, 11), Bobby Charlton (Man Utd, 32, 102), Emlyn Hughes (Liverpool, 22, 6), Alan Mullery (Tottenham Hotspur, 28, 27), Martin Peters (Tottenham, 26, 38), Nobby Stiles (Man Utd, 28, 28)
FWD: Jeff Astle (West Bromwich Albion, 28, 3), Allan Clarke (Leeds, 23, 0), Geoff Hurst (West Ham, 28, 38), Francis Lee (Man City, 26, 14), Peter Osgood (Chelsea, 23, 1)

SEMI-FINAL (17 June)

Brazil	(1) 3	**Uruguay**	(1) 1	Jalisco, Guadalajara; 51,261
Clodoaldo 44, Jairzinho 69, Rivelino 89		Cubilla 17		

THIRD-PLACE MATCH (2 June)

West Germany	(1) 1	**Uruguay**	(0) 0	Azteca; 104,403
Overath				

Three days later in Guadalajara, where they had the good fortune to stay for their entire campaign before the final, Brazil saw off Uruguay's resilient, if negative, challenge.

Uruguay started off well, shooting on sight, which seemed a reasonable policy against such a dire goalkeeper. Brazil looked jumpy, and Brito's awful pass put them in trouble. Morales immediately clipped the ball out to the chunky (I think that's the polite term) right-winger Cubilla. He had a lot to do and didn't do it spectacularly, lobbing a tame effort across Félix. Rather than save it, which seemed the obvious thing to do as the ball arced gently past him no more than three feet away, Félix left it, and seemed aghast when it bobbled inside the far post. Brazil poured into

attack but still seemed a little lacklustre – they weren't going to
have it easy against this defence, and it needed something a little
special on a free-kick to beat a goalkeeper as good as Mazurkiewicz
– he didn't just stop them, he caught them if they weren't up to
scratch.

The scorer Cubilla was an interesting figure; he looked
distinctly unathletic, but had a sharp burst of acceleration and
was a good crosser. Cubilla won four Uruguayan titles as a youngster and made his international debut as a teenager. He had an
unsuccessful spell with Barcelona and joined River Plate in
Argentina – he lost his international place during this time. A
return to Uruguay with Nacional brought him another four titles
(including another hat-trick) and a return to the Uruguay team in
time for this tournament. On his retirement he became a coach
and managed a number of big South America clubs, but the best
of his success came with Olimpia in Paraguay; he enjoyed three
spells there and won the league during each of them.

The game was in first-half injury-time when Brazil broke
through from an unlikely source. Usually Clodoaldo's job was to
shield the defence and win the ball for the more talented players
around him. Here he played a short pass to Rivelino and unexpectedly sprinted into the box for a return, which duly came with
perfect weight and accuracy. In one movement Clodoaldo swept
the ball home as if he were Pelé – he would reserve another
moment of uncharacteristic genius for the final.

The second half was all Brazil. Pelé went on one rampaging
run and it was only the third defender, Ancheta, who tried to cut
him down, who actually made contact; Brazil claimed a penalty
but the referee correctly noted the point of contact was on the
edge of the area. Midway through the half Jairzinho burst out of
his own half – he'd been quiet and a wee bit selfish to that point.
He fed the ball to Pelé who diverted it to Tostão who fed Jairzinho
again, continuing his run. The big winger outsprinted Matosas
and shot across the exposed Mazurkiewicz. Uruguay did absolutely nothing wrong, it was just fantastic, instinctive football.

Shortly after another piece of flapping from Félix gave
Uruguay hope, Pelé sprinted down the left, held the ball and
rolled it back for Rivelino to unleash another piledriver; this time

Mazurkiewicz got no more than a hand to it and the ball thumped into the corner. Game over. Rivelino knew it, he sprinted fully forty yards back to the Brazilian bench in the heat, fists pumping, seventies porn-star moustache bristling.

In the dying minutes Pelé sprinted onto a pass from Tostão with Mazurkiewicz hurtling off his line to meet him. Pelé instinctively knew that if he touched the ball the goalkeeper would tackle him, and if he touched it any harder the backtracking defender would intercept. So he left it; he dummied the 'keeper and ran round the back of him to retrieve the ball, just missing the far post with an instant shot. It doesn't look much on video until you stop and contemplate the football brain that worked out those angles in a split second while running at full pelt. That is the hallmark of genius – to do things no others can do; even simple things.

WORLD CUP CLASSIC No.8
17 June 1970, Azteca, Mexico City; 102,444

West Germany   **(0) (1) 3** Schnellinger 90, Müller 94, 110
Italy   **(1) (1) 4** Boninsegna 8, Burgnich 98, Riva 104, Rivera 111

Referee: **Arturo Yamasaki** (Mexico – but he used to be Peruvian!)
Coaches: **Ferruccio Valcareggi** (Italy) & **Helmut Schön** (West Germany)

West Germany (3–1–3–3): Sepp Maier (Bayern Munich); Berti Vogts (Borussia Mönchengladbach), Willi Schulz (Cologne), Karl-Heinz Schnellinger (AC Milan): Bernd Patzke (Hertha Berlin); Franz Beckenbauer (Bayern Munich); Uwe Seeler (Cpt, Hamburg), Wolfgang Overath (Cologne); Jürgen Grabowski (Eintracht Frankfurt); Gerd Müller (Bayern Munich), Hannes Löhr (Cologne). **Subs:** Siggi Held (Dortmund) 65m for Patzke; Reinhard Libuda (Schalke 04) 51m for Löhr
Italy (4–4–2): Enrico Albertosi (Cagliari); Tarcisio Burgnich (Inter), Roberto Rosato (Milan), Pierluigi Cera (Cagliari), Giacinto Facchetti (Cpt, Inter); Angelo Domenghini (Cagliari), Mario Bertini (Inter), Sandro Mazzola (Inter), Picchio De Sisti (Fiorentina); Roberto Boninsegna (Inter), Gigi Riva (Cagliari). **Subs:** Gianni Rivera (Milan) 45m for Mazzola; Fabrizio Poletti (Torino) 90m, for Rosato
Cautioned: Rosato (Ita) 36m, Müller (WGer) 66m, Albertosi (Ita) 73m, De Sisti (Ita) 104m, Domenghini (Ita) 114m

This has won polls as the best World Cup match of all time, which is stretching the point. It's a fan favourite because of the excitement and changeable nature of the game, rather than a critics' favourite because of the quality of the football. They both have a point; maybe it had the best half-hour of all time as the excitement was crammed into extra-time. Italy scored too early for the ninety minutes to be pulsating. It wasn't their way to go for the jugular, rather let the opponent bleed to death slowly, which is what West Germany did for ninety minutes until they conjured an unlikely equaliser from an unlikely source.

Mazzola was back in the side for Rivera, which surprised some, as Rivera had been highly influential in Italy's excellent second half against Mexico. It supports the theory Valcareggi was playing by numbers, especially when he swapped the two play-makers at half-time again.

It is fascinating to read the way in which this game is viewed with the benefit of hindsight in Italy and West Germany. The Italians, often so self-deprecating, have it as one of their great victories, coming through after a heartbreaking late equaliser and then going behind in extra-time. The Germans, normally pretty good at accepting defeat (except during their "posturing years" in the eighties and nineties), see it as a hard-luck story, a brave effort thwarted by Italian dark arts and a weak referee.

The last doesn't hold water. Yamasaki was a seasoned official – it was his third World Cup – and he did fine here with the exception of one call. West Germany claimed they should have had three penalties. In the first half Beckenbauer and Facchetti came together as Beckenbauer surged into the area; contact was minimal and Beckenbauer looked for the tumble; another surge later was stopped by a trip from Cera, but the TV footage shows the offence was a fraction outside the box – excellent decision. It did cost West Germany though, for Beckenbauer was injured as he tumbled and spent the rest of the game with his shoulder strapped, at first loosely and then actually held to his chest during extra-time. The one Yamasaki got wrong was when Seeler was held back chasing a rebound after Rosato made an excellent goal-line clearance.

Rosato had an exceptional game on Müller, but chances came elsewhere. Seeler missed a good chance, as did Grabowski, and Overath smashed a shot against the bar when he should have been on target with the 'keeper stranded. West Germany brought on a second winger in Libuda, for Löhr, who was nondescript, but he made little impact against Facchetti.

There was a lot of fuss made about Italian time-wasting and it was excessive and childish, but Yamasaki kept a lid on it and booked two players for taking the mickey, one of them goalkeeper

Albertosi. And Germans complaining about play-acting is too rich. Albertosi nearly paid for his slow-timing; forced to kick from his hand quickly, he hoofed one against the back of Siggi Held and the ball bounced slowly back towards the goal-line. Albertosi sprinted back while the predatory Müller sprinted forwards, and the Italian goalkeeper just got his toe in first to poke the ball past the post – good recovery.

Libuda's introduction allowed Grabowski to play on the left against Burgnich, slower than Facchetti, and it was his cross deep into injury-time that found the centre-half Karl-Heinz Schnellinger in unfamiliar territory. Schnellinger stretched and just got a toe to the ball – it was enough. There were suggestions he was insulted and threatened after scoring the goal (Schnellinger played in Italy for AC Milan) but that sounds a bit like tabloid tittle-tattle. The Italians protested about the extra-time played, but that, too, was a little rich.

The Germans, understandably, started extra-time a little more eagerly and got the first breakthrough. A cross from Libuda looked harmless enough until Poletti, on for Rosato, chested it down and Müller nipped in to scramble the ball past a furious Albertosi – the goalkeeper and Poletti got in each other's way trying to get to the ball as it crept over the line at a funereal pace. The lead lasted four minutes until Held mimicked Poletti's error, chesting a free-kick that Rivera tossed into the box straight into the path of Burgnich. Players were tired and marking slack, and Burgnich had time to let the ball sit at the right height to hammer home.

Now Italy were in the ascendancy, Rivera enjoying the extra space in midfield – Beckenbauer was a peripheral figure in his makeshift sling and the most defensive player, Patzke, had been substituted. Just before the break in extra-time he picked the ball up in space and threaded a pass to Domenghini, who had risked a sprint down the left. The winger curled in a first-time pass to Riva, lurking on the edge of the penalty area. He controlled the ball with his chest, pushed it outside the incoming Schnellinger with his next touch, balanced himself and hit a precise low shot beyond Maier. Quality finishing.

The Germans weren't done. Held tried to redeem himself with a surging run, and it started a spell of pressure. Italy cleared a free-kick and from the corner Seeler's downward header forced

Albertosi to tip over. Seeler won the second corner, too – the Italians lacked height in the middle without Rosato – and headed across for Müller, who diverted the ball away from the goalkeeper into the corner. Much was made of Rivera's rather feeble attempt to stop it, but his only chance really was to handle the ball and give away a penalty. All-square again.

Not for long. West Germany didn't touch the ball before Italy were back in front. The kick-off went to Facchetti, who squirted a pass out to Boninsegna. The centre-forward ran past the tiring Schultz (a weak link for West Germany), looked up and cut the ball back into space. Rivera strolled into the German box and passed the ball into the corner.

The Germans didn't have anything left. They pressed forward wearily but the equally weary Italians didn't have to run now, and they were able to soak up the crosses and quash Libuda and Grabowski with numbers.

Italy certainly had the rub of the green and there was a lot of time-wasting, but I've seen Italian and German sides behave much worse without widespread censure. Fun game, especially the last half-hour. Best game ever? Not by a long chalk (see Ten Best World Cup Matches).

WORLD CUP FINAL No.9
21 June 1970, Azteca Stadium; 107,412

Brazil   **(1) 4**   Pelé 18, Gérson 66, Jairzinho 71, Carlos Alberto 86
Italy   **(1) 1**   Boninsegna 37

Referee: **Rudi Glöckner** (East Germany)
Coaches: **Mário Zagallo** (Brazil) & **Ferruccio Valcareggi** (Italy)

Brazil (4–4–1–1): Félix (Fluminense); Carlos Alberto (Cpt, Santos), Everaldo (Grêmio), Wilson Piazza (Cruzeiro), Hercules Brito (Flamengo); Jairzinho (Botafogo), Clodoaldo (Santos), Gérson (São Paulo), Roberto Rivelino (Corinthians); Pelé (Santos); Tostão (Cruzeiro)
Italy (4–4–2): Enrico Albertosi (Cagliari*); Tarcisio Burgnich (Inter), Roberto Rosato (Milan), Pierluigi Cera (Cagliari), Giacinto Facchetti (Cpt, Inter); Angelo Domenghini (Cagliari), Mario Bertini (Inter), Sandro Mazzola (Inter), Picchio De Sisti (Fiorentina); Roberto Boninsegna (Inter), Gigi Riva (Cagliari). **Subs:** Antonio Juliano (Napoli) 74m for Bertini; Gianni Rivera (Milan) 84m for Boninsegna

* Cagliari were a Sardinian team and had just won the title for the first time. They had six players in the squad, the same as Internazionale. In more recent years Cagliari have been a bit of a yo-yo team between *Serie A* and *Serie B*.

This was a brilliant Brazilian side and they were fully into their stride. They played well in this match – though perhaps not quite so well as is remembered – but really they didn't have to play that well. Italy were a good side, but not by any means a great one (the second-best team in this tournament was England), and they were tired. Brazil had no extra rest but their semi-final against Uruguay lasted thirty minutes less and was played at a noticeably more measured pace. The Italy victory was emotionally and mentally exhausting too, as much a test of will as of ability, and they were playing the redoubtable Germans.

Brazil were awesome up front – it has to be repeated and re-emphasised, this was the best forward line ever put into the field, pressed close only by the 1958 version of Brazil. Pelé was the best player the game had ever seen and he was in imperious form, vision and leadership added to the multiple skills. There was no weakness; he was physically strong, deceptively quick for a player who strolled for most of a game, superb in the air, imaginative and a sharp finisher. Gérson, too, was so much more than the player seen in England in 1966; his ability to dictate the pace of the game and pick a pass were crucial to Brazil's ball retention, and he was always prepared to drop in deeper if he felt his colleagues were over-committed. A great player with good team discipline – I can't say player without ego, because he was a conceited so-and-so. Rivelino, too, was a hard-working player as well as a gifted one. Everyone remembers those vicious free-kicks, struck with the inside or outside of the boot, that swerved and dipped menacingly in the thin air, but his passing was a joy, too, and he could tackle better than expected. Tostão was a jewel, another player who played a role for the team and made things easier for those around him. Not really a centre-forward – his initial success at club level was as a ball-carrying playmaker – but prepared to adapt to the position, and he offered pace, movement and persistence rather than a towering presence of especially lethal finishing. The last member of the famous five, Jairzinho, definitely could finish. Strong and quick, he was an intimidating opponent running with the ball, but he could overplay sometimes – he was the least intelligent footballer of the five. He thrived in 1970 on

Pelé's ability to draw defenders and then play him in with a simple pass.

> *I don't know how much it is. My father told me that when you're*
> *working, don't stop to count your money.*
>   Pelé, on being asked what he thought his
>   transfer value might have been. Times change.
>   Or maybe he really was just a special one.

Four of these players were in the 1966 squad (Rivelino was the odd man out), but it took the appointment of Saldanho to blend them together, and the calm of Zagallo to give them the right framework to express themselves. The most remarkable aspect of this victory, from a personnel point of view, was that it was achieved with a quite awful goalkeeper.

It's easy to say Italy were the opposite of Brazil, all defence and no attack, but the Italians have never been that straightforward. The defensive mindset is a (football) cultural thing started in the 1960s, that the way to win games was to stop the opposition scoring, and that became paramount if the team was in the lead. It didn't mean they were short of attacking players – Riva, Mazzola and Domeghini were all established international players of the highest calibre – just that they were expected to put their creative urges to one side for the good of the system.

So, after an initial flurry from Italy saw Riva force a save (miracles never cease) out of Félix, the game of cat and mouse commenced. It was Italy's way – a quick start to try to force a lead, as against West Germany, then retreat to the trenches and prepare to repel the bombardment. But this wasn't an ageing Seeler, the finisher Müller and the lifeless Löhr, it was Brazil, and Brazil with a tactically astute coach. Zagallo knew how good Pelé was in the air, and with the impressive Rosato marking Tostão, they agreed the No.10 would target Burgnich on the far post. Brazil's first and third goals came from this ploy, the first an emphatic header from Rivelino's improvised cross.

Brazil would not have been Brazil without the odd shocker at the back and this time it was Clodoaldo, showboating even before half-time. His attempted back-heeled pass was cut out by Boninsegna – not a player to mess with, he was full of running and had a great attitude – who went straight at the heart of the defence, crashed through two tackles and beat his team-mate Riva to the loose ball to put Italy level. Félix was floundering around ten feet away, having committed ridiculously early. A really bad goal to concede.

Brazil controlled the ball superbly thereafter and drove Italy deeper and deeper, but at 1–1 there was always the sneaky feeling that their defence might just have another catastrophic error in it somewhere along the line. Mazzola was playing well – he stayed on after half-time – and Boninsegna ran as willingly as ever. Riva was quiet – Carlos Alberto, the Brazilian captain, had a good day all round. Brazil had chances – Rivelino proved he wasn't a one-trick pony by hitting the bar from a free-kick with his wrong foot.

It took twenty minutes of the second half to come and it was from a most deserving source. Gérson was the only one of the front five yet to score in the tournament, but the timing of his first was immense. Yet another Jairzinho run foundered against Facchetti's strength and athleticism, but the ball skewed off to Gérson, who stepped around another defender and shot into the corner from twenty yards. The game was effectively over five minutes later when Pelé beat Burgnich in the air again and Jairzinho forced the ball over the line through brute strength.

If Valcareggi could be forgiven for not bringing Rivera on at half-time, well as Mazzola was doing in keeping the ball for spells and stemming the tide towards his own goal, he surely erred in not bringing him on now for Bertini or De Sisti. Instead, he waited nearly ten minutes and brought on Juliano of Napoli for his first game of the tournament. Rivera got his "chance" with six minutes remaining, coming on for the exhausted Boninsegna.

There remained only the most famous goal in the history of football – don't shout it out loud but it was a bit meaningless in the context of the match. Bit of showboating from Clodoaldo (a little keepie-uppie dribble to get things moving), a little run from Jairzinho, slipped pass inside to Pelé, slide-rule ball inside the defence to Carlos Alberto – bang! Thank you very much, world champions again and we'll take that trophy for keeps now as it's our third time if you don't mind . . .

If you're too young to have seen these Brazilians, get some videos – the England game, Uruguay, the final, Peru if you want a giggle at some comical defending – they really did play some sublime stuff.

World Cup Heroes No.14
Mário Zagallo (1931–)
Brazil

The first man to win the World Cup as player and coach. After making his international debut as a twenty-seven-year-old in early 1958, Zagallo became a key player for Brazil in the 1958 and 1962 World Cup tournaments, a deep-lying winger who could augment both the midfield and attack. He was the kind of player Brazilian coach Feola liked, one who would listen to tactics and play to a system. Zagallo possessed a wicked left foot and his curling crosses for Vavá and Pelé were a rich source of goals for Brazil.

Injuries forced Zagallo to retire in 1964 and he quit club football with Botafogo the following year. It was only a couple of years before he was back in charge of the club, the first of five spells as Botafogo manager; he also had three spells in charge of Flamengo, the club with which he made his name as a player.

But it was at international level his coaching name was really made. When Saldanho's regular outbursts became too unpalatable for the Brazilian football authorities in 1970, Zagallo was drafted in as a safe pair of hands for the World Cup Finals. He didn't tinker too much with the personnel, just dropped a little more team ethic into a marvellous pool of talent. Zagallo was a mild-mannered man for the most part, and unfailingly courteous, but tales are told of a fearsome Fergie-esque blast the players suffered after their listless first half against Uruguay. Zagallo was still in charge four years later but there was no Pelé, no Gérson and no Tostão, and their replacements tried to play a more cautious game to release Jairzinho and co, but they simply weren't good enough.

Zagallo returned to the Brazilian squad in the early 1990s under Carlos Alberto Parreira, and was there when the 1994 trophy was won; he took full charge four years later when Brazil appeared to be coasting to another title until they misfired in the final.

In between, Zagallo helped the United Arab Emirates qualify for the Finals for the first time and helped develop football in Kuwait and Saudi Arabia.

1970 Team of the Tournament:

Banks (England)
Schnellinger (West Germany)   Ubiña (Uruguay)   Rosato (Italy)   Facchetti (Italy)
Mullery (England)   Pelé (Brazil)   Gérson (Brazil)
Jairzinho (Brazil)   Müller (West Germany)   Riva (Italy)

Leading scorers: Muller 10; Jairzinho 7; Cubillas 5.

The official team is listed as: Mazurkiewicz (Uruguay); Carlos Alberto (Brazil), Ancheta (Uruguay), Beckenbauer (West Germany – even though he played in midfield), Facchetti (Italy); Gérson (Brazil), Rivelino (Brazil), Charlton (England – now I love the Bobster, but he honestly truly did nothing special in this tournament); Pelé (Brazil), Müller (West Germany), Jairzinho (Brazil).

Heaven Eleven No.6

Brazil

Coach:
Vicente Feola (but really, who needs one with this lot?)

Goalkeepers:
Gylmar: star player in the 1958 team, even if few people know the name – also played in 1962 & 1966
Émerson Leão: goalie in the rather defensive '70s side – if he had played in 1970 they would have been even better

Claudio Taffarel: played more than 100 games for Brazil; World Cup winner in 1994

Defenders: (Oh, do we have to . . .?)
Cafu: remarkably consistent performer, played in three World Cup Finals and had a sixteen-year international career
Djalma Santos: scary, scary man
Nílton Santos: rated by many as the game's best-ever left-back
Branco: fulminating attacking back from the 1990s, much better than Leonardo or Roberto Carlos
Lúcio: towering central defender, could play a bit as well; good club career in Europe
Luís Pereira: hard man in the weak 1974 team; highly rated in Brazil
Bellini: captain and reassuring presence in the defence in 1962

Midfield & Wide:
Pelé: just Pelé
Gérson: wonderfully agile mind and persuasive left foot
Rivelino: I hear he took a mean free-kick . . .
Socrates: appeared lazy, maybe even was a bit, but . . .
Falcão: exciting, hard-running attacker from the '80s
Garrincha: a wizard
Didi: superb craftsman in the '50s and early '60s, a real general
Mauro Silva: I know, there are better players not here, but every team needs its workhorse and this man was a rock (better than Dunga) – ask Deportivo fans

Strikers:
Tostão: hard-working and committed attacker, chased lost causes and did the work of two
Ademir: ridiculously acrobatic and talented forward in the post-war team
Ronaldo: okay, so he occasionally put on a few pounds, but it never seemed to stop him scoring
Neymar: the Brazilians always find a space in their squad for "one for the future" – he's in just in case he makes this list look a bit lacking in 2014 – and he is some talent

Omissions: Too many to mention really. **Zico** was sacrificed for a defensive player, also unlucky were **Zagallo**, **Mauro Ramos**, **Ronaldinho**, **Rivaldo**, **Romário**, **Vavá**, **Luizinho**, **Jorginho** – looking at the list I would have to concede I have harboured a slight bias towards the old school. **Jairzinho** I left out as I always felt he was bit flattered by playing in such a great team; **Bebeto** and **Roberto Carlos** I left out because they weren't that great.

Likely first XI (not that the second XI would be much fun to play against . . .):

Gylmar

Cafu   Lúcio   Luís Pereira   N Santos

Mauro Silva

Garrincha   Didi   Pelé   Falcão

Ronaldo

Bloody Nora.

4.4 GOLDEN BOOTS
& BALLS OF GOLD

There are numerous trophies handed out every year in categories like the world's best player, Europe's top scorer, the World Cup's most valuable performer, the best goalkeeper in South East Asia and the best tea-lady in southern Azerbaijan.

The World Cup has two main awards, the Golden Boot, for the tournament's top scorer, and the Golden Ball for the tournament's outstanding player.

Here are the winners.

Golden Boot winners

1930	Guillermo Stábile (Uruguay)	8
1934	Oldrich Nejedly (Czechoslovakia)	5
1938	Leônidas da Silva (Brazil)	7
1950	Ademir (Brazil)	8
1954	Sándor Kocsis (Hungary)	11
1958	Just Fontaine (France)	13
1962	Flórián Albert (Hungary)	4
	Valentin Ivanov (USSR)	
	Garrincha (Brazil)	
	Vavá (Brazil)	
	Drazan Jerkovic (Yugoslavia)	
	Leonel Sánchez (Chile)	
1966	Eusébio (Portugal)	9
1970	Gerd Müller (West Germany)	10

1974	Grzegorz Lato (Poland)	7
1978	Mario Kempes (Argentina)	6
1982	Paolo Rossi (Italy)	6
1986	Gary Lineker (England)	6
1990	Salvatore Schillaci (Italy)	6
1994	Oleg Salenko (USSR)	5
	Hristo Stoichkov (Bulgaria)	5
1998	Davor Suker (Croatia)	6
2002	Ronaldo (Brazil)	8
2006	Miroslav Klose (Germany)	5
2010	Thomas Müller* (Germany)	5

Golden Ball winners

The Golden Ball winners for the first few tournaments have been awarded retrospectively. The first year the actual award was given after deliberation by a number of senior football writers, was 1978.

Year	Actual winner	Should have won
1930	José Nasazzi (Uruguay)	Andrade (Uruguay)
1934	Giuseppe Meazza (Italy)	Meazza
1938	Leônidas da Silva (Brazil)	Leônidas
1950	Zizinho (Brazil)	Obdulio Varela (Uruguay)
1954	Ferenc Puskás (Hungary)	Fritz Walter (West Germany)
1958	Didi (Brazil)	Didi
1962	Garrincha (Brazil)	Garrincha
1966	Bobby Charlton (England)	Bobby Moore (England)
1970	Pelé (Brazil)	Pelé
1974	Johan Cruyff (Holland)	Cruyff
1978	Mario Kempes (Argentina)	Daniel Passarella (Argentina)
1982	Paolo Rossi (Italy)	Marco Tardelli (Italy)
1986	Diego Maradona (Argentina)	Maradona
1990	Salvatore Schillaci (Italy)	Jürgen Klinsmann (West Germany)
1994	Romário (Brazil)	Roberto Baggio (Italy)

* Müller was the first winner of the award who finished level on goals with other players but won the award on the tie-breaker by counting back the number of assists he provided for other players. Diego Forlán, Wesley Sneijder and David Villa missed out.

1998 Ronaldo (Brazil)	Lilian Thuram (France)
2002 Oliver Kahn (Germany)	Ronaldo (Brazil)
2006 Zinedine Zidane (France)	Fabio Cannavaro (Italy)
2010 Diego Forlán (Uruguay)	Forlán

One defender (Nasazzi in 1930) and one goalkeeper is utter nonsense; easy to favour headline-grabbing attackers, but they are not always the defining influence within their team. Rossi, for example, was rightly the "story" of 1982, but Tardelli hauled Italy through a couple of tough spells, played well in the group games when Rossi was anonymous, and ran the final. In 2006 there was sympathy initially for Zidane and he was given this award despite his moment of madness in the final; actually it was unwarranted and cost his team dearly, so he should have got nowhere near an award – Cannavaro was colossal in every game.

Golden Glove award (the Yashin Award from 1994–2006) – for the tournament's best goalkeeper

1994 Michel Preud'homme (Belgium)
1998 Fabien Barthez (France)
2002 Oliver Kahn (Germany)
2006 Gianluigi Buffon (Italy)
2010 Iker Casillas (Spain)

Best Young Player – only inaugurated in 2006

2006 Lukas Podolski (Germany, 21)
2010 Thomas Müller (Germany, 20)

There are other awards, like the FIFA Fair Play award and the Most Entertaining Team award that are just too meaningless to bother with.

The football award that gets the FIFA suits most exercised is the annual nonsense that is the Ballon d'Or, the award for the best player in the world. Initiated in 1991, the award used to be the FIFA World Player of the Year until it merged with France Football's Ballon d'Or (European Footballer of the Year).

Ballon d'Or (as much for club football as international)

1956 Stanley Matthews (England)	1957 Alfredo Di Stéfano (Argentina)
1958 Raymond Kopa (France)	1959 Di Stéfano (2)
1960 Luis Suárez (Spain)	1961 Omar Sivori (Italy)
1962 Josef Masopust (Czechoslovakia)	1963 Lev Yashin (USSR)
1964 Denis Law (Scotland)	1965 Eusébio (Portugal)
1966 Bobby Charlton (England)	1967 Flórián Albert (Hungary)
1968 George Best (Northern Ireland)	1969 Gianni Rivera (Italy)
1970 Gerd Müller (West Germany)	1971 Johan Cruyff (Holland)
1972 Franz Beckenbauer (West Germany)	1973 Cruyff (2)
1974 Cruyff (3)	1975 Oleg Blokhin (USSR)
1976 Beckenbauer (2)	1977 Allan Simonsen (Denmark)
1978 Kevin Keegan (England)	1979 Keegan (2)
1980 Karl-Heinz Rummenigge (W.Ger)	1981 Rummenigge (2)
1982 Paolo Rossi (Italy)	1983 Michel Platini (France)
1984 Platini (2)	1985 Platini (3)
1986 Igor Belanov (USSR)	1987 Ruud Gullit (Holland)
1988 Marco van Basten (Holland)	1989 Van Basten (2)
1990 Lothar Matthäus (West Germany)	1991 Jean-Pierre Papin (France)
1992 Van Basten (3)	1993 Roberto Baggio (Italy)
1994 Hristo Stoichkov (Bulgaria)	1995 George Weah (Liberia)
1996 Matthias Sammer (Germany)	1997 Ronaldo (Brazil)
1998 Zinedine Zidane (France)	1999 Rivaldo (Brazil)
2000 Luís Figo (Portugal)	2001 Michael Owen (England)
2002 Ronaldo (2)	2003 Pavel Nedved (Czech Rep)
2004 Andriy Shevchenko (Ukraine)	2005 Ronaldinho (Brazil)
2006 Fabio Cannavaro (Italy)	2007 Kaká (Brazil)
2008 Cristiano Ronaldo (Portugal)	2009 Lionel Messi (Argentina)

FIFA World Player of the Year

1991 Lothar Matthäus (Germany)	1992 Marco van Basten (Holland)
1993 Roberto Baggio (Italy)	1994 Romario (Brazil)
1995 George Weah (Liberia)	1996 Ronaldo (Brazil)
1997 Ronaldo (2)	1998 Zinedine Zidane (France)
1999 Rivaldo (Brazil)	2000 Zidane (2)
2001 Luís Figo (Portugal)	2002 Ronaldo (3)

2003 Zidane (3)

2004 Ronaldinho (Brazil)

2005 Ronaldinho (2)

2006 Fabio Cannavaro (Italy)

2007 Kaka (Brazil)

2008 Cristiano Ronaldo (Portugal)

2009 Lionel Messi (Argentina)

Ballon d'Or

2010 Messi (2)

2011 Messi (3)

2012 Messi (4)

2013 Ronaldo (2)

TOTAL FOOTBALL

5.1 WORLD CUP 1974

FIFA made one of those special decisions in preparation for the 1974 Finals that seem to be their unique preserve. They did away with quarter-finals and initiated a second phase of groups. More money for the coffers, less tension and excitement for the specta-tors. Thus has it always been, thus will it always be. I believe, somewhere in a parallel dimension, football is played competi-tively and hard, but for the entertainment of the spectators, and it is run by an august body of good men and true whose sole aim is to preserve a balance between endeavour and skill and provide a safe and comfortable environment for the spectators, who pay only what they can afford to watch. But then I watch *Dr Who* and read Tolkien so I can be considered a fantasist.

West Germany was a sure bet as host, and their election was guaranteed after a deal with Spain that saw Spain awarded the 1982 tournament, much as Argentina and Mexico carved up 1970 and 1978. They had plenty of big stadia already in place and an excellent transport and logistical infrastructure in place after all the hard work rebuilding the country after the war.

The cities chosen to host matches were Berlin (the Olympic Stadium, home to Hertha Berlin), Munich (the 1972 Olympic Stadium, chosen for the Final and home to both Bayern and TSV Munich), Hamburg, Dortmund, Düsseldorf, Gelsenkirchen (home to Schalke 04), Frankfurt, Hannover and Stuttgart.

The social and economic climate had changed over the last few years in Europe, from the vibrancy and expectation of the 1960s to a more grim reality The three-day week and extensive power cuts in Britain weren't an isolated phenomenon; across

1974
WEST GERMANY

Like England in 1966 West Germany could call on a number of massive club stadia for their World Cup project; and, like England, these were pre-war terraced grounds with meagre facilities. The Germans used nine stadia in nine cities spread across the country.

Munich: Olympiastadion
Like Mexico four years earlier, West Germany had hosted the Olympic Games two years earlier and had a ready-made relatively modern stadium to offer for the final. In the final 75,200 people watched their team beat Holland.

The new stadium became the home of two local sides, Bayern Munich and Munich 1860, until it was supplanted by the new Allianz Arena in 2006.

West Berlin: Olympiastadion
This was an older stadium constructed by the Nazis to showcase the 1936 Olympics. Over 80,000 watched West Germany's opening game in the 1974 finals in a slightly re-jigged ground, and it was renovated and re-used for the 2006 finals.

Hamburg: Völksparkstadion
The main Hamburg stadium has been given various name changes to appease sponsors, but it will always be the Völkspark to fans. Built in 1953, Hamburg SV moved in for the 1963-64 season when the new Bundesliga started, and the club remains the ground's owners. The Völkspark hosted the famous game between West and East Germany at the 1974 finals.

Frankfurt: Waldstadion
Now officially the Commerzbank Arena, the Waldstadion was built as the home of Eintracht Frankfurt in 1925 and has remained on the same site ever since. In 1974 it hosted West Germany's semi-final with Poland, a match that was played in such atrocious conditions, it is sometimes referred to as the wasserschlacht (water battle) in Germany.

Düsseldorf: Rheinstadion
This ground, which housed 66,000 spectators for West Germany's first second-phase match in 1974, was the home of Fortuna Düsseldorf until 2002 when it was demolished and replaced with the Esprit Arena.

Dortmund: Westfalenstadion
Dortmund benefited from Cologne's withdrawal as a host city and the Borussia Dortmund stadium was hastily renovated for the purpose. For the 1974 tournament it had a capacity of 54,000, but has grown as the club's fortunes have soared.

Stuttgart: Neckarstadion
Now the Mercedes Benz Arena for sponsorship purposes, the famous Neckar has been home to Vfb Stuttgart since 1933. In the main, German clubs have re-built or expanded on existing sites rather than build new out-of-town stadia and, along with sensible pricing, it has benefited attendances in the Bundesliga. The ground filled its capacity of 68,900 for both the Italy games it hosted in 1974.

Gelsenkirchen: Parkstadion
This was home to Schalke 04, Germany's strongest club either side of the Second World War, until it closed in 2001 when Schalke moved into the Veltins-Arena next door. It was in the Parkstadion that Yugoslavia put nine goals past luckless Zaire in 1974.

Hanover: Niedersachsenstadion
This huge stadium had extra seats installed for 1974, but since then capacity has decreased to a mere 60,400. The original name means Lower Saxony Stadium, but the ground has acquired sponsors names like the AWD Arena and HDI-Arena (current title) in modern times.

Europe there was a wave of protest – and, much more chillingly, terrorism and a refusal to accept the status quo. Harold Wilson had spent a fair proportion of the last decade in power – he blamed his defeat in the 1970 election on England's World Cup failure – and the left-centre alliance the SPD held sway in Federal Germany under Helmut Schmidt, who took over from Willy Brandt a month before the tournament.

The terrorists were a major concern. At the 1972 Olympics in Munich, terrorists (the Black September group) had kidnapped and murdered eleven Israeli athletes, with all the concomitant escalation of tension. Black September had links to the Baader-Meinhof or Red Army faction, a group of extreme left-wing militants who had carried out a series of shootings and bombings over the previous few years. In Britain, the IRA were running a high-profile and aggressive campaign on the mainland, while Italy and Spain also had problems with militants and separatists. Security was tight and visible. Thankfully the tournament passed without serious incident.

Qualifying

The qualifying tournament was a fascinating affair in its own right. In South America the perennials all made it, but Uruguay started to show signs of decline, losing at home to Colombia. In North America, Mexico, who usually waltzed through, fell foul of a thumping by Trinidad and Tobago, which let in not their opponents but another Caribbean side, Haiti, for their first (and probably last) appearance. It helped the Haitian cause that the final game against Trinidad and Tobago was played at home in front of an intimidating crowd whipped up by the Haitian dictator Papa Doc Duvalier's armed lackeys. Port au Prince was a scary city under Duvalier; six people died as a result of a crowd stampede set off by an exploding firecracker in an earlier qualifier against Cuba. In Africa, too, virgin finalists came through in the form of Zaire, the former name of what is now the Democratic Republic of Congo; they did it in style, too, winning all four games in the final three-team group. The third debutants were Australia, who won through protracted Asian qualifying, squeezing past South

Korea in a play-off after their two-leg affair produced two tight draws. This wasn't modern Australia, full of émigrés to the European leagues, but a home-grown side, fit and willing but lacking finesse, for all the enthusiasm of their young Yugoslav coach Ralé Rasic.

The country simply known as Congo was involved in a heated tie with Cameroon. After a 2–2 draw in the Congo, Cameroon were trailing at home when they were awarded a penalty. Congo protested, both teams piled in and the Cameroon President decided the answer was to send in paratroopers. There were two fatalities as the army "restored order" – Cameroon were disqualified and Congo beaten in the next round. The Cameroon scorer was a young striker called Roger Milla. We haven't heard the last of Roger.

Europe had some fun times as well. The Soviet Union won their three-team group but were kicked out of the tournament when they refused to travel and play in Pinochet's Chile in a play-off. A noble gesture or rank hypocrisy? A bit of both ... Anyway, this is a football book not a game of *who was the most oppressive regime of the 1970s?* Holland and Belgium contested the tightest of groups, drawing 0–0 twice; the group was decided on goal difference and the Dutch mustered an impressive twenty-four goals against the group minnows Norway and Iceland. The final 0–0 draw rankled with the Belgians, who scored in the dying stages only to have the goal chalked off incorrectly for offside.

The biggest casualties were England. They won in Wales and then dropped a home point in the return. Wales did them a favour by beating Poland in Cardiff, but then England put in a shoddy performance in Chorzów and lost 2–0, with Alan Ball sent off. Peter Shilton was poorly positioned when beaten by a deflected free-kick from wide on the left for the first goal, and Bobby Moore, nearing the end of his extraordinary career, was embarrassed by Wlodi Lubanski for the second. The game descended into a kicking match, and Ball's decision to sort out a tiff without consulting the referee saw him asked to leave the field. He was only the second England player to be sent off in an international (the first was Alan Mullery) and it took eighteen months and a different manager before he was forgiven and selected again. Still, no harm done, for surely England would beat Poland on their own ground in the autumn.

WORLD CUP SHOCK No.3
17 October 1973, Wembley Stadium; 100,000

England (0) 1   Clarke 63 (p)
Poland (0) 1   Domarski 57

Referee: **Vital Loraux** (Belgium)
Coaches: **Alf Ramsey** (England) & **Kazimierz Gorski / Jacek Gmoch** (Poland)

England (4–3–3): Peter Shilton (Leicester City); Paul Madeley (Leeds United), Roy McFarland (Derby County), Norman Hunter (Leeds), Emlyn Hughes (Liverpool); Tony Currie (Sheffield United), Colin Bell (Manchester City), Martin Peters (Tottenham Hotspur); Mick Channon (Southampton), Allan Clarke (Leeds), Martin Chivers (Tottenham). **Sub:** Kevin Hector (Derby, for Chivers, 85)
Poland (4–3–3): Jan Tomaszewski (LKS Lodz); Anton Szymanowski (Wisla Krakow), Jerzy Gorgon (Górnik Zabrze), Adam Musial (Wisla Krakow), Miroslav Bulzacki (LKS Lodz); Lewslaw Cmikiewicz (Legia Warsaw), Kazimiercz Deyna (Legia Warsaw), Henryk Kasperczak (Stal Mielec); Grzegorz Lato (Stal Mielec), Jan Domarski (Stal Mielec); Robert Gadocha (Legia Warsaw)

By the time of the return Poland had, oddly enough, made more changes to their side than England. Moore had called it a day and Hunter was in. A striker, Mick Channon, replaced the suspended Ball, and Tony Currie, an attacking midfield player, replaced the destructive Peter Storey (who should never have been allowed to sniff an England cap, let alone wear one; he was a criminal off the pitch and a thug on it).

Poland's captain Wlodi Lubanski, had gone off with a serious injury in Chorzów – it cost him his place in the Finals – and Poland had reshaped their side around the composed and cultured Deyna in midfield, with two good wingers providing the attacking threat.

Press, pundits and the people expected an England victory; Austria had just been slaughtered 7–0 by the same XI and in Currie England seemed to have found a flair player who could make a more sustained contribution than the disappointing Rodney Marsh. In the BBC studio Brian Clough highlighted the Polish goalkeeper Jan Tomaszewski as a weakness; a couple of recent errors and a penchant for melodrama supported Clough's case.

In the opening minutes Tomaszewski dropped the ball attempting to throw it out, and Clarke nearly nipped in to score. Perhaps the dislocated finger *"the clown"* (Clough's words) suffered concentrated his mind, because he didn't make another mistake after that.

The game took the form of a siege; England poured forward, urged on by Colin Bell, who dominated the midfield, and created chance after chance only to be thwarted by last-ditch defending, bad finishing and superb goalkeeping – one first-half save, clawing away a savage hit from Bell after a goalmouth melee, was quite outstanding. With the Poles defending so deeply, Chivers and Clarke simply occupied each other's space, and most of the half-chances fell to the less adroit Tottenham man, whose strength was not as a goalmouth poacher. England were purposeful, but too narrow – Peters and Channon failed to drift wide enough to offer an extra option.

A rare Polish break early in the second half saw Lato almost clear on the left. Hunter had plenty of time to thrash the ball into touch, but he clumsily trod on the ball and Lato sprinted clear (Lato v Hunter in a foot race was barely a contest), cut inside and released Domarski in acres of space to fire past Hughes. Even then Shilton should have stopped the well-hit shot but it squirmed under his body and into the goal – alas, Shilton was not yet the magnificent goalkeeper he would become.

England, to their credit, kept coming, and were denied a well-worked equaliser from a long throw for no obvious reason. Moments later referee Loraux, perhaps sensing he had made a ricket, gave England a soft penalty when Peters went down under pressure from Musial. Clarke kept his nerve during the ensuing kerfuffle and chipped the ball one way while Tomaszewski threw himself with gusto in the opposite direction.

Finally, with minutes to go, Chivers was put out of his misery and withdrawn. Kevin Hector was brought on to offer the width England desperately needed. He nearly found the winner, too, with a thumping header that beat Tomaszewski but was cleared off the line – Clarke might have done better with the follow-up than nudge it past the post. Another piledriver from Bell was cleared by Bulzacki, and England finally ran out of time.

The result was greeted as a national disaster, but it wasn't the bumbling performance many remember. Poland weren't rubbish – they proved that in Germany the following year – and they had more than their share of luck. And of course there was Tomaszewski, whose inspired performance Brian Clough would never be allowed to forget.

Finals

GROUP 1

West Germany	(1) 1	**Chile**	(0) 0	14 June, West Berlin; 83,168
Breitner 18				
East Germany	(0) 2	**Australia**	(0) 0	14 June, Hamburg; 18,180
Own goal 58, Streich 72				
West Germany	(2) 3	**Australia**	(0) 0	18 June, Hamburg; 52,000
Overath 12, Cullmann 34, Müller 53				
Chile	(0) 1	**East Germany** (0) 1		18 June, West Berlin; 27,000
Ahumada 69		Hoffmann 55		
West Germany	(0) 0	**East Germany** (0) 1		22 June, Hamburg; 58,900
		Sparwasser 77		
Australia	(0) 0	**Chile**	(0) 0	22 June, West Berlin; 16,100

1. East Germany 5pts (4–1); 2. West Germany 4pts (4–1); 3. Chile 2pts (1–2); 4. Australia 1pt (0–5)

The favourites? Few could see beyond West Germany as winners of the 1974 Finals in their own country. They had won the 1972 European Championship with imperious ease, and Schön had tightened his defence by pushing Beckenbauer back to play as a *libero*, or creative centre-back, combining cute interception with forays forward to instigate German attacks. This left the fearsome Schwarzenbeck to deal with any unruly centre-forwards who had a notion to disrupt the great man's afternoon. Schön's main problem was fitting in the abundant skills of Günther Netzer, who had pulled the strings in midfield so wonderfully well in the European Championships. Holland were still a work in progress, viewed as a team of talented misfits (nothing has changed . . .), and not yet able to translate the brilliance of their club sides to international football. Brazil were rebuilding and missing players through injury – poor Tostão had retired early after his retinal problem became more acute – and Argentina looked short of world-class players, unless the highly thought of Brindisi could make his mark. Italy were still hard to beat but lacked exciting forwards with Riva and Boninsegna past their best. East Germany, Sweden, Scotland, Yugoslavia; all had good teams but none looked like World Cup winners.

Helmut Schön was miffed with Netzer because he had elected to play in Spain (for Real Madrid) against Schön's wishes. He also wanted to play the experienced Wolfgang Overath, who was injured for the latter stages of the European Championship, alongside Uli Hoeness. Netzer in addition to these two would have been a bit of a luxury. He was just about the only man in Germany who thought Netzer should be left out of the team.

The campaign started badly. A row between the players and the German FA over pay (what else?) nearly led to mutiny, and Schön and the officials had to scramble to get Beckenbauer onside before half the side would agree to play. This disaffection manifested itself in the performances in the group games against lightweight opposition; poor against Chile (who were awful, as they invariably are outside South America), the bare minimum against Australia and woeful against East Germany, where the West were beaten in the only international between the two. Not a single player from the East German side would have made the West XI, but a solid defensive display and a breakaway from the Magdeburg striker Jurgen Sparwasser was enough.

The German press corps was far from impressed, although they forbore, mostly, the rabid nonsense that the English tabloids would peddle in such circumstances. Maybe it was all a cunning plan – by finishing second the West Germans avoided the more unpleasant of the two second-phase groups. I'm kidding; the game may be a statistical footnote as far as the World Cup is concerned – both sides were likely to progress – but it had enormous political significance and was not taken lightly by either side. East Germany was still a new country and the intensive sports programme (or systematic cheating, as it is now known to have been) that the government initiated to promote a notion of East German well-being was yet to show full fruit. This victory was a triumph that could be trumpeted to the impressionable youngsters that the party was drawing into its programme; young men and women who didn't remember the old Germany.

East Germany were fooling no one; they looked no more than a competent, functional side and unlikely to trouble the better sides in the second phase. Australia made an undistinguished first appearance in the Finals, failing to score a goal and picking up a solitary point in a drab, meaningless game with an awful Chile team. Only once their better players started moving abroad would Australia prove more competitive – sadly the same migration has been the death of their domestic football and they find themselves slipping backwards again, unable to foster new talent in the face of so many other more popular sports.

GROUP 2

Brazil	(0) 0	**Yugoslavia**	(0) 0	13 June, Frankfurt; 61,500
Scotland	(2) 2	**Zaire**	(0) 0	14 June, Dortmund; 25,800
Lorimer 26, Jordan 34				
Brazil	(0) 0	**Scotland**	(0) 0	18 June, Frankfurt; 60,600
Yugoslavia	(6) 9	**Zaire**	(0) 0	18 June, Gelsenkirchen; 30,500
Bajevic 8, 30, 81, Dzajic 14,				
Surjak 18, Katalinski 22,				
Bogicevic 35, Oblak 61,				
Petković 65				
Scotland	(0) 1	**Yugoslavia**	(0) 1	22 June, Frankfurt; 54,000
Jordan 88		Karasi 80		
Brazil	(1) 3	**Zaire**	(0) 0	22 June, Gelsenkirchen; 35,000
Jairzinho 12, Rivelino 66,				
Valdomiro 79				

1. Yugoslavia 4pts (10–1); 2. Brazil 4pts (3–0); 3. Scotland 4pts (3–1); 4. Zaire 0pts (0–14)

In England's absence the home press latched on to Scotland, who had seen off Czechoslovakia to qualify for only the second time, and the first in sixteen years. The Scots had some decent forwards and two good full-backs but no creative spark to make it all run smoothly. With the young Celtic striker Kenny Dalglish a bit overawed in his first major tournament, and Denis Law past his use-by date, they were over-reliant on finding the towering head of Joe Jordan. It worked against Zaire, who were terrible at the back, but two goals was a weedy return for all the possession Scotland enjoyed. A 0–0 draw with Brazil was creditable enough

– but in truth Brazil were uninspired in '74 and seemed as happy with the draw as Scotland. On the same day Yugoslavia were more clinical than the Scots and racked up a hatful against Zaire, meaning Scotland would have to beat them in their final game. It was hard to see even this Brazil side failing to get more than two against Zaire – in the event they laboured to a 3–0 win. During the game Mwepu earned one of the World Cup's more bizarre yellow cards, rushing out from the Zaire wall at a free-kick to belt the stationary ball downfield. It was hilarious, but the African side was undeserving of the mockery heaped upon them for their naïve play in the tournament.

Scotland drew their last game and went home, a late Jordan goal insufficient. Much was made of the fact that they became the first team to be eliminated without losing a game but sympathy should be avoided. They were a plodding side and lacked pace and creativity and this was a poor group. It was a decade too late for Baxter and a decade too early for Souness or Strachan. It was sad for Billy Bremner, the captain, who worked his socks off in his only Finals appearance trying to spark his colleagues into life. The results of this group meant West Germany avoided Brazil in the second phase.

Not that Brazil were scaring anyone this time around. With Clodoaldo and Tostão out, Zagallo had only Piazza, Rivelino and Jairzinho left from the 1970 squad. He had a better goalkeeper (how could he not?), a rock-solid centre-half in Luís Pereira and hardworking defensive midfield players. Rivelino was still an influential player and was the main creative influence now Pelé and Gérson were gone, but Jairzinho was nowhere near as effective without those great players behind and around him. To score only three goals against this kind of opposition was most un-Brazilian, even if one of them was a thunderbolt from Rivelino that must count as one of the hardest-hit shots ever seen in the World Cup.

Yugoslavia bullied Zaire effectively, but there was no evidence the Slavic brittleness against better opposition had gone away, because the opposition here was so limp. Bajevic's strike rate in international looks good (twenty-nine in thirty-seven) but three came here against one of the weakest minnows ever to make the

Finals and five more against an awful Venezuela team. His coaching career in Greece is more impressive than his playing career – eight league titles inside twenty years.

There was patronising sympathy for the hapless Zaire players, the first black Africans to qualify for the Finals. Their country was governed by a military dictator, Joseph (or Sese Seko Nkuku Wa Za, as he liked to be known) Mobutu. After the tournament it became clear that the players were operating under ridiculous expectations, with all sorts of riches promised if they covered themselves in glory. Apparently glory meant beating Brazil and the best European teams; the players received nothing but threats and a shower of ****-all when they got home. Mobutu seized power with backing from the USA and Belgium in 1960, ousting the democratically elected President, Patrice Lumumba, and arranging his execution. African politics is a dangerous game in which to be involved.

Scotland Squad 1974:

GK: David Harvey (Leeds United, 26 years old, 7 caps), Thomson Allan (Dundee, 27, 2), Jim Stewart (Kilmarnock, 20, 0)

DEF: John Blackley (Hibernian, 26, 3), Martin Buchan (Manchester United, 25, 13), Willie Donachie (Manchester City, 22, 11), Jim Holton (Man Utd, 23, 11), Sandy Jardine (Rangers, 25, 16), Danny McGrain (Glasgow Celtic, 24, 12), Gordon McQueen (Leeds, 21, 1), Erich Schaedler (Hibernian, 24, 1)

MID & WIDE: Billy Bremner (Leeds, 31, 48), Peter Cormack (Liverpool, 27, 9), Don Ford (Heart of Midlothian, 29, 3), David Hay (Celtic, 26, 24), Tommy Hutchison (Coventry City, 26, 8), Jimmy Johnstone (Celtic, 29, 21), Peter Lorimer (Leeds, 27, 14), Willie Morgan (Man Utd, 29, 19)

FWD: Kenny Dalglish (Celtic, 23, 19), Joe Jordan (Leeds, 22, 11), Denis Law (Man City, 34, 54)

GROUP 3

Holland Rep 9, 86	(1) 2	Uruguay	(0) 0	15 June, Hannover; 53,700
Bulgaria	(0) 0	Sweden	(0) 0	15 June, Düsseldorf; 22,500
Holland	(0) 0	Sweden	(0) 0	19 June, Dortmund; 52,500

Bulgaria	(0) 1	**Uruguay**	(0) 1	19 June, Hannover; 13,400	
Bonev 75		Pavoni 87			
Holland	(2) 4	**Bulgaria**	(0) 1	23 June, Dortmund; 52,100	
Neeskens 5 (p), 44 (p),		Own goal 78			
Rep 71, de Jong 88					
Sweden	(0) 3	**Uruguay**	(0) 0	23 June, Dortmund; 28,300	
Edström 46, 77,					
Sandberg 74					

1. Holland 5pts (6–1); 2. Sweden 4pts (3–0); 3. Bulgaria 2pts (2–5); 4. Uruguay 1pt (1–6)

Holland had squeaked into the Finals but they looked like contenders here from the very first game. Their opponents, Uruguay, had Pedro Rocha, their missing playmaker from 1970, back in the side, but he was pretty much alone in trying to play football. But this sort of nonsense held no fear for the Dutch, who could look after themselves, and they won at a canter.

The first came early; Cruyff whipped in a left-footed cross from the right and the first head to it was Rep's, topped with a ridiculous and enormous mullet. Suurbier missed a great chance (what was he doing in the centre-forward position?), Jansen hit the post and Rensenbrink blazed over with a free hit from ten yards. How the game remained only 1–0 until the eighty-sixth minute I have no idea, it was just very Dutch. *"Chill out, man, don't panic, if we need another, we'll get another . . ."* Actually they didn't need another because the opposition were so bad, but it came anyway, from Rep again, a neat finish to round off a passing move between van Hanegem and Rensenbrink. Uruguay offered only thuggery in response; Montero Castillo was dismissed for a challenge so late the TV cameras missed it by a full second and Forlán (yes, it was Diego's dad) should have followed, he nearly decapitated Neeskens and had already been booked.

Holland took their foot off the gas for their second game – or maybe Sweden were just better than Uruguay. They certainly had a vastly experienced defence and Holland made few chances, but after two 0–0 draws Sweden would require a bit more from their attackers against Uruguay. It helped that Bulgaria and Uruguay drew 1–1 (imagine what a crowd-pleaser that was) – it meant any win would guarantee them a place in the second phase, and a draw would probably be enough as Bulgaria beating Holland was unlikely. The highlight of the Holland v Sweden game was a turn by Cruyff, flicking the ball between his own legs and spinning ninety degrees that had the pundits in raptures. It is an oft-shown bit of skill that came to embody the notion of Total Football.

Holland were superb against Bulgaria, creating a host of chances against a rugged defence. The only surprise was that Bulgaria scored, when Krol turned a cross into his own goal with the game all but won. Kolev started the rot by hacking down Cruyff as he threatened to cut in along the goal-line from the left. At the end of the half Vasilev hauled Jansen down as he sprinted on to a through ball. Neeskens put both penalties to the goal-keeper's right with unstoppable power; all three actually, the ref was having a *look at me* day and made him retake the first one. How like a Dutch player to put it in exactly the same place. Neeskens hit the post in between with another crashing drive. His big bushy sideburns made him look like Wolverine – he had claws, too, our Johan.

In the second half Vasilev completed his bad day by heading a free-kick straight to Rep, who volleyed it viciously past Staykov. Krol's aberration came soon after – in fairness Bonev was a foot behind him and would surely have scored had the defender not attempted a clearance – but de Jong, on for Neeskens, restored the three-goal lead with a diving header from another pinpoint Cruyff cross.

The table is misleading, Holland completely dominated this group, and Cruyff was massively impressive, even if he hadn't scored. West Germany were no longer such clear favourites. Sweden joined them in the second phase with an unexpectedly comfortable win over Uruguay. The first half was dull, the second a stroll as the young Eindhoven striker Ralf Edström put Sweden in front immediately after the break. Sandberg added a second after a clever dummy by Ahlström put him clear and Edström scored a second when Sweden broke up an attack and found themselves a man over.

GROUP 4

Italy	(0) 3	**Haiti**	(0) 1	15 June, Munich; 51,100
Rivera 52, own goal 64,		Sanon 46		
Anastasi 78				
Poland	(2) 3	**Argentina**	(0) 2	15 June, Stuttgart; 31,500
Lato 7, 62, Szarmach 8,		Heredia 60,		
Babington 66				
Argentina	(1) 1	**Italy**	(1) 1	19 June, Stuttgart; 68,900
Houseman 20		Own goal 36		
Poland	(5) 7	**Haiti**	(0) 0	19 June, Munich; 25,400
Lato 17, 88, Deyna 18,				
Szarmach 30, 35, 50,				
Gorgon 30				
Argentina	(2) 4	**Haiti**	(0) 1	23 June, Munich; 24,000
Yazalde 15, 68,		Sanon 63		
Houseman 18, Ayala 55				
Poland	(2) 2	**Italy**	(0) 1	23 June, Stuttgart; 68,900
Szarmach 38, Deyna 44		Capello 85		

1. **Poland 6pts (12–3); 2. Argentina 3pts (7–5); 3. Italy 3pts (5–4); 4. Haiti 0pts (2–14)**

The last group was expected to be a stand-off between the ageing, wily Italians and the new Argentina side under their former defender Vladislao Cap. Not much was really expected of Poland without their star striker Lubanski, despite their display against England, and Haiti were a weak side and playing, like Zaire, under severe pressure applied by an obnoxious regime.

It would make a great quiz question: who broke Dino Zoff's world record time in internationals without conceding a goal of nineteen hours and three minutes? Answer: Emmanuel Sanon, whose goals against Italy and Argentina earned him a spell with Belgian side Beerschot. Here he outpaced the Italian defence (as my mum would probably have done) and rounded the mighty Dino to penetrate the impenetrable at the start of the second half. It woke Italy up and they won easily enough, but it showed their faults for others to see.

In the second game Argentina got off to a rotten start. Mario Kempes, the new teenage sensation, missed a glorious one-on-one and a minute later his side were behind. Carnevali dropped a routine corner and Lato volleyed in the loose ball. Basic stuff; it took Cap five matches to work out Carnevali was rubbish, and he had Ubaldo Fillol on the bench, one of the best goalkeepers Argentina have had. A minute later Argentina gave the ball away in a bad zone and Lato played in the centre-forward Szarmach,

Lubanski's replacement, who scored with great confidence. The Górnik Zabrze striker was a complete unknown before the tournament; he was a star at the end of it. Argentina were in disarray and were almost overwhelmed. Deyna forced a sprawling save from Carnevali and Lato hit the post with a delicious curled free-kick while Szarmach had a shot cleared off the line and hit the post when he should have scored after another terrible defensive mix-up. It was a surprise when Argentina got a goal back, an excellent dipping strike from Heredia, but Poland scored again two minutes later. A free-kick was pushed to the massive centre-half Gorgon but his powerful strike was straight at Carnevali. The goalkeeper tried to launch a quick counter but succeeded only in freeing Lato to bear down on him and score inside the post. Four more minutes and a fine run and cross from Ayala and header back across goal from Kempes found Babington unmarked; Argentina had four efforts at goal from less than six yards before Babington finally scrambled the ball home. It was still Poland who had the better chances after that and they thoroughly deserved the win. The applecart was lying on its side.

Argentina and Italy cancelled each other out in Stuttgart. Houseman scored a sensational volley after twenty minutes from Babington's lovely long ball but Italy dug in and a suspect defence never looked secure. The own goal that brought Italy level was unlucky – Perfumo didn't expect Benetti's control to let him down and his thrust of the leg seemed almost involuntary – it was enough to turn the ball in. Argentina looked enthusiastic but dodgy, Italy looked reliable but unenthusiastic. Their great new hope, the striker Giorgio Chinaglia, raised in Wales and very British in style, big and powerful and direct, had a stinker, was taken off after sixty minutes and threw an epic tantrum, remonstrating with the bench and throwing stuff around in the changing rooms. The press had a ball.

Poland were both enthusiastic and exciting, and they ripped into Haiti. Lato end-stopped the scoring and in between there was a leisurely hat-trick for Szarmach, a goal for the excellent skipper Deyna and a free-kick from the man-mountain Gorgon that was greeted with hilarity by his team-mates, which seems a bit mean. He did give it a right old smack. Carnage.

Argentina needed to beat Haiti with some comfort and hope Poland did them a favour. The first part was easy, even without finishing as sharp as the Poles, and despite another good performance from Francillon, the Haiti goalkeeper who was their best player throughout.

Poland were in no mood to allow Italy easy passage and left them with a mountain to climb after taking a 2–0 half-time lead. Szarmach buried a fantastic header from Kasperczak's cross, despite the close attentions of his marker, and a few minutes later Kasperczak made as if to cross again, played the ball square to Deyna instead and watched his captain plant a fierce shot just inside Zoff's left-hand post. Poland's finishing was first rate. Chinaglia, back in the side, was lightweight again and substituted less visibly at half-time. Italy tried manfully to get back level but they were always vulnerable on the break and Capello's goal (yes, that one) came too late to make any difference.

Italy purged their team after the tournament; former greats like Riva, Rivera and Mazzola were history, and the next tournament saw the first flowering of one of their very best sides.

GROUP A

Brazil Rivelino 60	(0) 1	**E. Germany**	(0) 0	26 June, Hannover; 58,463
Holland Cruyff 11, 90, Krol 25, Rep 73	(2) 4	**Argentina**	(0) 0	26 June, Gelsenkirchen; 55,348
Argentina Brindisi	(1) 1	**Brazil** Rivelino 32, Jairzinho 49	(1) 2	30 June, Hannover; 38,000
Holland Neeskens 7, Rensenbrink 58	(1) 2	**E. Germany**	(0) 0	30 June, Gelsenkirchen; 67,148
E. Germany Streich 14	(1) 1	**Argentina** Houseman 20	(1) 1	3 July, Gelsenkirchen; 53,054
Brazil	(0) 0	**Holland** Neeskens 50, Cruyff 65	(0) 2	3 July, Dortmund; 52,500

1. Holland 6pts (8–0); 2. Brazil 4pts (3–3); 3. East Germany 1pt (1–4); 4. Argentina 1pt (2–7)

The two surviving South American sides faced East Germany and Holland. Brazil beat East Germany when Rivelino found the corner with a trademark vicious free-kick. Brazil still didn't convince; the team was full of very un-Brazilian athletic types with none of the subtle movement and finesse that characterised the earlier sides. Given what was at his disposal, Zagallo cut his cloth accordingly. The result was desperately disappointing.

Even with such threadbare resources, Brazil saw off Argentina. It was a poor game between two football nations of pedigree, but another swerving drive from Rivelino gave Brazil the lead, and a header from Jairzinho won it after Mario Brindisi, the golden boy of Argentina, equalised with a neat free-kick. Argentina were neat and pretty but had no thrust up front – Kempes and Ayala were too similar, technically gifted but neither a true centre-forward. And Brian Clough should have reserved his barbs for their goalkeeper. Carnevali flapped at crosses, rushed out of his goal too early whenever an attacker broke free and generally sent the heebie-jeebies throughout his defence. Five games too late they picked Fillol and drew their last game with East Germany – they should have won – when Kempes finally contributed something and beat two men before flighting an inviting cross for Houseman to finish. The failure of the team to fulfil their potential led to a managerial change; César Luis Menotti was the new broom and by the next World Cup all but Houseman, Kempes and Fillol were swept away.

Holland eased through. They crushed Argentina in a game played in pouring rain on a soaking pitch, their speed and precision and power leaving Argentina bemused and forlorn. Cruyff was imperious, scoring twice and crossing for Johnny Rep to head home; the attacking left-back Krol scored with a deflected rocket. In the next game they cruised past East Germany in third gear, retaining possession rather than looking for the killer blow. It was a trait that would cost them dearly. Neeskens hammered home another trademark rocket and Rob Rensenbrink, the left-winger who played for Anderlecht in Belgium, opened his account for the competition.

The decider against Brazil was a rough affair that had Mário Zagallo crying foul about the Dutch tackling. Amidst all the fluff about Total Football, it is easy to forget that this Dutch team were a hard bunch. Even without the powerful centre-half Hulshoff, who missed the tournament through injury, there were some fierce tacklers. The left-back Ruud Krol was a forefather of Stuart

Pearce; no wonder he was such an attacking force as the attacker was usually left breathless on the ground after colliding with those thighs. He was also a sumptuous passer of the ball. Jansen and Haan were uncompromising in defence, van Hanegem could tackle and Neeskens was just plain nasty, leaving a sly foot in and going for the ankles. Even the great artist Johan Cruyff was no stranger to the physical side of the game; watch him shield the ball and he's all elbows and knees, an impenetrable barrier. If the defender collided with one of those protruding limbs, so be it.

The coach of the Holland team was Rinus Michels, the genius who built up Ajax of Amsterdam into Europe's top team. Michels left Ajax to manage Barcelona (and took Cruyff with him two years later), but now he was back to make sure Holland maxim-ised their opportunity after their let-off against Belgium. Like Ajax, the Dutch were as much about keeping things tight as they were about scoring goals – look at the record of both sides and it is littered with 1–0s and goalless draws – including two 0–0s against Belgium which helped the Dutch squeeze into the finals. Their system has been described – by Brian Glanville amongst others – as Total Football, with complete fluidity and interchang-ing of positions. This is an exaggeration. The full-backs were full-backs. They were assured in possession and attacked – that was nothing new to world football – but their main job was to defend, and they knew how to do that, too, unlike some of the over-rated walkabout Brazilian full-backs we've seen over the years. Yes, occasionally Suurbier or Krol would pop up in the opposition penalty area, but then so did Facchetti, full-back with the utterly defensive Inter and Italy teams. Hulshoff's young replacement, Wim Rijsbergen, stayed in the middle (he was actually a full-back for his club) where he was abetted by Arie Haan and Wim Jansen; nominally half-backs, these two would share the duties of the extra centre-back, with Haan playing as a sweeper in front of the defence and Jansen as a more conventional defensive midfield player.

Johan Neeskens and Wim van Hanegem were in midfield and their job was to retain possession and make sure Cruyff and company got the supply they needed. Van Hanegem was a stroller, a bit one-paced and bandy-legged but with a great range of passing and a bit of aggression; he would act as deep-lying feeder (similar in position and style to Gérson of Brazil) while Neeskens, a brisker, sharper player would advance and look to add his ferocious shooting to the attacking mix (van Hanegem scored six times in fifty-two games, Neeskens seventeen in forty-nine games).

Much is made of the fluidity of the forwards Rensenbrink, Rep and Cruyff. Again, there was less unusual than we have been led to believe. Cruyff was the principal goalscorer but he was no one's idea of a traditional centre-forward. He was ungovernable, both as player and individual, so coaches left him to it, and he would fill the opposition half with his presence, his feints and dribbles and tricks and swivels; one turn against Sweden when he flicked the ball past a defender with his heel and turned in off the touchline was replayed again and again. Rep and Rensenbrink stayed central or moved wide to accommodate Cruyff's genius. Rensenbrink was skilful and sinuous and could beat players at will – he played in Cruyff's mobile position for Anderlecht but suppressed his ego for the Holland team (which makes him a rarity). Rep was strong and direct and attacked the ball well in the penalty area as well as dropping deep to engage his powerful shooting – he and Rensenbrink had similar scoring records but a much greater proportion of Rep's goals came in World Cup Finals matches.

The fluidity didn't come from the whole team, it came from Cruyff, just as it had at Ajax; he moved everywhere, demanding the ball, and, if he filled a colleague's space, they moved in or out accordingly, hence the belief of interchangeability. It wasn't a ploy, it was fluidity born partly and paradoxically of intractability, the refusal of stubborn players to adhere to a tactical plan. It was Holland. David Winner's fabulous 2000 book *Brilliant Orange* spends over 250 pages trying to explain and eventually concludes (I paraphrase and over-simplify) *Why do I bother, they're Dutch*, so what chance do I have in a paragraph?

Another myth: that the Dutch were just Ajax in orange shirts – the Amsterdam team had won three European Cups since the last World Cup. Six of the squad were from Ajax (make it seven, as Cruyff had been an integral part of the European Cup-winning squad before moving to Barcelona), seven were from their principal rivals Feyenoord. The team that played in the final had five from Ajax, three from Feyenoord, plus Cruyff, goalkeeper Jan Jongbloed (a late replacement) and Rensenbrink, who played for Anderlecht in Belgium.

They beat Brazil rather easily, by the way, hence Zagallo's protestations. The Brazilians missed a couple of early chances after an unusually slow start from Holland but once the Dutch found their rhythm it was one-way traffic, punctuated only by a series of appalling tackles from both sides. It would have ended eight men apiece thirty years on – Rep stayed on the field after a blatant elbow in the face earned only a booking. Both Dutch goals were sweet moves finished with aplomb by Neeskens and Cruyff – silk and steel.

GROUP B

Yugoslavia	(0) 0	**West Germany** (1) 2	26 June, Düsseldorf; 66,085	
		Breitner 39, Müller 82		
Poland	(1) 1	**Sweden**	(0) 0	26 June, Stuttgart; 43,755
Lato 44				
West Germany	(0) 4	**Sweden**	(1) 2	30 June, Düsseldorf; 67,861
Overath 51, Bonhof 52,		Edstrom 24,		
Grabowski 76,		Sandberg 53		
Hoeness 89 (p)				
Yugoslavia	(1) 1	**Poland**	(1) 2	30 June, Frankfurt; 53,200
Karasi 43		Deyna 24 (p), Lato 62		
West Germany	(0) 1	**Poland**	(0) 0	3 July, Frankfurt; 61,249
Müller				
Sweden	(1) 2	**Yugoslavia**	(1) 1	3 July, Düsseldorf; 31,700
Edström 29,		Surjak 27		
Torstensson 85				

1. West Germany 6pts (7–2); 2. Poland 4pts (3–2); 3. Sweden 2pts (4–6); 4. Yugoslavia 0pts (2–6)

The West German squad was in a dark place, and Helmut Schön took to his hotel room in a fit of pique/depression. It was the moment Beckenbauer stepped up to be top dog in the establishment; a hastily convened press conference was called to make up for a no-show by Schön at the previous one, and it was the captain, not the manager, who did most of the talking. Calm, unhurried, articulate, Beckenbauer made remarks about the side's level of performance that implied changes to the side; who can say whether Schön had already bought into this or whether Beckenbauer was forcing his hand?

West Germany were in an all-European group with Poland, Sweden and Yugoslavia; manageable, but they would have to up their levels. Of course they did, they're German, and they had five world-class players and a number of other very good ones. They were much improved against Yugoslavia, with Hoeness back in the starting line-up and Bonhof of Borussia Mönchengladbach adding some zest. Breitner thumped the opener from way out, and Müller added a late second to seal it, but the back four never gave Yugoslavia's talented but easily disheartened forwards a look-in. It was essentially the Bayern Munich defence that won the European Cup a few weeks earlier, only with Gladbach's Berti Vogts at right-back – maybe if Bayern's Johnny Hansen had been German instead of Danish, Schön would have picked him as well. I jest – Vogts was Mr Dependable and a key member of the team.

Poland were looking likely too. They beat Sweden in a tight encounter with few chances. Gadocha switched wings and hit a deep cross from the right, Szarmach headed back across goal and Lato nodded the ball in from two yards out. In the second half England's nemesis Tomaszewski kept Poland in front, making three excellent saves, including Tapper's penalty, hit hard but at a nice height.

Poland squeezed past Yugoslavia four days after, in Frankfurt. They were gifted a goal in a niggly game when Karasi needlessly kicked out at Szarmach as the players were clearing the area; today a referee would probably have carried on with play rather than award a penalty, then returned and sent off Karasi as the incident was well after the ball had moved on. Karasi survived and provided the equaliser just before half-time with a smart finish to round off an excellent, patient passing move. As usual Yugoslavia produced too little of the football they were capable of and they conceded a winner to Lato's header from another excellent corner from Gadocha. The Polish forwards weren't tall (Szarmach was five foot ten and Lato five foot nine) but they attacked the ball well in the air and Gadocha hit flat skimming corners that negated the extra height of the central defenders.

West Germany trailed Sweden 1–0 in their next game, but played their best half thus far to win the best game of the group

4–2 – and without Müller contributing a goal. Sweden were full of fight but West Germany simply had the better players. They dominated possession in the first half but the Swedes are invariably well organised and they kept their feet and didn't give away silly free-kicks and concede possession too easily. Herzog, who had come in on the wing for the second phase, was anonymous and the Germans struggled to make clear chances. It was Sweden who got the only goal of the half. A clearance was headed into the air, Edström watched it drop and executed a perfect dipping volley beyond Maier – the German defence should have done better than stand and watch.

West Germany immediately stepped up the pace in the second half and Beckenbauer forced a save from Hellström in the first minute. Müller made a nuisance of himself in the area – the ball wasn't cleared and Overath drove home with his "wrong" foot. Less than a minute later Müller chested the ball down for Bonhof to hit a terrific strike which Hellström could only divert onto the post – the ball rolled the width of the goal-line before sneaking in off the second upright. West Germany switched off momentarily, and a deep cross skimmed Schwarzenbeck's head and fell to Sandberg, who politely accepted the present. Vogts gave Schwarzenbeck a right earful, which was brave of him.

West Germany still looked the more likely and a persistent attack ended with Grabowski – on for Herzog and back in the team to stay – to fire across Hellström. Germany sensibly kept pressing and Sweden struggled to build attacks; when they did they found Beckenbauer in impassable mode playing just ahead of the other defenders. Hölzenbein hit a post, Müller poked a good chance narrowly wide and then made a meal of the slightest touch as he motored into the box to win a last-minute penalty, which Uli Hoeness buried.

Sweden had made a good contribution to the tournament and ended it well by beating Yugoslavia in their last game, Edström adding to his burgeoning reputation with his fourth goal of the competition.

Just as in the first group the tournament effectively had a semi-final with a crunch game between West Germany and Poland, albeit one in which West Germany only needed a draw. The match was played in appalling conditions – this was a pretty wet World Cup – in Frankfurt and West Germany coped marginally better. The Polish wingers were well policed by Vogts and Breitner and they used the energetic Bonhof to limit Deyna's influence. Sepp Maier made a couple of crucial saves from Lato as West Germany dug in. One was a spectacular salmon leap effort when the confident Polish winger went for an outrageous strike from a free-kick way out on the right. The other was something of a collector's item when Maier made a great double save from Gadocha and then Lato after Beckenbauer aimed a complete air shot at an attempted clearance. Banner headline – BECKENBAUER FALLIBLE AFTER ALL!

They had their moments in the game but the Poles missed the cavalry-officer moustache of the injured Szarmach bristling at the head of their attack; his replacement Domarski, who scored that vital goal in the qualifier at Wembley, was a good technical player but neither so aggressive nor so potent in front of goal. West Germany picked the Eintracht Frankfurt striker Bernd Hölzenbein for the second phase games. In the Bundesliga Hölzenbein, like England's Franny Lee, had a reputation as one adept at winning penalties. In uncouth parlance, he was a clever cheat. Here he lived up to his reputation with a nonsensical piece of theatrics, but justice was served when the ever-acrobatic Tomaszewski saved a rather tame spot-kick from Hoeness. Tomaszewski never repeated his heroics against England in West Germany, and he never cured his indecision on crosses, but he was a remarkable shot-stopper. It mattered little, West Germany were in control by this stage. Bonhof was put through by Hölzenbein's neat touch and then was challenged on the edge of the box; the ball broke to Müller, unmarked about twelve yards out and he made no mistake.

Poland went home with heads high; they won six games out of seven, even beating Brazil in the third-place play-off. In Deyna, the sweeper Zmuda (playing in the first of four World Cups at twenty), Lato and Szarmach they had world-class players – Lato scored seven in seven to win the Golden Boot – with willing accomplices in Kasperczak, the tireless winger Gadocha and the elegant Musial at the back. The strapping six foot four stopper

Jerzy Gorgon became something of a cult figure with his mythical name, silly mullet and enormous thighs. The Poles were beginning their best football decade; only when they started to lose their best players to wealthier foreign clubs did they slip back to the periphery. Gorgon and Szarmach's club side, Górnik Zabrze, captained by Wlodi Lubanski, had presaged the success of the national team by reaching the European Cup Winners' Cup Final in 1970, the first time a Polish side had reached a European Final. They lost on the big occasion, 2–1, to Manchester City, but wins over Rangers (very strong at the time) and AS Roma were a reminder that there were talented players in the country.

THIRD-PLACE MATCH

Poland	(0) 1	**Brazil**	(0) 0	6 July, Munich; 74,100
Lato 76				

World Cup Heroes No.15

Kazimierz Deyna (1947–89)

Poland

A debate on Poland's finest ever player is a debate on the merits of Kazimierz Deyna and Zbigniew Boniek. Deyna was a composed midfield "stroller" with an eye for goal and a super temperament, which benefited some of his more excitable colleagues.

Deyna made his debut for Poland at 20 years old and was a key member of the squad by the time of the 1972 Olympics, where Poland won the Gold Medal in the football. Deyna scored nine goals from midfield in the tournament, including both goals in the final against Hungary. Gradually the Poles improved their squad, adding in Lato, Kasperczak, Szymanowski and Zmuda to an already talented line-up. They crept in to the 1974 Finals under the radar as everyone assumed they would lose out to England, and were still under-rated at the start of the competition, with their captain and best player, Lubanski, out injured.

Except Lubanski wasn't their best player, he was just the totemic figure who dragged them out of the football wilderness. Deyna was their best player, unhurried on the ball, with a powerful shot and a long stride that took him clear of tacklers in a pace or two. In Lubanski's absence he was made captain and he remained the Poland skipper until the end of the 1978 World Cup Finals campaign. He ended his career with ninety-seven caps and forty-one goals – helluva strike rate for a midfielder (Frank Lampard has twenty-nine in the same number of games). In 1974 Deyna was third in the Footballer of the Year award – big deal, you think, until spotting that numbers one and two were Johan Cruyff and Franz Beckenbauer, which made Deyna the best mortal. He was a notch below those guys, but sill a fantastic footballer.

He spent most of his best years at Legia Warsaw then three years at Manchester City after the 1978 World Cup, but injuries meant City never saw the best of him. Deyna took the Yankee dollar and moved to the NASL with San Diego Shockers; he retired in California but was killed in a motor accident two years later aged only forty-one. Legia Warsaw no longer use the No.10 shirt – this was one of the first instances of a club retiring a shirt in a player's honour.

Deyna played the Polish prisoner-of-war Pavel Wolcheck in the camp team in the cheesy 1981 film *Escape To Victory*. His main thespian expression was one of bemusement – not dissimilar to the one worn by most who saw the film.

WORLD CUP FINAL No.10
7 July 1974, Olympiastadion, Munich; 75,200

West Germany (2) 2 Breitner 25 (p), Müller 43
Holland (1) 1 Neeskens 2 (p)

Referee: **Jack Taylor** (Eng)
Coaches: **Helmut Schön** (West Germany) & **Rinus Michels** (Holland)

West Germany (4–4–2): Sepp Maier (Bayern Munich); Berti Vogts (Borussia Mönchengladbach), Franz Beckenbauer (Bayern), George Schwarzenbeck (Bayern), Paul Breitner (Bayern); Jürgen Grabowski (Eintracht Frankfurt), Rainer Bonhof (Gladbach), Uli Hoeness (Bayern), Wolfgang Overath (Cologne); Gerd Müller (Bayern), Bernd Hölzenbein (Eintracht Frankfurt)

Holland (3–4–3): Jan Jongbloed (FC Amsterdam); Wim Suurbier (Ajax), Wim Rijsbergen (Feyenoord), Ruud Krol (Ajax); Wim Jansen (Feyenoord); Wim van Hanegem (Feyenoord), Johan Neeskens (Ajax), Arie Haan (Ajax); Johnny Rep (Ajax), Johan Cruyff (Ajax), Rob Rensenbrink (Anderlecht). **Subs:** Rene van der Kerkhof (PSV Eindhoven) for Rensenbrink, 45m; Theo de Jong (Feyenoord) for Rijsbergen, 69m
Cautioned: Vogts (WGer) 4m, van Hanegem (Hol) 23m, Neeskens (Hol) 42m, Cruyff (Hol) 45m

At least the two best sides made the final, played the day after Poland clinched third place with a dreary 1–0 win against Brazil – it was obvious which team regarded third place as a triumph and which saw it as failure.

Most reports of the Final preferred the angle of German implacability against Dutch invention but that's nonsense. It was the early seventies, youthful rebellion was still the *plat du jour,* so the Dutch weren't quite the iconoclastic mavericks they were painted – it was the Germans who almost refused to play in the tournament and Paul Breitner, their left-back, who liked to be seen reading Karl Marx. Apparently the irony of demanding playboy wages while reading Marx was lost on the big-haired boy.

Nor were the Dutch the upholders of progressive and creative football against the onrushing Teutonic machine. The Germans had Beckenbauer and Overath and (on the bench) Netzer, sublime technicians and wonderful players to watch. And the Dutch were just as happy to crunch into a tackle as Schwarzenbeck or Vogts. Holland had played better in the earlier rounds, but that counted for nothing in the final. Many World Cup winners have started slowly – Italy were rubbish in the group games in 1982, England were a bit wooden in '66, Spain ineffectual in their 2010 opener against Switzerland.

Most pundits felt that Holland would win if they played to their best. The German tabloids had more pressing concerns, printing a sensational (and unsubstantiated) piece about naked pool parties in the Dutch camp earlier in the proceedings. It probably made little difference to the Dutch, but it was a factor in their 1978 campaign . . .

The referee for the Final was England's Jack Taylor. Taylor made his presence felt in the right way before the match even started when he noticed there were no corner flags. Reassuring to see even the hyper-efficient Germans could make basic errors.

The opening to the game was even more dramatic, and again Taylor played a role. In the opening seconds Cruyff jogged back to his own centre-half and demanded the ball. A patient interchange of passes followed and Cruyff popped up in the inside-left channel. He beat Vogts with an exhilarating change of pace and was brought down by a rash challenge from Hoeness. Taylor had the courage to give a perfectly legitimate penalty award; Beckenbauer's hand-waving was – for now – merely arrogant and irrelevant. Neeskens' penalties were rarely stopped. It was the first penalty in a World Cup Final.

The second came twenty-three minutes later and showed Taylor's weakness. Beckenbauer had chirruped his way through the first twenty minutes, questioning every decision, and Taylor cracked. Hölzenbein was allowed to run into a crowded area from a position of no threat and he went over the first foot that came towards him. There was no contact, but Taylor fell for it – had he not watched the footage of the semi-final? After that apology for a penalty by Hoeness against Poland, Paul Breitner was allotted the job and he rolled it into the corner. Taylor was standing eight feet away and failed to notice that Breitner had not placed the ball on the spot.

Cruyff had disappeared, suppressed by his marker, Vogts, who let him go deep but picked him up as soon as he ventured into a threatening area. Some of the German tackling was hard but it could never be termed intimidatory, and Cruyff's protests at half-time as were ill-judged as Beckenbauer's earlier. Only once did he get room again in the first half and he put Rep clear on the left, but the striker shot hastily and unconvincingly at Maier. Moments later Bonhof ran clear on the right, beat Haan (he could have gone for another penalty but elected to stay on his feet) and crossed low to the near post. Müller took a touch to give him breathing space from Krol, and somehow hooked the ball from behind him with enough power to beat the goalkeeper – brilliant finishing, Krol did nothing wrong.

The second half consisted of a succession of Dutch attacks repelled without too many loud alarms by the Germans. When they did get possession West Germany showed they could keep the ball just as well as Holland, with Overath, playing in a deeper role, always a claiming influence and outlet for beleaguered defenders. What joy the Dutch did get came when they got the ball wide, but their lack of a true goalscorer told, as all too frequently no one got on the end of the cross. Rensenbrink was carrying an injury and was withdrawn at half-time for René van der Kerkhof, Rep had a poor game and van Hanegem went missing. He later claimed Holland overplayed in the first half to taunt the Germans but that reads as too glib; it's symptomatic of one of the weaknesses of Dutch football that they claimed they were just too good and forgot to win the match. They have never been good at analysing and learning from failure. (England have the same fault, oddly, lots of hair shirt and gnashing and wailing but no conspicuous attempt to do anything different.) It was their normal style of game to play keep-ball, so why is so much made of the fact they did it in a final? On the rare occasions Holland broke the German wall they found Maier in terrific form – the stand-out save was one great block at the near post when he stood tall to parry a fierce blunderbuss of a volley from Neeskens.

The truth was Holland thought they were going to win, but were outthought tactically. Vogts did a great marking job despite an early booking, and Cruyff was irritated rather than flattered and inspired by the attention. The rest were so dependent on Cruyff to make the play that no one stepped up to fill the void; Neeskens and van Hanagem were exceptional players but neither shone here. West Germany used Beckenbauer a little further forward alongside Overath to deny the playmakers room, leaving Schwarzenbeck and the full-backs to pick up the attackers if they wandered into the area. Hölzenbein played wider than usual and he and Grabowski pushed back the Dutch full-backs, reducing their efficacy as an attacking force. Müller did his thing, and behind him Bonhof covered quite awesome amounts of ground in both supporting the centre-forward and helping the defence – it was the game the Gladbach star really stepped up to belong in this august company.

Holland were a great side, man for man they were better than West Germany, but Holland never seem to have the team ethic the Germans can boast and the togetherness was crucial. West Germany had to be at their best, and were; Holland never came close to theirs after the first fifteen minutes. And West Germany had Gerd Müller, the finest predator the penalty area has known. Müller was rarely seen in wide positions and rarely ventured into his own half. Müller's territory was the penalty area and the land in a line between the area and the halfway line. He would prowl there, bandy-legged, innocuous-looking, ready to explode if his side mounted an attack. He wasn't exceptionally quick (except over ten yards and in his head), wasn't amazing in the air, didn't possess a hammer of a shot and didn't have the dribbling skills to take out two defenders in a mazy run. But still he scored sixty-eight goals in sixty-two internationals, few of them easy pickings against muppets. They key was anticipation – when the ball came to Müller he always knew what he was going to do with it, and prepared his body shape accordingly. His first touch was designed not to bring the ball to his feet necessarily, but to take it where a defender couldn't reach it, and his low centre of gravity gave him impeccable balance and he was able to get shots or headers away with only a fraction of the room lesser players required. Football writers and fans use an apparently meaningless term "he/she knows where the goal is" – it is used for strikers who can find the target without lifting their head to aim. Puskás had it, Jimmy Greaves had it, Davor Suker had it; Müller was the ultimate expression of knowing where the goal is.

Müller retired from international football at the top after West Germany won the World Cup and a year later went to play in the USA. He struggled with alcohol in the '80s until some of his former team-mates helped him clean up (togetherness, right?) and he still works at Bayern Munich. One of the all-time greats.

West Germany were the first, and deserving, recipients of the brand new FIFA World Cup Trophy designed and created by the noted Italian sculptor Gazzaniga. Defeat or no, Holland were hailed as one of the great teams and by all accounts their party after the match was an epic affair – unlike the Germans, who mostly boycotted their official "do" after the German FA, in typically misanthropic mode, refused to allow wives and partners to attend.

World Cup Heroes No.16
Wolfgang Overath (1943–)
West Germany

West Germany in 1974 had six world-class players, and by that I mean players of the very, very highest quality. Five of them were Sepp Maier, Paul Breitner, Franz Beckenbauer, Gerd Müller and Gunter Netzer, but Netzer didn't even make the team. The reason Netzer wasn't picked was Wolfgang Overath. At the 1972 European Championships Netzer was outstanding, dictating play and offering a goal threat with his powerful shooting.

But Helmut Schön was unconvinced. He (and, it is alleged, the caucus of Bayern Munich players within the team) preferred the less obvious but subtle skills of Overath alongside the graft of Hoeness and Bonhof. Less likely to do something sensational, unless one was an aficionado of deliciously curled left-foot passes, Overath was also less likely to give the ball away, which suited Schön's plan. Only in the unexpected and painful defeat by East Germany did Netzer get an airing, twenty minutes as substitute for Overath.

The press demanded the inclusion of the Gladbach player, but Schön (and Beckenbauer by this stage) stood firm, and Overath's game improved in the second phase, where his telling looped passes on stodgy pitches were one of the Germans' best assets.

Overath made his debut for West Germany in 1963, and was in the team during both the 1966 and 1970 World Cup Finals tournaments. His eventual nineteen appearances in the Finals by the end of the 1974 contest was second only to his countryman Uwe Seeler at the time. By the end of the tournament Overath had silenced the German press, and achieved a new status amongst German football fans – they loved him because he didn't play for Bayern Munich as well as for being gifted.

It is possible he is not rated as highly in England as some of his compatriots, because he was largely anonymous in the two memorable encounters between the two sides in 1966 and 1970; the hard-running England midfielders closed down space better than most opponents and Overath liked a bit of time to ply his trade. He was similar in style to Liam Brady, but played a little deeper than the Irishman. Like Gerd Müller he called time on his international career on the high note of winning the World Cup.

Overath was a one-club man, spending his entire career at 1.FC Köln (Cologne) and winning the league title in 1963–64, one of the three occasions Cologne lifted the trophy.

Team of the Tournament, 1974:

Maier (West Germany)

Vogts (West Germany)   Beckenbauer (West Germany)   Krol (Holland)   Breitner (West Germany)

Deyna (Poland)   Neeskens (West Germany)   Overath (West Germany)

Lato (Poland)   Müller (West Germany)   Cruyff (Holland)

Official Team of the Tournament: Most unusually, the official side differs from mine in only one position; they rather curiously selected **Rensenbrink** ahead of Müller. Both teams feature Krol in a central position, where he would later prove himself equally comfortable, to accommodate Breitner – if picking a true centre-half it would probably be the veteran **Björn Nordqvist** of Sweden.

Leading scorers: Lato (7); Szarmach & Neeskens (5)

Heaven Eleven No.7

Germany (including West & East):

Coach:
Sepp Herberger. Patriotic, crafty, good motivator, and wouldn't stand any nonsense from the troublemakers.

Goalkeepers:
Sepp Maier: World Cup winner who got better with age
Oliver Kahn: Germany's best player in their "wilderness years" either side of 2000

Harald Schumacher: remembered for one incident but was a better goalkeeper after that; a legend at Cologne

Defenders:
Franz Beckenbauer: the best ever
Matti Sammer: best East German player
Karl-Heinz Schnellinger: uncompromising defender, adept at right-back or in the middle
Berti Vogts: tough-tackling right-back, just don't let him near the manager's job . . .
Paul Breitner: attacking right-back, converted to midfield where he was never as effective
Philipp Lahm: wonderful modern attacking left-back
Karlheinz Förster: great stopper and man-marker

Midfield & wide:
Fritz Walter: creative, cultured, deep-lying playmaker
Helmut Rahn: aggressive goalscoring winger from the 1950s
Lothar Matthäus: good holding and box-to-box midfielder with a great shot, rubbish centre-back
Michael Ballack: great goalscoring midfielder, a combination of Lampard and Gerrard
Wolfgang Overath: sweet left foot, lovely, deceptively lazy style
Bernd Schuster: great all-round player – not always the best team-player
Günter Netzer: urgent, aggressive, ball-carrying playmaker
Pierre Littbarski: tricky winger with quick feet and good distribution

Strikers:
Gerd Müller: supreme predator
Jürgen Klinsmann: hard-working, charismatic and skilful, a complete modern forward
Uwe Seeler: great target man and hard running striker, super in the air
Karl-Heinz Rummenigge: striker-cum-wide-player, good finisher, lightning-quick over a few yards and on the turn
Rudi Völler: great positional player, good poacher

Omissions: Hardly anyone from the '80s and '90s – but then they just weren't quite at it: **Hassler, Andi Möller, Brehme, Kaltz, Kohler** – they were all a step short of this class, they just didn't realise it. Of the earlier generations **Jupp Posipal** was a top defender, and **Max Morlock** a crafty inside-forward with a good scoring record. We could as easily have included **Jürgen Grabowski** as Littbarski. Of the current crop Schweinsteiger has much to offer, while **Thomas Müller**, goalkeeper **Neuer**, **Mesut Özil** and the dominant defender **Mats Hummels** may all yet reach legendary status. Perhaps the unluckiest is **Miroslav Klose** – I just have a vague feeling that he is not quite as good as his goals record. The former East German **Joachim Streich** was considered – a top striker in a second-rate team. Recent retiree **Arne Friedrich** is not far behind Förster and Schnellinger at centre-back.

Likely first XI:

Kahn

Vogts Beckenbauer Förster Lahm

Rahn Matthäus Schuster Overath

Müller Rummenigge

5.2 REFEREES

It is a tough job, everyone tells us – players, managers, chairmen, FIFA suits, even referees themselves. Usually they tell us that shortly before complaining about the referee and how he has ruined their team's opportunity and spoiled their day ... blah blah blah ... Fergie, Wenger, Mourinho, all the high-profile managers do it, they needle and carp in the hope that next time that referee will remember not to upset them and earn their opprobrium. Often it works, referees are human and these are powerful, intimidating individuals. It is all part of the mind games.

And it's nothing new. The Italian manager in the 1930s, Vittorio Pozzo, was fond of pointing out to referees which opposing players were most likely to transgress. Bobby Moore was always unfailingly polite and respectful with referees – it perpetuated the notion that he was the perfect gentleman and would never, never commit a foul, your honour, not Bobby. Once, when a referee was pole-axed by a shot, Moore even did the decent thing and grabbed the whistle to bring the game to a halt – well that referee was hardly going to book him next time out, was he? Italian and South American captains in the 1960s liked to act as a second referee on the pitch, offering advice and guidance to the official official. Not all referees appreciated the help – Herr Kreitlein got so fed up of Rattin's "assistance" he sent him off in 1966. Eight years later Beckenbauer's innocent-seeming comment to Jack Taylor when he awarded an early penalty against West Germany – *"you are an Englishman"* – was delivered with such weight that it manifestly affected Taylor's judgement when he next had to make a decision, resulting in the penalty given for Hölzenbein's dive.

Referees can reasonably be divided into three types; authoritative, unobtrusive and visible. Most referees opt for the unobtrusive style, try to keep a low profile and let the players get on with it, intervene if necessary but don't make a big song and dance and try and be consistent. Dermot Gallagher, Avraham Klein, the great Israeli referee, and Arppi, the Brazilian who did a great job in the 1986 World Cup Final, were all referees who preferred to fly under the radar. The problem with the unobtrusive style is that if the game gets out of hand it can be hard for the referee to wrestle back control. In the 2010 World Cup Final Howard Webb was in no way to blame for the nonsense that took place – that would be the Dutch – but he wasn't the sort of figure to scare the players back into submission.

Those kind of figures are rare, they are the authoritative referees, the ones who keep control just because they are who they are. Strong personalities for the most part, they don't need a plethora of cards to keep a grip; Pierluigi Collina, Kim Milton Nielsen and the great Scottish referee Bobby Davidson all kept control through willpower and reputation rather than by flagrant wielding of power. Just occasionally these referees can be a little too convinced of their own rectitude (because they are usually right); Nielsen's dismissal of Beckham in 1998 was born of disdain for Beckham's persona rather than football common sense.

The visible referees are the ones to avoid. They embrace every rule change with great relish and feel the need to display their awareness of every nuance and ensure that not just the players, but the crowd and TV audience know exactly who is in charge. When the FA introduced a rule to the Premier League that stated goalkeepers had six seconds to release the ball from hand once it was under their control, the first instance of a goalkeeper being penalised for such an offence was when David Elleray awarded an indirect free-kick in a televised game between Newcastle and Bolton. Alan Shearer scored and it changed the course of the game, all because Elleray desperately wanted to be the centre of attention – he was the first referee to visibly enjoy being interviewed on *Match of the Day*. It is the same need that made Clive Thomas claim he had blown the whistle to end the first-half just as Zico was heading the ball into the goal. It is the same desire to be the centre of attention that led Jorge Larrionda to disallow Frank Lampard's goal against Germany in 2010 – one glance at the body language of the German defenders told him the ball was over the line, but where was the headline in that? There is a simple hard and fast rule – when the referee is the centre of attention, it is bad for the game.

Here are the nineteen gentlemen who have refereed a World Cup Final:

Year	Referee	Country
1930	John Langenus	Belgium
1934	Ivan Eklind	Sweden
1938	Georges Capdeville	France
1950	George Reader	England
1954	Bill Ling	England
1958	Maurice Guigue	France
1962	Nikolai Latyshev	USSR
1966	Gottfried Dienst	Switzerland
1970	Rudi Glöckner	East Germany
1974	Jack Taylor	England
1978	Sergio Gonella	Italy
1982	Arnaldo Coelho	Brazil
1986	Romualdo Arppi	Brazil
1990	Edgardo Codesal	Mexico
1994	Sándor Puhl	Hungary
1998	Saïd Belqola	Morocco
2002	Pierluigi Collina	Italy
2006	Horacio Elizondo	Argentina
2010	Howard Webb	England

England has provided four World Cup Final referees, France, Italy and Brazil two apiece, and nine other countries have supplied one.

For a long while there was an assumption within the British press that our own officials were in some way more impartial and accomplished than Johnny Foreigner. The abject performances of Arthur Ellis and Ken Aston in crucial World Cup matches should have scotched that but the notion persisted. Jack Taylor wasn't

Total Football

rubbish in the 1974 Final, but he did succumb to Beckenbauer's subtle promptings; later suggestions that he was overly fussy are unfair and mainly based on the delay to the start because Taylor insisted on corner flags being placed correctly. He was absolutely right to do so and the blame lay entirely with the organisers, although one of the officials might have spotted it earlier.

English referees have not had a glorious time in recent years either; Graham Poll (a decent referee who was given an unduly hard time by the media) made a basic error in the Croatia game in 2006 and Howard Webb (a really good referee) was much criticised for his handling of the 2010 Final. Maybe we could just accept that our lot are okay, but just as prone to error as any other.

Well, not quite any other. None of the British referees has been involved in any of the true shockers, where it was hard to watch the game without the impression that something odd was going on. Either that or the officials involved were just truly incompetent, in which case why were they there? I'm teasing, there is no widespread conspiracy, but there has always been bias towards the home nation (England were beneficiaries in 1966), conscious or otherwise. It makes commercial sense to keep the hosts in as long as possible and if it makes commercial sense then you can be sure it matters to FIFA.

Award for the worst decision in a World Cup Finals match

Hmmm, I'm English, so Ali Bin Nasser is up there for Maradona's Hand of God goal against England (1986) that our three-quarters-blind Siamese cat would have spotted, as is the aforementioned Mr Larrionda for failing to see Lampard's shot land about eighteen inches over the goal-line against Germany in 2010. If I were German I would probably put in a mention for Dienst and Bakhramov in the 1966 Final. Señor Aranda's sending-off of Laurent Blanc against Croatia in the semi-final in 1998 was one with really sad repercussions, while Charles Corver's refusal to censure Harald Schumacher's assault on France's Patrick Battiston in 1982 was one of the most cowardly decisions. For an all-out dire performance, the hapless Byron Moreno Ruales of Ecuador during Italy v South Korea in 2002 takes some beating, culminating in Totti's ridiculous dismissal for diving; if he'd sent him off for having a truly awful game, fair enough, but not for that.

Do you know what, I don't care if I am English, I am a reasonably impartial man and I can't find a worse decision than the Hand of God goal. It wasn't cheating (at least not by the referee) just a rank bad decision by an official who was hopelessly out of his depth. I know the referees pool needs to be reflective of the full FIFA membership, but don't give a big game between two sides with a history of animosity to a guy with limited experience.

5.3 WORLD CUP 1978

FIFA persisted with the awful second-phase groups, but this was the last World Cup with only sixteen sides in the Finals; the lure of ever more lucre meant twenty-four teams would turn up in Italy four years later. FIFA announced that in the knockout rounds (which in this format meant only the third-place match and the final) penalties would decide the winner if the scores were level after extra-time.

When the choice of host was made in 1966 Argentina seemed perfectly acceptable; they were the biggest South American football country yet to host the event and they had agreed to withdraw their application for 1970 in Mexico's favour in return for a reciprocal free run at the nomination, which they got. On football grounds they were an ideal host; enthusiastic, knowledgeable (if partisan) fans, big grounds (two in Buenos Aires and one each in Córdoba, Mar del Plata, Rosario and Mendoza). The final was scheduled for the Monumental in Buenos Aires, home of the River Plate club.

The problem lay in the fact that, two years prior to the start of the tournament, Argentina had suffered a military coup. President Isabel Peron, widow of Juan Peron, had ordered the elimination of the rebels, primarily left-wing guerrilla forces in the Tucumán province in the north of the country. The military campaign was brutal and effective, and the generals used it to expand the political situation into a general state of emergency, with the military taking precedence over the civilian government. The war on Tucumán was expanded to a general war on anything left-wing and, with the silent complicity of Washington, they proceeded to weed out any dissidents and protesters as well as the arms-bearing resistance. The operation is known now as the Dirty War and the junta (military dictatorship) retained control of the country until 1983, when they agreed to hand back power to a civilian government after suffering a costly defeat in the Falklands War.

Trace the path of football and you don't see the pattern of history emerging because football is just an edited highlights version, its contribution to history consequential, not causal. Football isn't a mirror of society – or, if it is, it is like the hall of mirrors in Orson Welles' *Lady from Shanghai*, a carnival of distortion and disproportion. Equally, to trace the history of football and ignore the socio-political context in which events took place is to do the game a disservice. The influence of the Nazi party on the fortunes of the Germany-Austria team in the 1930s, the use of the 1978 World Cup as a propaganda vehicle by the military junta in Argentina, the awarding of the 2018 tournament to a morally bankrupt oligarchy – these are moments where football and politics intertwine. Just let's not ever believe that what takes place on the field is ever the primary motivation for the power brokers of the game.

Prior to the tournament one or two European FAs questioned the wisdom of travelling to Argentina (Holland, Italy) in the face of incontrovertible evidence of abuse of power and torture brought forward by Amnesty International, but the left-wing youth movement, the Montoneros, declared a ceasefire for the duration of the competition. Even so there were bombings in Buenos Aires only weeks before the teams were due to arrive.

Another political upheaval had changed the balance of power within football since the last World Cup. In 1974 – just before the Finals tournament – Stanley Rous had lost the vote to elect the President of FIFA. The new incumbent was a charismatic, friendly, media savvy one-man PR machine called João Havelange. Havelange made a tour of all the smaller federations in the preceding months, fostering goodwill and promising a much bigger say for the non-Europeans in the running of the game. It worked; he won the election easily against an unimaginative and old-fashioned regime and football had a new world order. The starch

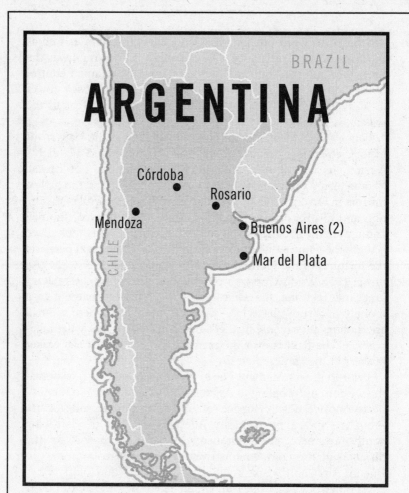

BRAZIL

ARGENTINA

Córdoba

Rosario

Mendoza

Buenos Aires (2)

Mar del Plata

CHILE

ARGENTINA

Six stadia in five cities hosted the 1978 finals, with two situated in the capital Buenos Aires.

Buenos Aires: Estádio Monumental
The national stadium currently has a capacity of 67,660, down from the near 72,000 that watched the 1978 final between Argentina and Holland. The ground was built in the 1930s, since when it has been the home of the River Plate club – in fact, many people refer to the ground simply as the 'River Plate stadium'.

Buenos Aires: Estádio José Amalfitani
Built in the 1940s, the second Buenos Aires ground used was that of Vélez Sársfield. It holds just under 50,000 spectators and also serves as the main home of Los Pumas, the Argentine rugby union team.

Cordóba: Estádio Cordóba
This was a new stadium prepared for the World Cup; it has subsequently undergone a name-change after Mario Kempes, hero of Argentina's victory in the 1978 finals. All the professional sides in the city rent the ground for big games.

Mar del Plata: Estádio José Maria Minella
Another new stadium in the coastal city to the south-east of the capital, this one held over 40,000, but the best attendance was 38,100 for Italy against France. The stadium is used largely for events and concerts as Mar del Plata has no major club.

Rosario: Estádio Gigante de Arroyito
This was an older stadium, built in the 1920s as the home to Rosario Central. Rosario hosted all Argentina's second-phase games. It is surprising that this wasn't the ground renamed in Kempes' honour as he was a local boy.

Mendoza: Estádio Ciudad de Mendoza
The stadium has since been renamed the Estádio Malvinas Argentinas to reflect the passions aroused by the Falklands War; it was the smallest of the World Cup grounds, holding under 40,000. The stadium has seen more use for football in recent years after Godoy Cruz reached the top flight of the Argentinian league.

and stiff upper lip had given way to gold teeth and self-aggrandisement. Only time would tell if the game would benefit – Havelange's bank account certainly did.

Qualifying

European qualification went largely with form, which meant no place for England, whose failure four years previously meant they ended up in a group with a strong seeded team, Italy. Halfway through their qualifying campaign manager Don Revie, whose tenure of the national side had been a disaster from start to finish, resigned in favour of a hefty pay-packet in the Middle East. Defeat in the opening match and lacklustre wins over the group minnows Finland and Luxembourg left with the impossible task of having to slaughter the best defensive side around in the last game. Ron Greenwood's reshaped side, built around a spine of Dave Watson, Trevor Brooking and Kevin Keegan, played well and won 2–0 but it wasn't enough. England had a decent enough defence – Watson was a quality old-fashioned stopper and there were other competent players around him – but they lacked punch up front. Trevor Francis, their best attacker, was horribly injury prone and the others were simply not international standard. It was a problem which would persist until the emergence of Gary Lineker in the mid-eighties.

It was Scotland who represented Britain. For the second successive competition they eliminated Czechoslovakia in qualifying – no mean feat, the Czechs were reigning European Champions after stunning West Germany in Belgrade. Scotland recovered from defeat in Prague to record an excellent 3–1 win at Hampden Park a year later. Joe Jordan caused havoc; the Czech defence couldn't deal with Willie Johnston's stream of crosses and that was meat and drink to a stomper like Jordan (this isn't disrespectful, Jordan was a fine no-prisoners centre-forward who would annihilate any defender who wasn't up for a tussle).

Wales did them a huge favour by beating the Czechs handsomely in Cardiff and Welsh protests that a dodgy penalty denied them a place in the final are well documented but way off mark.

In the game against Scotland at Anfield, Liverpool, a long throw was handled in the area and Scotland were given a penalty. The offender in the referee's eyes was Dave Jones but the real culprit appeared to be Scotland striker Joe Jordan. If Wales wanted a scapegoat they need look no further than their own FA, whose decision to play a "home" match at Anfield instead of a passionate Welsh crowd at Wrexham was born of nothing other than greed.

Poland would be back, with a new star in Zbigniew Boniek, an exciting attacking midfielder, to add to their 1974 roster, most of who were still around. Other than that the East European sides struggled, Romania, Bulgaria, the Soviet Union and Yugoslavia all failing to qualify.

Neither of the Irish teams got close; the North were in a horrid group with Holland and Belgium (Holland cruised through this time). They were a mixed bag, losing to Iceland but beating Belgium 3–0 at home, with a young forward called Gerry Armstrong getting his first international goals – we'll see him again. The Republic lost out to France, but did notch up a good win over the French in Dublin with an early Liam Brady goal. Sweden, Austria and Spain all won through comfortable groups. In a 9–0 thrashing of Malta the Rapid Vienna striker Hans Krankl helped himself to six goals; he would carry Austria's hopes into the competition.

In South America, Bolivia ambushed Uruguay (now in serious decline) and earned a spot in the final group with Brazil and Peru. They lost 8–0 to Brazil (Zico got four) and 5–0 to Peru, and were consigned to a play-off against Hungary. They got hammered in that as well, 6–0 – Hungary even won the away leg for good measure.

Asia and Africa both produced tournament debutants. Asia was getting tougher, with a lot more teams entering, and Iran had to come through an all-play-all group with Australia, South Korea, Hong Kong and Kuwait. They did so with distinction, winning six and drawing twice. Tunisia had a battle, beating neighbours Morocco (on penalties after two draws) and Algeria as well as Guinea before heading a three-team final eliminator with Nigeria and Egypt. They merited their place, having beaten all the strong sides in the region; the key win was a 1–0 victory in Lagos, sealed with an excellent defensive performance after an own goal gave them the lead. Mexico completed the line-up with the usual free place (nominally called the CONCACAF group).

Finals

Favourites? The press wrote up Brazil and the hosts – no European team had won in South America (still hasn't). West Germany were thought of as the strongest European side and Poland had most of their 1974 team. Even Scotland were attracting money at the bookmakers. The maverick team was Holland again; they would have been favourites if playing with a full deck, but they were missing their trump card – Cruyff. Cruyff announced that he wouldn't travel to Argentina immediately after the 1974 tournament, and he stuck to his guns. The story from 1974 about the pool party may have been a factor; Cruyff was very close to his wife, and a very private man – clearly that kind of tabloid tattle was not his cup of tea and it soured his relations with the press, which were never easy. That has always been the way with the tabloids; the dragnet of prurience catches many sleepy, unsuspecting fish as well as the gaudy ones who want to be on the front pages. (Who knows what Cruyff really wanted, he didn't always seem to know himself.) What is known is that he was missed. Rob Rensenbrink was a fantastic player – revered in Belgium, if not in his own country, where he was the superstar in one of the best sides in Europe, Anderlecht – but he wasn't Cruyff. Rensenbrink was an introverted, low-key character, and he didn't provide a spark that lit the whole team in the way Cruyff did in 1974. Maybe that's part of the difference between a top player and a genius. Van Hanegem didn't make the trip, either. He insisted to the coach, the Austrian Ernst Happel, who had managed van Hanegem at Feyenoord when they won the European Cup, that he must be assured of a place in the starting eleven, an assurance which Happel wasn't prepared to give. Happel was right, van Hanegem was not quite the player of old and Holland weren't short of combative players. So van Hanegem stayed at home.

GROUP 1

Italy	**(1) 2**	**France**	**(1) 1**	2 June, Mar del Plata; 42,653
Rossi 29, Zaccarelli 54		Lacombe 1		
Argentina	**(1) 2**	**Hungary**	**(1) 1**	2 June, Monumental; 76,909
Luque 14, Bertoni 83		Csapó 9		
Hungary	**(0) 1**	**Italy**	**(2) 3**	6 June, Mar del Plata; 26,533
A Tóth 81 (p)		Rossi 34, Bettega 36,		
		Benetti 61		
France	**(0) 1**	**Argentina**	**(1) 2**	6 June, Monumental; 76,909
Platini 60		Passarella 45 (p),		
		Luque 73		
Argentina	**(0) 0**	**Italy**	**(0) 1**	10 June, Monumental; 76,909
		Bettega 67		
France	**(3) 3**	**Hungary**	**(1) 1**	10 June, Mar del Plata; 23,127
Lopez 23, Berdoll 38,		Zombori 41		
Rocheteau 42				

1. Italy 6pts (6–2); 2. Argentina 4pts (4–3); 3. France 2pts (5–5); 4. Hungary 0pts (3–8)

Argentina had an unusually tough group for the host nation, with Italy, a developing France team and Hungary, full of attacking talent as usual. They won their opener against Hungary and it set the tone for the tournament. The Portuguese referee ignored a succession of niggling, provocative fouls, including one on the goalkeeper for the deciding goal, but was quick to punish any retaliation, sending off two Hungarian forwards. He never even used his card for Tibor Nyilasi; the Hungarian striker had had enough of Tarantini's constant hacking, clattered him into the running track and walked calmly off the field.

The opening game in Group 1 had a goal after thirty-nine seconds, from France's Bernard Lacombe. Italy were unfazed and came back to win 2–1. They looked decent and had a solid coach in Enzo Bearzot. The team leaned heavily on Juventus, dominant in *Serie A* (temporarily free of foreign stars, having banned clubs from hiring them at the start of the decade); it was the usual mix of skill (Scirea, Antognoni, Rossi) and brutality (Gentile, Benetti), with young Marco Tardelli, who had both in equal measure, looking a real find. France were an unfinished article, still building their great eighties team, and their young midfield star Michel Platini made no headway against this level of cynicism cum professionalism.

The win lifted Italy and they brushed Hungary aside before taking on the hosts. Argentina had a little more trouble with

France and required the help of some generous officiating. France
made a few changes, bringing in some younger players, including
Dominique Rocheteau, the bright new attacker from St Étienne.
After a tight first half Argentina got the breakthrough just before
half-time, but it was a disgraceful decision that allowed it. Luque
latched onto a lobbed pass and took a touch before shooting
weakly against the French captain Marius Trésor. The
Argentinians clamoured loudly for a penalty, the eleven in striped
blue shirts deliberately orchestrating the seventy-odd thousand in
the stands. A linesman with no clear view of the incident waved
his flag and a referee who seemed sure it wasn't an offence was all
too quick to give a penalty. Pathetic.

France, playing with some panache, were dealt another blow
when their goalkeeper Jean-Paul Bertrand-Demanes made a
leaping save from Valencia's long-range lob, but crashed his
back against a post as he came back down and had to go off.
Undeterred, France attacked and when Lacombe beat Fillol to a
through ball and lobbed it neatly over him, Platini was on hand
to crash the ball home when it came back off the bar. They
should have been ahead minutes later when Platini carried the
ball the length of the field and played in Didier Six; Six beat the
last man and pushed the ball past Fillol but it rolled just the
wrong side of the post. No argument about the winner. Luque
scored it with a fantastic hit from outside the area, but I'm sure
the French coach Hidalgo was curious to ask his team why no
challenge came in while the striker waited an age for the ball to
drop after his awkward first touch. A win in their last game
against Hungary was little consolation for France. The game
started with an odd incident, when it transpired both sides had
only white shirts with them – France had wrongly assumed they
would be asked to use their second strip as both normally played
in blue. A scrabble around local clubs ended with France playing in green stripes for the first and only time.

Italy beat Argentina with a fantastic goal by Roberto Bettega
after some pinball passing down the left. Passarella contested
every other decision and was politely but firmly ignored by a referee, Klein of Israel, who seemed oblivious to the demands from
the crowd for an Argentina win. Argentina should have been

relieved to have come through a tough group – Hungary lost all three games but probably played as well as Brazil or Poland in winning their respective groups. Klein was lined up to referee the final by FIFA – would it surprise you to learn he was withdrawn and given the third-place match after Argentina lodged a protest on some spurious grounds about his ethnicity?

Italy looked really impressive, not usually their way in the early games of a major tournament. The blend of silk and steel and experience and youth looked well balanced. The new attacking combination of the experienced Bettega of Juventus with the bright young Vicenza star Paolo Rossi showed great promise, and the new defenders, Gentile (without moustache), Cabrini (only twenty) and the sweeper Scirea, looked every bit as redoubtable as the old guard.

GROUP 2

Poland	(0) 0	**West Germany**	(0) 0	1 June, Monumental; 76,909
Tunisia	(0) 3	**Mexico**	(1) 1	2 June, Rosario; 17,396
Kaabi 55, Ghommidh 80, Dhouieb 87		Vázquez Ayala 45 (p)		
West Germany (4) 6		**Mexico**	(0) 0	6 June, Córdoba; 35,258
D Müller 14, H Müller 29, Rummenigge 38, 71, Flohe 44, 89				
Poland	(1) 1	**Tunisia**	(0) 0	6 June, Rosario; 9,624
Lato				
Tunisia	(0) 0	**West Germany**	(0) 0	10 June, Córdoba; 30,667
Poland	(1) 3	**Mexico**	(0) 1	10 June, Rosario; 22,651
Boniek 42, 83, Deyna 56		Rangel 51		

1. Poland 5pts (4–1); 2. West Germany 4pts (6–0); 3. Tunisia 3pts (3–2); 4. Mexico 0pts (2–12)

Two of the less fancied sides, Mexico and Tunisia, were drawn in a group with two tough European sides, West Germany and Poland, first and third four years earlier. Mexico were given a shout in the hot conditions but they were awful, losing all three matches and handing Tunisia the distinction of being the first African team to win a match at the World Cup Finals. All three goals in a 3–1 win were scored by their defenders, and the Africans' skill and fitness surprised most observers. The North African sides (Morocco, Algeria, Egypt, Tunisia) tend to be

technically good and quick, often quite defensive in their set-up;
the western African countries tend to be bigger and more
powerful, with a high level of individual skill but often less discipline or organisation. This is a generalisation, but serves as a
broad summary of the difference in style between the two
regions.

Poland and West Germany started the tournament with a
dreadful draw – no surprise there, it merely followed the pattern
of opening games. West Germany had lost an abundance of great
players and not yet replaced them. Rainer Bonhof was a footsoldier not a general, and there was no one at the back with even
a glimmer of Beckenbauer's talent. The new striker, twenty-two-
year-old Karl-Heinz Rummenigge of Bayern Munich, looked a
potential successor to Gerd Müller (albeit a very different kind of
player) but the others were ordinary. Hölzenbein was thirty-two
in 1978 and more of a tumbling clown than an international
player; Abramczik and Dieter Müller were a shadow of their
predecessors. Klaus Fischer of Schalke was prolific in the
Bundesliga and against poor opposition but lacking against the
very best; scoring a couple of spectacular goals on TV does not
make an international striker. The new much-vaunted playmaker,
Stuttgart's Hansi Müller was "the next big thing" in German
football for nearly a decade before everyone realised he was
twenty-six and hadn't done much.

Poland had many of the same faces as 1974, but lacked the
element of surprise second time around. Some of the faces were
a little more lined and a little less energetic, some just not in
such scintillating form. They found Tunisia a handful, only
some stubborn defending and a tidy finish from Lato earned
them a scarcely deserved 1–0 win. West Germany should have
beaten Tunisia more comfortably but left their shooting boots at
home – Fischer especially. Again the African side never looked a
class below their more vaunted opposition. Which is more than
can be said for Mexico, who were stuffed by West Germany and
beaten easily by Poland. It has proved a pattern for Mexico,
unless playing in their own country; easy qualification from the
cushiest region, big build-up pre-tournament, moderate
performances and an early flight home. It's a disappointing

return for a football-mad country with an enormous population. They made a really ordinary German team look like
world-beaters.

GROUP 3

Austria Schachner 10, Krankl 79	**(1) 2**	**Spain** Dani 21	**(1) 1**		3 June, Amalfitani; 40,841
Brazil Reinaldo 44	**(1) 1**	**Sweden** Sjöberg 37	**(1) 1**		3 June, Mar del Plata; 38,618
Austria Krankl 44 (p)	**(1) 1**	**Sweden**	**(0) 0**		7 June, Amalfitani; 41,424
Brazil	**(0) 0**	**Spain**	**(0) 0**		7 June, Mar del Plata; 34,771
Spain Asensi 76	**(0) 1**	**Sweden**	**(0) 0**		11 June, Amalfitani; 42,132
Brazil Roberto Dinamite 40	**(1) 1**	**Austria**	**(0) 0**		11 June, Mar del Plata; 35,221

1. Austria 4pts (3–2); 2. Brazil 4pts (2–1); 3. Spain 3pts (2–1); 4. Sweden 1pt (1–3)

So where was the outstanding team? It certainly wasn't
Brazil.

Brazil, who looked a shadow of the great teams of the previous
decade, scraped into the second phase with two draws and a
narrow victory over Austria, who were already through. The end
of their rather drab game against Sweden provided a moment of
comic relief – unless you happened to be Brazilian. They won a
corner in the dying seconds and thought they had an opening win
when Zico headed it home. Unfortunately for them the referee
was Clive Thomas, the Dickie Bird of football, who thought the
crowd paid all that money to watch him not the twenty-two international footballers running around him. Thomas decreed the
whistle was blown before the ball entered the goal; he had played
less than ten seconds over the ninety. He didn't referee another
Finals game, a rare correct call from FIFA.

The decision affected very little; Sweden were toothless and
lost their other games 1–0, while Austria proved the surprise
package by beating Spain as well as the Swedes. Their centre-
forward, Hans Krankl of Rapid Vienna, was good enough to
have invited an offer from Barcelona, and he proved his worth
with the winning goal in both games. There was more to come
from him.

GROUP 4

Peru	**(1) 3**	**Scotland**	**(1) 1**	3 June, Amalfitani; 40,841	
Cueto 43, Cubillas 70, 76		Jordan 19			
Holland	**(1) 3**	**Iran**	**(0) 0**	3 June, Mendoza; 33,431	
Rensenbrink 40 (p), 62, 79 (p)					
Holland	**(0) 0**	**Peru**	**(0) 0**	7 June, Mendoza; 28,125	
Iran	**(0) 1**	**Scotland**	**(1) 1**	7 June, Córdoba; 7,938	
Danaifar 60		Own goal 43			
Peru	**(3) 4**	**Iran**	**(1) 1**	11 June, Córdoba; 21,262	
Velasquez 2,		Roshan 42			
Cubillas 36 (p), 40 (p), 79					
Scotland	**(1) 3**	**Holland**	**(1) 2**	11 June, Mendoza; 35,130	
Dalglish 44,		Rensenbrink 34 (p),			
Gemmill 46 (p), 68		Rep 71			

The last remaining group looked a cakewalk for Holland and Scotland. Holland were still a terrific side, even without Cruyff and van Hanegem, and Scotland had their best squad for years.

Scotland's campaign was the most bizarre any British team has experienced in the Finals. It was an epic failure on a scale unmatched until France in 2010. The manager was Ally MacLeod, a former winger with a number of Scottish clubs and Blackburn Rovers in the English first division; he played in Rovers' 3–0 FA Cup Final defeat to Wolves in 1960. MacLeod was positive to the point of brashness and a self-declared winner.

MacLeod won his managerial spurs in a good spell at Ayr and when he had a positive influence at a larger club, Aberdeen, he was given the nod as successor to the dour and introverted Willie Ormond as manager of the national team.

Things started well as victory in the Home Championships was sealed with an excellent 2–1 win over England at Wembley. The performance was overshadowed by the behaviour of a large section of the Tartan Army who invaded the pitch, cut up large sections of turf and brought down the goalposts – all viewed now with an air of indulgent nostalgia, but had it been England fans the attitude would be very different. A repeat of the behaviour two years later led to changes in the way Scotland fans were monitored on away trips. A decent tour of South America was followed by victories in the last two qualification matches; defeat at home to England in the Home Championships did little to dampen the optimism of MacLeod and the Scottish supporters. A jaunty song by well-known comedian Andy Cameron entitled "Ally's Tartan Army" made the UK Top Ten, and MacLeod made extravagant promises to the press – tantamount to tying chunks of raw steak to his torso before diving into shark-infested waters. The squad made a celebratory tour of Hampden before being waved off at the airport by thousands of well-wishers.

It was a good squad, with plenty of experience. Only seven of the twenty-two played their domestic football in Scotland, most were plying their trade in the tougher English league, including the team's big star, Liverpool's Kenny Dalglish. The biggest concern was in goal, where Partick Thistle's Alan Rough combined spectacular flying saves with schoolboy errors. If all this sounds like we're setting up MacLeod and co for a fall, then my job is done, because it came, and it was a long way down, only last-minute redemption saving the team from the flames of utter ignominy. *(See next mini-chapter, Scotch missed.)*

Scotch missed

Scotland's history at the World Cup Finals is a litany of self-inflicted podiatric wounds. Having declined an invitation in 1950, they were really bad in 1954 and worse in 1958. They failed to qualify again until 1974, when they sent a competent squad to West Germany but were unable to negotiate a tricky group. They didn't lose a match in 1974 (for the only time) but went out because they failed to score more than two against Zaire. A draw with Brazil wasn't as impressive an achievement as it sounds; this was one of the worst Brazil teams to appear in a Finals tournament.

So to 1978 and Argentina.

Scotland had one piece of bad luck before the tournament started when Danny McGrain of Celtic was declared unfit. McGrain was an excellent right-back and one of the mainstays of the team. Before Scotland's first match Gordon McQueen was also injured and played no part in the tournament – McQueen was a solid defender, commanding in the air, but would have made little difference in Argentina.

Even without these two the squad was full of good players. McQueen's Manchester United team-mate Martin Buchan was an elegant and experienced defender and Kenny Burns had just been voted player of the season in England. In attack Kenny Dalglish had proved an astute replacement for Kevin Keegan at Liverpool and was a more complete player than in 1974 when he disappointed. Alongside him MacLeod had a choice of Derek Johnstone, prolific for Rangers, or the more experienced Joe Jordan. Some expected him to take Andy Gray of Aston Villa, a young and hungry striker, fearless and terrifically combative, but he opted for Joe Harper of his old club Aberdeen instead.

Midfield was where Scotland were strongest. MacLeod's best combination appeared to be Willie Johnston, the cussed but talented West Brom winger, with Bruce Rioch and Graeme Souness inside plus one from John Robertson, Asa Hartford or Archie Gemmill filling the other spot. The options proved too many for MacLeod, who made the fatal error of going into the tournament not knowing his best team.

The opening game was against Peru. Scotland's trickiest selection was at full-back where they were lacking without McGrain. The best bet seemed to be Willie Donachie at left-back (he was the only one in the squad) and Sandy Jardine; his best days were behind him but he offered nous and good distribution. MacLeod picked neither, opting for the inexperienced Stewart Kennedy of Aberdeen (retreat to the familiar of club players you know, another elementary mistake) and Martin Buchan, a centre-half playing out of position. Instances in the World Cup of players doing well out of position are few and far between. Peru's strength was the pace of their wingers, Muñante and Oblitas, and the ability of Teófilo Cubillas to get the ball out to them; the same Cubillas was dismissed in the British press as past it – he was twenty-nine. MacLeod stationed Rioch and Don Masson, now thirty-two, in the middle and Hartford and Johnston in the wider positions. Up front, calls in the Scottish papers for Johnstone's inclusion were ignored in favour of Jordan – one decision MacLeod did get right, Jordan was a threat in all three games.

Peru played neat little passing triangles all day and Scotland got nowhere near them. Rioch had few opportunities to get forward, he was too busy chasing the ball and Masson was a disaster. It started okay, Rioch hitting a typically fierce drive which Quiroga only half-stopped – Jordan put in the rebound, but then Peru took control and deservedly equalised before half-time, when a neat passing move picked its way through the Scotland defence.

It was hot in Córdoba and the Scots visibly tired in the second half, notably the ageing midfield and Buchan, unused to charging up and down the flank – Willie Johnston was no defender and provided little cover, even if he did offer Scotland's most potent threat. They should have gone ahead all the same, but it would have been fortuitous. Another surging run from Rioch seemed to be going nowhere when he took a heavy touch, but minimal contact from the back-tracking Cubillas was deemed enough for a penalty. Masson took the penalty and completed a miserable day's work when Quiroga saved to his right – the penalty wasn't hard enough and was at a comfortable height for the goalkeeper.

Peruvian midfielders were walking past their markers now, and Cubillas had no defender within eight yards when he took aim on forty minutes. He gave Rough absolutely no chance from twenty-five yards – past it indeed! Off came Rioch and Masson for fresh legs (Macari and Gemmill), but it was quarter of an hour too late. They couldn't stem the tide and minutes later Kennedy was caught out of position for the umpteenth time and fouled Oblitas on the edge of the penalty area. Much was made of the fact that five foot five Lou Macari was on the end of the Scottish wall but Rough left a huge area to his right and Cubillas simply toe-poked the ball around the wall (not over Macari as some attest) and into the corner of the goal. Simples, peeps.

MacLeod absolved himself of blame for the defeat, aiming his ire at his players, who he claimed had not performed (or eight of them – not sure which three he reckoned played well . . .). Things went from bad to worse overnight. The results of a sample taken from Willie Johnston came back positive; Johnston had taken some hayfever pep pills he used regularly at home, but there was no standardisation of proscribed drugs in those days and he was unaware they were banned at the World Cup. Johnston took responsibility for his error – the same could not be said of Ally MacLeod or the Scottish FA.

Drug-taking in sport was not the issue in 1978 that it is today. Viewers on TV just thought East Germans were good at running and swimming, not chock-full of steroids. There was genuine shock at Johnston's test and subsequent ban and the player was hung out to dry and treated as a pariah back home. Totally unfair. Players were unused to a system of testing like the World Cup and there should have been advice and assistance offered by the FA and management team. That was conspicuously not the case in the Scotland camp; Johnston provided a convenient scapegoat to deflect the press from writing about the shortcomings of the campaign. Johnston did himself no favours with a crass interview with Frank Bough on *Nationwide*, but he was certainly not the criminal he was portrayed to be. (He was a bit of a naughty boy, though, lots of red cards for retaliation, and he once mooned the opposing bench after scoring in an NASL match.)

The next game against the weakest team in the group, Iran, was a must-win. MacLeod brought in Jardine and Donachie, with Buchan moving into the middle instead of Tom Forsyth – odd as it was generally agreed that Forsyth was one of the least awful players against Peru. Macari and Gemmill stayed in and John Robertson, the other genuine winger in the squad, was the obvious replacement for Johnston.

The game was a train wreck. Scotland created absolutely nothing. None of the midfield players got forward into the box and Kenny Dalglish added to the growing list of World Cup matches in which he went missing. Robertson, so confident and destructive for Nottingham Forest, seemed reluctant to take on his man – his crosses should have been manna from heaven for Jordan. Scotland took a barely deserved lead as the Iranian goalkeeper and a defender combined to create a Laurel & Hardy own goal under pressure from Jordan. The equaliser wasn't even a surprise, Iran were the better side for much of the second half. Remember, this wasn't the Scotland squad of the 2000s, almost devoid of players of true international class; this was 1978, with Celtic and Rangers still amongst Europe's elite and the pick of the squad playing for top English sides.

Scotland were derided by the media – gleefully so by the English, still smarting from the memories of the triumphal Tartan Army at Wembley and the jibes from Scottish colleagues about their failure to qualify. How Scotland must have wished they had failed to qualify, too; anything was better than this humiliation. Even their loyal army of fans turned against them, jeering as the team bus arrived at the hotel.

The third match came with no optimism. The opponents were Holland, who had three points like Peru. Scotland's forlorn hope, if there was any, was to beat the Dutch by three goals. At last MacLeod started with Souness (for Macari) – his one hint of *mea culpa* was in admitting the Liverpool playmaker should have played from the first game. Rioch was back – for Robertson, with Hartford and Gemmill pushed wider – and Burns, woeful against Iran, was omitted in favour of Forsyth. Stuart Kennedy came back for Jardine, which seemed a needless change. Kennedy looked a decent player going forward but had the positional sense of a puppy.

WORLD CUP CLASSIC No.9
11 June 1978, San Martin, Mendoza; 35,130

| Scotland | (1) 3 | Dalglish 44, Gemmill 46 (p), 68 |
| Holland | (1) 2 | Rensenbrink 34 (p), Rep 71 |

Referee: **Erich Linemayr** (Austria)
Coaches: **Ally MacLeod** (Scotland) & **Ernst Happel** (Holland)

Scotland (4–4–2): Alan Rough (Partick Thistle); Stuart Kennedy (Aberdeen), Tom Forsyth (Glasgow Rangers), Martin Buchan (Manchester United), Willie Donachie (Manchester City); Asa Hartford (West Bromwich Albion), Bruce Rioch (Cpt, Derby County), Graeme Souness (Liverpool), Archie Gemmill (Nottingham Forest); Kenny Dalglish (Liverpool), Joe Jordan (Man Utd).
Holland (4–4–2): Jan Jongbloed (Roda JC); Wim Suurbier (Schalke 04), Wim Rijsbergen (Feyenoord), Ruud Krol (Cpt, Ajax), Jan Poortvliet (PSV Eindhoven); René van de Kerkhof (PSV Eindhoven), Wim Jansen (Feyenoord), Johan Neeskens (Barcelona), Willy van de Kerkhof (PSV Eindhoven); Johnny Rep (SEC Bastia), Rob Rensenbrink (Anderlecht). **Subs:** Jan Boskamp (Molenbeek) 10m for Neeskens; Piet Wildschut (Twente Enschede) 44m for Rijsbergen
Cautioned: Gemmill (Sco) 35m

Finally it all clicked. With Souness playing deep in midfield, Hartford and Gemmill buzzing purposefully ahead and Rioch launching up to join Jordan, with Dalglish free to take up wide positions or come off the centre-forward and look for the ball, Scotland had their formation. It was midfield diamond before anyone had the faintest idea such a thing existed and it caused Holland problems. Behind them Buchan looked much more assured as a deep centre / sweeper where his lack of pace was no issue, and Forsyth roamed eagerly, tackling and harassing attackers before they got near the goal.

Scotland got on the front foot and stayed there. Rioch hit the bar with a thumping header (and probably ought to have scored), while Dalglish thought he'd scored only to discover the referee blew for a foul not a goal. Even when Holland opened the scoring this rejuvenated Scotland didn't panic. The goal was Kennedy's fault; he gave the ball away and in his haste to atone he brought Rep down – Scottish protests that he got the ball were rightly waved away. Rensenbrink slid the penalty into the corner of the goal.

Holland were struggling with injuries. Neeskens attempted a crude and dangerous tackle on Gemmill and the Scot quite reasonably jumped out of the way, unfortunately landing on Neeskens' stomach; hoist with his own petard, the Dutch playmaker left the field on a stretcher. Shortly after Rijsbergen took a knock and was clearly struggling. The Dutch bench declined to replace him, presumably hoping he would make it to half-time. It backfired. Souness received the ball on the left edge of the Dutch area and put an inviting cross into the back post area, where Jordan steamrollered Krol and headed back into the middle. Just in the space where Rijsbergen should have been was Dalglish, unmarked and for once he finished in the manner to which Liverpool fans were accustomed, high and handsome past a helpless Jongbloed. The Dutch promptly replaced Rijsbergen. Stable door . . . horse . . .

The second half started as the first ended, with a Scotland goal. Again Jordan's presence caused panic in the Dutch defence, and when Souness tried to latch on to a loose ball he was bumped clumsily by Willy van de Kerkhof. Gemmill was coolness personified with the penalty. Now Scotland had the bit between their teeth.

The next goal was one of the greats and a personal favourite. Archie Gemmill was a great pro, a player with some skill and a lot of intelligence and a huge heart. He had an impressive haul of three League Championship medals; two with Derby and then with Nottingham Forest the previous season, where he had followed manager Brian Clough (no bad judge of a player's attitude). Good player then, but he had no right to score a goal like this. Picking the ball up in nowhere territory on the right wing, he attacked the Dutch area. Jansen lunged in lazily and was beaten easily, then Ruud Krol got his body shape wrong and allowed Gemmill to pass by on the outside. Jan Poortvliet was covering and Gemmill would have to either go wider still or back into the melee in the box. He did neither, he nutmegged Poortvliet and found space. Jongbloed advanced, and as was his tendency, committed early; Gemmill leaned to his right and calmly lifted the ball over the prostrate goalkeeper. His face was a picture. I still fight back the tears every time I watch the goal. There is something very heartwarming about a worthy but unremarkable player ascending briefly to a higher plane.

The belief that Scotland could pull off something quite extraordinary lasted all of three minutes until Johnny Rep produced a thirty-yarder out of nowhere – Rough merely twitched like a marionette as the ball rocketed past him. The Dutch shooting in this World Cup was a wonder to see. The game petered out after this, for all the Scottish effort. Their terrific display was in vain, but some redemption was achieved, for the players if not for their clueless manager.

The preamble was over the top and absurd and invited the fall, which duly came. MacLeod was an inexperienced manager who had no idea of how voracious the press wolves could be when they scented blood. He gave them a reason to want him to fail with his hubris and was oblivious to his own shortcomings. MacLeod lasted one more game – why?!? – then returned to club management. He died in 2003, convinced, if his autobiography is to be believed, that he was just a wee bit unlucky.

The Scots' failure let in Peru, who actually headed the group (which must have delighted Brazil and Argentina and Poland who avoided a dangerous Holland side). Both Peru and Holland brushed Iran aside – they used the old-fashioned notion of passing to people wearing the same shirt, such a bizarre idea seemed to have evaded Scotland – and they played out a lifeless 0–0 draw when they met in Mendoza.

Scotland returned in 1982 with another good squad and another hard luck story, losing out on goal difference in a tough group with Brazil and the USSR. They maybe had a case with bad luck, but were hugely culpable in allowing New Zealand to score twice – 5–0 rather than 5–2 would have seen them through.

The squads of 1986, 1990 and 1998 were lacking the quality players of '74, '78 and '82, and their failure was expected; even so, defeats to Costa Rica and a 3–0 whacking by Morocco in 1998 were undignified displays. Now, Scotland would give anything for a chance to get near the Finals. A weak and badly run domestic game, dearth of quality and low ranking inevitably means they are fighting their way past two or three decent sides in a qualifying group, and their next appearance in the Finals looks a distance away. A midfield of Souness, Rioch, Hartford and Gemmill is nowadays just a dream.

Scotland Squad 1978:
GK: Alan Rough (Partick Thistle, 26, 18), Jim Blyth (Coventry City, 23, 2), Bobby Clark (Aberdeen, 32, 17)
DEF: Martin Buchan (Manchester United, 29, 28), Kenny Burns (Nottingham Forest, 24, 11), Willie Donachie (Manchester City, 26, 30), Tom Forsyth (Glasgow Rangers, 29, 19), Sandy Jardine (Rangers, 29, 33), Stuart Kennedy (Aberdeen, 25, 3), Gordon McQueen (Man Utd, 25, 20)
MID & WIDE: Archie Gemmill (Nottm Forest, 31, 26), Asa Hartford (Man City, 27, 24), Willie Johnston (West Bromwich Albion, 31, 21), Lou Macari (Man Utd, 28, 22), Don Masson (Derby County, 28, 16), Bruce Rioch (Derby, 30, 22), John Robertson (Nottm Forest, 25, 2), Graeme Souness (Liverpool, 25, 6)
FWD: Kenny Dalglish (Glasgow Celtic, 27, 54), Joe Harper (Aberdeen, 30, 3), Derek Johnstone (Rangers, 24, 13), Joe Jordan (Leeds United, 26, 30)

GROUP A

Italy	(0) 0	West Germany	(0) 0	14 June, Monumental; 67,547
Holland	(3) 5	Austria	(0) 1	14 June, Córdoba; 25,059
Brandts 6, Rensenbrink 35 (p),		Obermayer 80		
Rep 37, 53,				
W van de Kerkhof 82				
West Germany	(1) 2	Holland	(1) 2	18 June, Córdoba; 40,750
Abramczik 3,		Haan 27,		
D Müller 70		R van de Kerkhof 82		
Italy	(1) 1	Austria	(0) 0	18 June, Monumental; 66,695
Rossi				
Holland	(0) 2	Italy	(1) 1	21 June, Monumental; 67,433
Brandts 49, Haan 76		Own goal 19		

1. Holland 5pts (9–4); 2. Italy 4pts (2–2); 3. West Germany 2pts (4–5); 4. Austria 2pts (4–8)

The second phase, as in 1974, saw the South American sides in together, and a strong all-European group containing Italy, Holland, West Germany (who surely would improve?) and the also-rans, Austria.

My comment in brackets is deliberately misleading. West Germany didn't improve; this was one of their poorest World Cup showings – played six, won one, drew four, lost one. They had the worst of a 0–0 draw with Italy, with the midfield anonymous in the face of Antognoni, Benetti and Tardelli. Next up was Holland, and the Germans sneaked an early lead when Schrijvers made a mess of a free-kick and allowed Abramczik to follow up and head home. Holland poured forward and an Arie Haan blockbuster put the Dutch level. The Germans dug in – this was much their best effort of the tournament – and went in front again from a Dieter Müller header. For a while it looked like a repeat of the 1974 Final (without so many great players), but the Dutch had another gear and René van deKerkhof, one of the two PSV Eindhoven twins in the squad, scored a fine equaliser. There was still time for the referee to make an atrocious decision, sending off Dutch substitute Dick Nanninga after a bit of handbags with Hölzenbein in which the German was clearly the more culpable. Hölzenbein keeps cropping up in World Cup history but his influence as a catalyst for controversy far outstrips his modest talent for playing football; forty caps for a strong team seems generous in the extreme.

WORLD CUP CLASSIC No.10
21 June 1978, Olímpico Chateau Carreras, Córdoba;
38,3318

| **West Germany** | **(1) 2** | Rummenigge 19, Hölzenbein 67 |
| **Austria** | **(0) 3** | Own goal 60, Krankl 66, 88 |

Referee: **Avraham Klein** (Israel)
Coaches: **Helmut Schön** (West Germany) & **Helmut Senekowitsch** (Austria)

West Germany (4–4–2): Sepp Maier (Bayern Munich); Berti Vogts (Cpt, Borussia Mönchengladbach), Rolf Rüssmann (Schalke 04), Manny Kaltz (Hamburg), Bernard Dietz (MSV Duisburg), Dieter Müller (Cologne), Rainer Bonhof (Gladbach), Erich Beer (Hertha Berlin), Rudi Abramczik (Schalke 04); Karl-Heinz Rummenigge (Bayern), Hans Hölzenbein (Eintracht Frankfurt). **Subs:** Hansi Muller (Stuttgart) 45m for Beer; Klaus Fischer (Schalke 04) 60m for D Müller
Austria (4–4–2): Friedrich Koncilia (SWW Innsbruck); Robert Sara (Cpt, Austria Vienna), Erich Obermayer (Austria Vienna), Bruno Pezzey (SWW Innsbruck), Heinrich Strasser (Admira Wacker); Eduard Krieger (Bruges), Josef Hickersberger (Fortuna Düsseldorf), Herbert Prohaska (Austria Vienna), Wilhelm Kreuz (Feyenoord); Hans Krankl (Rapid Vienna), Walter Schachner (Alpine Donawitz). **Sub:** Franz Oberacher (SWW Innsbruck) for Schachner, 71m
Cautioned: Prohaska (Aut) 69m, Abramczik (WGer) 69m, Sara (Aut) 85m

The Germans' final fixture seemed meaningless; there had been little evidence this side could beat Austria by four or more goals. There was equally little evidence that they would lose – Austria hadn't beaten their neighbours for forty-seven years and they had found it tough in the second phase – but that's what happened in a game that is remembered in Austria as the Miracle of Córdoba. This sounds a touch hyperbolic for a dead fixture; but it was Austria versus West Germany, with all the baggage of the Anschluss still hanging in the air.

West Germany's team looks a shadow of its predecessor; Maier, Vogts, Hölzenbein and Bonhof remained, but the replacements for the other greats of '74 were invariably weaker by comparison, with the exception of Rummenigge, and he was not yet the great player we saw the following decade. Austria had an experienced (but not old) team that had played together a lot. Their goalkeeper, Koncilia, was one of Europe's best, Hans Krankl was a livewire striker and the midfield string-puller, Herbert Prohaska of Austria Vienna, was more composed and authoritative than a twenty-two-year-old had a right to be.

Austria had the better of an ordinary first half but it was West Germany who scored. Rummenigge played a delightful double-one-two with Dieter Müller before sliding the ball past the advancing Koncilia – the only moment of real quality in the half. The start of the second half saw roles reversed as West Germany were on top yet conceded the next goal. Bonhof hit a couple of rasping free-kicks narrowly wide and Rummenigge – a handful all game, running from deep – forced Koncilia into an excellent save. It was an own goal by skipper Berti Vogts after an hour that brought things level, but Sepp Maier was at fault. The veteran 'keeper and two attackers all missed a cross from the right, the ball hit the unsighted Vogts and ended up in the back of the net.

The Germans, like the Italians and Dutch before, marked Hans Krankl closely, believing that to negate Krankl was to minimise the Austrian's attacking threat. It worked for Holland and Italy, but here he showed just why he was receiving such close attention. Krieger's cross from the left cleared the central defenders and Krankl had given himself a couple of yards. Krankl's first touch was neat, taking the pace off the cross, and his second was outstanding, cracking a volley across Maier with remarkable power and perfect technique. Now he looked like a player who had just scored forty goals in a season.

The lead lasted less than a minute and the equaliser was absurdly simple. A Bonhof free-kick into the mixer and Hölzenbein rose unchallenged to score. Krankl still had more in his locker. In the closing minutes he burned past Rüssmann, cut inside to leave Berti Vogts on his backside and stabbed the ball past Sepp Maier with his left foot for the winner. If you watch the footage on YouTube, make sure you check out the original Austrian commentary with Edi Finger going absolutely bananas (as was Krankl). It was an extravagant celebration of a particular moment charged with the weight of a century of history. It was entirely disproportionate to the tournament circumstances.

Not much sympathy due a poor German side, but respect due to the distinguished career of Helmut Schön and his distinctive flat cap; it was his last match as manager of the national team.

*   *   *

It was a triumphant win for Austria, but they were well beaten by Holland in their first match in the group and couldn't find an answer to the Italian marking in the second. Holland made enforced changes, bringing in Wildschut for Suurbier and Ernie Brandts for the injured Rijsbergen, with Haan recalled in midfield for Neeskens, also injured. Brandts made an instant impact (it was only his second international), scoring with a firm header from Arie Haan's free-kick, and the Dutch were three-up and cruising at half-time. Italy had equally little trouble with Austria, a 1–0 score was hugely misleading, the goal coming early when Paolo Rossi dispossessed a defender and scored across Koncilia (who was excellent again).

In the deciding fixture in the group, later the same day, Holland met Italy needing only a draw to reach a second successive final. Italy looked much the better team in the early stages and took a deserved lead when Brandts and Bettega chased a through ball, and the Dutch defender's outstretched leg diverted it past Piet Schrijvers. The Ajax goalkeeper had come in for the second phase and looked secure but now Holland were back to the veteran Jongbloed as Schrijvers was injured in the collision with Bettega and Brandts. Jongbloed was a surprise choice as goalkeeper in 1974 (apparently on Cruyff's recommendation), and was picked for his skill as a sweeper behind the defence as much as his handling. He did okay but had shown little form since and was a surprising selection for the '78 squad and not expected to play.

It's a good thing for Holland that Brandts was okay, as it was his terrific strike that got Holland back in the game shortly after half-time. The winner was outrageous. Johnny Rep's strike against Scotland was a long way out but this one from Arie Haan (a defensive midfield player, for goodness sake!) was over forty yards and flew like an arrow to crash against the inside of the post and into the goal. Haan later stated in an interview that he still got goose-bumps when he watched a video of the goal. It was the most spectacular long-range hit in World Cup history.

GROUP B

Brazil	(2) 3	**Peru**	(0) 0	14 June, Mendoza; 31,278
Dirceu 15, 27, Zico 72 (p)				
Argentina	(1) 2	**Poland**	(0) 0	14 June, Rosario 37,091
Kempes 16, 72				
Poland	(0) 1	**Peru**	(0) 0	18 June, Mendoza; 35,288
Szarmach				
Argentina	(0) 0	**Brazil**	(0) 0	18 June, Rosario; 37,326
Brazil	(1) 3	**Poland**	(1) 1	21 June, Mendoza; 39,586
Nelinho 13,		Lato 45		
Roberto Dinamite 58, 63				
Peru	(0) 0	**Argentina**	(2) 6	21 June, Rosario; 37,326
		Kempes 21, 49, Tarantini 43		
		Luque 50, 72, Houseman 67		

1. Argentina 5 pts (8–0); 2. Brazil 5pts (6–1); 3. Poland 2pts (2–5); 4. Peru 0pts (0–10)

Group A had some good stuff. Group B had very little and had one of the most controversial games in World Cup history as its conclusion. Brazil opened the group with a comfortable win over Peru. At last a team put pressure on the weak Peruvian defence, and Brazil were two-up in half an hour, both from Dirceu, the one player in the line-up who lived up to his heritage. Peru ran out of ideas and their wingers, so dangerous in the first phase, never really got a look in. Argentina beat a disappointing Poland later the same day. Kempes opened the scoring after sixteen minutes, timing his run perfectly to glance Bertoni's cross past Tomaszewski. So highly rated but often so impotent in front of goal, it was Kempes' first goal of the tournament, and his first in nearly 700 minutes of World Cup action.

A few minutes before half-time Poland were awarded a penalty when Kempes deliberately handled on the line; it was supposed to earn a booking but he didn't get one. Deyna missed the penalty, a symptom perhaps of their waning confidence; Fillol later made a much more difficult save from the Polish captain's curled free-kick. Kempes, full of belief after his goal, executed a cute drag back to take out the last defender and fire past Tomaszewski after a superb run from Ardiles had opened up the defence.

The Argentina – Brazil encounter was barely watchable. Neither side showed much interest in playing football, being far more interest in perpetuating an ancient rivalry by running their studs up each other and throwing punches. Four yellow cards – thirty years later that number would be trebled for a game like this. Brazil's uncompromising centre-half, Oscar, against the fiery River Plate centre-forward Leopoldo Luque was pay-per-view stuff. Poland beat Peru with Andrzej Szarmach's only goal of the competition but three days later they were well beaten by Brazil, who raised their game. Nelinho, the left-back, scored with a scorching free-kick, and Roberto Dinamite lived up to his name for the only time in a World Cup match. Dinamite is the all-time leading scorer in the premier Brazilian domestic competition, the *Campeonato Brasileiro*, and a legend at Vasco de Gama, but he never really shone on the big stage, despite a decent overall scoring rate for his country. Grzegorz Lato scored his ninth and final World Cup goal just before half-time but Poland were never really in it. Lato returned four years later, as did Zmuda, the outstanding central defender, and Boniek, but the rest of this team didn't.

Argentina played Peru later that evening, knowing exactly what was required to reach the final. All sorts of conspiracy theories surround the result; Quiroga, the Peruvian goalkeeper was bribed; the Argentinian authorities agreed to send financial aid to Peru if the Peruvian authorities leaned on the team to lose; aliens from space took over the Peruvian team for ninety minutes and agreed to throw the game in return for shelter from the Klingons. Okay, I made the last one up; the point I'm making is that we just don't know and never will.

While there is no question the Argentinian authorities would have stooped to dirty tricks to win the match had they thought it was feasible – this was a foul regime, deeply unpopular abroad and anxious to give their own populace something to distract from the widespread and appalling breaches of human rights taking place on a daily basis. But would Peru have played along? It takes both sides to rig a game and while Peru were weak there is no evidence that they were *deliberately* weak. The Peruvians put in more tackles than they had against Brazil (where they were lucky to concede only three) and their goalkeeper, far from having a dodgy game, made a couple of terrific early saves. They just had no answer to the exciting Argentinian forward line. *"There was never a more macho team,"* says Cris Freddi and its clear what he means. This was a gaucho team, you could imagine Kempes and Luque strutting across the ranch with spurs clanking and a bandolier strapped across their chest; they were almost a parody of the dashing Latino male with their thrust-out chests and their long, tumbling hairstyles. If the forwards were the cowboys, behind them was the diminutive, respectable ranch foreman Ardiles; always dapper, both in appearance and movement, and always alert to an opportunity to launch another charge. The defence was familiar to followers of South American football, full of guys who could pass a ball but were utterly merciless on any of the opposition who tried to do the same. The captain, Daniel Passarella, was short and chunky but surprisingly good in the air – he got great lift from immensely powerful thighs. He took the penalties, which he hit with savage power, and a lot of the free-kicks. Passarella came from a line of captains that included Monti and Rattin – I'm the toughest kid on the street so I'm in charge.

Kempes got the first goal against Peru, striding between two defenders to take a return pass and beating a third before sliding expertly past Quiroga; all the uncertainty in front of goal had gone and this was a player at the peak of his game. The second came from a more surprising source. The game was ambling towards half-time; Argentina's urgency had brought only one goal of the four they needed and they were starting to run out of ideas. A corner from the right was just too high for the intended targets, but behind them was full-back Tarantini, who stooped and pinged the ball into the goal. The ensuing goal celebration involved a forty-yard sprint and a lot of shouting – it would all have been mightily impressive but for the awful bubble perm. It was Tarantini's only goal for Argentina in sixty internationals. Well thought of in his own country, he is remembered in Britain for a strange season with Birmingham City, which once saw him sent off for fighting with a member of his own team.

The second half was a performance of great power and author-ity. Kempes scored almost immediately after the break, crashing home after a neat one-two in a packed area, and Luque added the vital fourth five minutes later when Passarella won the ball in the air and left him with an open goal. The fifth and sixth, for Houseman, on as a sub and tapping in after another aggressive run from Kempes, and for Luque again, after some terrible defending, were icing on the cake.

Watching the game, there's nothing obviously wrong with Peru until they go four-down; they were just a poor team defensively. The captain, Chumpitaz, was thirty-four and looked about sixty-four, overweight and laughably slow, strolling back when his team lost the ball in dangerous positions. Not the performance of one who doesn't care, just one who couldn't keep up.

Brazil cried foul, but in truth the better team reached the final. Brazil won the third-place match against Italy in a surprisingly entertaining game; Italy decided to forego the *catenaccio* and just play, while Brazil scored two spectacular goals through Dirceu and Nelinho.

World Cup Heroes No.17
Teófilo Cubillas (1949–)
Peru

These last games in the second phase heralded the end for Peru's finest-ever player. I can say that without fear of contradiction. Few countries have such an indisputable stand-out star, a player who stands head and shoulders above any other – the only European equivalent I can muster is Jari Litmanen for Finland.

Cubillas made his name in the 1970 World Cup where he arrived as a twenty-one-year-old unknown quantity (as did his team to European audiences), and left as a major world player, after scoring in every game and impressing with his range of passing and spectacular shooting. In between 1970 and his next World Cup he was instrumental in Peru winning the Copa América for only the second time – their first title since 1939.

Peru again impressed at the 1978 Finals, and they thrived on their superstar's ability to play long passes out to the express train wingers Muñante and Oblitas. Only in the second phase when teams marked him tightly did his influence recede and the team struggle. Cubillas returned to the World Cup Finals for a last hurrah in 1982 in Spain, but it turned out to be a cheerless farewell as the team went out with a whimper not a bang. That sad end notwithstanding this was a player who for almost a decade would have walked into any side in the world.

Cubillas made his name in South America with Alianza Lima before trying his luck in Europe with first Basel and then Porto. Cubillas was one of many international stars who played in the NASL (for Fort Lauderdale Strikers); the USA showpiece league was no forum for keeping your game at international level, which may explain his poor form at the 1982 World Cup. Later in the decade Cubillas returned to Lima and played for Alianza for free for a season after their entire playing staff was wiped out in an air crash; Cubillas was still good enough to score eighteen goals the following season.

THIRD-PLACE MATCH

Brazil   (0) 2   **Italy**   (1) 1   24 June, Monumental; 69,659
Nelinho 64, Dirceu 71   Causio 38

WORLD CUP FINAL No.11

Argentina   (1) (1) 3 Kempes 37, 103, Bertoni 115
Holland   (1) (1) 1 Nanninga 82

25 June 1978, Monumental, Buenos Aires, Argentina; 76,609

Referee: **Sergio Gonella** (Ita)
Coaches: **César Luis Menotti** (Argentina) & **Ernst Happel** (Holland)

Argentina (4–4–2): Ubaldo Fillol (River Plate); Jorge Olguín (San Lorenzo), Luis Galván (Talleres), Daniel Passarella (Cpt, River Plate), Alberto Tarantini (free agent); Daniel Bertoni (Independiente), Américo Gallego (Newell's Old Boys), Osvaldo Ardiles (Huracan), Oscar Ortiz (River Plate); Leopoldo Luque (River Plate), Mario Kempes (Valencia). **Subs:** Omar Larrosa (Independiente) 65m for Ardiles; René Houseman (Huracan) 75m for Ortiz
Holland (3–4–3): Jan Jongbloed (Roda Kerkrade); Ernie Brandts (PSV Eindhoven), Ruud Krol (Cpt, Ajax) Jan Poortvliet (PSV Eindhoven); Wim Jansen (Feyenoord), Johan Neeskens (Barcelona), Arie Haan (Anderlecht), Willy van de Kerkhof (PSV Eindhoven); René van de Kerkhof (PSV Eindhoven), Johnny Rep (SC Bastia), Rob Rensenbrink (Anderlecht). **Subs:** Wim Suurbier (Schalke 04) 72m for Jansen; Dick Nanninga (Roda Kerkrade) 59m for Rep
Cautioned: Krol (Hol) 15m, Ardiles (Arg) 41m, Larrosa (Arg) 94m, Poortvliet (Hol) 96m

The Dutch were convinced they would not be allowed to beat Argentina in the final. It wasn't a good way to start the game. Nor was the undignified delay, when Argentina objected to the cast René van deKerkhof was wearing to protect his injured arm – five other opponents had all played against him without any issue – likely to help their mood. Referee Klein of Israel, demoted to the third-place match, also at Argentina's insistence, would just have told them to get on with it, Gonella of Italy prevaricated and tugged his forelock and made van de Kerkhof add a pointless extra layer. It all had the feel of a preconceived plan to give Argentina an edge. On the touchline Menotti frowned and swept back his hair in a gesture that had become familiar to TV viewers – one never sensed he was comfortable with all the shenanigans surrounding his team, not in the way Passarella, his captain, seemed to be. Menotti was a footballing man, with a philosophy that took Argentina back to an earlier age when they used flair and speed to unlock defences.

Menotti was appointed to revive the team's fortunes in 1974 after their failure at the World Cup. He was helped by a curious turn of events the following year when the big Buenos Aires clubs initiated a policy of refusing to release their players for international duty. Menotti was forced to look to the provincial sides for his squad and it paid off as he introduced players of the calibre of Galván, Ardiles and Gallego to the team. As an articulate man of left-wing leanings, it was widely anticipated he would be replaced after the coup of 1976, but the authorities stuck with him, and by the start of their home World Cup he had forged a competitive and entertaining team.

That's all they ever were. None of the teams at this World Cup was extraordinary, but at least two of the best three reached the final; Italy were unlucky to lose out to Arie Haan's thunderbolt.

The first half was nip and tuck. Holland's best two chances fell to Rep, who should have done better with a free header and saw a snap shot saved athletically by Fillol. At the other end Passarella stayed up after a set piece and broke the Dutch offside trap, but blazed his half-volley wildly over the bar. It was Kempes who broke the deadlock, a good first touch nipping the ball between the central defenders and the long stride getting him there just before Jongbloed. The air filled with ticker tape – an annoying practice that blighted sporting events for the next twelve months – and the intimidating noise got much louder in Dutch ears.

Despite their fatalism the Dutch kept attacking, and Fillol had to be at his best to deny Rensenbrink just before half-time. In the second half Argentina tucked Kempes deeper and left Luque on his own while they defended on the edge of their area. The game became scrappy, with lots of niggling fouls and time wasting from Argentina – Gonella was far too tolerant.

With Nanninga on for the disappointing Rep, Holland were throwing a lot of crosses in to use his height, and eventually it paid off. The Argentina defence was sucked into the middle and René van de Kerkhof was given acres of space to stand up a cross just ahead of Nanninga, who attacked it and buried it to the manner born.

Extra-time started and Menotti raised Argentina, who came out of their shell and poured forward again. It was Kempes, the man of the moment, who put them into the lead, attacking the Dutch defence through the same inside-left channel and swerving around two challenges. Jongbloed came out and did well, blocking Kempes' initial attempt, but he was unlucky and the ball bounced up for the Argentina striker to have a second chance. Kempes nearly had a hat-trick but another run was half-stopped and Bertoni was on hand to profit from the loose ball and seal Holland's fate.

Holland were the first team to lose consecutive finals, although reaching the final here was probably as good as they expected. Argentina were the third host country to win in four tournaments – both the others had help from referees but nothing on this scale and certainly none of the political pressure that was visible here. My memory of watching the final at home is of my dad switching the TV off in disgust as General Videla, the head of the Junta, handed the trophy over with an ingratiating smile. He explained why. I never watched football with quite the same innocence again.

Happily the tournament did the Junta no favours. They hoped it would present a more positive image of their regime to the watching world, but it served only to highlight the iniquities of which they were guilty. Argentinian goalkeeper Ubaldo Fillol stated later that he first became aware of the atrocities being committed within the country through the foreign media he met during the World Cup. Hey, chalk one up for The Beautiful Game.

World Cup Heroes No.18
Mario Kempes (1954–)
Argentina

Mario Kempes was the "next big thing" of Argentinian football long before he became the "big thing". It took him ten games to score in a World Cup Finals match, but then the floodgates opened and he was unstoppable.

There was something especially exciting about Kempes in full flow. Tall and athletic, with big thighs, a chiselled jaw and long, curling black hair, he had the look of a matinee idol – or perhaps the black-clad bad guy who seeks to thwart the matinee idol.

In 1974 Kempes wasn't ready for the attention thrust on him. He was a raw, natural player and found experienced European defenders had the measure of him, especially playing in a team that favoured measured, cautious football. Four years later, with Menotti in charge, Kempes had rein to collect the ball deeper and embark on charging runs at the defence, exchanging passes at chancy, breakneck speed with his team-mates. The goal still took a while to come, but in Argentina's last four matches in 1978, Kempes scored six times, only blanking in the kicking match against Brazil. Four of the goals came from those irresistible cavalry charges, and the Valencia man thoroughly justified Menotti's decision to exempt him from a policy of not picking European-based players.

In 1982 it was back to the scoreless wonder. Kempes played well in the group games, dropping into an attacking midfield role to allow Maradona room to explode further forwards, but in the second phase he was anonymous against Italy and Brazil, confirming an impression that he struggled against the very best defenders.

Kempes wasn't a great player, taking his whole career into account, but for a couple of weeks in the summer of 1978 he was the pride of the Junta, and looked every inch a Prince.

Team of the Tournament, 1978:

Leão (Brazil)
Olguin (Argentina)   Scirea (Italy)   Passarella (Argentina)   Cabrini (Italy)
Causio (Italy)   Ardiles (Argentina)   Gallego (Argentina)
Bettega (Italy)   Kempes (Argentina)   Rensenbrink (Holland)

Official Team of the Tournament: Fillol, Vogts, Krol, Tarantini, Dirceu, Cubillas, Rossi were all in, along with Leão, Passarella, Bettega and Kempes from my team. I am right, they are wrong, you'll just have to trust me.

Leading scorers: Kempes (6); Cubillas & Rensenbrink (5); Luque & Krankl (4)

Heaven Eleven No.8

Holland (with some help from the Belgians)

Coach:
Rinus Michels

Goalkeepers:
Edwin van der Sar: safe hands, best Dutch goalkeeper.
Jean-Marie Pfaff*: excellent Belgian 'keeper in the '80s
Michel Preud'homme*: Pfaff's successor, unlucky to overlap for a few years

Defenders:
Wim Suurbier: one of the great '74 team
Ruud Krol: attacking left-back or sweeper, or pretty much anywhere

* indicates a Belgian player

Jaap Stam: dominant centre-half, untypical of a Dutch player
Ronald Koeman: sweeper and set piece specialist
Vincent Kompany*: one of the best contemporary defenders
Danny Blind: under-rated sweeper, part of the Ajax revival and absurdly under-used for Holland in a weak era
Eric Gerets*: super reliable right-back for the strong '80s Belgian team

Midfield & wide:
Ruud Gullit: the dreadlocked one could play anywhere but was at his best in an attacking midfield role
Johan Neeskens: hard-tackling, hard-shooting star of the '74 team
Frank Rijkaard: great defensive midfielder, part of the Milan–Holland trinity with Gullit and van Basten
Clarence Seedorf: just preferred ahead of Edgar Davids, a reliable all-round midfielder
Arjen Robben: inconsistent but match-winning winger
Wesley Sneijder: attacking playmaker in the side that reached the 2010 Final
Faas Wilkes: first great post-war Dutch attacking player
Paul Van Himst*: regarded by many as Belgium's best ever

Strikers:
Dennis Bergkamp: one of the most intelligent forwards of recent years
Johan Cruyff: genius
Rob Rensenbrink: wonderful left foot and great dribbling skills
Marco van Basten: fierce shooter and finisher, unlucky with injury
Jan Ceulemans*: dangerous Belgian attacker from the '80s, strong as an ox

Omissions:
We could have included **Frank De Boer** at the back, or the '50s great **Cor van der Hart**. **Edgar Davids** was unlucky, as were **Marc Overmars** and **Piet Keizer**, we went for Robben's trickery instead of pace. **Arie Haan** was a top player, just too similar

to Rijkaard; **van Hanegem** was a terrific player but more influential at club level. The Belgian **Enzo Scifo** was over-rated and rarely delivered in big matches, while **Ludo Coeck**, tragically killed at thirty, would be a sentimental choice rather than a pragmatic one.

None of the Belgian attackers from their heyday was quite in this class, and nor were **Johnny Rep**, **Patrick Kluivert**, **Ruud van Nistelrooy** or **Robin van Persie** (another great club player who was never quite as effective at international level); Kluivert had all the talent but rarely had his head on the right way round. Ask in a few years and Fellaini, Hazard, De Bruyne, Benteke or Lukaku might be pushing for a place – Belgium have an exciting crop of players at time of writing.

Likely first XI:

Van der Sar
Gerets   Stam   Koeman   Krol
Rijkaard
Gullit   Neeskens   van Himst
Cruyff   van Basten

HEROES & VILLAINS

6.1 WORLD CUP 1982

Spain underwent major changes in the years immediately before and immediately after the country served as host for the World Cup. After forty years of one-party rule (the fascist Falange party led by General Franco was the only legally permitted political party) in the Cortes Generales (Spanish Parliament), the dictator's death in 1975 precipitated a change. The King, a cipher under Franco's rule, became the Head of State and a new democratic constitution was put in place in 1978. Unsettled, the military tried to initiate a new coup in 1981, but King Juan Carlos' personal intervention and lack of public support nipped the mini rebellion in the bud.

During Franco's reign Spain pursued an isolationist policy in foreign affairs, although the 1960s saw greater inclination to court alliance with other western powers, particularly the United States, as paranoia about Communist infiltration crept in. In the early 1980s the new Spain was enthusiastically displaying its new democracy – they joined NATO two weeks before the tournament began – and embracing the unique cultural heritage of its regions in a more devolved system. The World Cup, embraced by Franco initially as a propaganda coup, became a very different symbol of national pride.

Spain was a football mad country, with a really powerful league whose best sides had a terrific record in European competition. Games drew big crowds, so the availability of large-capacity stadia was not an issue; no other European country could boast two grounds as big as the Camp Nou in Barcelona and the Santiago Bernabéu in Madrid, the homes of the two giant clubs

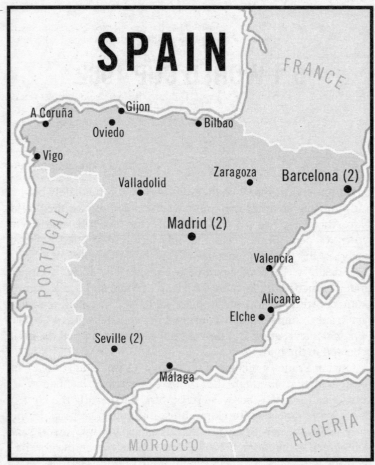

SPAIN

A Coruña

Gijon

Oviedo

Bilbao

Vigo

Zaragoza

Barcelona (2)

Valladolid

Madrid (2)

Valencia

Alicante

Elche

Seville (2)

Málaga

PORTUGAL

FRANCE

MOROCCO

ALGERIA

1982
SPAIN

The expansion of the number of clubs taking part meant more grounds were
needed and Spain used seventeen grounds in fourteen cities. They employed
a nicely egalitarian system, letting the smaller cities share the group matches,
only bringing Barcelona and Madrid into play for the second-group phase.

Madrid: Santiago Bernabéu
Real Madrid's magnificent stadium in the capital was the venue for the final
and also hosted Spain (and England's) second-phase matches. Only the Nou
Camp as a club stadium has a bigger capacity.

Madrid: Vicente Calderón
Opened in 1966, the Vicente Calderón was the second stadium in the capital and is the home of Atlético Madrid. The stadium never filled its 60,000-plus capacity during the tournament.

Barcelona: Nou Camp
Probably the most splendid football stadium in Europe, the glittering Nou Camp seems to reach into the sky these days, with a capacity for just under 100,000 people (all seated). At its peak, which encompassed this World Cup, the ground held a staggering 120,000 people, but didn't come close to filling it for the finals' matches.

Barcelona: Sarriá
The Sarriá was the home of Espanyol, the second Barcelona club, but was demolished in 2007. The club moved into a new stadium after a couple of years playing in the Barcelona Olympic Stadium.

Group 1 was shared between **Vigo** and **A Coruña** in the north west. The Balaídos had been home to Celta Vigo since the 1920s, while the **Estádio Riazor** was home to Deportivo de La Coruña. Until the last two or three years when Deportivo have struggled, the Riazor was a noted bogey ground for the mighty Real Madrid.

Further along the north coast to the east, **Oviedo** and **Gijon** hosted Group 2, using two smaller grounds; Sporting Gijon's El Molinón (opened in 1908) and Real Oviedo's **Carlos Tartiere**. The Carlos Tartiere was the smallest of the grounds used in the 1982 finals and was knocked down and re-built at the start of this century.

Group 3 was in the far south-east of the country in **Elche** and **Alicante**. The **Nuevo** stadium in Elche (since renamed after a former club president) and the **José Rico Pérez** in Alicante were the two grounds used, home to Elche FC and Hércules FC respectively. A lucky 23,000 in Elche watched Hungary score ten against El Salvador – a World Cup record.

England's group games in 1982 were played in the **San Mamés** (locally referred to as La Catedral) in **Bilbao** in the heart of the Basque country along the border with France. In 2013, one hundred years after the old stadium opened, a new San Mamés stadium opened in the city. Other games in Group 4 were played in **Valladolid**, at the smaller **José Zorrilla** stadium, built especially for the 1982 tournament.

Of the stadia used for the group games the biggest was the **Luis Casanova** (now Estádi Mestalla) in **Valencia**, opened the same year as the original Wembley. The spectators at the Luis Casanova looked on in shock as the host nation lost to Northern Ireland. Valencia shared hosting duties for Group 5 with **Zaragoza**, where the **la Romareda** stadium, home of Real Zaragoza, was renovated for the finals.

Two grounds in **Seville** saw service in 1982, the **Ramón Sánchez Pizjuán** and the **Benito Villamarín**. The larger Ramón Sánchez, home of Sevilla, hosted the classic West Germany versus France semi-final; the Benito Villamarín is the home of Real Betis. **La Rosaleda** in **Malaga** to the south-east shared Group 6 duties with Seville.

Barcelona and Real Madrid. The other games were dotted around the regions, in line with the new flavour of government, and there were two further grounds with capacity for over 50,000 fans in Sevilla in the south-west and Valencia on the east coast.

Elsewhere Argentina and Great Britain were at loggerheads over the Falkland Islands, so an England or Scotland game against Argentina was to be avoided if possible. England v Argentina games were passionate affairs without this new martial twist to the relationship.

The second-phase groups leading straight to the final was clearly unsatisfactory, so in 1982 FIFA introduced a new twist – second phase groups followed by semi-finals. It was marginally better, but as there were now twenty-four finalists (and commensurately more income for the FIFA coffers) some device was needed to whittle them down.

The biggest problem was the second phase groups – they each had three teams, which imbalance meant one team in the second and third matches had much less preparation time, and one team in the last match would probably have good reason to stifle the game and play for a draw. In three of the groups such fears were confirmed – in the other the system produced an out-and-out ripper.

Qualifying

UEFA changed their qualifying system quite dramatically, moving from three- and four-team groups to five teams with two going through from each section. (Plus one odd little three-team group with one qualifier, which made things very easy for Poland, drawn against a declining East Germany and Malta, who couldn't really decline because they were never any good.)

The British Isles came within a whisker of having five teams in the Finals.

England had the easiest task in a group including Romania, Hungary, Switzerland and Norway – no dross, but nothing intimidating. Easy or not, England's away form nearly saw them eliminated; defeats to Romania, Switzerland and Norway were only partially compensated by an excellent win in Budapest in June

1981 orchestrated by Trevor Brooking and Kevin Keegan. England's two best players were both past thirty and rarely fit at the same time – the match in Budapest was England's sixth game in the group and the first for which both were available. The defeat in Oslo three months later was a landmark win for the Norwegians, and is memorable for a historic rant by the Norwegian commentator Bjørge Lillelien.

> *We are the best in the world! We are the best in the world! We have beaten England 2–1 in football!! It is completely unbelievable! We have beaten England! England, birthplace of giants. Lord Nelson, Lord Beaverbrook, Sir Winston Churchill, Sir Anthony Eden, Clement Attlee, Henry Cooper, Lady Diana – we have beaten them all. We have beaten them all. Maggie Thatcher, can you hear me? Maggie Thatcher, I have a message for you in the middle of the election campaign,* [the Norwegian election of 1981] *I have a message for you: We have knocked England out of the football World Cup. Maggie Thatcher, as they say in your language in the boxing bars around Madison Square Garden in New York: Your boys took a hell of a beating! Your boys took a hell of a beating!*

Brooking was again absent and his replacement, Glenn Hoddle, the "great hope" of English football was anonymous. An anxious two months ensued while the other participants caught up with their games; Switzerland did England a huge favour by winning in Bucharest and a win over Hungary sneaked England into the Finals. Norway finished bottom for all Lillelien's rhetoric but their time was not so far away. Few people outside the tabloids were optimistic about England's chances. Young Bryan Robson and Manchester United colleague Steve Coppell provided great box-to-box energy and Brooking was still a crafty player, but the defence was pedestrian and while Paul Mariner worked commendably hard he was no one's idea of an international quality centre-forward. A record of won four, drew one and lost three didn't have the world's best teams quaking in their boots.

Scotland and Northern Ireland were in with Sweden and Portugal – sounds tough but those countries were at a low footballing ebb. Scotland won in Sweden in the autumn of 1980 with an excellent goal from Gordon Strachan, while Northern Ireland beat Portugal the following Spring when Gerry Armstrong headed the game's only goal fifteen minutes from the end. Neither of these results was a major surprise; Scotland still had a handful of top-class players and the Irish had their best team since the late 1950s. When Portugal lost twice to Sweden the two home nations were left in control of the group and could afford to play out a dreary 0–0 in October 1981. A humiliating 4–1 defeat for the Portuguese in Israel meant even a draw in their last match at home to Israel would see Northern Ireland join Scotland in the Finals. Another Armstrong goal saw them home with yet another 1–0 win. Northern Ireland were more than the sum of their parts – no superstars but a fantastic work ethic; they conceded only three goals in eight qualification matches, none of them at Windsor Park.

No one was holding their breath for the Scots after the debacle of 1978, but Souness and Dalglish were the axis of a great Liverpool team and the Aberdeen-based centre-half pairing of Alex McLeish and Willie Miller was a formidable barrier. They still didn't have a goalkeeper of any real quality.

Wales struggled manfully against the Soviet Union and Czechoslovakia. The Soviets were a top side, so Wales and the Czechs were battling for one place, hoping not to drop points against Turkey and Iceland (sounds like a Christmas shopping planner . . .). Both did, to Iceland, but Wales 2–2 home draw after leading twice proved costlier. It was a surprise, as Wales had not conceded at all in their first five games and had beaten Iceland 4–0 in Reykjavik. Coming off the back of a defeat in Prague the previous month, it left Wales with the stiff task of needing some sort of result in Tbilisi against the Soviet Union. It wasn't to be, the Soviets were in commanding form and won 3–0, and the Czechs got the point they needed at home to the Soviets in the last match to pip Wales on goal difference.

The Republic of Ireland were in a terribly difficult group containing France, rapidly improving, together with Holland and Belgium, who seemed magnetically attracted to each other in qualifying for the World Cup. Holland, finalists in the previous two World Cups, were clear favourites, with the other qualifier to come from France or Belgium; Ireland's allotted role was that of spoiler, capable of beating one of the fancied sides at Lansdowne Road but not consistent enough to make the top two.

The spoiling started in the second match when Ireland beat the Dutch with a late headed goal from a clever free-kick. Instead of shooting, Liam Brady executed a flop-shot (golf, look it up) over the wall and Mark Lawrenson, unmarked, headed tidily home – check out Lawro's beard on the video. Lawrenson made a significant contribution in the return too, a surging run and cross providing Frank Stapleton a chance to score with a typically brave header – Ireland came back twice to draw and leave themselves with a great chance of qualifying. Defeats in Belgium and France had made that unlikely; the Irish were especially unlucky in Brussels when the referee missed a blatant body-check on goalkeeper McDonagh for the late Belgium winner.

Ireland faced a crucial qualifier at Lansdowne Road against France and a packed stadium saw a fabulous match. An early lead was soon wiped out by Bellone's smart turn and finish, but some shoddy French defending saw Ireland go in 3–1 up at the break. France struggled to cope with the pace and power of Stapleton and Michael Robinson, who produced his best form for Ireland, despite not being Irish by anything other than expedience. It wasn't Jack Charlton who invented the notion of bolstering the Irish squad by playing the ancestry game – Lawrenson and Chris Hughton, both key players, were also English-born. A late goal by Platini was a consolation – now France had to win both their remaining games to head Ireland in the table. Intriguingly, Holland could also still qualify by beating France in Paris – the Irish were praying for a draw, not such an unlikely outcome. Holland had recalled Johan Neeskens for their win over Belgium (already qualified) but he held little sway as France turned up the heat in the second half and won 2–0. A routine win over the group whipping boys Cyprus (*nul points*, as they say in Eurovision) saw France, not Ireland, heading to Spain. Ireland, for all their qualities and the presence of the sublime Liam Brady, would not have matched France's achievements in Spain. Holland looked a spent force and were crucified in their own press. They had replaced coach Jan Zwartkruis with Kees Rijvers halfway through qualifying but it availed them little. In the next three years Rijvers would blood a new generation of Dutch stars, but it took a while before their impact was felt.

Elsewhere in Europe the usual suspects emerged. Reigning European Champions from 1980 West Germany won every game and scored for fun, but their group was weak – the second qualifiers were a moderate Austrian side. Yugoslavia and Italy also qualified easily from a weak group, though Italy gave their supporters momentary palpitations by losing for the first time to Denmark. Italy had been dealing with other concerns since the last Finals tournament – more of this in a moment.

In South America Uruguay showed their decline was deep-rooted as they failed to qualify again, beaten at home by Peru. Brazil looked much more like their old selves, and Chile qualified without conceding a goal, but – and this went also for Peru – looked unlikely to threaten with the competition held in Europe. Argentina would return as holders with many of the same players plus their new *wunderkind*, Diego Maradona. But they couldn't expect the same amount of assistance from the organisers and officials. In the CONCACAF section Honduras and El Salvador not only managed to avoid going to war during their matches, but they also both managed to qualify, at the expense of Mexico, for once; the USA didn't even make the final pool for CONCACAF qualification – soccer in the States was at a seriously low point. With two qualifiers each from Africa and the Asia/Oceania sections, the teams "making up the numbers" in the eyes of the European press were Cameroon, Algeria, Kuwait and New Zealand – all were making their debut in the Finals.

Finals

Brazil were everyone's favourites (aren't they always?), while West Germany and the Soviet Union had qualified with the most panache from Europe. Argentina could not be discounted with Menotti still in charge and Italy were expected to do well.

This World Cup was the first that felt like it was being thoroughly and voraciously exploited for commercial gain. Sponsors were conspicuous, as were empty seats after half-time while the prawn-sandwich brigade (Mr Keane's scoff has become common parlance for corporate hangers-on) finished wolfing down their freebies. David Goldblatt in *The Ball Is Round* cites the alarming statistic that this was the first tournament where the cost of flying in and housing FIFA officials exceeded the cost of flying in and housing the players. The trough was growing.

GROUP 1

Italy	**(0) 0**	**Poland**	**(0) 0**	14 June, Vigo; 22,000
Cameroon	**(0) 0**	**Peru**	**(0) 0**	15 June, La Coruña; 15,000
Italy	**(1) 1**	**Peru**	**(0) 1**	18 June, Vigo; 25,000
Conti 19		Díaz 85		
Cameroon	**(0) 0**	**Poland**	**(0) 0**	19 June, La Coruña; 12,000
Poland	**(0) 5**	**Peru**	**(0) 0**	22 June, La Coruña; 16,000
Smolarek 56, Lato 60,		La Rosa 83		
Boniek 62, Buncol 68,				
Ciolek 78				
Cameroon	**(0) 1**	**Italy**	**(0) 1**	23 June, Vigo; 17,000
Mbida	62	Graziani 61		

1. Poland 4pts (5–1); 2. Italy 3pts (2–2); 3. Cameroon 3pts (1–1); 4. Peru 2pts (2–6)

A tight group, with only one match of the six not drawn. The four sides played out two goalless draws for openers and followed up with two more, leaving the group still wide open. Italy and Peru had at least scored a goal each, although Peru left theirs till five minutes from time and needed a fortuitous deflection off Collovati from a Díaz free-kick to get it.

Cameroon exited with much sympathy when they drew their third match with Italy 1–1 but ceded second place to the Italians, having scored one goal less. The Italians, clearly not firing, still had the best of all three of their games, and Cameroon offered little up front apart from some dazzling smiles from the skilful and effervescent Milla. But he ploughed a lone furrow too often, and Cameroon's best player behind him was captain and goal-keeper Thomas Nkono.

The group was won by Poland, who scored five in a second half against Peru that contrasted with the other five hundred or so minutes of football. Poland had a new young side, with the vastly experienced Wladyslaw Zmuda, playing in his third World Cup Finals tournament, as captain. Kazi Deyna had retired, and the

new superstar and playmaker was Zbigniew (Zibi) Boniek, a
quick goalscoring attacking midfielder. Boniek was on his way to
Juventus in Italy and anxious to prove he was worth his £1.1m
transfer fee, a new record for an East European player.

Smolarek scored the first after Peru's centre-half Velasquez
needlessly gave the ball away and twelve minutes later it was 4–0.
Boniek put Lato through and when Quiroga came charging miles
out of his area all the veteran had to was pass the ball calmly past
him. Boniek scored the next himself after a free-kick on the edge
of the box caught Peru napping; instead of a shot the ball was
played to Smolarek, unmarked on the right, and his cross was
side-footed home. The best goal was the fourth; Lato started a
quick break on the right and found Andrzej Buncol with a long
crossfield ball. Buncol advanced and slipped a pass to Boniek in
the area; facing away from goal Boniek delivered a perfect back-
heel into Buncol's path and the midfielder belted the return past
Quiroga. Ciolek, on for Smolarek, added a fifth from Lato's pull-
back before La Rosa's consolation for Peru. It was a dull group,
but the two best sides qualified for the next phase.

GROUP 2

Austria Schachner	(1) 1	**Chile**	(0) 0	17 June, Oviedo; 22,000
Chile Moscoso 90	(0) 1	**West Germany** (1) 4 Rummenigge 9, 58, 67, Reinders 82		20 June, Gijon; 40,500
Algeria	(0) 0	**Austria** Schachner 56, Krankl 68	(0) 2	21 June, Oviedo; 22,000
Chile Neira 60 (p), Letelier 74	(0) 2	**Algeria** Assad 8, 31, Bensaoula 34	(3) 3	24 June, Oviedo; 18,000
West Germany Hrubesch 11	(1) 1	**Austria**	(0) 0	25 June, Gijon; 41,000

1. West Germany 4pts (6–3); 2. Austria 4pts (3–1); 3. Algeria 4pts (5–5); 4. Chile 0pts
(3–8)

The West Germany sides of the 1980s epitomised the decade;
unlovely and unloved – even their own journalists struggled to
heap praise on them beyond admiring their resolve in reaching
two World Cup Finals in the absence of more than a couple of
genuine world-class players. This was the side that earned the
reputation Germany suffered for two decades of mechanical

(above) Argentina before the 1930 Final. (Popperfoto/ Getty Images)

(left) Meazza (Italy) and Sárosi (Hungary) shaking hands before the 1938 Final. (Getty Images)

Joe Gaetjens, who scored the winning goal in the United States' 1–0 upset of England in the 1950 World Cup. (Popperfoto/Getty Images)

Puskás scores, but still loses in 1954. (Popperfoto/Getty Images)

Garrincha, the 'little bird'.
(Popperfoto/Getty Images)

Schiaffino, one of the unheralded
greats. (Getty Images)

The incomparable Pelé, as a teenager in 1958. (Popperfoto/Getty Images)

The Battle of Santiago, 1962. (Popperfoto/Getty Images)

The inimitable Bobby Charlton. (Popperfoto/Getty Images)

(left) 'Der Kaiser', Franz Beckenbauer. (Popperfoto/Getty Images)

(below) Pickles the dog, briefly the holder of the trophy. (Getty Images)

Hat-trick hero, Sir Geoff Hurst. (Popperfoto/Getty Images)

Braziiiiiiiiiil! 1970. Genius. (Popperfoto/Getty Images)

Cruyff, 1974. Genius. (AFP/Getty Images)

West Germany defy logic, and the Dutch, to win in 1974. (Getty Images)

Passarella wins for the Junta in 1978. (Getty Images)

Somebody's gonna get hurt …

… it was Battiston. (AFP/Getty Images)

Burruchaga, unsung hero.
(Bob Thomas/Getty Images)

'See, Peter, this is my right hand …' (Getty Images)

'… and this is my left.' (Bob Thomas/Getty Images)

Lineker doing what he did best. (Bob Thomas/Getty Images)

Shilton in 1990, still the world's No.1 at 40. (Bob Thomas/Getty Images)

Klinsmann gave one of the great displays against Holland in 1990.
(Bob Thomas/Getty Images)

US defender Alexi Lalas at the 1994 World Cup. (Bob Thomas/Getty Images)

The agony and the ecstasy of the penalty shoot-out: Baggio and Taffarel in 1994. (Bob Thomas/Getty Images; AFP/Getty Images; AFP/Getty Images; AFP/Getty Images)

Michael Owen en route to teenage glory in 1998. (Popperfoto/Getty Images)

Zizou (No.10) heads for victory in 1998. (AFP/Getty Images)

Coach Guus Hiddink took South Korea, who had never previously won a World Cup match, to the semi-finals in 2002. (Bongarts/Getty Images)

Grosso breaks German hearts in 2006. (Bongarts/Getty Images)

Rob Green howls after a howler in 2010. (AFP/Getty Images)

England expects (Jack Wilshere) ... (Getty Images)

... as does Germany (Mario Götze) ... (Getty Images)

... and Brazil (Neymar). (Getty Images)

efficiency without flair – they rarely lost, but they excited equally rarely. In 1982 they started the Finals shambolically, behaved shamelessly in their group, shuffled through the second phase, Schumacherred the French and then completed their alliterative journey by providing a touch of *schadenfreude* when they got stuffed in the final. Here is the shambles that started it all off:

WORLD CUP SHOCK No.4
16 June, 1982, El Molinón, Gijón; 34,000

Algeria	**(0) 2**	Madjer 53, Belloumi 69
West Germany	**(0) 1**	Rummenigge 67

Referee: **Enrique Labo Revoredo** (Paraguay)
Coaches: **Rachid Mekhloufi** (Algeria) & **Jupp Derwall** (West Germany)

Algeria (4–4–2): Mehdi Cerbah (RS Kouba); Chaabane Merzekane (Hussein Dey), Mahmoud Guendouz (Hussein Dey), Norredine Kourichi (Bordeaux), Faouzi Mansouri (Montpellier); Lakhdar Belloumi (GCR Mascara), Ali Fergani (Cpt, Tizi-Ouzou), Mustapha Dahleb (Paris St Germain), Salah Assad (RS Kouba); Rabah Madjer (Huseein Dey), Djamel Zidane (KV Kortrijk in Belgium). **Subs:** Tedj Bensaoula (MP Oran) 65m for Zidane; Salah Larbes (Tizi-Ouzou) 88m for Madjer

West Germany (4–4–2): Harald Schumacher (Cologne); Manni Kaltz (Hamburg), Karlheinz Förster (Vfb Stuttgart), Uli Stielike (Real Madrid), Hans-Peter Briegel (Kaiserslautern); Pierre Littbarski (Cologne), Wolfgang Dremmler (Bayern Munich), Paul Breitner (Bayern), Felix Magath (Hamburg), Horst Hrubesch (Hamburg), Karl-Heinz Rummenigge (Bayern). **Sub:** Klaus Fischer (Cologne) 83m for Magath
Cautioned: Hrubesch (WGer) 57m, Madjer (Alg) 83m

In their opening game the Germans were awful. Coach Jupp Derwall preferred the powerful Hrubesch to the sharper Fischer and the Germans were pedestrian in midfield where the recalled Breitner looked well past his sell-by date. Perhaps he believed his own pre-match prediction that West Germany would be too strong for Algeria.

Strength was the main thing with this German side. Kaltz and Briegel were enormous full-backs (Briegel a former decathlete) and their midfield players could run all day. The young Cologne winger Littbarski, a fantastic dribbler, was included, as was the elegant Magath, but the over-riding impression was one of athlet-icism and efficiency rather than movement and skill.

A goalless first half saw West Germany win a series of corners and set pieces and waste them all by lumping the ball at Hrubesch. They seemed so anxious to impose their physical presence on Algeria they forgot about playing football – a criticism aimed often at British rather than German sides. Algeria were giving the

German defence some cause for concern with their crisp passing, but created few clear openings in the first forty-five minutes.

That changed in the second half when the Algerians started to run with the ball in midfield and bring their wide players into the game. They deservedly took the lead after fifty-three minutes. A wonderful direct run from Zidane (no relation) sucked in the right of the German defence and left Belloumi in the clear for Zidane's pass. Belloumi's shot ballooned up off Schumacher's foot, evaded three German defenders and bounced kindly for Madjer to touch home at the far post.

West Germany responded with an unsophisticated assault, and equalised a quarter of an hour later when Rummenigge beat his man to a hard, low cross from Magath. It was "here we go again" in the press box as onlookers assumed the German machine would grind down the plucky underdogs and take control. Not so; these were talented underdogs and this machine was malfunctioning badly. Two minutes after Rummenigge's clinical finish, Algeria broke quickly through Zidane again. The ball reached Salah Assad who skinned Manni Kaltz down the left and hit an undefendable cross through the six-yard box to Lakhi Belloumi at the back post. Algeria were back in front. They nearly added a supreme third when full-back Merzekane broke and ran two-thirds the length of the field but he just ran out of steam and couldn't apply a finish. Back came West Germany but Hrubesch had a day to forget. He missed a golden opportunity when Stielike crept down the right and served up a gem of a cross, and missed again from a long, deep cross when the goalkeeper over-committed. West Germany thought they had scored direct from Breitner's corner, but the referee blew for pushing – guess who by? And it was Hrubesch who was dispossessed by Merzekane, who went on another great counter-attacking run and this time found Madjer on the edge of the area; the striker's rasping shot was only a whisker past the post. There was still time for Rummenigge to climb well at the back post and nod a cross against the bar before the whistle went and all of Algeria screamed its delight.

Just down the road in Oviedo a less exciting match was played out between Austria and Chile. Chile had the veteran Figueroa at centre-half, sixteen years after his World Cup debut as a nineteen-year-old in 1966, and he was still a redoubtable player, but the Chileans played too slowly and too predictably, and Austria looked stronger throughout. Austria scored with their first decent opportunity when Schachner converted a Bernd Krauss cross with a precise glancing header. Chile had a great chance to level within minutes, but Caszely missed the penalty his own run had won. There was little else to admire, some entertaining shooting from Hintermaier's bludgeon of a left foot aside.

Despite the peppering-in-print Derwall's team deservedly received from the press at home, the manager stuck with the same eleven against Chile and was rewarded with a much improved performance. Chile, a poor side, wilted in the face of some typically robust German tackling and offered little resistance as Rummenigge scored a hat-trick and West Germany won 4–1. Rummenigge already had two hat-tricks to his name from the qualifying tournament, against Finland and Albania, and this confirmed his reputation as a punishing finisher against weak or tired defences. The Chilean goalkeeper Osbén, who looked vulnerable against Austria, had another poor match and was at fault for two of the German goals, the first when he failed miserably to get down for Rummenigge's shot and allowed it to creep under his body.

Back in Oviedo, Austria marched on, defending better than West Germany against Algeria's quick counter-attacks and marking Fergani, the captain and playmaker, as well as keeping much tighter on Madjer and the much-vaunted Belloumi, who had a woeful game. Schachner scored again, when he was well placed to slot home a rebound from Welzl's shot, and Welzl then set up Krankl for a fierce swerving drive into the far corner; great finish but the tormentor of Germany from 1978 looked horribly out of sorts.

On 24 June, in the same venue, Oviedo, Algeria proved their performance against West Germany was no fluke and ran amok in the first half against Chile, who were having a nightmare tournament. Assad gave Algeria the lead after only eight minutes; Madjer's hard run down the left and excellent cross found Bensaoula, who unselfishly stopped the ball for Assad rather than take on a tricky volley; Assad coolly finished high past Osbén.

Assad added a second after a neat interchange and Bensaoula exploited Osbén's weakness against low shots. It could have been worse, Madjer hit the woodwork with a terrific shot and Osbén tipped another one just past the same upright. The second half was very different, as Chile hit back against tired opponents; Yáñez was brought down for a penalty which Neira converted (Caszely was off the field but one assumes his colleagues would not have let him risk another miss) and then Letelier scored with an excellent dribble and finish. Algeria were hanging on at the end, but they deserved the win – little did they know how costly the two Chilean goals would prove.

The group was still in the balance; Austria had four points, as did Algeria, while West Germany needed to beat Austria to match that total. They did, but in the most disappointing manner. If the oppro-brium that greeted their performance in the opening game was intense, it was nothing to the vilification the team received after the sham of their match against Austria. Needing a victory to proceed, West Germany scored early and that was pretty much that. Austria, all but through after wins against Chile and Algeria, seemed happy to play along and avoid a disastrous three-goal defeat as the match was played out at walking pace. It was a far cry from Krankl's hero-ics of 1978. The complete lack of energy from both sides suggested – still does – an element of collusion in engineering a result that suited both teams, but suggestion is not proof and no one has ever come forward and admitted the game was manufactured. A more charitable explanation is that both sides were afraid to press forward and risk a result that left them more exposed.

The world's press ranted and railed, none more so than the embarrassed Germans. Algeria and their supporters (and many neutrals) cried foul but there was nothing they – or FIFA – could do. No rules were broken, but the game left a sour taste. Derwall was stony-faced, claiming professionalism had won the day, but no one was impressed.

It was tough on Algeria, who had some talented players and, unlike many African sides, weren't afraid to have a go and attack the European sides – contrast with an equally talented Morocco in 1986. Fergani, Madjer, Belloumi and Assad were all exciting players – Belloumi went on to win 147 caps, many of them in admittedly low-quality, meaningless fixtures (at least in the context of the world game). Most of the squad chose to stay in Algeria to play domestic football; an exception was Salah Assad, who signed for Mulhouse in France when they enjoyed (?) a rare single season in Ligue 1 in France. Assad had an excellent season and was picked up by Paris St Germain but spent most of his time there on the bench. Assad had a mighty fine line in acrobatic goal celebrations, back-flips, somersaults, you name it.

GROUP 3

Belgium Vandenbergh 63	(0) 1	**Argentina**	(0) 0	13 June, Camp Nou; 95,000
Hungary Nyilasi 4, 83, Pölöskei 11, Fazekas 24, 55, Tóth 51, Kiss 69, 73, 77, Szentes 71	(3) 10	**El Salvador** Ramírez Zapata 65	(0) 1	15 June, Elche; 6,000
Argentina Bertoni 27, Maradona 28, 57, Ardiles 61	(2) 4	**Hungary** Pölöskei 76	(0) 1	18 June, Alicante; 32,093
El Salvador	(0) 0	**Belgium** Coeck 18	(1) 1	19 June, Elche; 6,000
Belgium Czerniatynski 76	(0) 1	**Hungary** Varga 27	(1) 1	22 June, Elche; 22,000
Argentina Passarella 23 (p), Bertoni 54	(1) 2	**El Salvador**	(0) 0	23 June, Alicante; 18,000

1. **Belgium** 5pts (3–1); 2. **Argentina** 4pts (6–2); 3. **Hungary** 3pts (12–6); 4. **El Salvador** 0pts (1–13)

The tournament's opening game, between Argentina and Belgium, finished 0–0 . . . oh, hang on, no it didn't. I've become so used to saying the opening game was 0–0 I almost forgot – this one had a goal. It was scored by Erwin Vandenbergh for Belgium – he was in so much space he could afford to wait an age for the ball to drop after a clumsy first touch, but he slotted it past Fillol smartly enough. The result was a surprise, but hardly seismic; Belgium had a good crop of players and finished runners-up at the 1980 European Championships, losing only to a very late Horst Hrubesch winner.

The result in the group's other opening game, played two days later in Elche on the south-east coast near Alicante, meant Argentina were looking nervously over their shoulders. The group's weakest team, El Salvador, played Hungary, who had headed England's group in qualifying. Their manager was Kálmán Mészöly from their exciting 1960s side, and they looked worthy successors here, with expert finishing to some neat build-up play. Nyilasi, the Hungarian captain, powered in the first after only four minutes and left-winger Pölöskei added a second on the break a few minutes later. The veteran Fazekas was allowed the freedom of the pitch to advance and curl in a nice third before half-time.

In the second half the real carnage began. Tóth added a fourth and Fazekas scored again – again with all the room in the world to aim a shot into the corner. Centre-forward Torocsik must have been livid to be taken off but his replacement Laszlo Kiss made history, becoming the first substitute to score a hat-trick in a World Cup Finals match. He remains the only one and his nine-minute triple remains the fastest in the Finals. His second was the pick of Hungary's goals, a lovely lob after his team-mates had worked him the ball on the left edge of the area. Szentes and Nyilasi (with another thumping header) completed the scoring but the wildest celebrations were for the goal at the other end, scored by Luis Ramirez Zapata – it briefly made the score a mere 5–1.

Argentina needed to beat Hungary – they weren't going to make up that goal difference – and met them next in Alicante. Kempes, who looked lost against Belgium, played in midfield and looked happier, seeing much more of the ball, and Valdano replaced the disappointing Diaz, just as he had in the opening game – at least, Valdano played until he himself was replaced, injured, after twenty-five minutes. Three minutes later Argentina were two-up, Bertoni scoring from Passarella's knock-down and Maradona touching in a loose ball. Argentina were completely in control now. Maradona added a typical solo third and Ossie Ardiles scored one of his infrequent goals when he finished off a move he started in his own half.

Belgium only managed a single goal against El Salvador (they lacked the imagination of the Hungarians, and El Salvador played much better), but they got the point they needed against Hungary to clinch their second-round place. Hungary, for all their style and panache, had been exposed by the two better sides and went home. Argentina managed a mere two against El Salvador the following day, for all their attacking potency, and they now faced a horrible second-phase group.

GROUP 4

England	(1) 3	**France**	(1) 1	16 June, Bilbao; 44,172	
Robson 1, 67,		Soler 25			
Mariner 83					
Kuwait	(0) 1	**Czechoslovakia** (1) 1	17 June, Valladolid; 12,000		
Al-Dakhil 58		Panenka 21 (p)			
Czechoslovakia	(0) 0	**England**	(0) 2	19 June, Bilbao; 44,182	
		Francis 63, own goal 66			
France	(2) 4	**Kuwait**	(0) 1	21 June, Valladolid; 30,043	
Genghini 31, Platini 43,		Al-Buloushi 75			
Six 48, Bossis 90					
Czechoslovakia	(0) 1	**France**	(0) 1	24 June, Valladolid; 28,000	
Panenka 84 (p)		Six 66			
England	(1) 1	**Kuwait**	(0) 0	25 June, Bilbao; 31,000	
Francis 27					

1. England 6pts (6–1); 2. France 3pts (6–5); 3. Czechoslovakia 2pts (2–4); 4. Kuwait 1pt (2–6)

England's campaign got off to a sublime start. Maybe the French players were still dwelling on the tabloid tales about Jean-François Larios and Michel Platini's wife – Larios left the French squad when the papers exposed his *affaire du coeur* with Mme Platini. Whatever the reason, the French switched off in the early seconds. England kicked off, Wilkins found Coppell, who won a throw-in. Using a ploy that was far from unique, Coppell's long throw found Terry Butcher, who advanced for just that purpose, and Butcher's flicked header found Bryan Robson unmarked. The England man did well to get over the volley and guide it past Ettori.

Robson had an excellent game, tackling and running and always prepared to get into the box and get hurt going for crosses. Just as well he did play his best, for England were outgunned elsewhere, where the slick French passing exposed the limitations of the English left-side combination of Sansom and Rix. France came back through Soler, who finished well from Giresse's wonderful through ball. The French bossed the next thirty minutes either side of half-time but failed to pick Robson up again in the second half and he scored his second with a rampaging header from Trevor Francis' cross. Towards the end, with France looking a bit weary, Coppell's long cross found Wilkins, who cleverly cushioned the ball into the path of Francis. Francis miscued his shot but it ricocheted to the unmarked Mariner, who scored with ease. It was a good performance from England against slightly disappointing opposition.

Next up for England were Czechoslovakia, a pale shadow of some of the sides they had sent to past tournaments. The Czechs started with a 1–1 draw against Kuwait, and that form continued into this match. England were criticised at home for a modest performance, but sometimes, in the early stages, if that's all that is needed then modest is a good way of avoiding expending energy and peaking too soon. A tap-in from Trevor Francis, England's best player, and an own goal sealed a comfortable, but boring victory.

France's second game featured one of the more bizarre incidents in World Cup history. Kuwait were enterprising against Czechoslovakia, and deserved at least their draw, but here they were outclassed. France brought in a pair of Bernards (not an insult, they were both called Bernard!), Lacombe and Genghini for Larios and René Girard. All the impetus came from the midfield, as usual, and Genghini and Platini provided the goals that gave France a comfortable half-time lead. When Didier Six was put in by Platini for a third three minutes after the interval, it seemed to be the end of it. Kuwait scored a consolation goal when the French defence lost concentration, but Alain Giresse scored a fourth and . . . utter chaos ensued. The Kuwaiti defence appeared to stop on hearing a whistle from the crowd and they mobbed the referee in protest when Giresse carried on and scored. The brother of the Kuwaiti ruler and President of their FA, Sheikh Fahad Al-Ahmad Al-Sabah, in full formal robes, called his players off. There were huddles and hugger-mugger and confusion and lots of posturing and lots of dithering from the Soviet referee before the game was resumed. Thankfully the outrageous decision (play to the whistle, fellers) to chalk off the goal didn't affect the outcome; both sides scored one more and it finished 4–1. Michel Hidalgo, the French manager, was apoplectic (he had every right to be) and had to be removed from the pitch by the

Spanish police, who were never the most subtle presence. Mr Stupar wasn't asked to referee another game. The Sheikh met a sad end, murdered by invading Iraqi troops as he defended the Royal Palace after the Emir and most of his family had fled. A man of some presumption, but also a man of enormous personal courage.

France needed a point against Czechoslovakia to qualify alongside England. Didier Six scored after a huge mix-up in the Czech penalty area, and the penalty that drew the Czechs level was a debatable one. Amoros headed off the line in the closing moments, but it would have been sad for the tournament if Czechoslovakia had progressed at France's expense – only one team looked as if there was more in their locker. England headed the group comfortably after a 1–0 in another tedious match against Kuwait. Glenn Hoddle came in for Bryan Robson, but did little to support the extravagant claims for his inclusion from his many admirers; it was the injured Keegan's buzz and energy around the opposition penalty area that was missed most.

GROUP 5

Honduras	**(1) 1**	**Spain**	**(0) 1**	16 June, Valencia; 49,562
Zelaya 8		López Ufarte 65 (p)		
N. Ireland	**(0) 0**	**Yugoslavia**	**(0) 0**	17 June, Saragossa, 18,000
Spain	**(1) 2**	**Yugoslavia**	**(1) 1**	20 June, Valencia; 50,000
Juanito 14 (p), Saura 67		Gudelj 10		
Honduras	**(0) 1**	**N. Ireland**	**(1) 1**	21 June, Saragossa; 15,000
Laing 60		Armstrong 10		
Yugoslavia	**(0) 1**	**Honduras**	**(0) 0**	24 June, Saragossa; 12,000
Petrovic 87 (p)				

1. Northern Ireland 4pts (2–1); 2. Spain 3pts (3–3); 3. Yugoslavia 3pts (2–2); 4. Honduras 2pts (2–3)

Spain's group, on paper, contained the weakest side in each of the top three seeding groups, plus an unknown quantity in Honduras. Spain were expected to qualify – they would have struggled to do so from any other section. The hosts were unfortunate in that their turn to hold the tournament on home soil coincided with a dearth of quality players. Only the goalkeeper and full-backs can in any way be counted as greats of Spanish football.

Honduras provided stiffer opposition than anticipated in Spain's first game, taking the lead after eight minutes. A number of the Hondurans won contracts with Spanish clubs (mostly at a level below the big teams) after their performances here – the central defender Anthony Costly and midfielder Héctor Zelaya, who scored that early goal, were amongst those who impressed watching scouts, as did Gilberto Yearwood, who was already playing in Spain, with Valladolid.

Like Spain, Yugoslavia didn't bring a vintage crop of players, and they were held to a 0–0 draw with Northern Ireland, well organised and prepared to graft, as always. Yugoslavia were better against Spain; they started positively and took the lead when Gudelj headed home a free-kick. With Spain in trouble the home bias factor kicked in. Not the Simpsons patriarch, but the World Cup factor that dictates that for the sake of the coffers the home nation must be given every chance to reach the latter stages. It has worked in every World Cup except South Africa, and it worked here when Sørensen, the Danish referee, gave a penalty for a foul that was clearly a foot outside the area. The defender stayed completely still and was clearly standing out of the penalty area; the most charitable explanation is that Mr Sørensen was feeling the pressure from the partisan crowd in the Luis Casanova stadium (Valencia). Sørensen even compounded his error and ordered the kick re-taken when López Ufarte missed with the first attempt. In fairness the goalkeeper clearly left his line, but plenty of other instances of the same offence went unpunished. Spain changed kicker and Juanito scored. Dodgy, dodgy stuff.

Yugoslavia still created chances – Arconada made a fantastic double save from Petrovic and Susic, while Slijvo skimmed the outside of the post from twenty-five yards. Spain did slightly better in the second half, and López Ufarte clipped the top of the bar with a free-kick, but it was still Yugoslavia who created the best chances; Vujovic put a header an inch wide of the post with Arconada beaten and Susic fired hard into the side netting when clear. Even Spain's winning goal had an element of fortune; Quini, on for the limp Satrústegui, made a hash of a shot from López Ufarte's corner, but the ball spun through to Saura, who

scored at the far post. The goal seemed to take the stuffing out of
Yugoslavia and the game subsided.

Over in Zaragoza the Northern Ireland squad expected to pick
up their first win against Honduras, but, like Spain, found the
debutants hard to break down. Newspaper reports of the Irish
squad partying all night were laughed off by Billy Bingham, and
there were no hangovers apparent as the Irish started on top.
Martin O'Neill should have scored with a free header, but it
wasn't his strong point and his effort sailed over the bar. Sammy
McIlroy's free-kick hit the bar, and so did Chris Nicholl's follow-
up header, but Gerry Armstrong put the third attempt in the
back of the net – he headed a queue of three players waiting to
knock the ball in. Honduras looked tidy on the ball and created an
opening for Betancourt to hit the post with a left-foot volley, but
Northern Ireland dominated the midfield and pushed Honduras
deeper. Whiteside and Hamilton went close, and Armstrong hit
the post after making room for a shot.

Whiteside had the ball in the net early in the second half, but
Armstrong, who provided the knock-back, was wrongly penalised for a foul. Honduras were still in the game, and Jennings
made an incredibly agile one-handed save from Betancourt's
header – remarkable reflexes for a thirty-seven year old. The
resultant corner did produce a goal, Laing's header came from a
sharper angle and Jennings had no chance. Northern Ireland
pressed – they didn't fancy having to beat Spain – and Armstrong's
fantastic turn created a chance which was denied by a good save
from Arzu. Jennings still had one more save to make, tipping
Figueroa's fierce free-kick around the post – the referee wasn't
impressed, he gave a goal-kick!

Honduras could still make the second phase if they beat
Yugoslavia and they came close. Yugoslavia needed Pantelic to make
two good one-on-one saves, and their late goal was fortunate. Sestic
cut in off the right-hand touchline, beating three men in an exciting
run, then spoiled it by diving over the next challenge and rolling
around as if shot. He got up smartly enough – as the cheats invariably do – when he realised the referee had given a penalty. Gilberto
was sent off shortly afterwards for venting his frustration. For the
Irish the goal was irrelevant – they still needed to beat Spain.

WORLD CUP SHOCK No.5
25 June 1982, Luis Casanova, Valencia; 49,562

Spain	**(0) 0**	
Northern Ireland	**(0) 1**	Armstrong 47

Referee: **Héctor Ortiz** (Paraguay)
Coaches: **José Santamaria** (Spain) & **Billy Bingham** (Northern Ireland)

Spain (4–4–2): Luis Arkonada (Cpt, Real Sociedad); José Camacho (Real Madrid), Miguel Tendillo (Valencia), José Alexanko (Barcelona), Rafa Gordillo (Real Betis); José Sánchez (Barcelona), Miguelo Alonso (Real Sociedad), Roberto López Ufarte (Sociedad), Enrique Saura (Valencia); Jesús Satrústegui (Sociedad), *Juan Gomez, known as* Juanito (Real Madrid). **Subs:** *Enrique Castro, known as* Quini (Barcelona) 45m for Satrústegui; Ricardo Gallego (Real Madrid) 78m for López Ufarte
Northern Ireland (4–4–2): Pat Jennings (Arsenal); Jimmy Nicholl (Toronto Blizzard), Chris Nicholl (Southampton), John McClelland (Glasgow Rangers), Mal Donaghy (Luton Town); Martin O'Neill (Cpt, Norwich City), David McCreery (Tulsa Roughnecks), Sammy McIlroy (Stoke City), Norman Whiteside (Manchester United); Gerry Armstrong (Watford), Billy Hamilton (Burnley). **Subs:** Tommy Cassidy (Burnley) 50m for McIlroy; Sammy Nelson (Brighton & Hove Albion) 73m for Whiteside
Cautioned: Juanito (Spa) 20m, Hamilton (NIre) 41m, McIlroy (NIre) 42m
Dismissed: Donaghy (NIre) 61m

I had to include this game because it was one of the great backs-to-the-wall performances. Whether it was that much of a shock is debatable – Spain had a poor tournament and the Irish were a decent side who, at the risk of repeating myself, were much better than the talent of the component parts. World-class players – one, the goalkeeper; international standard players – five, and that's being generous to both Nicholls; players prepared to give their last breath in the cause – eleven plus another eleven on the bench. It constitutes a shock because they didn't just beat Spain, they beat Spain + massively partisan Valencia crowd + weak referee (who spoke Spanish but not English, surely not a coincidence). It was joyous and unexpected; Northern Ireland's build-up included 4–0 hammerings by England and France and a 3–0 defeat by Wales.

The game was tight throughout; Spain were conspicuously more comfortable on the ball but also conspicuously nervous about the height and strength of the Northern Ireland forwards. Spain kept possession well early on, with the hardworking Miguel Alonso the platform for their best work. He is the father of Xabi Alonso, later of Liverpool and Real Madrid, and played a similar deep role, but without his son's fantastic passing ability. Alonso was one of four players from Real Sociedad, who were enjoying their best-ever spell in *La Liga* and had just won a second consecutive title, the only occasion they won the league. The statistic is perhaps more a comment on the relative weakness of Real Madrid and Barcelona, normally the source of over half a Spanish squad – here they supplied only two each of the starting line-up and nine within the squad.

López Ufarte came close twice, one run between the central defenders thwarted by Pat Jennings and another curling effort hit with too little power to trouble the Northern Ireland goalkeeper. Jennings was an immense comfort to the Irish under pressure. As he got older he eradicated the errors to which he was prone, and became a goalkeeper of the very highest quality. He ate crosses (another weakness he worked hard to improve), was extremely agile and had superb positional sense, working principally from the edge of the six-yard box in the manner of all the great British 'keepers of that era.

The biggest threat to the Irish came not from the weak Spanish forwards, but from the centre-halves Tendillo and Alexanko, both of whom went close with headers before half-time. Northern Ireland hung on until the break, but more was needed. More came two minutes into the second half when Armstrong got the ball in his own half and ran at the heart of the Spanish defence. The midfield, shorn of Zamora (out injured), parted like the Red Sea and Armstrong made forty yards before finding Hamilton to his right. The Burnley man did superbly well, taking the ball past Tendillo before the Spaniard got his balance right, and whipping in a good cross. Armstrong hadn't quite the energy to get on the end of it, so Arconada inexplicably gave him a helping hand, palming the ball out instead of catching it. Armstrong didn't panic, he just slotted the ball calmly back past the goalkeeper and two despairing defenders. If they could hang on the Northern Irish were through, and both sides knew the top-placed team avoided a nasty second-round group containing England and West Germany.

Spain, with the assistance of Señor Ortiz of Paraguay, the referee, went in search of an equaliser. Free-kick after free-kick went against the Irish rearguard, some genuine, some sought. Northern

Ireland, marshalled wonderfully by Jennings and the vastly experienced Chris Nicholl, stayed on their feet and repelled everything that was thrown at them, at first with some ease. Their task was made difficult when Mal Donaghy's shove on Camacho was followed by the teensiest little reaction from both players and the officials leapt at the chance to give the home side an edge. Watch the video now and we think, "oh maybe, he sort of raised his hand" – but in the context of some of the marking and tackling in the tournament as a whole it was barely a booking.

Out of their comfort zone now, Northern Ireland merely stepped up their efforts. The left hand side of the defence was under pressure without Donaghy, so Billy Bingham turned to the experience of Sammy Nelson, now thirty-three and winning his fiftieth cap. Billy Hamilton dropped into midfield and worked tirelessly, while Armstrong stayed up on his own, and never gave the Spanish defence a moment's peace.

The atmosphere inside the stadium was electrifying, and the performance of the Northern Ireland side under the most intense pressure was little short of heroic. It was their greatest-ever night.

GROUP 6

Brazil	**(0) 2**	**USSR** (1) 1	14 June, Seville; 50,000
Sócrates 75, Éder 87		Bal 34	
Scotland	**(3) 5**	**New Zealand** (0) 2	15 June, Malaga; 22,000
Dalglish 18, Wark 30, 34,		Sumner 54,	
Robertson 73, Archibald 79		Wooddin 65	
Brazil	**(1) 4**	**Scotland** (1) 1	18 June, Seville; 47,379
Zico 33, Oscar 49		Narey 18	
Éder 65, Falcão 88			
New Zealand	**(0) 0**	**USSR** (1) 3	19 June, Malaga; 17,000
		Gavrilov 25, Blokhin 48,	
		Baltacha 69	
USSR	**(0) 2**	**Scotland** (1) 2	22 June, Malaga; 30,000
Chivadze 60, Shengalia 84		Jordan 15, Souness 88	
Brazil	**(2) 4**	**New Zealand** (0) 0	23 June, Seville; 32,000
Zico 28, 31, Falcão 55,			
Serginho 69			

1. Brazil 6pts (10–2); 2. USSR 3pts (6–4); 3. Scotland 3pts (8–8); 4. New Zealand 0pts (2–12)

If Scotland were full of hubris and got their come-uppance in the 1978 World Cup, here they were unlucky from the start. The draw, so kind to Spain (and England) found them grouped with arguably the strongest teams in the top two seeded pools, Brazil and the Soviet Union.

These two strong sides met in the opening game, and the first half was cagey, with both feeling their way into the tournament, Brazil looking sluggish, the USSR cautious. The Soviets took the lead, but only through a shocker from Brazilian goalkeeper Waldir Peres, who should have made a routine save from Andrei Bal's far-from-unstoppable long-range effort. Instead, it hit Peres on the shin and bounced in, the goalkeeper showing the reactions and suppleness of an oak tree.

Brazil left it late to wake up, scoring twice in the last fifteen minutes, but the goals were worth the wait. First Sócrates side-stepped two defenders and unleashed a fantastic shot into the top left-hand corner of the goal – the ball went like a tracer bullet and swerved late. Three minutes from time Falcão stepped over a pass as Éder called from behind him; Éder flipped the ball into the air in front of him and hit a shot that left Dasaev a stunned spectator. No goalkeeping error for either of these, Dasaev was one of the best in the world.

In Malaga the next day Scotland delivered a performance of two halves, commanding in the first, stuttering in the second. They turned around 3–0 to the good. Gordon Strachan tormented the New Zealand defence and Kenny Dalglish and John Wark scored from his crosses – Wark stealing in between the defenders with a late run familiar to Ipswich fans. Wark also tucked away a rebound when van Hattum could only half save a Dalglish shot.

In the second half New Zealand had a bit of a go and got some joy. McGrain hit a weak back-pass to Alan Rough, who dithered – he was a great shot-stopper but a liability in any other situation – and let in the Kiwi centre-forward Sumner. Ten minutes later Steve Wooddin ran on to a hit and hope ball with Alan Hansen out of position and tucked it past Rough. Scotland's blushes were spared by a neat free-kick from John Robertson and a looping header by substitute Steve Archibald from Strachan's corner; the Aberdeen wide man was the shining light in a mixed bag of a performance.

Scotland's suspect defence faced a much bigger test in their next game in Seville, against Brazil, now warmed up. The first goal was top drawer, a lobbed pass headed back into the path of the onrushing right-back, who pushed it ahead of him and unleashed a screamer into the corner. The surprise was the scorer: full-back David Narey scoring his only goal for Scotland in thirty-eight games. Brazil were level by half-time through a curled free-kick from Zico, but Scotland had done pretty well, keeping the Brazilians at arm's length – not that this side were incapable of scoring from an arm's length and more.

The floodgates opened in the second half when Oscar got ahead of his marker to head in a corner at the near post. The last two goals were pure Brazilian. Éder, released on the left, shaped to smack one and then slowed his foot into the ball, drifting a pitching wedge over the stranded Rough (who was too far out). Three minutes from time another intricate move made space for Falcão to rifle a low shot off the inside of a post. Without hitting top gear Brazil had shown their power and Scotland's goal average took a dent, which left them needing to beat the Soviet Union, who beat New Zealand 3–0 without really breaking sweat.

Scotland recalled Joe Jordan for a bit of physical presence, and partnered him with Steve Archibald, even though Dalglish was fit again. Dalglish, such a great player at club level, was merely a good one for Scotland and never brought his A-game to a World Cup; the same could be said of Graeme Souness, that 1978 game against Holland apart. Not so Joe Jordan, the best British centre-forward of his era. Jordan had endured a torrid year, relegated with AC Milan, a great team in a lean spell, and out of the Scotland side for the first two games. He opened the scoring here, pouncing on a rare mistake by the elegant sweeper Aleksandr Chivadze, drawing Dasaev and ramming the ball into the corner. Scotland still led at half-time, but the USSR had the bulk of possession and the Scottish forwards were isolated. After an hour a neat passing Soviet move ended with a tame shot from Gavilrov; Rough flapped it away instead of catching it and Chivadze made amends by chipping neatly over the grounded 'keeper. Scotland's fate was sealed when Hansen misjudged a long ball down the left and headed it backwards. Retreating, the Liverpool defender collided with Miller, running across to cover and the ball bounced clear for Shengalia, the skilful Dinamo Tbilisi forward. Hansen was never likely to catch him and Shengalia rounded Rough with ease and scored. Souness's late strike, impressive as it was, meant the statistics implied Scotland came close to qualifying for the second phase. They didn't and another rather flat campaign was over.

Scotland's big problem in this tournament was not knowing their best defence. Stein may have been better to pick the Aberdeen pairing of Miller and McLeish – neither had Hansen's ability, but they knew each other's game and neither of them, individually, understood how to compensate for Hansen's lack of pace or power in the way his Liverpool partners Thompson and Lawrenson were able to do.

Scotland Squad 1982:
GK: Alan Rough (Partick Thistle, 30 years old, 48 caps), George Wood (Arsenal, 29, 4), Jim Leighton (Aberdeen, 23, 0)
DEF: George Burley (Ipswich Town, 26, 11), Allan Evans (Aston Villa, 25, 3), Frank Gray (Leeds United, 27, 22), Alan Hansen (Liverpool, 27, 14), Danny McGrain (Glasgow Celtic, 32, 60), Alex McLeish (Aberdeen, 23, 15), Willie Miller (Aberdeen, 27, 17), David Narey (Dundee United, 26, 13)
MID & WIDE: Asa Hartford (Manchester City, 31, 49), Davie Provan (Celtic, 26, 10), John Robertson (Nottingham Forest, 29, 21), Graeme Souness (Liverpool, 29, 25), Gordon Strachan (Aberdeen, 25, 11), John Wark (Ipswich, 24, 15)
FWD: Steve Archibald (Tottenham Hotspur, 25, 14), Alan Brazil (Ipswich, 22, 7), Kenny Dalglish (Liverpool, 31, 86), Joe Jordan (AC Milan, 30, 51), Paul Sturrock (Dundee United, 25, 7)

GROUP A

Poland	(2) 3	**Belgium**	(0) 0	28 June, Camp Nou; 30,000
Boniek 4, 27, 53				
Belgium	(0) 0	**USSR**	(0) 1	1 July, Camp Nou; 25,000
		Oganesian 49		
USSR	(0) 0	**Poland**	(0) 0	4 July, Camp Nou; 45,000

An unsatisfactory format saw Poland earn a semi-final place on goal difference. They owed it to Zibi Boniek, who scored a quite outstanding hat-trick against Belgium. After only three minutes Lato went past his man on the right and cut the ball back at forty-five degrees to the edge of the area where Boniek met it with an instant right-foot shot that flew past Custers. Just before the half-hour a cushioned header by Buncol from Kupcewicz's deep cross hung in the air long enough for Boniek to nod it over Custers, who was in no man's land. Belgium may have wished they had found a better punishment for regular goalkeeper Jean-Marie Pfaffs' poolside prank with a journalist than leaving him out of this game.

In the second half Boniek started a move wide on the right and continued his run; Smolarek and Lato kept the ball cleverly and Lato nudged it through for Boniek to waltz round the goalkeeper and score his third.

Three days later the Soviets couldn't match Poland's score. Belgium played better and were unlucky to lose at all, to a scrappy second half goal from Oganesian. For all their good possession and midfield talent, the Soviets lacked punch up front, where the former European Footballer of the Year, Oleg Blokhin, failed dismally to live up to his reputation.

The Soviet coach, Konstantin Beskov, was really part of a triumvirate with two influential club coaches, Nodar Akhalkatsi of Dinamo Tbilisi and Valeri Lobanovsky of Dynamo Kyiv. This explains the dominance of those two sides in the make-up of the side; the starting line-up for the first game included four Tbilisi players and five from Kyiv. The Soviet league champions in 1982 were Dynamo Minsk, who had one player, full-back Sergei Borovsky, in the twenty-two, while the 1983 champions, Dnipro Dnipropetrovsk, were not represented at all. The Soviets were regarded as a disappointment in 1982, the defeat by Brazil their only loss in a sequence that lasted three years, but still no major progress. More accurately, they were a work in progress and had yet to find the collective system that would realise their potential. They came closer in 1986 and 1988. Khoren Oganesian, the scorer against Belgium, was an Armenian, that country's finest player. Sergei Baltacha, the other central defender alongside Chivadze, was the first Soviet player to move to England when he joined Ipswich Town in 1988. Baltacha later played for St Johnstone and Inverness Caledonian Thistle in Scotland, and he and his wife, Olga, a pentathlete, had a daughter, Elena, who became a professional tennis player and was British No.1 for much of the first decade of this century.

In 1982 the Soviet Union was still set in its Cold War ways, and the regime's intolerance of opposition was highlighted in an ugly manner when, at their request, the Spanish police removed any tokens of support for the banned trade union, Solidarity, during the Poland v USSR match. The police waded in with a relish that was hard to stomach.

While violence simmered and then boiled in the stands, the game was tepid. Poland played deep and ran hard, and Blokhin had another stinker – his place in the team seemed to be untouchable, if the mystifying substitution of the lively Shengalia in his place was anything to go by. The result suited Poland – a stupid booking for Boniek didn't, as it meant they would face the winners of Group C without him.

GROUP B

W. Germany	(0) 0	England	(0) 0	29 June, Bernabéu; 75,000
Spain	(0) 1	W. Germany	(0) 2	2 July, Bernabéu; 90,089
Zamora 83		Littbarski 50, Fischer 75		
England	(0) 0	Spain	(0) 0	5 July, Bernabéu; 65,000

Dull, dull, dull. The first game between England and West Germany was determined by fear; two ordinary attacks (Rummenigge hit the bar late on but he was clearly not fully fit) failed to break down two well-drilled defences. Mills, the England captain, showed what an under-rated player he was and Terry Butcher dominated the penalty area. At the other end the Förster brothers negated Mariner and Francis, and Robson, like Rummenigge, was lacklustre by his standards.

For their next match against Spain, Derwall brought Littbarski back for the inadequate Reinders. Littbarski scored the opening goal at the beginning of the second half when Arkonada again failed to hold a ball he should have smothered – for such a good goalkeeper he really did have a disastrous tournament. Breitner's run after seventy-five minutes cut into the Spanish defence; he found Littbarski, who spun dexterously, drew Arkonada and laid the ball sideways for Fischer, who sealed Spain's fate. Zamora's late header flattered the Spanish, who were well beaten by an improved West Germany.

England still had a chance to qualify by bettering West Germany's score against a despondent and eliminated Spanish side. They barely even tried. It was a lifeless end to a depressingly negative campaign. Ron Greenwood took over as England manager with a reputation for attacking football born of his involvement in the flair-driven, exciting West Ham sides of the 1960s. His assistant was Don Howe, a former international right-back and acolyte of the "if they don't score we can't lose" school of coaching. Howe's influence was clear and Greenwood seemed to lack the will to resist falling back on English "virtues". The defence was excellent, admittedly, but that's irrelevant when the job in hand is to win by two goals.

England's central midfield was Ray Wilkins as the holding player – never as poor as people made out, the Deschamps of his age – and Bryan Robson. On the flanks were Steve Coppell and Graham Rix, neither a committed attacking player. When Coppell failed a fitness test England had limited options; Keegan was still unfit, as was Brooking, and Glenn Hoddle was poor against Czechoslovakia and Kuwait. England's answer looked adventurous, picking the Cologne attacker Tony Woodcock in a front three, using Trevor Francis as a roving forward.

Woodcock contributed little; neither he nor Mariner managed to fluster the Spanish central defenders like Armstrong and Hamilton had, yet England never looked to use Peter Withe of Aston Villa, whose power might have disturbed their equilibrium. Withe probably felt pretty good having scored the winner in the European Cup Final a few weeks earlier. Until the last twenty minutes neither of the England full-backs ventured forward – Sansom's best qualities were wasted sitting behind a defensive, character-less player like Rix. The press had clamoured for Keegan and he came on for Woodcock, but was woefully under-prepared and missed England's one gilt-edged chance, putting a header wide from Robson's cross. Brooking's introduction made a more noticeable difference – he should certainly have been risked from the start instead of Rix.

Mark Pougatch's book *Three Lions Versus the World* quotes various England players claiming they were the best team in the group and desperately unlucky to be going home without losing and conceding only one goal. They go to great lengths to defend Ron Greenwood, too – he was adored by his players. But all this is more an indication of the cocoon in which football squads are kept, bolstering their self-belief and convincing each other that setbacks are never of their making. Ex-pros are fond of telling lay pundits they don't understand the game and have no valid opinion. Twaddle. If companies struggle they bring in outside help; the panoramic view is far more revealing than the one at ground level.

Ron Greenwood got it wrong; England were too cautious and not quite good enough.

England Squad 1982:
GK: Peter Shilton (Nottingham Forest, 32, 37), Ray Clemence (Tottenham Hotspur, 33, 58), Joe Corrigan (Manchester City, 33, 9)
DEF: Viv Anderson (Nottm Forest, 25, 10), Terry Butcher (Ipswich Town, 23, 4), Steve Foster* (Brighton & Hove Albion, 24, 2), Mick Mills (Ipswich, 33, 37), Phil Neal (Liverpool, 31, 37), Kenny Sansom (Arsenal, 23, 23), Phil Thompson (Liverpool, 28, 35)
MID & WIDE: Trevor Brooking (West Ham United, 33, 46), Steve Coppell (Manchester United, 26, 36), Glenn Hoddle (Tottenham, 23, 11), Terry McDermott (Liverpool 30, 25), Graham Rix (Arsenal, 24, 8), Bryan Robson (Man Utd, 25, 19), Ray Wilkins (Man Utd, 25, 47)
FWD: Trevor Francis (Man City, 28, 28), Kevin Keegan (Southampton, 31, 62), Paul Mariner (Ipswich, 29, 21), Peter Withe (Aston Villa, 30, 6), Tony Woodcock (Cologne, 26, 22)

---

* Foster was an extraordinary selection. Dave Watson, although thirty-five, had done sterling service and won sixty-five caps without playing in a Finals tournament and it seemed a cruel cut to leave him out after he featured in virtually all the qualifiers. Especially for a player so desperately short of international quality as the headband-wearing Foster.

GROUP C

Italy	**(0) 2**	**Argentina**	**(0) 1**	29 June, Sarriá, 39,000
Tardelli 57, Cabrini 67		Passarella 83		

This had the potential to be a dour affair; Italy's disciplined and tough defence against Maradona and his cavalry charges. The cavalry charges never materialised, the runs were cut off in their prime as Italy's feared man-marker Gentile got a grip on the young maestro, often very literally in some uncomfortable regions of his anatomy. The full-backs harassed Bertoni and Kempes, and Tardelli, almost as intimidating as Gentile, was in Ardiles' face from the first minute. The Romanian referee, Mr Rainea, got some stick in the press, but there were five bookings in the first half (but only two to Italians) and a late red card for Gallego (pure frustration). The game never got out of hand, it was just cynical. Argentina never settled, and when Italy started to play in the second half they had no answer.

A good Italian passing move ended with Antognoni's perfectly weighted ball into the inside-left channel and Tardelli shot precisely across Fillol's body. Ten minutes later another break found Italian attackers queuing up to finish with the Argentinian defence panicking – it was the outstanding left-back Cabrini who administered an excellent left-footed finish high into the goal. Passarella's thunderous free-kick gave Argentina hope but there were only seven minutes remaining and the dark-blue wall tightened and held.

WORLD CUP CLASSIC No.11

Brazil	**(1) 3**	Zico 12, Serginho 68, Júnior 74
Argentina	**(0) 1**	Díaz 89

2 July 1982, Sarriá, Barcelona; 44,000

Referee: **Rubio Vázquez** (Mexico)
Coaches: **Telê Santana** (Brazil) & **César Luis Menotti** (Argentina)

Brazil (4–2–3–1): Waldir Peres (São Paulo); José Leandro (Flamengo), José Oscar (São Paulo), *Luiz Carlos Ferreira, known as* Luizinho (Atlético Mineiro), Leogevildo Júnior (Flamengo); Toninho Cerezo (Atlético Mineiro), Sócrates *de Souza Vieira* (Cpt, Corinthians); Paulo Roberto Falcão (AS Roma), *Arthut Coimbra, known as* Zico (Flamengo), Éder *Aleixo de Asiss* (Atlético Mineiro); Serginho *Chulapa* (São Paulo). **Subs:** Edevaldo *de Freitas* (Internacional) 82m for Leandro; João Batista (Grêmio) 84m for Zico
Argentina (4–4–1–1): Ubaldo Fillol (River Plate); Jorge Olguín (Independiente), Luis Galván (Talleres de Córdoba), Daniel Passarella (Cpt, River Plate), Alberto Tarantini (River Plate);

Daniel Bertoni (Fiorentina), Juan Barbas (Racing Club), Osvaldo Ardiles (Tottenham Hotspur), Mario Kempes (River Plate); Diego Maradona (Boca Juniors); Gabriel Calderón (Independiente). **Subs:** Ramón Díaz (River Plate) 45m for Kempes; Santiago Santamaría (Newell's Old Boys) 64m for Bertoni
Cautioned: Passarella (Arg) 33m, Waldir Peres (Bra) 77m, Falcão (Bra) 85m
Dismissed: Maradona (Arg) 87m

Argentina was in a bit of a pother. General Leopoldo Galtieri had initiated the invasion of the Islas Malvinas, the disputed territory held by Britain and known as the Falkland Islands. It was a populist (and popular) cause, as most Argentinians felt Los Malvinas were, by right, Argentinian. Margaret Thatcher, another politician in need of an electoral lift, disagreed and Britain sent her better trained and better equipped navy and forces to take back the islands. They did so, easily, in two months. Galtieri resigned and his successor, General Bignone, succumbed to calls for free elections – they finally took place in October 1983, when Raúl Alfonsin won the Presidency. The team shared the national sense of self-doubt during the World Cup of 1982, plagued by uncertainty and no little despondency; Osvaldo Ardiles, resident and employed in England, felt it keenly; he would spend the next season on loan at Paris St Germain before returning to Tottenham. Argentina had arguably a better squad than when they won the tournament four years earlier. Kempes would never reproduce the exciting form of 1978 but most of the team was still under thirty and the new superstar, Diego Maradona, could shred even the tightest defences with his pace and close control. It just never clicked for them; Menotti erred in picking the over-hyped Díaz and Calderón ahead of Valdano, who linked with Maradona so effectively four years later in Mexico. Their playmaker, Ardiles, a huge hit in English football, stated later he played his worst football at this tournament, his mind in turmoil over the conflicts the war had caused him.

Brazil was still ruled by generals in 1982, but they too were undergoing a steady transition to democracy; the age of the military dictators in South America was coming to an end, although any hope that the attendant economic and social problems would disappear with them proved wildly optimistic. Brazil's coach, Telê Santana, appointed in 1980, had put the joy back into Brazilian football, and team had rediscovered the attacking samba football of their glory years.

The game reflected these different attitudes and moods. Brazil attacked from the start – they knew no other way – but could have gone behind when a roll-back-the-years run from Kempes set up Barbas, whose header was too close to Peres. Brazil didn't have to wait long for their first goal. Éder hit a free-kick from thirty-five yards – Argentina weren't taken by surprise, they had a four-man wall. The ball brushed the fingertips of Fillol, at full stretch, and bounced back off the bar. There were no other Argentinians on the TV screen apart from the grounded goalkeeper when Zico nipped in ahead of his colleague Serginho to poke in the rebound. The difference in energy and desire was marked. The only shock of the first half was that Brazil didn't add further goals. Falcão went close twice, the second time after a delightful headed one-two with Sócrates set up a fierce volley that dipped just too late. Peres tipped over a Passarella header just before half-time but one sensed that Argentina were hanging on by their fingernails.

For Kempes it was an anti-climactic end to his World Cup career, substituted at half-time by Díaz. Díaz, the young River Plate forward so widely touted as one of the stars of the game for years to come, won his last cap here at the age of only twenty-two. The same wasn't true of Maradona, the one player who seemed up for this challenge, and he should have had a penalty at the beginning of the second half when he got past Júnior and the Brazilian full-back chased him and brought him down. The watching Italian coach noted how easily the full-backs were taken out when Brazil were not in possession.

The second Brazilian goal was a masterpiece, at once clinical and beautiful. Sócrates advanced and squirted a pass to Éder, immediately running towards the area, creating space behind him. Zico, normally ahead of his captain, filled the space and received the return from Éder. The No. 10 slid the ball carefully between two defenders for Falcão, overlapping on the right in familiar style. Falcão's cross was inch perfect, Serginho barely had to move to head home – good job, he usually missed when he had to move. It was the São Paulo centre-forward's only goal of the tournament. Serginho looked cumbersome, especially in comparison with the fluidity and grace of his colleagues. Brazil's hottest new forward talent, Careca, was injured before the tournament, but Santana liked the big front man, and would probably have picked Serginho anyway, in spite of the catcalls from the press box.

The last goal was just as good, but involved only two players. Left-back Júnior started the move with a purposeful run and finished it like a born striker with a sprint into the box and nonchalant prod past Fillol; the man in the middle was Zico, who received the ball with one touch and played it back into Júnior's path through a forest of players. This was a different Zico from the wastrel talent who did so little at the 1978 tournament.

A few minutes later we saw the other side of Júnior, messing about in his own penalty area and nearly letting in Maradona, whose clever chip just cleared the crossbar. Maradona was involved again moments later when the Brazilian substitute Batista went in high on Barbas; Maradona didn't wait for the referee to pronounce judgement but flew in waist high at the Brazilian and got a deserved red card. It was the kind of reckless response to frustration and perceived injustice that let Maradona down a number of times throughout his career. Yes, he was subjected to some excessively physical marking, but so were Pelé and Puskás and Stanley Matthews before him, and they managed restraint. Maradona had a bigger weapons rack even than Pelé, but they misfired more often and more disastrously.

Argentina went home and rebuilt their political system and their football team. Brazil moved on to a showdown with an Italian side that had discovered a little self-belief and, more importantly, had a defence that might have some answers to the Brazilian attack.

WORLD CUP CLASSIC No.12

Brazil   (1) 2   Sócrates 12 Falcão 68
Italy   (2) 3   Rossi 5, 25, 75

5 July, 1982, Sarriá, Barcelona; 44,000

Referee: **Avraham Klein** (Israel)
Coaches: **Telê Santana** (Brazil) & **Enzo Bearzot** (Italy)

Brazil (4–2–3–1): Waldir Peres (São Paulo); José Leandro (Flamengo), José Oscar (São Paulo), Luizinho (Atlético Mineiro), Leogevildo Júnior (Flamengo); Toninho Cerezo (Atlético Mineiro), Sócrates (Corinthians); Paulo Roberto Falcão (AS Roma), Zico (Flamengo), Éder

(Atlético Mineiro); Serginho (São Paulo). **Sub:** Paulo Isidoro (Grêmio) 69m for Serginho
Italy (1–4–3–2): Dino Zoff (Cpt, Juventus); Gaetano Scirea (Juventus); Gabriele Oriali
(Internazionale), Fulvio Collovati (AC Milan), Claudio Gentile (Juventus), Antonio Cabrini
(Juventus); Bruno Conti (AS Roma), Marco Tardelli (Juventus), Giancarlo Antognoni
(Fiorentina); Paolo Rossi (Juventus), Francesco Graziani (Fiorentina). **Subs:** Giuseppe
Bergomi (Internazionale) 34m for Collovati; Giampiero Marini (Internazionale) 75m for
Tardelli
Cautioned: Gentile (Ita) 13m, Oriali (Ita) 78m

This was a undisputable classic, a serious candidate for the
greatest match ever in the World Cup. In any other circumstances
it would have been billed as beauty versus the beast, the exponents of beautiful attacking football against the cynical defenders
of the legacy of *catenaccio*. Some of the press mistakenly did take
this line, forgetting that the Italians needed to win, and could not
afford to play on the back foot against this quality of opposition.

The Italian coach was the pipe-smoking Enzo Bearzot. Bearzot
had only a year's experience of club management on his retirement as a player, electing instead to join the national coaching
set-up. He was Head Coach of the Italian Under-23 side for a few
years and part of Valcareggi's set-up during the 1974 World Cup
Finals. After three years as assistant to Fulvio Bernardini,
Valcareggi's successor, Bearzot became Head Coach of the
national team in 1977. He cemented his reputation with good
showing at the 1978 World Cup Finals and the 1980 European
Championships, when little was expected of the team.

Before the 1982 Finals had even started Bearzot was under fire
from the Italian press, largely for selecting Paolo Rossi. Rossi had
a good World Cup in 1978 and was widely accepted as one the
best strikers around, but in 1980 he was implicated in the *totonero*
scandal, an investigation that rocked Italian football when it
revealed matches were being rigged by a betting syndicate. The
scam was initiated by a restaurant manager, Alvaro Trinca, who
owned a trattoria frequented by many of the Lazio squad. Trinca
and his associate Massimo Cruciano, were trying to defraud the
totcalcio (the Italian pools) but their scheme was far from fool-
proof, and they ended up losing significant amounts of money
and getting in debt to a number of bookmakers – not a good idea
in any country. The pair panicked and the police got wind of
something illegal, especially when a Lazio player not involved in
the fraud started airing his suspicions. Trinca and Cruciano even

consulted an attorney about whether they had any legal redress against the players who accepted their money and failed to deliver the promised result!

The end result was the demotion of Lazio and Milan from *Serie A* and punishments for various other clubs, as well as a number of bans handed out to some high-profile players, including Albertosi, the former international goalkeeper. Easily the most high profile was Paolo Rossi; Rossi always denied involvement and the evidence against him was largely circumstantial and he-said-she-said. It is possible Rossi was a high-profile scapegoat and deterrent, and it is possible he was involved. Whatever the justice of it, Rossi was banned for three years. The sentence was later commuted to two, which got him back on the field in time for the World Cup Finals, but he had time for only three matches for Juventus before the tournament.

Nonetheless, Bearzot persisted with picking Rossi in the face of all the criticism, even when he produced some rusty and ragged performances in the opening games. Even in the win over Argentina Rossi struggled – it was the high-quality Italian defenders and the in-form winger Bruno Conti who carried that day. Bearzot got fed up with the press carping, and stopped any communication between the squad and the media. It was under these tense circumstances they were expected to match the best team in the world.

And make no mistake about it, Brazil were the best team at this tournament. The eighties was a boring football decade, and tactical innovation was rare. Virtually every team played 4–4–2 or a variant and the subsequent match-up produced a lot of dull, unimaginative football. Even Brazil played a variant, but it was a variant that seemed to offer much more fluidity than other teams. Two big centre-halves protected Waldir Peres, a jumpy 'keeper, if not so flagrantly awful as Félix in 1970. Outside were two full-backs, Leandro and Júnior, who liked to attack; Júnior in particular, gave the impression he was a frustrated inside-forward.

In front of the defence was the babysitter, Cerezo, strong, powerful and not without skill. Alongside him was Sócrates, the playmaker, who liked to receive the ball early and start the fun. Zico played in front of Sócrates, and would zip forward to form a second prong in attack, as well as dropping deeper to cover Sócrates' occasional forays. Zico's exceptional passing ability and shooting meant he was both scorer and creator – his weakness was a tendency to disappear when things weren't going so well. Outside were Falcão to the right and Éder to the left – but it wasn't unusual for either to pop up in the penalty area or on the opposite wing. Falcão was a quick, lively player, two footed and with great movement and intelligence. He was familiar to the Italians, having signed with Roma in 1980. Éder's left foot earned him the nickname *The Cannon* (no explanation needed, surely?), and he was tough and strong; just as well, he was often needed to defend behind Júnior when the wanderer got a little over-excited.

In front of this array of genius was the powerfully built Serginho. No one quite knew why he was picked – maybe the others liked having a big lad to occupy the centre-halves – but it was doubtful he would worry the Italian No.5 Collovati.

Against this glittering array was the world's best defence in front of the world's most experienced goalkeeper. Dino Zoff may not have been as supple as he was, at forty years old, but he was a commanding presence in the area with over 100 caps behind him. Collovati, who had just crossed the city to join Inter from relegated Milan (they were dark times for the black and reds, two relegations in three years), was the ball-winner in the middle of the defence, Scirea the hoover behind him, unflappable and graceful. The left-back Cabrini was a veteran at the ripe old age of twenty-four, and on the other side Oriali, a midfield player, played almost an attacking full-back role while Gentile sat just inside him as the team bouncer. Benetti, the attack-dog from 1978, had gone, but his replacement, Tardelli, was just as steely and a much better footballer. These six were the dark-blue wall, and ahead of them were the flair players: Conti, the winger, Falcão's team-mate at Roma, who was having a terrific World Cup, flitting from one flank to the other; Antognoni, the balletic Fiorentina captain, who seemed to glide over the grass; Rossi, the sharp-shooter, so good at moving off the shoulder of his marker; Graziani, the willing runner, nominally a second forward but one who frequently pulled wide to take defenders out of position or dropped into the space behind the centre-forward. With the wisdom of hindsight, it was madness to write off such a team, packed with quality and tough as tungsten.

Italy needed something special to happen before Brazil could impose their rhythm on the game, and they got the perfect start. You could hear the groans from the Italian press area when Rossi miskicked an inviting cross from Tardelli, but the complaints dried up a minute later. Conti wriggled away from his marker on the halfway line and made inroads up the right before switching play to Cabrini in acres on the left. Cabrini's swinging cross was a gem, Júnior's marking was pathetic and Rossi's header was emphatic. Now you could hear the groans from the press of every country – a goal to the good, surely, Italy would entrench.

They couldn't, the lead didn't last long enough. Zico went clear only for Serginho to pinch the ball off his toes and scuff it wide of the post – Zico shrieked in frustration at the big man. Moments later Zico evaded Gentile again, this time with a stunning back-heel and swivel, and played a smart ball for Sócrates down the inside-right channel. Sócrates took a touch to get clear of Scirea, who didn't dare dive in, and beat Zoff with a hard shot at his near post.

The game was poised again, and, for all Brazil's brilliance, the early goal had given Italy a measure of self-belief. It had certainly done wonders for Rossi and he struck again when he cut out a rare loose ball from Cerezo, nipped past Luizinho and fired home – Waldir Peres should have done better than wave the ball past him. More shouting from Zico ensued.

Brazil had a lot of the ball in the rest of the first half, but couldn't make it count. Zico screamed for a penalty when he slipped clear of Gentile again – he had proved harder to suppress than Maradona for the Italian enforcer – but he did the honest thing and got his shot away instead of going down, which swayed the referee.

The second half continued in the same vein – now, at last, we had the confrontation everyone expected. Brazil were scintillating, hitting heights of imagination and movement rarely seen, but the Italians were outstanding in their way, too. The referee was Klein of Israel, who had stood firm against Argentina in 1978, and the Italians knew they had to play it clean. They lost Collovati early to an injury and the replacement was the eighteen-year-old Inter defender Giuseppe Bergomi. Alongside Scirea Bergomi was superb, an unbelievably cool presence for a teenager. Outside them Cabrini and Oriali worked like demons to combat the Brazilian runners, while Tardelli and Conti were everywhere, hounding and tackling and trying to disrupt the Brazilian rhythm. For all the defensive skill shown chances came and went. Falcão shot across the goal and wide from the right, Zoff launched himself out of his six-yard-box to thwart Cerezo and Serginho tried a clever back-heel when he should have turned and thumped the ball. Brazil needed something out of the top drawer, the one reserved for Sunday best. It came from Falcão.

The midfielder had a lot of help from Cerezo. Sócrates fed Falcão the ball with a wall of Italian defenders in front of him. Cerezo, who knew he owed his team after his earlier error, set off a lung-bursting sprint around the back of Falcão to the Italian left. Cabrini left the middle to watch the overlap, and Scirea stayed put to cover him. The movement left the merest gap inside, so Falcão took a pace in to his left and hit a screamer past Zoff's right hand. Sensational stuff.

The radio and TV commentators greeted this second equaliser as if that was that; the Italians had resisted manfully but genius will have its day. They underestimated Italy. Even while Brazil dominated Italy always looked dangerous. They left Rossi and Graziani well forward, and the latter's work rate and running caused the Brazilian full-backs a dilemma; if they were too adventurous Graziani would fill in behind them and if Italy regained possession, he provided an immediate outlet for a long clearing pass. It was an option Júnior afforded them all game with a brainless performance. Italy won a corner from one such clearance. Conti swung it high into the box and the ball dropped from the aerial challenge to Tardelli, who hit half a shot with his left foot. Waldir Peres had the shot covered, so Rossi stuck out a leg and sent it the other way past his left shoulder. Italy were ahead again, and the misfit, who according to the astute readers of the game in the press box should not have been in the squad, had a hat-trick. Júnior stuck his hand up to claim for something, but he was out of position when the corner was won, played Rossi onside and wandered off the line just as the Italian hit the ball towards that corner. The second most over-rated Brazilian left-back of all time.

Italy might have sealed the game a few minutes later, when another break saw Rossi charge down the right and cut back for Oriali; Oriali unselfishly clipped the ball over for Antognoni, but he was ruled offside as he gleefully shot home – the linesman was wrong, a let-off for Brazil. In the last minute Éder took a free-kick from the left, which swung over everyone except Oscar at the back post. Oscar stooped and the ball flew towards the left-hand corner – where it was stopped by a diving forty-year-old. Zoff took the ball behind him, and not only saved it but held onto it, a miraculous save from the veteran. The Brazilians appealed, but the ball was nowhere near over the line. It was a dramatic end to an awesome game. That word, so overused, is entirely justified. I can genuinely say that every time I watch it (and I never tire of doing so) I am filled with awe at the ability on display, both attacking and defensive.

GROUP D

France	(1) 1	**Austria**	(0) 0	28 June, Vicente Calderón; 30,000
Genghini 39				
Austria	(0) 2	**N. Ireland**	(1) 2	1 July, Vicente Calderón; 24,000
Pezzey 43,		Hamilton 28, 74		
Hintermaier 67				
N. Ireland	(0) 1	**France**	(1) 4	4 July, Vicente Calderón; 30,000
Armstrong 75		Giresse 33, 80,		
		Rocheteau 46, 69		

France were without Michel Platini for their game against Austria, but his replacement, Jean Tigana from Bordeaux, was no slouch. Austria were light up front with Krankl's miserable form continuing, and they gave France little trouble. Tigana and Giresse linked well, and France peppered Koncilia's goal. The Austrian 'keeper was their best player but he had no chance with Genghini's superb left-footed free-kick. Michel who?

Northern Ireland started well against the Austrians in the Vicente Calderón stadium in Madrid. They had the best of the first half and led through a Billy Hamilton header, made by another selfless run and cross from the indefatigable Armstrong. Austria reshaped and improved after half-time, and Pezzey

cleverly diverted a drilled shot from Baumeister past Jennings for
an equaliser. Northern Ireland were struggling in intense heat –
both sides were, to be fair, the game was played at a ridiculous
time – and fell behind from a set piece. The ball was touched to
Hintermeier and at last his explosive shooting paid off as he
belted the ball into the inside netting. As well no one in the wall
got in the way, a doctor would have been required. This Northern
Ireland team never lay down, and, when Martin O'Neill's shot
squirted loose off a defender, Jimmy Nicholl chased the lost
cause, reached the ball ahead of Koncilia and lobbed it back into
the middle for Hamilton to nod home his second.

Beating France, however, was a lot to ask even of this heroic
Northern Ireland team, and it proved a bridge too far. France had
found their feet – England would not have brushed them aside a
second time – and they controlled most of the game, but the 4–1
score was flattering, and Northern Ireland had their chances.
Martin O'Neill had the ball in the net but it was ruled out for offside
– a decision somewhere between marginal and wrong. The move
typified Northern Ireland's verve; Whiteside cheekily back-heeled
the ball between two defenders to O'Neill, who played a one-two
with Armstrong and burst into the box to clip the ball over Ettori.

Within a few minutes France were ahead. Platini got behind
the beleaguered Northern Ireland defence and cut the ball back
for Giresse, who made no mistake. The second half had barely
started before France made the task nearly impossible, Rocheteau
bursting clear from halfway to sprint past Chris Nicholl and hit a
hard strike past Jennings at the near post – the only hint of an
error the Northern Ireland goalkeeper made.

France were playing some superb football now and Rocheteau,
a sublime player when fit and in the mood, tricked his way past
three defenders to score a third. Northern Ireland got one back
– Armstrong started the move on halfway and was at the far post
to convert Whiteside's cross when both Ettori and Hamilton
misjudged it. Northern Ireland were pressing and vulnerable to
the counter-attack. The impressive Tigana took advantage and
crossed for Giresse to crash home a header – Giresse looked
thrilled, at five foot four the Bordeaux midfielder probably didn't
get too many with his head.

Northern Ireland were out but went home with heads held high to a deserved heroes' welcome. They travelled out the least fancied of the European squads and went toe-to-toe with some good sides without taking a step backwards. Their team included a couple of guys playing in North America, a seventeen-year-old with two first team games for Manchester United, and two forwards who had played in just the second and third tier of the league. They had a real go, and put England and Scotland's flaccid efforts into perspective.

Northern Ireland Squad 1982:
GK: Pat Jennings (Arsenal, 37, 91), Jim Platt (Middlesbrough, 30, 14), George Dunlop (Linfield, 26, 0)
DEF: Mal Donaghy (Luton Town, 24, 12), John McClelland (Glasgow Rangers, 26, 10), Chris Nicholl (Southampton, 35, 41), Sammy Nelson (Brighton & Hove Albion, 33, 49), Jimmy Nicholl (Toronto Blizzard, 26, 43), John O'Neill (Leicester City, 24, 17)
MID & WIDE: Noel Brotherston (Blackburn Rovers, 25, 14), Tommy Cassidy (Burnley, 31, 23), Jim Cleary (Glentoran, 26, 2), Tommy Finney (Cambridge United, 29, 13), Johnny Jameson (Glentoran, 24, 0), David McCreery (Tulsa Roughnecks, 24, 39), Sammy McIlroy (Stoke City, 27, 56), Martin O'Neill (Norwich City, 30, 44), Norman Whiteside (Manchester United, 17, 0)
FWD: Gerry Armstrong (Watford, 28, 37), Bobby Campbell (Bradford City, 25, 2), Billy Hamilton (Burnley, 25, 17), Felix Healy (Coleraine, 26, 2)

It was a flat end for Austria and, in common with Northern Ireland, the last time they went past the group stage in a World Cup Finals tournament. I can't help agreeing with various writers who think the hangover from the vilification of both teams after the Austria v West Germany debacle affected them in the second round. They had some good players, regarded as all-time greats in Austria. Bruno Pezzey, who played in Germany, and Erich Obermayer, the captain, were solid defenders; Obermayer was a one-club man who played over 600 games for Austria Vienna. The playmaker, curly-haired, lazy-looking Herbert Prohaska, was a throwback to the 1930s team; a beautiful passer who expected lesser talents to do the hard yards. Prohaska was good enough to win *Serie A* with Roma the season after this tournament, but he returned to his first club, Austria Vienna, to finish his career. Hans Krankl, disappointing here, had his best moments in 1978. He enjoyed a superb first season at Barcelona on the back of that success but was plagued by injuries for a year or two and never looked quite as sharp again. Krankl was Austria's leading scorer until overtaken by Toni Polster.

World Cup Heroes No.19
Gerry Armstrong (1954–) & Billy Hamilton (1957–)
Northern Ireland

Citation for conspicuous work rate, devotion to duty, passion in response to the call to the colours and utter heroism goes to Gerard Joseph Armstrong, born Belfast, 23 July 1954, and William Robert Hamilton, born County Down, 9 May 1957.

Gerry Armstrong was having a good year. He had just won promotion with Watford and returned to England after the World Cup to score the club's first ever top-flight goal. A spell at Real Mallorca followed before Armstrong slipped back into the lower echelons.

Armstrong never looked much in England, just another hard-working forward with a predictable game and a poor scoring record. But in the 1982 World Cup Finals he stepped up his game like few other players of such questionable pedigree have ever managed. Playing a counterattacking game, Northern Ireland needed forwards who would work hard and always be on offer to receive the ball. Armstrong covered acres of ground for his team, dropping deep to look for the ball and launching attacks with raking balls out to the wide players before sprinting into the box to try to get on the end of them. He scored three times in the tournament – a much better return than he ever achieved in the league – and caused problems for every team he faced.

Armstrong was still in the Northern Ireland team for Mexico 1986, although he couldn't make the same impact in a fading team, but he should sleep well with the memories of Spain and the accolades his braveheart displays drew.

Alongside Armstrong was Billy Hamilton of third division Burnley. Hamilton was another journeyman who raised his game in Spain. It was his cross that led to Armstrong's goal against Spain and his double against Austria gave Northern Ireland a glimmer before they met France. Hamilton looked about twelve years old, and played with a coltish vigour and a deal of skill in the tournament that surprised the assembled football press.

Hamilton played over 200 games for Burnley before moving to Oxford, who were in the top flight at the time; Hamilton never held down a regular place and left to return to football in Northern Ireland. Like Gerry Armstrong, he shone only briefly, but it was a glorious couple of weeks.

Just before the World Cup ended, a Barcelona newspaper printed a commentary, pointing out that the presence of the world's best footballers was merely putting a gloss on Spain's domestic and economic problems. The article read, without any irony: *"Next week World Cup superstars Zico, Maradona and Hamilton will have gone home, but Spain will still be bankrupt."* I do hope Billy has that on his wall.

WORLD CUP CLASSIC No.13
8 July 1982, Sánchez Pizjuán Stadium, Seville; 66,400

West Germany	(1) (1) **3**	Littbarski 19, Rummenigge 103, Fischer 108
France	(1) (1) **3**	Platini 27 (p), Tresor 93, Giresse 99

Shoot-out:

France		West Germany	
Giresse	S 1–0	Kaltz	S 1–1
Amoros	S 2–1	Breitner	S 2–2
Rocheteau	S 3–2	*Stielike*	*M 3–2*
Six	*M 3–2*	Littbarski	S 3–3
Platini	S 4–3	Rummenigge	S 4–4
Bossis	*M 4–4*	Hrubesch	S 4–5

Referee: **Charles Corver** (Holland)
Coaches: **Michel Hidalgo** (France) & **Jupp Derwall** (West Germany)

West Germany (1–4–4–1): Harald Schumacher (Cologne); Manni Kaltz (Hamburg); Bernd Förster (Stuttgart), Karlheinz Förster (Stuttgart), Uli Stielike (Real Madrid), Hans-Peter Briegel (Kaiserslautern); Pierre Littbarski (Cologne), Wolfgang Dremmler (Bayern Munich), Paul Breitner (Bayern), Felix Magath (Hamburg); Klaus Fischer (Cologne). **Subs:** Horst Hrubesch (Hamburg) 73m for Magath; Karl-Heinz Rummenigge (Bayern Munich) 97m for Briegel
France (4–4–2): Jean-Luc Ettori (Monaco); Manuel Amoros (Monaco), Gerard Janvion (St Etienne), Marius Trésor (Bordeaux), Max Bossis (Nantes); Jean Tigana (Bordeaux), Alain Giresse (Bordeaux), Michel Platini (St Etienne), Bernard Genghini (Sochaux); Dominique Rocheteau (Paris St Germain), Didier Six (Stuttgart). **Subs:** Patrick Battiston (St Etienne) 50m for Genghini; Christian Lopez (St Etienne) 60m for Battiston
Cautioned: Giresse (Fra) 35m, Genghini (Fra) 40m, B Förster (WGer) 46m

Another match that has garnered countless column inches over the years, most of it about one incident in the second half, so let's get the incident out of the way. Harald Schumacher's challenge on Patrick Battiston was a shocker; as Battiston waited for a cute lob from Platini to land, Schumacher sprinted from his goal and launched himself, both feet off the ground, at the oncoming Frenchman. In modern times it was an instant red card and possibly a lengthy ban – the challenge was high, late and perpetrated at high velocity. Battiston had to have teeth capped as a result and he was lucky his injuries weren't more serious. Schumacher and his colleagues' lack of sympathy both at the time of the incident and subsequently did little to win over neutrals already disinclined to see them succeed.

Schumacher (known as Toni, from his middle name) was a good goalkeeper, and he and the obdurate Förster brothers presented a formidable obstacle; West Germany's problem was that the players in front of them were a tired vintage, especially without their injured skipper, Rummenigge. France had the opposite problem: their midfield was sublime, especially now Hidalgo had hit on the most effective quartet of Platini, Genghini, Giresse and Tigana. The attack was lightweight, but the fitful Rocheteau had skill to spare and Six was a willing runner. The defence was so-so, the admirable Trésor apart, prone to individual errors and lacking an authoritative goalkeeper. All four fullbacks in the game – Kaltz and Briegel, Amoros and Bossis – liked to attack and left gaps behind them. Hidalgo made a clever swap, using the better defender Amoros, against Kaltz to cut off his crosses, and Bossis' aggression to drive Briegel back into his own half.

It was a gap in the middle of the French defence that West Germany exploited after eighteen minutes when Klaus Fischer beat the offside trap. Ettori was quick off his line to save but the ball ran kindly for Littbarski, who picked his spot. The lead lasted less than ten minutes. Platini showed a side of his game we didn't see often, climbing well to knock down a free-kick for Rocheteau, who was fouled by Bernd Förster as he cocked the trigger. Platini put the penalty well out of Schumacher's reach. France moved the ball well and looked the better side throughout normal time, but West Germany were disciplined and the nearest France came (Battiston's ill-fated foray apart) was when right-back Manuel Amoros advanced and crashed a shot against the bar in the final minute.

The first ninety minutes was full of good play, but the real fun started in extra-time. France scored after only three minutes. Giresse cleverly made room for a cross on the right side of the penalty area and centre half Marius Trésor was criminally unmarked about ten yards out. Trésor had time for a touch but didn't bother; instead he leaned back and powered an acrobatic volley high into the roof of the net – a quality finish from a defender. Giresse scored what everyone assumed would be the decisive goal six minutes later, driving home Platini's square pass with the West Germany defence at sixes and sevens. Derwall responded by making the only change that made any sense, bringing on a half-fit Rummenigge for the full-back Briegel, who had been outplayed by Bossis down the Germans' left. France were unable to respond; the injured Battiston was a substitute and lasted only ten minutes before Schumacher's assault necessitated the use of France's second sub as his replacement.

Rummenigge made an instant impact. He had been on the pitch four minutes before he threw himself at a cross from the left; amid the melee Rummenigge got the vital touch that took the ball past Ettori. The French went from serene to shaky in that moment and another deep cross at the start of the second period of extra-time found Hrubesch climbing at the far post; the tall striker did well to turn the ball back into the danger area and

Fischer did even better to balance himself and execute a controlled overhead kick into the French net – a party trick he had proved he could pull off on more than one occasion in the *Bundesliga*.

It was a terrific game, and it was shame it had to be the first World Cup Finals match to go to a penalty shoot-out. The Germans won. Quel surprise. It looked bad for them when Uli Stielike missed his penalty – there were a few tears from the tough Real Madrid sweeper, it was a bit like watching the Grim Reaper stroking a kitten. Didier Six missed the next one, Bossis also missed and it was left to Horst Hrubesch to administer the coup de grace.

World Cup Heroes No.20

Marius Trésor (1950–)

France

By the time this talented French squad got their deserts and won something (the 1984 European Championship), Marius Trésor had retired from international football. There can be no doubt that he was a major factor in the success of the French national team in that era.

They were a pretty lightweight bunch when he made his international debut against Bulgaria in 1971, but a formidable outfit by the time he played his last international in late 1983.

Trésor got his chance in the French league with AC Ajaccio, during one of the periods they were holding their own in *Ligue 1*; he made his debut for France with the unfashionable Corsican side. He started eight years at Olympique Marseille in 1972 – they were the league champions for the last two years – but he never managed to win a title and moved to Bordeaux to spend his last years as a professional. Bordeaux provided a good core of the 1982 squad, including Giresse, Tigana and Bernard Lacombe.

By the time France qualified for a World Cup Finals, in 1978, Trésor was a fixture in the side and the captain, the first black player to captain France (he was born in Guadeloupe). France failed to get through a tough group, but showed great promise, with a young Michel Platini and the skilful Dominique Rocheteau as well as Trésor.

Four years later Platini was the superstar and the captain, but Trésor was still the organiser at the back. He was big and powerful, but had ability on the ball too – most defenders of that era are classed either as a stopper or sweeper, but Trésor was equally comfortable in either role. In 1982, after Christian Lopez was left out following a poor game against England, Trésor found a reliable partner in another Caribbean-born player, Gérard Janvion of St Etienne. With Bossis and the exciting Monaco player Amoros at full-back, France had a decent springboard for their brilliant midfield. The only thing missing was a consistent goalkeeper.

Trésor's goal against West Germany looked as if it might clinch a place in the final, but nerves and Rummenigge saw the dream implode. He may have missed out on the medal he deserved, but Marius Trésor was the daddy of a great generation of Les Bleus.

There is a nice ending; in the same year as France won the Euros he won the league title for the first time with his club Bordeaux, and promptly retired.

SEMI-FINAL (8 July)

Italy	(1) 2	Poland	(0) 0	Camp Nou, Barcelona; 55,000
Rossi 22, 73				

THIRD-PLACE MATCH (10 July)

Poland	(2) 3	France	(1) 2	José Rico Pérez, Alicante, 28,000
Szarmach 42, Majewski 45, Kupcewicz 47		Girard 14, Couriol 75		

The other semi-final was much more straightforward. Poland, missing Boniek's drive, were disappointing and Italy won in third gear. The only downside was an injury to the graceful Antognoni – being Italy, they replaced him after half an hour with Marini, another grafter, as they were already one-up after Poland failed to pick up Rossi at a set piece. Rossi added a second after superb work from Conti on the left.

Poland won an entertaining third-place match against the French reserves but it was the end of their best era and the last World Cup match for both the old warriors Lato and Szarmach. The new faces weren't quite in the same league, Boniek apart.

World Cup Heroes No.21

Grzegorz Lato (1950–)

Poland

The third-place match against France saw the end of one of the best World Cup careers, spanning three tournaments. When Poland surprised England in qualification for the 1974 Finals, no one clicked that England had been beaten by a very good side. And they kept on improving, none more so than Grzegorz Lato, an unheralded goalscoring winger from Stal Mielec in south-east Poland.

When Poland's star and captain, Wlodi Lubanski, was injured before the Finals, Poland changed their system, using two fast attacking wingers (Lato and Gadocha) either side of a single striker (Szarmach). They had stumbled across a great twenty-first-century tactical innovation thirty years too soon. Lato was the chief beneficiary; a more natural goals-corer than Gadocha, it was the lightning fast, balding winger who would be the one to get beyond the centre-forward and pick up the flicks and passes from Kazi Deyna and his midfield colleagues. Lato ended his first World Cup with seven goals and the Golden Boot; Szarmach was joint-second with five as Poland earned great plaudits for their adventurous attacking game.

Four years later Lato added a couple more goals as the Poles reached the second stage again, but they found the climate and Brazil and Argentina a little too hot for their liking. Another fourth place in 1982 owed more to the brilliance of new star Zibi Boniek than the old guard, but Lato added another to his tally to reach double figures in all World Cup Finals matches, level with another great goal-scoring winger, Helmut Rahn.

Lato's great asset was blistering pace, which frequently carried him clear of defences who appealed in vain for offside, usually because it seemed scarcely credible he could have covered so much ground so quickly. He was unselfish, or might have had even more goals, and adept at reaching the byline and whipping in crosses, usually hard and low.

After a decade with Mielec, Lato tried his luck in Belgium with Lokeren (Polish players were allowed to play abroad once they reached thirty – an exception was made only for Boniek). Immediately after the 1982 Finals he made an even more adventurous move – to Mexico, to play for Atlante.

Lato played his last game for Poland in 1984 and finished with 100 caps (FIFA disbarred some Olympic appearances, so his original figure of 104 has been officially reduced). His tally of forty-five goals is second only to Lubanski. More than any of his talented colleagues, Lato's career can be seen to have book-ended the finest era in Polish international football.

Intelligent and articulate, Lato was a Senator in Poland at the beginning of this century, representing a centre-left party, and he is the current head of the Polish FA.

WORLD CUP FINAL No.12
11 July 1982, Bernabéu, Madrid; 90,000

Italy	(0) 3	Rossi 56, Tardelli 68, Altobelli 80
West Germany	(0) 1	Breitner 83

Referee: **Arnaldo Coelho** (Brazil)
Coaches: **Enzo Bearzot** (Italy) & **Jupp Derwall** (West Germany)

Italy (4–4–2): Dino Zoff (Juventus); Giuseppe Bergomi (Inter), Fulvbio Collovati (AC Milan), Gaetano Scirea (Juventus), Antonio Cabrini (Juventus); Gabriele Oriali (Inter), Claudio Gentile (Juventus), Marco Tardelli (Juventus), Bruno Conti (Roma); Paolo Rossi (Juventus),

Francesco Graziani (Fiorentina). **Subs:** Alessandro Altobelli (Inter) 7m for Graziani; Franco Causio (Udinese) 89m for Altobelli
West Germany (1–4–3–2): Harald Schumacher (Cologne); Uli Stielike Real Madrid), Manni Kaltz (Hamburg); Bernd Förster (Stuttgart), Karlheinz Förster (Stuttgart), Hans-Peter Briegel (Kaiserslautern); Pierre Littbarski (Cologne), Wolfgang Dremmler (Bayern Munich), Paul Breitner (Bayern); Karl-Heinz Rummenigge (Bayern), Klaus Fischer (Cologne). **Subs:** Horst Hrubesch (Hamburg) 62m for Dremmler; Hansi Müller (Stuttgart) 70m for Rummenigge
Cautioned: Conti (Ita) 31m, Dremmler (WGer) 61m, Stielike (WGer) 73m, Oriali (Ita) 73m, Littbarski (WGer) 88m

Italy, superb against Brazil and efficient against Poland, were determined and unstoppable in the Bernabéu. The pre-match story was of two injured players; one, Antognoni, was missing for Italy, the other, Rummenigge, started for West Germany. The first serious action was another injury, to the willing Graziani and it ended his World Cup Final after seven minutes. Undeterred, Italy kept to their game plan and Altobelli worked manfully, as you would need to to fill Graziani's boots.

The Italian back four were unruffled and utterly dominant – aren't they always when the Italians are on song? In front of them Gentile prowled menacingly, moustache bristling, alert to any danger and throwing in the odd heavy tackle – best just to check if Rummenigge really is injured, eh, Claudio? The gap left by Antognoni's absence was filled admirably by Tardelli, playing slightly further forward than usual; the Juventus player was transformed in his second World Cup from a battling defensive midfielder to a genuine world-class box-to-box all-rounder. With Bruno Conti drifting in from the left to add guile, Antognoni was missed less by the team than the purists.

Italy were together now, completely united and with the bit firmly between their teeth. West Germany were a mess; Jupp Derwall had lost control of his squad, and there was resentment of both the captain Rummenigge, who seemed to have dispensation to decide whether or not he wanted to play, and of Breitner, the returning prodigal, and still a troublesome presence. Reports in the press of arguments in the dressing room and a rift between the captain and Stielike, the senior pro, can't have helped their mood.

Italy's midfield moved the ball quickly and neatly; it was as if Brazil had passed on some of their mojo during the enthralling game a week before. The Germans were static and unimaginative;

if their policy of working hard, tackling hard and shooting hard didn't work, then so be it. It didn't. The midfield had no idea how to penetrate the Italian wall, Littbarski looked frightened of Gentile, and Rummenigge, noticeably less than 100 per cent fit, was a shadow of the player he could be.

Italy should have scored after twenty-four minutes when Conti switched wings and ghosted past Briegel who responded by upending him for a penalty. Kaltz and Briegel, the German full-backs, were heralded as a new breed of footballer, toned and athletic, full of running and stamina and coached in basic technique. Here their footballing deficiencies were exposed; Cris Freddi picks out Briegel (a former athletics champion) as especially culpable, by-passed for all the Italian goals, but Kaltz was equally ineffectual, the Italian game-plan negating the hard, swinging crosses that created so many goals for Hrubesch at Hamburg and Rummenigge for the national team. The excellent Antonio Cabrini took the penalty, but it was horribly mishit and went wide; so the elegant defender took his place in the history books as the first man to miss a penalty in a World Cup Final. Given the outcome, he probably couldn't give a monkey's.

Italy knew they had the measure of their opponents and the goals came in the second half. Rossi was at the front of a queue waiting to convert Gentile's cross ten minutes after the restart, and then a clever flick from Scirea – on a rare foray into the opposition penalty area – set up Tardelli for a second. No one deserved a goal more and the midfielder's face as he turned away shrieking with excitement was the picture in every paper the next day – a mixture of pride and passion and joy. The Italians knew a two-goal cushion was enough against such uninspired opposition, and Altobelli's third after eighty minutes was the icing on the cake. Breitner drove in an impressively precise consolation for West Germany but a goal flattered them, they were comprehensively outplayed. (It flattered Breitner, too, he had a poor tournament.)

Italy won the cup by dint not just of their outstanding defensive work – a perennial feature of good Italian sides, but by playing cannily and cleverly and imaginatively on the break, and because their destructive players, for all the negative press they received, could pass and move and provide a platform for the creative elements ahead of them. And of course they had Rossi, whose redemptive hour had come. Some critics mourned that Brazil's vibrancy and artistry hadn't ended centre stage, but these Italians were no shabby understudies.

World Cup Heroes No.22
Marco Tardelli (1954–)
Italy

The "story" of the 1982 World Cup was the return of Paolo Rossi and his return to favour and form. Rossi would be the first to acknowledge that you didn't beat a Brazilian team of that quality and then brush aside Poland and West Germany without good team-mates.

The pick of them in this tournament was Marco Tardelli. Tardelli had something for everyone. He bit into tackles, sometimes with a little too much relish, and ran hard. When he joined the attack he could pick a pass and cross and get behind defenders. When Italy needed the dark-blue wall, Tardelli would drop in front of the defence and provide sweeping cover across the line, letting Claudio Gentile pick up the key danger man and administer his own unique brand of restraint. When Italy needed to be offensive Tardelli would morph into the complete box-to-box midfielder, with stamina and pace to offer. One of the great all-round midfielders and one of the great team players. If Tardelli had a weakness it was a shortage of goals. It might explain the exuberance of his reaction when he scored in the 1982 Final – that goal was one of only six he scored in eighty-one internationals.

Like Rossi, Tardelli showed great promise in Argentina in 1978, and he also travelled as an unused member of the 1986 squad. Tardelli wasn't in great form and was thirty-two, but he would surely have raised the commitment levels of the team in what was a flat defence of their title.

Tardelli was at Inter by 1976 but his best years were spent at Juventus where he won the lot; five *Serie A* titles, two Italian cups and one each of the three big European trophies. He missed out on only the European Championship, reaching the semi-finals in 1980. Nice haul.

Team of the Tournament, 1982:

Zoff (Italy)
Amoros (France)   K Förster (West Germany)   Scirea (Italy)   Cabrini (Italy)
Falcão (Brazil)   Giresse (France)   Sócrates (Brazil)   Tardelli (Italy)   Conti (Italy)
Rossi (Ita)

Official Team of the Tournament: Completely different and nonsensical, we agree only on Zoff, Falcão and Rossi. The Brazilian **Luizinho** was in at the back along with the wrong two Italians, **Collovati** and **Gentile**. **Júnior** was included, ludicrously, his defensive contribution was inept. **Boniek** got in on the basis of one match and **Platini** was picked on reputation, not performance. **Zico** was selected instead of Sócrates, and **Rummenigge**, who was only half-fit throughout the tournament, was in alongside Rossi. Nonsensical.

Leading scorers: Rossi (6); Rummenigge (5); Boniek & Zico (4)

Heaven Eleven No.9

British Isles

Coach: Billy Bingham

Goalkeepers:
Neville Southall (Wal): ninety-two caps in fifteen years, arguably Wales' best-ever player
Packy Bonner (Ire): Jack Charlton's last line of defence, underrated in England because he played for Celtic
Pat Jennings (NI): huge, huge hands and he knew what to do with them (in a good way . . .)

Defenders:
Kevin Ratcliffe (Wal): cultured defender, captain of title-winning Everton side in '80s
Paul McGrath (Ire): best centre-back from British Isles after Bobby Moore

Denis Irwin (Ire): Mister Reliable
Jackie Blanchflower (NI): cut off by Munich air crash, as highly rated as his brother
George Young (Sco): comfortable as a full-back or centre-half in the tight Rangers and Scotland defence after the war
Danny McGrain (Sco): quick, aggressive attacking full-back, sorely missed in 1978
John Greig (Sco): hard as nails and a great motivator

Midfield & wide:
Roy Keane (Ire): drive and panache, if overly irascible
Danny Blanchflower (NI): great passing ability, pace of my mum
Dave Mackay (Sco): he could play as well as tackle – even intimidated Billy Bremner
Ryan Giggs (Wal): what more is there to say . . .?
Liam Brady (Ire): wonderful left foot, who cares if he couldn't use the other? He deserved better team-mates
George Best (NI): an apt surname
Martin O'Neill (NI): clever player, brought out the best in others
Jim Baxter (Sco): gifted, strolling playmaker
Billy Bremner (Sco): gritty, determined character, rarely wasted the ball

Strikers:
John Charles (Wal): emergency centre-half as well, but at his best as an imposing target man
Denis Law (Sco): great poacher and a skilful dribbler
Gareth Bale (Wal): exciting player, shame we'll never see him in a World Cup tournament
Kenny Dalglish (Sco): never quite as good as he was for Liverpool, but still a handful

Omissions: Shay Given – it was a toss-up between him and Bonner. The eighties defenders for Scotland, **Hansen**, **Willie Miller** and **Alex McLeish** never quite convinced at the top level, and **Richard Gough** was a shade short of the players here, as was **David O'Leary**. **Jimmy Johnstone** is unlucky not to be included, one of a host of good Scottish wingers, as is **Gordon Strachan**, a much better player for Scotland than Graeme Souness. **Johnny Giles** was Ireland's best player in a weak generation, and **Frank Stapleton** was a great target man. **Craig Bellamy** might have made the squad but for the emergence of Gareth Bale, **Joe Jordan** is the unluckiest of the other Scottish forwards. Many of the most-capped for these sides were ordinary players, picked for lack of an alternative than for any great qualities.

Likely first XI:

Southall

McGrain   McGrath   J Blanchflower   Irwin

Best   D Blanchflower   Keane   Giggs

Law   Charles

6.2 SUBSTITUTES

It seems bizarre, from a twenty-first-century perspective, to think football matches once didn't have substitutes. We're not talking pre-war here, but as recently as the 1960s, before teams were allowed to replace injured players. Prior to that, injured players who were not entirely incapacitated would often hang around on the wing and try to be a nuisance to the opposition without getting too physically involved. In the 1962 World Cup Pelé pulled his groin in the second match of the tournament against Czechoslovakia and wandered off to graze on the left wing; later he spoke about how touched he was that the Czech right-side defenders Jan Lála and Jan Popluhár declined to hammer into tackles and cause him further injury. Not all defenders were as courteous.

Substitutes were introduced to the English league in 1965; Charlton's Keith Peacock was the first to be used when he replaced injured goalkeeper Mike Rose after ten minutes of a second division game against Bolton at Burnden Park. Sadly for Charlton, Peacock wasn't a goalkeeper – an outfield player went in goal and they lost 4–2. FIFA still hadn't embraced this innovation for the World Cup the following year.

By 1970 substitutes were permitted at the World Cup Finals. The first to take the field was Anatoly Puzach of the USSR, who replaced Viktor Serebrianikov at half-time in the opening game of the tournament against Mexico at the Azteca Stadium. In Mexico's very next game we had the first instance of a substitute replacing a substitute. Mexico's Horacio Lopez replaced Enrique Borja at half-time, but was injured half an hour later and himself replaced by Juan Ignacio Basaguren. Basaguren became the first sub to get on the scoresheet when he scored Mexico's fourth goal.

In 1970 substitutes were named players, and could not be selected from any member of the team's squad. In the modern tournaments any member of a team's squad of twenty-three who does not start the game is de facto available as a substitute, unless suspended for disciplinary reasons.

Substitutes seem a logical contribution to the rules; why should a team suffer because a player is injured through no fault of his or her own and through no fault of the team – often, in fact, through deliberate foul play from the opposition? The expression *kicking someone out of the game* came from attempts to do literally that.

Even tactical substitutions can enhance the game; it is a test of a coach's skill at using his available resources, as well as a test of a club or team's strength in depth. Helmut Schön for West Germany was a good early example of using a specific player to turn a game. His winger, Jurgen Grabowski, was a tricky little beggar, but tended not to play so well if used for a full ninety minutes. Schön used the substitute rule to introduce Grabowski at key moments – he did so with devastating effect against England in the quarter-final in 1970. For many modern coaches, brought up in an era of three permitted substitutes, their use and timing is a key skill.

Some coaches like to use subs early, so they can get into the game; Italian coach Valcareggi in 1970 used the rules to give his two playmakers Rivera and Mazzola part of a game each – a strange solution (cop-out?) to a selection headache. Other coaches prefer to use their starting XI for as long as possible unless things are going disastrously wrong, bringing on replacements when they know which players are tiring late in the game. The most popular time span for substitutions is between fifty-five and seventy minutes. Ebbe Sand came on for Denmark after fifty-nine minutes of their 1998 game against Nigeria; sixteen seconds later he was on the scoresheet. Impact sub indeed.

There are certain players who get a reputation for their impact as a substitute; David Fairclough and Ronnie Rosenthal with the great Liverpool side of the eighties, and the greatest impact sub in football, Ole Gunnar Solskjaer at Manchester United. There are others who get used a lot off the bench, either because they are more effective not playing ninety minutes, or they just aren't worth a starting place. Denilson, the Brazilian midfielder, played in the World Cup campaigns of 1998 and 2002. In 1998 he started one match and came off the bench in all six of the others. In 2002 he missed two games entirely, but was used as a substitute in five. At least he got on in the final, even if coach Scolari did leave it until the very last minute to give him a run. Denilson's eleven appearances as a substitute is a World Cup Finals record.

As with most rules the modern game has distorted the original intention and used substitutions as a negative tactic. The substitute used as a device to run down the clock. How often have we seen, with a minute or so left, the dreaded board come out to signal to the player furthest from the dugout that he should trudge wearily back, stopping to applaud the supporters and re-tie the laces on the boots he no longer needs? Or a substitute used just at the moment a penalty is awarded to disrupt the thought processes of the penalty taker. These devices could be easily dealt with – no subs after a dead ball has been blown until play resumes again, unless to replace an injured goalkeeper; no subs in the last five minutes of a match, even for an injury.

Sadly, as with so many of the issues that blight the game, FIFA lack the will to address these issues. Instead, they leave loopholes so farcical that friendly internationals can proceed with ten substitutes either side and managers can hand out caps like fairground trinkets.

6.3 WORLD CUP 1986

The 1970 World Cup in Mexico had been an exciting affair, but there were issues with the altitude, some of the stadia and the ticket pricing. So why did FIFA choose the same country as host only sixteen years later? The fault lay largely with Colombia, who were accepted as the hosts at a vote in 1974, but left it eight years before they withdrew, conceding they couldn't afford to fulfill all that FIFA's criteria demanded of the host nation, most of which involve filling FIFA's pockets. Colombia withdrew their candidacy and the Americas were due the tournament, so Mexico announced their availability. A strong bid from the USA was ignored in Mexico's favour, with no satisfactory explanation offered as to why the debutants should be ignored in favour of a country who hosted the event with only moderate efficiency sixteen years previously.

With twenty-four teams now taking part in the Finals, the five stadia offered for the last tournament in Mexico were clearly not adequate, particularly as the final round of matches in each preliminary group now had to be played simultaneously. The old Olympic stadium from 1968 was added to the roster – it wasn't used in 1970 – as was a third Mexico City stadium in the suburb of Nezahualcoyotl. Two stadia were added in the Monterrey region, another in Queretaro, one in Irapuato and a second in the Guadalajara area.

An earthquake late in 1985 did Mexico no favours, but none of the stadia was affected, and it was too late to change venue again at this eleventh hour, so the competition went ahead in the exhausting heat. And in appalling playing conditions; short notice

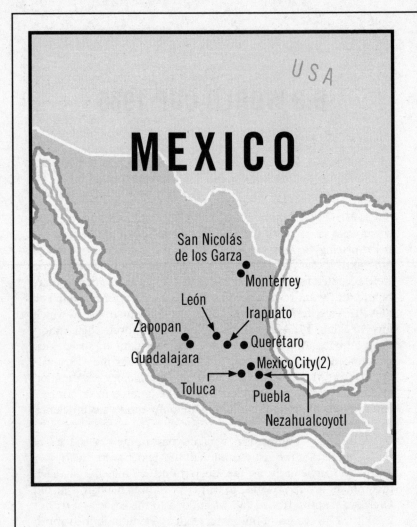

1986
MEXICO

With more teams involved, Mexico needed more than five grounds for their next job of hosting, and managed to find the extra venues and capacity in the three years between Columbia's resignation as hosts to the opening match on 31 May 1986.

Mexico City: Estádio Azteca
Now holding well over 100,000, the Azteca remained the centre-piece of the 1986 competition, hosting the final as well as witnessing the infamous 'Hand of God' intervention against England.

Mexico City: Estádio Olímpico Universitario
The Olympic Stadium, built for the 1968 games, wasn't used for the 1970 World Cup (it still wasn't suitable for football), but by 1986 it had entered the equation as a secondary venue in the capital, holding 72,000 spectators.

Guadalajara: Estádio Jalisco
The Jalisco was until recently very much the country's best stadium outside the capital, and hosted the semi-final between West Germany and France.

Léon: Estádio Nou Camp
Leon was no longer such a prestigious venue as in 1970, but it hosted group games and a fabulous second-round match between the USSR and Belgium.

Puebla: Estádio Cuauhtémoc
The games here were overpriced yet again and even for Argentina versus Italy the stadium was only two-thirds full.

Toluca: Estádio Luis Dosal
By now renamed officially as the Estádio Nemesio Diaz, La Bombonera was reduced to an also-ran role for the 1986 finals; it didn't even get a second-round game.

Monterrey and nearby **San Nicolás de los Garza** boasted two big stadia, the **Estádio Tecnologico** and the **Universitario**. England played their group games on the dreadful pitches in Monterrey. Other cities which hosted matches in 1986 were:

- **Querétaro: Estádio La Corregidora.**
- **Nezahualcoyotl** (a suburb of Mexico City): Estádio Neza 86.
- **Irapuato: Estádio Sergio León Chávez.**
- **Zapopan** (part of the Guadalajara municipality): Estádio Tres de Marzo.

it may have been but some of the training facilities and pitches were non-league quality.

At least the crowds could enjoy the cavorting of the World Cup mascot, a moustachioed jalapeño pepper called Pique. And the wave, of course. If they got bored they could always practise the latest craze to sweep sports stadia, which took its name from this tournament, the Mexican Wave. Is it just me who wants the ground to open up and swallow entire stands of people when the tiresome wave starts rippling around at a World Cup game or Test Match or break in play at Wimbledon?

Qualifying

England, under new manager Bobby Robson, who had turned Ipswich Town from also-rans into title contenders, much as Alf Ramsey had with the same club, qualified with some ease, despite a couple of drab draws with ordinary sides. Some better attacking players had come through since the last World Cup, but the defence was short on quality apart from the commanding Terry Butcher.

The second team through from England's group would be either Romania or Northern Ireland. Northern Ireland started badly by losing to Helsinki in Finland, but solid home form meant they were still in contention with two matches to go. Both were away, to the best two sides, Romania and England. Romania were a few years away from developing their excellent team of the 1990s, but had the twenty-year-old genius Gheorghe Hagi for inspiration. Hagi was team captain by the time of the tie in Bucharest but Romania couldn't break down a typically stubborn Northern Ireland defence and a first-half goal by Blackburn's Jimmy Quinn, a journeyman striker who never made the top division, gave the Irish hope they could qualify. They got the point they needed at Wembley, but they needed all Pat Jennings' skill and some ordinary finishing to get it. England were all over Northern Ireland but didn't do enough up front – a couple of misses by Kerry Dixon had even the Chelsea fans in the crowd hanging their heads in dismay. Romania cried foul but England had nearly twenty shots at goal – hardly the performance of a team settling for a draw.

Scotland were in an intriguing group with Spain and Wales and Iceland; the first three were very evenly matched. Wales had a horrible start, losing in Iceland and getting hammered by Spain in Seville; disappointing results for a team that could call on top-class players such as Neville Southall, Kevin Ratcliffe, Ian Rush and Mark Hughes. The group went with form until the following March when Wales turned up at Hampden Park needing a result and got it. Mark Hughes, still an international novice, cleverly chested the ball into Rush's path and the Liverpool striker thrashed it home.

The return game in September found Wales needing another win to progress, and they were optimistic when Mark Hughes gave them the lead after thirteen minutes. A superb block tackle and cross by Peter Nicholas (no great footballer but, boy, could he tackle) as Scotland tried to clear the ball found Hughes in a couple of feet of space; he finished as hard and fiercely as Rush had six months before. The Scots equaliser was another handball decision which rankled with the Welsh, eight years after the infamous Joe Jordan incident. The ball struck David Phillips' hand but the intent to handle was debated; in today's game the fact that Phillips' arm was raised above his head would have meant a certain penalty, but back in the '80s plenty of those weren't awarded. Davie Cooper's penalty was hard and accurate and went in the corner, despite a valiant fingertip from the great Neville Southall.

Scotland's relief at the result was palpable but their celebrations were short-lived. As the crowd dissipated after the match, news came through that Scotland manager Jock Stein, the legendary gaffer who had brought Celtic Britain's first European Cup, had suffered a heart attack at the end of the game and died in the Hampden medical room. It was the harshest of reminders of the stressful nature of the manager's job. His assistant took over the reins on a temporary basis after being given permission by Aberdeen where he had a day-job as manager. His name? Alex something-or-other. Oh yes, that's it – Ferguson. Alex Ferguson. Stein's death hung over the Scottish campaign, though, the sombre mood a far cry from the *hoots, mon, where's yer troosers* comedy turn of Ally McLeod eight years before.

There was still a game to go in this exciting group and Welsh hearts lifted when Iceland took a shock lead against Spain in Seville. Spain now needed two goals to win and top the group otherwise Scotland were off to Mexico and Wales were in the play-offs; the goals came, either side of half-time, and Welsh hopes were crushed.

Scotland faced a play-off against Australia, and took a 2–0 lead to Melbourne after second half goals at Hampden from Cooper and Frank McAvennie. The Aussies didn't lie down and launched a furious assault on the Scots goal, but a fine performance from Ferguson's club goalkeeper Jim Leighton kept them at bay and Scotland had made it by the skin of their teeth.

There were minor surprises elsewhere in Europe. Hungary banished Holland to the play-offs when most people thought the Hungarians' best days were over. (They were right – Holland just weren't that great, either.) A great win in Rotterdam for Hungary, after going a goal down, was the key result; the only reason Holland reached the play-offs was they won the return in Budapest after Hungary had already qualified. It availed the Dutch little. In the play-off they met Belgium yet again in a World Cup qualifier; they looked on their way to Mexico until a goal from Georges Grün five minutes from the end of the second leg meant the Belgians sneaked it on goal difference.

Denmark qualified for the Finals for the first time, heading a group that included the strong Soviet side – the Soviets poor away form cast a doubt over their likely form in Mexico. The attacking combination of the subtle Michael Laudrup with the quick and rangy Preben Elkjaer looked potent for Denmark – Elkjaer got eight goals in a group that didn't have a really lousy team in it. Finishing second led the Soviets to replace former World Cup star Eduard Malofeyev with the Kyiv coach, Lobanovski. Lobanovski had just led his team to victory over Atletico Madrid in the European Cup Winners' Cup in a display reminiscent – no exaggeration – of Ajax at their scintillating best. Where Malofeyev was regarded as the exponent of pure, attacking football, Lobanovski was a football scientist, a believer in method and system above individual talent. But the talent was unavoidable, the Soviets had some brilliant players, especially in Ukraine, and their ability and fitness allied to Lobanovski's aggressive pressing game made them a formidable outfit.

Portugal qualified for the first time in twenty years, finishing second behind West Germany, eliminating Sweden and Czechoslovakia in the process. West Germany won through easily, but suffered a hiccough at the end, losing at home to Portugal – their first-ever defeat in a World Cup qualifying match. They nearly lost their next one, against Czechoslovakia as well, a late Rummenigge equaliser sparing their blushes. France and Bulgaria qualified ahead of East Germany and Yugoslavia from a group where home form dominated. France won all four home games without conceding a goal; Bulgaria nearly matched them, conceding only one.

It was "as you were" in South America with the three traditionally powerful sides, Brazil, Argentina and Uruguay, heading the three groups. None of them looked invincible in doing so. Paraguay won a play-off section, beating Colombia and then Chile over two legs – it was their first successful qualifying campaign since 1958. Their star was Julio César Romero, an attacking midfield player with Brazilian side Fluminense; unusually Romero made his name in the NASL with New York Cosmos, normally the last port of call in a career rather than a launchpad.

The North African sides dominated the CAF section again, with all five of the countries with a Mediterranean coastline making the last eight – their game was still better developed than the West African and southern teams. Algeria and Morocco progressed, beating Tunisia and Libya respectively in the final stage. Algeria had most of their stars from 1982 still available; Morocco were more of an unknown quantity

Canada sprung a surprise in the CONCACAF region, winning a deciding group against Costa Rica and Honduras to join Mexico as the North American representatives. They were a boring team but didn't let in many goals. Iraq and South Korea made up the numbers, winning the Middle East and South East Asia zones; it was to be a disappointing tournament for the emerging nations.

Finals

The tournament lacked an obvious favourite, although the media built up an ageing Brazil side. France, winners of the 1984 European Championship, were the classiest European side, but no European team had ever won in the Americas, and France still lacked a centre-forward of genuine international class – a fate that seems to haunt them each time they assemble a back-up cast of stellar quality. France's best two strikers of the latter part of the twentieth century, Jean-Pierre Papin and Eric Cantona, were destined to play in poor (and poorly managed) sides that couldn't even qualify for major tournaments.

Argentina were widely regarded as a one-man team (although the one man was a singular talent), while West Germany were as prosaic as four years previously, which probably meant they would reach the final. Holders Italy were in no sort of form – it was a good job they didn't have to qualify, their campaign in qualifying for the 1984 European Championships was abysmal. The dark horse appeared to be a resurgent Uruguay, with new hero Enzo Francescoli. One or two pundits even whispered the suggestion that England might be a threat. Are you mad, sirs?!

The format changed again. FIFA finally cottoned on that second phase group matches were a dreadful idea and reintroduced a straight knockout; with six groups of four, it meant the four third-placed teams with the best record made the knockout stage – a strange reward for inadequacy – but it was still better than the second group idea. FIFA also decided, and it was another decision where common sense for once prevailed, that the last round of group matches in each group must be played simultaneously. After the suspicion aroused by the Argentina v Peru game in 1978 and, especially, the stalemate played out by Austria and West Germany in 1982, it offered a fairer deal to all.

GROUP A

Bulgaria	(0) 1	**Italy**	(1) 1	31 May, Azteca; 95,000
Sirakov 85		Altobelli 43		
Argentina	(2) 3	**South Korea**	(0) 1	2 June, Olímpico; 40,000
Valdano 6, 46, Ruggeri 18		Park Chang-sun 73		

Italy	**(1) 1**	**Argentina**	**(1) 1**	5 June, Puebla; 32,000
Altobelli 6 (p)		Maradona 33		
South Korea	**(0) 1**	**Bulgaria**	**(1) 1**	5 June, Olímpico; 45,000
Kim Jong-boo 69		Getov 10		
Italy	**(1) 3**	**South Korea**	**(0) 2**	10 June, Puebla 20,000
Altobelli 18, 73,		Choi Soon-ho 62,		
Own goal 82		Huh Jung-moo 89		
Argentina	**(1) 2**	**Bulgaria**	**(0) 0**	10 June, Olímpico; 45,000
Valdano 3, Burruchaga 79				

1. Argentina 5pts (6–2); 2. Italy 4pts (5–4); 3. Bulgaria 2pts (2–4); 4. South Korea 1pt (4–7)

Argentina and Italy had a deal of luck with the draw, pulling out two sides who had yet to win a World Cup Finals match. Italy had a workaday squad, with the usual sound defence, pretty much the same bunch as in 1982, with Vierchowod for Collovati. They were careless in the opener, allowing Bulgaria to steal a late equaliser. Bulgaria barely ventured out of their own half – hardly the ambition of a team desperate to win at the thirteenth attempt. Italy looked heavily dependent on Altobelli, who had gone from gallant sub in 1982 to leader of the line four years later.

Argentina brushed aside South Korea, who avoided defeat for the first time in a Finals match against Bulgaria three days later – fourteen and counting for the East Europeans, who scored early but were too cautious again. On the same day in Puebla, Argentina and Italy cancelled each other out, Maradona equalising after Altobelli scored from the spot. It may surprise you to learn that the game had a lot of fouls.

Italy avoided any indignity against the hardworking and physical South Koreans. They scored first when a cross found Altobelli at the far post – he took the ball on his chest, feinted to blast it with his left but instead floated it over the goalkeeper who was deceived into a premature dive. Cheeky boy. Altobelli restored Italy's lead in the second half, was on hand when Cho Kwang-rae poked a De Napoli cross into his own goal and then missed a penalty. Korea's second goal was mere consolation but their first was a cracker, Choi Soon-ho stepping inside a tackle and rifling a terrific shot just under the bar from twenty yards. South Korea were out but gave notice of their potential nuisance value – they have qualified for every Finals tournament since this one.

Bulgaria were, if anything, even more defensive, and lost 2–0 to Argentina with one early and one late goal. Under the odd rules they still made the second stage – they didn't deserve to. Argentina looked okay, but were heavily reliant on Maradona to make things happen in the opposition half. It remained to be seen whether they would miss the veteran Passarella; the former captain had been ill and later complained about a conspiracy to keep him out of the team after he recovered. Passarella was the only left-over from Argentina's 1978 success.

GROUP B

Mexico	(2) 2	**Belgium**	(1) 1	3 June, Azteca; 110,000
Quirarte 23, Sánchez 39		Vandenbergh 45		
Paraguay	(1) 1	**Iraq**	(0) 0	4 June, Toluca; 24,000
Romero 35				
Mexico	(1) 1	**Paraguay**	(0) 1	7 June, Azteca 114,600
Flores 3		Romero 85		
Belgium	(2) 2	**Iraq**	(0) 1	8 June, Toluca; 10,000
Scifo 16, Claesen 19 (p)		Rhadi 59		
Iraq	(0) 0	**Mexico**	(0) 1	11 June, Azteca; 103,763
		Quirarte 54		
Paraguay	(0) 2	**Belgium**	(1) 2	11 June, Toluca; 10,000
Cabañas 50, 76		Vercauteren 31, Veyt 59		

1. **Mexico 5pts (4–2)**; 2. **Paraguay 4pts (4–3)**; 3. **Belgium 3pts (5–5)**; 4. **Iraq 0pts (1–4)**

Three evenly matched teams and one poor one. Iraq were very physical and negative, but they were never overwhelmed – teams handing out thrashings to the minnows were becoming a rarity. Mexico looked much better than when they hosted in 1986. Their coach was Bora Milutinovic, a former Yugoslavia international; his name will appear again. And again. And again. Their "Superstar" was Hugo Sánchez, the tricksy Real Madrid attacker. A purveyor of party tricks and somersaults, Sánchez was less competent at delivering good performances for his country, although he scored here, with a far-post header from all of two yards. Paraguay's own star, Romero, scored the goals that gained them a win over Iraq and a late point against Mexico. The best game was the last one, a 2–2 draw between Belgium and Paraguay that saw both progress alongside Mexico. There were two amusing moments. Firstly Enzo Scifo, Belgium's Italian-born playmaker, scored a beauty from a free-kick, turned to acknowledge the acclaim, and then discovered the free-kick was indirect. Pay attention, boy! The second came when the Bulgarian referee showed the Paraguay coach Cayetano Ré a yellow card for excessive protestation from the touchline. Ré looked stunned – he later claimed he didn't even know coaches could be booked!

GROUP C

France Papin 79	(0) 1	**Canada**	(0) 0		1 June, León; 35,748
USSR Yakovenko 2, Aleinikov 3, Belanov (p) 24, Yaremchuk 66, own goal 75, Rodionov 83	(3) 6	**Hungary**	(0) 0		2 June, Irapuato; 16,500
France Fernandez 62	(0) 1	**USSR** Rats 54	(0) 1		5 June, León; 36,540
Hungary Esterházy 2, Détári 75	(1) 2	**Canada**	(0) 0		6 June, Irapuato; 13,800
France Stopyra 30, Tigana 63, Rocheteau 84	(1) 3	**Hungary**	(0) 0		9 June, León; 31,420
Canada	(0) 0	**USSR** Blokhin 58, Zavarov 75	(0) 2		9 June, Irapuato; 14,200

1. USSR 5pts (9–1); 2. France 5pts (5–1); 3. Hungary 2pts (2–9); 4. Canada 0pts (0–5)

Canada had no football pedigree and no players of any note. Many of the side were amateurs, some not officially registered with a club, including captain Bruce Wilson. Their coach was Tony Waiters, a former Blackpool goalkeeper capped by England in the 1960s. Waiters worked in Canada with Vancouver Whitecaps at the height of the NASL, famously winning the 1979 Soccer Bowl for the Canadian side (which included Alan Ball) after beating favourites New York Cosmos in the penultimate round. He did well to get the national side this far but all they could offer was toil and a blanket defence.

A 1–0 defeat to France was a minor triumph, owed in no small part to profligate finishing by the French attackers, and Jean-Pierre Papin in particular. Papin had just signed for Olympique Marseilles, where his career would blossom, but he still looked a bit green in this tournament. Canada's second game followed a similar pattern; no disgrace in a 2–0 defeat to

Hungary, but no real sense they could pull off a shock. The last game was lost by the same score, but only because the USSR put out their reserves.

Hungary were always struggling to qualify after their first game, which ended with a 6–0 hammering by the USSR. After qualifying reasonably comfortably, the USSR had suffered four straight defeats coming into the tournament. Once they reached Mexico, the new coach Lobanovski fell back on what he knew and filled the team with his old Dynamo Kyiv players – eight of them started against Hungary. Six of these players had only twenty-one caps between them – only the defenders Bessonov and Demyanenko, the captain, were experienced internationals – but their familiarity at club level delivered an instant rapport. It worked, six goals and six different scorers (one of them the Hungarian substitute Dajka) and an emphatic start to their campaign.

They were two-up inside four minutes. Yakovenko shot home after the ball fell kindly when a free-kick was blocked, and then Aleinikov (of Dynamo Minsk, not Kyiv) powered in an absolute rocket when Belanov teed him up with a deft touch. Belanov converted a penalty he won after chasing a long ball through the middle – none of this placement nonsense, he just wellied the penalty down the middle just under the bar; unstoppable. The fourth goal came from Yaremchuk after a fabulous run from Yakovenko, supposedly the defensive midfield player, and Dajka put the ball in his own net trying to prevent Yaremchuk breaking through again. Yevtushenko missed a penalty that probably shouldn't have been given, and Rodionov, a substitute, completed the rout when he followed up after Disztl in the Hungarian goal thwarted Aleinikov. Impressive.

The USSR against France was the pick of the matches in the group stages. Both teams had an abundance of talent in midfield; the Soviets were technically sound, quick, eager, full of running and the French were older, craftier and full of imagination. Three of the excellent French quartet had hit thirty, but Luis Fernandez (born in Spain) added zest and bite aplenty. The approach play was patient and excellent, but Bossis and Battiston dealt with Belanov better than Hungary, and, with Stopyra and Papin equally well policed, clear chances were rare. The Soviets opened the scoring when Vassily Rats scored with what could hardly be described as a chance at all, exploding a shot into the top corner with his left foot from fully thirty-five yards. France's equaliser came after a flowing passing move; Giresse played the killer ball, a chip into the penalty area where Fernandez scored with an adroit two-touch finish. The right result.

France completed the last rites on Hungary with an easy 3–0 win that included Jean Tigana's only goal for France in fifty-two internationals. He had the most defensive role of the midfield quartet, and fantastic stamina, but finishing was presumably not his strongest point. The goal was a good one, a thumping finish after a neat passing triangle; his team-mates' celebration was delirious and sincere. They respected the tiring shifts that Tigana contributed to the team. Stopyra headed the first goal after half an hour from right-back Ayache's excellent cross and the veteran Rocheteau scored the final goal just before the end. This was no intricate passing move; Platini chased down a punt from Joel Bats, flicked the ball across the goal for the unmarked Rocheteau. No one would fancy facing either France or the USSR in the knockout rounds.

GROUP D

Brazil Sócrates 61	(0) 1	**Spain**	(0) 0	1 June, Jalisco, Gua; 35,748
N. Ireland Whiteside 6	(1) 1	**Algeria** Zidane 59	(0) 1	3 June, TdM, Gua; 22,000
Algeria	(0) 0	**Brazil** Careca	(0) 1	6 June, Jalisco, Gua; 47,000
Spain Butragueño 1, Salinas 18	(2) 2	**N. Ireland** Clarke 46	(0) 1	7 June, TdM, Gua; 28,000
Algeria	(0) 0	**Spain** Calderé 15, 68, Eloy 71	(1) 3	12 June, Tecnológico; 23,980
Brazil Careca 15, 87, Josimar 41	(2) 3	**N. Ireland**	(0) 0	12 June, Jalisco; 46,500

1. Brazil 6pts (5–0); 2. Spain 4pts (5–2); 3. Northern Ireland 1pt (2–6); 4. Algeria 1pt (1–5)

In the opening game Spain looked an improvement on the 1982 version. They had a sound defence, which included Andoni Goikoetxea, the Butcher of Bilbao, so named after he gave Maradona a hammering in a game for Athletic Bilbao against

Barcelona three years earlier. Ahead of them Michel of Real Madrid was an excellent wide midfield player, and young Emilio Butragueño looked a hard-working and inventive striker. They were unlucky to lose to a slightly jaded Brazil – Michel had a shot bounce down off the bar and wrongly ruled as no goal. Brazil didn't offer the promise they had four years earlier, but they were sound at the back, with Júlio César looking an authoritative stopper and Branco an excellent attacking full-back. Brazil seemed to have finally realised Júnior wasn't a defender, he played here in a left-sided midfield role.

Northern Ireland's triumph was getting here – they had even less in their locker than in 1982, and surely couldn't expect the same players to raise their game as spectacularly as in that campaign. If they did expect it, they were disappointed; a draw with Algeria was Northern Ireland's only point. They left themselves a mountain to climb against Spain, conceding twice in the first twenty minutes, and were well beaten by Brazil, who produced three showpiece goals. Careca got two, smashing home Müller's superb low cross and then playing a one-two with Zico (recovered from injury and on as a substitute) and firing home. The middle one was a punt from Josimar from miles out that left Pat Jennings clutching at thin air on his forty-first birthday. The downside for Brazil was that Josimar tried a repeat every time he got within forty yards of the goal throughout the rest of the tournament, but it was a good way to introduce yourself on your international debut.

Algeria were disappointing after their encouraging 1982 campaign – they had looked easily the strongest African team in qualifying but were eclipsed by Morocco in Mexico. Some of the classy players from 1982 looked a little less eager now, and the team lacked the zest it had shown four years previously. Algeria's squad contained the first player with an English club to represent an African team at the World Cup Finals – Rachid Harkouk of Notts County played a game and a half in the group.

There was a footnote to Spain's easy win over Algeria that strikes more of a chord now; Spanish striker Ramón Calderé, who scored two goals, was discovered to have ephedrine in his system. Spain's plea that the drug was in a remedy administered by a local hospital for a stomach upset was given more credence than it would today and the player escaped without a ban.

Brazil qualified for the next round as the only team to win all three games, but no one was feeling intimidated.

Northern Ireland Squad 1986:
GK: Pat Jennings (Tottenham Hotspur, 41 years old, 116 caps), Jim Platt (Coleraine, 35, 21), Philip Hughes (Bury, 21, 0)
DEF: Mal Donaghy (Luton Town, 28, 42), Alan McDonald (Queens Park Rangers, 22, 5), John McClelland (Watford, 30, 38), Bernard McNally (Shrewsbury Town, 23, 1), Jimmy Nicholl (West Bromwich Albion, 29, 70), John O'Neill (Leicester City, 28, 36), Nigel Worthington (Sheffield Wednesday, 24, 8)
MID & WIDE: David Campbell (Nottingham Forest, 20, 1), David McCreery (Newcastle United, 28, 53), Sammy McIlroy (Cpt, Manchester City, 31, 84), Steve Penney (Brighton & Hove Albion, 22, 8), Paul Ramsey (Leicester, 23, 9), Ian Stewart (Newcastle, 24, 26), Norman Whiteside (Manchester United, 21, 26)
FWD: Gerry Armstrong (West Brom, 32, 62), Mark Caughey (Linfield, 25, 2), Colin Clarke* (Bournemouth, 23, 3), Billy Hamilton (Oxford United, 29, 39), Jimmy Quinn (Blackburn Rovers, 26, 11)

This tournament was the end of the road for a great generation of Northern Ireland players; Gerry Armstrong, Pat Jennings, Billy Hamilton, Jimmy Nicholl, John O'Neill and reserve goalkeeper Jim Platt retired or weren't picked again, and Sammy McIlroy bade farewell at the next match against England.

GROUP E

Uruguay	(1) 1	**W. Germany**	(0) 1	4 June, Queretaro; 30,500
Alzamendi 4		Allofs 83		
Denmark	(0) 1	**Scotland**	(0) 0	4 June, N'hualcoyotl; 18,000
Elkjaer 57				

* Clarke scored Northern Ireland's goal against Spain and went on to score thirteen goals, a national record, albeit an unimpressive one, until passed by David Healy.

Scotland	(1) 1	W. Germany	(1) 2	8 June, Queretaro; 25,000
Strachan 17		Völler 22, Allofs 49		
Denmark	(2) 6	Uruguay	(1) 1	8 June, N'hualcoyotl; 26,500
Elkjaer 11, 69, 79,		Francescoli 45 (p)		
Lerby 41, M Laudrup 51,				
J Olsen J 88				
Uruguay	(0) 0	Scotland	(0) 0	13 June, N'hualcoyotl; 20,000
Denmark	(1) 2	W. Germany	(0) 0	13 June, Queretaro; 28,500
J Olsen 43 (p), Eriksen 62				

1. Denmark 6pts (9–1); 2. West Germany 3pts (3–4); 3. Uruguay 2pts (2–7); 4. Scotland 1pt (1–3)

The Germans had done the unthinkable in 1984 and fired their coach for the first time, after an underwhelming European Championships. The new man in the hot seat was no less than Franz Beckenbauer. Beckenbauer declared no interest in the job until a national newspaper unilaterally threw a hat into the ring on his behalf. Or so he claimed. Originally he took the job on a caretaker basis waiting for the availability of Stuttgart manager Helmut Benthaus, but Stuttgart had a shocking season and Benthaus' appointment was untenable. Beckenbauer made no rash promises – he warned the German officials that the team was nowhere near good enough to compete at the World Cup. There were some good players in the squad, but only one of proven world class, the striker and captain Karl-Heinz Rummenigge, and, just as in 1982, he wasn't fully fit. There was another, but unfortunately for Beckenbauer and West Germany he was one of the most cussed and awkward players the game has known; Bernd Schuster was staying in Barcelona with his wife-cum-manager, Gaby. The defence was robust but limited, and in Rummenigge's Bayern Munich colleague Lothar Matthäus they had a strong running midfield player – more Bonhof than Netzer but a step on from the class of '82. The creative burden fell on the thirty-three-year-old (and ever so slightly portly) Felix Magath. The fans' favourite was the Werder Bremen striker Rudi Völler, one of those rare characters even opposition fans seemed to appreciate.

West Germany were, frankly, awful in their group games. They conceded a lead to Uruguay, who had a legitimate goal not given after the ball hit the bar, crossed the line and bounced out. Germany introduced a half-fit Rummenigge and the experienced Littbarski and scraped a draw. They conceded another lead against Scotland, to an excellent strike by Gordon Strachan, but came back to win through Allofs and Völler. It was a second defeat for Scotland – they lost their opener 1–0 to a strong Danish side – and they faced elimination at the group stage yet again unless they could beat Uruguay. They didn't, despite José Batista's sending-off in the very first minute. It remains the fastest dismissal in the Finals; some reports suggested the referee took out the wrong card, but it was a dreadful tackle, intended to hurt and intimidate Scotland's best player (Strachan, by a country mile), and fully deserved a straight red. Scotland huffed and puffed but Uruguay looked much more solid than in their previous match and held out with relative ease. Alex Ferguson kept shuffling his forward pack throughout the tournament, but none of his five strikers was international class, and his supposed playmaker, Graeme Souness, gave two wretched displays. His insistence on picking the stomping bruiser Aitken ahead of either his more gifted Celtic colleague Paul McStay or the Rangers winger Davie Cooper did the team no favours. Some sympathy is due – a bruiser did seem to be appropriate against Uruguay, who were a disgrace; dirty, cynical and abusive towards the officials, they were handed an official reprimand by FIFA.

The best team in this group by a distance was Denmark, the first European team to have more than half their squad in a Finals tournament playing in leagues outside the country. The Danish league was mediocre, so fifteen of the squad earned their living in Belgium, England, Germany, Holland or Italy. They put down a marker when they annihilated Uruguay in their second match, a result no one predicted. Uruguay had a man sent off (Bossio) after less than twenty minutes – the ferocious and indiscreet tackling of the sixties teams had not gone away – but they were already a goal down and the Danish strikers pulled their much-vaunted defence all over the pitch. This wasn't one of the along-for-the-ride teams Denmark slaughtered, but a team regarded as a sneaky outside bet for a tournament played in conditions that suited them. Uruguay's tiny consolation came from a penalty converted by Francescoli, but it was a painful tournament for the No.10.

Francescoli was a huge success with River Plate in Argentina and did well in France and Italy after this tournament, but he never flourished in a World Cup.

Denmark had a great combination up front, the passing and positioning of Michael Laudrup alongside the inexhaustible running and powerful finishing of Elkjaer. Laudrup led his markers a merry dance while Elkjaer galloped through the empty spaces he left and helped himself to a hat-trick. Denmark confirmed their supremacy by beating West Germany 2–0 in the game to decide who won the group, despite the Germans raising their game from their first two efforts. It is a quirk of World Cup Finals tournaments that winning the group isn't always rewarded, and Denmark would surely have preferred Germany's last sixteen match against Morocco to their own encounter with Spain.

Scotland Squad 1986:
GK: Jim Leighton (Aberdeen, 27 years old, 26 caps), Andy Goram (Oldham Athletic, 22, 3), Alan Rough (Hibernian, 34, 53)
DEF: Arthur Albiston (Manchester United, 28, 13), Richard Gough (Dundee United, 24, 23), Maurice Malpas (Dundee Utd, 23, 10), Alex McLeish (Aberdeen, 27, 43), Willie Miller (Aberdeen, 31, 48), David Narey (Dundee Utd, 29, 28), Steve Nicol (Liverpool, 24, 8)
MID & WIDE: Roy Aitken (Glasgow Celtic, 27, 20), Eamonn Bannon (Dundee Utd, 28, 9), Jim Bett (Aberdeen, 26, 17), Davie Cooper (Glasgow Rangers, 30, 14), Paul McStay (Celtic, 21, 14), Gordon Strachan (Man Utd, 29, 34), Graeme Souness (Sampdoria, 33, 15)
FWD: Steve Archibald* (Barcelona, 29, 26), Graeme Sharp (Everton, 25, 6), Frank McAvennie (West Ham United, 26, 2), Charlie Nicholas (Arsenal, 24, 15), Paul Sturrock (Dundee Utd, 29, 17)

---

* Archibald must rank as one of Barcelona's most bizarre signings. Terry Venables took him from Tottenham in 1984 to general amazement. He was surprisingly popular and scored twenty-four goals in just over fifty *La Liga* appearances. He was less successful for Scotland, with only four goals in his twenty-seven appearances, the last of them against Brazil at this World Cup.

GROUP F

Morocco	**(0) 0**	**Poland**	**(0) 0**	2 June, Universitário; 19,694
Portugal	**(0) 1**	**England**	**(0) 0**	3 June, Tecnológico; 19,998
Carlos Manuel 75				
England	**(0) 0**	**Morocco**	**(0) 0**	6 June, Tecnológico; 20,200
Poland	**(0) 1**	**Portugal**	**(0) 0**	7 June, Universitário; 19,915
Smolarek 68				
Portugal	**(0) 1**	**Morocco**	**(2) 3**	11 June, TdM, Gua; 18,000
Diamantino 79		Khairi 18, 27, Krimau 61		
England	**(3) 3**	**Poland**	**(0) 0**	11 June, Universitário; 22,600
Lineker 9, 14, 34				

1. Morocco 4pts (3–1); 2 .England 3pts (3–1); 3. Poland 3pts (1–3); 4. Portugal 2pts (2–4)

England found themselves in a winnable group. English football needed a fillip. Their clubs were serving an indefinite ban from European competition after the tragic events at the European Cup Final at the Heysel Stadium in Brussels the previous year. The hooligan effect was less conspicuous at club level than in the late seventies, but a nasty element with racist undertones had attached itself to the England team and officials held their breath every time the team travelled abroad. In 1980 fans had rioted after a match in Turin and Italy, and the riot police of Europe – some of them also little more than hooligans, but uniformed – had their cards marked. Fortunately Mexico was a long way away.

England plus one of Poland or Portugal, it was widely thought. Not after two rounds of matches they didn't; England were bottom of the group and the whipping boys, Morocco, hadn't conceded a goal. They hadn't scored one either, admittedly, but they had the best of their first match against Poland and kept England at arm's length easily enough.

The games were a disaster for England. This was a good squad, with an excellent core in Shilton, Butcher, Bryan Robson, the playmaker Hoddle and exciting new striker Gary Lineker. The tactics didn't match it. Wilkins, a passable holding player in 1982, was now just pedestrian and Mark Hateley, his Milan colleague, didn't have enough subtlety against international defences. And there was a gap in the centre of the defence, where Robson hadn't found a consistent partner for Butcher. He had tried Alvin Martin (in the squad) of West Ham and Mark Wright of Derby, but had settled for the Finals on the converted full-back Terry Fenwick.

Despite masses of possession, England didn't hurt Portugal in the opening game and, when Diamantino skinned the laboured Sansom and crossed, no one picked up Carlos Manuel. It was a sucker punch and a scarcely deserved win for Portugal, who were very defensive and just as uninspired as England.

In that first game Ray Wilkins was just anonymous, in the second he became the first England player to be dismissed in a World Cup Finals match. Wilkins was booked on forty minutes, and then Bryan Robson left the field after aggravating a shoulder injury. Stoic to the last, Robson spent a few moments trying to click the shoulder back into place; *it's a bit painful, this* was the extent of his moaning about an injury that would have had lesser men weeping. When a decision went against England a minute or so later, Wilkins hurled the ball towards the official. He surely didn't mean to hit him but it was a bit school playground and clear dissent so Wilkins took the long walk. He only played a few more games, and it was a tame end for a man who started at Chelsea as an attacking, goalscoring midfield player of untold potential.

Morocco should have gone on and won the game and put England out but they were too scared of losing. The point meant England could guarantee qualification by beating Poland in their last group game.

Poland, not the force of the last three tournaments, beat Portugal in their second game, and now topped the group. In another poor game Smolarek's breakaway goal decided things, but neither the Poles nor Portugal looked up to much and the one supposedly great player on the pitch, Boniek, looked disinterested.

England needed replacements for Wilkins and the injured Robson, and they found them in Peter Reid and Trevor Steven, both of Everton, champions and then runners-up in the past two seasons. Steve Hodge came in on the left for the disappointing Chris Waddle, and Peter Beardsley came in up front as a more subtle foil to Lineker.

The feisty Reid and the more conservative selection of Hodge allowed Glenn Hoddle to play further forward – he had just pottered around on the right side of midfield in the first two matches – and actually hurt the opposition, while Lineker exploded into life. England went two-up inside fifteen minutes. After some neat passing Trevor Steven received the ball in the centre and immediately slipped the ball to his Everton colleague, right-back Gary Stevens, overlapping down the right. Stevens' cross was hit first time and Lineker, as was his wont, read it better than the defenders and bundled it in. Five minutes later Kenny Sansom cleared up the left and found Peter Beardsley who spun and hit a great pass in front of Steve Hodge. Again the cross was instant, and again Lineker was first on the spot, crashing home on the half volley. A class goal; defence to back of the net in four seconds. The third, which effectively ended the game before half-time, was a gift from Poland goalkeeper Mlynarczyk, who dropped a corner – perhaps he felt Polish goalkeepers owed England one after Tomaszewski in 1973. Lineker swivelled and rocketed the ball into the roof of the net – another great piece of finishing and England's first Finals hat-trick since Sir Geoff. Panic over – inhale, breathe deep, relax.

Over in Guadalajara Morocco became the first African team to reach the second round with a fine win over Portugal. Abderazzak Khairi scored twice, the second a class finish from a long, hanging cross and Krimau scored a third when put clear with no defenders within shouting distance. Portugal, under their old warrior centre-forward Jose Torres, were poor against England, worse against Poland and indescribably awful against Morocco. Morocco even headed the group with that win.

SECOND ROUND

Thankfully FIFA dispensed with the hideous second-round group phase for 1986, but it did mean a complicated system whereby the third-placed teams in the initial groups scrambled through to the last sixteen, which seemed an inappropriate reward for failure. The system produced an unexpected semi-finalist. The others were less unexpected – would it surprise you, dear reader, to learn that West Germany was one of them?

A word about the heat, here is as good a place as any. World Cup games (any major game) are played to suit TV channels, not players – TV channels give FIFA money. The TV channels that cough up most for soccer are in Europe, so the games were played, in Mexico, at times to suit peak-time audiences in a completely different time zone. This meant kick-off times were midday and four o'clock, when the sun was highest and temperatures reached forty degrees; temperatures which are exaggerated in sports stadia, where the heat gets trapped in the lowest area – the playing surface. Players lost between six pounds and a stone per game (2.5–6 kilos) – no, not an exaggeration, a stone. Gerry Armstrong claimed it made him the player he was in 1982, as he tended to carry too much weight and stripping down made him leaner and quicker. Not all were as positive about the experience; John Aldridge recalls a game in the United States in 1994 when he was asked to give a urine sample after the game and had to wait nearly two hours before he could produce a drop.

Nutrition and hydration techniques have improved hugely in the last thirty years – in 1986 it was still pretty basic. Here you go, son, have a salt tablet and a drink of water. The strong running European sides wilted visibly in the heat – except for the bloody Germans, of course, they never wilt.

WORLD CUP CLASSIC No.14
15 June 1986, Campo Nuevo, León; 32,277

Belgium	(0) (2) 4 Scifo 54, Ceulemans 77, Demol 101, Claesen 108
USSR	(1) (2) 3 Belanov 27, 69, 111 (p)

Referee: **Erik Fredriksson** (Sweden)
Coaches: **Guy Thys** (Belgium) & **Valeri Lobaonvsky** (USSR)

Belgium (4–4–2): Jean-Marie Pfaff (Bayern Munich); Eric Gerets (PSV Eindhoven), Michel Renquin (Standard Liège), Stéphane Demol (Anderlecht), Georges Grün (Anderlecht); Enzo Scifo (Anderlecht), Jan Ceulemans (Cpt, Bruges), Patrick Vervoort (Beerschot), Francky Vercauteren (Anderlecht); Nico Claesen (Standard Liège), Daniel Veyt (Waregem). **Subs:** Lei Clijsters★ (Waterschei) 99m for Grun; Leo van der Elst (Bruges) 112m for Gerets
USSR (4–5–1): (all Dynamo Kyiv unless stated): Rinat Dasaev (Spartak Moscow); Vladimir Bessonov, Oleg Kuznetsov, Anatoly Demyanenko (Cpt), Andrei Bal; Pavel Yakovenko, Zavarov, Aleinikov (Dinamo Minsk), Yaremchuk, Rats; Belanov†. **Subs:** Sergei Rodionov (Spartak Moscow) 71m for Zavarov; Vadim Yevtushenko 78m for Yakovenko
Cautioned: Renquin (Bel) 65m

★ Clijsters is the father of Kim Clijsters, the former world No.1 tennis star and three-time US Open winner.
† Belanov's exciting performances in this tournament and in European competition earned him the European Footballer of the Year award for 1986.

On paper this looked one of the less interesting games. Belgium hadn't looked that great in the group – they clearly didn't like the heat – and the USSR had looked a mean machine. It turned out to be a minor classic, full of excellent attacking play and great goals. I remember watching the match in my damp basement flat in York, my girlfriend baffled by my excitement at a match between two teams in whom I had no emotional investment. I had no rational explanation back then but now I think I do. All the football matches that I have enjoyed the most are ones where I have no emotional investment. Watching Bolton is too stressful and tense – not to say downright dispiriting in the last three years – and watching England is sometimes little short of masochism. Watching two teams without being too concerned about the outcome allows a much greater degree of objectivity and – an inevitable consequence – a more thorough understanding of the dynamics of the game. Here endeth the pomposity, back to the football . . .

The first half hour was all about Dynamo Kyiv – I'm sorry, I meant the Soviet Union. They were outstanding, a repetition of the annihilation of Atletico Madrid in the Cup Winners' Cup Final but without the killer touch. Belanov's first contribution was an embarrassing swing and a miss at a cross from blond Kuznetsov, the centre-back, who showed all his sides positional versatility with a piece of deft skill in the opposing penalty area. Yaremchuk produced an even worse miss from six yards out after a goalmouth scramble – his miscued shot wasn't even close.

Belanov proved rather better from twenty-odd yards. He received the ball with his back to goal at the end of a quick Soviet counter-attack, swivelled and punched the ball with his right foot high against the left-hand upright of Pfaff's goal. You could hear the ball thump off the back stanchion of the goal above the noise of the crowd. Long-range shooting was a feature of this tournament in the rarefied air and high temperatures, and both sides were prepared to pepper the goal. That was it for a first half dominated by the USSR, but Belgium had served warning with a couple of dangerous deep crosses which the Soviets had not dealt with well.

At the start of the second half Belgium came into the game a little more. They made sure that Enzo Scifo, the skilful young Anderlecht midfielder, saw more of the ball, and coach Guy Thys made sure they got as many crosses in as possible to test a perceived weakness in the Soviet defence. Still the Soviets had the best chance of the opening minutes, when Zavarov hit the post after ghosting into the box to meet Rats' cross; he should have scored, and the shot from the rebound hit was cleared off the line.

Belgium were level a minute later when a long, raking cross from Vercauteren found Scifo unmarked (possibly in an offside position) with enough time to take a touch and prod past Dasaev. Yaremchuk just let Scifo run; the Soviets played an aggressive offside game, even in their own area, but it backfired here with some poor officials on duty.

Belanov continued to be a thorn in Belgium's side, and he restored the USSR's lead when Zavarov slipped him the ball twelve yards out on the right. He feinted to blast the shot, committing Pfaff, and then cleverly steered the ball past the goalkeeper's feet. The turning point came eight minutes later when Vervoort's long punt found Ceulemans free beyond the Soviet defence. The Belgium captain was two yards offside but no flag came – maybe the American linesman had been reading up on the Cold War – and Ceulemans' neat finish was allowed to stand. Ceulemans had a good game and a good tournament and a good career, most of it with his socks rolled around his ankles and his shoulders hunched. He was strong as an ox and could run all day, and finished well from any range – he scored nearly a goal every two games from midfield in a distinguished career with Bruges, and played nearly 100 times for Belgium. Paul Van Himst is regarded as Belgium's best player, but Ceulemans surely runs him close.

The Soviet bad luck continued when Yaremchuk's fierce shot bounced up and over off the bar rather than back down to the lurking Belanov. The USSR were nearly caught out in the air at the back again when Scifo sneaked in at the far post, but Dasaev saved bravely at the cost of a bump on the head.

The USSR were a system team, and when it worked it was a

well-oiled machine; in some way they reflected the Soviet state, a plausible model based on sound philosophy but vulnerable to human fallibility. The Soviet defence showed its fallibility twice in extra-time. They stood and watched as a Vercauteren cross went all the way to Demol at the far post – the twenty-year-old's header was emphatic – and then failed to close down Nico Claesen as he waited for Clijsters' header to drop so he could volley home. Belanov's penalty to complete his hat-trick came too late and a furious late assault was in vain. The Soviets had been the most entertaining side in the competition, but it was Belgium who progressed.

Mexico Negrete 34, Servin 61	(1) 2	**Bulgaria**	(0) 0	15 June, Azteca; 114,580
Brazil Sócrates 29 (p), Josimar 56, Edinho 78, Careca (p) 83	(1) 4	**Poland**	(0) 0	16 June, Jalisco, Gua; 45,000
Argentina Pasculli 41	(1) 1	**Uruguay**	(0) 0	16 June, Puebla; 26,000
France Platini 15, Stopyra 57	(1) 2	**Italy**	(0) 0	17 June, Olimpico; 71,449
West Germany (1) 1 Matthäus 88		**Morocco**	(0) 0	17 June, Universitário; 19,800
England Lineker 31, 72, Beardsley 56	(1) 3	**Paraguay**	(0) 0	18 June, Azteca; 98,728
Spain Butragueño 43, 57, 79, 88 (p), Goikoetzea 68 (p)	(1) 5	**Denmark** J Olsen 32 (p)	(1) 1	18 June, Queretaro; 38,500

Impossible to pre-arrange the draw with such a complicated group system, but if the hosts, Mexico, could have handpicked their second-round opponents they would surely have plumped for Bulgaria; no World Cup pedigree, hated the soaring temperatures, no qualify attackers and a really cautious coach. I'm not building up to an "ah, but . . ." moment here – Mexico drew Bulgaria, Bulgaria were shockingly bad again and Mexico won at a canter, scoring two excellent goals in the process. For the first time in a Finals tournament a CONCACAF side was justifying its presence; it was certainly a much better performance than they gave as hosts in 1970. Negrete's spectacular volley in the first half woke the crowd up after a somnolent first half-hour, and he took the corner that led to the second; I'm sure I'm mistaken but I've watched the video a couple of times and I'm not sure

Servin didn't just trip and accidentally head-butt the ball into the goal . . .

Brazil survived a couple of early scares to overwhelm Poland. Tarasiewicz's through ball evaded everybody and caught goal-keeper Carlos on his heels; he was lucky it hit the post instead of drifting into the net. A few minutes later a persistent Poland attack was finally cleared only for Jan Karas to hit a screamer which rebounded a long way off the bar. Brazil started to get into their stride, and the full-backs started to advance and cause Poland problems – the Poles lacked the wide players to get in behind them or make them defend. Júnior fed Careca down the inside-left channel, but he was baulked before he could shoot; Sócrates just pushed the penalty into the corner with no fuss; it was a touch of arrogance that would come back to haunt him. Penalties were a slow process in this World Cup; one of FIFA's new instructions for the referees was to stop encroachment into the area while a penalty is being taken. They like to sweat the small stuff.

Normal service was resumed in the second half, with Brazil adding three more goals. Josimar made it two in two games with a sensational strike, wriggling between two defenders before hitting a shot high past Mlynarczyk from an unlikely angle; normally the 'keeper has to be culpable with those but Mlynarczyk was beaten by sheer pace. The Brazilian captain added a third, shortly after a spectacular overhead kick from Boniek whizzed past the post with Carlos a spectator. Edinho cleared a Polish foray then sprinted sixty yards to collect Careca's clever back-heel; Edinho twisted inside the last defender and finished inside the post as if to the manner born. A fantastic goal from a central defender. Careca worked really hard up front with only fitful support from the talented but showy Müller, and he deserved his goal, another penalty after Zico was brought down. It was the last the World Cup saw of Zibi Boniek; his star flickered only briefly on the biggest stage but his hat-trick against Belgium in 1982 was a thing of beauty.

Argentina had just enough to see off Uruguay, who were neutered by a FIFA warning after their tawdry showing and two red cards in three group matches. Without the kicking and intimidation they had little to offer and weren't missed. Maradona looked really up for the game, but the goal came from a mistake by the experienced Uruguay defender Eduardo Acevedo, who miskicked straight to Pedro Pasculli. Argentina were stodgier than in '78 and '82, largely because their coach, Carlos Bilardo, was mechanical and cautious – the antithesis of the free-thinking Menotti, his predecessor.

Italy, with the same coach as in 1982, Bearzot, were a huge let-down. They had a good defence and still had tidy attackers such as Conti and Altobelli, but they appeared tired and apathetic. Bearzot looked worn down by the constant carping of the media – not just the English, then – and, if Altobelli didn't score, no one else looked capable. France replaced Papin with Rocheteau and he had a hand in both goals, first putting Platini through for a classy chipped finish, and then playing in Tigana, who crossed for Stopyra to score a second and end the game as a contest. It was the last we saw of Scirea in the World Cup, one of the greats and the model for the greatest Italian central defender of the lot, Franco Baresi. Baresi's brother, Giuseppe, played in the match against France, selected, unsuccessfully, to mark Platini. Scirea was dead by the time the Finals were played next, killed in a car accident in Poland while on a scouting mission for Juventus. Bruno Conti never played for Italy again either and Cabrini was gone within a year. It was the end of the great winning team from 1982, only Bergomi, the teenage sensation, remained through to 1990.

Morocco weren't a pushover, they had talented players and kept possession well in stifling heat, but they lacked punch and maybe a bit of courage. A 1–0 defeat to a late Lothar Matthäus strike against West Germany earned them much sympathy, but failing to score for the third time in four games was not suggestive of a team gambling to win the match. West Germany had that grim, determined air that suggested, modest side as they were, they intended to go all the way. A draw that saw them meet Morocco and Mexico was hardly strewing their path with insurmountable obstacles.

Grim is an equally apt description of Paraguay in their game against England, they seemed more interested in inflicting pain than defeat. Bobby Robson stuck with the side that beat Poland and it produced an identical scoreline. There was an early scare when Shilton had to tip Cañete's shot over the ball, and Butcher had to be rescued by his goalkeeper after a careless pass-back. England took control after that, with Reid watchful of the play-maker Romero and the wide players causing problems for Paraguay's full-backs. Trevor Steven was a revelation; he had ten caps coming into the tournament without ever being a regular, but looked a terrific player here, full of running off the ball and rarely wasteful with it.

After half an hour, Hoddle, enjoying the freedom (if not the Paraguayan tackling), put in a wicked curling ball, which evaded Lineker and his marker, but stayed in play for Hodge to turn back into the middle. Lineker had regained his feet, his marker hadn't, and England were ahead. Moments later the England man sport-ingly applauded Fernández in the Paraguay goal when he bril-liantly tipped over a volley from Beardsley's cross.

In the second half Lineker needed treatment off the field when he was cynically elbowed by the Paraguayan captain, Delgado. It was a completely unprovoked attack on a player who never retali-ated, and could have caused serious injury. One improvement football has seen in recent years is retrospective punishment on video evidence. Delgado was lucky, but the watching world knew his behaviour was that of a thug and a coward. Justice was done when England scored while Lineker was having treatment. Hoddle's corner was met by Butcher with a deft control-and-shoot worthy of a Brazilian – Beardsley popped in the rebound when Fernández saved.

Paraguay should have had a penalty when Martin pulled back Cabañas – they were incensed and muttered darkly afterwards, but taking the moral high ground after this performance was a bit rich. Beardsley nearly got a second when he insolently pushed the ball one way round Delgado and nipped round the defender on the other side – sadly the finish didn't match the lead-up. Lineker, happily recovered and back on the field, did get a second when Hoddle played a terrific ball between two defenders for Stevens to cross. England deserved the win, Paraguay deserved to go home; file alongside Bulgaria and Uruguay under good riddance.

The last match provided the most surprising result. Denmark took the lead against Spain when Jesper Olsen converted a penalty after a foul by Gallego. Two minutes from half-time Olsen was involved again, nonchalantly rolling a square ball into the path of Butragueño, who scored with ease. The only problem was that Butragueño was on the other team; it was a catastrophic error from Olsen and Denmark never recovered. Denmark fell apart in the second half. They gave away two penalties and conceded two more goals to crosses (provided by Spaniards), both scored by Butragueño, who helped himself to four. It was a sad end for the great Danish sweeper, Morten Olsen, now thirty-six and who first played for Denmark in 1970. He carried on until he was nearly forty and won more than 100 caps, but this was his only World Cup. The result meant at least one unexpected semi-finalist, as Spain would now meet Belgium in the quarters.

QUARTER-FINALS

WORLD CUP CLASSIC No.15
21 June 1986, Jalisco, Guadalajara; 65,777

Brazil	**(1) (1) 1**	Careca 17
France	**(1) (1) 1**	Platini 40

Shoot-out:

Brazil		**France**	
Sócrates	*M 0–0*	Stopyra	S 0–1
Alemão	S 1–1	Amoros	S 1–2
Zico	S 2–2	Bellone	S 2–3
Branco	S 3–3	*Platini*	*M 3–3*
Júlio César	*M 3–3*	Fernández	S 3–4

Referee: **Charles Corver** (Holland)
Coaches: **Telê Santana** (Brazil) & **Henri Michel** (France)

Brazil (4–4–2): Carlos Roberto (Corinthians); Josimar Higino (Botafogo), Júlio César da Silva (Guarani), Edinho Nazareth (Cpt, Udinese), *Claudio Ibrahim vaz Leal, known as* Branco (Fluminense); *Ricardo Rogerio, known as* Alemão (Botafogo), Sócrates (Cpt, Flamengo), Elzo Aloísio (Atlético Mineiro), Leodevildo Júnior (Torino); *Antonio de Oliveira, known as* Careca (São Paulo), *Luís Corrêa, known as* Müller (São Paulo). **Subs:** Zico (Flamengo) 71m for Müller; Paulo Silas (São Paulo) 90m for Júnior
France (4–4–2): Joel Bats (Paris St Germain); Manuel Amoros (Monaco), Patrick Battiston (Bordeaux), Maxime Bossis (Racing Club Paris), Thierry Tusseau (Bordeaux); Jean Tigana (Bordeaux), Alain Giresse (Bordeaux), Michel Platini (Cpt, Juventus), Luis Fernández (Paris St Germain); Yannick Stopyra (Toulouse), Dominique Rocheteau (Paris St Germain). **Subs:** Jan-Marc Ferreri (Auxerre) 84m for Giresse; Bruno Bellone (Monaco) 99m for Rocheteau
Cautioned: None

This was definitely one for the romantics, the last hurrah for two great midfields, the ageing Brazilians and the French *Carré Magique* (Magic Square). Brazil didn't quite have the glitz of 1982 – no Falcão, Éder or Cerezo, but Elzo was a powerful fetch-and-carry man, Júnior was playing in his best position and full of imagination and Alemão was an exciting player with a typically explosive swerving shot. The real find was twenty-two-year-old Branco, an attacking full-back with exceptional pace and good crossing ability as well as a fierce shot. Branco had all Júnior's attacking instincts with the pace and discipline to get back and perform his defensive duties.

Brazil enjoyed the better of the first half. Sócrates was in splendid form, dictating the pace of the game without ever getting above a stroll. Müller started brightly and caused the French problems early on, and after seventeen minutes he twisted away from his marker(s), played an intricate one-two with Júnior and put one on a plate for Careca. Careca finished high and hard into the roof of the net. Later in the half, just as France were imposing some rhythm of their own, Careca made a great chance for Müller but he drilled his shot against the post when he ought to have scored.

France drew level shortly after. Giresse found Rocheteau in space on the right and his cross was a tough one to defend. Goalkeeper Carlos and Yannick Stopyra collided as they both went for it and the ball ran through to Platini, in space on the far post. Platini had a quiet game and an ordinary tournament but it seemed fitting he scored on his birthday. Saint Michel, as the French press called him, saved his very best for the 1984 European Championships, when he dominated the tournament every bit as much as Maradona dominated this 1986 World Cup. Platini's nine goals in five games was a phenomenal return for a midfield player. He was almost the antithesis of Maradona as a player. Where Maradona received the ball and immediately looked to run at defenders and take them out of the game, Platini received the ball with the angle for the next pass already in his head, along with the exact piece of ground he next intended to occupy. When the ball was loose in or around the penalty area, he just seemed to be there, with no one marking him. He was the chess player to Maradona's gunslinger, but on his day he could be every bit as devastating; a different breed of super-hero.

France gave as good as they got in the second half and extra-time, but goalkeeper Joel Bats had to be alert. The centre of the French defence was weak in the air – neither Max Bossis nor Patrick Battiston was an old-fashioned centre-half – and Brazil caused problems with crosses. A combination of good positioning and poor heading meant Bats was never too uncomfortable. The exception came in the seventy-third minute. Zico who came on for Müller to a rapturous welcome sent Branco into the area in the inside-right position (I know, I know, what was the left-back doing there . . . this is Brazil, remember). Bats was quick off his line, tangled with the full-back and a penalty was given. Zico took the kick – Brazil's third penalty taker already this tournament – and hit it too close to Bats.

Extra-time was a ding-dong do, each team creating chances against tired defenders. Bellone, on for Rocheteau, was brought down just outside the box – the French were still claiming a free-kick (in Platini territory) when Sócrates missed a glorious chance at the other end. It was that sort of half-hour.

Penalties always seem an unedifying way to settle a good contest, but in fairness to FIFA (and you will have noticed I am reluctant in that regard) there was no better way to decide the outcome. Previous tournaments (especially 1958) had shown that teams having to get through a replay were at a massive disadvantage in the following round.

Sócrates did his team no favours here. He looked like he was running on sand during that extra half-hour; maybe the fatigue fogged his brain for it was a dumb act from a smart man to try a repeat of his cocky penalty against Poland. Bats saw it coming and pushed the ball away with his left hand. Zico took a penalty, having missed during the game, which took a bit of nerve. He scored, happily; it would have been a sad way for him to go missing twice from the spot. Zico was a great player, two-footed, sublime passer, good finisher, but he was punished by the media for not being as good as everyone wanted him to be. The media wanted a new Pelé, and that was too much to ask. As Pelé, Zico was inadequate; as Zico he was pretty damn good.

Platini conceded France's advantage by missing his spot-kick, but Júlio César promptly handed it back to France. Luis Fernandez scored under extreme pressure, and France were through, and had buried the ghost of their defeat on penalties to West Germany in 1982. Last observation: why on earth did Careca not take a penalty?

West Germany   **(0) 0**   **Mexico**   **(0) 0**   21 June, Universitário; 44,386
(West Germany won 4–1 on penalties)

Next up for the hosts Mexico were West Germany, through to the quarter-final without actually doing much. The game was a stinker, the Mexicans responding with play-acting and referee baiting to some rough German tackling. The game teetered on the brink of chaos and we had a liberal sprinkling of cards, including two reds.

West Germany were the better team amid the nonsense. Larios kept the Mexicans in the game with a great point-blank save from Allofs' volley, and the referee decided the game was too one-sided so sent off Berthold for a glimmer of retaliation when Quirarte brought him down as he roared up the right touchline. Quirarte, already booked, rolled around as if shot and the Colombian referee bottled the decision and favoured the home team. Risible; Matthäus agreed and was booked for clapping sarcastically and patting the referee on the back.

Mexico were buoyed and poured forward but their strikers were powder-puff and the vaunted Sánchez was laughably bad. The referee evened up the numbers in extra-time when Aguirre got a second yellow for a cynical block on Matthäus. One wonders if Beckenbauer had a word at ninety minutes.

The West Germans kept their nerve in the penalty shoot-out (it won't be the last time I type that) but the Mexicans lost theirs in front of 40,000 frenzied fans. Quirarte and Servin missed and Littbarski finished things off.

Mexico were out but not disgraced, for which much of the credit was due to their coach, the former Yugoslavia defender Bora Milutinovic. It was the start of a remarkable journey for Bora.

World Cup Heroes No.23
Sócrates Brasileiro Sampaio de Souza
Vieira de Oliveira (1954–2011)
Brazil

One of the real greats, Sócrates graced two World Cups with his brand of cerebral, minimum physical effort football. Bearded and cool, sometimes sporting a headband, *The Doctor* (he was qualified as one) was an educated, articulate man who took an active interest in politics and was an admirer of Che Guevara and John Lennon. Sócrates is appreciated by historians of the game in Brazil as much for his stance against the military government of the time as for his marvellous football.

Sócrates only turned professional aged twenty – he played for Botafogo and later, during his best years, for Corinthians – but he was good enough and smart enough to be an international player within a year. He had great vision and range of passing (with either foot), and would wander forward from a deep-lying position to unleash fierce shooting or get into the box and use his height and strength.

His weakness was obvious; Sócrates wasn't especially athletic and showed reluctance to track back, which didn't endear him to his coach at times. He was a heavy smoker, too, which made his stamina suspect, a factor in the 1986 game against France. In the great Brazil sides of 1982 and 1986 the weaknesses could be glossed over; the team was so adept at keeping possession they could afford a Sócrates, as long as he had a minder (Cerezo in 1982, Elzo in 1986).

Sócrates didn't win a lot – Brazil never won the World Cup or the Copa América during his time – but the contribution he and his midfield colleagues made to two World Cup tournaments are indelible. Above any results, Sócrates' generation restored the heroic beauty of Brazilian football after the desecration of the awful defensive sides of 1974 and 1978. Brazil don't have to win for us to love them, they just have to be Brazil. Sócrates was really Brazilian and we loved him for it.

The Doctor died young in 2011, a victim of his nicotine habit and alcohol abuse. His demise drew tributes from the President of Brazil as well as from the football world as far away as Florence (where he played for a year with Fiorentina). There was a particularly fulsome tribute from Garforth Town in the north-east of England; in 2004 the fifty-year-old Sócrates had coached the side for a month, appearing for twelve minutes as a substitute against Tadcaster Albion.

WORLD CUP CLASSIC No.16
22 June 1986 Azteca, Mexico City; 114,580

Argentina	(0) 2	Maradona 51, 56
England	(0) 1	Lineker 81

Referee: **Ali Ben Nasser** (Tunisia)
Coaches: **Carlos Bilardo** (Argentina) & **Bobby Robson** (England)

Argentina (3–5–1–1): Nery Pumpido (River Plate); Joe Luis Cuciuffo (Velez Sarsfield), Oscar Ruggeri (River Plate), José Luis Brown (Atletico Nacional); Ricardo Giusti (Independiente), Sergio Batista (Argentinos Juniors), Héctor Enrique (River Plate), Jorge Burruchaga (Nantes), Julio Olarticoechea (Boca Juniors); Diego Maradona (Cpt, Napoli); Jorge Valdano (Real Madrid). **Sub:** Carlos Tapia (Boca Juniors) 75m for Burruchaga
England (4–4–2): Peter Shilton (Cpt, Southampton): Gary Stevens (Everton), Terry Butcher (Ipswich Town), Terry Fenwick (Queens Park Rangers), Kenny Sansom (Arsenal); Trevor Steven (Everton), Glenn Hoddle (Tottenham Hotspur), Peter Reid (Everton), Steve Hodge (Aston Villa); Peter Beardsley (Newcastle United), Gary Lineker (Everton). **Subs:** Chris Waddle (Tottenham) 69m for Reid; John Barnes (Watford) 74m for Steven
Cautioned: Fenwick (Eng) 9m, Batista (Arg) 60m

This was a game that had bad blood in its veins. Four years previously the two countries were at war – Argentinians understandably made no distinction between Britain and England. The Falklands were so far away from Britain that a year or two after the war it was little more than a footnote in history for most people in the country. In Argentina the nearby Malvinas were a territory they had coveted and claimed since Argentina gained independence, and it was an issue the military government used to rouse popular nationalist feeling. (Even today the Peronist

parties – nationalists – under Cristina Kirchner still keep owner-
ship of the islands on the political agenda.)

It is a pattern, the new world's dislike of the colonial European
powers and it has fostered many a bitter football match. The
players tried to play it down in the Azteca, but you could sense
it.

The game was a good one. This was a competitive England
team and they had players who could hurt. Argentina went with
a three-man back line and used wing-backs to counter Steven
and Hodge, with three in midfield and Enrique negating Hoddle,
who reverted to disappointing mode and disappeared after twenty
minutes.

The first half came and went in a succession of niggly fouls
and half chances. Fenwick – out of his depth at this level – was
booked for a lunge at Maradona and should have been sent off
for elbowing the same player, only the referee didn't see it. It
wasn't the first thing Mr Ben Nasser missed. England's best
chance of the half came when Pumpido tripped over his own
feet and Beardsley pinched the ball, but the Newcastle man
should have looked up and crossed instead of shooting into the
side netting from a tight angle – Lineker was unmarked in the
middle.

The match was settled in a five-minute spell early in the
second half. Every Argentina attack was coming through
Maradona – not that you could stem the tide by man-marking
him, his close control was simply too good, and his body strength
awesome. The No.10 started another attack, and Hodge's
attempted clearance was towards rather than away from his own
goal. Shilton and Maradona went for the ball and it ended up in
the back of the net. At full speed it's just about possible to accept
Ben Nasser might not have seen it. But even a moment's pause
to assess the situation tells him that Maradona could not have
feasibly reached the ball and diverted it past Shilton with his
head, and that ten English players running towards him weren't
acting telepathically in concert and claiming handball on some
secret signal. Ben Nasser floundered, near drowning, in a sea of
his own inadequacy throughout the match – late in the game he
stood two feet from the end of the Argentina wall at an England

free-kick, virtually making an extra man – but it wasn't him that cheated.

So, okay, the referee was culpable, but what about Maradona? Why did he choose to cheat and punch the ball in the net? Did his hatred of the English extend to soiling his reputation as a sportsman? Because no impartial observer could find that acceptable, just as no one found Thierry Henry's handball in a later match acceptable. It was a shabby incident; this and his various flirtations with illegal substances put Maradona, an astonishing talent, a step below other great sportsmen. More Lance Armstrong than Michael Phelps.

His second goal showed the other side of the coin. Maradona received the ball just inside his own half, sprinted away from a knackered Peter Reid, ran past Fenwick as if he wasn't there and evaded Sansom's despairing lunge as he pushed the ball past Shilton. A fantastic goal, by anyone's measure, but as an Englishman it still hurts me to acknowledge it.

England belatedly brought on their wide players and began to push Argentina back. John Barnes produced a piece of skill on the left edge of the box worthy of Maradona when he jinked past Enrique and Giusti and stood a perfect cross off for Lineker to finish. Barnes offered England some belated hope, as he was walking round Giusti, exposed on the right side of the Argentina midfield with Burruchaga substituted. Argentina responded instantly with another surge form Maradona and some clever interplay leading to Valdano hitting the post – the lone frontman was excellent, always available and sure-footed on the ball.

Another Barnes cross evaded the diving Lineker at the far post by centimetres, and Argentina hung on with Burruchaga and Batista strong to the end in the middle and the backs committed and hard behind them. The better team – just – won the day, but their captain cheated to make it happen, and all the post-match nonsense about The Hand of God helping him score just made the offence smell more rank. You're not the Messiah, Diego, you're just a naughty boy.

Robson got some stick for not playing the wingers, but he had no reason to expect Bilardo to change formation and neither Barnes nor Waddle had done enough to merit selection ahead of guys who had just won two games 3–0. Maybe one of them should have come on earlier. Barnes could have replaced Beardsley and allowed Hodge to tuck in and help combat Maradona. The football writers also devoted many column inches about how much more effective England were without Robson and Wilkins; Wilkins, yes, past his sell-by date; however, Robson was sorely missed in this match. But overall it was a good campaign from England, who were a quarter-final sort of team, and have been for the subsequent twenty-five years.

England Squad 1986:
GK: Peter Shilton (Southampton, 36 years old, 81 caps), Chris Woods (Norwich City, 26, 4), Gary Bailey (Manchester United, 27, 2)
DEF: Viv Anderson (Arsenal, 29, 21), Terry Butcher (Ipswich Town, 27, 40), Terry Fenwick (Queens Park Rangers, 26, 15), Alvin Martin (West Ham United, 27, 15), Kenny Sansom (Arsenal, 27, 65), Gary Stevens (Everton, 23, 9), Gary A Stevens (Tottenham Hotspur, 24, 6)
MID & WIDE: John Barnes* (Watford, 22, 27), Glenn Hoddle (Tottenham, 28, 33), Steve Hodge (Aston Villa, 23, 3), Peter Reid (Everton, 29, 6), Bryan Robson (Cpt, Manchester United, 29, 51), Trevor Steven (Everton, 22, 10), Ray Wilkins (29, AC Milan, 80), Chris Waddle (Tottenham, 25, 16)
FWD: Peter Beardsley (Newcastle United, 25, 5), Kerry Dixon (Chelsea, 24, 6), Mark Hateley (AC Milan, 24, 18), Gary Lineker (Everton, 25, 13)

* Jamaican-born Barnes announced himself on the international scene with a stunning solo goal against Brazil in a 1980 friendly. It remained his finest individual moment in a career that brought great success at club level with first Watford and then Liverpool. Barnes seemed to feel the weight of expectation more than most when playing for England and it froze some of that great natural ability. He could have been great, but is remembered only as a very good player.

Belgium   (1) (1) 1 **Spain**   (0) (1) 1   22 June, Puebla; 45,000
Ceulemans 34   Señor 84

Tight and tense. Belgium scored with a superb diving header
from Ceulemans and it looked like they were on their way through
in ninety minutes until Señor's late volley flew in the top corner.
Until then Pfaff and his defence stood firm; twenty-year-old
Stephane Demol was quite outstanding in marking Butragueño
out of the match. Belgium looked the more likely in extra-time,
but had to live through the tension of a penalty shoot-out before
taking their place in the semi-finals. A good series of penalties left
Belgium 5–4 winners, with Pfaff saving the one tamely hit effort
from Sporting Gijón winger Eloy.

SEMI-FINALS

West Germany   (1) 2   **France**   (0) 0   25 June, Jalisco, Gua; 47,500
Brehme 9, Völler 89
Argentina   (0) 2   **Belgium**   (0) 0   25 June, Azteca; 110,420
Maradona 51, 63

One semi-final was a repeat of the 1982 match against France,
but this wasn't as good a contest. France seemed spent after their
efforts against Brazil four days earlier, and their best striker,
Dominique Rocheteau, was injured (as usual). The midfield
quartet of Giresse, Fernandez, Platini (not fully fit) and Tigana
was quelled by the power of Matthäus and his cronies and when
the French did find a way through they found their old nemesis
Schumacher in defiant form. There was no quibble this time;
goals at the beginning and of the match from Andreas Brehme (a
horrible blunder by Joel Bats) and Rudi Völler (a cheeky finish)
settled it and yet again an unfancied German team was in the
World Cup Final.

In Mexico City Maradona had the Azteca Stadium in uproar
with his outrageous talent. Belgium had sent three attackers
home injured and Claesen had neither the pace nor the height
to worry Brown and Co. Enrique, the man-marker, was put on
Ceulemans and Belgium had little else to offer. Argentina
nearly got another assist from God in the first half, but this time
the linesman spotted Valdano using his arm to score; Maradona

set up the chance with a sizzling volley which Pfaff could only palm back into play. Giusti missed the best chance of the half when another incisive run from Maradona created an opening.

The first goal came early in the second period, from an inevitable source. Burruchaga, rangy and skilful, was excellent in this match, helping his captain dictate the pace of the game. It was his clever disguised pass with the outside of his right foot that gave Maradona the merest hint of a chance. The finish, with the outside of the left foot, was masterful, the timing of the shot as Pfaff came out was perfect.

Enrique missed a chance created by Maradona's deft chip, and Olarticoechea had a shot well saved by Pfaff. It was one-way traffic, Belgium were working overtime just to stay in the game. After sixty-three minutes they weren't. Maradona's second goal was a reprise of the solo effort against England. There is a famous picture of Maradona, ball at his feet, poised to run at a massed Belgian defence. It looks inconceivable that he could pick his way through, but he did, at pace, ball glued to his feet. The general consensus is this was the better goal of the two. In the previous game against England the defenders were a bit shell-shocked after the award of the controversial first goal; no such scenario against Belgium and these were better defenders than England's, the centre-backs Renquin and Demol had been superb all tournament.

THIRD-PLACE MATCH

France				Belgium			
France	(2) (2) 4			**Belgium**	(1) (2) 2	28 June, Puebla; 21,500
Ferreri 27, Papin 43,				Ceulemans 11,		
Genghini 104,				Claesen 73		
Amoros 111 (p)						

An entertaining game; France played their reserves and they had fun, Belgium didn't and looked a bit more deflated. Belgium had a good tournament, their best ever, but the crop of players that did so well in the 1980s was ageing and they weren't replaced. The coach, Guy Thys, who had been in charge of the national team since 1976, was gone by the next World Cup (although he returned for a brief caretaker spell after a poor show in the Finals). Only now, in the 2010s, have Belgium unearthed a new generation of players who look capable of the sort of results they pulled off here against the USSR and Spain.

It was the end for this glorious generation of French stars, too, but France would have their moment in the following decade.

WORLD CUP FINAL No.13
29 June, 1986, Azteca, Mexico City; 114,580

Argentina	**(1) 3**	Brown 23, Valdano 55, Burruchaga 85
West Germany	**(0) 2**	Rummenigge 74, Völler 82

Referee: **Romualdo Arppi** (Brazil)
Coaches: **Carlos Bilardo** (Argentina) & **Franz Beckenbauer** (West Germany)

Argentina (4–4–1–1): Nery Pumpido (River Plate); Joe Luis Cuciuffo (Velez Sarsfield), Oscar Ruggeri (River Plate), José Luis Brown (Atletico Nacional); Ricardo Giusti (Independiente), Sergio Batista (Argentinos Juniors), Héctor Enrique (River Plate), Jorge Burruchaga (Nantes), Julio Olarticoechea (Boca Juniors); Diego Maradona (Cpt, Napoli); Jorge Valdano (Real Madrid). **Sub:** Marcelo Trobbiani (Elche) 89m for Burruchaga
West Germany (5–3–2): Toni Schumacher (Cologne); Thomas Berthold (Eintracht Frankfurt), Ditmar Jakobs (Hamburg), Karlheinz Förster (Stuttgart), Norbert Eder (Bayern Munich), Hans-Peter Briegel (Verona); Lothar Matthäus (Bayern), Andreas Brehme (Kaiserslautern); Karl-Heinz Rummenigge (Cpt, Internazionale), Klaus Allofs (Cologne). **Subs:** Rudi Völler (Werder Bremen) 45m for Allofs; Dieter Hoeness (Bayern) 61m for Magath
Cautioned: Maradona (Arg) 17m, Matthäus (WGer) 21m, Briegel (WGer) 62m, Olarticoechea (Arg) 77m, Enrique (Arg) 81m, Pumpido (Arg) 85m

This was an odd match-up and not the one most neutrals would have chosen. The official Team of the Tournament selected only Maradona from either of these two sides; while that is a silly judgment, both had other excellent contributors, it is a reflection of the fact that both teams were "winning ugly". West Germany scraped past Morocco and Mexico, then met an exhausted French team who had given everything against Brazil. Argentina sneaked a win against Uruguay, held on against an England comeback and dismissed Belgium through the genius of one man.

Both sides had good players, but the focus was on Maradona and his opposite team captain, Karl-Heinz Rummenigge, anxious not to be the first man to captain two losing sides in World Cup Finals. West Germany's other top-notch player,

Lothar Matthäus, who had a good tournament, was sacrificed to mark Maradona; he did so to good effect, but it didn't work as a tactic, for it left West Germany bereft of ideas going forward as the rest of their midfield contributed little. Presumably Franz Beckenbauer remembered the success Berti Vogts made of marking Cruyff in 1974 rather than the way his own role of tracking Bobby Charlton reduced his impact on the 1966 Final.

The opening was cagey, neither side wanted to make an error, but one came anyway. Burruchaga took a free-kick from near the right touchline, Schumacher came to meet the cross and got nowhere near it, and Jose Luis Brown headed into an empty net. See if you can guess how many goals Brown scored in his thirty-six international appearances? Yup – one. Brown had a good tournament, playing as sweeper behind Ruggeri and Cuciuffo in a three-man back line.

The first half consisted mainly of stoppages for niggly trips and pushes; delays that were lengthened by an awful lot of moaning and carping from both teams. The second half was better. The game looked dead and buried just before the hour when Enrique advanced and set Valdano free of some uncharacteristically shabby German marking. The Real Madrid striker coolly slotted the ball past Schumacher with his right foot. Two-nil down and showing nothing up front (did Franz Beckenbauer ever wonder what might have been if Schuster could have been brought back into the fold?), West Germany were deep in the mire.

But even deep in the mire West Germany could not be discounted. With Völler already on for Allofs, they threw on Dieter Hoeness, brother of seventies star Uli. Hoeness wasn't much cop, but he was big and decent in the air and the Germans fancied throwing a few crosses into the mix, especially with Brown carrying his arm in a sling after he fell awkwardly. (Bilardo, normally so tough, should have made him go off as he had Oscar Garré in the squad, a perfectly serviceable centre back who had played all three group games.)

West Germany pushed Berthold and Briegel further on to the Argentinian wing-backs. This created space for Matthäus, free of his marking role, and Brehme, to try get in some quality balls. The direct approach paid off. West Germany won a series of corners, and Brehme took all of them. Argentina looked shaky at all of them with Brown ineffective. Rummenigge forced home Völler's flick-on, and eight minutes from time Völler got the equaliser from Berthold's firm header back across goal. The Germans, outplayed for most of the game, now fancied they were going to win it. Maradona had other ideas. The little master had been quiet for a spell, apart from one outrageous trick when he controlled the ball in the small of his back before flipping it forward and taking a shot.

Three minutes after Völler's goal Maradona got the ball in the centre circle and pinged an instant pass to Burruchaga, charging through the middle with half the German defence still upfield. Burruchaga outstripped Briegel, itself no mean feat, ignored Valdano to his left and hit the ball low past Schumacher, who took an age to come off his line. West Germany couldn't raise themselves again and the World Cup was Argentina's for the second time in three tournaments.

The focus, inevitably, was on Maradona, but others played their part. They had a decent goalkeeper (Pumpido), a tough, discipline defence, willing runners in midfield with tough little Batista grafting behind Burruchaga and a good front man (Valdano) with terrific movement and a bit of nous. Add Maradona and it wasn't at all the poor side many remember – it was certainly better than the 1978 vintage and won the cup without as much help from the officials, a certain Mr Nasser apart.

Team of the Tournament, 1986:

Pfaff (Belgium)
Berthold (West Germany)   Demol (Belgium)   Brown (Argentina)   Brehme (West Germany)
Burruchaga (Argentina)   Tigana (France)   Fernandez (France)
Maradona (Argentina)   Ceulemans (Belgium)
Lineker (England)

Official Team of the Tournament: The official team obviously felt the largesse had to spread around the teams. **Josimar** was in (laughable), as was Manuel Amoros (better as a youngster in 1982) and the Brazilian central defender **Júlio César**. Tigana and **Platini** were both in, despite Platini having a poor competition – he was clearly preparing for his career as a football administrator. **Elkjaer** and **Butragueño** were both in on the basis of scant evidence,

although Elkjaer was impressive while Denmark were still in the competition. We agreed on Pfaff, Tigana, Maradona, Ceulemans and Lineker – one Argentinian and one German seems a poor reflection of which teams got to the final. The team of the tournament should reward overall contribution, not just being easy on the eye. Berthold, for example, was excellent in every game, including the one where he was given a laughable red card.
Leading scorers: Lineker (6); Butragueño, Careca & Maradona (5)

Heaven Eleven No.10

The Soviet Union (and its constituent nations)

Coach:
Valeri Lobanovski (Ukraine) – the appliance of science

Goalkeepers:
Lev Yashin (USSR): probably the greatest-ever Soviet footballer
Rinat Dasaev (USSR): super 'keeper in the 1980s team, one of the few not from Dynamo Kyiv
Mart Poom (Estonia): really steady goalkeeper with over 100 caps

Defenders:
Kakha Kaladze (Georgia): held down a place at Milan for a few years and they know a thing or two about defending
Viktor Onopko (Russia): most capped Russian player, elegant ball-playing defender
Anatoliy Demyanenko (USSR/Ukraine): captain of Lobanovski's '80s team
Vladimir Bessonov (USSR/Ukraine): attacking right-back in the 1980s
Murtaz Khurtsilava (USSR/Georgia): tough defender in the '60/70s
Aleksandr Chivadze (USSR/Georgia): first Georgian to captain the Soviet side
Vladimir Kaplichny (USSR/Ukraine): excellent right-back in the side that played in the 1970 World Cup
Albert Shesternyev (USSR/Russia): dominant stopper in the 1960s

Midfield & wide:

Anatoly Tymoschuk (Ukraine): consistent midfielder in the last decade and won the Champions League with Bayern Munich in 2013

Aleksandr Mostovoi (USSR/Russia): the first great maverick of the post-Soviet era

Sergei Aleinikov (USSR/Belarus): best of the bunch from the terrific '80s midfield

Igor Chislenko (USSR/Russia): tireless, nippy winger in the 1960s

Valentin Ivanov (USSR/Russia): goalscoring winger from the first Soviet side to emerge into the global game

Eduard Streltsov (USSR/Russia): the best player you never heard of

Igor Netto (USSR/Russia): playmaker and later sweeper in the 1950s teams

Vladimir Muntian (USSR/Ukraine): playmaker and craftsman in the 1970s Soviet side

Strikers:

Andriy Shevchenko (Ukraine): forget the guy you saw at Chelsea, this is the Milan version, sharpest striker in Europe for a few years

Igor Belanov (USSR/Ukraine): exciting forward with explosive shot

Anatoliy Byshovets (USSR/Ukraine): quick feet and a good eye for goal; talented, under-rated forward in the early 1970s

Oleg Blokhin (USSR/Ukraine): the first international superstar from the Soviet Union – nicknamed the Ukraine Train, he was really, really quick

Omissions: Some good defenders didn't make it; **Anyukov** and **Berezutsky**, the current full-backs, **Dzodzuashvili**, the Georgian from the '60s/70s team, **Oleg Kuznetsov**, the central defender who smashed his cruciate and was never the same after he joined Rangers. **Banishevsky** and **Malofeyev**, the centre-forward and playmaker with the 1966 World Cup team, were fine players, as were most of the talented midfield players from the

Kyiv and USSR teams of the 1980s: **Zavarov**, **Rats**, **Yaremchuk** and **Protasov** were all top performers.

In more recent times **Sergei Rebrov** dovetailed brilliantly with Shevchenko, while **Georgi Kinkladze** was an outstanding playmaker for Georgia for a while.

Likely first XI:

Yashin
Bessonov Shesternev Chivadze Demyanenko
Chislenko Netto Streltsov Ivanov
Shevchenko Blokhin

6.4 APPEARANCES

Only one team (Brazil) has appeared in every World Cup Finals tournament. They are unlikely to relinquish that record with the five qualifiers from ten nations system that CONMEBOL enjoy – hard to see five other South American sides heading the Brazilians in a round-robin table.

Italy and Germany (including West Germany) have played in seventeen each, Argentina in fifteen, Mexico in fourteen and England, Spain and France in thirteen each. Mexico stand out like a sore thumb – they get a free ride from the weak CONCACAF section and the distorted FIFA rankings. The USA back this theory – nine appearances in the Finals without really threatening. The only European side with a significant number of appearances but no marked progress is Switzerland, also with nine (yes, I was surprised, too).

In total seventy-six nations have made one or more appearance in the World Cup Finals – to reach this figure FIFA considers both the Czech Republic and Slovakia in adding to the statistics of Czechoslovakia, Serbia as the continuation of Yugoslavia's record and Russia as the successor to the Soviet Union. Confused? FIFA like it that way, it makes them seem a lot cleverer than they are.

Brazil and Germany have each reached seven finals, but Brazil won five compared to Germany's three. Germany have reached an impressive twelve semi-finals (Brazil eight). England's most telling statistic is eight eliminations at the quarter-final stage (see the later article *England at the World Cup*).

Eighteen countries have made just a solitary appearance in the Finals; at time of writing (September 2013) Senegal and Ukraine look best placed to make a second, while Ethiopia and Burkina Faso are one play-off away from a debut, and Jordan will play off against the fifth-placed South American nation, either Uruguay, Ecuador or possibly Chile. In Europe Bosnia-Herzegovina are well placed to make the Finals, while Montenegro, Albania and Iceland are all still in with a sniff.

On an individual level only two players, Antonio Carbajal, the Mexican goalkeeper, and Lothar Matthäus of Germany, have appeared in five Finals tournaments; quite a few, including Bobby Charlton and Scotland goalkeeper Jim Leighton, have travelled to four.

Matthäus also heads the list of matches played in the Finals, with twenty-five (impressive), two ahead of Paolo Maldini, with Maradona, Uwe Seeler and Wladyslaw Zmuda on twenty-one. On the list of players with fifteen or more matches played there are fourteen Germans – a testimony to their success and also to their consistency of selection. England have one player, Peter Shilton, on that list. Brazil have twelve, Italy six, France four, Argentina, Belgium and Poland three each, Spain two and South Korea one.

Here they all are:

25 Lothar Matthäus (Germany)
23 Paolo Maldini (Italy)
21 Diego Maradona (Argentina); Uwe Seeler (West Germany); Wladyslaw Zmuda (Poland)
20 Cafú (Brazil); Grzegorz Lato (Poland)
19 Miroslav Klose* (Germany); Wolfgang Overath (West Germany); Ronaldo (Brazil); Karl-Heinz Rummenigge (West Germany); Berti Vogts (West Germany)
18 Franz Beckenbauer (West Germany); Thomas Berthold (West Germany); Antonio Cabrini (Italy); Fabio Cannavaro (Italy); Dunga (Brazil); Mario Kempes (Argentina); Pierre Littbarski (West Germany); Sepp Maier (West Germany); Gaetano Scirea (Italy); Claudio Taffarel (Brazil)

* Both could add in 2014. Klose is still scoring for Germany at thirty-five years old. If he played in every match in the Finals and Germany reached the semi-finals, he would overtake his countryman, Lothar Matthäus, at the head of this table.

17 Fabien Barthez (France); Thierry Henry (France); Jürgen Klinsmann (Germany); Lúcio (Brazil); Roberto Carlos (Brazil); Karl-Heinz Schnellinger (West Germany); Enzo Scifo (Belgium); Peter Shilton (England); Dino Zoff (Italy)

16 Roberto Baggio (Italy); Giuseppe Bergomi (Italy); Andreas Brehme (West Germany); Jan Ceulemans (Belgium); Gilberto Silva (Brazil); Myung-Bo Hong (South Korea); Jairzinho (Brazil); Oscar Ruggeri (Argentina); Lilian Thuram (France); Andoni Zubizarreta (Spain)

15 Bebeto (Brazil); Zbigniew Boniek (Poland); Max Bossis (France); Iker Casillas[*] (Spain); Didi (Brazil); Nílton Santos (Brazil); Rivelino (Brazil); Hans Schäfer (West Germany); Francky Van der Elst (Belgium)

[*] Casillas will end up much higher on this list. Despite losing his place in the Real Madrid side in 2012–13, he remains first choice and captain of his country. At thirty-three in 2014, he feasibly has two more World Cups in him, and Spain will start as one of the favourites in 2014.

6.5 WORLD CUP 1990

One of the worst tournaments in the competition's history. The goals per game ratio hit a record low, which still stands, and negativity was so rife that it prompted the introduction of the back-pass law. From now on, if a defender deliberately played the ball back to his goalkeeper, the goalkeeper was not allowed to pick it up, only kick it. The punishment for transgression was an indirect free-kick at the point where the ball was picked up. For the next World Cup, teams would be awarded three points for a win in the group stages in both qualifying and the Finals. England had experimented with this in 1981 and found it satisfactory and a few other nations had followed suit, but most waited until FIFA adopted the three-point rule to follow suit. The red-card count shot up in 1990 as well, but rule changes were largely responsible for this as FIFA tried to clamp down on really bad tackling and professional fouls.

In 1990 the World Cup was back in Italy after fifty-six years, the first time a European nation has hosted the tournament twice, a record matched since by France and Germany. The only other candidates were the Soviet Union, who shot themselves in the foot by withdrawing from the 1984 Olympic Games in Los Angeles not long before the final vote, which was won very comfortably by Italy. Italy had one of the most prestigious and wealthy leagues in the world, and as such could offer ready-made stadia and media resources. Most of the grounds required some updating and expansion, but only two (the Stadio San Nicola in Bari and the Stadio delle Alip in Turin) were built from scratch.

1990
ITALY

Italy needed more grounds than in 1934, and used twelve cities instead of eight. Seven of those cities also hosted matches in 1934, the exception being **Trieste**.

Rome: Stadio Olimpico
The stadium used for the Olympic games of 1960 became the showpiece of Italia '90, and hosted the final. Over 73,000 souls were forced to watch a dire, bad-tempered affair between West Germany and Argentina. The stadium is the home of both major Rome clubs, Lazio and Roma.

Milan: Stadio San Siro
The San Siro was actually the biggest stadium used in the competition, but was overlooked for the semi-finals.

Naples: Stadio San Paulo
Maradona's home ground was the source of some controversy when he asked them to support him rather than Italy, but few Neapolitans succumbed to the appeal.

Florence: Stadio Artemio Franchi
Fiorentina's ground was down to a 41,000-capacity in 1990, and so it missed out on the bigger games. As an added insult, the Florentines had to endure an atrocious quarter-final between Argentina and Yugoslavia.

Genoa: Stadio Luigi Ferraris
Bologna: Stadio Renato Dall'Ara
Both grounds were playing host to their second World Cup finals tournaments, having both undergone extensive refurbishment to make them fit for purpose. Bologna saw David Platt score a late winner for England against Belgium.

Turin: Stadio delle Alpi
It does seem an extravagance to build a new stadium for a World Cup and then knock it down only sixteen years later, but that's what happened to the Stadio delle Alpi, the scene of England's defeat to West Germany on penalties in 1990.

Bari: Stadio San Nicola
If Italy is shaped like a boot, as it is often described, Bari is roughly where the Achilles tendon would be. The San Nicola was a 58,000-capacity extravagance built for the World Cup, but the stadium has never been completely filled for a match.

Verona: Stadio Marc'Antonio Bentegodi
The Marc'Antonio is home to both Verona clubs, Chievo and Hellas. Hellas regained their Serie A status for 2012–13. Considering they were given an unattractive group, the games at both Verona and Udine were well-attended.

Udine: Stadio Friuli
Udine is in the Friuli-Venezia region to the north-east of Italy, only twenty-five miles from the border with Slovenia. The stadium was opened in the 1960s and tarted up for the 1990 finals; its tenant, Udinese, have punched above their weight in Serie A for almost twenty years.

Cagliari: Stadio Comunale Sant' Elia
The main city on the island of Sardinia, Cagliari was used as a dumping ground for trouble by the Italian authorities, hosting all three England group games. The ground was built after the club won Serie A in 1970, but they have never since matched those glory days.

Palermo: Stadio La Favorita
This atmospheric stadium hosted the other games in England's group. The local team, Citta di Palermo, has been strong in recent years but was surprisingly relegated from Serie A in 2013; the club plans to build a new ground which it doesn't have to rent from the city.

The construction and engineering for the stadia and surrounding infrastructure became the subject of a massive investigation two years later when it was discovered that the entire project was a mass of kickbacks and profiteering. *Tangentopoli*, the Italians called it (Bribe City is a rough translation), and the follies included an underground railway in Rome that was rendered obsolete the moment the tournament ended. Hundreds of labourers were injured and twenty-four died, but there were no significant prosecutions.

Not that the competing nations were concerned with any of that; there was significantly less griping about facilities and playing conditions in a country that had a settled and wealthy football establishment. Footballers (sportsmen in general) have always been able to gloss over the political and social background to their competition; perhaps that isn't necessarily a bad thing.

Qualifying

With Argentina guaranteed a place as the holders, Brazil, Uruguay and Colombia made up the South American quartet. Colombia needed to see off Israel (mystifyingly placed in the Oceania section) in a tight two-leg play-off settled by a solitary goal.

The group containing Brazil, Chile and Venezuela finished in extraordinary fashion. Chile, needing a victory in Rio to qualify, were a goal down with just over twenty minutes to play. Their goalkeeper, Roberto Rojas, suddenly fell to his knees in his own penalty area, bleeding profusely from a wound apparently inflicted by something thrown from the crowd. The Chileans left the field and refused to continue, but their ploy to have the game annulled or awarded to them was rumbled by a subsequent investigation that revealed Rojas had a razor blade concealed in his glove and his wound was self-inflicted. For once FIFA acted swiftly and correctly; Rojas was banned for life along with his manager, and Chile were told they would play no part in qualification for the 1994 Finals tournament.

Uruguay qualified on goal difference after both they and Bolivia disposed of Peru rather easily – Peru were a spent force after their excellent decade from 1970. Uruguay seemed to have discovered a goalscorer to go with the approach play of Francescoli; Ruben Sosa of Lazio scored five times in four matches. Arnoldo Iguarán was similarly influential as Colombia squeezed past Paraguay and Ecuador. Both strikers travelled to Italy (not that Sosa had far to go as he lived in Rome!) with exciting things expected of them.

A North American place was thrown open by the disqualification of Mexico for fielding ineligible players in a youth tournament. In a five-team group that also counted as the CONCACAF championship Costa Rica (who were in the final pool by dint of Mexico's expulsion) finished their games early and seemed sure to qualify. Second place was a straight contest between the USA and Trinidad & Tobago and it all came down to a winner-takes-all match in November, 1989. US defender Paul Caligiuri's goal settled it and the USA were in the Finals for the first time since 1950. With typical overstatement the US media used the careworn phrase *"the shot heard around the world"* to celebrate Caligiuri's goal and proclaim the re-emergence of US soccer. The phrase was actually coined to herald a miracle shot by Gene Sarazen at the 1935 US Masters when he holed his second at the monster par-5 fifteenth on the way to winning the trophy. The rest of the world, US media hyperbole notwithstanding, wasn't quaking. The Americans were solid and hard-working but scored only six goals in eight games in this pool. Costa Rica had a little more flair but a leaky defence.

South Korea and the United Arab Emirates (for the first time) represented Asia, having finished the top two in a six-team group, which was played out as a mini-tournament in Singapore. South Korea looked much the most accomplished side, while the Emirates qualified with four draws and a 2–1 in over China courtesy of two late goals. They were the *we'll have them, please* team in the draw.

African qualification was tainted with tragedy and violence. During one of the groups used to determine the four qualifiers for the final stage, Nigeria's Sammi Okwaraji collapsed and died from heart failure during a game against Angola. The game was abandoned with ten minutes on the clock and the result stood; neither side qualified. The last four were Cameroon and three

North African sides and the draw threw Egypt and Algeria, never the best of friends, together. The first game in Constantine was a 0–0 draw, and the return in Cairo was played in front of a capacity crowd. Egypt scored after four minutes through Hossam Hassan, but the Algerians claimed their goalkeeper was baulked by another Egyptian forward (they were right). The referee Ali Ben Nasser (of Hand of God) fame gave the goal and pretty much every other decision the home team claimed. At the end of the game he was mobbed by furious Algerian players and officials and there was a huge ruckus in the changing rooms and in the media room. When the Egyptian team doctor was hit in the eye and blinded by a broken bottle, the finger was pointed at Lakhdar Belloumi, the Algerian striker, who was handed a prison sentence in his absence by an Egyptian court. The court order for his arrest was only rescinded twenty years later in 2009; the real culprit was reported as the team's reserve goalkeeper. All a bit unsavoury. Cameroon won through with far less fuss, beating Tunisia home and away.

Most of the usual suspects from Europe turned up. West Germany and Holland were drawn together, but with the top two from all but one European group to qualify, it was a coast for both teams and they played out what for them were two quiet draws. This didn't give much of a clue about what was to come in the Finals. Wales never lost by more than the odd goal, but most of their quality players were a bit long in the tooth and they finished bottom of the group behind Finland.

France were in transition after the retirement of the *Carré Magnifique*, and they were the most high-profile casualty of the qualifying stage. A dropped point away to Cyprus proved fatal, and Scotland pipped them to second place by a point; they earned victory in Cyprus with a last-minute goal from Richard Gough. Scotland's crucial match was a two-nil win over the French at Hampden with a brace from Mo Johnston, whose six goals were crucial in qualifying. Johnston's partnership with Ally McCoist was Scotland's main cause for optimism. A gifted Yugoslavia team waltzed away at the top of the group and went to Italy with some confidence, boasting talents like Stojkovic, Vujovic and the mercurial Savicevic.

Scotland were joined in the Finals by England, who qualified without conceding a goal but still finished second behind Sweden in their group by dint of three 0–0 draws. They needed a draw from their last game in Poland and got it – just; Poland hit the bar with seconds to go. The most memorable image of the campaign was Terry Butcher, head covered in blood-stained bandages after suffering a nasty head wound during the vital draw in Stockholm. Butcher probably wouldn't have been allowed to continue nowadays, but he did, and earned iconic status with the fans. Sports fans will always appreciate a player putting it on the line for the cause, far more than they will admire a dilettante match winner who produces one in every three matches.

Changes had been demanded after the debacle of England's early exit from the 1988 European Championships, and, although they weren't huge, they were crucial. Des Walker was installed as a replacement for Tony Adams – Adams was not yet the towering influence he became the following decade. Stuart Pearce was immediately picked and Kenny Sansom retired – Sansom played a year or two too long. Up front Peter Beardsley provided a foil for Lineker's predatory instincts and behind them, instead of Glenn Hoddle there was the energy and drive of Paul Gascoigne, the man Hoddle never forgave for displacing him. Few players divide critics as much as Hoddle. Some remember him as a great player misused and played out of position at international level – and it is true that the English style and system never really suited him. Others (me included) remember too many games when much was expected and little received – a tendency to go missing on the big occasion. Hoddle is in good company in this regard; World Cup history is littered with big name club players who didn't enjoy the party. He was undoubtedly gifted – his passing was the equal of Johnny Haynes – he just lacked that little bit extra needed to impose himself on a game at the very highest level. And Bobby Robson never solved the conundrum of how to play Hoddle and Bryan Robson in the same side. The answer was three at the back, but England only adopted the system in panic during the 1990 campaign – too late for Hoddle. Gascoigne came to the tournament on the back of a superb display against Czechoslovakia – a timely performance as

Robson was frustrated by Gascoigne's childish antics and indiscipline.

Belgium and Czechoslovakia headed a tough group that left an improving Portugal team stranded. Both qualifiers earned a draw in Lisbon, which ultimately cost Portugal. The Czechs had high hopes of their centre-forward, the long-haired Tomás Skuhravy, while Belgium had their captain Jan Ceulemans, one of their all-time greats, playing in his third World Cup Finals tournament and still a major performer at thirty-three.

Both Ireland teams were in a group with Spain and Hungary, and this time it was the south who emerged strongest. After a poor start in which they failed to find the net in their first three games they won a run of three home games in the spring of 1989 and crushed Northern Ireland 3–0 in October to virtually clinch their place. Ireland weren't a particularly gifted or attractive side but they did their "thing" well, and had the unsentimental manager they needed to implement their direct game. England's World Cup-winning centre-half Jack Charlton had no more than a decent record as a club manager when he was approached by the FA of Ireland as a surprise choice for the national team. They qualified for their first major championship (Euro '88) two years later and comfortably outperformed England (not difficult). Ireland had a good crop of players, especially in defence where Charlton could choose from Paul McGrath, one of the best in the world, the experienced David O'Leary and the uncompromising and consistent Mick McCarthy, a natural leader.

The Soviet Union, finalists in the 1988 European Championships, and perennial dark horses who always fell short, made it through again, the last time the Communist amalgam of states would compete as a combined entity. Lobanovsky still had the core of the fine team from 1986, and had the added luxury of Alexei Mikhailichenko, who had emerged as a genuine world-class midfield player. Austria qualified with them from a weak group.

Denmark were favourites to qualify from the top group and went to Bucharest for their last match needing a draw to win the group. They had beaten Romania, their hosts, comfortably in Copenhagen only a month earlier. The game was a minor classic.

Denmark took the lead after six minutes when a brilliant Brian Laudrup run set up a tap-in for Flemming Poulsen. The younger Laudrup was still only twenty but he and his brother promised great things to come for their country.

Romania had some good young players of their own, mostly with Steaua Bucharest, who had just finished runners-up in the 1989 European Cup. The two best of them combined to find an equaliser when Gheorghe Hagi's flat cross was won in the air by Marius Lăcătus; Balint hooked in the knock down. The second came from an incisive run by right-back Dan Petrescu; Peter Schmeichel came out to quash the threat, the ball broke free and Ioan Sabau put home the loose ball. The battered old Steaua stadium was in uproar with the entire 30,000 bouncing up and down in unison and making the noise of three times that number.

A sublime piece of skill in the second half nearly brought a third for Romania. A beautiful curled pass from Hagi found Lăcătus twelve yards out on an angle; the winger killed the ball with his first touch and, realising Schmeichel was charging out to block, slowed his foot through the ball and lifted a perfect lob over the 'keeper – no easy task, Schmeichel was massive. The ball dropped towards the goal but slowly enough that a defender was able to get behind his goalkeeper and head off the line.

Poulsen missed Denmark's best chance of an equaliser, putting Laudrup's cut-back into the side netting, and a minute later another curled pass from Hagi caused problems in the Danish defence. Sabau nicked the ball past the last defender and again Schmeichel's block fell kindly for a Romanian attacker – Balint – to slide home. Hagi, never one for the easy option, managed to get himself sent off for a crude tackle, but his colleagues dug in for the last twenty-odd minutes and Romania were top of the group and on their way to Italy – only their second post-war appearance in the Finals and first for twenty years. Denmark were the unlucky second-placed team – they had fewer points than the others and didn't make the cut. If that was bad luck it evened out two years later when the expulsion of Yugoslavia from the 1992 European Championships gave them a late passport to the Finals – they grasped the opportunity with both hands.

Finals

The draw, held in Rome in 1990, was a glitzy affair with Sophia Loren and Luciano Pavarotti. It was a bile-inducing sight, watching the FIFA officials preen and simper in the presence of genuine stars. And how we loved Ciao, the ghastly little stick man who was to be the tournament's symbol. We did, didn't we?

The draw was kind to Brazil, England and West Germany. West Germany was about to become plain old Germany again; the Berlin Wall was breached in the Autumn of 1989, and officially dismantled while the tournament was taking place. East Germany re-adopted the Deutschmark in 1990, and this World Cup was the last major sporting event where the two competed as separate countries. Italy had a testing group, while Belgium, the fifth seeds after their exploits in the 1980s, had a tricky section with Spain and Uruguay. The shortest straws were pulled out by the teams in Group B, where Argentina, the holders, the Soviet Union, Romania and Cameroon, the best of the teams from the wannabes pot, would face off.

The favourites were Holland, the European Champions from 1988; Brazil were always contenders, as were West Germany, and Argentina still had Maradona. The Italians had some good young players and the usual tight defence and they couldn't be discounted on home ground. The Soviets were many people's tip, while Yugoslavia, so full of talent, had their admirers.

GROUP A

Italy Schillaci 80	(0) 1	**Austria**	(0) 0	9 June, Olimpico; 72,303
USA Caligiuri 60	(0) 1	**Czechoslovakia** Skuhravy 26, 79, Bílek 39 (p) Hasek 50, Luhovy 89	(2) 5	10 June, Florence; 33,266
Italy Giannini 11	(1) 1	**USA**	(0) 0	14 June, Olimpico; 73,423
Czechoslovakia Bílek 29 (p)	(1) 1	**Austria**	(0) 0	15 June, Florence; 38,962
Italy Schillaci 10, Baggio 78	(1) 2	**Czechoslovakia**	(0) 0	19 June, Olimpico; 73,303
Austria Ogris 49, Rodax 63	(0) 2	**USA** Murray 84	(0) 1	19 June, Florence; 34,857

1. **Italy** 6pts (4–0); 2. **Czechoslovakia** 4pts (6–3); 3. **Austria** 2pts (2–3); 4. **USA** 0pts (2–8)

Italy had bags of talent in midfield – Donadoni, De Napoli, the Roma playmaker Giannini – but didn't score many goals. Gianluca Vialli had just helped Sampdoria win their first (and hitherto only) *Serie A* title, but his game was about space and movement and threat rather than finishing. Alongside him, Napoli's Andrea Carnevale was the current preference without really looking like the answer to the problem. The Juventus striker, Toto Schillaci, had made the squad after a good first season in the top flight and was the only obvious goalscoring back-up, with young Roberto Baggio as the alternative to Vialli.

The first game served only to highlight Italy's problem. Carnevale missed chances galore, one a ghastly spoon over the bar from six yards out with the goalkeeper beaten. Vialli played well, but for all his movement and running didn't look a major goal threat. Off came Carnevale with fifteen minutes to go, replaced by Schillaci for only his second international appearance. A few minutes later Vialli did wonderfully well to twist and fire over a superb cross. Schillaci timed his jump between the centre-halves perfectly and bulleted a header past Lindenberger. In four minutes on the pitch Schillaci had saved his manager, the articulate and likeable Azeglio Vicini, a torrent of abuse from the Italian media.

The next game against the USA followed the same pattern except the solitary goal came earlier, from Giannini. Graceful and fluid, Giannini was known as *Il Principe* (The Prince) by his admirers – not for his Machiavellian capacity for intrigue but for his grace and bearing on the pitch. Giannini is an icon at Roma, where he played over four hundred games in a fifteen-year stint after taking a while to establish himself, but he never fully scaled the heights as an international. Here he burst into the area after Vialli cleverly and unselfishly let the ball run through his legs and finished with a powerful left-foot drive. Nicola Berti won a penalty after thirty-three minutes but Vialli's kick pinged off the post and away, and the Italians had a goal debatably chalked off for offside. Zenga made an excellent double save from a free-kick and the follow-up, but that apart the *Stati Uniti* offered as little in attack as the Austrians.

Austria and the USA were equally impotent against Czechoslovakia, who put five past the Americans, with Skuhravy confirming his promise with a couple of good goals, ending a flowing counter-attack for the Czech's opener and beating goal-keeper Tony Meola to a right-wing corner for the fourth. The USA scored the best goal of the game when Caligiuri ran from the halfway line, beat the last defender and finished expertly. The US media were less bombastic about this effort, although it was a far better piece of work than the *"shot heard around the world"*. The game against Czechoslovakia's neighbours, Austria, was a dour and niggly affair settled by Michal Bílek's second penalty in two games – he didn't muck about but just hammered the ball into the middle of the goal and dared the goalkeeper to get in the way. Bílek is now the current coach of the Czech Republic team (although his position is precarious as they are unlikely to qualify for the 2014 Finals). Most of this Czechoslovakia side was Czech rather than Slovakian – the defenders Kocian and Moravcík were the exception in these first two games. Vladimir Weiss, who started against Italy after coming off the bench twice, would later manage Slovakia in their own World Cup Final appearance in 2010.

Italy made changes for this final group match; Schillaci started and Baggio replaced the luckless Vialli. Carnevale never played for Italy again – his final futile gesture was a rude one towards the coach when he was again substituted after another ineffectual display against the USA. Carnevale left Rome that summer after winning two league titles alongside Maradona at Napoli. He was suspended after five games for narcotic use, and was soon playing with the up-and-comings and the other also-rans in *Serie B*.

Italy were lively and imaginative, with Baggio's dribbling adding an extra dimension alongside Giannini's skill. They were buoyed by an early goal when Schillaci headed home after Giannini's shot had bounced up off the ground at a convenient height. Ferri and Baresi controlled Skuhravy well – one saving tackle from Baresi when the big man looked clear was a master-class in timing. Baresi was thirty already, but had only been first choice at the back since Scirea retired, however he looked a class act here, and would do so again in four years' time. Stejskal saved well from Schillaci (twice) and Giannini had a shot kicked off the line but there was nothing the Czech defence could do when

Baggio played a one-two with Giannini and ran at the heart of the defence, sending Hasek every which way but the right way before sliding the ball under the diving goalkeeper.

The other game in Florence between Austria and the USA was another poor game littered with bad tackles between two limited sides. The USA were a disappointment in their first Finals appearance for forty years and would need a big improvement to impress their home supporters four years later.

USA Squad 1990:

GK: Tony Meola (contracted to US Soccer Federation, 21 years old); Kasey Keller (Portland Timbers, 20), David Vanole (Los Angeles Heat, 28)

DEF: Des Armstrong (Baltimore Blast, 25), Marcelo Balboa (San Diego Sockers, 22), Jimmy Banks (Milwaukee Wave, 25), Brian Bliss (Albany Capitals, 24), John Doyle (San Francisco Bay Blackhawks, 24), Steve Trittschuh (Tampa Bay Rowdies, 25), Mike Windischmann (Cpt, Albany Capitals, 24)

MID & WIDE: Paul Caligiuri (Meppen, 26), Neil Covone (College soccer, 20), Eric Eichmann (Fort Lauderdale Strikers, 25), John Harkes (Albany Capitals, 23), Chris Henderson (College soccer, 20), Paul Krumpe (Chicago Sting, 27), Tab Ramos (Miami Sharks, 23), John Stollmeyer (Washington Stars, 27)

FWD: Bruce Murray (Washington Stars, 25), Chris Sullivan (Gyori, Hungary, 25), Peter Vermes (Volendam, 23), Eric Wynalda (SF Bay Blackhawks, 20)

WORLD CUP SHOCK No.6
8 June 1990, Giuseppe Meazza (San Siro), Milan; 73,870

Argentina	(0) 0	
Cameroon	(0) 1	Omam-Biyik 67

Referee: **Michel Vautrot** (France)
Coaches: **Carlos Bilardo** (Argentina) & **Valeri Nepomniachy** (USSR)

Argentina (5–3–1–1): Nery Pumpido (Real Betis); Nestór Fabbri (Racing Club), Roberto Sensini (Udinese), Juan Simón (Boca Juniors), Oscar Ruggeri (Real Madrid), Nestór Lorenzo (Bari); Sergio Batista (River Plate), Jorge Burruchaga (Nantes), José Basualdo (Stuttgart); Diego Maradona (Cpt, Napoli); Abel Balbo (Udinese). **Subs:** Claudio Caniggia (Atalanta) 45m for Ruggeri; Gabriel Calderón (Paris St Germain) 69m for Sensini

Cameroon (4–5–1): Thomas N'Kono (Español); Stephen Tataw (Cpt, Tonnerre Yaoundé), Victor Ndip (Canon Yaoundé), Benjamin Massing (Creteil), Bertin Ebwelle (Tonnerre Yaoundé); Émile Mbouh (Le Havre), Cyrille Makanaky (Toulon), Emmanuel Kundé (Prévoyance Yaoundé), André Kana-Biyik (Metz), Louis Paul Mefede (Canon Yaoundé); François Omam-Biyik (Stade Lavallois). **Subs:** Thomas Libih (Tonnerre Yaoundé) 65m for Mfede); Roger Milla (JS Saint-Pierroise) 82m for Makanaky
Cautioned: Massing (Cam) 10m, Ndip (Cam) 23m, Sensini (Arg) 27m, Mbouh (Cam) 54m
Dismissed: Kana Biyik (Cam) 61m (serious foul play); Massing (Cam) 88m (second yellow)

Was it such a surprise? Yes. Some point to the poor recent form of the holders and the fact that Cameroon were a decent side with plenty of players with league experience in Europe. It doesn't wash. Argentina were the holders and had the bulk of the side who won in 1986; sides with this level of experience are usually able to raise themselves for a big tournament, especially with the best player in the world in their ranks, playing in the country where he now lived. And the Cameroonians who did earn their living in Europe were mainly with second-tier sides in France; the biggest exception was Thomas N'Kono, the goalkeeper with Español in La Liga.

Argentina dominated the early stages when Cameroon showed a bit too much respect and sat too deep. Burruchaga was slow to react when sent clear, allowing N'Kono to block, and Ruggeri made a pig's ear of a free header from a free-kick. For all Argentina's possession Cameroon created the best chance of the first half when Makanaky stole between two defenders to get on the end of a raking pass from Omam-Biyik. The striker nudged the ball past Pumpido but Lorenzo just got back to make an excellent goal-line clearance.

The odds swung in Argentina's favour after an hour when referee Vautrot sent off Kana-Biyik for tripping Claudio Caniggia, on at half-time to inject some pace into the Argentinian front line. Caniggia was a long way from the goal area and a defender was covering immediately behind Kana-Biyik, but Vautrot deemed it a professional foul. FIFA had introduced the red card for a professional foul ruling at the eleventh hour, and Vautrot, who had a reputation as a good, tough referee, looked like he was claiming his own personal bit of history rather than judging the situation dispassionately. It was an awful decision.

Six minutes later Cameroon, even more defensive now, sent a hopeful free-kick into the box. Omam-Biyik was alone amid a sea of blue and white shirts but jumped the highest and sent a firm downward header straight at Pumpido, who managed only to feebly help the ball on its way into the goal.

While the European commentators still patronisingly referred to "little Cameroon", the Africans, who were massive and unsubtle in defence, started to kick lumps out of the Argentinian forwards. Having erred in sending off Kana-Biyik, the French referee seemed unwilling to hand out further punishment. With two minutes to go he had no alternative. After a Cameroon attack broke down, Caniggia sprinted clear from inside his own half. The first defender pulled out of a tackle, the second clipped Caniggia's heel and the third, Massing, took him out as comprehensively as if he had been hit by a tractor. None of Massing's colleagues protested the dismissal; he had already been booked, but even without the earlier offence this was a red card – it was perilously close to assault.

The best chance in injury-time still fell to Cameroon, when their substitute, the venerable and skilful thirty-eight-year-old Roger Milla, engineered an excellent opportunity for Mbouh, who blasted his shot excitedly over the bar.

It was a desperate performance by Argentina – Balbo must have had sleepless nights over a missed header in the second half with the goal at his mercy. They were unsure at the back, unresponsive to their captain's efforts in midfield and, Caniggia apart, toothless up front. Cameroon had shown they were not there to make up the numbers and were prepared to mix it to get a result.

GROUP B

Romania	(1) 2	**USSR**	(0) 0	9 June, Bari; 42,907	
Lăcătus 41, 55 (p)					
USSR	(0) 0	**Argentina**	(1) 2	13 June, Naples; 55,759	
		Troglio 27, Burruchaga 78			
Cameroon	(0) 2	**Romania**	(0) 1	14 June, Bari; 38,687	
Milla 76, 87		Balint 88			
Romania	(0) 1	**Argentina**	(0) 1	18 June, Naples; 52,733	
Balint 68		Monzón			
USSR	(2) 4	**Cameroon**	(0) 0	18 June, Bari; 37,207	
Protasov 20, Zygmantovich 29,					
Zavarov 52, Dobrovolsky 63					

1. **Cameroon 4pts (3–5); 2. Romania 3pts (4–3); 3. Argentina 3pts (3–2); 4. USSR 2pts (4–4)**

The other opening match in this group also produced a surprise, though not on the scale of Cameroon's win. Romania were without Hagi, suspended after his red card against Denmark. The USSR, just as significantly, were forced to leave Mikhailichenko at home with an injury. The rest of the Soviet side were runners – skilful but not desperately imaginative – and they hadn't replaced the brilliant Belanov at centre-forward.

Lăcătus, Romania's other star, opened the scoring with a fierce drive that nearly took Dasaev into the goal with the ball, and then got a fortunate penalty for an offence clearly – to everyone but Señor Cardellino and his linesman – committed outside the area. Lăcătus converted, and later missed a glorious opportunity for a hat-trick, sidefooting past the far post with the goal at his mercy.

These chances aside, the USSR were much the better side in the first half. Intricate passing created chances for Protasov, Zavarov and Aleinikov, but the Romanian captain, Lung, was equal to the challenge and blocked all three. The goals knocked the stuffing out of the Soviets and Romania could have added more late on. The attendance at this match was given as nearly 43,000; the reality was about a third of that figure, but FIFA declare ticket sales as the attendance. The stadium in Bari held nearly 60,000, a tad extravagant for a club side that even in *Serie A* only drew more than 10,000 for the really big games.

A game later and the USSR were out, beaten 2–0 again, this time by Argentina. An early chance for Shalimov from Dobrovolski's cleverly placed cross caused a collision between Olarticoechea and his goalkeeper, which left Pumpido with a broken leg; he never played for his country again, a nasty way to go. Argentina had a decent replacement in Sergio Goycochea. With the new goalkeeper understandably nervous, Maradona decided to give him a helping hand, literally, when he stopped Kuznetsov's flicked header at the near post. He was a devious little tinker was the world's best player. The referee was badly placed and probably knew giving a penalty against Saint Diego in Napoli was a bad idea – all will be explained!

Argentina scored first from a Troglio header after some good work from left-back Olarticoechea, and added a second from a mistake by Kuznetsov. In between Bessonov was red-carded for yet another foul on Caniggia, only this time the decision was correct. The Soviets still played the more methodical football, even with ten men, but were unable to convert chances into goals and paid the price.

The next day in Bari Cameroon's party continued with a two-one win over Romania. Lăcătus was bullied by the big Cameroon defenders and Hagi was strangely subdued, one searing shot tipped over by N'Kono apart. The star of the show was Milla, who scored twice, both times taking out the last defender, first with strength and then with speed, before finishing with confidence – a commodity he was never short of. Both goals were celebrated with a flamboyant, hip-wiggling dance around the corner flag – it was to be one of the images of the tournament.

Romania and Argentina played out a draw in their last match, both teams clearly holding something in reserve, while the USSR thrashed Cameroon, a result not entirely explained by the fact that Cameroon were definitely through and the Soviets out. As in 1986, the USSR were better than their results suggested and would be missed.

GROUP C

Brazil Careca 40, 63	**(1) 2**	**Sweden** Brolin 78	**(0) 1**	10 June, Turin; 62,628
Costa Rica Cayasso 49	**(0) 1**	**Scotland**	**(0) 0**	11 June, Genoa; 30,867
Brazil Müller 33	**(1) 1**	**Costa Rica**	**(0) 0**	16 June, Turin; 58,007
Sweden Strömberg	**(0) 1**	**Scotland** McCall 10, Johnston 81 (p)	**(1) 2**	16 June, Genoa; 31,823
Costa Rica Flores 74, Medford 87	**(0) 2**	**Sweden** Ekström 31	**(0) 1**	20 June, Genoa; 30,223
Scotland	**(0) 0**	**Brazil** Müller 81	**(0) 1**	20 June, Turin; 62,502

Scotland Squad 1990:

GK: Jim Leighton (Manchester United), Andy Goram (Hibernian), Bryan Gunn (Norwich City)
DEF: Gary Gillespie (Liverpool), Richard Gough (Glasgow Rangers), Craig Levein (Heart of Midlothian), Maurice Malpas (Dundee United), Alex McLeish (Aberdeen), Stewart McKimmie (Aberdeen), Dave McPherson (Hearts)
MID & WIDE: Roy Aitken (Cpt, Newcastle United), Jim Bett (Aberdeen), John Collins (Hibernian), Gary McAllister (Leicester

City), Stuart McCall (Everton), Murdo McLeod (Borussia Dortmund), Paul McStay (Celtic)
FWD: Gordon Durie (Chelsea), Robert Fleck (Norwich), Mo Johnston (Rangers), Ally McCoist (Rangers), Alan McInally (Bayern Munich)

1. **Brazil 6pts (4–1); 2. Costa Rica 4pts (3–2); 3. Scotland 2pts (2–3); 4. Sweden 0pts (3–6)**

There were doubts about the Brazilian defence, and doubts about the un-Brazilian tactics adopted by coach Lazaroni. The defence was never sorely tested in a poor group. Careca's sharp finishing won the first match against Sweden, and both Costa Rica and Scotland packed their defence and hoped for the best. Against Costa Rica, Brazil were thwarted by the woodwork and good goalkeeping from Conejo, while against Scotland they looked unimpressive but benefited from a terrible late error from Jim Leighton in the Scotland goal – an error which cost them a place in the second round.

In fairness, it was a terrible display against Costa Rica in the first game that cost Scotland. Bora Milutinovic, who had so galvanised Mexico in 1986 now did the same with the Central American side, instilling discipline and nous along with some inherent flair. A neat move between Marchena and Jara created a goal for Cayasso just after half-time and Scotland didn't test Luis Conejo nearly enough. The prolific Mo Johnston was easily suppressed and there wasn't the wit in the Scotland midfield to open up an unremarkable defence. The pre-match assertion by Scotland manager that Costa Rica would provide comfortable first opposition was made to look remarkably dim.

Sweden were a disappointment, apart from the exciting little forward Thomas Brolin (not yet the overweight shambles who appeared in England). Gordon Durie and Robert Fleck offered a little more vigour and pace to the Scotland attack, and in that perverse way the Scots have in World Cup Finals they followed a shambolic performance with an encouraging one. Good discipline against a timid Brazil nearly saw them through. Costa Rica deserved their place in the second round after coming from behind against Sweden, whose young team would enjoy better times.

GROUP D

Colombia	(1) 2	**UAE**	(0) 0	9 June, Bologna; 30,791
Redín 50, Valderrama 85				
Yugoslavia	(0) 1	**West Germany**	(2) 4	10 June, Milan, 74,765
Jozic 55		Matthäus 28, 63, Klinsmann 39,		
		Völler 69		
Colombia	(0) 0	**Yugoslavia**	(0) 1	14 June, Bologna; 32,257
		Jozic 75		
UAE	(0) 1	**West Germany**	(2) 5	15 June, Milan; 71,167
Khalid Ismail 47		Völler 35, 75, Klinsmann 37,		
		Matthäus 48, Bein 58		
West Germany	(0) 1	**Colombia**	(0) 1	19 June, Milan; 72,510
Littbarski 88		Rincón 90		
Yugoslavia	(2) 4	**UAE**	(1) 1	19 June, Bologna; 27,833
Susic 4, Pancev 7, 46,		Juma'a 20		
Prosinecki 90				

1.West Germany 5 pts (10–3); 2.Yugoslavia 4 pts (6–5); 3.Colombia 3 pts (3–2); 4. UAE 0 pts (2–11)

West Germany's modus operandi in recent World Cups had been to start off slowly and improve gradually throughout the tournament, scraping results, while more exciting teams knocked each other out. It had got them to the final in 1982 and 1986 but they had finally encountered sides with the same degree of self-belief but more talent. Finally, in 1990, for the first time since the 1970s, West Germany had abundant talent to go with the self-belief.

They started the juggernaut rolling with a dominant performance in their opening game against Yugoslavia, an extravagantly gifted but brittle side. Lothar Matthäus, a more complete player than in 1986, opened the scoring with a piledriver and his Internazionale colleague Jürgen Klinsmann added a second, glancing a header across the goal off his floppy barnet – he looked a bit surprised when it went in. A header from a free-kick by Davor Jozic pulled one back but the Germans didn't even pause for breath. Two minutes later another surging run and brutal finish from Matthäus restored their advantage and Yugoslavia melted away. Matthäus combined scoring goals with completely subduing the dangerous Stojkovic in midfield – it was his greatest performance in a World Cup match. Völler added a late fourth, following in after the goalkeeper made a hash of Brehme's cross. West Germany looked a complete side. The five-man defence was marshalled by the veteran Klaus Augenthaler and the big, strapping, athletic

Buchwald advanced into midfield when the Germans had the ball,
allowing Matthäus to play further forward. This brought Matthäus'
formidable shooting into play more, and the new, exciting left-back
Andreas Brehme packed a lethal shot as well. Thomas Hässler was
a skilful, clever player (with Andreas Möller and Olaf Thon in
reserve; West Germany had great options in midfield), and the
Italian-based front two of Klinsmann – all power and edge – and
the experienced Völler were a dynamic combination.

The United Arab Emirates, enterprising but just not good
enough, were brushed aside and only Colombia provided decent
opposition, albeit depressingly negative. Littbarski's late goal
seemed to have punished their time-wasting and histrionics, but
an even later one from Freddy Rincón earned the disappointing
Colombians a place in the last sixteen. Yugoslavia joined them
after recovering from their pounding by the Germans to beat
Colombian (narrowly) and the UAE (easily). The Slavs had
dropped Savicevic, who looked shell-shocked against West
Germany, and brought in his Red Star colleague, the Macedonian
striker Darko Pancev; he looked the real deal against the UAE,
scoring twice and tormenting the defenders.

GROUP E

Belgium	(0) 2	**South Korea**	(0) 0	12 June, Verona; 32,790
Degryse 53, De Wolf 63				
Uruguay	(0) 0	**Spain**	(0) 0	13 June, Udine; 36,713
Belgium	(2) 3	**Uruguay**	(0) 1	17 June, Verona; 33,759
Clijsters 15, Scifo 22,		Bengoechea 72		
Ceulemans 46				
Spain	(1) 3	**South Korea**	(1) 1	17 June, Udine; 32,733
Michel 23, 63, 82		Hwang 44		
Spain	(2) 2	**Belgium**	(1) 1	21 June, Verona; 35,950
Michel 26 (p), Gorriz 38		Vervoort 29		
Uruguay	(0) 1	**South Korea**	(0) 0	21 June, Udine; 29,039
Fonseca				

1. Spain 5pts (5–2); 2. Belgium 4pts (6–3); 3. Uruguay 3pts (2–3); 4. South Korea 0pts
(1–6)

South Korea weren't very good, which didn't reflect well on
Asian football, as they were comfortably the best side in the region.
They committed more fouls in three matches than Uruguay, which
takes some doing, and showed little going forward.

The Koreans held Belgium for forty-five minutes, but the introduction of Ceulemans at half-time changed things. The big man's power threw the Koreans into reverse and Belgium won comfortably enough. Spain needed an inspired display from José Miguel González Martín del Campo to counter Korea's aggression. Michel, as he preferred to be known, was a consistent and assured performer for Real Madrid and Spain, but this was his best day. He hit a sweet cushioned volley to give Spain the lead and restored it with a superb free-kick after Hwang Bo-kwan had equalised with an equally good strike. Spanish coach Luis Suárez, a star for them in the early 1960s, sat in his chair shaking his head for a good five minutes after Hwang's hammer of a shot. The last goal was another gem, as Michel killed an awkward bouncing ball with a touch that completely flummoxed one defender, twisted past another and finished hard across Choi with his left foot – a hat trick to equal Boniek's against Belgium in 1982.

Belgium had Eric Gerets, their veteran right-back, sent off after only thirty-six minutes against Uruguay. Fortunately they were already two-nil ahead and had a good enough defence to hold on with some ease; Ceulemans put them three-up before Uruguay found a solitary response.

Spain edged the final game against Belgium, but, if Scifo's penalty had gone under the bar instead of rebounding from it, Belgium, not Spain, would have headed the group. Not that either of them had an easy second-round tie, but both would fancy their chances. Spain finally looked as if some of their club success was rubbing off, and they had goals in them with Butragueño leading the line and Michel coming off the right wing to such effect. Belgium were very experienced, and had a knack of maximising their resources under canny Guy Thys. Uruguay were decidedly ordinary and looked ideal opponents for the hosts in the next phase. Francescoli looked a weary and demotivated player, not a great one.

GROUP F

England Lineker 9	(1) 1	**Ireland** Sheedy 72	(0) 1	11 June, Cagliari; 35,238
Egypt Abdelghani 82 (p)	(0) 1	**Holland** Kieft 58	(0) 1	12 June, Palermo; 33,288
Holland	(0) 0	**England**	(0) 0	16 June, Cagliari; 35,267

Ireland	(0) 0	Egypt	(0) 0	17 June, Palermo; 33,288
Egypt	(0) 0	England	(0) 1	21 June, Cagliari; 34,959
		Wright 58		
Holland	(0) 1	Ireland	(0) 1	21 June, Palermo; 33,288
Gullit 10		Quinn 71		

Seven goals in six games, no wonder the Italian press were so rude about the football coming out of the group. The authorities didn't help. They were worried about the hooligan element in the support from the three European sides and carted the entire group off to Sardinia, where the local *carabinieri* (riot police) treated the fans with markedly less respect than they afforded the local gangsters. And bracketing the Irish supporters with the English yobs and the Dutch extremists was an insult, as was chartering a plane and randomly arresting exactly the same number of England fans as seats in Rimini before the second-round match in nearby Bologna and forcibly repatriating them. This was a cretinous response to the trouble, and typical of the reaction of the police in southern Europe at the time; instead of enlisting the help of the English police, who enjoyed great success in combating hooliganism, they reacted to violence and indiscretion with violence and indiscretion and exacerbated the problem, turning bystanders into participants. I'm not excusing the hooligans who poisoned the game for a decade (I didn't attend a league match between 1982 and 1990), I'm simply suggesting that providing other hooligans in uniforms for them to clash with was not the answer.

Back to the football, what there was of it. England versus Ireland was unspeakable, but at least England avoided defeat, unlike in the parallel fixture at the 1988 European Championships. Sheedy's equaliser was just about deserved and came from a bad mistake by Steve McMahon. A predicted Dutch landslide against Egypt never materialised; Holland looked a pale imitation of the team that won the Euros, and Egypt were most certainly not flattered by a draw. They got another in their next match against Ireland, a stultifying game.

England adopted a sweeper system against Holland, which seemed unnecessary as Holland were awful again and couldn't worry a defence in which Mark Wright was excellent as the deep-lying defender. Peter Beardsley, who had a rotten game against

Ireland, made way. Van Basten destroyed England in 1988 but here he was easily restrained by Des Walker and appeared fed up long before the end.

Van Basten got no more change from McCarthy and McGrath, never mind that both lacked outright pace; Niall Quinn's route one equaliser got the Irish their third draw and a place in the last sixteen. England needed a win to top the group. They reverted to a back four, leaving Butcher out, with McMahon replacing the injured (again) Robson and Steve Bull, who played in the second division with Wolverhampton Wanderers, coming in alongside Lineker. England got the win courtesy of Mark Wright's only goal in forty-five internationals, but watching Paul Gascoigne trying to get into the game while his colleagues failed to string three passes together was painful stuff.

The best players in the group were Walker, McGrath, Frank Rijkaard and the twenty-one-year-old Egyptian sweeper Hani Ramzy. All centre-backs. 'Nuff said.

SECOND ROUND

Cameroon Milla 106, 109	(0) (0) 2	**Colombia** Redin 116	(0) (0) 1	23 June, Naples; 50,026
Costa Rica Gonzalez 56 Kubik 77	(0) 1	**Czechoslovakia** Skuhravy 11, 62, 82,	(1) 4	23 June, Bari; 15,100
Argentina Caniggia 80	(0) 1	**Brazil**	(0) 0	24 June, Turin; 61,381

Colombia's goalkeeper was bound to play a part at some stage. René Higuita fancied himself as a character; he liked to take penalties, and he liked to stroll out of his goal and play the ball around like a seasoned *libero*. In later years he developed his scorpion kick, delighting the Wembley crowd during a friendly by launching himself forward parallel to the ground and clearing a crossfield ball with his heels. Higuita missed the next World Cup – he was in prison after playing a part – that of an unwitting dupe, it appears – in a kidnapping saga.

Here he was just silly. Posing on the ball miles out of his goal (with no cause) he stumbled over a return pass from a team-mate and gave the ball away to Roger Milla, who was in the sort of form that made a mockery of his age. Milla had already scored once, cruising past a poor challenge from the Colombian sweeper and crashing a shot in at Higuita's near post; the second goal settled the match and Colombia's response was no consolation. The Milla wiggle was competing with Schillaci's impassioned run-around as the celebration of the tournament.

Cameroon were the first African team to reach the quarter-finals, and they deserved it. The first ninety minutes of the match were dull, but they defended resolutely and showed the greater purpose in extra-time. And they had a good goalkeeper, not a circus clown.

Colombia were a big disappointment. Their captain, Carlos Valderrama, arrived with a reputation as big as his blonde afro hair, but left having made negligible impact; his fellow midfielder Freddy Rincon was more impressive – he was unlucky against Cameroon when an explosive shot cannoned off the bar to safety in normal time.

It didn't take a genius to work out that Costa Rica were weak against crosses, so the Czech coach, with his Doctorate in PE and Sports Psychology, was unlikely to miss it. Dr Venglos resigned after the tournament and took up an offer to coach Aston Villa, some time before overseas coaches became fashionable in England. He didn't understand the manic English game, and his players didn't understand his halting English – it would be down to others to cement the reputation of European managers in the English league.

Czechoslovakia hurled cross after cross into the penalty area, where Skuhravy was just the man to feed off such service. South and Central American goalkeepers tended to stay on their line and at a muscular six foot four Skuhravy was too much for the centre-backs. Costa Rica were as enterprising as ever going forward and equalised in the second half when González produced a terrific header from a free-kick, but Skuhravy put Czechoslovakia back in front a few minutes later, stooping low to cleverly turn a mishit shot into the corner. Kubik's free-kick curled into the corner with the goalkeeper (Barrantes – Conejo was injured) motionless, and Skuhravy finished his hat-trick of headers to make it four. Costa Rica had done themselves proud getting this far. It remained to be seen if Skuhravy could cause the same problems for Augenthaler, Kohler and Co.

The match between Argentina and Brazil was billed as the

heavyweight clash of the round, but the reality was a poor game between two deeply ordinary teams. Brazil should have run away with the game as they dominated possession and created half a dozen good chances in the first half-hour. The score remained nil-nil through a combination of sloppy finishing and good goalkeeping – plus a smidge of ill luck when Dunga's fine header rebounded off the post. The injury to Nery Pumpido appeared serendipitous for Argentina by the end of this game (though probably not to Pumpido). His replacement Goycochea made a series of excellent saves; one second-half effort from Alemão was right out of the top drawer.

Argentina, starved of possession, created next to nothing, but they always had Maradona, who was a threat even carrying injuries. A late run at the narrow Brazilian defence found the Brazilian right-back Jorginho awol and Caniggia running free. Maradona slipped the ball through and the blond striker rounded Taffarel and scored. Robbery, but Brazil's wounds were partly self-inflicted, the five-man defence overly cautious against a team with one forward. And surely Bebeto might have done better than Müller, whose tricks and flicks in this World Cup were an indulgence not an asset. Brazil's best attacking player was their left-back Branco, which says plenty.

WORLD CUP CLASSIC No.17
24 June, 1990, Giuseppe Meazza (San Siro), Milan; 74,559

| West Germany | (0) 2 | Klinsmann 50, Brehme 84 |
| Holland | (0) 1 | R Koeman 88 (p) |

Referee: **Juan Carlos Loustau** (Argentina)
Coaches: **Franz Beckenbauer** (West Germany) & **Leo Beenhakker** (Holland)

West Germany (4–4–2): Bodo Illgner (Cologne); Thomas Berthold (Roma), Jürgen Kohler (Bayern Munich), Klaus Augenthaler (Batern), Andreas Brehme (Internazionale); Guido Buchwald (Stuttgart), Lothar Matthäus (Cpt, Internazionale), Stefan Reuter (Bayern), Pierre Littbarski (Cologne); Rudi Völler (Roma), Jürgen Klinsmann (Internazionale). **Sub:** Karl-Heinz Riedle (Werder Bremen) 78m for Klinsmann
Holland (4–3–2–1): Hans van Breukelen (PSV Eindhoven); Berry van Aerle (PSV Eindhoven), Ronald Koeman (Barcelona), Frank Rijkaard (AC Milan), Adri van Tiggelen (Anderlecht); Jan Wouters (Ajax), Aron Winter (Ajax), Robert Witschge (Ajax); Ruud Gullit (Cpt, AC Milan), Johnny van't Schip (Ajax); Marco van Basten (AC Milan). **Subs:** Wim Kieft (PSV Eindhoven) 67m for van Aerle; Hans Gillhaus (Aberdeen) 78m for Witschge
Cautioned: Völler (WGer) 21m, Rijkaard (Hol) 21m, Wouters (Hol) 32m, van Basten (Hol) 72m, Matthäus (WGer) 77m
Dismissed: Völler (WGer) 22m (fighting); Rijkaard (Hol) 22m (fighting)

West Germany versus Holland in the second round revisited an old enmity, a rivalry more poisonous than England and Germany ever shared. The Dutch had left themselves this tricky tie by being lazy and complacent in their group, and they came into the game with a sour attitude. They still looked a good side on paper but on the field they were disjointed and out of sorts. West Germany added muscle to the midfield by pushing Buchwald further forward and bringing in Jürgen Kohler to mark Marco van Basten.

Holland had marginally the better chances in the opening twenty minutes – Winter should have done better with an header from six yards out – but the game's talking point was an incident between Frank Rijkaard and Rudi Völler. Rijkaard fouled Völler as he broke through from a deep position and was booked – he seemed to think Völler "bought" the booking and decided the best response was to spit at his opponent. Völler, bizarrely, was booked for protesting and trying to show the referee the spit in his poodle coiffure. From Brehme's free-kick for the original foul, the ball bounced through to goalkeeper van Breukelen. Völler, following up as good strikers do, had to take evasive action to avoid a collision. Van Breukelen took exception – he received the merest clip – and Rijkaard joined in, pushing and prodding Völler as he tried to get up, even grabbing his ear. Rijkaard – rightly – was dismissed for being an arse, but the referee pusillanimously evened things out by also dismissing Völler. As they started to leave the field Rijkaard spat again, voluminously, at a flabbergasted Völler.

It was that Dutch thing again. Why did Rijkaard behave that way? He was an articulate, intelligent footballer who became an articulate, intelligent coach. A spat with the arrogant, boastful Matthäus would maybe have been understandable, but Völler was the least Teutonic and most likeable of the German squad. Rijkaard did later accept responsibility and apologise to the German, and they made an advert in later years which riffed on the incident, but it was a wildly aberrant moment from a fine player and remains a blot on his otherwise hot CV. FIFA – no surprise here – chose not to act and Rijkaard escaped without the significant ban he deserved.

West Germany, and Klinsmann especially, made light of Völler's absence, while the Dutch never found any rhythm. In the second half Germany found another gear; a purposeful break from Matthäus sent Klinsmann racing down the right but his cross was fractionally over-hit and Matthäus' header was easily saved. Moments later an impressive driving run and cross from Buchwald found Klinsmann sprinting ahead of his marker to the near post; the finish, angling the ball across the goalkeeper while still at full tilt, was sumptuous. A beautifully struck long pass from Brehme found Klinsmann clear again, and the striker's instantaneous shot belted back off van Breukelen's post. At the other end Gullit, of all people, failed to get over an awkward bouncing volley. With twelve minutes to go Klinsmann left to a deserved ovation from the Germans and the neutrals – the Dutch hatred of the Germans forbade them the courtesy of acknowledging a truly epic performance. Karl-Heinz Riedle was no mean replacement, and West Germany kept looking for a second goal. They got it when Brehme turned inside and curled a peach inside the far post with his right foot – he was granted absurd amounts of space to do so, space that Rijkaard would surely have filled.

Van Basten, subdued easily by Kohler, decided a balletic dive was the order of the day and Mr Lostau completed a bad day at the office by giving an eighty-eighth-minute penalty. Ronald Koeman was as reliable as ever from the spot, but it made little difference as the Dutch lacked the urgency to mount a rousing finale.

The English press was more sympathetic to Holland than they deserved. They were the most talented team in the tournament but went home early without winning a game, a far cry from the majesty and surety of the European Championships.

Ireland	(0) 0	**Romania**	(0) 0	25 June, Genoa; 31,818
Ireland won 5–4 on penalties				
Italy	(0) 2	**Uruguay**	(0) 0	25 June, Olimpico; 73,303
Schillaci 65, Serena 83				
Yugoslavia	(0) (1) 2	**Spain**	(0) (1) 1	26 June, Verona; 34,822
Stojkovic 77, 93		Salinas 83		
Belgium	(0) (0) 0	**England**	(0) (0) 1	26 June, Bologna; 24,520
		Platt 119		

Romania sorely missed Lăcătus (suspended) in their match against the massed green ranks of Ireland. McGrath played at the front rather than behind a back four – almost a modern holding position – and neutralised Hagi. On the one occasion Hagi got a shot away Bonner made a splendid save. Ireland showed little intent but plenty of resolve, and they took five excellent penalties, while Bonner's save from Timofte made the difference. Much was made of the "heroic resistance" but the Irish were in the quarter-finals without actually winning a game, a poor reflection on the six-group system. David O'Leary dined out for years on his nerveless winning spot-kick; the veteran centre-half did seem an unusual choice for such a mission.

Italy versus Uruguay was a cautious affair between two teams who always put avoiding defeat before enterprise. Italy won because they were more purposeful in the second half and had Schillaci, who was on a hot streak and finished ruthlessly from the first clear chance the Uruguayans allowed him. Uruguay managed only one significant shot on target, and that after a howler from De Napoli; Zenga saved well from Aguilera, who seemed surprised to have a sight of goal. The Italian back four were immaculate. They still hadn't conceded a goal and their next opponents were another safety-first team, Jack Charlton's Ireland.

Yugoslavia and Spain provided the most entertaining match of the round without delivering anything spectacular. Spain were the better team in the first half as the direct, aggressive running of Michel and Martin Vázquez put the Yugoslavs on their heels. Ivkovic looked shaky in goal – he made his best save with his face from a flicked header off Michel's whipped cross. The second half started in similar manner and Martin Vázquez should have done better when a brilliant, weaving run took him through the defence – alas, he blasted his shot the wrong side of the post. Martin Vázquez looked like he should have joined the Spanish Armada not the football team with his neatly coiffured hair and beard, but the Real Madrid star had a superb game and didn't deserve to end up on the losing side. He looked a good player here, but a move to Torino in Italy stalled his progress and he won his last cap in 1992, aged only twenty-six.

Yugoslavia improved after Savicevic came on for Pancev – if only they could both have played well at the same time! – but Spain still created more. Villaroya's searching cross found Butragueño unmarked in the middle but his header came back off the post straight to the grateful Ivkovic. Sounds unlucky, but in truth the Spanish captain should have buried the header. Ivkovic made a better save from Butragueño five minutes later; he was perfectly positioned to smother the striker's shot from the edge of the area.

Moments later Yugoslavia were in front. Vujovic was strong enough to hold off Sanchis down the left and his cross was flicked on by Katanec to Stojkovic, lurking beyond the far post. Stojkovic declined the risky volley, and instead he killed the ball dead while wrong-footing the covering defender before calmly stroking the ball into the goal. Dennis Bergkamp would perform almost exactly the same piece of sublime skill in a later World Cup. No wonder Marseille had just offered £5m for Stojkovic's services.

The last thirteen minutes were played at a frantic pace in the heat. Spain shouted for a penalty when Vulic tackled Salinas in the area; significantly the only player who didn't protest was Salinas. Two minutes later the same player was well placed at the far post to tuck in the loose ball when Martin Vázquez's shot was half blocked by a defender.

Yugoslavia were back ahead three minutes into extra-time, and it was Stojkovic who scored, with another piece of brilliance, bending a twenty-five yard free-kick around the wall. Tony Gubba described the goal as "soft" and blamed the wall but he was talking nonsense – the ball swung in six or eight feet from well outside the post and gave Zubizarreta no chance. Spain were exhausted and beaten and the last half hour was full of elegant possession football from the skilful Yugoslavs, especially Savicevic, who showed some of the form that lit up Milan after a near-£10m transfer in 1992.

England made the quarter-finals with a resilient rather than convincing performance. Robson reverted to a five-man defence, who twiddled their thumbs while the Belgians tested Shilton from distance; Scifo and Ceulemans both beat the big man but saw their efforts hit the post. At the other end Barnes had one of his best England games and he and Stuart Pearce down the left caused problems for the veteran Gerets. Barnes had the ball in the net, volleying in Lineker's beautifully weighted cross but the linesman flagged offside. He was wrong; Barnes came from a yard behind the last defender.

Robson replaced McMahon, a good player for Liverpool but out of his depth here, with David Platt, who the tabloids didn't like but the proper football journalists rated. He also, mystifyingly, replaced Barnes with Steve Bull. Bull was an honest pro and a great one-club player but he was a million miles from being an international centre-forward. England had a dearth of quality forwards, but surely even an out-of-form Beardsley was a better bet. Even better would have been Alan Smith of Arsenal, only belatedly recognised as a player with the intelligence (like Sheringham) to make up for a perceived lack of pace. Smith wasn't in the squad.

As the game drifted towards extra-time Gascoigne was booked (harshly) for a foul on Scifo, who made a meal of it. In the extra half-hour England did most of the pressing, but both sides were tired and Des Walker, with both substitutes already used, finished the game as a limping passenger. Fortunately Walker on one leg was good enough to mark Claesen, who ended seven years of being the "next big thing" with another damp squib of a performance.

England had one more trick up their sleeve. With two minutes on the clock Gascoigne took a free-kick from a distinctly unpromising central position thirty-five yards out. He lofted the ball into the area beyond the Belgian back line, which was high. David Platt stole around the back, and as the ball came over his shoulder he volleyed it beyond Preud'homme. Had the finish been by a Brazilian, poems and eulogies would have followed. It was a class bit of technique and the first of twenty-seven England goals for Platt – nearly one in every two games – and he would be one of the few quality performers (add Pearce, Woods and Adams) for England over the next five years.

QUARTER-FINALS

Argentina	**(0) (0) 0**	**Yugoslavia**	**(0) (0) 0**	30 June, Florence; 38,971
Argentina won 3–2 on penalties				
Ireland	**(0) 0**	**Italy**	**(1) 1**	30 June, Olimpico; 73,303
		Schillaci		
West Germany	**(1) 1**	**Czechoslovakia**	**(0) 0**	1 July, Milan; 73,347
Matthäus 24 (p)				
England	**(1) (2) 3**	**Cameroon**	**(0) (2) 2**	1 July, Naples; 55,205
Platt 25,		Kunde 61 (p), Ekeke 65		
Lineker 83 (p), 104 (p)				

These were really bad games of football for the last eight of a World Cup Finals tournament. Yugoslavia started really well against Argentina in Florence, with the highly promising Robert Prosinecki prominent. Prosinecki was the latest star off the Red Star Belgrade production line. Red Star (they are often referred to now by their Serbian name of Crvena Zvezda) were formed at the end of the Second World War and rapidly grew to become a major, later pre-eminent force in Yugoslav and Serbian football. The year after this World Cup they became the first Balkan side to win the European Cup. Ironically that success was the beginning of the end of the club's halcyon days – within two years every single member of the line-up in the European Cup Final, ten Yugoslavs and the Romanian centre-half Belodedici, was playing in another country for more money as civil war ripped the old Yugoslavia apart.

The game turned on the half hour when Sabanadzovic was booked for fouling Maradona; it was his second yellow and off he went. Yugoslavia dug in and Argentina ventured further forward without risking exposure. Bilardo was such a cagey manager that even against ten men he stuck with his sweeper system until into the second half, when he subbed Olarticoechea, who was already booked and struggling against Stojkovic. Argentina hit the bar but Maradona was subdued and they had the bulk of possession without creating too much – the opposite of their game against Brazil. In the penalty shoot-out Stojkovic thumped his kick against the bar only for saint Diego, of all people, to surrender the initiative with a feeble effort. A poor-quality shoot-out went Argentina's way when Goycochea, who was an acrobatic goalkeeper, stopped Hadzigebic's penalty high to his left. The

Yugoslav captain Vujovic took some stick for not taking a penalty himself.

Another unremarkable game in Rome's Olympic Stadium saw Italy seal a semi-final place against Ireland. The atmosphere was intense and the Italians were playing under immense pressure. Ireland had already exceeded expectations. Nerves were settled after twenty minutes when Aldridge was dispossessed, Baggio carried the ball deep into the Irish half and Donadoni thumped a shot towards the near corner of the goal. Bonner blocked the shot effectively but the ball came back to the player Ireland least wanted it to. Toto Schillaci wasn't in the sort of form to miss an open goal, even in this cauldron. Ireland fought manfully – McGrath was outstanding again and Andy Townsend ran himself dizzy harassing the Italian midfield. But the quality wasn't there and the Italian defence dealt fairly comfortably with long angled balls into the box. Schillaci – who else? – thundered a free-kick against the bar. The ball bounced down inches from Bonner's backside and then up and out to safety. In the dying moments the Sicilian ran clear of the defence only to be called back for a very debatable offside flag. He was a yard on – just too quick for a tired and ageing defence. Ireland had done well but they hadn't actually won a game and scored only twice in five matches; the better side was in the semi-final.

West Germany against Czechoslovakia was a bit muted. The Germans were exemplary at the back and didn't give Skuhravy a sniff, but they were less exuberant going forward than in the earlier games and were grateful to Klinsmann's ability to go to ground convincingly for the penalty that won them the game. Maybe they were conserving energy for tougher tasks ahead.

England against Cameroon wasn't exactly a technical masterclass but it outdid the other three matches for excitement. The crowd in Naples saw more incident in two hours than those in Florence, Milan and Rome did in five. England set up in the same formation as against Belgium, but with Platt in for McMahon at last. If they expected Cameroon to be similarly cagey they were wrong, as the Cameroonians came at them from the off, flooding the midfield and driving England into a flat back five. They had a handful of early shots, but Shilton was off his line quickly to block Biyik when he had the best chance of the lot.

It was England who took the lead, against the run of play and with just about their first coherent attack. Butcher sent Pearce up the left for the first time and the full-back's excellent driven cross found Platt unmarked at the far post. The Villa man's finish was emphatic. The rest of the half was nip and tuck, with England a little more settled but Cameroon still dangerous – Libih missed their best chance when he headed over after he lost Des Walker.

Milla came on for his usual forty-five minutes (it ended up a longer run-out than he expected) and bought a penalty when Gascoigne carelessly brushed him in the box. It was one of those grey-area moments where no one criticises the striker for going down, although he probably could have stayed on his feet. Shilton nearly reached Emanuel Kundé's penalty but it just brushed his fingertips instead of his palms.

Cameroon created two more chances in the next few minutes as England reeled. A poor pass from Waddle let in Omam-Biyik, who set up Makanaky, who hit it into Row Z, as the cliché goes. A minute later Milla got the ball with his back to goal and was allowed to turn and slide the ball into the path of Ekeke, who got away from Platt and rocketed a shot past the exposed England goalkeeper. Ekeke had only been on the pitch three minutes. Shilton was incandescent with his central defenders, but it was through the midfield that the runners were coming. England just didn't have a good sitting midfield player in their squad since Peter Reid retired. It is a position that a succession of England coaches have failed to solve. Again, more anon.

It nearly got worse. Omam-Biyik fed Milla and took a lovely back-heeled return, stumbled, seemed to lose control, but recovered to get in another back flick, which Shilton did well to block. Then it did get worse. England had brought on Peter Beardsley for an anonymous John Barnes at half-time and then Trevor Steven to add to the midfield, sacrificing the tiring Butcher. Before they had time to work out the new formation, Mark Wright got a whack on the head from Milla and had to retreat to the wing, clearly dizzied. Parker moved into the middle and Steven was forced into service as an emergency right-back. This did England an unexpected favour – Steven's energy proved valuable, and Parker kept Milla quiet.

England looked better going forward and Gascoigne urged them on – he was a tireless runner, especially for a player who always looked a few pounds over fighting weight. A free-kick was cleared and turned back in by Parker. Wright, making a nuisance of himself, flicked the ball on and Lineker swivelled on the edge of the area and had his trailing foot caught by the defender. The England striker tucked away the penalty nervelessly. There were seven minutes to go – long enough for Shilton to be called into action again with a sprawling save from the livewire Omam-Biyik.

Omam-Biyik continued to be a threat in extra-time. Shilton had to be positioned well to save his header after Trevor Steven did wonderfully well to turn away Makanaky's initial cross, and then Biyik sauntered past England's midfield and thumped a shot past the post. It took a combination of Gascoigne and Lineker to finish it. Gascoigne picked up the loose ball when a Cameroon attack broke down, drove hard at the centre of the Cameroon defence and played a perfect ball for Lineker. Debate raged about whether N'Kono touched the England striker as he went past him, but he went down and the penalty was given. Lineker's second penalty was hard and low to the other side of the goalkeeper.

Cameroon were finally broken and England dominated the last fifteen minutes, Gascoigne showing his enormous desire with a lung-bursting run that should have led to Lineker's hat-trick only for the striker to whip his shot past the post. England were in the semi-finals but they knew they had been in a game – their goalkeeper was their Man of the Match. Cameroon deserved great credit for their campaign, some naïve and brutal defending apart.

Republic of Ireland Squad 1990:
GK: Pat Bonner (Glasgow Celtic, 30 years old, 38 caps), Gerry Peyton (Bournemouth, 34, 28)

DEF: John Byrne (Le Havre, 29, 19), Chris Hughton (Tottenham Hotspur, 30, 50), Mick McCarthy (Cpt, Millwall, 31, 42), Paul McGrath (Aston Villa, 30, 36), Kevin Moran (Blackburn Rovers, 34, 55), Chris Morris (Celtic, 26, 21), David O'Leary (Arsenal, 32, 51), Steve Staunton (Liverpool, 21, 13)
MID & WIDE: Ray Houghton (Liverpool, 28, 29), Alan McLoughlin (Swindon Town, 23, 1), Kevin Sheedy (Everton, 30, 28), John Sheridan (Sheffield Wednesday, 25, 8), Andy Townsend (Norwich City, 26, 12), Ronnie Whelan (Liverpool, 28, 38)
FWD: John Aldridge (Real Sociedad, 31, 30), Tony Cascarino (Aston Villa, 27, 21), David Kelly (Leicester City, 24, 6), Niall Quinn (Manchester City, 23, 15), Bernie Slaven (Middlesbrough, 29, 4), Frank Stapleton (Blackburn, 33, 71)

World Cup Heroes No.24

Roger Milla (1952–)

Cameroon

One of the great World Cup characters. Milla was already twenty-six when he played his first game for Cameroon in 1973. He moved to France, with Valenciennes, and then Monaco, for a season, and Bastia, where he scored the winner in the French Cup Final in 1981. He was with Bastia when Cameroon took their bow at the 1982 World Cup.

When Cameroon missed out on qualification for the 1986 Finals, Milla called it a day, and by 1990 he was in semi-retirement playing for a low-level team on the island of Réunion. Cameroon had a decent squad for the 1990 Finals, but were short of fire-power, and the story goes that the Cameroon President personally called Milla to persuade him to join the squad for one last hurrah.

Some hurrah. The old boy still had a turn of pace and could still finish, and he rattled the net twice against Romania and Colombia and caused problems for England in the quarter-final, each time coming off the bench to do late damage.

His appetite revived, Milla returned to Cameroon and played for four years for Tonnerre (Thunder) in Yaoundé, scoring as regularly as ever. He was still chipper enough to make the Cameroon squad for the 1994 World Cup, and when he scored against Russia he broke the record as the oldest goalscorer in the World Cup Finals. The previous holder of the record was himself, four years earlier!

Always smiling and popular with the media, Milla was a great advert for African football and one of its first global stars. His goal celebration, the endearing corner-flag wiggle, was used by Coca-Cola for an advertising campaign during the 2010 World Cup.

More recently, Milla has been fighting against corruption and incompetence in the administration of Cameroon football – he was dismissed from an honorary post with that august body for one outburst too many in 2012. A true entertainer, Milla has lived longer in the memory than many a better footballer.

SEMI-FINALS

Argentina		**(0) (1) 1 Italy**	**(1) (1) 1** 3 July, Naples; 59,978
Caniggia 67		Schillaci 17	

Shoot-out

Italy		Argentina	
Baresi	S 1–0	Serrizuela	S 1–1
Baggio	S 2–1	Burruchaga	S 2–2
De Agostini	S 3–2	Olarticoechea	S 3–3
Donadoni	*M 3–3*	Maradona	S 3–4
Serena	*M 3–4*		

Not a classic, but then no one expected one between these two sides. Italy had kept ten successive clean sheets and Argentina had shown they were prepared to sneak through the competition by any means possible. In this instance, it meant fouling and niggling and spoiling and slowing down the game to deny their opponents any rhythm. That and try to get the ball to Maradona, their one player capable of hurting the opposition, but he was well policed by De Agostini and De Napoli.

Before the game Maradona implored the Neapolitans to support him and Argentina instead of Italy, asserting (with some justification) that the wealthier northerners looked down on the south of the country. Maradona as working-class hero. Discuss. Imagine Messi asking the Barcelona fans to support Argentina against Spain ... actually, hang on, that isn't so far-fetched ...

Italy were much the better team in the first half and should have turned around more than one to the good. Argentina were just dirty. The goal, from you-know-who, came after Goycochea saved Vialli's shot. Vialli was back in the side but he still looked goal-shy and the omission of Baggio was odd. Argentina's equaliser came from nowhere, Olarticoechea's cross presented no apparent danger until Zenga came halfway and then backtracked, ending up nowhere when Caniggia's back header went in at the far post. Italy were far too cautious and Argentina were on top until extra-time, when both sides went into their shell and looked content to play out time, wasting plenty of it and hardly mustering a serious attempt on goal.

The shoot-out was tense but they always are. Donadoni, the best wide player in the competition, hit his kick straight at Goycochea, Maradona avoided a repetition of his feeble effort against Yugoslavia, and Serena never looked like scoring, he was fidgety and nervous before he took the kick. Why didn't Schillaci take a penalty?

Argentina would be missing four players through suspension for the final. Maradona moaned throughout the tournament about how the competition was "fixed" for Italy to win (rich coming from an Argentinian after 1978) and now he moaned about the suspensions. Every one of the yellow cards Vautrot handed out in this match was justified. Giusti was sent off for two offences – the second was worth a straight red; Olarticoechea, the least physical of the Argentinian defenders, was booked for a cynical trip, Batista for going through his man and Caniggia for deliberate handball – it was his third offence, Vautrot had been patient.

WORLD CUP CLASSIC No.18
4 July 1990, delle Alpi, Turin; 62,628

West Germany	(0) (1) 1 Brehme 59
England	(0) (1) 1 Lineker 80

Shoot-out:

England		West Germany	
Lineker	S 1–0	Brehme	S 1–1
Beardsley	S 2–1	Matthäus	S 2–2
Platt	S 3–2	Riedle	S 3–3
Pearce	*M 3–3*	Thon	S 3–4
Waddle	*M 3–4*		

Referee: **Ramiz Wright** (Brazil)
Coaches: **Bobby Robson** (England) & **Franz Beckenbauer** (West Germany)

West Germany (4–4–2): Bodo Illgner (Cologne); Thomas Berthold (Roma), Jürgen Kohler (Bayern Munich), Klaus Augenthaler (Bayern), Andreas Brehme (Internazionale); Guido Buchwald (Stuttgart), Lothar Matthäus (Cpt, Internazionale), Thomas Hässler (Cologne), Olaf Thon (Bayern); Rudi Völler (Roma), Jürgen Klinsmann (Internazionale). **Subs:** Karl-Heinz Riedle (Werder Bremen) 38m for Völler; Stefan Reuter (Bayern) 68m for Hässler
England (1–4–3–2): Peter Shilton (Derby County); Mark Wright (Derby); Paul Parker (Queens Park Rangers), Des Walker (Nottingham Forest), Terry Butcher (Cpt, Glasgow Rangers), Stuart Pearce (Nottm Forest); David Platt (Aston Villa), Paul Gascoigne (Tottenham Hotspur), Chris Waddle (Olympique Marseille); Peter Beardsley (Liverpool), Gary Lineker (Tottenham). **Sub:** Trevor Steven (Rangers) 70m for Butcher
Cautioned: Parker (Eng) 66m, Gascoigne (Eng) 99m, Brehme (WGer) 109m

The best game of the tournament by a distance, and one of the few where both sides set out to win the game from the start. England left out Barnes and brought back Beardsley, while Wright played with a head injury after his knock against Cameroon. For West Germany, Völler was back from suspension and returned for Riedle, and Hässler and Thon played instead of Bein and Littbarski. They added more energy and creativity while Matthäus kept a watchful eye on Gascoigne.

The first half was cat and mouse without being boring. Gascoigne probed away at the German reaguard, which looked secure, while Klinsmann and Völler (until he picked up a knock and had to go off) tried to stretch England to get behind the wing-backs. They struggled, largely due to the excellence of both those full-backs, Parker and Pearce. The second half continued in the same vein for a while, although West Germany showed a little more urgency and Matthäus came into the game a little more. It did seem as if it would take an error to produce a goal, but it was actually a piece of bad luck that unlocked England's defence.

Brehme's free-kick was hit hard but straight at Paul Parker, who ran to charge down the kick, and Shilton, on his six-yard box, was helpless as the ball looped up off the defender's outstretched leg and over his head.

England tried manfully to get on terms, and Gascoigne started to run past the German midfield players as Matthäus, in particular, tired. England withdrew Butcher again for Steven and went to four at the back with Waddle wide on the left. Beckenbauer added a sixth defender in Reuter in an attempt to hang on, but a momentary lapse let the Germans down. Parker crossed from the right and Kohler and Augenthaler indulged in some "after you, Jürgen, no, no, I insist, Klaus". Very un-German and the lurking Lineker wasn't a chap to refuse such largesse when offered. Extra-time beckoned – the third time in a week for England.

Extra-time served up a pulsating half-hour. Shilton saved brilliantly low down from Klinsmann's firm header as West Germany pressed, but Gascoigne and Waddle were breaking quickly at the other end. One Gascoigne run ended when he pushed the ball too far ahead and a silly lunge after it caught Berthold and brought that famous booking. Had England won, it may not have been a bad thing that Gascoigne would miss the final – he wore his heart on his sleeve, Gazza, and the Argentinians were adept at pushing buttons.

Waddle swayed into the German area in that hunched, deceptively languid way of his and unleashed a terrific cross-shot that came back off the post just out of reach of Lineker, and just after the turnaround Buchwald hit the same post with a fierce right footer. England fans were out of their seats when Platt found the net, but he was offside and knew it.

The shoot-out is burned into the consciousness of any England supporter, the first of numerous exits on penalties that haunted the team over the years. Lineker, Beardsley and Platt scored the first three, and Stuart Pearce was a regular penalty taker for Nottingham Forest and was a racing certainty to score – no wobbly legs for old Psycho. He hit the ball cleanly but straight at Illgner, who saved with his legs. When Chris Waddle spooned England's next kick over the bar they were out.

Robson was already on his way to PSV Eindhoven after the FA had given notice they were ready for a change. A terrific club manager, he never coped well with the tabloid abuse as England manager. A kind, gentlemanly sort, he could never understand journalists who arrived at England matches boasting about how their article would be the one that got the manager the boot. His tenure as manager was ordinary, and he never really discovered how to best harness his most talented players. England reached the semi-finals in Italy – beyond anyone's expectations – but they stumbled from game to game rather than orchestrate a coherent campaign. His replacement, Graham Taylor, the Watford manager, was most definitely a man with a plan. Unfortunately it wasn't a very good one.

England Squad 1990:
GK: Peter Shilton (Derby County, 40, 118), Chris Woods (Glasgow Rangers, 30, 16), David Seaman* (Queens Park Rangers, 26, 2), Dave Beasant* (Chelsea, 31, 2)
DEF: Terry Butcher (Cpt, Rangers, 31, 72), Tony Dorigo (Chelsea, 24, 3), Paul Parker (QPR, 26, 5), Stuart Pearce (Nottingham Forest, 28, 24), Gary Stevens (Rangers, 27, 39), Des Walker (Nottm Forest, 24, 18), Mark Wright (Derby, 26, 24)
MID & WIDE: John Barnes (Liverpool, 26, 53), Paul Gascoigne (Tottenham Hotspur, 23, 11), Steve Hodge (Nottm Forest, 27, 22), Steve McMahon (Liverpool, 28, 12), David Platt (Aston Villa, 23, 5), Bryan Robson (Manchester United, 33, 85), Trevor Steven (Rangers, 26, 26), Chris Waddle (Olympique de Marseille, 29, 52), Neil Webb (Man Utd, 27, 24)
FWD: Peter Beardsley (Liverpool, 29, 40), Steve Bull (Wolverhampton Wanderers, 25, 7), Gary Lineker (Tottenham, 29, 51)

THIRD-PLACE MATCH

Italy	(0) 2	England	(0) 1	7 July, Bari; 51,426
Baggio 71, Schillaci 85 (p)		Platt 81		

---

* Under new rules late replacements for injured goalkeepers were allowed and Beasant was drafted in for the injured Seaman.

A reasonably entertaining game with an appropriate ending as Schillaci signed off with the winning goal. England missed Gascoigne and gave a few of the reserves a game. Shilton signed off less happily with a rare error for Baggio's goal, but he was a truly great goalkeeper, second only to Banks in England's history, and a close second at that. David Platt ended a tournament of great promise with a header from a left wing cross – a near replica of his goal against Cameroon, but this time the provider was Tony Dorigo of Chelsea, given a run-out in place of the despondent Pearce.

World Cup Heroes No.25

Salvatore "Toto" Schillaci (1964–)

Italy

Some players enjoy fabulous club careers but don't deliver when it comes to the big international tournaments. Others emerge from a cocoon of ordinariness to make the most of their big day out. Toto Schillaci is firmly in the latter category.

Schillaci was twenty-five years old at the start of the 1990 World Cup and had a solitary cap to his name. Ahead of him in the queue to play were Andrea Carnevale, Gianluca Vialli, hailed as the best Italian striker since Luigi Riva, and Roberto Baggio, the young, gifted ball-player from Fiorentina. Very much fourth in line was the bricklayer's son, Schillaci, selected on the back of a successful first season in *Serie A* with Juventus.

Juve had fallen on hard times after dominating the eighties, and were trying to get back on terms with the Milan giants and the new pretenders, Maradona's Napoli. They had turned to Schillaci after impressive performances for Messina, the Sicilian *Serie B* side. Schillaci had played for Messina since he was a teenager, despite his allegiance to the rival city, Palermo, where he was born. Very definitely a boy from the wrong side of the tracks – Schillaci's brother was arrested for thieving during the tournament – the striker was a very different type of Italian from the chic urban northerners Vialli and Baggio. His playing style was very different, too, more direct and aggressive than his skilful compatriots.

With Italy struggling for goals and Carnevale blotting his copybook, Schillaci got his opportunity and repaid his coach with a series of exciting performances and, more importantly, goals. His impassioned, raised fist, mad-eyed goal celebrations made him an instant folk hero in Italy, and the undoubted star of the tournament. He scored in very game he started and all but one in which he got on the pitch, finishing as winner of the Golden Boot with six goals. In a sterile and low-scoring tournament he was a breath of fresh air.

Schillaci lost form as quickly as he found it, struggling at Juventus and never cementing a place at Inter. He played only eight more games for Italy and scored only one more goal. At thirty years old Schillaci became the first Italian international to move to the J-League in Japan, where he rediscovered his goal touch for Jubilo Iwata.

WORLD CUP FINAL No.14
8 July 1990, Olimpico, Rome; 73,603

Argentina	(0) 0	
West Germany	(0) 1	Brehme 84 (p)

Referee: **Edgardo Codesal** (Mexico)
Coaches: **Carlos Bilardo** (Argentina) & **Franz Beckenbauer** (West Germany)

Argentina (4–4–1–1): Sergio Goycochea (Millionaros); José Serrizueal (River Plate), Roberto Sensini (Udinese), Juan Simón (Boca Juniors), Oscar Ruggeri (Real Madrid), Nestór Lorenzo (Bari); Pedro Troglio (Lazio), Jorge Burruchaga (Nantes), José Basualdo (Stuttgart); Diego Maradona (Cpt, Napoli); Gustavo Dezotti (Cremonese). **Subs:** Pedro Monzón (Independiente) 45m for Ruggeri; Gabriel Calderón (Paris St Germain) 53m for Burruchaga
West Germany (4–4–2): Bodo Illgner (Cologne); Thomas Berthold (Roma), Jürgen Kohler (Bayern Munich), Klaus Augenthaler (Bayern), Andreas Brehme (Internazionale); Guido Buchwald (Stuttgart), Lothar Matthäus (Cpt, Internazionale), Thomas Hässler (Cologne), Pierre Littbarski (Cologne); Rudi Völler (Roma), Jürgen Klinsmann (Internazionale). **Sub:** Stefan Reuter (Bayern) 73m for Klinsmann
Cautioned: Dezotti (Arg) 5m, Völler (WGer) 52m, Troglio (Arg) 84m, Maradona (Arg) 88m
Dismissed: Monzón (Arg) 65m, Dezotti (Arg) 87m

Because it's a World Cup Final we're expected to give it due respect with a full report, blow by blow. But the heart's not in it. So begins Cris Freddi's account of the 1990 Final. Amen to that.

An awful, awful game was won by the less deplorable of the two teams. Look on the internet at some of the feeds and a huge conspiracy theory exists amongst Argentinian fans that they were "robbed" of this World Cup. How deluded can you get? They spoiled and fouled their way to the final via two penalty shoot-outs and showed no enterprise or attacking desire throughout the tournament. Finally they came across a team who were just as versed in (rather different) dark arts and it's a conspiracy. The Italian crowd certainly showed no mercy, heckling Maradona for his comments before the Italy match and, less forgivably, whistling the Argentinian anthem.

If you want statistics to back up my assertion that Argentina were nowhere near the best side in this competition, here are some:

Argentina	Played 7	Won 2	Drew 3	Lost 2	Goals 5–4
England	Played 7	Won 3	Drew 3	Lost 1	Goals 8–6
Italy	Played 7	Won 6	Drew 1	Lost 0	Goals 10–2
Argentina	Played 7	Won 5	Drew 2	Lost 0	Goals 15–5

The prosecution rests, your honour.

Having played really well to reach the final the Germans decided a bit of gamesmanship was in order to get the Argentinians going, so Klinsmann, Völler, Hässler and the rest started rolling and writhing. It worked a treat. This Argentina side was much more suited to a fight than a game of football so they responded with hacking and spitting and threats. Maradona was lucky to escape censure for an elbow on Buchwald, who went down as if poleaxed. For those of you who don't remember him, Guido Buchwald was six foot two and built like the proverbial brick privy. It's a miracle Maradona could reach his face, let alone damage it. Minutes later came Monzón's tackle on Klinsmann that led to the first red card. It was late and a bit reckless but was probably a yellow by the day's standards. The reason Codesal, the Mexican referee, gave it was Klinsmann's reaction. You may be familiar with the infamous spear tackle in rugby; this is when a player tackles an onrushing opponent and upends him to land him on his head. Very dangerous and very frowned upon. Here Klinsmann spear-tackled himself, with a spectacular somersault and expertly cushioned shoulder landing. No wonder he was hurt, most people would kill themselves attempting such a manoeuvre. Monzón was the first player to be sent off in a World Cup Final.

The ITV commentary with Brian Moore and Ron Atkinson is hilarious – check it out. Talk about sour grapes after the England defeat. They just get the whole scenario wrong. Yes, the Monzón sending off was harsh, but they then claim Codesal gets the penalty decision wrong seven minutes from time. Völler went down easily but Sensini's challenge was late and he got a lot more of Völler than N'Kono had of Lineker. Argentina protested for a full three minutes and Brehme was spat at while he waited to take the kick. Undeterred he put it in the corner out of Goycochea's reach. Brehme took free-kicks and corners with his left foot, but penalties with his right. Odd.

Two minutes later the ITV boys are up in arms again. Kohler hangs on to the ball after conceding a throw and earns severe opprobrium from Upright Ron. Sympathy is forthcoming for the Argentinian who "tried to get the ball off him". For goodness sake, Dezotti grabbed Kohler round the throat and pulled him backwards! And he had already been booked. The old sourpusses were still moaning about the Germans until the end. Fellers, you were talking claptrap, the team that won was the only one who played football throughout the tournament.

Maradona was booked for a teary protest – at least two other Argentinians should have walked for manhandling the referee. All the bitterness and bile that had tainted their football for twenty years came to a head in this match. The paranoia and conviction they stood alone against the world was manifest and ugly and I am not alone in rejoicing they didn't win this tournament. And I would admit to a touch of *schadenfreude* (an appropriately German expression); Maradona was a genius, an extravagant talent, but he was also a cheat, and it's nice when cheats get their come-uppance.

World Cup Heroes No.26
Rudi Völler (1960–)
West Germany

The German team of the 1980s and 1990s were not an especially loveable bunch. Even my friend Ulrich acknowledges this in *Tor!* Rummenigge, Matthäus, even the engagingly articulate Klinsmann, they all put people's backs up. Rummenigge was just a little too Teutonic, too blond, Matthäus too full of himself and the sound of his own voice, Klinsmann a little too knowing and too expert with the diving and gamesmanship. The rest of the team were, by and large, athletic, powerful men with big thighs and limitless stamina, unsmiling and professional and not . . . you know . . . loveable.

The exception was Rudi Völler. A genial, engaging man, he expressed himself well on the pitch and off. He was a tough player who took his share of kicks and bumps without complaining too much – except where Frank Rijkaard was involved. He smiled when he scored and played with the freedom of a volunteer not a conscript.

Völler's partnership with Klinsmann was dynamic. Both players liked to move across the line and take up wide positions, and they would swap sides regularly, making them hard to pick up. The movement and speed of thought was exceptional, and Völler's control and ability to pick a pass was a great foil for Klinsmann's pace and directness.

Völler represented West Germany in two World Cups, 1986 and 1990, and reunified Germany as a wily thirty-four-year-old in 1994 – although defeat in that tournament was a less than happy ending. He reached two finals. In 1986 he scored as a substitute as West Germany roared back into the game with Argentina. In the rematch in 1990 he played the full ninety minutes, but spent most of it looking on as a bemused spectator while the referee lost control of a tempestuous game.

Völler's performances in 1986 earned him a big-money move to *Serie A* with AS Roma, after his years with Werder Bremen brought him tantalisingly close to the *Bundesliga* title, but only as far as second; Bremen finally won the title the year after Völler left. From Roma he went to Olympique Marseille, where he played in the 1993 European Cup-winning side. The club was later stripped of their French league title after their part in a bribery scandal and sent down a division, so Völler went back to Germany with unfashionable Bayer Leverkusen.

Perhaps partly because he never played for one of the big city clubs (especially Bayern Munich, who were loathed elsewhere), Völler was popular with crowds across the whole of the country – a good comparison in England would be the respect in which Chelsea's Gianfranco Zola was always held by opposing fans.

Völler played his last international at the 1994 World Cup, and packed in completely two years later. He finished with forty-seven international goals – behind only Gerd Müller at the time. Appropriately Klinsmann finished four years later on the same total and only Miroslav Klose has gone past them since.

At every ground Völler played in the second half of that last 1995–96 season he was cheered as his name announced by both sets of fans, and after his last game saw Leverkusen avoid relegation, the opposing captain, his former German team-mate Andreas Brehme, walked to the halfway line, raised Völler's hand and led him around the ground to a standing ovation.

In 2000 Völler was handed the job as coach of the national team without any club experience. He had the worst squad in living memory to handle and suffered the indignity of a mauling by England and near failure to qualify for the 2002 World Cup before rousing the team to exceed expectations and reach the final. A dismal showing at the 2004 European Championships saw Völler replaced by his former strike partner Jürgen Klinsmann. Even when Völler memorably lost his rag with a journalist during a 2003 interview the German public supported him. Beckenbauer, Rummenigge, Matthäus, Breitner, Klinsmann; they were all better footballers than Rudi Völler, but none of them was . . . you know . . . loveable.

Team of the Tournament, 1990:

Shilton (England)
Bergomi (Italy)   McGrath (Ireland   Kohler (West Germany)   Olarticoechea (Argentina)
Donadoni (Italy)   Matthäus (West Germany)   Gascoigne (England)   Omam-Biyik (Cameroon)
Klinsmann (West Germany)   Schillaci (Italy)

Supersub: Milla (Cam)

Official Team of the Tournament: Goycochea and **Conejo** were jointly given the nod – both were flawed but spectacular as opposed to Shilton's reassuring competence. The official team had **Maldini**, **Brehme** and **Baresi** at the back – a sweeper and two left-backs. Hmmm. Both the Italian defenders were excellent but both played better against superior opposition four years later; the non-inclusion of McGrath, the best defender in the tournament, is laughable. The official team included **Maradona** – of course it did. His contribution was fitful and occasional, his team's progress down more to sharp defending and sackfuls of luck than his genius. Omam-Biyik was outstanding; he showed amazing energy levels and was the heartbeat of Cameroon's midfield.

Leading scorers: Schillaci (6); Skuhravy (5); Michel, Milla, Matthäus & Lineker (4)

Heaven Eleven No.11

Argentina

Coach:
César Luis Menotti

Goalkeepers:
Ubaldo Fillol: World Cup winner, widely regarded as Argentina's best ever
Sergio Goycochea: great shot-stopper and penalty stopper – less fond of crosses
Antonio Roma: solid 'keeper behind the 1966 defence

Defenders:
Julio Olarticoechea: cultured left-back and winner in 1986
Daniel Passarella: captain of the 1978 winning team, thighs like steel girders
José Luis Brown: heroic sweeper from 1986, discarded prematurely
Oscar Ruggeri: big, no-nonsense stopper from the Maradona era
Javier Zanetti: quick, alert full-back – played about a million games for Inter and they don't appreciate bad defenders
Silvio Marzolini: lightning-quick attacking left-back from the '60s
Roberto Perfumo: one of the less scary members of the '60s team, captain in 1974

Midfield & wide:
Diego Maradona: himself
Antonio Rattin: a tall commanding defensive midfield player, not one to mess with
Néstor Rossi: first great midfielder of the post-war years
Jorge Burruchaga: Maradona's lieutenant
Juan Román Riquelme: great playmaker who never quite made the mark he should at international level
Javier Mascherano: stubborn midfielder, neat and aggressive, can play at the back
Osvaldo Ardiles: ball-carrier and prompter, World Cup winner in 1978
Juan Sébastian Verón: undervalued in England, terrific in Italy

Strikers:
Lionel Messi: unplayable on his day, may yet deliver on the biggest stage in 2014
Gabriel Batistuta: rabbit killer
Luis Artime: gifted artiste in a vicious side in the 1960s
Mario Kempes: taking his overall career not an all-time great but a wow in 1978
Carlos Tévez: awkward customer for managers and defenders alike

Omissions: Hernán Crespo had his moments up front, as did Kempes' strike partner **Leopoldo Luque**. **Ariel Ortega** was an exciting attacking midfield player in the Maradona mould. **Diego Simeone** was a knowing and much-capped enforcer around the turn of the century, while **Sergio Batista** was a willing runner alongside Maradona and Burruchaga. **Juan Pablo Sorín** was a terrific wing-back but Argentina are over-stocked there, while **Pablo Aimar** never quite matched his early promise as a dashing winger. The jury is still out on the likes of **Higuaín** and **di María**.

Likely first XI:

Fillol

Zanetti Ruggeri Passarella Marzolini

Ardiles Rattin Verón

Maradona

Messi Batistuta

6.6 WORLD CUP MOVIES

Sports movies are terribly hit and miss, mostly miss. Most don't have the budget or expertise to film credible sport scenes. Most of them, especially if Hollywood producers get their hands on them, present a sentimental and distorted view of the sport they purport to portray.

There have been a handful of films based around the World Cup (and probably a few more I haven't seen). Here are the small few I found worth watching.

Africa United (2010) dir: Deborah Gardner-Paterson
The story of four children who make a journey across half the African continent from Rwanda to Johannesburg for the 2010 World Cup Final. The film is warm-hearted but still throws a few punches about the plight of children and the threat of AIDS in Africa. 7/10

The Game of Their Lives (2005) dir: David Ansbaugh
The story of the players who made up the USA squad that unexpectedly beat England in the 1950 World Cup Finals. Again, a wee bit sentimental, but not too cloyed with Hollywood saccharine, although it fails to follow up with the story of how Haitian Joe Gaetjens was neglected and left to die in poverty. Director Ansbaugh had previous success with sports movies as the director of *Hossiers* (basketball) and *Rudy* (American football). 6.5/10

La Gran Final (*The Great Match*) (2006) dir: Gerardo Olivares
Released in time for the 2005 Finals, Olivares' engaging movie follows three groups of people (Amazon Indians, Mongolian

tribesmen and North African tuareg nomads) attempting to travel 500 km each to find a TV so they can watch the 2002 World Cup Final. Some great photography and stand-out moments, even if a little far-fetched and simplistic. 7/10

The Miracle of Berne (Das Wunder von Bern) (2003) dir: Sönke Wortmann
An excellent account of West Germany's victory in the 1954 World Cup Final seen through the eyes of a young boy and his ex-POW father. A little bit sentimental but also an interesting study of post-war Germany and the way that unexpected victory changed the mood of a nation. 7.5/10

Offside (2006) dir: Jafar Panahi
Iranian film about a young girl who disguises herself as a boy in order to watch the 2006 World Cup qualifying match between Iran and Bahrain. Laugh-out-loud funny in parts, censorious about the attitudes that make football matches male-only in many Islamic countries. Panahi filmed two endings to cover both possible outcomes to the match, which was a real event. 8/10

Sixty Six (2006) dir: Paul Weiland
Really sweet period piece about a young Jewish boy in London in 1966 who has the misfortune to have his Bar Mitzvah on the same day as the World Cup Final. Helena Bonham-Carter (that well-known Jewish actress) and Eddie Marsan are terrific as the parents and Gregg Sulkin magnificent as the put-upon Bernie. 7/10

Beyond this the only advice I can offer is to avoid any football film endorsed or made with the co-operation of or approved by FIFA. And avoid watching *Zidane;* slow-motion footage of a man spitting a lot is not art, it's just unhygienic.

GLOBALISATION

7.1 WOMEN'S WORLD CUP

The next soccer World Cup to take place after Italia '90 was the inaugural FIFA Women's World Cup in 1991. I use the word soccer in deference to the United States, who were the competition's first winners. The tournament was the brainchild of João Havelange (or more likely one of his underlings), who was the head of FIFA at the time. FIFA were determined to have control over the premier women's football tournament, after China had experimented with an international competition (on an invitation only basis) in 1988.

For this first tournament in China twelve teams competed in the Finals; three from Asia (the hosts, China, Chinese Taipei and Japan), five from Europe (the most successful teams from the first European Championships, held earlier the same year) and one each from Oceania, South America, Africa and North/Central America.

The USA were clear favourites for the first edition. The women's game was well established in the USA with roots much deeper than the men's game and less likelihood that prime athletes would be lost to American football, basketball or baseball – all bastions of male domination.

The competition was expected to come from China and the north European teams, and so it proved, with the three Scandinavian sides and Germany joining the hosts, Taipei, the USA and Italy in the quarter-finals. The expected winners of these games all prevailed, the hosts going down by a single goal against Sweden, much to the disappointment of the organisers and the locals.

The stars of the women's game at the time were the experienced American forwards Carin Jennings and Michelle Akers, along with the captain April Heinrichs and the young teenage star Mia Hamm. All except Heinrichs went on to make over 100 appearances for the US women's team – Hamm reached a staggering 275. (Worth noting here that most senior women's fixtures were internationals, there was little organised league football.) Akers finished as top scorer (she netted five against Taipei in the quarter-final), while Jennings was voted the best player in the tournament. Two other youngsters stood out, both of whom are now viewed as greats of the women's game; the German midfielder Bettina Wiegmann and the Chinese striker Sun Wen.

Wiegmann scored for Germany in the semi-final, as did Germany's best striker, Heidi Mohr, but Jennings scored a hat-trick and Heinrichs chipped in with two as the USA won easily, 5–2. Norway won the all-Scandinavian semi-final equally easily, beating Sweden 4–1.

Linda Medalen, Norway's biggest star, equalised Michelle Akers opener for the USA in the final, in front of an official crowd of over 60,000 in Guangzhou. Akers added a second twelve minutes from time and Norway couldn't find a response.

The second tournament in 1995 was held in Sweden and the line-up was very nearly as-you-were, with only three different qualifiers. Asia lost a place as the contest was held in Europe, so North America got a second and Canada effectively replaced Taipei. Australia qualified ahead of New Zealand and this time all the European participants were from the north of the continent as England replaced Italy in the Finals. England's best players were the veteran captain Gillian Coultard, midfielder Hope Powell and the Doncaster Belles forward Karen Walker. Powell later became team manager and also served as manager of the side that played under the GB banner at the 2012 London Olympics. The 1995 side also included Clare Taylor, who was a member of the England side that won the 1993 Women's Cricket World Cup.

In the group stage Norway, the United States and China looked the most impressive; England beat Nigeria and Canada (just) but could make no impression on a rock-solid Norwegian defence. Concerns that England weren't at the level of the very top sides were confirmed when they were brushed aside by Germany in the quarter-finals. China got their revenge on Sweden, knocking the Scandinavians out of their own competition just as Sweden did them four years earlier. The USA remained the favourites; Akers and Hamm were back, and, although Jennings had gone, the competition saw the emergence of Kristine Lilly as a driving force. Lilly was destined to become professional football's most-capped player of either sex with 352 appearances between 1987 and 2010.

The USA got a shock in the semi-final when they were shut out by that iron Norwegian defence. Norway conceded one goal in the tournament and that a late consolation for Denmark in the quarter-final, and they kept quality forwards such as Walker, Akers and Mohr subdued. The defence included twins Anna and Nina Nymark Andersen. Ann Kristin Aarønes scored the decisive goal after ten minutes (she finished as tournament top scorer), while a late strike from Wiegmann was enough to see Germany past China and into the final. The final followed the same pattern. Germany saw a lot of the ball but couldn't get through and goals from Hege Riise, the player of the tournament, and Marianne Pettersen meant Norway were the second world champions.

The third competition, in 1999, was held in the United States, and the US media machine meant it was easily the most high-profile women's competition to date. Three years earlier women's football had started at the Olympic Games, and FIFA were determined not to be upstaged. The number of combatants was increased to sixteen and England were the only side to appear in 1995 but not in 1999; Italy were back in, and Russia, Mexico, Ghana and North Korea were added to the mix.

The USA, the Olympic champions, dominated their group, as did Norway, the holders, and China, Olympic silver medallists. The other group was closer and headed by Brazil, making their presence felt for the first time. This condemned group runners-up Germany to a tough quarter-final against the USA, which they only just lost, the US coming back from 2–1 down at half-time. American defender Brandi Chastain scored at both ends – she was to emerge as one of the tournament's stars.

The Americans had too much experience for Brazil in the semi-final, and China tore apart a Norwegian side that was nowhere near as tight as in 1995. The final was an anti-climax, a rather tense game with few chances – the USA were wary of Sun Wen's skill and pace, and the Chinese side were a counter-attacking team. The Chinese kept a tight watch on Mia Hamm, by now the game's leading player, and the best passer of the ball and football brain the women's game had seen. The game came down to a penalty shoot-out and it was up to Chastain to score the winning penalty kick. The tabloids, who had barely given the tournament an inch of coverage, were more than happy to print the picture of the delighted goalscorer whirling her shirt around her head.

China were due to host the 2003 Finals, but the SARS outbreak caused a hasty switch to the USA, the best equipped to deal with the problem at such short notice. The usual suspects turned up. Europe lost a place to accommodate the disappointed original hosts alongside newbies South Korea. Still no England, no Italy again and no Denmark for the first time, but France took their bow in the Finals, as did Argentina and South Korea at the expense of Mexico.

The United States were the favourites again, even though Norway pipped them to the Olympic title in Sydney in 2000. Germany and China were both contenders and Brazil were still improving.

Brazil had the precocious talents of seventeen-year-old Marta at their disposal, the heir apparent to Hamm as the world's leading player, but they were still less focused as a team than the Europeans and were edged out by a disciplined Sweden side in the last eight. Both Germany and the USA had a prolific goalscorer and Abby Wambach got the only goal of the game as the US beat Norway, while Birgit Prinz scored twice as the Germans overwhelmed Russia. A young Canadian team sprang the competition's biggest surprise, eliminating China with captain Charmaine Hooper's early goal. Canada took the lead in their semi-final, too, but Sweden found two late goals. The USA lost 3–0 to Germany, but the game, which many felt featured the best two teams, and is regarded as one of the classic of the women's game, was tight right until the end. Germany scored twice on the break in injury-time as the USA threw caution to the wind, and would face Sweden in the final.

Germany, with Wiegmann, a veteran now, as captain and the powerful Renate Lingor alongside her, were worthy tournament winners, but it took extra-time to see off a hard-working Sweden team, who had their own superstar now in Hanna Ljungberg. Ljungberg gave them the lead just before half-time when she outpaced the German defence, but the Germans scored immediately after the break through Maren Meinert, persuaded out of retirement to play in the tournament. Substitute Nia Künzer scored the decisive goal in the eight minute of extra-time, a powerful header from Lingor's long free-kick.

In 2007, China were given the chance to host the tournament, after missing out in 2003. There were, as usual, few changes in the make-up of the contestants. England made their second appearance and Denmark were also back – out went France and Russia.

The groups were a little closer than in previous tournaments, suggesting some of the also-rans were catching up a little. Only Brazil won all three games, including an impressive 4–0 demolition of China; the Chinese were not as good as in previous years but they were no pushover. The USA were surprisingly held to a draw by North Korea, Norway were held by Australia, and England got a very creditable 0–0 draw with Germany, especially so after a shaky first match which saw them draw 2–2 with Japan – both England goals scored by their star player, Kelly Smith. A thrashing of Argentina saw them through in second place.

Normal service was resumed in the semi-finals as the four top seeds all prevailed. England held the USA until half-time but three second half goals finished them off. Norway edged out China, Germany cruised past North Korea and Brazil edged out Australia 3–2 with a late Cristiane goal after they carelessly let a two-goal lead slip.

It was no surprise when Germany beat Norway rather easily – they looked an awesome unit, and were yet to concede a goal. Brazil beating the Olympic Champions, the United States, was a bit more of a shock, Shannon Boxx's sending off, while harsh, was irrelevant as Brazil were already three-up by half-time. Marta was simply wonderful, a bag of tricks and sashays and slaloms – she scored twice to end the tournament as top scorer and Golden Ball winner as best player. But even Marta's genius was not enough against the machine that was the German defence and Birgit Prinz's clinical second half finish from her first real chance of the game sent the German on their way; Simone Laudehr added a late second.

In 2011 the Women's World Cup came back to Europe for only the second time, to Germany, with the final earmarked for the Commerzbank Arena (formerly Waldstadion), home of Eintracht Frankfurt.

Asia lost a place in 2011 and it was China who surprisingly missed out for the first time, leaving a fast-improving Japanese side and an athletic Aussie team to lead the way for the continent. Mexico got the spare place, and Colombia and Equatorial Guinea made their debuts at the expense of Argentina and Ghana. France qualified from the European zone, not Denmark; England appeared in successive Finals tournaments for the first time.

The favourites were the usual ones; the USA were the Olympic champions, Germany the holders and European Champions and Brazil still had the unfettered brilliance of Marta.

Germany won all their group games but they did actually let in goals, which gave the other sides hope. The German squad was getting on a wee bit, and they had lost Lingor to retirement; she had been a powerhouse in their winning sides of 2003 and 2007.

England topped their group; a disappointing draw with Mexico was followed by a narrow win against New Zealand courtesy of Jessica Clarke's late winner and an excellent 2–0 victory over Japan. Brazil and Sweden topped the other two groups, Sweden with a terrific 2–1 in over the United States.

It is the fate of English football teams to lose in the quarter-finals, and the women are no different from the men in that regard, nor are they any better at winning penalty shoot-outs. Veteran defender Faye White had the misfortune to miss the crucial spot-kick against France. France, a much-improved side, did well against the USA in their semi; the game was 1–1 until the last ten minutes when the prolific Abby Wambach and new star Alex Morgan scored two goals in three minutes to settle the tie.

The USA had squeezed past Brazil in the previous round in another classic. Lauren Cheney gave the USA the lead but Marta equalised from the penalty spot after Rachel Buehler hauled her back and earned a red card for doing so. Marta's first penalty was saved superbly by Hope Solo (what a fantastic name!!), but the Australian referee ordered the kick retaken for encroachment and Marta made no second mistake. With two minutes of extra-time gone, things looked bad for the USA as they found themselves a goal down. A cross from the left found the US defence appealing for offside instead of concentrating, and Marta snuck in to hit a clever volley across Solo and in off the far post. The USA never gave up and in extra-time of extra-time Wambach secured legend status when she beat the goalkeeper to a deep cross and sent the contest into a penalty shoot-out. Daiane missed her kick for Brazil and Ali Krieger scored the last and decisive fifth penalty of an excellent set of kicks from the USA.

Karina Maruyama's goal in extra-time put paid to the hosts as a resilient Japanese defence kept them at bay. Japan's fourth place in the Olympics in 2008 had served notice they were improving and the three years since had seen them come on still further. Two goals from Nahomi Kawasumi, one a brilliant lob from nearly forty yards out, helped Japan see off Sweden 3–1 in the semi-final.

The final was a close match played at a furious tempo – there had been a general shift to faster more physical game throughout women's football in the twenty-first century. In an even first half, the Americans were more direct and purposeful but the Japanese were neat and kept their shape – their captain and midfield general looked the best player in the tournament. The USA started the second half better, with more threat now that Morgan was on to partner Wambach. The whippet-like youngster had already hit the post before she put the USA in the lead, running on to Rapinoe's through ball and drilling home. Japan equalised with ten minutes to go when Buehler and Krieger made a mess of clearing a cross and Aya Miyama accepted the easy pickings on offer.

Just before half-time in extra-time it seemed as if Wambach had done it for the second game running; a natural poacher she was in the perfect position to convert Morgan's cross after another great run from the young substitute. This time it was the Americans' turn to suffer late heartbreak; there were three minutes left when Sawa, appropriately enough, made the scores level again, cleverly flicking home a corner at the near post.

There was still drama to come. In time added on in extra-time Iwashimizu brought down the rampant Morgan on the edge of the area and was sent off. The danger was cleared and it was yet another penalty shoot-out for the USA. This time their nerves failed them. Boxx and Carli Lloyd, who both scored against Brazil, missed their kicks, and only Wambach of four US takers managed to score. Japan were the unexpected World Champions. The same two teams played out another tense final the following year at the London Olympics, but a late Japan charge was not quite enough and the USA turned the tables with a 2–1 victory to win their third consecutive Olympic title.

It is a moot point which tournament is the pinnacle of the women's game. For a game that isn't just about money, unlike the men's game, it would be nice if the Olympics could somehow become the ultimate goal of women's soccer. Not that FIFA would ever let that happen.

In 2011 Canada was chosen as the host country for the 2015 tournament. The only competition was from Zimbabwe, but that was withdrawn before a vote could be taken. Zimbabwe. Hmm. About as appropriate as electing, let's see . . . Qatar, maybe, as the host for the men's World Cup. That would just be madness, wouldn't it? Plain daft?

7.2 WORLD CUP 1994

There was a lot of curmudgeonly old world whingeing about the award of the World Cup to the USA in 1994. The truth was it was the turn for a non-European host and of the three candidates the USA had by far the best infrastructure; the delegates weren't quite ready for Morocco and the Brazilian bid was a bit of a shambles – they polled only two votes to Morocco's seven and the United States' ten. In return for the privilege of hosting the competition, the US promised to establish a professional league, a bargain that was kept with the launch of Major League Soccer in 1996. The stadia were excellent and the crowds plentiful and enthusiastic if occasionally ignorant of nuance; there were conspicuously more families and youngsters than would be seen at a World Cup game in Europe. The World Cup attracted average crowds way in excess of any previous tournament – the total number of spectators exceeded the total at the four subsequent tournaments, all of which had thirty-two teams in the Finals rather than the twenty-four that turned up in the US. And there was a legacy of sorts; as well as the MLS there was a significantly higher level of interest in the game amongst American youngsters. The challenge now is not to lose the best young players to other sports.

On the downside the gimmickry and glitter that inevitably surrounded an American sporting occasion spilled over into some really bad decisions. Some of the stadia chosen were entirely inappropriate, given the availability of hundreds of high-capacity sports grounds in this vast and wealthy country. Some of the owners of those grounds weren't above pricing themselves out of a deal or simply rejecting the notion of a soccer tournament on their hallowed turf.

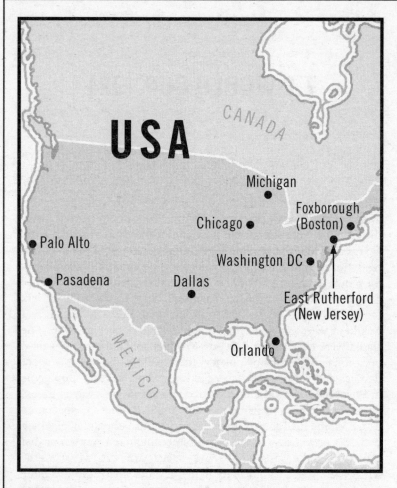

1994
UNITED STATES

The USA was ideally equipped to host a World Cup, with a number of vast sports arenas already in existence. With soccer not being such a big deal in the USA, however, there was a reluctance to commit capital to renovations and so some of the grounds were not as impressive as the freshly built stadia offered by other host countries.

Pasadena, California: Rose Bowl
A famous old California landmark, the Rose Bowl is the home of the annual

College Football bowl game – American football, that is. Any complaints about its ramshackle appearance should be weighed against the 90,000-plus spectators the ground accommodated for all six of the games played there in the 1994 finals, even the irrelevant third-place play-off.

Palo Alto, California: Stanford Stadium
The other West Coast ground was the 85,000 capacity stadium in Stanford, Palo Alto (home of the great research university). The football stadium was adapted for the 1994 World Cup and later knocked down and rebuilt without its original athletics track.

Michigan: Pontiac Silverdome
The Silverdome is a multi-sports arena built in the 1970s principally for the Detroit Lions gridiron franchise. The record attendance was over 93,000, but that was for Pope John Paul II, not a sporting event.

Chicago, Illinois: Soldier Field
With a capacity of just over 60,000, Soldier Field is small for a US gridiron stadium, but is the oldest extant venue, and has been the home to the Chicago Bears since 1971.

Foxborough (Boston), Massachussetts: Foxboro Stadium
The Foxboro was built in the 1970s as home to the New England Patriots, but it was knocked down in 2002 (replaced by the Gillette Stadium) and is now an outdoor shopping mall.

Washington DC: Robert F Kennedy Memorial Stadium
The RFK was opened in 1961 as the home of the Washington Redskins, but they left in 1996 and the stadium is now the home of the Major League Soccer team, D.C. United. It is a frequently used venue for the US national team as support is high for soccer in the area.

East Rutherford, New Jersey: Giants Stadium
One of America's most evocative sporting arenas was finally closed in 2010 and replaced with a new purpose-built ground on an adjacent site. The ground was home at times to both the New York Jets and the New York Giants, two of the big names in gridiron. The Giants Stadium was awash with colour and ex-pats for the clash between Italy and Ireland in 1994.

Dallas, Texas: The Cotton Bowl
Another 90,000 capacity stadium, this time in the heart of Texas, was host to the famous college bowl game that gave it the name. The bowl has no major tenant, but hosts innumerable one-off matches and annual fixtures and major events.

Orlando, Florida: The Citrus Bowl
Similar in usage to the Cotton Bowl, the Citrus Bowl hosted five games in the 1994 finals and was at or near capacity for all of them, even though they were unglamorous fixtures.

Normally so good at the glitz, the United States gave us a ghastly, saccharine-tasting opening show. Jon Secada sang on like a trooper after dislocating his shoulder when a trapdoor malfunctioned, Whoopi Goldberg tripped without a defender in sight and Diana Ross missed an open goal from a few feet with a plastic football, no goalkeeper and a collapsible net, which went on ahead and collapsed anyway as the Munchkins sang in celebration of a goal that wasn't. Kill me, kill me now, please, before I have to watch any more.

Qualifying

There was some sensational stuff in the qualifying competition, some more noteworthy than anything the Finals offered.

Without the USA, who automatically qualified as hosts, Mexico had an even easier stroll than usual through to the Finals. Canada went through to a complicated play-off scenario, where they were beaten on penalties by Australia after both sides won their home match 2–1. Australia still had a hurdle to overcome, and it was high one, taking on the fourth placed South American team, who, rather surprisingly, happened to be Argentina. Argentina had won the Copa América twice since the last World Cup Finals, but they didn't carry that form into the qualifiers. Defeat in Colombia and a stale 0–0 draw at home to Paraguay left the team that reached three of the last four World Cup Finals needing to win their last home game against Colombia in Buenos Aires.

WORLD CUP SHOCK No.7
5 September 1993, Estadio Monumental, Buenos Aires; 53,400

Argentina	(0) 0	
Colombia	(1) 5	Rincón 41, 73, Asprilla 50, 75, Valencia 86

Referee: **Ernesto Filippi** (Uruguay)
Coaches: **Alfio Basile** (Argentina) & **Francisco Maturana** (Colombia)

Argentina: Sergio Goycochea (River Plate); Julio Saldaña (Boca Juniors), Jorge Borelli (Racing Club), Oscar Ruggeri (Cpt, San Lorenzo), Ricardo Altamirano (River Plate); Gustavo Zapata (Yokohama Marinos), Fernando Redondo (Tenerife), Diego Simeone (Sevilla), Leonardo Rodriguez (Borussia Dortmund); Ramón Medina Bello (Yokohama Marinos), Gabriel Batistuta (Fiorentina). **Subs:** Claudio Garcia (Racing Club) 54m for Rodriguez; Alberto Acosta (Boca Juniors) 69m for Redondo

Colombia: Óscar Córdoba (América de Cali); Luis Herrera (Atlético Nacional), Luis Perea (Atlético Junior), Alexis Mendoza (Atlético Junior), Wilson Pérez (América de Cali); Leonel Álvarez (América de Cali), Gabriel Gomez (Atlético Nacional), Carlos Valderrama (Cpt, Atlético Junior), Freddy Rincón (Palmeiras); Faustino Asprilla (Parma), Adolfo Valencia (Bayern Munich)

Colombia had possibly their best-ever team. They had performed respectably enough at the 1990 Finals, and had the bones of the same squad with a couple of important additions. The 1990 goalkeeper, René Higuita, was serving his prison sentence, and his replacement, Córdoba, was less eccentric and marginally more reliable. Up front there was the exciting attacker Faustino Asprilla, playing with Parma in Italy. Asprilla, as Newcastle fans would attest, was a fruit nut loop but he was also a dangerous opponent, with pace to burn and brilliant close control, although his finishing was erratic.

Argentina's form had stood up well under Alfio Basile since defeat in 1990 and they still hadn't lost a World Cup qualifying match at home. But there was no Maradona, he had retired from international football, and without him Argentina's midfield was merely workmanlike. The new Golden Boy was the striker Gabriel Batistuta, who was banging in goals and generally being adored at Fiorentina; the city of Florence and Batistuta's glamorous film-star looks and charm were an ideal union.

The game started with the usual hail of ticker-tape, but by the end it was distraught Argentinian defenders littering the pitch. Colombia had a good mix. An experienced defence sat behind a terrific midfield, where Leonel Álvarez and Gabriel Gómez acted as runners and minders for the big-haired playmaker Valderrama and the electrifyingly quick Freddy Rincón. Asprilla and Rodolfo Valencia up front both liked to peel off into wide areas and attack the penalty area from wide. Argentina tried to use Redondo and Simeone to stifle Valderrama, but the Colombia captain was in the mood.

The game was played at a hectic pace for a South American match; Argentina under Basile liked to get forward quickly and use the pace of Batistuta and Medina Bello. They pressed heavily in midfield, believing it would restrict Valderrama's influence, but the result was acres of space behind the defence, and Colombia had the legs of the one-paced Argentinian defence. It was all pretty even as half-time approached. A twisting run by Asprilla had forced Goycochea into a sprawling save by his near post, and at the other end Batistuta's touch let him down when clear. Córdoba's defenders had to help him out on one occasion when he had a touch of the Higuita's and came wandering out of his goal. There was little hint of the carnage to come.

On forty-one minutes Valderrama pounced on a loose ball and sprinted away from two Argentinian players. I say sprinted, it was the merest acceleration, Valderrama didn't do undignified things like sprint – but it was enough. Rincón was charging up on his right; the pace of Valderrama's pass was perfection and whether Rincón's first touch was heavy but lucky or brilliant is irrelevant. It took the ball clear of the last defender and Rincón left him and the goalkeeper for dead as he finished brilliantly.

Just after half-time it was Asprilla's turn. Taking a long ball down with instant control, he turned Saldana inside out before squeezing the ball under Goycochea. Argentina were in trouble and made changes but Córdoba saved well from Batistuta's vicious shot and Argentina had shot their bolt.

Colombia cleared their lines and Valderrama set Asprilla going down the left. And he just kept going, all the way to the byline. His initial cross was cleared but Álvarez followed up and drove the ball in again; Rincón's shot was hit straight into the ground but the odd bounce was enough to take it past Goycochea. Saldana, the Argentinian right-back had a nightmare and was never picked again, he probably still wakes in the night with visions of Asprilla running past him. He was robbed by Asprilla for the fourth and the Colombian raced clear of the defence. Goycochea came out, did nothing wrong and watched helplessly as Asprilla checked on his shot and floated it up and over the goalkeeper. Quite brilliant – worthy of the little man watching forlornly in the stands in an Argentina shirt with No.10 on the back. It yet was another run from Asprilla that finished the scoring, as he drew the defenders and played in Valencia for a fifth; there was a hint of offside but the demoralised Argentinians could barely muster a complaint – that would *not* have pleased the little No.10.

The little No.10, who was, of course, Diego Maradona, was so displeased he allowed himself to put his personal battle against cocaine addiction to one side and be talked out of retirement and put his efforts behind the World Cup campaign.

Argentina made it, just, but only because Paraguay failed to win in Peru and allowed Argentina to sneak second place. They met Australia in a two-legged affair and won the home game 1–0 after a 1–1 draw in Sydney. Maradona looked ring-rusty and contributed only fitfully, but his presence clearly galvanised his colleagues.

Another qualifying record disappeared alongside Argentina's unbeaten home run. Brazil had never lost a qualifying match until now, but after a 0–0 draw in Ecuador they came a cropper against Bolivia after another unimaginative performance. The Bolivian hero was Marco Etcheverry, an attacking midfielder with the matador style and flowing mane of Mario Kempes. Etcheverry tormented the Brazilians. In the first half he won a penalty but belted it straight at the goalkeeper, who held on well. Taffarel did less well with three minutes to go; Etcheverry rampaged down the left, tricked his way to the byline and sent in a low, hard cross. The ball went straight at Taffarel with no significant power, but the Brazilian goalkeeper bent to collect and let the ball clip his heel, whence it deflected into the goal. The stadium went berserk, and had hardly calmed down ninety seconds later when Bolivia added a second, substitute Peña finishing off after Etcheverry set him clear with a delicious curled pass.

Bolivia won all their home games and with one round to go they were level on points with Brazil and Uruguay, who met in Rio while Bolivia travelled to Ecuador knowing a draw would be enough as their goal difference was vastly superior to Uruguay's. They got it, and made the Finals for the first time since 1950; Brazil beat Uruguay with a brace from Romário.

Saudi Arabia and South Korea made it through the Asian qualifying; the AFC repeated their idea of playing the final group as a round robin mini tournament, this time in Doha. The pick of the games was the Saudi's win over Iran by the odd goal in seven which sealed their debut appearance in the Finals.

Cameroon's heroics in 1990 meant the Africans got an extra qualifying place. Cameroon saw that justice was done by claiming one of them – two goals from one of the 1990 heroes, Omam-Biyik, sealed a crucial 3–1 win over Zimbabwe. The other places went to Morocco, who looked less accomplished than in the eighties, and an exciting young Nigeria squad, who would play in the Finals for the first time.

It might have been interesting to see how the American crowds reacted to the presence of an England team but they were denied the opportunity. Not by perfidious refereeing, as Graham Taylor would have us believe, but by a mixture of ineptitude and poor selection. Taylor was in thrall to the Charles Hughes methodology of getting the ball forward in as quick a time as possible and relying on second ball possession to create opportunities. He favoured athleticism over artistry and set too little store by touch and technique. One or two of the defenders aside, the rest were short of what was required; Premier League "legends" like Les Ferdinand and Ian Wright looked much more ordinary in international company. Paul Ince was a good player, and was to have one truly great World Cup day, but he couldn't boss sides around at this level, and David Platt was a lieutenant not a general. Carlton Palmer became a symbol of the team's inadequacy – not poor Carlton's fault, he didn't pick the team but he and Geoff Thomas and Andy Sinton were symptomatic of Taylor's breed of player. Lacking instant touch and awareness, England tried to win games on crumbs of possession.

England qualified for the 1992 European Championships but, shorn of the injured Paul Gascoigne, didn't make it past the group stage, two 0–0 draws and a defeat by Sweden sending them home. The neutrals in the Swedish crowds jeered their dismal style and the tabloids posted pictures of a turnip instead of Graham Taylor's head (Swedes beat turnips, geddit?). Taylor took a squad to a major tournament without a recognised right-back and played three different players there, two midfield players and a centre-half. Dearie me. England's best player, Gary Lineker, saw the writing on the wall and retired.

Come the World Cup in 1994 and there wasn't even the comfort of a successful qualifying campaign as England made an early, and humiliating, exit. Norway and Holland took the top two places in the group. Norway under Egil Olsen were a salutary lesson to England in how to play the direct game. They got the ball forward just as quickly but they had the forwards to hold up the ball and let the supporting players move into position and create problems around the box – England's forwards were too isolated and lacked the technique to shield the ball adequately – only when Terry Venables made Teddy Sheringham an automatic pick did England acquire this skill.

England drew at home to Norway – a trifle unluckily, they dominated the game but conceded a late equaliser to a thunderous strike from Kjetil Rekdal. They then gave away a two-goal lead against Holland – the usual Wembley jitters defending a well-earned lead – and lost badly in Oslo. The two Norway games, eight months apart, illustrated how much morale and form had dipped; dominant in the first, England were never at the races in Oslo. England would have to win in Rotterdam to qualify, and they would have to do it without Gascoigne, whose fitness could no longer be relied upon. This was by no means a great Dutch side, but Holland controlled the game, and had a goal wrongly chalked off. Much was made of the referee's failure to dismiss Ronald Koeman for a professional foul (Koeman scored the opener minutes later), but that was a smokescreen. England, semi-finalists four years earlier, were back amongst the also-rans. England's final game was a 7–1 win over San Marino; all very routine but after twenty minutes England were still a goal down after Stuart Pearce's back-pass allowed David Gualtieri to score the fastest goal in World Cup competition on eight and a half seconds. A subsequent fly-on-the-wall documentary made Taylor and his hapless assistant Phil Neal a laughing stock; Taylor didn't deserve that.

Graham Taylor's record at club level was thoroughly laudable. He took a nothing club and put them in the upper echelons of the top division – and Watford were never as preposterously one-dimensional as, say, Wimbledon under Bobby Gould; they were direct but intelligent. But even this doesn't wash at international level. Possession is the law, and Taylor's England teams never got it.

Scotland were in even worse disarray under Andy Roxburgh. They tried to play but didn't have the talent or firepower to worry the decent sides any longer. Their only victories in a tricky group were against Malta and Estonia. To many pundits' surprise it was Switzerland, not Portugal, who qualified alongside Italy, reaching the Finals for the first time since 1966. The Portuguese coach, who brought on many of the "Golden Generation" in his time as the Under-20s coach, was Carlos Queiroz, later assistant to Alex Ferguson at Manchester United, and the Swiss coach was one Roy Hodgson.

Wales did rather better in a competitive group that included Belgium, Romania and Czechoslovakia (competing as the Republic of Czechs and Slovaks – they knew they were about to split into two nations but hadn't yet sorted out the paperwork!). In an everybody-can-beat-everybody-else group it came down to Belgium's game against the RCS and Wales' last home match against Romania, who had thrashed them in Bucharest. Wales had a good side, some top-class players alongside the willing workers who always made up the numbers for a country of that size. Even without the suspended Mark Hughes they could call on Gary Speed, Ian Rush (past his best), Neville Southall, Dean Saunders and a nippy youngster by the name of Giggs. Belgium and the RCS would draw, so without knowing it, Wales simply needed to win.

Gheorghe Hagi was pulling the strings for Romania, and they missed a couple of good chances before Hagi opened the scoring with a long range shot; Neville Southall should have done better. Wales came back and started to trouble Romania from set pieces, one of which produced a poacher's goal for Saunders. Moments later Gary Speed was hauled down by Dan Petrescu and Wales had a penalty. Left-back Paul Bodin was the penalty taker, and a good one – he scored a crucial one for Swindon to win a play-off match the previous summer and had scored all three he took for Wales. The BBC switched from the dull procession of Ian Wright scoring goals against San Marino to this pulsating encounter. Cue complaints from thousands of England fans who either had no feel for the pulse of sporting tension or simply no pulse at all. Bodin didn't score and Wales' chance had gone. A late goal from Florin Raducioiu put the Romanians through instead, and they would illuminate the competition, but it was heartbreaking for a generation of Welsh stars. One, Gary Speed, is tragically no longer with us after taking his own life in 2011. He was manager of Wales at the time.

The closest fight of all came in Ireland's group, where they had to face Spain and Denmark, the reigning, if unexpected, European Champions, as well as facing the extra challenge of playing their northern counterparts. Wor Jack still had his abrasive defence and had added the even more abrasive Roy Keane to his strong midfield. Up front was trickier, where his main options were the gangling Niall Quinn (not yet matured) and the ageing John Aldridge, never a major force at this level. Still, that defence was redoubtable and they engineered draws in Denmark and Spain. A horrible defeat at home to Spain, when they uncharacteristically let in three goals in the first half, meant everything came down to the last two games in the group. Ireland's opponents? Northern Ireland, with the Troubles still boiling and anti-Republican feeling at an incendiary level. Jimmy Quinn's volley seventy-two minutes into a desperate and error-strewn game meant the Republic were going out. Alan McLoughlin's equaliser four minutes later meant they were still in with a chance. The game had one moment of pure farce; Jack Charlton summoned the giant Tony Cascarino from the bench when Quinn scored, only to discover Cascarino had forgotten to put his shirt on! Not *The Times'* football analyst's finest moment. Ireland went through by the narrowest of calculations, having the same points and goal difference as Denmark but with more goals scored.

A win for either side in the Spain versus Denmark game and Ireland would qualify; a drawn game meant they were out. When Zubizarreta, Spain's experienced goalkeeper, was sent off for a professional foul after ten minutes things looked bleak for Spain – their substitute was a twenty-three-year-old debutant, Santiago Canizares of Celta Vigo. Spain defended well and Canizares was inspired, making save after save to thwart the Danes – Brian Laudrup could have had a hat-trick against a mere mortal. Ireland were probably praying for a Danish breakthrough but it was Spain who grabbed an unlikely winner with their only serious chance when Fernando Hierro, so dangerous from set pieces, bulleted a header from a corner past Peter Schmeichel. Ireland were through and Denmark were out; sacrilege to say this in Dublin, but the Finals tournament would be the worse for it.

The only group that was over before the last round of matches saw Greece and Russia qualify comfortably from an easy section; the sad demise of Hungary as a football force was partly responsible, but the main reason was the absence of Yugoslavia or any of its progeny, still banned until the hideous civil wars and ethnic purges could be brought to a halt. Greece would make their first appearance in the Finals. Russia competed for the first time as plain old Russia, without any help from the Ukrainians or Georgians or any of the other nationalities that helped constitute the Soviet Union. Seeing how since the break-up of the Soviet state and Yugoslavia a number of those nations have remained competitive in European football, it makes us realise just how little they achieved as composite sides – invariably less than the sum of their parts.

WORLD CUP SHOCK No.8
17 November, 1993, Parc des Princes, Paris, France; 48,402

France	(1) 1	Cantona 32
Bulgaria	(0) 2	Kostadinov 37, 90

Referee: **Leslie Mottram** (Scotland)
Coaches: **Gerard Houllier** (France) & **Dimitar Penev** (Bulgaria)

France (4–4–2): Bernard Lama (Paris St Germain); Alain Roche (PSG), Marcel Desailly (Milan), Laurent Blanc (St Etienne), Emmanuel Petit (Monaco); Paul LeGuen (PSG), Didier Deschamps (Olympique de Marseille), Reynald Pedros (Nantes), Frank Sauzée (Atalanta); Eric Cantona (Manchester United), Jean-Pierre Papin (Cpt, AC Milan). **Subs:** David Ginola (PSG) 69m for Papin; Vincent Guérin (PSG) 81m for Sauzée
Bulgaria (4–4–2): Boris Mihailov (Cpt, Mulhouse); Emil Kremenliev (Levski Sofia), Trifon Ivanov (Neuchâtel Xamax), Petar Hubchev (Hamburg), Tsanko Tzvetanov (Levski Sofia); Zlatko Yankov (Levski Sofia), Yordan Lechkov (Hamburg), Krasimir Balakov (Sporting), Emil Kostadinov (Porto); Lyuboslav Penev (Valencia), Hristo Stoichkov (Barcelona). **Subs:** Petar Aleksandrov (Aarau) 82m for Tzvetanov; Daniel Borimirov (Levski Sofia) 82m for Lechkov

Inept as England were, and as unlucky as Denmark were, the prize for the biggest qualifying cock-up, possibly in World Cup history, has to go to France. By September 1993 France were all but through. They led the group by a point and had two home games to go, one against Israel, who had yet to win a match in the group and had lost 4–0 at home to the French the previous

February. France weren't yet the side that won the trophy in 1998 but they had talent in abundance. No Zidane but there was Cantona, and Deschamps, Desailly and Laurent Blanc were all in a side captained by the prolific Jean-Pierre Papin.

Israel played well – they were an improving team – and took the lead when Ronnie Rosenthal, the Liverpool "supersub", turned his man and arced over a dangerous cross. It seemed to have cleared everyone until Reuven Atar dived and turned it back across goal with his head – Harazi applied the finish. France took over and found a rhythm, with their best work coming through the enigmatic David Ginola, the darling of Paris St Germain. He rolled a square pass for Frank Sauzée to slot home a slide rule shot and then did it all himself, cutting in from the left before hitting a sizzler past Ginzburg; it was a textbook shot, with pace, precision and swerve. Then it all went belly-up. Israeli substitute Eyal Berkovic (yes, that one, but still a newbie here) started a flowing move and Rosenthal's acceleration took him past two defenders before Nimni nipped the ball off his toes and poked it goalwards; Lama made a good save but the ball popped up to Berkovic, who finished with the outside of his foot. It was Rosenthal again who caused the final piece of the damage, three minutes into injury-time. A quick break found him wide left where he scorched past Lizarazu and crossed for Atar to volley home.

Still, no big deal; even if Bulgaria beat Austria (which they did) and Sweden picked up four points against Austria and Finland (which they did), France were still through if they avoided defeat against Bulgaria. It looked a good bet just past the half-hour. A right-wing cross found Papin peeling off his marker to head back into the path of Cantona. The Manchester United striker adjusted that idiosyncratic upright stride and belted it past Mihailov; it was a goal that would become familiar to Premiership viewers over the next few years. Bulgaria didn't give up and levelled with a thumping header from Kostadinov from a well-taken corner. The second half was tense, but France looked pretty secure at the back and kept the ball well. The game was in its death throes when a free-kick on the right was rolled to Ginola, whose cross was overhit. Bulgaria pinged the ball quickly down the right and Penev found Kostadinov on the edge of the French penalty area; his shot was instantaneous and fierce. France were out. Their coach, Gerard Houllier, moaned that Ginola should have kept the ball instead of crossing; he was right, and it was the sort of lazy error that came between Ginola and greatness. But how like Houllier to pass the blame elsewhere – it became a familiar refrain at Liverpool.

The events of that night, 17 November, across Europe meant the World Cup was denied a view of either Eric Cantona or Ryan Giggs. It was also the single most exciting and tense night in World Cup qualification history.

The Finals

In recent years the holders of the World Cup have a chance to assess their form before the next tournament as they are now required to qualify for the Finals. In 1994 Germany went into the competition having not played a competitive game since 1992 when they were ambushed by Denmark in the final of the 1992 European Championship. While Franz Beckenbauer's assessment after the 1990 final that Germany would be unstoppable once the stars from the East were moulded into a united side had been shown as misplaced, they still looked the strongest European entrants. Italy had their fabulous Milanese defence, and both Argentina and Brazil were contenders in America, especially with Maradona back in the frame. Pelé thought Colombia would win – surely the kiss of death, the great man's predictions are invariably nonsense. Sweden or Spain were probably a better shout as an outsider.

The draw was kind in the first instance, matching them against Mexico in the vast Giants Stadium in New Jersey. Mexico were well-supported and used to the heat, but they lacked quality; their one superstar, Hugo Sánchez, was thirty-six and some way past his peak, and of the rest only Luis Garcia was good enough to cut the mustard in a top European league. That may sound dismissive of the Mexican leagues, but in an odd way – and in stark contrast to the situation with the top African sides – the well-funded Mexican domestic set-up has set them back internationally. With no serious competition on the continent, the best Mexican players lack experience of crunch games, so, while they always qualify, the step-up to a major tournament finds them wanting.

The referee (from Syria) made a pig's ear of the match. He handed out ten yellow cards (two each to Bulgarian right-back Kremenliev and Luis Garcia), and gave a penalty for nothing in particular – Kremenliev had a bad day, he was the victim here, as well. Stoichkov's seventh-minute goal was almost worth the admission alone. After Mexico bossed the opening, a careless pass let Kostadinov take possession in the centre circle and he threaded a superb ball inside the last defender for Stoichkov, running from deep. The striker took one touch to push the ball ahead of him, wound that lethal left foot back and hit a hammer blow past Jorge Campos in the Mexican goal. Kostadinov hit the post from a free-kick (the surprise here being that Stoichkov let someone else take one) but neither side could find a way through. Mexico had a horrible time in the penalty shoot-out. Garcia Aspe, who converted the penalty during the match, shot high and wide with the first kick and Mihailov saved two tame efforts from Bernal and Rodriguez. Campos, whose flamboyant self-designed jerseys were a feature of the competition, saved superbly from Balakov but could do nothing about the next three penalties and Lechkov administered the coup de grace – Stoichkov's dead-eye precision wasn't even needed.

So. Germany v Bulgaria. No contest, surely, especially as the champions had three extra days to prepare and Bulgaria played extra-time in stifling heat against Mexico. Germany fielded nine players who owned winners' medals from 1990; they were vast on experience but short on pace.

GROUP A

Switzerland Bregy 39	(1) 1	**USA** Wynalda 44	(1) 1	18 June, Detroit; 73,425
Romania Raducioiu 16, 90, Hagi 34	(2) 3	**Colombia** Valencia 43	(1) 1	18 June, Pasadena; 91,865
Switzerland Sutter 16, Chapuisat 52, Knup 66, Bregy 72	(1) 4	**Romania** Hagi 35	(1) 1	22 June, Detroit; 61,428
USA Own goal 34, Stewart 52	(1) 2	**Colombia** Valencia 89	(0) 1	22 June, Pasadena; 93,194
Colombia Gaviria 44, Lozano 89	(1) 2	**Switzerland**	(0) 0	26 June, Palo Alto; 83,769
Romania Petrescu 17	(1) 1	**USA**	(0) 0	26 June, Pasadena; 93,869

1. Romania 6pts (5–5); 2. Switzerland 4pts (5–4); 3. USA 4pts (3–3); 4. Colombia 3pts (4–5)

The United States, under Bora Milutinovic, looked much sharper than in 1990. They had managed to export a few of their better players and the experience of playing in the European leagues gave them a bit more know-how, tactical acumen and guile. American teams are always fit and these stadiums were hot, hot, hot – none more so than the indoor affair in Detroit where the USA played their opener against Switzerland. A draw was about right – both goals came from well-struck free-kicks.

The other opener in the group saw Romania face the much-hyped Colombians in the Rose Bowl, the famous venue for the annual collegiate American Football final. You know I've been carping about official FIFA figures distorting the crowd numbers? Not here, the place was packed and it was rocking.

The game was billed as a contest between the two No.10s, Hagi and Valderrama. Hagi won hands down. After sixteen minutes he released Raducioiu down the left. The big striker might not have been able to get in Milan's first team (no disgrace) but he finished really well here, cutting in past two men on to his right foot and belting the ball past Córdoba. The Romanian playmaker's next offering was Pelé-esque, a brilliant chip from fully forty yards that Córdoba did well to fingertip away. Córdoba didn't learn his lesson. He liked to hover on his six-yard line or just past and Hagi had spotted it; his next effort was from miles out on the left touchline and it flew past the Colombian 'keeper with height and power to dip in the far corner. Gorgeous Gheorghe. Valencia's near post header gave Colombia hope, but Romania looked comfortable, with Valderrama shackled by Popescu and Asprilla a nonsensical parody of the player who destroyed Argentina. It was Romania who scored the last goal, a breakaway from Raducioiu, released by yet another Hagi pass.

Colombia were even worse against the United States, disheartened and short of desire, Rincón and Álvarez apart. Valderrama was kept quiet by Harkes and Ramos, and Asprilla was replaced at half-time. The own goal which gave the USA their lead had appalling ramifications. The culprit, Andrés Escobar, was later murdered in Medellin, Colombia's capital, apparently because his error cost some gangster a lot of money at the bookmakers. A lot of soul-searching went on and it cast a cloud over the tournament, but the incident said a lot more about Colombia than it did about the World Cup.

Back in the hothouse of the Pontiac Silverdome (sounds like *Mad Max IV*), Switzerland beat Romania with something to spare. The stadium was a ludicrous choice, with specially flown in grass and no air conditioning, and seating just a few feet from the playing surface – it was a downright health hazard for the players. The Swiss were an unremarkable team but – and it is a feature of Hodgson's teams – they were well organised and difficult to break down and worked for each other. The defence was vastly experienced – skipper Alain Geiger was approaching 100 caps – and up front Stéphane Chapuisat of Borussia Dortmund was a mobile and intelligent target. Defeat to Colombia in the final game was irrelevant but it did show a couple of cracks in what had looked an impressive façade. Romania clinched top place in the group by beating the USA with a goal from their England-bound attacking full-back Dan Petrescu. The United States were happy to make the second phase, when most pundits predicted they would finish at the bottom of the group. Colombia went home. Sorry, Pelé.

GROUP B

Cameroon	(1) 2	**Sweden**	(1) 2	19 June, Pasadena; 83,959
Embe 31, Omam-Biyik 47		Ljung 8, Dahlin 75		
Brazil	(1) 2	**Russia**	(0) 0	20 June, Palo Alto; 81,061
Romário 26, Rai 53 (p)				
Cameroon	(0) 0	**Brazil**	(1) 3	24 June, Palo Alto; 83,401
		Romário 39, Marcio Santos 66,		
		Bebeto 73		
Russia	(1) 1	**Sweden**	(1) 3	24 June, Detroit; 71,528
Salenko 4 (p)		Brolin 38 (p), Dahlin 59, 81		
Russia	(3) 6	**Cameroon**	(0) 1	28 June, Palo Alto; 74,914
Salenko 16, 41, 44 (p),		Milla 47		
73, 75, Radchenko 82				
Sweden	(1) 1	**Brazil**	(0) 1	28 June, Detroit; 77,217
K Andersson 23		Romário 47		

1. Brazil 7pts (6–1); 2. Sweden 5pts (6–4); 3. Russia 3pts (7–6); 4. Cameroon 1pt (3–11)

Cameroon were managed by a French coach, Henri Michel. Michel was in charge of France when they won the 1984 European

Championships, although many claimed Michel Platini called the shots, and nothing subsequent had suggested he was a top-notch manager. His side here were too old but, paradoxically, too naïve. Alongside the old guard Michel insisted on picking the raw seventeen-year-old centre-back Rigobert Song, and he was a liability, tormented by the Swedish forwards and sent off after an hour of chasing Romário. Roger Milla created a piece of history by scoring against Russia, aged forty-two, but the Russians scored six at the other end, and Milla's inclusion was an indication of Cameroon's shortage of quality. Salenko's five goals against Cameroon, plus a penalty against Sweden in a 3–1 defeat, was enough to give him a share of the Golden Boot. Salenko, who played for Logroñés, a small club enjoying a rare spell in the Spanish top flight, was never picked again after this tournament, and these were the only goals he scored for his country. Not the stuff of legend.

Russia were hampered by a pre-tournament mutiny which led to the dropping of a number of key players, including the dangerous wingers Dobrovolski and Kanchelskis and the playmaker Kiriakov. They were no match for Brazil or Sweden, whose forward combination of Kennet Andersson, Thomas Brolin and Martin Dahlin looked a tasty treat. Brazil were very un-Brazilian, strong at the back, sharp up front but a tad pedestrian in midfield; they were also very competent. Both would represent awkward second-round opposition.

GROUP C

Germany Klinsmann 61	(0) 1	**Bolivia**	(0) 0	17 June, Chicago; 63,117
South Korea Hong 85, Seo 89	(0) 2	**Spain** Salinas 51, Goikoetxea 56	(0) 2	17 June, Dallas; 56, 247
Spain Goikoetxea 14	(1) 1	**Germany** Klinsmann 48	(0) 1	21 June, Chicago; 63,113
Bolivia	(0) 0	**South Korea**	(0) 0	23 June, Boston; 53,456
South Korea Hwang 52, Hong 63	(0) 2	**Germany** Klinsmann 12, 37, Riedle 20	(3) 3	27 June, Chicago; 63,089
Spain Guardiola 19 (p), Caminero 66, 71	(1) 3	**Bolivia** Sánchez 67	(0) 1	27 June, Dallas; 63,998

1. Germany 7pts (5–3); 2. Spain 5pts (6–4); 3. South Korea 2pts (4–5); 4. Bolivia 1pt (1–4)

When Germany lined up for the tournament's opener against Bolivia, competing in the Finals for the first time in forty-four years, there was only one player from the former East Germany in the starting line-up, the powerful and skilful sweeper Matthias Sammer. Germany were still using the 1990 mould; strapping athletes with good basic skills and endless stamina, augmented by the occasional silky touch from Hässler, Möller or Klinsmann. When the match kicked off, all twenty-two players were probably still giggling after the catastrophic opening ceremony. Germany won a dull game 1–0 and came from a goal down to draw 1–1 with Spain. Both German goals were scored by the excellent Klinsmann, but him aside they looked colourless against defensive opponents. South Korea, fit and relentless in the heat, came back from 2–0 down against Spain, albeit against ten men after Nadal, the Spanish enforcer, saw red – not an unfamiliar experience for the man nicknamed *The Beast* at Barcelona. They nearly went one better against Germany, who took their foot off the gas at half-time when three goals to the good (including two more from Klinsmann). South Korea kept running and scored two good goals, and with half an hour to go Germany's main rivals must have enjoyed seeing how panicky they became under pressure. England fans are familiar with their team hoofing the ball aimlessly upfield as a means of relieving the defence – for German supporters it was an unfamiliar and dispiriting sight. More significantly still, Germany's star midfielder, Stefan Effenberg, who played for Italian club Fiorentina, was sent home after the match. Never a popular player in his own country – he was notoriously arrogant and played for the hated Bayern Munich – Effenberg was booed by sections of the German support when substituted against South Korea. He responded by giving them the finger and it was all the excuse the German management team needed to get rid of a player they saw as unpredictable and unsupportive. Spain saw off Bolivia to join the Germans in the last sixteen.

GROUP D

Argentina	(2) 4	**Greece**	(0) 0	21 June, Boston; 53,486
Batistuta 2, 44, 89 (p), Maradona 60						

Nigeria	(2) 3	Bulgaria	(0) 0	21 June, Dallas; 44,932
Yekini 21, Amokachi 43, Amunike 55				
Argentina	(2) 2	Nigeria	(1) 1	25 June, Boston; 54,453
Caniggia 22, 29		Siasia 8		
Greece	(0) 0	Bulgaria	(1) 4	26 June, Chicago; 63,160
		Stoichkov 5 (p), 55 (p), Lechkov 66, Borimirov 89		
Bulgaria	(0) 2	Argentina	(0) 0	30 June, Dallas; 63,998
Stoichkov 61, Sirakov 89				
Nigeria	(1) 2	Greece	(0) 0	30 June, Boston; 53,001
George 45, Amokachi 90				

1. Nigeria 6pts (6–2); 2. Bulgaria 6pts (6–3); 3. Argentina 6pts (6–3); 4. Greece 0pts (0–10)

This group was effectively a three-way affair because Greece were embarrassingly bad. I mean really bad, as bad as any of the emerging countries who were mocked by European scribes in previous years. They barely mustered a shot worthy of the name and conceded ten in three matches.

Argentina looked rejuvenated as they destroyed Greece and beat Nigeria; Maradona looked fit and slim and Caniggia's two goals against Nigeria were sharply taken for a man who had just served a lengthy ban for cocaine use. Maradona scored against Greece and had a hand in both the cleverly worked free-kicks that brought the goals against Nigeria, where he equalled the record of twenty-one appearances in the Finals. He never broke the record because before Argentina took the field against Bulgaria their captain and inspiration was banned after ephedrine and various other substances were found in his urine sample. Now we knew how he lost the weight. Oh, Diego, so great and yet so flawed. He was really quite Shakespearean in the heights and depths to which he was capable of climbing or stooping.

Nigeria had been brutally efficient in brushing aside Bulgaria in their first match, and recovered to beat Greece and ensure they reached the next round. Both Bulgaria and Argentina joined them after Bulgaria beat Greece (quite abysmal) and Argentina (understandably subdued). Even after Bulgaria had a man sent off, Argentina struggled to find a way past the giant Ivanov and his colleagues.

The best moment of the group came in the final minute of the last match of the group when Daniel Amokachi surged past a

crowd of defenders and blasted a shot into the top corner. The
Nigerian forwards were massive – they just went through defenders rather than round them.

WORLD CUP SHOCK No.9
18 June 1994, Giants Stadium, New Jersey; 74,826

Republic of Ireland	**(1) 1**	Houghton 12
Italy	**(0) 0**	

Referee: **Mario van der Ende** (Holland)
Coaches: **Jack Charlton** (Ireland) & **Arrigo Sacchi** (Italy)

Ireland (4–4–1–1): Pat Bonner (Glasgow Celtic), Denis Irwin (Manchester United), Phil Babb
(Coventry City), Paul McGrath (Aston Villa), Steve Staunton (Villa); Ray Houghton (Villa),
Roy Keane (Man Utd), Andy Townsend (Villa), John Sheridan (Sheffield Wednesday), Terry
Phelan (Manchester City); Tommy Coyne (Motherwell). **Subs:** Jason McAteer (Bolton
Wanderers) 67m for Houghton; John Aldridge (Tranmere Rovers) 89m for Coyne
Italy (4–4–2): Gianluca Pagliuca (Sampdoria); Mauro Tassotti (AC Milan), Alessandro
Costacurta (AC Milan), Franco Baresi (Cpt, AC Milan), Paolo Maldini (AC Milan); Roberto
Donadoni (AC Milan), Dino Baggio (Juventus), Demetrio Albertini (AC Milan), Alberigo
Evani (Sampdoria); Roberto Baggio (Juventus), Beppe Signori (Lazio). **Subs:** Daniele
Massaro (AC Milan) 45m for Evani; Nico Berti (Internazionale) 83m for Signori
Cautioned: Phelan (Ire) 30m, Coyne (Ire) 52m, Irwin (Ire) 80m

We football writers do carp a little about Ireland's World Cup
Finals campaigns. It's probably the "brave little Ireland"
nonsense that was bandied about in the tabloids; this was a well-
organised outfit that knew exactly what it was doing, from the
cynical exploitation of Irish heritage to secure a stronger squad
than in previous years to the defensive formation and aerial
tactics designed to discomfort more technically adept
opposition.

Let's give credit where it is due – it worked. Up to a point. And
how good could they have been? Look at this team. A really good
goalkeeper, the best full-back in the first ten years of the
Premiership, one of the best centre-halves any British Isles team
has seen, and a world-class box-to-box midfield leader. Four top-
level international players. Add Staunton, a player of great
temperament and consistency, the grafters Townsend and
Houghton, and the passing ability of the rather one-paced but
creative John Sheridan. Had they played football, would they
have done even better? Or would the lack of a true international
striker have cost them? Who knows?

This was Ireland's finest night, even surpassing, for achievement if not emotion, beating England at the 1988 European Championships. It wasn't a David against Goliath occasion. Arrigo Sacchi, the Italian coach, got his tactics wrong and picked a light, nimble side who struggled against the physical Irish. The Italians didn't use the heat to their advantage as Mexico later did, and the Irish were able to defend deep and comfortably; Roberto Baggio playing at centre-forward just made him easy to mark, when he preferred to play in the elusive "hole".

The crowd was preponderantly Irish, mostly Irish American, who had managed to acquire most of the tickets earmarked for the equally numerous New York Italian contingent. The atmosphere was loud, but – as is usually the case with Irish soccer fans – good natured. By the end it was a big green party.

The decisive goal came early, when Coyne challenged Costacurta for a high ball and the ball lobbed up to Baresi. The Italian captain's header was a weak one, straight to Ray Houghton, and the Glaswegian's shot rose and then dipped sharply to beat a surprised Pagliuca. Ireland were calm, accomplished and hard-working (Coyne covered miles in the heat and needed treatment on the team bus); Italy were pretty awful.

GROUP E

Norway	(0) 1	**Mexico**	(0) 0	19 June, W'ton DC; 52,359
Rekdal 85				
Italy	(0) 1	**Norway**	(0) 0	23 June, New Jersey; 74,624
D Baggio 59				
Mexico	(1) 2	**Ireland**	(0) 1	24 June, Orlando; 61,219
L García 43, 66		Aldridge 84		
Norway	(0) 0	**Ireland**	(0) 0	28 June, New Jersey; 76,322
Italy	(0) 1	**Mexico**	(0) 1	28 June, W'ton DC; 53,186
Massaro 48		Bernal 58		

1. Mexico 4pts (3–3); 2. Ireland 4pts (2–2); 3. Italy 4pts (2–2); 4. Norway (1–1)

This was the only occasion all four teams in a group finished on the same number of points. There wasn't a hair between them. Norway were indebted to another fierce strike from Rekdal for their opening win, but Mexico recovered to beat Ireland in staggering heat in Orlando. The match was played at midday, which was just suicidal in those temperatures. The need for water was intense, and there were heated scenes on the touchline in every sense when Jack Charlton thought the officials were stopping his players taking on fluid (they weren't). Less clever was an unnecessary and officious delay in allowing John Aldridge to take the field as a substitute. The touchline microphones picked up some choice vernacular from both the Scouse striker and his manager. Aldridge scored Ireland's goal, made by fellow Scouser Jason McAteer, who impressed coming off the bench. By then Ireland were two-down, as Luís Garcia scored two crisp goals, both set up García Aspe, who gave Irwin a tough time.

Over in New Jersey Italy conducted a famous rearguard action against Norway. Goalkeeper Gianluca Pagliuca was sent off after only twenty-one minutes and Sacchi, to the astonishment of the watching media, took off his best player, Roberto Baggio, to accommodate Luca Marchegiani, the reserve goalkeeper. There was method in the madness, as Sacchi explained; Signori was fitter and physically stronger and better able to take on the lone forager role the situation demanded. There was no mention of why Casiraghi, not Baggio, was withdrawn into midfield . . .

That the Lazio 'keeper had little to do owed much to Italian resilience and much to the shortcomings of Olsen's Norway. Italy lost Baresi to injury three minutes into the second half and moved Maldini into the middle. Italy were reeling but Norway had no Plan B. They kept on knocking long balls up to a defence that had retreated to the edge of the penalty area – meat and drink to classical interceptors like Maldini, Berti and Dino Baggio. A rare Italian break led to a free-kick on the left and Signori's excellent cross was met by Dino Baggio with a towering header. Now the *Azzurri* were in their element. Even when Maldini was rendered a passenger after a knock to his ankle, the winger Daniele Massaro filled in at left-back with commendable assurance – but Norway never got the quick-footed Leonhardsen to run at him or get behind him.

The permutations in the last two matches were many, as every team stood a similar chance of qualifying. Norway and Ireland played out a stultifying 0–0 draw; Ireland's defence looked as untroubled by Norway's directness as it had by Italy's passing and movement. Mexico's late equaliser against Italy changed the complexion of the group and eliminated Norway. Olsen's team were a little unlucky to go out with four points, but they were a one-trick pony and their manager wasn't the genius his outspoken observations suggested he believed himself to be.

GROUP F

Belgium	(1) 1	Morocco	(0) 0	19 June, Orlando 60,790
Degryse 11				
Saudi Arabia	(1) 1	Holland	(0) 2	20 June, W'ton DC; 52,535
Amin 19		Jonk 50, Taument 86		
Holland	(0) 0	Belgium	(0) 1	25 June, Orlando; 62,387
		Albert 65		
Morocco	(1) 1	Saudi Arabia	(2) 2	25 June, New Jersey; 72,404
Chaouch 27		Al-Jaber 8 (p), Amin 45		
Holland	(1) 2	Morocco	(0) 1	29 June, Orlando; 60,578
Bergkamp 43, Roy 78		Nader 47		
Saudi Arabia	(1) 1	Belgium	(0) 0	29 June, W'ton DC; 52,959
Al-Owairan 6				

1. Holland 6pts (4–3); 2. Saudi Arabia 6pts (4–3); 3. Belgium 6pts (2–1); 4. Morocco 0pts (2–5)

Saudi Arabia were mightily impressive. Quick and neat, they gave Holland a scare, leading 1–0 at half-time before the Dutch woke up and applied some pressure in the second half. The Saudis' goalkeeper, Al-Deayea was horribly culpable on Holland's winning goal, completely missing a deep cross that Taument nodded into the empty net. The first Dutch goal was a ripper from Wim Jonk, who did that sort of thing regularly for Ajax and Internazionale. In their second game the Saudis beat Morocco with the help of some equally appalling goalkeeping by Al-Deayea's opposite number. Morocco had already lost to Belgium and were now out.

In the Saudis' game against Belgium, they scored early, and it was one of the great World Cup goals, a sensational solo effort by Said Al-Owairan. The midfielder was fed the ball in space in his own half and set off on the attack; bursting between two opponents with a little change of pace, he found himself attacking back-pedalling defenders afraid to lunge in and risk a red card so early in the match. De Wolf pulled out of a challenge and allowed Al-Owairan to run, Smidts was turned inside out and Albert made only a belated and token attempt to cover as the Saudi midfielder shot high past Preud'homme. (How familiar that must sound to Newcastle fans – a great footballer, Philippe Albert, but who on earth told him he should play at the back?) The Saudis had a number of good players; the goalkeeper Al-Deayea (his faux-pas in the first game notwithstanding), right-back Al-Khilaiwi, the captain Majed Abdullah, enjoying a well-deserved swansong and the new striker Sami Al-Jaber all won over 100 caps for their country.

Preud'homme took some beating, he was a top goalkeeper and unlucky that his early career coincided with the second half of the great Jean-Marie Pfaff's. Preud'homme put in a great shift in the previous match when Belgium beat their old rivals Holland. It was a good game – the winners knew they were through to the next round – with lots of chances at either end and some defending that had prospective opponents salivating. Ed De Goey in the Holland goal also had a fine match but had no chance with a strong finish from Albert, showing the attacking quality that was in stark contrast to some of his work at the back. Holland came back strongly after Albert's goal, substitute Marc Overmars giving Smidts a torrid time down the left, but Preud'homme stopped everything they threw at him, two saves from a Bergkamp skimmer and a typical Ronald Koeman rocket standing out from a number of good ones.

Holland missed the injured van Basten and Gullit (who wouldn't?), who was having a prickly time with the coach, Dick Advocaat. They still had some talent, with Bergkamp, shipped in – literally, to counter his fear of flying – after a nightmare season with Inter and speedy youngster Overmars, both of whom would find their way to Arsenal.

SECOND ROUND

Germany	**(3) 3**	**Belgium**	**(1) 2**	2 July, Chicago; 60,246
Völler 6, 40, Klinsmann 11		Grün 8, Albert 89		
Spain	**(1) 3**	**Switzerland**	**(0) 0**	2 July, W'ton DC; 53,121
Hierro 15, Luis Enrique 74,				
Beguiristain 87 (p)				
Sweden	**(1) 3**	**Saudi Arabia**	**(0) 1**	3 July, Dallas; 60,277
Dahlin 6,		Al-Ghesheyan		
K Andersson 51, 89				

Saudi Arabia's reward for beating Belgium in the group match was to avoid Germany in the second round. It was not such good news for Belgium. It was another decent match, especially a pulsating opening. Rudi Völler, restored to the starting line-up, finished economically giving Germany the lead, and he combined brilliantly with his old strike partner Klinsmann for the second – cue manic fist-pumping from Jürgen. In between Germany made a hash of clearing a free-kick and Belgian captain Georges Grün poked home. Germany had what looked a comfortable two-goal cushion before half-time when Rudi Völler was unmarked from a corner; Preud'homme might have done better with Völler's downward header but he was entitled to ask what his central defenders were doing. Belgium gave it their all in the second half and were denied the clearest of penalties when Helmer brought down Weber when he was clear on goal. A penalty and red card might have changed things, but Albert's subsequent goal – a calm finish after some excellent passing – came too late to save his team. Exit with honour for Belgium, progress with reservations for Germany.

It was the end of the road for two of the unfancied sides. Switzerland were well beaten by Spain. Over half the Spanish team were from a terrific Barcelona side under Johan Cruyff. Barca had just won four consecutive *La Liga* titles with a good blend of home stars and imports, as well as the 1992 European Cup. Spain's first two scorers were from Barca's great rivals Real Madrid. Fernando Hierro, playing in midfield, not in the *libero* position he adopted at Real Madrid, scored the first when Switzerland's offside trap back-fired. The second finished the Swiss off with fifteen minutes to go. Sergi was allowed to run a long way off the left wing and with everyone expecting the shot he poked the ball to Luis Enrique who turned and fired home.

Saudi Arabia played their usual neat, quick game but they were unable to hold the Swedish front line, with Andersson in particular in destructive form. After only six minutes the big striker swivelled and pumped in an undefendable swinging cross; Martin Dahlin just jumped and used the pace of the ball to divert it into the goal. Andersson's first goal was a textbook display of power and purpose. He hooked the ball over a defender, controlled it, muscled the defender away a second time, beat another and drove a left-foot shot into the very corner of the goal. Sweden created other chances but missed them and Saudi Arabia came more into the game as the Texas heat took its toll in the Cotton Bowl. Ravelli made two cracking saves but could do nothing about Al-Ghesheyan's goal when the winger cut in from the right and cracked a left-footer high past the goalkeeper's shoulder. Hope lasted two minutes plus a few seconds; Brolin to Dahlin to Andersson to the corner of the goal, in off the post. Game over.

WORLD CUP CLASSIC No.19
3 July 1994, Rose Bowl, Pasadena, CA; 90,469

Romania	**(2) 3**	Dumitrescu 11, 19, Hagi 56
Argentina	**(1) 2**	Batistuta 16 (p), Balbo 75

Referee: **Pierluigi Pairetto** (Italy)
Coaches: **Anghel Iordănescu** (Romania) & **Alfio Basile** (Argentina)

Romania (4–4–2): Florin Prunea (Dinamo Bucharest); Dan Petrescu (Genoa), Daniel Prodan (Steaua Bucharest), Miodrag Belodedici (Valencia), Tibor Selymes (Cercle Bruges); Ioan Lupescu (Bayer Leverkusen), Gheorghe Popescu (PSV Eindhoven) Gheorghe Mihali (Dinamo Bucharest), Dorinel Munteanu (Cercle Bruges); Gheorghe Hagi (Cpt, Brescia); Ilie Dumitrescu (Steaua Bucharest). **Subs:** Constantin Gâlca (Steaua Bucharest) 86m for Hagi; Corneliu Papura (Universitatea Craiova) 88m for Dumitrescu
Argentina (4–4–2): Luis Islas (Independiente); Roberto Sensini (Parma), Fernando Cáceres (Real Zaragoza), Oscar Ruggeri (Cpt, San Lorenzo), José Chamot (Foggia); Ariel Ortega (River Plate), Diego Simeone (Seville), Fernando Redondo (Tenerife), José Basualdo (Vélez Sársfield); Abel Balbo (Roma), Gabriel Batistuta (Fiorentina). **Sub:** Ramón Medina Bello (Yokohama Marinos) 63m for Sensini
Cautioned: Ruggeri (Arg) 33m, Popescu (Rom) 50m, Redondo (Arg) 55m, Chamot (Arg) 56m, Selymes (Rom) 68m, Cáceres (Arg) 83m, Dumitrescu (Rom) 85m

The Rose Bowl might have been a bit shabby and run-down for some tastes but concerns about safety were ill-founded and the huge bowl provided a wonderful setting for this cracking game.

Both sides had notable omissions. Argentina had removed their captain Maradona from their squad to try to avoid action from FIFA, while Romania had to play without Raducioiu, their best striker, who got a second yellow card for brainlessly kicking the ball away in their last group match. The focus shifted from the Argentinian No.10 to his Romanian counterpart, often found wanting in the past but seemingly up for the cup on this occasion.

The first goal came out of the blue. Balbo had already missed a good chance for Argentina when a weaving run from Simeone created an opening. The lead lasted five minutes after Batistuta won a penalty for a soft challenge by Prodan. Perhaps the referee felt he deserved it for a cheeky back-heeled turn. Another two minutes, another goal. A superb threaded ball from Hagi, from the right this time, found Dumitrescu, who opened his body to execute the coolest finish at the near post.

Ten minutes into the second half Dumitrescu returned the favour. He dispossessed Basualdo and ran at the Argentinian defence. Selymes decoyed to his left, and Dumitrescu cleverly held the ball and released Hagi, who was running hard to his right. The finish was with Hagi's weaker right foot but was still unstoppable.

In between the Argentinians pressed hard. Romania's wing backs were pushed back and made a five-man defence and Argentina enjoyed a lot of midfield possession, allowing Simeone and Ortega to run at the Romanians. It was in the centre that Romania stayed strong, where Gica Popescu and Miodrag Belodedici resisted all Argentina could throw at them. They needed to be, guys like Hagi and Dumitrescu didn't set much store by chasing back.

The sweeper Belodedici was an interesting character. Of Serbian extraction (he was born right on the border between the two countries), he had won the European Cup with both Steaua Bucharest and Red Star Belgrade, the first player to win with two clubs. Now with Valencia in Spain, Belodedici was a deep-lying central defender with pace and an uncanny ability to time a tackle. He and Prodan negated the threat from Batistuta and Balbo in the second half, while Popescu sat in front of them and stemmed the runs and reduced Argentina to pot shots from distance. Balbo's tap-in owed more to Prunea's fumble than his own skill, which was short of what was needed in an Argentinian shirt.

Romania played out the last fifteen minutes amidst a cacophony of noise from the largely Hispanic, Argentina-supporting crowd, but there were few alarms. Iordănescu allowed himself the luxury of substituting Hagi (tired) and Dumitrescu (booked and flaky) – he would have been mortified had Argentina sneaked a goal and his side faced extra-time without their two most creative players

Ireland	**(0) 0**	**Holland**	**(2) 2**	4 July, Orlando; 61,235
		Bergkamp 11, Jonk 40		
Brazil	**(0) 1**	**USA**	**(0) 0**	4 July, Palo Alto; 84,147
Bebeto 73				
Nigeria	**(1) (1) 1**	**Italy**	**(0) (1) 2**	5 July, Boston; 54,367
Amunike 26		R Baggio 88, 102 (p)		
Mexico	**(1) (1) 1**	**Bulgaria**	**(1) (1) 1**	5 July, New Jersey; 71,030
García Aspe 18 (p)		Stoichkov 7		

Ireland's campaign came to a subdued end. Bergkamp's early goal, set up by Overmars' pace, settled any Dutch nerves. Jack Charlton left out young McAteer, who had been one of the team's best players, and restored Phelan, who hadn't. And McGrath at last had an opponent (Bergkamp) who knew how to avoid him and tax his creaky knees by making him run around. Keane and Sheridan and Rijkaard and Jonk cancelled each other out, but the Dutch wide players gave them an edge. The second goal was a catastrophic error from Pat Bonner, who let Jonk's shot slip through his hands, but Ireland didn't seem to have much idea how to chase a game after going behind early.

Brazil and the United States met on the fourth of July, but there was to be no holiday celebration for the Americans. Brazilian boss Carlos Alberto Parreira was not the chap who captained them in 1970, but a career coach who made his name in the Middle East, taking first Kuwait and then the United Arab Emirates to the World Cup Finals. He took a bold decision here, leaving out Raí, his captain. Raí was Sócrates' younger brother by eleven years, but he looked out of sorts here, maybe feeling the effects of a first full season in European football with Paris St Germain.

The USA defended well, with their long-haired central defender Alexei "Jesus" Lalas in excellent form again. The nick-name was a reference to his physical similarity to inaccurate Western representations of Jesus in Renaissance art, a white guy with long flowing locks and occasionally a wispy beard. A couple of last-ditch tackles by Lalas made him a saviour of sorts. The American forwards, with the crafty and quick (but lazy) Roy

Wegerle on the bench, were out of their depth and even after Leonardo was sent off just before half-time they made little impression on this brick wall of a Brazilian defence. Leonardo took no further part in the tournament after his elbow poleaxed Tab Ramos, fracturing his skull – a horrible attack, albeit hugely out of character. Romário, withdrawn a little deeper to help in midfield with Brazil a man down, made the only goal for Bebeto. The Brazilians brought on a young right-back, Cafú, for his Finals debut in the second half.

The Americans had cause to be pleased with their campaign. They had made big strides since 1990, and showed good team-work and tactical awareness. Any American sports team will have good conditioning and fitness, and they showed superb commitment in the heat. Another couple of international-class players and they might give the big boys something to think about.

Italy came within a whisper of going out against Nigeria. A goal behind after some un-Italian defending at a corner let in Amunike, they were down to ten men after seventy-six minutes. Gianfranco Zola, only on the pitch for twelve minutes, was mysti-fyingly sent off by the Mexican referee, Brizio Carter, a hopeless official who made a habit of this sort of nonsense. In this instance he had a partner in crime – the Nigerian right-back Eguavoen was guilty of a shocking piece of play-acting to engineer Zola's dismissal. It was Zola's only appearance in the World Cup Finals. Two years later he joined Chelsea and enjoyed the best spell of his career, appreciated more in West London than he ever was in Italy.

Italy dominated the game against a surprisingly timid Nigeria, for whom Finidi George and a young Jay-Jay Okocha were anony-mous. Okocha remained a brilliant but frustrating and inconsist-ent player, George remained an over-rated and unfulfilled one. Dominating the game is all very well, but not if you don't score and the Italians couldn't find a way through a massed defence and on-form goalkeeper, Nigerian captain Peter Rufai. There were only two minutes left when right-back Roberto Mussi strong-armed his way past a couple of defenders and cut back a nicely weighted ball for Roberto Baggio. The European Footballer of the Year had looked all puff and wind so far in the tournament, contributing little except a major pout when he was taken off against Norway. He seized the moment here, placing a wonderfully controlled shot past a couple of defenders and Rufai's outstretched hand.

Eguavoen got his come-uppance for his faking in extra-time, upending Antonio Benarrivo and giving Baggio the opportunity to slot away the winner from the penalty spot. They left it late, but the better team went through.

Bulgaria, in the knockout rounds for the first time, got a kind draw in Mexico. Hristo Stoichkov, the temperamental Barcelona striker, gave them an early lead, but a terrible decision gave Mexico a penalty and an equaliser and Bulgaria started to get a little stroppy. A poor game, refereed by a Syrian official who would have struggled to control an Under-12s game, dragged through extra-time to a penalty shoot-out. Half of the eight penalties were missed, Mexico making a hash of their first three (even García Aspe, who scored one in the match). Yordan Lechkov, the game's best player, put Mexico out of their misery and out of a second consecutive Finals tournament on penalties. We Englishmen feel your pain, Mexico.

Republic of Ireland Squad 1994:

GK: Pat Bonner (Glasgow Celtic, 34, 73), Alan Kelly (Sheffield United, 25, 3)

DEF: Phil Babb (Coventry City, 23, 5), Denis Irwin (Manchester United, 28, 26), Gary Kelly (Leeds United, 19, 5), Alan Kernaghan (Manchester City, 27, 11), Paul McGrath (Aston Villa, 34, 65), Kevin Moran (Blackburn Rovers, 38, 69), Terry Phelan (Man City, 27, 22), Steve Staunton (Villa, 25, 47)

MID & WIDE: Ray Houghton (Villa, 32, 58), Roy Keane (Man Utd, 22, 22), Jason McAteer (Bolton Wanderers, 22, 5), Eddie McGoldrick (Arsenal, 29, 12), Alan McLoughlin (Portsmouth, 27, 17), John Sheridan (Sheffield Wednesday, 29, 19), Andy Townsend (Villa, 30, 45), Ronnie Whelan (Liverpool, 32, 50)

FWD: John Aldridge (Tranmere Rovers, 35, 57), Tony Cascarino (Chelsea, 31, 50), Tommy Coyne (Motherwell, 31, 14), David Kelly (Wolverhampton Wanderers, 28, 16)

United States Squad 1994:
GK: Tony Meola (Cpt, Buffalo Blizzard, 25), Jürgen Sommer (Luton Town, 25), Brad Friedel (Newcastle United, 23)
DEF: Marcelo Balboa (Léon, 26), Mike Burns (Viborg, Denmark, 23), Paul Caligiuri (Freiburg, 30), Fernando Clavijo (St Louis Storm, 37)*, Tom Dooley (Bayer Leverkusen, 32), Cle Kooiman (Cruz Azul, Mexico, 30), Alexei Lalas (no contract, 24)†, Mike Lapper (Wolfsburg, 23)
MID & WIDE: John Harkes (Derby County, 27), Cobi Jones (Coventry City, 24), Hugo Perez (San Diego Sockers, 30), Tab Ramos (Real Betis, 27), Claudio Reyna (Virginia Cavaliers, 20), Mike Sorber (UNAM Pumas, Mexico, 23)
FWD: Frank Klopas (AEK Athens, 27), Joe-Max Moore (Saarbrücken, 23), Earnie Stewart (Willem II Tilburg, 25), Roy Wegerle (Coventry City, 30), Eric Wynalda (Saarbrücken, 25)

QUARTER-FINALS

Italy	(1) 2	**Spain**	(0) 1	9 July, Boston; 54,605
D Baggio 25,		R Baggio 88		
Caminero 59				
Holland	(0) 2	**Brazil**	(0) 3	9 July, Dallas; 63,998
Bergkamp 64, Winter 77		Romário 52, Bebeto 62,		
		Branco 81		

The tournament, pretty ordinary so far, briefly sprang to life in the quarter-finals, producing four good matches between evenly matched sides.

Italy might have struggled against this quality of opposition with ten men, even with eleven it was never easy. Roberto Baggio was thwarted early on but was generally kept quiet by Nadal and company. It was his unrelated namesake Dino Baggio's classical long-range strike that put the Italians ahead. Caminero's equaliser was the result of a fine counter-attack, but it was an Italian leg

---

* Clavijo became the oldest player sent off in a World Cup Finals match when he got his marching orders late in the match against Brazil.
† Lalas is mistakenly listed in some sources as playing for Padova, but that deal was only done after his impressive performances in the Finals. He became a cult figure among fans everywhere, with his bizarre hairstyle and buccaneering tackling, but he never really cut the mustard in European soccer.

that took the ball up and over Pagliuca. Late on Salinas was one on one with the Italian 'keeper but lost his nerve, and Pagliuca leaped high to tip over a long-range hit from Hierro. Italy were under intense pressure for the last half-hour but survived through a combination of good goalkeeping and typically resolute last-ditch defending.

Baggio (Roberto) kept his nerve where Salinas didn't. Nicola Berti's chip forward bounced loose as Italy attacked and Signori just reached it ahead of Nadal (who should have seen red for his challenge). The referee did well to play on and Roberto Baggio, who had disappeared so completely it was easy to forget he was playing, took the ball around Zubizarreta and scored from a tough angle. On this occasion the better team didn't win, but it left many people wondering if Italy's name was on the trophy.

The referee missed a blatant elbow in the match. To be fair so did all the TV commentators; there was barely a mention of it in the coverage. Tassotti's assault on Luis Enrique was as danger-ous as Leonardo's against the USA, a fact reflected in a lengthy post-match eight-game ban. If FIFA had clamped down on play-acting and cheating in the 1990s as hard as they clamped down on serious foul play, it might not have become as endemic as it is today.

Holland and Brazil played out a cagey first half in Dallas, before sharing five goals in a half-hour burst in the second half. Romário volleyed home Bebeto's cross with Koeman trailing sluggishly behind him and then watched his strike partner skim the post. On the hour Bebeto waltzed through the Dutch back line, beat De Goey and scored. Holland stood still, hoping for an offside against Romário – Koeman still had his hand up when Bebeto scored. Play to the whistle, son. We were then "treated" to the ghastly baby-cradling goal celebration that Bebeto bequeathed to the football world. Had the referee sent him off there and then he would have done the game a huge service.

The Dutch needed a quick response and got one, Bergkamp running on to a clever throw and beating Taffarel, who was slow to come out. The goalkeeper, who looked past his best, didn't come at all for De Boer's corner twelve minutes later and Winter couldn't miss. The Brazilian defence looked vulnerable, having been near impassable for four and a half games.

With Leonardo suspended Brazil recalled the veteran Branco and he offered up his free-kick skills in the last few minutes. The first, hard and high, was tipped over superbly by De Goey; the second, harder and low, flew just inside the far post.

Here's a thought. Had Advocaat picked Danny Blind, the Ajax sweeper, instead of Koeman, a good passer and set piece kicker but a suspect defender, they might have dealt better with the Brazilian forwards.

WORLD CUP SHOCK No.10
10 July 1994, Giants Stadium, NJ; 72,416

Bulgaria	**(0) 2**	Stoichkov 75, Lechkov 79
Germany	**(0) 1**	Matthäus 48

Referee: **José Torres Cadena** (Colombia)
Coaches: **Dimitar Penev** (Bulgaria) & **Berti Vogts** (Germany)

Bulgaria (4–4–2): Boris Mihailov (Cpt, Mulhouse); Ilian Kiriakov (Melida), Trifon Ivanov (Neuchâtel Xamax), Petar Hubchev (Hamburg), Tsanko Tzvetanov (Levski Sofia); Zlatko Yankov (Levski Sofia), Yordan Lechkov (Hamburg), Nasko Sirakov (Levski Sofia), Krasimir Balakov (Sporting); Hristo Stoichkov (Barcelona), Emil Kostadinov (Porto). **Subs:** Petar Aleksandrov (Aarau) 82m for Tzvetanov; Daniel Borimirov (Levski Sofia) 82m for Lechkov
Germany (4–4–2): Bodo Illgner (Cologne); Thomas Berthold (Stuttgart), Thomas Helmer (Bayern Munich), Jürgen Kohler (Juventus), Michael Wagner (Kaiserslautern); Thomas Hassler (Roma), Guido Buchwald (Stuttgart), Lothar Matthäus (Bayern), Andreas Möller (Juventus); Rudi Völler (Olympique de Marseille), Jürgen Klinsmann (Monaco). **Subs:** Thomas Strunz (Stuttgart) 59m for Wagner; Andreas Brehme (Kaiserslautern) 83m for Hassler
Cautioned: Helmer (Ger) 14m, Wagner (Ger) 15m, Ivanov (Bul) 22m, Hassler (Ger) 49m, Klinsmann (Ger) 50m, Stoichkov (Bul) 82m, Mihailov (Bul) 85m, Völler (Ger) 89m

Further progress for Germany looked likely, as Berti Vogts' men drew Bulgaria, the weakest of the quarter-finalists. This meant virgin territory for Bulgaria, through to the knockout stages. They had some good players, just no pedigree at this level. Many of their stars played abroad, but only one of them was a "name" player; that was Hristo Stoichkov, the highly strung Barcelona striker. Stoichkov was a great player, a left-sided striker with strength and some pace and a fine crosser of the ball; he was also lethal from free-kicks and rarely missed penalties, which he was adept at winning. He could be a liability; a major brawl in a 1985 Cup Final in Bulgaria led to a life suspension, which was eventually repealed to one month – a fairly extreme change of heart by the authorities. Had the ban stood Bulgaria would have lost its finest-ever player. Not that Stoichkov learned his lesson; he continued to berate officials, and in his first season at Barcelona (1990–91) he was suspended for two months for treading on the referee's foot. He was as brash and unapologetic as his country's later superstar, Dimitar Berbatov, was unassuming.

There were other good players. Borislav Mihailov (Mulhouse in France), the goalkeeper with the – ahem, shall we say, distinctive? – hair transplant was the captain and a reassuring presence. In front of him giant stopper Trifon Ivanov (Neuchatel Xamax in Switzerland) was anything but reassuring to his opponents; his scary beard and ragged eighties mullet made him look like a cross between Trevor Hockey, the cult sixties hatchet-man and Nick Rhodes from Duran Duran. The balding midfield playmaker Yordan Lechkov, the busy winger Emil Kostadinov and the curly-haired Krasimir Balakov were all international quality, all playing abroad, but not well known outside Bulgaria or the club where they played (Hamburg, Porto and Sporting Lisbon respectively). But how would this mish-mash of expats and players from Levski Sofia, the dominant domestic club, fare at the business end of a major tournament?

Pretty well was the answer. Bulgaria started brightly, and Stoichkov stung Illgner's palms with a shot from a tight angle. The Barcelona man then set up Balakov for a low drive, which hit the outside of Illgner's post. Klinsmann, who put a free header straight into Mihailov's arms in the first half, made the breakthrough early in the second, but he did it in unsavoury fashion, throwing himself to the ground after a fifty-fifty challenge with Lechkov. How a perennial diver like Klinsmann could fool a referee who presumably was regarded as one of the game's top officials is mystifying. Maybe a FIFA refereeing committee which four years earlier had appointed one of its members' son-in-law to a key game could explain . . .

The Germans thought they were two-up soon after. Hässler hit the post and Völler controlled the rebound and drilled home. The offside decision from the linesman was a good one – Völler was offside when Hässler, the last man to touch the ball, hit his shot.

Bulgaria showed great resolve against intimidating opponents.
Stoichkov won a free-kick on the edge of the box and swung it
gracefully over the wall and into the side of the goal Illgner had
vacated. Three minutes later Yankov twisted inside past a defender
and chipped a tempting ball into the middle. The Germans had
been sucked across the right and Lechkov stole in behind the
centre-backs to send a flying header into the top corner. Brian
Glanville analyses the goal in his World Cup history. The Germans
had decided to play with a sweeper, but instead of putting Matthias
Sammer there, who played the position for Borussia Dortmund,
they used Matthäus, a midfield player. Matthäus thought he was
good enough to play anywhere, but he was *in absentia* when
Lechkov crept in to beat five foot five Thomas Hässler to the ball.

Germany looked stunned. The rest of the world screamed for
Bulgaria to hold on, and they did. Beckenbauer's arrogant prediction from 1990 had come to roost, and an ageing side full of self-
belief but little else, was out of the competition. It was the end of
the road for a whole generation of uncompromising German
athletes; Buchwald, Berthold, Illgner, Riedle, Brehme and Völler
all played their last game in the Giants Stadium. It must have
seemed a long flight home.

Sweden   **(0) (1) 2 Romania**   **(0) (1) 2** 10 July, Palo Alto; 81,715
Brolin 79,   Raduciou 88, 101
K Andersson 115
Sweden won 5–4 on penalties

Another good game, though it was without the charged atmosphere of Romania's game against Argentina. The Palo Alto
stadium was huge, but more austere and distant than the Rose
Bowl.

Most of the action was packed into the last half of the match,
although, had Dahlin's header gone inside of the post instead of
hitting it after three minutes, there might have been more drama
early on. There were only ten minutes remaining when Brolin
sneaked behind the wall to get on the end of Mild's well-rehearsed
and clever free-kick, and only two left when Raducioiu belted
home a lucky deflection that came his way. When Raducioiu
pounced on another loose ball in the first period of extra-time

and Stefan Schwarz was sent off a minute later for a second bookable offence the game was surely up for Sweden. Kennet Andersson had other ideas, beating Prunea, who was slow to come, to a long punt into the area. Substitute Henrik Larsson, complete with outrageous dreadlocks, missed a great chance to finish Romania off, but it went to penalties. Mild missed the first one badly and then all the classy attackers on view scored until Dan Petrescu hit a tame effort straight at Ravelli. Petrescu had looked a terrific player going forward and played only one season at Sheffield Wednesday before Chelsea picked him up and he became an integral part of their upgrade. Dumitrescu kept Romania in the hunt with a bottle penalty and Larsson atoned for his earlier miss by slotting home the first sudden-death kick. Romania's great sweeper, Belodedici, missed the vital kick to hand a semi-final place to Sweden; he never looked confident, stuttering twice in a long run up and Ravelli got a good palm to the ball. Belodedici would be in good company – another great defender was about to miss a penalty.

SEMI-FINALS

Italy R Baggio 20, 25	(2) 2	**Bulgaria** Stoichkov 44 (p)	(1) 1	13 July, New Jersey; 77,094
Sweden	(0) 0	**Brazil** Romário	(0) 1	13 July, Pasadena; 84,569

THIRD-PLACE MATCH

Sweden Brolin 8, Mild 30, Larsson 37, K Andersson 39	(4) 4	**Bulgaria**	(0) 0	16 July, Pasadena; 83,716

The semis were something of an anti-climax after those quarter-finals. Italy won their game through Baggio's inspirational strikes, Brazil theirs through organisation and patience.

Roberto Baggio scored two outstanding goals. For the first he wandered in at a leisurely pace off the left wing, strolled around a couple of defenders and bent a shot inside the post, for the entire world as if he were playing on the park against a bunch of kids. The expression on his face as the ball went in told us otherwise, as did the pandemonium in the cacophonous Giants Stadium

– no Irishmen poaching the Italians' tickets this time. For the second goal he hit an instant shot across Mihailov from Albertini's pass.

Bulgaria kept their heads up and Sirakov won a penalty when he turned Costacurta and was brought down. Stoichkov scored it – he rarely missed from the spot. The goal left him joint top scorer with Salenko, but he would have bigger and better memories of the tournament than the Russian. The game was easier for the Italians than 2–1 suggests, but Baggio limping off after seventy minutes was a worrying sight for Sacchi and the Italian fans.

Brazil, too, won more comfortably than their scoreline suggests; Sweden just looked a bit spent after their exertions in the quarter-final. Brazil missed chances, Ravelli made three very good saves – he had an excellent tournament – and it needed another quality finish from Romário, reading a long cross better than the Swedish defenders, to settle the issue.

Sweden recovered some energy and composure in time for the third-place game and beat a listless Bulgaria 4–0. Both sides had cause to be pleased with their campaign.

World Cup Heroes No.27

Yordan Lechkov (1967–)

Bulgaria

Lechkov is one of those excellent football characters we would never hear about were it not for the quadrennial bunfight that is the World Cup. Lechkov started with his local club, Sliven, as a teenager, and he scored in their momentous (and solitary) Bulgarian Cup win in 1990. His form for Sliven earned him international selection and a move to CSKA Sofia and after a single season he joined Hamburg in the Bundesliga, taking advantage of the freedom of movement offered in the post-Communist Eastern Europe.

An attacking player at home, he played a more conventional midfield role at Hamburg, and his probing runs from deep and excellent passing made him a key player. No one noticed outside Germany and Bulgaria. No one actually noticed Bulgaria were any good until they knocked France out. Lechkov played well in the group matches in the USA, and his energy and fitness were a great asset in the heat as many of the European sides struggled. His crowning moment was unquestionably the headed goal that eliminated Germany; it remains Bulgaria's greatest victory. Lechkov lived up to his enhanced reputation with some good showings in the 1996 European Championships.

Lechkov had a reputation as a grumpy so-and-so and a move to Olympique de Marseille in 1996 was short-lived when he fell out with Gérard Gili, the coach. A move to Besiktas was even worse, when a dispute with John Toshack, himself a stubborn individual, meant Lechkov missed three years, including the 1998 World Cup Finals, when FIFA blocked his registration.

Lechkov spent the time building up a successful business and after a brief return to football he ended his career back at Sliven, where he later became Mayor, surviving a couple of scandals along the way. My Bulgarian is non-existent so I am afraid I can provide no detail of these episodes!

Hardly an all-time great, even many who saw him may not remember his name – but they probably remember the bald geezer who knocked out the cocky Germans.

WORLD CUP FINAL No.15
17 July 1994, Rose Bowl, Pasadena; CA. 91,194

Brazil	(0) 0
Italy	(0) 0

Shoot-out:

Italy		Brazil	
Baresi	M 0–0	*Márcio Santos*	M 0–0
Albertini	S 1–0	Romário	S 1–1
Evani	S 2–1	Branco	S 2–2
Massaro	M 2–2	Dunga	S 2–3
R Baggio	M 2–3		

Referee: **Sándor Puhl** (Hungary)
Coaches: **Carlos Alberto Parreira** (Brazil) & **Arrigo Sacchi** (Italy)

Brazil (4–4–2): Claudio Taffarel (Reggiana); *Jorge de Amorim, known as* Jorginho (Bayern Munich), Aldair *Nascimento* (Roma), Márcio Santos (Bordeaux), *Claudio Vaz de Leal, known as* Branco (Fluminense), Mauro *da* Silva *Gomes* (Deportivo La Coruña), *Iomar do Nascimento, known as* Mazinho (Palmeiras), *Carlos Beldorn, known as* Dunga (Stuttgart), *Crizam de Oliveira, known as* Zinho (Palmeiras); Romário (de Souza) (Barcelona), *José Gama, known as* Bebeto (Deportivo La Coruña). **Subs:** *Marcos Evangelista, known as* Cafú (São Paulo) 21m for Jorginho; *Paulo Sérgio Rosa, known as* Viola (Bayer Leverkusen) 105m for Zinho

Italy (4–4–1–1): Gianluca Pagliuca (Sampdoria); Roberto Mussi (Torino), Franco Baresi (Cpt, AC Milan), Paolo Maldini (AC Milan), Antonio Benarrivo (Parma); Roberto Donadoni (AC Milan), Dino Baggio (Juventus), Nicola Bert (Internazionale), Demetrio Albertini (AC Milan); Roberto Baggio (Juventus), Daniele Massaro (AC Milan). **Subs:** Luigi Apolloni (Parma) 34m for Mussi; Alberigo Evani (Sampdoria) 94m for D Baggio

Cautioned: Mazinho (Bra) 4m, Apolloni (Ita) 40m, Albertini (Ita) 42m, Cafú (Bra) 87m

A weary end to an exhausting tournament played in debilitating conditions at the behest of clueless buffoons in suits and greedy TV moguls.

Some of the game's best players were patched up and struggling; Baggio's thigh was strapped, Baresi had an operation, incredibly, twenty-four hours before the game and Romário had to pass a late fitness test. Both right-backs were off the field just after the half-hour, Jorginho replaced by Cafú and Mussi by Apolloni. Maldini stayed in the middle in lieu of the suspended Costacurta – how unlucky, to miss both the European Cup Final and World Cup Final through cards given earlier in the tournament. Dunga and Mauro Silva held the Brazilians together, stifling Albertini and starving Baggio and Massaro of possession, so the Italians created little of note. Romário missed a chance that he might have put away if fit, while Baresi and Maldini had Bebeto in their pocket. Pagliuca was equal to the long-range stuff he was peppered with – his one fumble came back to him off the post.

Everyone, every single football writer going, complains about penalties as a means of settling a game, as does every commentator in every language you can think of. None of them ever suggest a better idea. The replays which left one team exhausted for the next round were unfair. The Golden Goal was gimmicky and took away the excitement of a comeback. Penalties are harsh on the losing team, but they are an equal test, they are dramatic, they require skill and nerve and some thought. Why not? Another half an hour of this match would have been tedious indeed – and someone would have collapsed from the heat.

Baresi and Baggio put their penalties over the bar, that's what everyone remembers. Two of Italy's greatest players cost them. Gross over-simplification. Italy did well to reach the final. Sacchi made the correct decisions on team selection most of the time (although he should have included Vialli in the squad) and Baggio was heroic in the latter stages of the competition. How unfair it must have seemed that the newspapers all carried a picture of him, ponytail drooping, shoulders slumped, while Taffarel, an average goalkeeper, was Brazil's hero. Brazil's hero was the manager, actually. Carlos Parreira had made them into a World Cup-winning side; they may have been the least exciting Brazilian side to do so, but Parreira could only play the hand he was dealt and there weren't oodles of brilliant attacking players sitting at home wondering why they weren't playing.

A little footnote: Brazil took a youngster to this World Cup for experience, after only half a season with Cruzeiro, a young lad they hoped would become a truly great player. He was Ronaldo Luis Názario de Lima. Remember the name.

World Cup Heroes No.28
Roberto Baggio (1967–)
Italy

The most gifted Italian player of his generation only played fifty-six times for the *Azzurri*, a statistic not explained away just by injury. He made his debut in 1988 and played the bulk of those games over the next decade, although his final appearance was a special friendly against Spain in 2004 to mark his retirement from the game.

A difficult player, who fell out at some point with pretty much every coach he worked with, Baggio was still a great trier and never did his sulking on the pitch. He developed at Vicenza, improved and was revered at Fiorentina and won the title at Juventus. He won another at Milan a year after being discarded by Juventus, which must have been satisfying. Moved on to Bologna he responded with his best goal tally in a season as a team earmarked for the drop finished eighth and Baggio won back his place in the Italy squad in time for the 1998 World Cup. It was a disappointing campaign, but like Stuart Pearce for England in 1996 Baggio had the guts to bury a ghost and score a penalty in a shoot-out to atone for a famous miss.

Baggio's resilience in coming back from injury was remarkable. He suffered five serious fractures at Juve, and in his last years at Brescia came back from a ligament injury at thirty-five to save the club from relegation. Baggio called time in 2004: fittingly his last match was at one of the great stadia, the San Siro, and a full house (unheard of for a match against unfashionable Brescia) gave him a wonderful ovation when he was taken off on eighty-eight minutes.

Michel Platini once described Baggio as a number nine-and-a-half. He meant that while Baggio wasn't a straight goalscorer, nor was he a withdrawn second forward. Baggio was a bit different. He had brilliant close control and liked to take defenders on, but didn't have the flat-out pace to leave them for dead, so it made sense for him to play slightly withdrawn, where there was space, but not too withdrawn, because he liked defenders near him to turn and flummox. In his later years he played deeper still and showed a fine range of passing and awareness of movement.

While never regarded as a goalscorer, Baggio's strike rate for Italy (almost one in two games) is better than most of their contemporary strikers (Vieri, Rossi, Vialli, Altobelli, Inzaghi) and much better than that of his natural successor Alessandro Del Piero.

Loved by fans, if not by coaches, Baggio was Italy's greatest attacking player of the last forty years.

Team of the Tournament, 1994:

Ravelli (Sweden)
Jorginho (Brazil)   Belodedici (Romania)   Marcio Santos (Brazil)   Maldini (Italy)
Lechkov (Bulgaria)   Dunga (Brazil)   Hagi (Romania)
Baggio (Italy)   Romário (Brazil)   Stoichkov (Bulgaria)

Official Team of the Tournament: Very little difference, for once. The official team had only three defenders – don't really see Hagi or Brolin putting in a shift at wing-back, myself. They always weight these teams towards attacking players. It's a team, fellers, look the word up. They had **Preud'homme** for Ravelli (not much in it) and **Brolin** and **Balakov** for Belodedici and Lechkov (Balakov was a better player than Lechkov over his career, but not here).

Leading scorers: Salenko & Stoichkov (6); Klinsmann, Baggio, Romário & K Andersson (5)

Heaven Eleven No.12

Italy

Coach:
Vittorio Pozzo: I know, we said post-war, but I only meant the players . . . and there's always Bearzot if you don't like it.

Goalkeepers:
Gianluigi Buffon: tough choice between him and Zoff
Dino Zoff: see above
Enrico Albertosi: part of 1970 team, definitely third choice here

Defenders:
Giuseppe Bergomi: cool teenager to old hand
Giacinto Facchetti: first great attacking back in the *catenaccio* system
Paolo Maldini: awesome
Gaetano Scirea: grace under pressure
Franco Baresi: also awesome
Fabio Cannavaro: colossal, massive heart
Gianluca Zambrotta: mobile, adaptable, reliable
Claudio Gentile: if there's a man to mark . . .

Midfield & wide:
Alessandro Del Piero: creative talent to burn
Bruno Conti: excellent winger on either flank

Marco Tardelli: enforcer who could also play
Andrea Pirlo: great deep-lying playmaker, a footballer's footballer
Sandro Mazzola: great energy and vision and passing
Gianni Rivera: effortless air and an eye for goal
Roberto Donadoni: gave the team great width without ever just being a winger
Francesco Totti: has been an excellent, sometimes undervalued servant

Strikers:
Roberto Baggio: everyone's favourite Buddhist
Luigi Riva: cracking left foot and serious pace
Paolo Rossi: great opportunist, great movement
Roberto Bettega: forceful attacker and did well when the team were struggling

Omissions: Some quality defenders, amongst them **Nesta, Costacurta, Cabrini, Burgnich**. What other country could leave Antonio Cabrini out? It is just possible that the game's best three left-backs have all been Italian. **Antognoni** was a fine midfielder, **Romeo Benetti** was a terrifying presence (but we ain't short of them) and **Franco Causio** was a dangerous winger with a dangerous moustache. Up front **Vialli** never quite scored enough and **Graziani** was a tiny bit short of this level, but with the heart of a lion.

Likely first XI:

Buffon
Bergomi Cannavaro Baresi Maldini
Tardelli Pirlo
Baggio Del Piero Riva
Rossi

7.3 OVER-RATED PLAYERS

Time for a bit of fun.

Here are two selected elevens, chosen carefully by a panel of experts. (Me and my friend, Guy.)

In the unlikely event of any of the players reading this: fellers, don't worry, you have a World Cup Winner's medal, which is more to show for your career than I, or any other bitter scribe will have. Except Tarantini, you really were rubbish.

The Worst XI to own a World Cup Winner's medal:
Goalkeeper: Félix (Brazil, 1970) – by a mile, a complete travesty.
Right-back: Djalma Santos (Brazil, 1962) – in 1954 he was massive and scary, in 1958 he was scary and brilliant, in 1962 he was just massive.
Left-back: Alberto Tarantini (Argentina, 1978) – a thug with a thumbnail of talent.
Centre-back: Klaus Augenthaler (West Germany, 1990) – I never got him, he was slow and easily brushed off the ball, but had massive guys like Köhler and Buchwald to babysit.
Centre-back: Frank Leboeuf (France, 1998) – not Frank's fault Blanc was suspended, but deeply unfair he got the medal instead of his skipper. Nice guy, though.
Midfield: Mazinho (Brazil, 1994) – a right-back used as an extra defensive midfielder, Pelé must have shuddered at the sight.
Midfield: Héctor Enrique (Argentina, 1986) – one of a number of sub-standard players carried by Maradona in that team.

Midfield: Nobby Stiles (England, 1966) – did a job, but wasn't really an international-standard footballer, let alone a World Cup winner; one of a breed/generation who would be in Division 2 nowadays.

Forward: Bernd Hölzenbein (West Germany, 1974) – not much good and unsporting.

Forward: Stéphane Guivarc'h (France, 1998) – lucky to get the gig, Dugarry was marginally better, and even had a stinker while France dominated the Final.

Forward: Pedro (Spain, 2010) – two years later Spain played without a proper striker rather than play Pedro, 'nuff said.

Over-hyped XI
An XI who have arrived at the World Cup and not been as good as either the press, or maybe the player, think they are.

Goalkeeper: Jorge Campos (Mexico, 1994, 1998) – oh, but he was such a character, he sometimes played at centre-forward and he designed his own jerseys . . . Yes, but he was a terrible goalkeeper and the jerseys looked like something a colourblind kid with a random basket of crayons might have come up with.

Right-back: Maicon (Brazil, 2010) – touted as the best right-back in the world, within a couple of years was the third-choice right-back at Manchester City.

Left-back: Roberto Carlos (Brazil, 1994, 1998 & 2002) – the free-kicks were laughably bad and a waste of possession, his crossing was amateur hour and he was a woeful defender. The single most over-rated footballer in the history of the international game.

Centre-back: Ronald Koeman (Holland, 1990 & 1994) – good passer, nice free-kicks, but slow and often out of position in defence. If Holland had picked Danny Blind they may have beaten Brazil in 1994.

Centre-back: Taribo West (Nigeria, 1998 & 2002) – well, he must be good, he plays for Inter . . . except that Inter weren't very good in the late '90s. Don't draw attention to yourself by putting ribbons in your dyed hair unless you're very, very good.

Midfield: Miguel Angel Brindisi (Argentina, 1974) – he was the big bad, coming to take the World Cup away from Brazil . . .

or get dropped after the first game and play little part until Argentina were already out.

Midfield: Enzo Francescoli (Uruguay, 1986 & 1990) – great player, a legend in the Copa América, but so disappointing in his two World Cup appearances. His only defence is that his colleagues were worse, but he was meant to set the standard.

Midfield: Hidetoshi Nakata (Japan, 1998, 2002 & 2006) – the new big thing when he came to France in 1998 but he was awful, wasteful in possession and terrible defensively. He improved in 2002 & 2006 but by then less was expected and he was just another decent footballer.

Midfield: Johnny Haynes (England, 1958 & 1962) – maybe the best passer of the ball in the world game at the time, but never got to work in either tournament; his successor in the 1980s, Glenn Hoddle, suffered the same fate in 1986, flattering to deceive.

Forward: Sylvain Wiltord (France, 2002 & 2006) – so many caps, so little impact.

Forward: Gabriel Batistuta (Argentina, 1994, 1998 & 2002) – happy to bang them in against the Muppets, invariably missing when the opposition was a bit more real. Cris Freddi describes him as a *rabbit killer*, and it's a neat epithet.

7.4 WORLD CUP 1998

Thirty-two teams. Blimey. In all, 174 entered the qualifying process, with thirty to join France and Brazil in the Finals – that means nearly one in six went through. It meant anyone who was anyone would surely win through, didn't it? Sort of – but it also meant more countries with no serious chance of winning made the Finals. Still, a liberal scattering of banana skins is always fun isn't it? Yes, but an equally liberal scattering of dull group games is less so. One definite improvement was the fact that finishing third in a first-phase group meant you were out – no more reward for failure.

Another huge improvement was the outlawing of the tackle from behind. Medical analysis had told football's administrators that these were the dangerous tackles, the ones that ended careers, and they did nothing for the game as a spectacle. Critics bemoaned the loss of the old-fashioned crunching tackle, but the art of tackling was never meant to be the art of hurting. Defending would become a new art form, one where the best practitioners stayed on their feet. The downside (there always is one) was the need for a new breed of forward to use the rules to buy free-kicks and cards for their opponents by exaggerating the seriousness of a challenge.

So no crashing tackles from the back, no back-passes, we were in for a feast . . .

France seemed a solid and unobjectionable choice as host, and ten cities were chosen from various applicants as the main venues. Two of the stadia were in the environs of the capital; the old Parc des Princes, formerly a velodrome and home to Paris St Germain, and the brand-new national stadium (for both football and rugby union), the Stade de France. The other major venue was the Vélodrome in Marseille, which would host a semi-final.

There were still concerns about hooligans, with the violent element in the English game attaching itself to the national team after finding the police attention a little hot at domestic fixtures. And what better than to beat on Johnny Foreigner, eh? All sorts of solutions were proposed, mostly draconian and stupid. In the end it was the same diligent methods of identifying and eliminating the ringleaders that weeded out the worst culprits and curtailed this poison. A lot of mud gets slung at the British police (some merited, the vilification of their actions at Hillsborough included) but they have done a really good job against hooliganism.

After the ghastly razz-a-matazz in some of the American stadia in 1994, it was the turn of the players to embarrass themselves and make us look away. There was a selection of hideous footwear, with Blanco of Mexico's tri-coloured pair taking first prize for ostentation. The goalkeeping jerseys were a right old state – I believe I have already passed opinion on Campos' designer gear, And some of the haircuts, well I know I'm a curmudgeonly middle-aged Northern man, but honestly, there were ponytails of all descriptions, some loose, some braided, there were dreadlocks, Mohicans, tonsures shaved into patterns and messages, ringlets, poodle heads (Valderrama was still with us) and dyed hair of various hues. Jay-Jay Okocha with green hair – imagine if he'd done that at Bolton . . . They say it's a man's game, but some of these lads were surely bought a My Little Princess Make-Up and Hair Set by mistake when they were little.

Qualifying

It was a long and complicated road to qualification for some teams. Iran played six matches in an initial group, eight in a final group and then three more play-off matches, one which they lost against Japan, and another two draws against Australia, which saw them through on away goals. It was tough on the Aussies, but they switched off at 2–0 up in Melbourne and goals from Karim

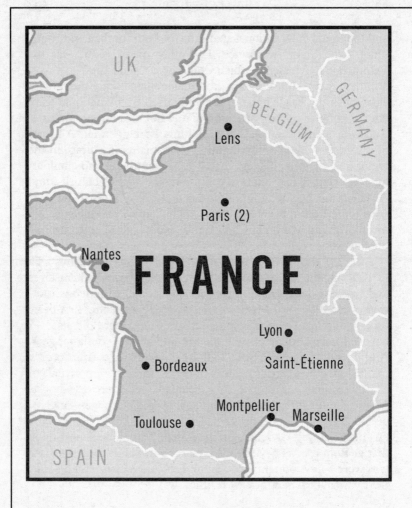

1998
FRANCE

Of the nine grounds used for the 1938 finals in France, only three were used again in 1998. Seven new venues were added to make ten in all.

Paris: Stade de France and Parc des Princes
The Parc des Princes was still a fine venue, but was forced to play second fiddle to the brand-new Stade de France, a stadium for both the national football and national rugby union teams. It was built with a capacity of

80,000 and every seat was taken for the final between the hosts and Brazil. The Stade de France is in Saint-Denis, a northern suburb of the city.

Bordeaux: Parc Lescure
The old Bordeaux ground is earmarked for closure in 2015, but it served in two World Cups and stood for over seventy years. It was filled to capacity (31,800) for all five matches it hosted in the 1998 Finals.

Toulouse: Stade Municipal de Toulouse
The same stadium, with a bit of modernization that served in the 1938 Finals.

Marseille: Stade Vélodrome
The biggest club ground in France served a second term as a World Cup venue and hosted the semi-final between Brazil and Holland. The Vélodrome is currently undergoing refurbishment to increase the capacity to 67,000 for the 2016 European Championships.

Lyon: Stade de Gerland
Home of the successful Olympique Lyonnais club, the Gerland missed out in 1938, but hosted six matches in 1998.

Lens: Stade Felix Bollaert
Now the Stade Bollaert-Delelis, this ground is the home of Racing Club Lens. The capacity is 40,000, more than the city's official population, but the cities of Picardie are close together and form a large semi-urban sprawl so that statistic is deceptive. France played their second-round match against Paraguay in Lens.

Nantes: Stade de la Beaujoire
Situated in the city of Nantes at the mouth of the Loire, this stadium was built for the 1984 European Championship and hosted six games at the 1998 World Cup, including Brazil's classic quarter-final win over Denmark.

Montpellier: Stade de la Mosson
Wealthy Montpellier volunteered to double the size of its ground for the 1998 finals from 16,000 to 32,900 and was rewarded with six finals matches, and a few games at the 2007 Rugby World Cup.

Saint-Étienne: Stade Geoffroy-Guichard
Home to the famous Les Verts of Saint Étienne, the G-G was the venue for England's brilliant and heartbreaking rearguard action against Argentina in 1998, the team's finest World Cup moment since winning in 1966.

Bagheri and Khodada Azizi sent them out. Both scorers, along with Iran's most famous player, the striker Ali Daei, played in the *Bundesliga* in Germany for Arminia Bielefeld (Bagheri and Daei) and Cologne (Azizi). Saudi Arabia and South Korea headed the two final groups and also travelled to France. The four Asia sides would muster five points from twelve games at the Finals, which didn't augur well for Japan and Korea in 2002.

Africa had five teams in the Finals and the five qualifiers all won their groups with something to spare; Nigeria finished only a point ahead but had the luxury of switching off in their last match against Guinea and duly lost. Tunisia, Cameroon, Morocco and South Africa would join them in the Finals. Algeria, normally one of the strongest African sides, screwed up big time, losing to Kenya in an initial play-off and not even making the group stage.

North American qualification produced three finalists and was really about who joined Mexico and the United States. It was Jamaica, a new face, who won through in third place in the final group. In the autumn of 1997 they put together a crucial run of games, beating Canada and Costa Rica 1–0 and earning a 1–1 draw against the USA in Washington. All three goals were scored by the young English-born striker Deon Burton, of Derby County. Burton and a few other English pros, including the experienced Wimbledon midfielder Robbie Earle, had swelled the Jamaican ranks to good effect. Jamaica had qualified the Irish way.

For the first time CONMEBOL introduced the idea of a large round-robin group to decide their four entrants (and to generate more cash, of course).

Argentina topped the section, with Paraguay a surprise package in second place. Paraguay got an excellent point in Buenos Aires. Batistuta beat José Luis Chilavert in the Paraguay goal with a superb free-kick, but Chilavert extracted the perfect revenge, bending in a twenty-five-yard free-kick for the equaliser. The World Cup had a character coming. They also had one of the world's best defenders in Carlos Gamarra, who had just endured a miserable season with Benfica – he never excelled in Europe – but was a colossus for his country in the qualifiers. Colombia also won through comfortably – it was last chance for Valderrama and his generation to live up to the hype on the biggest stage. The last place went to Chile on goal difference from Peru. Chile effectively sealed their fate with a 4–0 win over Peru, a superb hat-trick from Marcelo Salas sealing the deal. They finished off with an equally comfortable 3–0 win over Bolivia. Salas had just signed a deal at Lazio, and his compatriot Iván Zamorano was at Internazionale after a fine spell at Real Madrid in the first years of the decade. Like Colombia, they had to prove they could perform outside South America.

A new qualifying system within UEFA meant only the group winners won through to the Finals automatically, plus the second placed team with the best record. The other runners-up had to get through two-legged play-offs against each other to earn a place. Europe had a lot more countries in the zone after the break-up of Yugoslavia and the Soviet Union. The new sides had low rankings, so it meant there were dangerous floaters like Croatia and Slovakia in the third pool of seeds and even some good sides in the fourth pool (Ukraine and Yugoslavia, effectively Serbia and Montenegro).

Some of the top sides won through easily enough. Norway romped away with the easiest section, while Spain, Romania and Germany won their groups without losing a game. Romania were especially impressive, scoring for fun and conceding only four in their group while winning every game except a draw in Dublin – a result most sides would take in the 1990s. The Irish did seal second place with a 2–1 win in Lithuania courtesy of two goals from Tony Cascarino, a much-improved player after a late career stint in France with Marseille and now Nancy. The Irish fell at the last hurdle, beaten 2–1 in Brussels by Belgium with a goal from PSV's Luc Nilis, who also scored the Belgians' equaliser in Dublin.

Belgium were just squeezed into second in their group by their neighbours Holland – these two are like England and Poland in World Cup qualifiers, magnetically attracted. To be fair, Holland beat Belgium home and away – it was Turkey who gave them problems, their win in Istanbul demonstrated how much they had improved in recent years. We shall draw a veil over Wales' contribution. They started well, winning their first two matches easily; unfortunately their opponents were San Marino, who got no points and no goals. Wales won no more matches and got a pasting in Holland.

Yugoslavia finished second to Spain, ahead of the Czech Republic and Slovakia. Some of the class of 1990 were still there – Stojkovic, now thirty-five, and Savicèvic, and they had Savo Milosevic, mocked in his three years at Aston Villa but happier in the more patient Balkan style. Spain's win in Valencia over the Slavs, with goals from Pep Guardiola and the fizzy new striker Raúl, meant Spain headed the group and stayed there.

Hungary finished second to Norway in their weak group – more impressive was Norway's 4–2 defeat of Brazil in a friendly in Oslo. Hungary got hammered home and away by Yugoslavia in the play-offs. Another ordinary fivesome saw Bulgaria edge Russia into second place. Ivanov's goal in a 1–0 win in Sofia gave them breathing space and rendered Russia's win in Moscow irrelevant.

The Laudrup brothers helped Denmark put the disappointment of 1994 behind them and win their section, while the Ukraine edged out Portugal, who drew too many games they should have won. Would they ever deliver? Northern Ireland managed only a single win over Albania; their ranking was plummeting and their contribution reduced to that of occasional spoiler. Croatia won the battle of the newbies for a place in the Finals, but Ukraine had cause for future optimism in the form of their strikers, Andrei Shevchenko and Sergei Rebrov, both still in their early twenties. Croatia's best forward, Alen Boksic, was injured just before the Finals; he was a great player but too often injured.

Group 4 contained a very strong Swedish side, a well-managed and hard-working Scotland team and a similarly well-organised Austrian squad. Three former Soviet states, Estonia, Latvia and Belarus made up the numbers. A cold group. The 1994 quarter-finalists started well but then inexplicably lost at home to Austria, to a goal by Andy Herzog of Werder Bremen after a shocking mistake in the Swedish defence. Kennet Andersson had a penalty saved by Konsel – there was justice there, as the kick was given for a superb saving tackle, not a foul. The Swedes lost their next game, too, to a seventh minute goal from John McGinlay for

Scotland. Now Sweden were struggling, because Austria and Scotland were gritty sides and were grinding out results against the weaker teams. Sweden needed a result in Vienna.

The game was rough, and Austria's Pfeffer saw red just before half-time, but things evened up when Roland Nilsson followed for a debatable professional foul. That man Herzog (later he became Austria's most capped player) came up trumps again, scoring the only goal with a glorious run and left-foot strike. There was more drama to come when Konsel was sent off for another professional foul with eight minutes left but Austria hung on. There was nothing Sweden could now do but hope one of the other two sides dropped silly points. They didn't, and a team that should have gone to France and would have been fancied to do well were out. Scotland qualified automatically as the best second-placed team. Good job, there were some tasty sides in the play-off pot.

The weirdest game for Scotland came when they were due to play Estonia in Tallinn. Scotland objected, not unreasonably, to the poor-quality floodlights temporarily rigged up on a lorry in each corner. FIFA ordered the kick-off time to be moved forward, but Estonia had a strop and didn't turn up. Scotland kicked off and were promptly awarded the game. Estonia cleverly did turn up for the second kick-off, claiming they had asked for confirmation of FIFA's decision and received none. FIFA were soft and ordered the game replayed and it finished 0–0 – just was well it didn't affect Scotland's qualification. The best moment came when the assembled Tartan Army (the real sufferers here) stood forlornly in one end of the ground for the earlier kick-off chanting *"One team in Tallinn, there's only one team in Tallinn . . ."* (Only funny if you go to local derbies – an explanation would spoil it.)

And England? Oh, you know, nothing to fret about, just the usual roller-coaster. They were excellent in Euro '96, albeit on home turf. Under Terry Venables they showed a new grasp of a modern way of playing, keeping the ball for longer until an opportunity to attack at pace presented itself. They had a team filled with players who were comfortable on the ball and Venables used Teddy Sheringham to complement Alan Shearer's strength and aggression, and the partnership clicked, releasing Shearer as a genuine threat at this level.

But Venables had gone, ousted by the FA suits who didn't think he was the "right sort of chap", and in his place was Glenn Hoddle, who had done well at Swindon and Chelsea, and certainly understood the need for patient, sophisticated football at the top level. Qualification was fraught, a home defeat to a Gianfranco Zola goal for Italy seemed to have condemned England to second place at best, and Hoddle was lambasted (rightly) for picking only one proper centre-half.

England did have talent coming through, especially at Manchester United, and a briefly renascent Gascoigne helped engineer a good away win in Poland, where Italy dropped a point. The big result for England was Italy's 0–0 draw with Georgia in Tbilisi, which meant they only needed a point in Rome, not a victory. They got it, on a teeth-grindingly tense night, due in part to a good defensive performance and in the main to the innate caution of the Italians. Italy joined England in France after scraping a draw and a 1–0 win against Russia, but, like England, they hardly looked contenders.

So who did? Brazil were hard to discount, even without the injured Romario, for the seventeen-year-old from 1994 was now one of the world's most feared attackers. Argentina looked a good side in qualifying, and these two seemed the most likely threat to the best European sides; Germany, as always, France, the host, disappointing at Euro '96, Holland (ditto), Spain (ditto) and Romania, an exciting team if maybe a bit past their very best. There were a few wagers placed on Norway and Yugoslavia, too.

GROUP A

Brazil César Sampaio 4, own goal 73	(1) 2	**Scotland** Collins 37 (p)	(1) 1	10 June, Stade de France; 80,000
Morocco Hadji 38, Hadda 60	(1) 2	**Norway** Own goal 45, Eggen 61	(1) 2	10 June, Montpellier, 28,750
Norway H Flo 46	(1) 1	**Scotland** Burley 66	(1) 1	16 June, Bordeaux; 30,236
Morocco	(0) 0	**Brazil** Ronaldo 8, Rivaldo 45, Bebeto 51	(2) 3	16 June, Nantes; 33,266
Scotland	(0) 0	**Morocco** Bassir 22, 84, Hadda 47	(1) 3	23 June, St Étienne; 35,500
Brazil Bebeto 77	(0) 1	**Norway** TA Flo 82, Rekdal 88 (p)	(0) 2	23 June, Marseilles; 60,000

1. Brazil 6pts (6–3); 2. Norway 5pts (5–4); 4. Morocco 4pts (5–5); 4. Scotland 1pt (2–6)

Scotland had the honour of kicking off the new World Cup against Brazil. Against expectations they did rather well, equalising an early goal with a debatable penalty (coolly converted by John Collins). In the second half a blanket defence did well to stifle a Brazil team that ran out of ideas. Against the blistering pace of Ronaldo, Scotland's ancient central defenders dropped deep and made Brazil play passes in, which they intercepted and cleared with great skill and enthusiasm. In front of them the Scottish midfield tried to keep the ball when they finally got it, and Gordon Durie put in a heroic shift as the lone front man. Tom Boyd, who had an exceptional game, was the unfortunate scorer of the own goal which settled the game, inadvertently knocking the ball into the net after Leighton saved well from Cafú. For once Scotland were not the architects of their own downfall, although worse was to follow.

Morocco earned a well-deserved point off Norway, twice taking the lead. Mustafa Hadji scored a fabulous goal coming off the left and shooting past Grodås and Hadda's volley was almost as good. Norway had little to offer but hefty crosses towards Flo, but they scored from two of these, both as a result of goalkeeping misjudgements.

Olsen responded to Norway's poor performance by dropping a striker (Solskjaer, his most skilful player) and picking an extra midfielder. He was that good a coach. Scotland again ate up the long balls thoughtfully pumped in at their dominant centre-halves. Early in the second half Håvard Flo sneaked some space to stoop and nod in a loose ball, but Norway were undone by a mirror of their own tactics when Weir's long ball found Burley with space and time to look up and lob Grodås.

Brazil, still massive and intimidating in the centre of their defence, but more skilful at the other end than in 1994, made short work of Morocco. Which makes it odd that Scotland, so redoubtable in defence thus far, should be torn apart by Morocco in their last match. The defenders, forced to play up the pitch as Scotland needed a win were at last exposed for lack of pace. Hendry and Weir had a nightmare, Leighton, so good against Brazil, let in a soft strike from Hadda, and Burley was sent off for a crude tackle from behind. A very painful night and it was the last agonising night

Scotland experienced in the World Cup Finals. They haven't qualified since and it looks a pipe dream at the time of writing, for all the
galvanising effect on morale of the admirable Gordon Strachan.

Egil Olsen had not been too complimentary about the Brazilians,
mocking their defending and insisting he was a better coach than
Mario Zagallo. His team strove to back up his boasting in their last
group match, needing a win to grab second place in the group.

Ronny Johnsen was superb against Ronaldo, timing his tackles
well and not allowing the quicksilver striker to turn; not a huge
surprise, he was brilliant at Manchester United for a couple of
years until injury hampered his career. The midfield ran and ran
against Rivaldo and company, and the huge Júnior Baiano was
made to look a bit of a clodhopper by Tore André Flo. Flo was a
hugely under-rated player, probably because his goals-per-game
ratio was below the very best, but he led the line really effectively.
Mobile and strong as well as tall, he shrugged Baiano off on
numerous occasions while his colleagues flooded up in support.
(*If that's Júnior Baiano I wouldn't like to meet Senior Baiano*,
quipped Ron Atkinson – he had a point, the man was colossal.)

Brazil scored first when Denilson recovered from a fall when
fouled and crossed for Bebeto while Norway expected the referee
to intervene. Bebeto had a woeful tournament but couldn't miss
this. The lead lasted five minutes until Flo beat Baiano again and
scored with a shot across Taffarel. Another five minutes and Flo
had his shirt pulled by the Brazilian defender. Rekdal blasted the
penalty into the side of the goal so hard it was irrelevant which
way Taffarel went (he chose correctly but got nowhere near the
ball). For now Olsen's self-aggrandising baloney seemed justified,
but I'm unconvinced Norway would have won had Brazil needed
something from the game, for all their heroics.

Scotland Squad 1998:

GK: Jim Leighton (Aberdeen, 39 years old, 86 caps), Neil
Sullivan* (Wimbledon, 28, 3), Jonathon Gould (Glasgow Celtic,
29, 0)

* Neil Sullivan took over as No.1 after the tournament; he was a solid
'keeper but is, unfortunately for him, best remembered as the bloke who
was beaten from the halfway line by David Beckham in 1996.

DEF: Tom Boyd (Celtic, 32, 55), Colin Calderwood (Tottenham Hotspur, 33, 28), Matt Elliott (Leicester City, 28, 3), Colin Hendry (Cpt, Blackburn Rovers, 32, 32), Tosh McKinlay (Celtic, 33, 19), Jackie McNamara (Celtic, 24, 6), David Weir* (Heart of Midlothian, 28, 5), Derek Whyte (Aberdeen, 29, 8)

MID & WIDE: Craig Burley (Celtic, 26, 25), John Collins (Monaco, 30, 49), Christian Dailly† (Derby County, 23, 10), Scott Gemmill (Nottingham Forest, 27, 13), Darren Jackson (Celtic, 31, 24), Paul Lambert (Celtic, 28, 12), Billy McKinlay (Blackburn, 29, 25)

FWD: Scott Booth (Utrecht, 26, 16), Simon Donnelly (Celtic, 23, 8), Gordon Durie‡ (Glasgow Rangers, 32, 40), Kevin Gallagher (Blackburn, 31, 36)

GROUP B

Chile	(1) 2	**Italy**	(1) 2	11 June, Bordeaux; 31,800
Salas 45, 51		Vieri 10, R Baggio 85 (p)		
Austria	(0) 1	**Cameroon**	(0) 1	11 June, Toulouse; 37,500
Polster 90		Njanka 77		
Chile	(0) 1	**Austria**	(0) 1	17 June, St Étienne; 30,392
Salas 69		Vastic 90		
Italy	(1) 3	**Cameroon**	(0) 0	17 June, Montpellier; 35,000
Di Biagio 8, Vieri 75, 89				
Austria	(0) 1	**Italy**	(0) 2	23 June, Stade de France; 75,000
Herzog 91 (p)		Vieri 48, R Baggio 89		
Cameroon	(0) 1	**Chile**	(1) 1	23 June, Nantes; 39,000
Mboma 55		Sierra 20		

1. **Italy 7pts (7–3)**; 2. **Chile 3pts (4–4)**; 3. **Austria 2pts (3–4)**; 4. **Cameroon 2pts (2–5)**

This group was closer than it looked on paper. Italy had qualified with less than their usual comfort, and such was their shortage of class forwards they brought back a slightly creaky Roberto Baggio. Their opening match against Chile was a cracker, a real game of two halves.

* Still a bit of a clunk here, Weir improved massively at Everton in his thirties, and was still playing for Scotland in his fortieth year, and for Rangers a couple of years after that. Scotland's most consistent player of the last decade.

† Another who improved with age. Picked here as a workmanlike defensive midfielder, he dropped back to become a polished central defender at West Ham. Saw him at Charlton in Division One in his mid-thirties; ran the game from sweeper without breaking sweat. Under-rated.

‡ Known in the game as Jukebox, one of the great nicknames.

Italy were all over it in the first half; Baggio looked purposeful and sharp and after only ten minutes his expert touch from Maldini's long ball put in Vieri, who scored easily. Maldini was captain now, with his father as manager, but accusations of nepotism don't wash when the son is as good as Maldini. The game turned just before the break when Chile got a lucky break at a corner and Salas equalised. In the second half he and Zamorano started to move the Italian backs around and create space. Acuña used it and sent in a wicked cross for Salas to attack and score. Italy looked shell-shocked, but Baggio kept playing football and brought two great saves out of Tápia (which is Spanish for wall, a perfect name for a goalkeeper). Italy's equaliser was jammy, a penalty scored by Baggio (which took nerve after his miss in 1994) after he belted a cross at a defender's arm, but they deserved it.

Austria against Cameroon was abrasive, to say the least, and it was generous on the referee's part to let the game finish eleven-a-side. Polster's forty-fourth goal for Austria remains a record, but didn't disguise the fact that he and his team were out of their depth. Cameroon, The Indomitable Lions, were a pale imitation of the 1990 side, once excitingly direct and robust they were now just dirty. Italy sorted them out, the team and Vieri in particular resisting retaliation in favour of humiliation. Cameroon could – and should – have finished with eight men. I must repeat Cris Freddi's summary for you: *For once, Christian had devoured the Lions.* Nice one.

Italy beat Austria as well, to top the group, but at a cost, Alessandro Nesta injured his knee, and was out – his replacement was the thirty-four-year-old veteran Giuseppe Bergomi. Robert Baggio, injured against Cameroon, came back as a sub against Austria but didn't look fluent.

Chile drew all three games to clinch second. Vastel denied them a win with Austria's second injury-time equaliser, and Cameroon gave them (a) a bit of a runaround and (b) a bit of a kicking in their last match. Cameroon finished the match, and their tournament, with nine men, after Rigobert Song became the first man to get two red cards in the World Cup Finals, and Laureano Etame-Mayer joined him six minutes after coming on as a late substitute. Etame Mayer later played for Arsenal as plain old Lauren, but he wasn't very good there either.

GROUP C

Denmark	(0) 1	**Saudi Arabia**	(0) 0	12 June, Lens; 38,140
Rieper 68				
France	(1) 3	**South Africa**	(0) 0	12 June, Marseilles; 55,077
Dugarry 34,				
own goal 78, 91				
South Africa	(0) 1	**Denmark**	(1) 1	18 June, Toulouse; 36,500
McCarthy 52		Nielsen 14		
Saudi Arabia	(0) 0	**France**	(1) 4	18 June, Stade de France; 75,000
		Henry 36, 77, Trezeguet 67,		
		Lizarazu 84		
France	(1) 2	**Denmark**	(1) 1	24 June, Lyons; 43,500
Djorkaeff 13 (p), Petit 56		M Laudrup 43 (p)		
Saudi Arabia	(1) 2	**South Africa**	(1) 2	24 June, Bordeaux; 34,500
Al-Jaber 45 (p),		Bartlett 19, 90 (p)		
Al-Turiyan 73 (p)				

1. **France 9pts (9–1); 2. Denmark 4pts (3–3); 3. South Africa 2pts (3–6); 4. Saudi Arabia 1pt (2–7)**

A stroll in the park for the hosts. South Africa tried hard in the opening game, but their goalkeeper, Hans Vonk was vacillatory and they offered little up front. Dugarry beat Vonk, to a cross for the first and Issa scored a clumsy own goal for the second. He played for Olympique de Marseille and wouldn't have enjoyed looking a klutz on his home ground. Thierry Henry added a third in injury-time – Issa actually put this one over the line but Henry's chip was going in. Over in Lens, Denmark struggled past Saudi Arabia in Michael Laudrup's 100th international, the solitary goal in a dire game coming from the strong centre-half Marc Rieper from Brian Laudrup's cross.

The Danes were poor again in Toulouse against South Africa, conceding an equaliser to a good opportunist strike from Benni McCarthy and losing two men, Molnár and Wieghorst, to red cards, along with Phiri of South Africa. Denmark owed their point to a shocking miss by Mkhalele; South Africa theirs to Lucas Radebe, who just about held a porous defence together. Alongside him Mark Fish was greyhound quick but prone to losing his man, while the full-backs were awful.

France beat Saudi Arabia easily but had Zidane sent off for a crude foul. He claimed a personal slur had goaded him – not the last time we would hear that sort of lame excuse from Zizou. He had already set up Henry's opener with a brilliant piece of sleight of foot, and his dismissal merely evened up the numbers after Al-Khilaiwi's debatable red for a tackle on Lizarazu. In his defence the Bayern Munich full-back didn't make a meal of it but Brizio Carter, a FIFA favourite despite being an appalling referee, was quick to flash red and appease his masters. South Africa avoided last place with a 2–2 draw against Saudi Arabia, but they would have won but for more shoddy refereeing. The Saudis, disappointing again, were given two soft penalties and created nothing. France beat Denmark to top the group, but only because Denmark were awful again. Some of the Danes were clearly unhappy with their Swedish manager; Schmeichel was publicly critical. The midfield, even Michael Laudrup, looked stale and unimaginative, but Per Frandsen, who had just had an outstanding Premier League season with Bolton, was left on the bench.

GROUP D

Bulgaria	**(0) 0**	**Paraguay**	**(0) 0**	12 June, Montpellier; 27,650
Nigeria	**(1) 3**	**Spain**	**(1) 2**	13 June, Nantes; 33,257
Adepoju 24, own goal 72, Oliseh 77		Hierro 20, Raúl 46		
Bulgaria	**(0) 0**	**Nigeria**	**(1) 1**	19 June, Parc des Princes; 48,500
		Ikpeba 26		
Spain	**(0) 0**	**Paraguay**	**(0) 0**	19 June, St Étienne; 35,300
Bulgaria	**(0) 1**	**Spain**	**(2) 6**	24 June, Lens; 41,275
Kostadinov 56		Hierro 5 (p), Luis Enrique 18, Morientes 53, 80, own goal 88, Kiko 90		
Paraguay	**(1) 3**	**Nigeria**	**(1) 1**	24 June, Toulouse; 37,500
Ayala 1, Benitez 58, Cardozo 86		Oruma 10		

1. Nigeria 6pts (5–5); 2. Paraguay 5pts (3–1); 3. Spain 4pts (8–4); 4. Bulgaria 1pt (1–7)

Bulgaria against Paraguay wasn't a great game, but it had a couple of Chilavert free-kicks to liven things up. Bulgaria didn't look anywhere near as good as in 1994, and Stoichkov was in petulant mode, not match-winning mode, not that the two were necessarily mutually exclusive with him. They went out with a whimper, beaten by Nigeria and crushed by Spain.

By then Spain were desperate. A defeat by Nigeria after a catastrophic error from the great Zubizarreta was followed by a dull draw against Paraguay, in which Chilavert displayed his goal-keeping talents – he was much more than a show-pony.

Bora Milutinovic left out half his first eleven against Paraguay having already qualified for the second stage (and won the group). The Spanish press cried foul but that was sour grapes; Nigeria had every right to rest players, and they still came back from a goal down (scored in the first minute) to level and then dominate the rest of the first half. They found Chilavert in good order again, and Paraguay came back strongly – their need was greater. There was a feeling Spain hadn't picked their best side, and there had been some disappointing performances, Hierro and Luis Enrique honourably excepted. The fact is they went out because of their own shortcomings, not through poor officiating or bad luck. But I'm pretty sure France would rather have lined up against Paraguay in the next round.

GROUP E

Mexico	(0) 3	**South Korea**	(1) 1	13 June, Lyons; 37,588
Peláez 51,		Ha Seok-ju 28		
Hernández 74, 83				
Holland	(0) 0	**Belgium**	(0) 0	13 June, Stade de France; 75,000
Belgium	(1) 2	**Mexico**	(0) 2	20 June, Bordeaux; 34,750
Wilmots 43, 49		Garcia Aspe 56 (p),		
		Blanco 62		
South Korea	(0) 0	**Holland**	(2) 5	20 June, Marseilles; 55,000
		Cocu 37, Overmars 41,		
		Bergkamp 71, van Hooijdonk 79,		
		R de Boer 82		
Holland	(2) 2	**Mexico**	(0) 2	25 June, St Étienne; 35,500
Cocu 4, R de Boer 18		Peláez 74, Hernández 90		
Belgium	(1) 1	**South Korea**	(0) 1	25 June, Parc des Princes; 48,500
Nilis 6		Yoo Sang-chul 71		

1. Holland 5pts (7–2); 2. Mexico 5pts (7–5); 3. Belgium 3pts (3–3); 4. South Korea 1pt (2–9)

Easy. Dull. Dull. Easy. Easy (preposterous scoreline). Dull.

South Korea were very ordinary and when their goalscorer was red-carded a minute after giving them the lead against Mexico, they fell apart. Belgium and Holland plodded at each other in a laborious parody of previous brilliant incarnations. Collina, not an easy referee to fool, sent off Kluivert for the merest brush against Staelens. Kluivert's brooding demeanour did him no favours in these incidents but that doesn't excuse Staelens' cheating. Belgium let a two-goal lead slip against Mexico, while Holland looked more the part as they crushed South Korea. Holland also let a two-goal lead over Mexico slip after an embarrassingly one-sided first half. The embarrassment at the end was all over the face of Jaap Stam, the world's most expensive centre-half, who slipped and let in Hernández for the equaliser. Belgium should have had a hatful against a Korean side who had just had their popular coach sacked, but they missed chances and Yoo Sang-chul scored from a free-kick and knocked them out.

GROUP F

Yugoslavia	**(0) 1**	**Iran**	**(0) 0**	14 June, St Étienne; 30,392
Mihailovic 73				
USA	**(0) 0**	**Germany**	**(1) 2**	15 June, Parc des Princes, 43,815
		Møller 9, Klinsmann 64		
Germany	**(0) 2**	**Yugoslavia**	**(1) 2**	21 June, Lens; 41,275
Own goal 73,		Own goal 13,		
Bierhoff 79		Stojkovic 53		
Iran	**(1) 2**	**USA**	**(0) 1**	21 June, Lyons; 44,000
Estili 40, Mahdavikia 83		McBride 87		
Germany	**(0) 2**	**Iran**	**(0) 0**	25 June, Montpellier; 35,500
Bierhoff 50, Klinsmann 57				
Yugoslavia	**(1) 1**	**USA**	**(0) 0**	25 June, Nantes; 39,000
Komljenovic 3				

1. Germany 7pts (6–2); 2. Yugoslavia 7pts (4–2); 3. Iran 3pts (2–4); 4. USA 0pts (1–5)

Another boring group, with never a shred of doubt which two sides would go through, even though neither played well. Germany looked strong, as always, resilient, as always, and full of themselves, as always when Matthäus played. Yugoslavia looked talented, as always, capricious, as always, and argumentative, as always when Mihailovic played.

Klinsmann was still sharp for a thirty-three-year-old, but Bierhoff, a hero in 1996 with two goals in the European Championship Final, looked wooden. The midfield had too many players like Hassler and Møller who tended to flit in and out of a game. Yugoslavia were too slow despite their immaculate technique, and desperately needed someone who could run with the ball as well as pass.

The USA had gone backwards since the tournament in their country, and had nothing up front where Brian McBride, a hard-working target man rather than a goalscorer, toiled with minimal support. Iran were negative and disappointing. The match between the two weaker sides, billed as a potentially explosive affair, was defused by the common sense of both sets of officials and the players, not by the asinine rhetoric of the politicians and FIFA dignitaries. An exchange of gifts and no bad tackles; job done, can we get on with the football now, please? If only real threats were this easy to defuse.

Beating up Caribbean island teams in qualifying is very different from taking on top European and South American sides, as the USA found out here. They needed to get more players up to a standard where they could play in the top leagues in Europe and get experience against class opposition. The MSL had just got going in the USA, but it needed longer to bed in before it started to yield a generation of players capable of making that transition.

United States Squad 1998:
GK: Brad Friedel (Liverpool, 27, 56), Jürgen Sommer (Columbus Crew, 29, 8), Kasey Keller (Leicester City, 28, 33)
DEF: Jeff Agoos (DC United, 30, 87), Marcelo Balboa (Colorado Rapids, 30, 126), Mike Burns (New England Revolution, 27, 73), Tom Dooley (Cpt, Columbus Crew, 36, 77), Frankie Hejduk (Tampa Bay Mutiny, 23, 11), Alexei Lalas (Metro Stars, 28, 98), Brian Maisonneuve (Columbus Crew, 24, 7), Eddie Pope (DC United, 24, 23), David Regis (Karlsrühr, 29, 2)
MID & WIDE: Chad Deering (Wolfsburg, 27, 10), Cobi Jones (LA Galaxy, 27, 107), Pedrag Radosavljevic (Kansas City Wizards, 34, 24), Tab Ramos (Metro Stars, 31, 80), Claudio Reyna (Wolfsburg, 24, 59), Earnie Stewart (NAC Breda, 29, 47)
FWD: Brian McBride (Columbus Crew, 25, 21), Joe-Max Moore (New England Revolution, 27, 68), Roy Wegerle (Tampa Bay Mutiny, 34, 39), Eric Wynalda (San Jose Clash, 29, 100)

GROUP G

England Shearer 42, Scholes 89	(1) 2	**Tunisia**	(0) 0	15 June, Marseilles; 54,587
Colombia	(0) 0	**Romania** Ilie 45	(1) 1	15 June, Lyons; 37,572
Tunisia	(0) 0	**Colombia** Preciado 83	(0) 1	22 June, Montpellier; 35,500

Romania	(0) 2	England	(0) 1	22 June, Toulouse; 37,500
Moldovan 46, Petrescu 89		Owen 83		
England	(2) 2	Colombia	(0) 0	26 June, Lens; 41,275
Anderton 20, Beckham 29				
Romania	(0) 1	Tunisia	(1) 1	26 June, Stade de France; 80,000
Moldovan 72		Souayeh 10 (p)		

1. Romania 7pts (4–2); 2. England 6pts (5–2); 3. Colombia 3pts (1–3); 4. Tunisia 1pt (1–4)

I shall do more than pay this lip service, as with the last two groups, but only because England were involved. The excitement level was nil, the football was ordinary and two teams were so clearly better than the other two there was little tension, unless you were an England fan who refused to believe Hoddle's team could beat a pedestrian and unambitious Colombian side.

The opening match was played in the miserable aftermath of some disgraceful behaviour in the centre of Marseilles, a violent enough city without a thousand hooligans adding to the mix. Awful scenes, and in the first instance some of the draconian measures bandied about by the *Daily Mail* fraternity didn't seem so ridiculous. England made their customary heavy weather of seeing off the group minnows, but the goal came eventually, Shearer powering a header past a goalkeeper who reacted late. Scholes added a late second to complete a sound performance and England were on their way.

A banner paying tribute to Andrés Escobar was the most positive thing Colombia produced in their opening match, and Hagi's only significant contribution set up Adrian Ilie for a terrific run and finish. Ilie looked an exciting prospect when he first came on to the scene, but his career was one of diminishing returns rather than gradual improvement.

England and Romania were evenly matched in the second match. The first half was a stalemate; the wing-backs cancelled out and Ilie's shot that hit the bar looked suspiciously like a misplaced cross. Hagi, kept quiet by Ince and Batty in the main, created a goal with his only major contribution again, a lovely cross which Moldovan controlled and volleyed with great technique. England improved when Owen's pace was added to Shearer's strength – Sheringham looked out of form and confidence – and a good move ended with the ball breaking kindly for the eighteen-year-old to score.

Hoddle was criticised for not starting with Owen in the match against Romania, but it was good use of the youngster to use him as an impact substitute initially. The manager's comments about Owen's immaturity to the media, however, were crass and typical of his total lack of man-management skills. With mature, confident players, Hoddle was an ideal coach, technically sound, tactically intelligent and sophisticated. With more brittle individuals, he was a disaster – insensitive and tactless and oblivious to lack of confidence when he had so much faith, both in his God and himself. The trait had manifested in his treatment of Paul Gascoigne, prior to the tournament; Hoddle's decision to leave him out was correct, the manner in which he did it was humiliating, summoning players to his room one by one for a show-and-tell moment. Kindergarten stuff. And if Hoddle was right about Gascoigne, he ruined Matthew Le Tissier as an international player. The Southampton player was a genius, but a smidge small-minded. Rather than ease him in gently to international football, Hoddle threw him in against Italy in a World Cup qualifier and then carped when Le Tissier didn't deliver. Giving him a "last chance" in a B international, Hoddle then ignored the results – Le Tissier scored a hat-trick and stole the show – and ignored Le Tissier. A major opportunity lost to capitalise on the form of one England's most talented mavericks of the last forty years. And further indication that Hoddle had a problem with players he knew had talent the equal of his own – stories abound of the manager's burning need to show off his own skills in training. A major talent as a player, and a potentially great manager, Hoddle was let down in both careers by his failings as a character.

Wanting to beat Colombia rather than settle for a draw, Hoddle got it right. (See, not all criticism . . .) David Beckham, who should have played from the first game, replaced David Batty, and Owen came in from the start. Contrary to what some pundits claim, Owen and Shearer were not an ideal partnership, they both wanted to head the line, but at least England had an extra dimension with Owen's searing pace, and it meant the midfield had more space as defenders were reluctant to press high and leave space in behind them.

Anderton and Beckham interchanged cleverly at wing-back and right side of a midfield three, and when Bermúdez failed to clear Owen's cross, Anderton thumped a volley past Mondragon. The goalkeeper was equally helpless to stop Beckham's awesome dipping free-kick at the end of what had become a comfortable night for England. So it was goodbye to Valderrama and Valencia, and the last we would see of Rincón in the big time. Asprilla had already gone, sent home for insulting the coach; he would play a few more games but Colombia haven't been seen in the Finals since, although they look good to make 2014.

Romania played out a draw with Tunisia, proceedings enlivened by the appearance of ten of the Romanian team with dyed yellow hair. The exception was the shaven-headed goalkeeper, Stelea, so coach Iordanescu joined in by joining him in hairlessness. All very silly. They nearly paid for it by losing control of the group, although the choice of a quarter-final against Argentina or Croatia was a bit devil-and-the-deep-blue-sea.

WORLD CUP CLASSIC No.20
14 June 1998, Félix Bollaert, Lens; 38,058

Croatia	(1) 3	Stanic 26, Prosinecki 52, Suker, 68
Jamaica	(1) 1	Earle 45

Referee: **Vitor de Melo Pereira** (Portugal)
Coaches: **Miroslac Blazevic** (Croatia) & **René Simôes** (Jamaica)

Croatia (4–3–2–1): Drazen Ladic (Croatia Zagreb); Dario Simic (Croatia Zagreb), Igor Stimac (Derby County), Slaven Bilic (Everton), Robert Jarni (Real Betis); Zvonimir Soldo (Stuttgart), Robert Prosinecki (Croatia Zagreb), Aljosa Asanovic (Napoli); Zvonimir Boban (Cpt, AC Milan), Mario Stanic (Parma); Davor Suker (Real Madrid). **Subs:** Goran Vlaovic (Valencia) 72m for Simic
Jamaica (4–4–2): Warren Barrett (Cpt, Violet Kickers); Frank Sinclair (Chelsea), Ian Goodison (Olympic Gardens), Onandi Lowe (Harbour View), Ricardo Gardner (Harbour View); Peter Cargill (Harbour View), Robbie Earle (Wimbledon), Theodore Whitmore (Seba United), Fitzroy Simpson (Portsmouth); Deon Burton (Derby County), Paul Hall (Portsmouth). **Subs:** Andrew Williams (Columbus Crew) 72m for Earle; Walter Boyd (Arnett Gardens) 81m for Hall
Cautioned: Soldo (Cro) 5m, Simic (Cro) 59m, Burton (Jam) 62m

This wasn't about the match it was about the crowd. Jamaica, with their pot-pourri of English league journeymen and eager locals, were never likely to match a seasoned side like Croatia, who had top-class defenders in Jarni, Stimac and Bilic, and guys who could hurt at the other end.

The stadium was a picture. Small enough that it looked full, even with two of the less well supported sides playing, the contrast between the pink and white flags of the Croatians and their face-painted fans, with the bustling Jamaican crowd, all yellow and gold and tea cosy hats, was a fantastic spectacle. The Jamaicans had their own reggae band, and there was none of the nasty racist stuff that has marred some Croatian games since, the pink and white army just joined in the party. The neutrals just watched, amazed, eyes glued to the stands as much as to the pitch.

Croatia controlled the first half, although Jamaica harried and hounded, and Earle threatened at set plays. After sustained pressure Jamaica didn't clear properly, and Igor Stimac cannoned a shot against the bar; Mario Stanic was on hand to poke in the loose ball. On forty-five minutes came the moment everyone except the Croatians wanted. The nineteen-year-old Jamaican wing-back Ricardo Gardner, whose pace was Jamaica's biggest threat, lost Soldo down the left and whipped in a terrific cross. Robbie Earle rose above the central defenders and powered home his first goal for his adopted country.

The Jamaican crowd went potty. The reggae drums doubled in volume, horns blew and the ladies started dancing. During the entire half-time break the entire stadium was bouncing and cheering and pointing and laughing and dancing. You didn't dare go to the loo in case you missed a trumpet solo or a new explosion of conga rhythms. At the end of the half-time break, after a brief moment to acknowledge the return of the teams, the fans in the rest of the ground, including most of the Croatians, gave the Jamaican support a huge round of applause. Maybe I'm being overly sentimental, but it was a lovely reminder of just how much fun sport played in the right spirit can be.

Back on the field, Croatia re-assumed control in the second half and scored when Prosinecki fired in from a seemingly impossible angle. Suker added a third with a typically calm finish, although a deflection took his shot over the goalkeeper. Burton must have left his shooting boots in the Caribbean; here we saw the shaky finishing that blighted his league career when he missed a very good headed chance.

GROUP H

Argentina Batistuta 28	**(1) 1**	**Japan**	**(0) 0**	14 June, Toulouse; 33,400
Croatia Suker 76	**(0) 1**	**Japan**	**(0) 0**	20 June, Nantes; 39,000
Argentina Ortega 31, 54, Batistuta 72, 76, 83 (p)	**(1) 5**	**Jamaica**	**(0) 0**	21 June, Parc des Princes; 48,500
Croatia	**(0) 0**	**Argentina** Pineda 36	**(1) 1**	26 June, Bordeaux; 36,500
Jamaica Whitmore 39, 54	**(1) 2**	**Japan** Nakayama 74	**(0) 1**	26 June, Lyons; 43,500

1. **Argentina** 9pts (7–0); 2. **Croatia** 6pts (4–2); 3. **Jamaica** 3pts (3–9); 4. **Japan** 0pts (1–4)

The most fun group, even if the pecking order was as predictable as most of the others.

Batistuta's header gave Argentina a win over Japan, who were neat and tidy and had lots of possession but no goal threat. Argentina improved markedly in their second game, and Ariel Ortega started to throw off the next Maradona millstone and look a proper player in his own right. He scored twice, both after startling bursts of acceleration worthy of the master, and laid on another for Batistuta. By then Jamaica were down to ten men and struggling, and Batistuta was able to add two more. For the second Finals tournament running Argentina's glamour puss had scored three against defensively weak opposition; would he do better than last time when the real defenders were in the way?

Suker's movement and finishing were too much for Japan, who again played well without ever looking like getting a result. The Real Madrid striker hit the bar before he scored with an economical far post finish.

In two fairly meaningless matches – there wasn't much between England and Romania, the next round opponents for the qualifiers from this group – Argentina narrowly beat Croatia in a listless game and Jamaica got the win they wanted against Japan with two goals from Theodore Whitmore. They had a blast, except against Argentina, and Whitmore earned a few years with Hull City, while Bolton snapped up the lively Gardner and turned him into one of the best attacking backs in the Premier League.

SECOND ROUND

Italy Vieri 18	(1) 1	**Norway**	(0) 0	27 June, Marseilles; 60,000
Brazil César Sampaio 11, 26, Ronaldo 45 (p), 70	(3) 4	**Chile** Salas 68	(0) 1	27 June, Parc des Princes; 48,500
France Blanc 113 (gg)	(0) (0) 1	**Paraguay**	(0) (0) 0	28 June, Lens; 41,275
Denmark Møller 2, B Laudrup 11, Sand 59, Helveg 76	(2) 4	**Nigeria** Babangida 77	(0) 1	28 June, Stade de France; 79,500
Germany Klinsmann 74, Bierhoff 86	(0) 2	**Mexico** Hernández 47	(0) 1	29 June, Montpellier; 35,000
Yugoslavia Komljenovic 48	(0) 1	**Holland** Bergkamp 37, Davids 90	(1) 2	29 June, Toulouse; 37,500
Croatia Suker 45 (p)	(1) 1	**Romania**	(0) 0	30 June, Bordeaux; 34,700

Only three of these eight matches were worth the exorbitant admission.

Italy squeezed the life out of Norway, who created only one chance for Tore André Flo, which Pagliuca saved. Olsen failed to bring on Solskjaer, the most lethal substitute in world football, until eighteen minuets from the end, and when he did his team just kept thumping long crosses at Flo. Good riddance.

Brazil easily saw off Chile in an entertaining match. Chile worked hard and created a few chances, but Brazil finished clinically, the powerful defensive midfielder César Sampaio setting them in on their way with two goals from set pieces. He now had three goals in four games in France, the same as he scored in his other forty-three internationals. Ronaldo scored the other two, one from the spot and one to seal the game two minutes after a Salas header gave Chile a glimmer. Comedy moment: Rivaldo twisted away from a defender, went between two more and pushed a through ball to Júnior Baiano, who surprisingly found himself one on one with the 'keeper. So surprisingly that he fell over the ball. I would swear that even one or two of the Brazilians were giggling.

Paraguay had a good defence and Gamarra and Chilavert both enhanced big reputations. France had no forward worth the name (Thierry Henry was still playing as a wide attacker). So a stalemate was no surprise. France kept plugging away – Paraguay didn't, they played for penalties; Fabien Barthez might as well have read his birthday cards and eaten his cake in the penalty area. France got their reward for at least trying when Laurent Blanc, their captain and centre-half, hit a volley from Trezeguet's knock down. Chilavert nearly stopped even that. That was game over – the Golden Goal had come into play for the first time. There was a lot of confusion in the crowd – clearly many of them hadn't twigged that the first goal in extra-time wins the game. France had let in one debatable penalty in nearly six and a half hours.

Denmark were not a happy bunch and received wisdom had it that Nigeria would roll them over. Hmmm. Peter Møller scored after two minutes, a fierce left-foot drive from Michael Laudrup's flick-on. Another Møller left-footer, this time from a free-kick, was half saved by Rufai and knocked in by Brian Laudrup. Eleven minutes gone and received wisdom wasn't looking very wise at all. Now Kanu, Okocha, George and the rest started attacking, but the Danes were fired up by this point, and they had Schmeichel behind them and he hoovered up anything that got through Nielsen and two centre-backs. Ebbe Sand came on for Møller and showed a bit of class, cleverly nudging Laudrup's bobbling pass to the side of Taribo West and hitting it smartly as it landed. A late starter at twenty-five, it was his first goal for Denmark, but he was a stalwart for the next few years. The match was over, the last two goals a footnote.

Mexico looked lively and up for it, but they were just ground down by Germany, who won the game on self-belief. They certainly didn't win it with talent, they were ponderous and one-dimensional, hoping Bierhoff would get on the end of crosses and Klinsmann would reach the ball first. Vogts kept changing his pack but they were all the ten of clubs; in this game he started with seven defensively minded players – against Mexico, for goodness sake! Mexico deserved their lead and would have gone two-up had Hernández taken an easier chance than the one he scored.

Holland against Yugoslavia should have been a cracker but neither side was at their best and it was all a bit messy and spiteful. Three yellow cards, all to Yugoslavia, was generous and a tad myopic from Scottish referee Hugh Dallas.

Bergkamp showed his strength – not always what he is remembered for – to hold off a defender and score from Frank de Boer's raking pass. Just after half-time Komljenovic, who had scored with a fine header against the USA repeated the dose from a free-kick. The goals represented two-thirds of the big defender's international haul. Yugoslavia were briefly on top, and when Hugh Dallas awarded a penalty for Stam's shirt-pull (he missed a few others on both sides, so why give that one?) they should have taken the lead. Mijatovic, a star at Real Madrid that season, had a rank bad tournament and hit the penalty against the bar. The game was open for someone to seize, and it was Edgar Davids who rifled a shot in after a spell of Dutch pressure.

Romania ran out of steam against Croatia, who should have finished wilting opponents off long before the end. Suker's penalty was given for what looked like a fifty-fifty tangle. Popescu howled his frustration and earned himself a booking but referees tend not to overturn decisions. You would think footballers would realise that after all these years, would you not?

A signature of this round was the lack of potency in attack of most of the protagonists. Ronaldo was an obvious exception, but Bebeto, his partner, looked well past his use-by date and Klinsmann was not the force of old for Germany. There were good strikers still in: Bergkamp, the Laudrups, Vieri, Batistuta, but none looked in prime form. Flo and Salas and Hernández were all out and the hosts might as well have had me up front. So maybe Suker, who looked an ordinary footballer at times but had that strikers' instinct for being in the right place, could make the difference.

WORLD CUP CLASSIC No.21
30 June 1998, Geoffrey Guichard, St Étienne; 30,600

| Argentina | (2) (2) 2 Batistuta 6 (p), Zanetti 45 |
| England | (2) (2) 2 Shearer 10 (p), Owen 15 |

Shoot-out:

Argentina		England	
Berti	S 1–0	Shearer	S 1–1
Crespo	*M 1–1*	*Ince*	*M 1–1*
Verón	S 2–1	Merson	S 2–2
Gallardo	S 3–2	Owen	S 3–3
Ayala	S 4–3	*Batty*	*M 4–3*

Referee: **Kim Milton Nielsen** (Denmark)
Coaches: **Daniel Passarella** (Argentina) & **Glenn Hoddle** (England)

Argentina (4–4–1–1): Carlos Roa (Mallorca), José Chamot (Lazio), Nelson Vivas (Lugano), Roberto Ayala (Napoli), Javier Zanetti (Internazionale); Matías Almeyda (Lazio), Juan Sebastián Verón (Sampdoria), Diego Simeone (Cpt, Internazionale); Ariel Ortega (Valencia); Gabriel Batistuta (Fiorentina), Claudio López (Valencia). **Subs:** Hernán Crespo (Parma) 68m for Batistuta; Sergio Berti (River Plate) 91m for Simeone
England (4–4–2): David Seaman (Arsenal); Gary Neville (Manchester United), Tony Adams (Arsenal), Sol Campbell (Tottenham Hotspur), Graeme Le Saux (Chelsea); David Beckham (Man Utd), Paul Ince (Liverpool), Paul Scholes (Man Utd), Darren Anderton (Tottenham); Alan Shearer (Newcastle United), Michael Owen (Liverpool). **Subs:** Gareth Southgate (Aston Villa) 71m for Le Saux; David Batty (Newcastle) 97m for Anderton
Cautioned: Seaman (Eng) 5m, Ince (Eng) 10m, Verón (Arg) 44m, Simeone (Arg) 47m, Almeyda (Arg) 73m, Roa (Arg) 120+m
Dismissed: Beckham (Eng) 47m (retaliation)

This was the best game of the round and one of only two truly great games in the entire tournament. England may not have played the prettiest football in World Cup history but they have been involved in more than their fair share of high drama roller-coaster games. Maybe it's the punishing pace we try to play at, but it seems to produce end-to-end epics every now and then.

The whole game was good, played between two sides with good technique who wanted to win the game. England? Good technique? Well, yes, actually, all these players could trap and pass, the odd heavy touch from Adams and Ince apart, and those two had other admirable qualities. There was obvious animosity, especially after the sending off, but it never spilled over into anything vicious.

The big match up was reckoned to be in the middle where Ince, Beckham and Scholes had to outwit the formidable combination of Verón, Simeone and Ortega. I've just re-read that – five world-class players (or soon-to-be) and one who truly had drunk of the peyote that night.

Three goals in the first fifteen minutes set the stadium alight. (Not literally, the yobs had calmed down a little.) Seaman brought down Batistuta unnecessarily and a bit clumsily and the long-haired one put the penalty away – just. Five minutes later and Shearer was celebrating a penalty at the other end after Owen was clipped by Ayala as he ran into the area. A further five minutes and Owen was in World Cup history with one of the really great goals. Ince tackled back and fed Beckham who spotted Owen on the move. Owen took the pass in his stride and roared across and away Chamot, giving the defender no chance to recover. Ayala was the last man on the edge of the area and Owen took him out to the right and without spoiling his angle too much, such was the speed he was moving. The shot, taken on the run, was hit high and hard past Roa with the fearlessness of youth. "*Just think what he'll be like when he grows up,*" said the BBC commentator. Not sure he ever got any better than this. Maybe the Germans would disagree.

If Paul Scholes had taken a tough half-chance minutes later that might have been it, but he pushed it wide of the post. Argentina levelled just before half-time. Verón bought a soft free-kick, and after Batistuta dummied a shot Verón pushed the ball down the side of the England wall to Zanetti, who spun and fired in a cracking equaliser. Two minutes after the break the entire complexion of the game changed when referee Kim Milton Nielsen made a shocker of a decision, sending off David Beckham after an innocuous tangle with Simeone. Simeone went down as if shot, and Verón and Batistuta were immediately in Nielsen's face waving cards. Loathsome stuff; perhaps Batistuta was bored, because he had contributed nothing since his penalty.

Now we came to it. What could England offer a man down against the team who were now favourites for the World Cup? Guts, passion, hard work and a lot of skill; for once we got the full *Three Lions on a Shirt.* For the last seventy-five minutes of this pulsating match England went toe-to-toe with a top side and gave as good as they got – and they had a man less. Shearer was the captain, and he put a stint in, his power alongside the threat of Owen's pace meaning Argentina were reluctant to commit defenders forward in numbers. Shearer was the captain, but the leaders were behind him. At the back Gary Neville, playing an unfamiliar role in a back three, was calm and collected alongside the immense Adams (who should have been captain) and Sol Campbell, who became a big boy. Anderton belied his nickname (*"Sicknote"*) with a skilful display until replaced by the waspish Batty, and Le Saux worked equally hard down the left until replaced by Gareth Southgate. In the middle Scholes, all precision and bite, gave way to Paul Merson, whose ability to run with the ball and keep possession were invaluable in extra-time. Seaman made up for his impetuous tackle earlier with a fine late save. And in the middle, loving every minute of it, was Paul Ince. Ince, the first black player to captain England, gave the performance of his career, a demonic, frenzied air about him as he chased every ball, made tackle after tackle, and, in the dying minutes, still had the energy to burst through a couple of weak tackles and get a shot in. If that had gone in I think I would have cried. Ince was faced with Simeone, one of the great South American hard men, and Almeyda, a notorious enforcer with Lazio, and they backed down; Simeone, the captain, was substituted. Batistuta was already off, replaced by Crespo, utterly quashed by Campbell. For one day, Incey, you truly were *The Guv'nor*.

England thought they had won it with a Golden Goal, but Sol Campbell's fine header was ruled out because Shearer fouled the goalkeeper. It was a good decision, although Roa might not have reached the cross, but habits are hard to break, and Shearer had been fouling goalkeepers at set plays and getting away with it for a decade.

Of course it was inevitable that England would lose the penalty shoot-out. Maybe if Hoddle had used Lee or McManaman instead of Batty, particularly as they weren't struggling to hold the line . . . but that's carping. Mind you, either of these two would have taken a better penalty than poor old Batty – but then, so would I. That Ince was the other player who saw his shot saved was unjust.

When Argentina beat England in 1986, it was a shrug of the shoulders and acknowledgement that the better team won. Not this time. This hurt. England were terrific and courageous and deserved to go through. Within a year the manager was gone, let down by his propensity for airing his rather self-righteous personal opinions. England had lost two good managers in succession to character judgements, so now they went for a good old-fashioned patriot in Kevin Keegan.

England Squad 1998:
GK: David Seaman (Arsenal, 34, 40), Nigel Martyn (Leeds United, 31, 7), Tim Flowers (Blackburn Rovers, 31, 11)
DEF: Tony Adams (Arsenal, 31, 51), Sol Campbell (Tottenham Hotspur, 23, 16), Rio Ferdinand (West Ham United, 19, 3), Martin Keown (Arsenal, 31, 18), Graeme Le Saux (Chelsea, 25, 20), Gary Neville (Manchester United, 23, 27), Gareth Southgate (Aston Villa, 27, 25)
MID & WIDE: Darren Anderton (Tottenham, 26, 18), David Batty (Newcastle United, 29, 31), David Beckham (Man Utd, 23, 15), Paul Ince (Liverpool, 30, 39), Rob Lee (Newcastle, 32, 17), Steve McManaman (Liverpool, 26, 21), Paul Merson (Middlesbrough, 30, 18), Paul Scholes (Man Utd, 23, 7)
FWD: Les Ferdinand (Newcastle, 31, 17), Michael Owen (Liverpool, 18, 5), Alan Shearer (Cpt*, Newcastle, 29, 31), Teddy Sheringham (Man Utd, 32, 33)

QUARTER-FINALS

France	(0) 0	Italy	(0) 0	3 July, Stade de France; 77,000
France won 4–3 on penalties				
Germany	(0) 0	Croatia	(1) 3	4 July, Lyons; 39,100
		Jarni 45, Vlaovic 80, Suker 85		

You can imagine how this went. I fell asleep after about an hour and haven't bothered watching the video since. Very unprofessional of me, but life's too short . . .

---

* Hoddle made Shearer captain because, ostensibly, he felt it would help him win more penalties. Utter rot – the only man who should have captained this team was Adams, a natural leader and a man who had learned the tough way about taking responsibility after battling through alcohol addiction. Shearer was too passive as a captain, and his contributions in TV studios demonstrate he was never the greatest match analyst.

WORLD CUP CLASSIC No.22
3 July 1998, La Beaujoire, Nantes; 35,500

Brazil   (2) 3   Bebeto 10, Rivaldo 26, 61
Denmark   (1) 2   Jørgensen 2, B Laudrup 50

Referee: **Gamal El-Ghandour** (Egypt)
Coaches: **Mário Zagallo** (Brazil) & **Bo Johansson** (Sweden)

Brazil (4–4–2): Claudio Taffarel (Atlético Mineiro); *Marcos Evangelista, known as* Cafú (Roma), Aldair *Nascimento* (Roma), *Raimundo Ferreira, known as* Júnior Baiano (Flamengo), Roberto Carlos *da Silva* (Real Madrid); *Carlos* César Sampaio (Yokohama Flügels), Leonardo *Nascimento de Araújo* (Milan), *Carlos Bledorn, known as* Dunga (Cpt, Júbilo Iwata), Rivaldo *Vitor Borba* (Barcelona); Ronaldo *Nazário* (Internazionale), *Roberto Gama, known as* Bebeto (Botafogo). **Subs:** Denilson *de Oliveira* (São Paulo) 64m for Bebeto; Emerson *da Silva* (Bayer Leverkusen) 71m for Leonardo); *José Roberto da Silva, known as* Zé Roberto (Flamengo) 87m for Rivaldo
Denmark (4–4–2): Peter Schmeichel (Manchester United); Søren Colding (Brondby), Jes Høgh (Fenerbahçe), Marc Rieper (Celtic), Jan Heintze (Bayer Leverkusen); Thomas Helveg (Udinese); Martin Jørgensen (Udinese), Allan Nielsen (Tottenham Hotspur), Michael Laudrup (Cpt, Ajax); Brian Laudrup (Rangers), Peter Møller (PSV Eindhoven). **Subs:** Stig Tøfting (MSV Duisburg) 45m for Nielsen; Ebbe Sand (Brondby) 66m for Møller; Michael Schjønberg (Kaiserslautern) 87m for Helveg
Cautioned: Roberto Carlos (Bra) 11m, Helveg (Den) 19m, Aldair (Bra) 37m, Colding (Den) 40m, Tøfting (Den) 72m, Cafú (Bra) 81m

This was a belter. Like the England game in the previous round, it was kick-started by early goals and never let up.

This wasn't as good a Danish team as the eighties version. They had the creative influence of the Laudrup brothers and a great goalkeeper (who had an average tournament and a poor game), but they didn't have anywhere near as good a defence as that overseen by Morten Olsen and they didn't have a scary centre-forward like Elkjaer. But then this wasn't a vintage Brazilian side either, just a very good one.

Michael Laudrup started the fun with a quick free-kick to his bro, who knew exactly where Martin Jørgensen was and cut the ball back for the winger to ram home. Good goal, good start, Brazil would have to play properly.

Ronaldo was only passed fit to play in the morning, and he only looked seventy per cent, but even that was pretty good. France would have picked him at forty per cent. His first contribution here was a little dart to the left and reverse pass into the space he had created for Bebeto. Bebeto produced his one classy moment of the competition with a pinpoint finish. Brazil enjoyed a good spell, but attacks kept breaking down because Ronaldo was sluggish or Bebeto wasn't up with the game. When Dunga robbed Helveg and fed Rivaldo the Barcelona player dispensed with the guys ahead of him, took a few strides and chipped the ball over Schmeichel as he came out; with Rieper getting across quickly there was no need for the goalkeeper to come, Rivaldo had only one angle so Schmeichel just needed to guard his near post.

Denmark didn't quail, and they were still in contention at half-time, and more so five minutes into the second half. For twenty minutes the Danish midfield had kept the ball really well and Brazil had struggled to get much change. Jørgensen drove through the middle and chipped the ball out to the right, where Brian Laudrup hammered a thoroughbred finish past Taffarel. As the ball came over Roberto Carlos could easily have jumped and headed the ball away or for a corner or at least made it hard for Laudrup. What did he do? He tried an overhead kick. Silly boy.

Rivaldo had clearly decided this one was down to him, and he ran fully thirty yards before pumping a long range effort past Schmeichel, who was a bit late getting down. Denmark replaced Møller, who had done very little, with Sand and immediately looked threatening again. Helveg took a pass from the right and played an instant ball to Sand, who had slipped Roberto Carlos; Sand immediately picked out Marc Rieper on the penalty spot and cut the ball sharply to him. The ball was fractionally behind Rieper but he screwed his foot around it and jammed it only just wide of the post. It happened in the blink of an eye and took out seven Brazilian players; it was superb football. Rieper, playing as a supplementary forward in the closing stages, missed Denmark's last chance when he headed Brian Laudrup's cross onto and over the crossbar.

It was a breathless game where both sides had the beating of the opposition defence. Denmark were desperately unlucky to lose but it would have been equally hard to begrudge Brazil a place in the last eight, they looked the most complete team.

WORLD CUP CLASSIC No.23
4 July 1998, Vélodrome, Marseilles; 55,000

Argentina	**(1) 1**	López 18
Holland	**(1) 2**	Kluivert 12, Bergkamp 89

Referee: **Arturo Brizio Carter** (Mexico)
Coaches: **Daniel Passarella** (Argentina) & **Guus Hiddink** (Holland)

Argentina (4–4–1–1): Carlos Roa (Mallorca), José Chamot (Lazio), Roberto Sensini (Parma), Roberto Ayala (Napoli), Javier Zanetti (Internazionale); Matías Almeyda (Lazio), Juan Sebastián Verón (Sampdoria), Diego Simeone (Cpt, Internazionale); Ariel Ortega (Valencia); Gabriel Batistuta (Fiorentina), Claudio López (Valencia). **Subs:** Mauricio Pineda (Udinese) 67m for Almeyda; Abel Balbo (Roma) 90m for Chamot
Holland (4–4–2): Edwin van der Sar (Ajax); Michael Reiziger (Barcelona), Jaap Stam (PSV Eindhoven), Frank de Boer (Cpt, Ajax), Artur Numan (PSV Eindhoven); Ronald de Boer (Ajax), Edgar Davids (Juventus), Phillip Cocu (PSV Eindhoven), Wim Jonk (PSV Eindhoven); Patrick Kluivert (AC Milan), Dennis Bergkamp (Arsenal). **Sub:** Marc Overmars (Arsenal) 64m for R de Boer
Cautioned: Stam (Hol) 10m, Numan (Hol) 17m, Chamot (Arg) 22m, Sensini (Arg) 60m
Dismissed: Numan (Hol) 76m (second yellow); Ortega (Arg) 87m (diving + attempted headbutt)

Not as good a game as England against Argentina, despite the obvious high skill quotient involved when these two meet. Argentina had the best of the first half, with Ortega hitting the post with a snorter and Batistuta going close with his standard solitary contribution. It was level at half-time after Bergkamp knocked down a Ronald de Boer cross for Kluivert to score; otherwise Kluivert had a nothing game, he was still only twenty-one and not quite ready for this. Argentina responded quickly with a López goal from Verón's long pass – it was a great ball but the marking was dire.

The game stayed tense in the second half, but it seemed to be drifting towards extra-time when Arthur Numan, already booked, went tanking into Diego Simeone. About time too, watching England fans shouted, but it was a reckless moment from a player who had a really good tournament up to now.

If there was a moment for Argentina to seize the game that was it, but they stayed in the same gear. Phillip Cocu was the archetypal utility player, but without the pejorative connotation of jack-of-all-trades-master-of-none that phrase implies, and he dropped effortlessly into the defence. Crucially, the Dutch had watched England and saw how more effectively England defended with two forwards still on the pitch, so they left Kluivert and Bergkamp on.

With three minutes left on the clock, Ortega did a belly flop in the penalty area, and lifted his hands in the time-honoured gesture. Referee Carter lifted his, to issue a caution for diving. Edwin van der Sar must have offered some choice observation because Ortega rather comically tried to head-butt a man at least ten inches taller than himself. The card turned to red.

Two minutes later Frank de Boer hit one of his auto-targeted missiles (best long passer out of defence the game has seen? Discuss . . .) about fifty yards towards Dennis Bergkamp, charging into the right-hand side of the penalty area. There were three touches with the right foot from about eight yards out at a tight angle with Roberto Ayala breathing down his neck. The first persuaded the ball to lie, the second to turn and sit up, the third, with the outside of the boot, told Roa to go fetch it out of the back of his net. One man and his ball control; absolutely brilliant. And buckets of *schadenfreude* across the living rooms of England. Is that a mixed metaphor? Or just nonsense? Just go with it, I'm excited having just watched the footage for the umpteenth time. For me, Maradona scored the second-best goal in World Cup history in 1986. This topped it. *Buenos noches*, Argentina.

Germany were hampered by a red card for Wörns for a late tackle on Suker, and they worked over-time to compensate, giving their best performance of the tournament, despite the scoreline. (This wasn't the view aired commonly at the time, but watching the match again Germany were competitive and in the game until the second goal, despite the Croatian's superior technique and pace.) But they created no real clear chances, apart from Hamann's stinger that hit the post. Croatia had more edge, and scored two good goals from wide positions as well as a rare right-footer from Suker, who looked a bit shocked when it went in. It was the end of a generation for Germany, and they would have to keep papering over the cracks for the next few years. There was some blue sky; Hamann and Jens Jeremies looked players for the future and there was a good goalkeeping replacement for Köpke in Oliver Kahn (some felt he should have played in France).

Croatia were solid at the back, accurate in midfield and razor sharp in the penalty area, and worth their place in the semi-final.

SEMI-FINALS

Brazil	(0) (1) **1 Holland**	(0) (1) **1**	7 July, Marseilles; 54,000
Ronaldo 46	Kluivert 86		
Brazil won 4–2 on penalties			
France	(0) **2** **Croatia**	(0) **1**	8 July, Stade de France; 76,000
Thuram 48, 69	Suker 46		

The Brazil–Holland game was a strange affair. Both teams played well, but both seemed to be holding something in reserve. Maybe a few players were carrying injuries, and a few were on a yellow card, but no one got hold of the game and said *mine, I'm gonna win this*!

Kluivert had his best game yet; he equalised with a superb header from Ronald de Boer's cross and gave Júnior Baiano almost as torrid a time as had Flo. Alongside him, however, Bergkamp was oddly subdued, as was Rivaldo at the other end, although Ronald de Boer diligently offered cover to Reiziger to help deal with the threat.

Frank de Boer and Stam were excellent, marshalling Ronaldo well except in two key moments, once when he slipped the pair of them and scored from Rivaldo's clever pass, the other when Edgar Davids got back to make an outstanding saving tackle, which Ronaldo declined to try to turn into a penalty. Bebeto, anonymous, was replaced by Denilson, and for Holland van Hooijdonk came on from Zenden – an odd change as Zenden, in for the injured Overmars, had provided great ammunition for the strikers and roasted Zé Carlos (in for Cafú) on half a dozen occasions.

Brazil were the better – or marginally less tired – team in extra-time, and Holland are always the worse team in a penalty shoot-out, with a record even worse than England. How very Dutch. Cocu and Ronald de Boer were the unfortunates. Maybe Ronald and Frank should have swapped shirts, they were pretty much indistinguishable except for the name and number on the back and Frank scored his penalty.

World Cup Heroes No.29

Lilian Thuram (1972–)

France

One hundred and forty-two games Lilian Thuram played for France, first at right-back then in the middle of the defence. Those games spanned fourteen years, from 1994 to 2008, including four European Championships and three World Cup Finals tournaments. In all that time, in all those games, he scored two goals for his country. How unlucky were Croatia?

Forget what you may have read about the 1998 World Cup being dominated by Zidane's brilliance; that was just the final. The 1998 World Cup was dominated by great defenders, mainly French, and Thuram was one of them. The balance in that defence was perfect: a bulwark ball-winning centre-half (Desailly), a ball-playing sweeper (Blanc), a speedy attacking full-back (Lizarazu) and a balancing Mr. Reliable on the other side (Thuram).

The semi-final against Croatia was boring. Most of France's games in the 1998 World Cup were boring. The first half was stale, the second flared into life when Suker scored for Croatia almost immediately after the break. Thuram replied almost immediately for France when a certain goal-shy defender dispossessed Boban, the Croatian captain, played a one-two with Youri Djorkaeff and beat Ladic on the angle. The game remained interesting for another twenty minutes until Thuram cut inside Robert Jarni and scored with his other foot. After that France slammed the door shut on Croatia, even after Laurent Blanc was so unjustly sent off, victim of a spiteful (and out of character) bit of play-acting by Slaven Bilic.

Thuram played for only four clubs, Monaco, Parma, Juventus and a last hurrah at Barcelona. He was integral to each of his main clubs, one of the first names on the team sheet week in, week out. He was like watching a defender with Gary Neville's brain and Rio Ferdinand's physique and ability. He rarely got injured, rarely complained and rarely had a bad game.

When France failed at the 2002 World Cup and the 2004 European Championships, coach Raymond Domenech called upon a few of the old guard to come out of retirement – they were Zidane, Makélélé and Thuram. Now playing at centre-half alongside the younger, quicker William Gallas, Thuram helped France get to the final. He was as good at thirty-three as he was in 1998 at twenty-six.

Thuram retired in thirty-eight when the same heart defect that killed his brother prematurely was detected. He has spent much of his time since espousing equal rights in France, supporting same-sex rights and immigrant rights. A bit more imaginative than the usual post-career bit of punditry.

THIRD-PLACE MATCH (11 July)

Croatia	(2) 2	Holland	(1) 1	Parc des Princes, Paris, 45,500
Prosinecki 13, Suker 36		Zenden 21		

Croatia seemed to want it more than Holland. The winning goal secured the Golden Boot for Suker, but Zenden's was special, cutting inside Jarni and spanking a rising shot past van der Sar.

WORLD CUP FINAL No.16
12 July 1998, Stade de France, Paris; 75,000

France	(2) 3	Zidane 27, 45, Petit 90
Brazil	(0) 0	

Referee: **Saïd Belqola** (Morocco)
Coaches: **Aimé Jacquet** (France) & **Mário Zagallo** (Brazil)

France (4–3–2–1): Fabien Barthez (Monaco); Lilian Thuram (Parma), Marcel Desailly (Milan), Frank Leboeuf (Chelsea), Bixente Lizarazu (Bayern Munich); Christian Karembeu (Real Madrid), Didier Deschamps (Juventus), Emmanuel Petit (Arsenal); Youri Djorkaeff (Internazionale), Zinedine Zidane (Juventus); Stéphane Guivarc'h (Auxerre). **Subs:** Alain Boghossian (Sampdoria) 57m for Karembeu; Christophe Dugarry (Olympique de Marseille) 66m for Guivarc'h); Patrick Vieira (Arsenal) 75m for Djorkaeff
Brazil (4–4–2): Claudio Taffarel (Atlético Mineiro); *Marcos Evangelista, known as* Cafú (Roma), Aldair *Nascimento* (Roma), *Raimundo Ferreira, known as* Júnior Baiano (Flamengo),

Roberto Carlos *da Silva* (Real Madrid); *Carlos* César Sampaio (Yokohama Flügels), Leonardo *Nascimento de Araújo* (Milan), *Carlos Bledorn, known as* Dunga (Cpt, Júbilo Iwata), Rivaldo *Vítor Borba* (Barcelona); Ronaldo *Nazário* (Internazionale), *Roberto Gama, known as* Bebeto (Botafogo). **Subs:** Denilson *de Oliveira* (São Paulo) 45m for Leonardo; Edmundo Alves de Souza (Fiorentina) 74m for César Sampaio
Cautioned: Júnior Baiano (Bra) 33m, Deschamps (Fra) 39m, Desailly (Fra) 48m, Karembeu (Fra) 56m
Dismissed: Desailly (Fra) 68m (second yellow)

There were more column inches devoted to the pre-match hysteria than to the game itself. Ronaldo was having a nap in the afternoon before the game and had a seizure – probably induced by stress, the medics later said. His room-mate, Roberto Carlos, called the team doctors rather than the manager, which doesn't speak volumes for Zagallo's standing with the players, although it was Roberto Carlos, so who knows. The doctor's couldn't find anything physically wrong, but Ronaldo was packed off to hospital for a check-up, where he was given the all-clear.

With the wisdom of hindsight he shouldn't have played, even if he was physically able, and it's debatable whether doctors now would have allowed it, after incidents like Marc Vivien Foé's death and Fabrice Muamba's near-fatal experience. His head cannot have been in the right place; he wanted to play and one can only assume Zagallo couldn't bear the consequences of leaving him out and Brazil losing. The obvious replacement, Edmundo, had hardly featured and had a reputation for losing it at crucial moments (his nickname was *The Animal!*). Zagallo went for the cosy option and Edmundo stood down.

Things never clicked for a Brazilian team clearly unsettled by the pre-match incident and France's five-man midfield took control of the game. Deschamps did his thing, Petit burst from one end to the other with vigour and panache, and Zidane had room to play his little passes and go past a player here and there.

The first two goals came from corners and both were scored by Zidane, a good header of the ball but not exactly a massive guy. He met Petit's right-side corner firmly and it went into the goal in precisely the spot Roberto Carlos was supposed to be. He wasn't. But you knew that.

The second header was even more powerful and just went too quickly for the man on the line to react.

Brazil had moments, but only one or two, and Ronaldo hit his one good chance straight at Barthez. Zagallo didn't even do him the kindness of taking him off. He was still better than the French strikers; both Guivarc'h and Dugarry missed when one-on-one with Taffarel. Desailly was sent off for a second yellow with twenty-three minutes remaining, but Brazil were gone by then and it was barely noticeable that France were missing both first choice central defenders. Denilson showed flashes in the second half after replacing Leonardo, and he hit the bar in injury-time after deceiving Leboeuf. France went up the other end and banged in the final nail, Petit rounding off an incisive break with a left-foot shot.

I probably haven't given France enough credit. In a tournament dominated by good defenders, they had the best, with a tight shielding midfield in front. They conceded only one goal in open play and two in all in eleven and a half hours of football. The defence, Deschamps and Emmanuel Petit were thoroughly excellent, Zidane was intermittently brilliant but not as good as you think you remember he was. The other forward players were nondescript, and the coach Aime Jacquet always put caution first; Karembeu, a defender as an extra shielding midfielder was overkill with all those good tacklers, and France could and should have used Patrick Vieira more – he and Petit had just won the double with Arsenal. Another Arsenal player, Nicolas Anelka, although only nineteen, would surely have made more impact than any of the forwards Jacquet picked in his squad.

But the right team won. Maybe. Oh, you decide . . .

World Cup Heroes No.30
Carlos Caetano Bledorn Verri,
known as Dunga (1963–)
Brazil

Eric Cantona used the term "water-carrier" to describe Didier Deschamps' role in the French team. Cantona wasn't being polite (he rarely was), but the term has stuck as a description of an ego-free midfield player who is prepared to do the dirty work while other more creative players take the glory. Claude Makélélé developed and defined the role and the likes of Busquets and Khedira perform it admirably and athletically.

The first quality water carrier in international football was Dunga. Poor in 1990 he was criticised for being a Brazilian without flair, but the coach, Carlos Parreira, manager of the 1994 squad, knew that, for better or worse, the game was changing and the pure attacking football of old wouldn't wash, especially as Brazil simply didn't have enough players of that quality. So he needed Dunga again for the 1994 campaign, to sit in front of the defence and protect and serve. When Parreira dropped Raí, he turned to the unassuming but reliable Dunga as captain. A couple of weeks later he lifted the World Cup. Dunga wasn't a goals-corer, but he didn't abdicate any responsibility; when the 1994 Final went to penalties he stepped up and scored his kick, and did it again in the 1998 shoot-out against Holland. And he was tough; in a group game when against Morocco he nearly came to blows when he admonished Bebeto and the veteran striker questioned his authority.

Dunga's club career started in Brazil, moved to Italy for a few years, then a couple of seasons with Stuttgart; by the 1998 World Cup he had spent three years in the relatively low standard of the J-League in Japan. But he was fit and he knew what the World Cup was about, so he kept his place and went to France as captain again, aged thirty-four. Nor did he disgrace himself, offering a solid defence alongside César Sampaio to allow Rivaldo and Ronaldo freedom to practice their art. Only when Zidane woke up for the final did Dunga finally look off the pace.

Dunga returned as manager of the Brazilian team at the 2010 World Cup, but they didn't win, and we know what happens to Brazilian managers when they don't win. A real trooper, though he would never say so himself.

Team of the Tournament, 1998 (they changed it to a squad of 16):

Van der Sar (Holland)

Thuram (France)   Desailly (France)   F de Boer (Holland)   Jarni (Croatia)

Deschamps (France)

Verón (Argentina)   Di Biagio (Italy)   Rivaldo (Brazil)

Ronaldo (Brazil)   Suker (Croatia)

Subs: Chilavert (Paraguay); Gamorra (Paraguay);
Asanovic (Croatia); Zidane (France); Vieri (Italy)

Official Team of the Tournament: Barthez (for Chilavert); **Roberto Carlos** (for Jarni, disgraceful decision, all fur coat and no knickers); **Dunga** (better in 1994), **Davids** (hardworking but not sensational) and **Michael Laudrup** (one good game – a retirement present) for Deschamps, Di Biagio, Verón and Asanovic with **Bergkamp** (maybe . . .) plus **Brian Laudrup** (patchy) up front, no room for Vieri, who carried Italy's forward line.

Leading scorers: Suker (6); Vieri & Batistuta (5)

Heaven Eleven No.13

France

Coach:
Arsène Wenger: well why not, at least he wouldn't just let the player run riot and call the shots like they usually try and do

Goalkeepers:
Fabien Barthez: never seemed to make as many mistakes as you expected him to . . .
Joel Bats: another flawed but still good one
Julien Darui: post-war 'keeper, and a really good one by all accounts

Defenders:
Lilian Thuram: Mr Reliable
Manuel Amoros: fast attacking back from the '80s
Bixente Lizarazu: ditto, '90s
Laurent Blanc: captain of the World Cup winning team
Marcel Desailly: the Rock
Robert Jonquet: cool ball-playing defender in the '50s
Marius Trésor: great sweeper in the late '70s early '80s
Max Bossis: the boss-man, nearly 100 caps before it became meaningless

Midfield & wide:
Zinedine Zidane: great at his best, but too easy to mark
Michel Platini: could play deep, could play almost in attack, complete midfield player
Alain Giresse: unselfish box-to-box midfield player
Claude Makélélé: set the standard for the modern holding midfield player
Jean Vincent: elegant winger in the '58 team
Luis Fernández: forceful wide midfielder alongside MP
Raymond Kopa: goalscoring inside-forward with Real Madrid and France
Roger Piantoni: another slick inside-forward from the '50s

Strikers:
Jean-Pierre Papin: unlucky to miss the two great teams
Just Fontaine: goal machine, often underestimated because he retired early
Thierry Henry: quick, great finisher, but better for Arsenal than France
Eric Cantona: King Eric, so cool, but often unmanageable

Omissions: Defenders **Patrick Battiston** and **William Gallas**, midfielders **Jean Tigana** (we needed some width), **Didier Deschamps** (Makélélé was a little bit better), **Emmanuel Petit** and **Franck Ribéry** (just a bit too inconsistent). **Dominique Rocheteau** – we'll pretend he's injured, he usually was – and **Nicolas Anelka**. I ignored most of the current lot, they're all show and wind.

Likely first XI:

```
                    Barthez
       Thuram  Desailly  Blanc  Lizarazu
                    Makélélé
       Kopa  Giresse  Platini  Zidane
                     Henry
```

THE BRIDESMAID
UP THE AISLE

8.1 WORLD CUP 2002

As the vote for the hosts of the 2002 World Cup drew near (South American and European entries were not accepted) three countries were still in the frame: Mexico, Japan and South Korea. The two Asian countries began to get nervous that they would miss out if their vote was split, even though it seemed absurd that Mexico might get a third tournament just because there were few alternatives outside Europe and South America.

The solution was for Japan and South Korea to combine their bid – a solution that was deemed acceptable as it won a unanimous verdict from the committee. It was the first time two countries would co-host, and the first time the Finals were held in Asia. Logistics were no problem – the two countries were no further apart than the East and West coast of the United States. FIFA have since stated they will not consider another co-hosting bid. Although I'm sure the right amount of ready cash would persuade them.

The whole hosting issue has become an accountant's dream/ nightmare, with FIFA deciding a policy of rotating between continents is best and then changing their mind a few years later. And they do make a song and dance of it all, I suppose because the TV companies demand it be an event. The next three could be horrendous. Brazil might be a bit of a cock-up, and an awful lot of the population don't want it. Russia is huge and the travel will be horrendous and punitively expensive and the fans will get ripped off and the racists will boo the black players and all the money will go to a few gangsters . . . I mean businessmen . . . but I guess it's their turn. Qatar was just the worst decision ever.

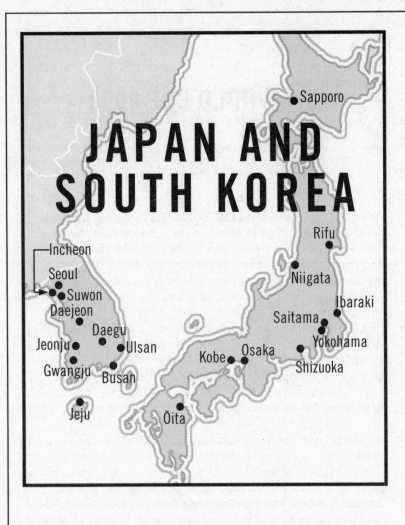

JAPAN AND SOUTH KOREA

- Sapporo
- Rifu
- Niigata
- Ibaraki
- Saitama
- Yokohama
- Shizuoka
- Kobe
- Osaka
- Ōita
- Incheon
- Seoul
- Suwon
- Daejeon
- Daegu
- Ulsan
- Jeonju
- Gwangju
- Busan
- Jeju

2002
JAPAN & SOUTH KOREA

South Korea

The ten stadia used in Korea weren't very imaginatively named, at least not in translation: take name of city, add 'World Cup Stadium' – job done! Almost all were constructed especially for the finals, and even the older ones were refurbished so as to be unrecognizable; Korea wanted to impress.

The cities used were: **Seoul**, the capital in the north-west of the country, and a satellite city, **Suwon**, as well as **Incheon** nearby. Down the western side of the country were the cities of **Daejeon**, **Jeonju** and **Gwangju**, and the city of **Jeju** on an island to the south of the Korean mainland. Towards the south-east there was **Daegu**, and further to the south-east on the coast the cities of **Busan** and **Ulan** also hosted matches. Daejeon saw Korea beat Italy, and Gwangju saw them beat Spain on penalties; they finally succumbed to West Germany in Seoul.

Japan

Japan also offered ten stadia, eight of them on the main island of Honshu, but none, oddly enough, actually in the capital, Tokyo.

Yokohama International: the venue for the final was in **Yokohama**, a satellite city south of Tokyo. The stadium was trialled at the previous year's Confederations Cup (the money-spinning joke invented by FIFA to fill their coffers when there is no World Cup).

Also in the same part of the country as the capital were **Saitama Stadium**, in **Saitama**, a large Tokyo suburb and the **Kashima Soccer Stadium** in the **Ibaraki** prefecture slightly to the north.

Along the east coast were **Miyagi Stadium** in the city of **Rifu**, and over on the west coast was the Niigata Stadium in the city of that name, where England beat Denmark in the last sixteen. Far to the north, on the island of Hokkaido, was the **Sapporo Dome** in the city of that name, now used for the city's strong baseball team as well as for football.

To the south-east was the **ECOPA Stadium** in **Shizuoka**, and on the very far south of Honshu were the **Kobe Wing Stadium**, **Kobe**, and the **Nagai Stadium** in **Osaka**, Japan's third largest city after Tokyo and Yokohama. The Nagai was an odd one out in being an existing sports stadium. Across the water from Osaka was the **Ōita Stadium** in Kyushu island's biggest city.

I hope they move it; I really do, not because I don't want to see it in the Middle East, but just choose a country that has football pedigree as well as money. I know the North African nations are off-limits at the moment, but why not Egypt in twelve years, or Turkey? Use somewhere like Korea or England or the USA as a short-notice back-up if necessary.

Both countries offered up ten major stadia, all with a capacity of over 40,000. Only two were already in existence, the Nagai athletics stadium in Osaka, and the Kashima stadium, home of the J-League team, Kashima Antlers. The other eight stadia in Japan, and ten in South Korea, were all built from scratch, which is pretty impressive, but these two countries stake their international reputation on being pretty damned smart at building stuff. Eight of the Japanese stadia were on the main island of Honshu, with three in the Tokyo area; one was in Ōita on Kyushu Island to the south and one in Sapporo on Hokkaido to the north. Nine of the Korean stadia were on the mainland, with three to the north east in the Seoul / Incheon are, and the tenth was on the island of Jeju south of Korea and south-west of Japan.

FIFA had other concerns. Just before the tournament the General Secretary of FIFA, Michel Zen-Ruffinen, a lawyer, produced a document which he claimed held proof of widespread corruption within the organisation, going to right to the top, including President Sepp Blatter. To cut a long story short the report was suppressed, another legal team was drafted in to refute Zen-Ruffinen and he ended up the subject of an internal investigation which resulted in the suspension of numerous committee members who supported his claims. Only later did it become clear that corruption was indeed widespread within FIFA. Nothing has ever been proven against Sepp Blatter. No doubt the truth will come out years later, as is often the way with these stories. In the meantime a lot of lawyers made a lot of money. They like a lawyer, do FIFA, they make sure small street vendors aren't allowed to trade near a *FIFA World Cup Stadium* even if they've had their stall there for league matches for the last twenty years. And they make sure the TV cameras don't show people eating *the wrong brand of snack*. All useful stuff and integral to the soul of football, wouldn't you agree?

Qualifying

With two host nations and holders France already in the draw, there were twenty-nine slots to divvy up. Europe got a further thirteen, South America four, Africa five, CONCACAF three and Asia two more. Europe, South America, Asia and Oceania would all contribute one further team to two intercontinental play-offs to determine the final two qualifiers.

In Asia, two final groups of five produced Saudi Arabia as one group winner and China, who would make their first Finals appearance, as the other. China were particularly convincing, winning all their home games without conceding and losing only to Uzbekistan. The runners-up in the Saudi Arabia group, Iran, would have to beat a European team over two legs.

In the last phase in Africa five groups of five would be headed by the five eventual qualifiers. Cameroon, Tunisia and South Africa got through quite comfortably, although South Africa were aided by Guinea getting kicked out for excessive governmental interference.

With three rounds to go in group C, Morocco led with twelve points (two to play), with Senegal in second on nine (also two to play) and Egypt on nine with three to play. The first round made things tough for Egypt as they lost to Morocco, while Senegal didn't play. Next up Egypt creamed Namibia, and Senegal nabbed a crucial win over Morocco with a goal from El Hadji Diouf. It seemed perfectly plausible that all three teams would finish level on fifteen points and it would come down to goal difference. Advantage Egypt, whose goal difference was nine, while Senegal's was seven – and bad news for Morocco, who had a goal difference of five and could do nothing about it. On the downside for Egypt they were playing their bitter rivals Algeria away from home, while Senegal only had to travel to play the group whipping boys, Namibia.

When Mido (yes, him, but less broad in the beam than in his time in England) scored for Egypt after an hour everything was level on goal difference, as Senegal were three-up in Namibia. But it was slightly advantage Egypt again, they had the better head-to-head record.

Yacine Bezzaz scored for Algeria and swung things in Senegal's favour, while goals from Fadiga and N'Diaye gave Senegal a 5–0 win. Egypt couldn't muster a winner, so Algeria had a good gloat and Senegal qualified.

Nigeria qualified with a point to spare but had to pull their finger out and win their last three games to edge past Liberia, who unexpectedly beat them in Monrovia. Two matches in July, 2001 swung it. Liberia lost at home to Ghana while Nigeria walloped Sudan in Omdurman. A last win over Ghana was enough to get home by a point. Nigeria still had muscle aplenty in the side, but an improved Okocha and Kanu added a bit of subtlety. Liberia's exit meant we would never see the excellent George Weah in the World Cup. Weah, who had spells at Monaco, Paris St Germain and AC Milan, plus a few strange months on loan in the Premier League, was one of the first African players to make a serious impact in Europe – a real pioneer if not quite the world-beater he was cracked up to be.

North America produced the USA, Mexico and Costa Rica as qualifiers – how terribly novel. The only surprise was that it was Costa Rica who powered through the final group, losing only in the USA and winning seven of ten matches. The key win for them was a 2–1 victory in Mexico City having been one-down. The goals were scored by Rolando Fonseca and Hernán Medford, which was good, because they had been big players for Costa Rica for a decade; Fonseca is third in the all-time appearances list and is Costa Rica's leading goal scorer, two ahead of Paolo Wanchope who was also in this squad.

You may remember reading about Brazil losing a qualifying match for the first time in 1993. Well the new round-robin format changed all that nonsense. They lost six matches this time around as they went through big changes of personnel between the 1998 and 2002 tournaments. Their home form got them through the section in third place, but away from home they won two, drew in Colombia and lost six. And Japan was a long way from home. Argentina headed the table in fine style, losing only once (in São Paulo) and scoring over forty goals, with fifteen different scorers, chief amongst them Hernán Crespo, of Lazio, one of the most lethal strikers in European football.

Sandwiched between these two big beasts was Ecuador, qualifying for the first time with their own Golden Generation, while
Paraguay were still a good side and only behind Brazil on goal
difference. Uruguay got the chance to play-off against Australia
and won 3–1 on aggregate despite defeat in Melbourne, where a
vast crowd filled the famous old cricket ground. Unsurprisingly
Uruguay had a man sent off in that match, and six booked in the
return, but two goals from Richard Morales saw them home.

Ecuador's hero was Agustin Delgado, who scored winning
goals against Brazil, Paraguay, Chile, Bolivia and Peru. Delgado
was registered to play for Southampton, but curiously seemed to
always be fit for international duty and injured when he came
back to England. He managed eleven games in three seasons for
the Saints, and had Gordon Strachan tearing his hair out.
Qualification was sealed with a 1–1 draw at home to Uruguay
with a goal from Jaime Kaviedes, who once played four games on
loan at Crystal Palace.

Colombia didn't make it despite winning the Copa América
the previous year (which didn't include a lot of the European-
based players), while Chile, who had played quite well at the last
tournament, were bottom of the pile.

In Europe, UEFA and FIFA came up with a brilliant new
system for seeding the groups, based on all sorts of coefficients
and modifiers. It was about as comprehensible as a David Lynch
movie in Sanskrit. (I am, of course, dear reader, assuming you are
not fluent in Sanskrit – my apologies if I have erred.) Of the nine
teams in the top seeded pot, only two won their group and two
more came through the play-offs, while six sides made it from pot
two, two from pot three and one, Slovenia, from the fourth tier of
seeds. Which, actually, is not a complaint, I think it's a good thing
– the same old teams every time gets boring.

Of the top seeds, Spain won a poor group with ease, Austria in
second. Spain won their four home games rattling up a goal
difference of 15–1 and dropped only two points overall, as did
Sweden, who let in only three goals in ten games. Turkey reached
the play-offs in Sweden's group, and had a highly rated striker,
Hakan Şükür, thirty now, but a danger. The most remarkable
goalscoring feat for the Turks came in the 3–3 draw with

Macedonia. Two-down at half-time, Turkey hit back with two strikes from Aston Villa's Alpay. Macedonia scored again, but Alpay was having none of that and completed his hat-trick. Alpay was Turkey's centre-half. Turkey beat Austria 6–0 on aggregate (5–0 in Istanbul) and made the Finals for the first time since 1954 when they made up the numbers.

Italy qualified comfortably ahead of Romania, scoring more goals than is their wont. The first choice front three of Del Piero, Inzaghi and Totti looked very accomplished. Inzaghi (then of Juventus, but with Milan by the time the Finals came round) scored both goals in their best performance, a 2–0 win in Bucharest.

Slovenia, with their tempestuous playmaker Zlatan Zahovic, had done really well to reach Euro 2000 and not disgraced themselves in the Finals, but they really weren't expected to qualify here ahead of Russia and Yugoslavia, especially when they drew their first game 2–2 with the Faroe Islands, conceding twice in the last three minutes. After five games they had one win and four draws, one of these a good result in Moscow. In September, on the day England played Germany in Munich, Slovenia played Russia at home. Milan Osterc opened the scoring in a scrappy game with a terrific back-header from Acimovic's cross. Milenko Acimovic was Slovenia's best player in the absence that night of Zahovic; he played for Red Star Belgrade but moved to Tottenham later in the summer, where he spent two years on the bench and in the treatment room. In the closing minutes the referee, England's Graham Poll, spotted some shirt tugging at a set piece, and Acimovic put the penalty away. As the old cliché goes, there was dancing in the streets of Ljubljana. Why Poll didn't give penalties for all the shirt pulling that went on throughout the entire match, only he can tell you. A point ahead of Yugoslavia, they needed a point in Belgrade, and got it courtesy of an early goal. No mistakes in the last home game against the Faroes, and then the small matter of a play-off against Romania. Romania weren't the force they were in the '90s and a 2–1 win in Ljubljana and a draw away was enough. Good effort from the team seeded fourth in their group.

The best second placed team got an easier play-off, against Iran, and the lucky ones were Ireland. Not lucky in that they didn't deserve it, but it was better than playing Turkey or Germany. Their group contained Holland and Portugal, so they were up against it, as well as three lesser sides, Estonia, Cyprus and Andorra. It became two mini groups as, unusually, none of the top three dropped a single point against the weaker sides.

Ireland started with a draw in Amsterdam. Jason McAteer set up Robbie Keane – he was still doing that silly forward roll into a bow-and-arrow posture goal celebration – and then McAteer scored a belter, rounding off a superb counter-attack with a lovely left-foot strike. Ireland conceded a poor goal from a cross and an outrageous thirty-five yarder from Giovanni van Bronckhorst, but it was still a good result. Another good draw followed in Lisbon; Ireland conceded first this time, but Matt Holland, a second-half substitute, equalised with a stunning strike low into the corner.

Definitely advantage Ireland and when Conceição and Pauleta gave Portugal victory in Holland, the Dutch were in major trouble. In Lisbon the following spring, Jimmy Floyd Hasselbaink played for, and got, a penalty early on against Portugal, and when Patrick Kluivert added a second minutes after half-time from Overmars' fantastic cross, the Dutch were right back in the frame. Portugal mounted one last, desperate attack and Frank de Boer, normally so calm, buffeted Pauleta in the area. Urs Meier, the Swiss referee, gave a penalty, quite rightly, and Figo scored it. The Dutch made a stink, but with no cause. Ireland and Portugal were hard to separate. Figo's header cancelled Roy Keane's tidy finish and honours were even again in Dublin. So to a showdown with Holland. Portugal looked likely to win the group, but if Ireland could avoid losing in Dublin, and the other games all went with form, they could at least reach the play-offs. Ireland were largely outplayed and had Gary Kelly sent off for a tackle from behind after an hour, minutes before the referee turned down a penalty appeal from van Nistelrooy when he collided with Shay Given. The Gods were with Ireland; Roy Keane broke a tackle and played in Steve Finnan as he was clattered by the second defender. Finnan switch the ball back to the left and McAteer was unmarked to score against the Dutch again. Holland (Stam, Cocu, Overmars, van Nistelrooy, de Boer, Davids, Kluivert, Seedorf) were out.

Ireland did their job against Iran and took their place in the Far East.

Norway were in with the top seeds but they were a poor side now. Egil Olsen had left after the 1998 Finals and had been spending his time getting Wimbledon relegated after fourteen years in the top flight while reminding us how good a coach he was. Most of the good players were gone, too. Poland took advantage and won the group, with Ukraine second; Wales made as little contribution as Norway, they finished fifth and fourth behind Belarus. Emmanuel Olisadebe, a quick young striker, had become the first black player picked by Poland as soon as he adopted citizenship in 2000, and he scored eight goals in qualifying, one fewer than Shevchenko for Ukraine.

Denmark started with a lot of draws in their cosy-looking group, but got going in spring 2001 when they took four points off the Czechs, their nearest rivals. Jon Dahl Tomasson, once of Newcastle (and unsuccessful there) but now a much more complete player, and Ebbe Sand were a dangerous forward combination. Northern Ireland added little except a couple of creditable draw with the Danes.

England and Scotland were both in five-team groups, both tricky. Scotland had Belgium and Croatia; England had their old nemesis, Germany. Scotland started well but were undone by a run of results in spring 2001. At 2–0 up against Belgium they were in control of the group only to concede a last-minute equaliser to the giant centre-half Daniel Van Buyten. When Croatia also got a point at Hampden it meant Scotland needed something from their game in Brussels. They lost 2–0 and that was it; Croatia beat Belgium in their last game with a goal from Alen Boksic, thirty-two now but anxious to make up for missing the 1998 Finals. Belgium lost their play-off against the Czech Republic.

England were making a drama out of crisis, as usual. After a truly appalling showing and a 1–0 defeat at home to Germany in their opening game of this campaign, Kevin Keegan had bid a teary farewell to a job he wasn't remotely qualified to do. Less involved in the game than most managers who eat, sleep and breathe football, Keegan didn't watch enough players and didn't watch enough football outside England to know how to prepare a team at this level. Caretaker manager Howard Wilkinson took the team to Finland, dropped Michael Owen and got a 0–0 draw.

In came England's first overseas coach, Sven-Göran Eriksson, a studious looking Swede with a bit of nous, a lot of experience, and, we would learn, a canny bedside manner. The first thing Sven did was to restore Owen and the Liverpool man scored in the next two games as England started to pick up points. Germany matched England's ordinary result in Finland, which helped – they had to come from 2–0 down to get even a draw after Mikael Forssell struck twice in the first half. A good win in Athens left England with two soft home games to finish, but there was still the big test to come; Germany in Munich.

WORLD CUP SHOCK No.11
1 September 2001, Olympiastadion, Munich, Germany; 63,000

Germany	**(1) 1**	Jancker 6
England	**(2) 5**	Owen 12, 48, 65, Gerrard 45, Heskey 73

Referee: **Byron Moreno** (Ecuador)
Coaches: **Rudi Völler** (Germany) & **Sven Göran Eriksson** (England)

Germany (1-4-3-2): Oliver Kahn (Cpt, Bayern Munich); Christian Wörns (Borussia Dortmund); Thomas Linke (Bayern), Jens Nowotny (Bayer Leverkusen), Marko Rehmer (Hertha Berlin), Jörg Böhme (Schalke 04); Sebastian Deisler (Hertha Berlin), Didi Hamann (Liverpool), Michael Ballack (Leverkusen); Carsten Jancker (Bayern), Oliver Neuville (Leverkusen). **Subs:** Gerald Asamoah (Schalke 04) 45m for Wörns; Miroslav Klose (Kaiserslautern) 64m for Ballack; Sebastian Kehl (SC Freiburg) 79m for Neuville
England (4-4-2): David Seaman (Arsenal); Gary Neville (Manchester United), Sol Campbell (Arsenal), Rio Ferdinand (Leeds United), Ashley Cole (Arsenal); David Beckham (Cpt, Man Utd), Steven Gerrard (Liverpool), Paul Scholes (Man Utd), Nick Barmby (Liverpool); Michael Owen (Liverpool), Emile Heskey (Liverpool). **Subs:** Steve McManaman (Real Madrid) 64m for Barmby; Owen Hargreaves (Bayern Munich) 79m for Gerrard; Jamie Carragher (Liverpool) 84m for Scholes
Cautioned: Heskey (Eng) 54m, Hamann (Ger) 79m

When Germany scored a ridiculously simple goal after six minutes English hearts sank. Ballack's cross was nodded on by the diminutive but unmarked Neuville for Jancker to knock past Seaman. England fans started looking up who the other likely second placed teams were going to be.

England had Sven's first choice team out. Owen was a hard player to partner, and he seemed to enjoy playing with Emile Heskey, so Heskey it was; Liverpool bought the goal-shy striker for just that reason. Why else pick a player with a heavy first touch who couldn't finish his dinner? Barmby got the nod as the more left-sided of a midfield quartet.

The lead only lasted six minutes. A silly foul by Deisler gave Beckham a chance to whip in a free-kick. Germany never cleared it and Gary Neville's intelligent headed lob reached Barmby, who nodded it into Owen's path; the striker's finish was expert, getting his foot high over the awkward bouncing ball. Deisler made another error at the other end minutes later, falling over his feet and screwing the ball wide when presented with an open goal. Both sides looked capable of scoring; a silly back-pass (Deisler again) gave England an indirect free-kick, but it's hard to beat a wall formed on the line and both Beckham's first shot and Neville's follow-up were charged down. On forty minutes David Seaman had to be at his best to reach a drive from Jörg Böhme and tip it round the post, but in the main Campbell and Rio Ferdinand had got a grip on the German forwards.

As half-time approached, and the players were starting to wind down for the break, Gary Neville tried one more charge up the line and was found by a deft lob from Beckham. Neville's cross was blocked but as Beckham tried to nick the follow-up past Novotny he was brought down. Beckham's first kick was unusually poor and charged down, his second attempt, left-footed was headed out. Steven Gerrard, hovering on the edge of the penalty area, took the ball on his chest and hit a marvellous low drive into the corner of the goal. It was the perfect time to score the second goal.

Three minutes into the second half England were in dreamland. Beckham harried on the right, won the ball and chipped left footed, into the middle. Heskey rose well and did what he was there to do – give the ball to Owen. His strike partner's volley was instant and beat Oliver Kahn for pace.

Germany's best player, Michael Ballack missed their best chance to get back into the game, blasting Jancker's clever knockdown high into the night sky.

At the other end an England attack broke down but before the Germans could settle into possession Gerrard won the ball back and played an instant pass to Michael Owen, who, like a predatory in-form striker should, still hovered on the shoulder of the last defender. Owen moved up a gear, went clear, and hammered the ball high past Kahn for a brilliantly taken hat-trick. Eight minutes later Scholes played a good one-two with Beckham and put Heskey clear. On any other occasion Kahn would have been too big a presence for such a nervous finisher, but on that night Heskey took one touch to put the ball in front of him and stroked it calmly past Kahn.

Germany were awful, surely, worst team they ever had etc, etc. Er . . . no, that was 2004. Rudi Völler had forged a half-decent side and they had been playing well. In the very even first half they created chances and could easily have gone in 2–1 ahead not 2–1 down. Jancker was in great form and was a real handful, with a good touch for a big feller, and Ballack was establishing a repu-tation as a world-class attacking midfield player. Admittedly there were a few journeymen in the team, but this was essentially the group that (SPOILER ALERT) got all the way to the World Cup Final a few months later.

England were really good, a couple of moments in the middle of the defence and down the left apart. Beckham and Neville sliced the German left flank open time after time and Owen had the beating of either centre-back on the floor. England passed their way through; they didn't bang the ball hopefully over the top. This was the Golden Generation, that over-used phrase – but they looked it here. Gerrard played a little further back, behind Scholes, and they rarely wasted a pass. They needed a better left-sided option than the lightweight Barmby, and Heskey couldn't stay, but it would do for now: a team with six world-class players and three very good ones could not be ruled out in a major tournament.

After the euphoria of that epic win, England nearly failed to finish the job. They beat Albania easily enough, without playing at all well, and needed to match or better Germany's result in the last game. It had to be assumed Germany would beat Finland at home.

Greece were not a good side – coach Otto Rehhagel hadn't yet hit on the formula that would win them the 2004 European

Championship – but they could be obdurate and England tended to get jittery at Wembley if the crowd started whistling and getting impatient, which they usually did. And England were missing Gerrard and Owen.

The crowd had cause to whistle in this game. England were terrible; disjointed and sluggish. Paul Scholes, normally such a crisp passer, gave the ball away every time, Nicky Barmby did the same and what Danny Murphy was doing there, Sven only knows. Good club player but ... Michael Owen was sorely missed – the front two of Heskey and Fowler were woeful. (Fowler was another good Premiership player who could not make that next rung.)

Charisteas gave Greece the lead with an angled shot past an unsighted Nigel Martyn, and Martyn had to make two good saves to keep it to 1–0. One man alone was playing to his potential for England. David Beckham was everywhere, passionate, skilful, prompting, exhorting his colleagues.

Martyn made the second of his saves and threw the ball intelligently to the England captain. Beckham twisted and turned, lost one man and was brought down by the second. Thirty-five-year-old Sheringham came on for Fowler as Beckham prepared to take the free-kick – desperate measures. Sheringham's first touch flicked the ball over the goalkeeper for an equaliser. Greece were back in front a minute later, Nikolaidis knocking in a smart snap-shot while England dozed off. Sven went three at the back and brought on McManaman but Greece wouldn't cave in. News filtered through that the Germans couldn't break down Finland either (Antti Niemi had a blinder in goal), but England just couldn't get their game together. Nikopolidis was playing well in the Greek goal too, he made one sprawling stop from a Beckham free-kick in the first half and couple of excellent interventions as England pressed for a second goal. Beckham sent a second free-kick sizzling just wide, and Sheringham won another one with the game in injury-time. The Germany game had finished 0–0.

It was one of the greatest free-kicks in football history. I'm not being silly, the quality of the strike, given the situation and the pressure, was a quite outstanding display of skill and technique, worthy of Platini. It was Beckham's finest moment and confirmed his elevation from pantomime villain in 1998 to national hero in 2001.

Then came the metatarsal moment. A few weeks before the tournament England's superstar broke a bone on the top of his foot. He underwent some serious surgery and recuperation and was passed fit to travel; but just how fit was he?

Finals

Argentina were most people's favourites for the title, along with Italy, maybe Spain (always maybe Spain and always disappointment). The holders France had most of the same team, as did Croatia, and if Owen played well and Beckham's foot was okay, then England couldn't be discounted at their best. Surely Brazil and Germany? Not this time, they just didn't have the players. Or so went the general opinion of almost every scribe and TV pundit in the land.

WORLD CUP SHOCK No.12
31 May 2002, Seoul World Cup Stadium, 62,561

France	(0) 0	
Senegal	(1) 1	Bouba Diop

Referee: **Ali Mohammed Bujsaim** (United Arab Emirates)
Coaches: **Roger Lemerre** (France) & **Bruno Metsu** (Senegal)

France (1–4–3–2): Fabien Barthez (Manchester United); Lilian Thuram (Juventus), Marcel Desailly (Cpt, Chelsea)), Frank Leboeuf (Olympique de Marseille★), Bixente Lizarazu (Bayern Munich); Sylvain Wiltord (Arsenal), Emmanuel Petit (Chelsea), Patrick Vieira (Arsenal), Youri Djorkaeff (Bolton Wanderers); David Trezeguet (Juventus), Thierry Henry (Arsenal). **Subs:** Christophe Dugarry (Bordeaux) 60m for Djorkaeff; Djibril Cissé (Auxerre) 81m for Wiltord
Senegal (4–1–4–1): Tony Sylva (Monaco); Ferdinand Coly (Lens), Pape Malick Diop (Lorient), Lamine Diatta (Rennes), Omar Daf (Sochaux); Aliou Cissé (Cpt, Montpelier); Moussa N'Diaye (Sedan), Salif Diao (Sedan), Pape Bouba Diop (Lens) Khalilou Fadiga (Auxerre); El Hadji† Diouf (Lens)
Cautioned: Petit (Fra) 47m, Cissé (Sen) 51m

★ Leboeuf was the only member of France's starting line-up playing in France and he had only just gone back. Every one of Senegal's players played in France until English and Italian clubs started hoovering them up after the tournament.
† A couple of writers point out that this is an honorific, not a forename, but, if it's how everyone knows him, then it's just wilfully perverse to use a name with which no one is familiar instead.

What a start to the tournament. Just as in 1990, when Argentina came a cropper, an African team upset the holders' welcome party.

Senegal won this because they got their tactics spot on. They knew France, without Zidane, would struggle to make clear chances for their forwards if they stifled the midfield, so they did just that, positioning their captain, Cissé, just behind a four-man midfield with instructions to defend first and worry about scoring later.

But not too much later. Diouf, who was a thorn in the French defence's side all afternoon, beat Leboeuf for pace down the left and crossed. There was no obvious danger, but, in trying to clear, Manu Petit only kicked the ball against his own goalkeeper. Barthez, surprised, could do nothing with it and Bouba Diop said thanks very much and tapped it into the goal.

France tried their hardest – that accusation was levelled at them but was unfair – and yet couldn't create clear opportunities let alone good ones. Fadiga nearly doubled Senegal's lead, but his shot clattered the crossbar – he could hit a ball really hard, and minutes later France came closest to a goal when Henry's shot also hit the woodwork.

Coly and Daf blocked the channels, and France didn't have the aerial threat to trouble the central defenders; far from a rousing backs-to-the-wall performance, Senegal were coasting towards the end. They were fit too, they didn't use any substitutes in the heat.

France had problems. They had brought Zidane, but hadn't intended to use him in the group stage. Djorkaeff was supposed to provide the guile (he had spent the last season at Bolton on loan and done well enough to force his way back into the squad) but he was a support act and struggled to impose himself on difficult games. Vieira was a wonderful athlete and imposing presence, but he couldn't do it all, and he got precious little from Wiltord or Petit. Henry tried but didn't see enough of the ball, and Trezeguet was anonymous.

Senegal looked a genuinely good side, not just a minnow having its day; Denmark and Uruguay would do well not to take them lightly.

GROUP A

Denmark	(1) 2	**Uruguay**	(0) 1	1 June, Ulsan; 30,157
Tomasson 44, 83		Rodriguez 47		
Uruguay	(0) 0	**France**	(0) 0	6 June, Busan; 38,289
Denmark	(1) 1	**Senegal**	(0) 1	6 June, Daegu; 43,500
Tomasson 16 (p)		Diao 51		
France	(0) 0	**Denmark**	(1) 2	11 June, Incheon; 48,100
Rommedahl 22,				
Tomasson 67				
Senegal	(3) 3	**Uruguay**	(0) 3	11 June, Suwon; 33,681
Fadiga 20 (p),		Morales 46, Forlán 69,		
Bouba Diop 26, 39		Recoba 87 (p)		

1. Denmark 7pts (5–2); 2. Senegal 5pts (5–4); 3. Uruguay 2pts (4–5); 4. France 1pt (0–3)

Jon Dahl Tomasson confirmed his improvement to watching English fans with both Denmark goals in a win over Uruguay. Chelsea fans, used to speed and a disappointing end product from Jesper Gronkjaer, would have been astonished at his precise cross for the first. Uruguay's equaliser was special. Two men were hovering on the edge of the box when a corner was cleared; one of them, García juggled the ball and flipped it to his mate, Rodríguez, who volleyed it handsomely in at the near post. Denmark deserved their win though.

France should have been out after two games. Henry was sent off for a dangerous late tackle – some English TV guys defended him but it was a definite red card. Uruguay didn't really take advantage – their Internazionale star Álvaro Recoba, did little to justify his reputation.

Senegal produced more of the same against Denmark in a physical encounter. Their full-backs were excellent again, and negated Jørgensen and Rommedahl, the speedy Danish wingers. Salif Diao contributed a well-deserved equaliser and a red card for a nasty studs-up tackle. The two shaven-headed Danish midfielders, Stig Tøfting and Thomas Gravesen didn't flinch in the face of the rough stuff and handed out their fair share in return.

Denmark beating France and knocking them out was no longer a surprise. Zidane came back but with this much bite in the Denmark midfield he would have struggled even if fully fit. Wiltord had another shocker and Trezeguet vanished after hitting the bar early on. Rommedahl volleyed in after twenty minutes and Tomasson bullied Desailly off the ball to score the second – he wouldn't have done that four years earlier, but he looked the business here, strong and full of thoughtful running and always looking like he would take the chances if they came his way.

The fun was happening over in Suwon, where Senegal ran up a three-goal lead against Uruguay with two more goals from Bouba Diop and a penalty after a preposterous dive from Diouf. Had he done that a few years later when his reputation went before him he would have been yellow carded and laughed at, but he got a decision from the Dutch referee. Pua, the Uruguay coach, sent on two fresh attackers at half-time and got an instant response. Recoba woke up, sending in Silva from the kick-off. His shot was saved but Morales, on the pitch for less than a minute, scored with his first touch. Forlán, the other substitute – a position with which he was familiar having warmed the bench throughout his first season at Manchester United – then cracked home a fine volley. Senegal were panicking and it was hard to keep up with the yellow card count. Amazingly no one was asked to leave the field, although another yellow card for diving would have been the right response to a tumble by Morales, but the referee gave a penalty instead. How even-handed of him. Senegal just about held out, but by now they had a stack of players with yellow cards to their name.

GROUP B

Paraguay	(1) 2	**South Africa**	(0) 2	2 June, Busan; 25,186	
Santa Cruz 39, Arce 55		T Mokoena 63, Fortune 90 (p)			
Spain	(1) 3	**Slovenia**	(0) 1	2 June, Gwangju; 28,598	
Raúl 44, Valerón 74		Cimirotic 82			
Hierro 87 (p)					
Paraguay	(1) 1	**Spain**	(0) 3	7 June, Jeonju; 24,000	
Own goal 10		Morientes 53, 69,			
		Hierro 82 (p)			
South Africa	(1) 1	**Slovenia**	(0) 0	8 June, Daegu; 47,226	
Nomvete 4					
Spain	(2) 3	**South Africa**	(1) 2	12 June, Daejeon; 31,024	
Raúl 4, 56,		McCarthy 31, Radebe 53			
Morientes 45					
Slovenia	(1) 1	**Paraguay**	(0) 3	12 June, Seogwipo; 30.176	
Acimovic 45		Cuevas 65, 84, Campos 73			

1. Spain 9pts (9–4); 2. Paraguay 4pts (6–6); 3. South Africa 4pts (5–5); 4. Slovenia 0pts (2–7)

Spain won a really weak group at a canter without looking an exceptional team. The established guys were good but they had no one new and exciting to convince they were going to change their habit of doing well early and then going out in the last sixteen or last eight.

Paraguay did well in their last match, beating Slovenia despite playing with ten men for seventy minutes. Slovenia were awful – their big player, Zahovic, had a shocker against Spain, was taken off and then sent home for firing a volley of choicest Slovenian insults at the coach. South Africa were out of their depth – their big player, Benni McCarthy, should just have been sent home for being a waste of space; more *buffoon buffoon* than *bafana bafana*.

GROUP C

Brazil	(0) 2	**Turkey**	(1) 1	3 June, Ulsan; 33,842
Ronaldo 50, Rivaldo 87 (p)		Şaş 45		
China	(0) 0	**Costa Rica**	(0) 2	4 June, Gwangju; 27,217
		Gómez 61, Wright 65		
Brazil	(3) 4	**China**	(0) 0	8 June, Seogwipo; 36,750
Roberto Carlos 15,				
Rivaldo 32, Ronaldinho 45 (p),				
Ronaldo 55				
Costa Rica	(0) 1	**Turkey**	(0) 1	9 June, Incheon; 42,299
Parks 86		B Emre 56		
Costa Rica	(1) 2	**Brazil**	(3) 5	13 June, Suwon; 38,524
Wanchope 39, Gómez 56		Own goal 10, Ronaldo 12,		
		Edmilson 38, Rivaldo 62,		
		Júnior 64		
Turkey	(2) 3	**China**	(0) 0	13 June, Seoul; 43,605
Şaş 6, Bülent 9,				
Davala 85				

1. Brazil 9pts (11–3); 2. Turkey 4pts (5–3); 3. Costa Rica 4pts (5–6); 4. China 0pts (0–9)

Turkey gave Brazil a wake-up call in their opening game. Brazil had plenty of opportunities, and Ronaldinho showed why he was being touted as the next big thing for Brazil. Ronaldo, a bit chubby but still a natural goalscorer, converted Rivaldo's cross, and Rivaldo's left foot saw to the penalty after Alpay was red carded for a professional foul. Popular opinion said the game showed how poor this Brazilian team was; hindsight tells us Turkey were better than Brazil and the experts had believed.

FIFA made a big noise about clamping down on simulation before the tournament. Simulation, by the way, is FIFA-speak for cheating. This match set the tone for the tournament. In the closing minutes Rivaldo won a corner on the right. The defender Hakan Ünsal kicked the ball towards the Brazilian with the merest hint of aggression and a huge amount of *get on with it, pal, and stop time-wasting*. The ball hit Rivaldo's leg and he went down as if poleaxed, clutching his face. The referee sent off the Turkish defender while a linesman, who was a few feet away, said nothing. FIFA, with the benefit of a TV replay, fined Rivaldo £5,000. Had they given the cheating so-and-so a two-match ban the game would be a better product now than it is. But it was FIFA, and they blew it.

Turkey were poor in their second game, and allowed Costa Rica to sneak a late equaliser, which left the Turks needing a favour from Brazil so they could go through on goal difference. They got it, Brazil beat China and Costa Rica with something to spare and their stars all got a goal or two to get them going; even one of Roberto Carlos's free-kicks went in the goal instead of the further reaches of the stand behind it. Turkey beat China easily to confirm their place – but it was another dull first phase group, the first game excepted. Even watching Brazil is unexciting if the opposition are as supine as China and Costa Rica. It sounds harsh, but in the World Cup you're playing with the big boys so you have to come up with a plan to match them and try and neutralise them and give yourselves a chance, however small. China couldn't do that; they had a vastly experienced coach (the ubiquitous Milutinovic) but no players good enough to create openings and no defenders who could match quality strikers like Ronaldo, Ronaldinho and Hasan Şaş, the scary-looking Turkish left-sided attacker. I discount Şükür, my mum could have marked him in this form. He only kept his place because he was an icon in Istanbul and Günes, the coach may have been lynched if he'd left him out.

GROUP D

South Korea		(1) 2	**Poland**	(0) 0	4 June, Busan; 48,670
Hwang 26, Yoo 53					

Portugal	**(1) 2**	**USA**	**(3) 3**	5 June, Suwon; 37,306
Beto 39, own goal 71		O'Brien 4, own goal 29,		
		McBride 36		
USA	**(1) 1**	**South Korea**(0) 1		10 June, Daegu; 60,778
Mathis 24		Ahn 78		
Poland	**(0) 0**	**Portugal**	**(1) 4**	10 June, Jeonju; 31,000
Pauleta 14, 65, 77,				
Rui Costa 88				
Portugal	**(0) 0**	**South Korea**(0) 1		14 June, Incheon; 50,239
		Park		
Poland	**(2) 3**	**USA**	**(0) 1**	14 June, Daejeon; 26,482
Olisadebe 3,		Donovan 83		
Kryszalowicz 5,				
Marcin Zewlakow 66				

1. South Korea 7pts (4–1); 2. USA 4pts (5–6); 3. Portugal 3pts (6–4); 4. Poland 3pts (3–7)

This was more like it, a bit of controversy, a few goals, one of the better sides getting turned over. That's what the World Cup is about, not shooting practice against sides who wouldn't beat your third XI.

South Korea took Poland apart. They were unworried by the heat – they were phenomenally fit, as well as accustomed to the climate – and the Poles were a big, slow team, perfect opposition for the lively Koreans, who preferred ninety minutes of helter skelter. Their top scorer, Hwang Sun-hong was thirty-three now, but he got their first goal with a near-post volley. His replacement Ahn Jung-hwan, looked sharper still, and came close twice. The second goal was one man's work as Yoo Sang-chul drifted through Kaluzny and Waldoch and cracked a fierce shot in by the post. Great start for the hosts, and great support from a sea of red in the stands – the Koreans had given away enough replica shirts to fill Seoul.

A day later in Suwon the group had an upside down look after the USA beat Portugal. The Portuguese, gifted players all, just didn't look like a team. With only half an hour gone Figo was shouting at his colleagues to get him some possession, while Pauleta made run after run only to watch his wide players try and beat a man and lose the ball. McBride's strength in the air gave USA their advantage; his header was saved by Baia and knocked in by O'Brien for the opener. The USA so unnerved the Portuguese defence on high balls that Jorge Costa didn't look where his header was going and he put it in his own net. McBride added a third with a cleverly controlled header off balance.

Beto got one back after a poor clearance and Agoos hacked into his own net in the second half, but the Portuguese ran out of ideas, and Donovan and Beasley both had chances to extend the Americans' lead.

Against the USA, Ahn replaced Hwang to good purpose again, heading the equalising goal after Lee Eul-yung missed his chance from the penalty spot. Portugal took out their frustration on a lousy Polish side. Pauleta helped himself to a good hat-trick and Rui Costa, awful in the first match and left out from the start, came on and scored the fourth.

Poland beating the USA would have been a result most people predicted before the tournament, but after the events of the previous ten days it almost qualified as a shock. Two goals in the first five minutes finished the game – the USA weren't so clever at chasing when they went behind.

In Incheon, Portugal made life very difficult for themselves with some shocking indiscipline. João Pinto got his marching orders for a wild two-footed lunge on Park Ji-sung and the rest of the team surrounded the referee for a full five minutes. Fernando Couto actually had the ref's face in his hands but somehow managed to stay on the pitch. Today he would have been given a massive ban after the match and deserved it. After sixty-five minutes Portugal were down to nine when Beto tripped Lee Yung-pyo and received a second yellow. Again the referee had little option.

Had the nine men held on they would have scraped through with Poland's help, but Park Ji-sung administered the coup de grace with a brilliant finish. Lee Yong-pyo's cross came to him high up beyond the far post; he chested the ball down, volleyed it to the left of Conceição with his right foot as it dropped and hit it on the volley again, with his left foot this time, hard and low past Baia. The benefit of two-footed players – great goal. Portugal, fractious and over-rated, weren't mourned.

GROUP E

Cameroon	(1) 1	**Ireland** (0) 1	1 June, Nigata; 33,679
Mboma 39		Holland 52	
Germany	(4) 8	**Saudi Arabia** (0) 0	1 June, Sapporo; 32,218
Klose 20, 25, 69, Ballack 40,			
Jancker 45, Linke 72,			
Bierhoff 84, Schneider 90			
Ireland	(0) 1	**Germany** (1) 1	5 June, Ibaraki; 35,854
Keane 90		Klose 19	
Saudi Arabia	(0) 0	**Cameroon** (0) 1	6 June, Saitama; 52,328
		Eto'o 65	
Cameroon	(0) 0	**Germany** (0) 2	11 June, Shizuoka; 47.085
		Bode 50, Klose 79	
Ireland	(1) 3	**Saudi Arabia** (0) 0	11 June, Yokohama; 65,320
Keane 7, Breen 61,			
Duff 87			

1. **Germany** 7pts (11–1); 2. **Ireland** 5 pts (5–2); 3. **Cameroon** 4pts (2–3); 4. **Saudi Arabia** 0pts (0–12)

Ireland had a bit of baggage to deal with before the tournament even started. Their training facilities were second rate and the hotel a bit shabby, so Roy Keane kicked up about it to a journalist and was taken to task by Mick McCarthy, the manager. So far, no big deal; Keane had a right to moan, but not to the press – the Irish FA are cheapskates and always short change their players. McCarthy, for his part, knew there was nothing he could do about the facilities at that stage and didn't want Keane rocking the boat.

Keane did more than rock the boat, he damn near sank it. Instead of dealing with the matter quietly Keane bawled his manager out with a foul-mouthed tirade, making reference to the fact that he didn't think McCarthy was a genuine Irishman and that he was a crap player and a crap manager (only the first was true). To cut the rest of the story short, Keane went home and Ireland had lost their best player. The pair buried the hatchet a few years later when they were forced to meet as managers of clubs in the same division.

We talked about having a plan to combat sides with better players. Clearly no one talked to Saudi Arabia about it, they got annihilated by the Germans. The Polish-born Kaiserslautern striker Miroslav Klose got a hat-trick of headers and ... oh, I can't be bothered, it was a turkey shoot. They were better against

Cameroon and Ireland – or maybe Cameroon and Ireland just weren't as potent as Germany – but still lost all three and failed to score.

Against Cameroon in their opener, the Irish had a bit of a hangover from the incident, and were poor in the first half. An early goal in the second half settled them, and they could have won it towards the end. Matt Holland, on whom Ireland were now depending as a midfield general, scored with a fine low shot.

Ireland struggled against Germany, who looked solid but unspectacular, and the new star Klose scored with yet another header. Damien Duff had Ireland's best effort but it brought a great save out of Oliver Kahn. The equaliser was a throw-back to Jack Charlton's tactics; Steve Finnan launched a long ball towards the gangling Niall Quinn – thirty-five now and used as a sub, but a much better player than he was at twenty-five. Quinn got some head on it, and the ball fell nicely for Robbie Keane, who chested it down and smashed it straight through Kahn, who did well to get a glove on it but couldn't keep it out.

Ireland knew that even though they lay third in the group, if they beat Saudi Arabia by two or more goals they were through whatever the result in Shizuoka. It was a laborious performance but they got the job done; McCarthy puffed out his cheeks in relief as Damien Duff scored the third goal that meant a sneaky breakaway from the Saudis was meaningless. As it happened, any win would have sufficed as Germany beat Cameroon (very disappointing) with two second half goals. It was a rough-house affair that left Germany with a lot of players on a yellow card, among them their captain and goalkeeper, Kahn, and their best creative player, Michael Ballack. Ziege, Hamann, who had been excellent so far and Ramelow (sent off against Cameroon) would all miss the next match.

GROUP F

Argentina Batistuta 63	(0) 1	**Nigeria**	(0) 0	2 June, Ibaraki; 34,050
Sweden Alexandersson 60	(0) 1	**England** Campbell 24	(1) 1	2 June, Saitama; 62,561
Nigeria Aghahowa 27	(1) 1	**Sweden** Larsson 35, 62 (p)	(1) 2	7 June, Kobe; 36,194

England	**(1) 1**	**Argentina**	**(0) 0**	7 June, Sapporo; 35,927
Beckham 44 (p)				
Argentina	**(0) 1**	**Sweden**	**(0) 1**	12 June, Miyagi; 45,777
Crespo 88		A Svensson 59		
England	**(0) 0**	**Nigeria**	**(0) 0**	12 June, Osaka; 44,864

1. Sweden 5pts (4–3); 2. England 5pts (2–1); 3. Argentina 4pts (2–2); 4. Nigeria 1pt (1–3)

This was a scandalous group. All four of these sides would have qualified from any of the other groups – it was born of making the draw based on geography rather than competence. Argentina looked good in their first match, keeping the ball superbly against Nigeria, with Verón outstanding, in direct contrast to his struggles in the Premier League – they weren't all of his managers' making, as some suggest, he found the tempo difficult. The Argentinian full-backs, Sorin and Zanetti, were especially threatening, as Argentina's dominance of the midfield sucked in Nigeria's wide players and left room down the flanks. Batistuta converted the third of three good opportunities he was handed from crosses.

Saitama saw the proverbial game of two halves. England were smooth and measured and in control in the first half, and ragged and inaccurate and panicky in the second. Sweden were lifeless and unadventurous in the first half and purposeful and aggressive after the break. All the newspapers stated England should have lost, but over ninety minutes the result wasn't too unfair. Campbell scored England's goal with a replica of his header against Argentina; Sweden's goalkeeper, Magnus Hedman complained that he had been fouled but it was his own centre-forward, Marcus Allbäck, who baulked him.

An injury to Gary Neville left England really short at right-back; Danny Mills was the only specialist in the squad and his temperament was highly suspect, as well as his defending. Both left-backs were only twenty-one, and both were better going forward than defending. The idea was mooted of playing wing-backs and using Owen Hargreaves or Kieron Dyer on the right, Cole on the left, and playing Beckham in the middle. Eriksson, a confirmed 4–4–2 man, rightly decided to stick with what he and the players knew.

Nigeria were unlucky to lose to Sweden. They had a young side and being the captain seemed to suit Okocha, who was much more committed and involved than previously. With the trickster pulling the strings Nigeria had the better of the early exchanges and scored through a powerful header from Julius Aghahowa, the twenty-year-old who played in the Ukraine with Shakhtar Donetsk. Henrik Larsson cut inside a defender and finished well, as he did week in, week out for Celtic, and it woke Sweden up. His winning penalty with three minutes left was a correct decision but harsh on Nigeria's performance.

England really needed something from their game against Argentina, which required a big improvement in midfield. It was a lot to ask with one of your three best players (Gerrard) missing through injury, another (Beckham) only about eighty per cent fit and a third (Scholes) struggling for his best form. England left out Darius Vassell, who was anonymous against Sweden (and was, for my money, the worst selection ever by an England manager for a World Cup match), stiffened the midfield with Nicky Butt and put Heskey back up front instead of wandering about like a lost puppy on the left.

It was another good game, though without the intensity of the knockout round in France. Eriksson got his tactics right, and was actually helped by an early injury to Hargreaves. The Bayern Munich player's inclusion meant Scholes was operating in a role he didn't much like, coming in off the left; Sinclair, Hargreaves' replacement, was a genuine wide player, so Scholes could move inside and threaten, knowing Butt would sit behind him.

Butt snuffed out Verón, who was taken off, Cole had a good game against the lively Ortega, and Batistuta spent an hour in Ferdinand's pocket before giving way to Crespo. The goal came from the penalty spot when Owen tumbled over Pocchettino's ill-judged challenge. It wasn't a dive, as Argentina protested, but it wasn't much of a foul either – a lot of them are given, it's why the phrase "bought a penalty" exists, a halfway house between cheating to get one and a clear foul. See the foot, make sure there's contact and don't make a meal of it. It is why the very best defenders see the rabbit before they release the ferret. Pocchettino, by the way, is the same guy who was appointed manager of Southampton in 2013.

Beckham had to endure some nonsense from Simeone before taking the penalty, as the man who got him sent off four years before hovered around him offering his hand, and then had the effrontery to look offended when Beckham told him where to go. Beckham scored. He looked happy.

Instead of knuckling down, Argentina got tetchy instead, and spent the second half trying to get a reaction instead of a goal. They had only one really good chance, a header from Pocchettino that Seaman did well to hold. Eriksson left himself open to criticism, even after such a good performance, by taking off Owen and bringing on not Vassell or Robbie Fowler, not even an attacking midfield player like Dyer, but another left-back, Wayne Bridge. Sven really was terrible at substitutions.

England needed a point from their last game and got it, with a conservative but competent performance in infernal temperatures. It was fair enough, but they would have cause to regret it. Argentina exited the tournament they started as favourites in a flurry of protesting, moaning and diving. Batistuta, captain for the day, spent another afternoon not scoring against a proper defence. Svensson gave Sweden the lead with a well-struck free-kick and Crespo's goal was a futile late gesture.

GROUP G

Mexico Blanco 60 (p)	(0) 1	**Croatia**	(0) 0	3 June, Nigata; 32,239
Italy Vieri 7, 27	(2) 2	**Ecuador**	(0) 0	3 June, Sapporo; 31,081
Croatia Olic 73, Rapaic 76	(0) 2	**Italy** Vieri 55	(0) 1	8 June, Ibaraki; 36,472
Ecuador Delgado 5	(1) 1	**Mexico** Borgetti 29, Torrado 56	(1) 2	9 June, Miyagi; 45,610
Mexico Borgetti 34	(1) 1	**Italy** Del Piero 85	(0) 1	13 June, Oita; 39,291
Ecuador Méndez 48	(0) 1	**Croatia**	(0) 0	13 June, Yokohama; 65,862

1. Mexico 7pts (4–2); 2. Italy 4pts (4–3); 3. Croatia 3pts (2–3); 4. Ecuador 3pts (2–4)

After two games the group looked done and dusted. Italy played really well against Ecuador; Totti was inventive, the defence typically mean and Vieri looked razor sharp, taking both goals superbly. He was a handful for a guy who occasionally looked as if he might trip over his own feet. Croatia looked tired and past their best. So how to explain Croatia beating Italy? Boksic played much better, which helped, and they were enlivened by the introduction of Ivica Olic just before the hour, but Italy just didn't play well. Vieri scored his third goal of the opening week with a pounding header, but he missed a glorious opportunity to make the game safe. Olic equalised when the defence switched off and let Jarni's cross travel right across the box, and Materazzi, on for Nesta, sold himself early and let Rapaic beat his challenge for the winner.

Jared Borgetti would go on to become Mexico's highest scorer, and he gave his team the lead against Italy with a glancing header. He had scored their first in the win over Ecuador when they came from behind to win more comfortably than the scoreline suggests. Italy made numerous chances, but Vieri, Inzaghi, Montella and Vieri again missed them all. Del Piero came on for Totti, who created most of the chances, and he got the vital goal, latching on to Montella's hopeful cross to head home.

Italy got their first bit of luck in the group after the final whistle. Croatia had reverted to useless mode and lost to Ecuador, Méndez tucking away a knock down from Gordon Strachan's favourite striker, Delgado.

GROUP H

Belgium Wilmots 57, Van der Heyden 75	(0) 2	**Japan** (0) 2 Suzuki 59, Inamoto 68	4 June, Saitama; 55,256
Tunisia	(0) 0	**Russia** (0) 2 Titov 59, Karpin 64 (p)	5 June, Kobe; 30,957
Russia	(0) 0	**Japan** (0) 1 Inamoto 51	9 June, Yokohama, 66,108
Belgium Wilmots 13	(1) 1	**Tunisia** (1) 1 Bouzaiene 17	10th June, Oita, 37,900
Tunisia	(0) 0	**Japan** (0) 2 Morishima 48, H Nakata 75	14th June, Osaka; 45,213
Russia Beschastnykh 52, Sychev 88	(0) 2	**Belgium** (1) 3 Walem 7, Sonck 78, Wilmots 82	14 June, Shizuoka; 46,640

1. Japan 7pts (5–2); 2. Belgium 5pts (6–5); 3. Russia 3pts (4–4); 4. Tunisia 1pt (1–5)

The second hosts enjoyed a much kinder draw than South Korea got. Belgium were strong and good in the air, Japan were a bit lightweight but quick and clever. A draw was fair. Tunisia never tested Russia, and when Japan did, they were found wanting. Junichi Inamoto scored in consecutive games, taking a nice flick from Yanagisawa to score the only goal. The Russian centre-forward Vladimir Beschastnykh rounded the 'keeper in the closing stages but contrived to miss. Poor from Russia's leading scorer. Belgium and Tunisia drew a stinker – no points each would have been fair.

Japan beat Tunisia, who had offered little except some solid defensive work. Their six foot four phone box of a centre-half Radhi Jaidi ended up at Bolton under Sam Allardyce and didn't look out of place in the Premier League. In the final match Belgium scored twice late on to beat Russia and steal second place. Five goals flattered another ordinary match – the highlight was Wesley Sonck's acrobatic goal celebration; even the biased Russian judge would have given it 5.8 – just a little bit off for a minor stumble on landing.

SECOND ROUND

Germany Neuville 88	(0) 1	**Paraguay**	(0) 0	15 June, Seogwipo; 25,176
England Own goal 5, Owen 22, Heskey 44	(3) 3	**Denmark**	(0) 0	15 June, Nigata; 40,582
Sweden Larsson 11 *golden goal	(1) (1) 1	**Senegal** H Camara 37, 104*	(1) (1) 2	16 June, Oita; 39,747
Ireland Keane 89 (p) Spain won 3–2 on penalties	(0) (1) 1	**Spain** Morientes 8	(1) (1) 1	16 June, Suwon; 38,926
USA McBride 8, Donovan 66	(1) 2	**Mexico**	(0) 0	17 June, Jeonju; 36,380
Belgium	(0) 0	**Brazil** Rivaldo 67, Ronaldo 86	(0) 2	17 June, Kobe; 40,440
Japan Davala 12	(0) 0	**Turkey**	(1) 1	18 June, Miyagi; 45,666

Germany against Paraguay was another safety-first affair. Oliver Neuville saved us the unappetising prospect of another half hour with a smart volley two minutes from the end. Arrivederci Chilavert, an entertaining addition to the World Cup pantheon. Neuville, only five foot seven was a busy, skilful player who never let a defence rest. Völler was criticised for persisting with him – he wasn't a prolific scorer – but he repaid his faith in this tournament.

The English newspapers insisted England were comprehensively outplayed by Denmark, but they were 3–0 up at half-time and took the foot off the pedal to conserve energy in the heat. What more did they want? Ferdinand got the opener when Sorensen made a pig's ear of his tame header and the ball crept shamefacedly over the line. When Gravesen failed to clear Butt's flick on, the ball fell to Owen – harsh and full punishment for a half-mistake was duly dispensed. Heskey got the third just before half-time with a skidding shot on a greasy surface – again Sorensen's handling let him down. The game was over and petered out. Yes, Denmark had better technique on a dreadful surface then England, but Sand had a weak game and Campbell got a strong grip on the dangerous Tomasson; 3–0 is never lucky.

The scribes said Sweden were unlucky, too, but they should have beaten Senegal, even in the heat. Larsson (dreadlocks gone – all hair gone, in fact) scored a fine header to give them the lead, but they sat back too deep and let Senegal come at them. Senegal responded by pushing Camara up alongside Diouf – had Sweden tried to apply more pressure he may well not have in the right place to score the two excellent goals he did. Diouf won a long ball in the air, Camara controlled it, took it to the right of a defender and belted it past Hedman from twenty yards. Camara's second goal was even better, running from deep past static defenders to fire home off the post with his left foot. Camara showed flashes of this brilliance in his years in the Premier League but was injury-prone and inconsistent. Diouf proved a more resilient performer in England – especially with Bolton after a tricky spell at Liverpool – but his on-and-off field antics made him one of the least-liked opposing players at every ground he visited. He just never grasped the notion of personal responsibility and role model. Svensson had hit the post a few minutes earlier, and Zlatan Ibrahimovic missed one glorious opportunity to win the game. He would improve as a player and grow up.

Spain gave Ireland a bit of a runaround in the early stages of their match, but the same pattern emerged as elsewhere. An early lead tempted sides to sit back in the withering sun and conserve fluid and energy levels. Spain had a Raúl strike chalked off for offside correctly, and then got a bit defensive and let Damien Duff run at them. Duff won a number of free-kicks as Spain persistently brought him down and eventually one of them was in the penalty area. It was a soft award but Spain had invited it. Harte's kick was weak and easily saved by the twenty-one-year-old Casillas, already established as number one at Real Madrid and for Spain. Kilbane's miss from the rebound was worse than the penalty miss – there wasn't even a goalkeeper to beat, he was still on the floor.

With little time on the clock Ireland got a lifeline when Hierro was penalised for shirt-tugging – another generous decision, both sides had been at it all afternoon with no intervention from the referee. It's another grey area that FIFA haven't sorted. Do you just accept argy-bargy at set plays or do you give a penalty every time? Here's one from Holtie's 100 Ideas To Improve Football – if a defender shirt-pulls or blocks in the area, have the kick re-taken with that player off the field until the ball goes dead again. Harte was off the field – he must have been relieved – but Robbie Keane made light of the pressure and put his kick right in the corner.

Extra-time passed at walking pace and the game went to penalties. No heroics from Irish centre-backs this time; Holland, David Connolly and Kilbane all missed (as did Juanfran and Valerón for Spain) and Gaizka Mendieta finished it. Robbie Keane scored his penalty; he looked so nonchalant for a twenty-one-year-old playing in his first big tournament. He's an odd player, Keane, he never stays with a club for very long and his record for most of them is unremarkable, but he has sixty international goals at almost one every two matches. To put that record into perspective the next highest scorer for Ireland is Niall Quinn, who retired after this tournament, with twenty-one. No one else comes close to Keane's strike rate.

Had Roy Keane been around Ireland may – probably would – have won this game. And I'm not sure they would have found South Korea such hard work as the Southern European teams. What ifs, buts and maybes – utterly meaningless but a writer's dream.

The USA beat Mexico with surprising ease. McBride and Donovan were too direct and far too good in the air for the Mexican defence, and the Americans' five-man defence snuffed out Blanco and Borgetti. The Mexicans became very petulant towards the end and their captain, the Monaco centre-back Rafael Márquez, was sent off for an appalling tackle on Cobi Jones.

Brazil against Belgium was another to add to the growing list of disappointing games in this World Cup. Belgium growled and grunted and perspired, while Brazil looked short of confidence. Rivaldo's opening goal took a big deflection past De Vlieger and Ronaldo barely deserved his after a limp performance. Brazil owed much to their excellent centre-halves and their defensive midfielders Gilberto and Edmilson.

Japan were toothless against Turkey; they had done well to get out of their group, but had nothing further to offer the tournament. Rüstü didn't have to make a serious save, but was a spectator when Alex's superb free-kick clipped the bar. Ümit Davala's header from a corner in the twelfth minute won the match – it was more impressive than his Mohican.

WORLD CUP SHOCK No.13
18 June 2002, Daejeon, Korea; 38,588

South Korea	(0) (1) **2** Seol 88, Ahn 116*
Italy	(1) (1) **1** Vieri 18

*golden goal

Referee: **Byron Moreno** (Ecuador)
Coaches: **Guus Hiddink** (South Korea) & **Giovanni Trappatoni** (Italy)

South Korea: Lee Woon-jae; Choi Jin-cheul, Hong Myung-bo, Kim Tae-yung; Song Shung-gug, Kim Nal-il, Park Ji-sung, Yoo Sang-chul, Lee Young-pyo; Seol Ki-hyeon, Ahn Jung-hwan.
Subs: Hwang Sung-hong 65m for Kim Tae-yung; Lee Chun-soo 70m for Kim Nam-il; Cha Du-ri 85m for Hong Myung-bo
Italy: Gianluigi Buffon (Juventus); Christian Pannucci (Roma), Damiano Tommasi (Roma), Paolo Maldini (AC Milan), Francesco Coco (AC Milan); Gianluca Zambrotta (Juventus), Mark Iuliano (Juventus), Francesco Totti (Roma), Cristiano Zanetti (Internazionale);

Alessandro Del Piero (Juventus); Christian Vieri (Internazionale). **Subs:** Gennaro Gattuso (AC Milan) 61m for Del Pier); Angelo Di Livio (Fiorentina) 72m for Zambrotta
Cautioned: Coco (Ita) 4m, Kim Tae-yung (SKor) 17m, Totti (Ita) 22m, Tommasi (Ita) 56m, Zanetti (Ita) 60m, Song Shung-gug (SKor) 81m, Lee Chun-soo (SKor) 100m, Choi Jin-cheul (SKor) 116m
Dismissed: Totti (Ita) 104m (second yellow, for diving)

The Italians have it down as one of the great injustices. Everyone else has it down as them failing to kill off a weaker team. Italy were convinced there was a conspiracy afoot to eliminate them and let the hosts through. Evidence? Yes, that much. Korea harboured ambitions to get into the knockout phase, which was why they employed a crack coach like Hiddink and paid him a king's ransom. Anything else was a bonus, but not the sort that comes in a brown envelope.

As early as the fifth minute Italy showed that their defence was not the impregnable stronghold of old. From a set piece both Coco and Panucci were manhandling Korean attackers; it seemed to be Panucci who was penalised. Ahn's penalty wasn't the worst seen in the Finals, but Buffon pulled off a spectacular save to his right. A few minutes later Totti's vicious, swinging corner was met by Vieri and the scribes were writing Korea's epitaph.

Forget the controversy for a moment. This was a rip-roaring match. Korea only had one speed – breakneck – and Italy had to dig in to match them for fitness and urgency.

Here are the edited highlights:

- Ahn executes a nifty heel flick to make space for a shot but the shot doesn't match the set-up.
- Totti's peach of a through ball reaches Tommasi (excellent match) but Lee Woon-jae was quick off his line to block.
- Vieri is put through by another sublime pass from Totti, but hammers his shot wide.
- The veteran Hwang, on as a substitute, lofts a deep ball into the penalty area with two minutes of normal time remaining; Panucci takes the ball on his thigh but topples backwards and Seol nips in to drive the loose ball past Buffon.

- Still in normal time Tommasi, still full of running, gets clear down the left and sticks one on a plate for Vieri, who, stretching, scoops the ball wide.
- Cha Du-ri forces Buffon into a save with a classical overhead kick.
- Sung's free-kick sneaks under the jumping Italian wall and an unsighted Buffon does brilliantly to tip it round the post.
- Totti is through on the right side of the penalty area and comes thigh to thigh with a defender. No penalty and a red card for diving, said the Ecuadorian referee. This was the decision that so incensed the Italians, and it was a poor one. Not the penalty, that was debatable, but the red card was really harsh. Totti had one of his best games in a major tournament.
- Gattuso charges up the right; Seol, tracking back (good) tries to back-heel the ball out of trouble (very, very bad) and Gattuso robs him and cracks in a shot. Lee makes another good save.
- Lee Young-pyo hits a cross deep into extra-time, it evades Maldini but Ahn, behind him, diverts it into the corner of the goal.

The post-match analysis in Italy was hysterical and prolonged. Every two-bit pundit from Palermo to Lugano had an opinion on exactly how and why Italy were cheated. The match-winner, who played for Perugia, was publicly told he wouldn't play for them.

South Korea deserved great credit. They were playing a team that man-for-man, was in a different class but they ran for two hours and never gave up.

Republic of Ireland Squad 2002:
GK: Shay Given (Newcastle United, 26 years old, 39 caps), Dean Kiely (Charlton Athletic, 31, 6), Alan Kelly (Blackburn Rovers, 33, 34)
DEF: Gary Breen (Coventry City, 28, 43), Kenny Cunningham (Wimbledon, 30, 34), Richard Dunne (Manchester City, 22, 14),

Steve Finnan (Fulham, 26, 13), Ian Harte★ (Leeds United, 24, 40), Gary Kelly[*] (Leeds, 27, 46), Andrew O'Brien (Newcastle, 22, 5), Steve Staunton (Cpt, Aston Villa, 33, 38)
MID & WIDE: Lee Carsley (Everton, 28, 19), Damien Duff (Blackburn, 23, 26), Matt Holland (Ipswich Town, 28, 19), Roy Keane (Manchester United, 30, 58), Kevin Kilbane (Sunderland, 25, 31), Mark Kinsella (Charlton, 29, 28), Jason McAteer (Sunderland, 30, 47), Steve Reid (Millwall, 21, 5)
FWD: David Connolly (Wimbledon, 24, 33), Robbie Keane (Leeds, 21, 33), Clinton Morrison (Crystal Palace, 23, 7), Niall Quinn (Sunderland, 35, 88)

QUARTER-FINALS

Brazil	(1) 2	**England**	(1) 1	21 June, Shizuoka; 47,436
Rivaldo 45,		Owen 23		
Ronaldinho 50				
Germany	(1) 1	**USA**	(0) 0	21 June, Ulsan; 37,337
Ballack 39				
South Korea	(0) (0) 0	**Spain**	(0) (0) 0	22 June, Gwangju; 42,114
South Korea won 5–3 on penalties				
Turkey	(0) (0) 1	**Senegal**	(0) (0) 0	22 June, Osaka; 44,233
Ilhan 94†				

Just before half-time in Shizuoka, the Brazilian centre-back Roque Júnior cleverly dragged back the ball before it could go over the line. He found Ronaldinho, who skipped a weak challenge from Scholes and sold Ashley Cole a dummy that allowed him to play in Ronaldo, who scored easily – he could still finish, it was the other stuff like running and jumping that he found a bit much.

Five minutes after the break, England, still a bit shell-shocked, gave away a free-kick wide out of the left about forty-five yards from goal. Ronaldinho beat Seaman with a huge up-and-under – the England goalkeeper had previous against Nayim of Real Zaragoza in the 1995 European Cup Winners' Cup Final. England barely had another shot at goal and Sven made horrible substitutions again. (I don't care how tired Owen was, even with one leg sawn off he was better than Darius Vassell.) Even after

---

★ Kelly was Harte's uncle.
† golden goal

Ronaldinho was sent off (he received much misplaced sympathy for a nasty challenge, for some reason) England just didn't get at their opponents. Cafú and Roberto Carlos were both better attackers than defenders but England never got at them, and Eriksson didn't use Joe Cole, the one player in the squad who knew how to beat a man.

Before that it was a cakewalk. England kept possession well, Beckham seemed less fragile than in the previous games and was stopping Roberto Carlos from raiding down the left, and Owen looked like he had the beating of the Brazilian backs. Owen's goal was a little fortunate – he wouldn't have reached Heskey's pass but for an inadvertent knock-on from Lúcio. It's about the only error I remember the big central defender making all tournament.

A few months earlier it seemed highly unlikely that Germany would go deeper into the tournament than England. They had a tricky time of it against the USA and were grateful to Kahn for two great first half saves from Landon Donovan after the striker got behind a sluggish back line. Michael Ballack stole into the box to score with a firm header from Ziege's swinging cross. Klose should have added a second a couple of minutes later but he headed against a post with the goal gaping.

In the second half Eddie Lewis had a free header from Reyna's corner but Kahn half stopped it. The ball squirmed under his body and bounced up to hit Torsten Frings' arm on the line. The referee consulted the linesman and said no penalty. It was a brave decision and technically correct as Frings' arm was never raised and the ball moved towards him not vice versa. Most refs would have given the penalty; does that make them or Hugh Dallas right? In the dying moments Mathis (no relation to Johnny) crossed from the right and Tony Sanneh smacked a header just the wrong side of the post. Tough on the States, who were the better team on the day, but typically resilient of Germany.

South Korea produced more of their thing against Spain, running and running and tackling and tackling. Fernando Morientes had a goal disallowed in extra-time because Joaquin was ruled to have carried the ball over the line before he crossed it; a really bad decision, although the referee's whistle can clearly be heard before Morientes heads the ball.

Joaquin was man of the match in most of the papers, but his final ball apart from this one was not accurate enough and on at least three occasions he took a pot-shot with his head down instead of passing to a better positioned colleague. And his penalty in the shoot-out was awful. Ahn was brave to take one on after the miss against Italy, and he scored, and a young Spanish midfielder with three caps plus a couple of substitute appearances stepped up to take one, and he also scored. A warm World Cup welcome, please, for Señor Xavi Hernández, ladies and gentlemen. The final kick went to Hong Myung-bo, the captain.

The man of the match, by the way, wasn't Joaquin, it was Korea's goalkeeper, Lee Woon-jae, who was colossal here, and had a really excellent tournament. The standard of goalkeeping was a feature of this World Cup; Kahn, Buffon, Casillas, Rüstü, Friedel, Given and Lee were all top class, as was David Seaman, his horror moment apart. Even Brazil had a good goalkeeper; Marcos only won twenty-nine caps but he looked pretty good here. He nearly signed for Arsenal after the tournament, but opted to stay with Palmeiras, who had just been relegated; he never left, playing for the one club for his entire twenty-year career. I do love a one-club player.

Turkey against Senegal was another non-event (unless you happen to be Turkish or Senegalese, of course, in which case seeing your country become the first team from Asia (sort of) or Africa (definitely) to reach a World Cup semi-final was a huge thing). Turkey dominated possession and Alpay and Bülent and Ergün dealt with Diouf and Camara better than anyone else so far. The Besiktas midfielder Ilhan scored the Golden Goal from a corner, flicking the ball cleverly across Sylva and into the far side of the goal. Before that most of Turkey's best chances fell to Hakan Şükür, who was an embarrassment.

SEMI-FINALS

Germany	(0) 1	**South Korea**	(0) 0	25 June, Seoul; 65,625
Ballack 75				
Turkey	(0) 0	**Brazil**	(0) 1	26 June, Saitama; 61,058
Ronaldo 49				

THIRD-PLACE MATCH

Turkey	(3) 3	**South Korea**	(1) 2	29 June, Daegu; 63,483
Şükür 1, Ilhan 12, 32		Lee EY 9, Song 90		

Two really boring semi-finals were settled by a solitary goal. South Korea's thing didn't work against Germany, who weren't fazed by the scurrying and tackling and didn't get wound up by the odd decision going against them. Amazing what you can do by starting the game without conspiracy theories racing around in the head.

Korea couldn't do much about Ballack's goal; it was a class finish after a great initial save from Lee. Kahn also made a couple of decent saves and generally looked impregnable. Germany's new superstar Klose had a poor game for once, well policed by Hong and company, who did well to cut off the supply of crosses.

The other significant moment also involved Ballack; he picked up a yellow card that would keep him out of the final. No Gazza tears, he just rolled up his sleeves and made sure his colleagues were there for him to watch – impressively professional.

Turkey were really disappointing in their match against Brazil – they gave them a much tougher game in the group stage. Ronaldinho was suspended after his red card against England, Kléberson offered little as his replacement and Ronaldo was in and out of the game again. His goal was a toe-poke, which sneaked guiltily past the goalkeeper in a cluttered penalty box.

Şükür nicked a goal his miserable contribution didn't merit in the third-place match, and with it a place in the record books for the fastest ever goal in the Finals, as Ilhan robbed Hong and fed the striker a few yards out. It was still a surprise when he hit the target. The game was entertaining, in a park game sort of way. Neither of the third or fourth placed teams will reach the semi-finals again anytime soon.

World Cup Heroes No.31
Hong Myung-bo (1969–)
South Korea

Hong Myung-bo received high praise for his performances in the 2002 competition. Fine, some of the awards – third-best player in the tournament – were a nod to the co-hosts, but he had not looked out of place amongst the world's best defenders.

Hong first played in the World Cup in 1990 in Italy, but Korea looked a poor side and went home without winning a game. Four years later Hong and the Koreans were back, and he got some attention with his sweeping passes out of defence and his goalscoring. He scored with a deflected free-kick in the comeback against Spain, and hit a rising twenty-five-yarder past Bodo Illgner in the next match, but Korea still came home early. 1998 was a step backwards and critics predicted embarrassment for both host nations in 2002.

Korea were a revelation. They had some better, younger players and a clever coach in the Dutchman, Guus Hiddink. Using Hong as part of a three-man defence with wing-backs meant his lack of pace wasn't exposed and it also left him free to step out and start attacks with his clever distribution. Korea conceded only three goals in six meaningful games. Hong, the team captain, kept his nerve in the penalty shoot-out against Spain, hitting his penalty high into Casillas' goal to eliminate the Spanish.

He retired immediately after the tournament, with a record 136 caps to his name, a total which Korea's excellent goalkeeper Lee Woon-jae came within four of before he also retired in 2010.

Hong played all his domestic football in Korea, unlike Ahn, Park and other high-profile Korean players. He remains one of Asia's greatest players, the only one in a list of players with fifteen or more World Cup appearances.

Hong studied for his coaching badges, and after some success with the Korean U-20 team he was appointed, in 2013, to the task of leading the full national team to the 2014 Finals. It seems highly unlikely they will emulate the class of 2014, but at least Hong knows what it takes to compete in a World Cup.

Korea is a long way away, and we know little of public opinion or their domestic game. In Korea, this man is held in the esteem in which Bobby Moore is held in England, or Beckenbauer in Germany.

WORLD CUP FINAL No.17
30 June 2002, International Stadium, Yokohama, Japan, 69,029

Brazil	**(0) 2**	Ronaldo 67, 79
Germany	**(0) 0**	

Referee: **Pierluigi Collina** (Italy)
Coaches: **Luis Felipe Scolari** (Brazil) & **Rudi Völler** (Germany)

Brazil (4-4-1-1): Marcos *Silveira* (Palmeiras); *Marcos Evangelista, known as* Cafú (Cpt, Roma), José Roque Júnior (AC Milan), *Lucimar da Silva, known as* Lúcio (Bayer Leverkusen), Roberto Carlos *da Silva* (Real Madrid); José Kléberson (Atlético Paranaense), *José* Edmilson *Gomes* (Lyon), Gilberto *Silva* (Atlético Mineiro), Rivaldo *Borba* (Barcelona); *Ronaldo de Assis, known as* Ronaldinho (Paris St Germain); Ronaldo *Nazário Lima* (Internazionale). **Subs:** *Osvaldo Júnior, known as* Juninho Paulista (Flamengo) 85m for Ronaldinho; Denilson *de Oliveira Araújo* (Real Betis) 89m for Ronaldo
Germany (3-4-1-2): Oliver Kahn (Cpt, Bayern Munich); Thomas Linke (Bayern), Christoph Metzelder (Borussia Dortmund), Carsten Ramelow (Bayer Leverkusen); Torsten Frings (Werder Bremen), Jens Jeremies (Bayern), Didi Hamann (Liverpool), Marco Bode (Bremen); Bernd Schneider (Leverkusen); Oliver Neuville (Leverkusen), Miroslav Klose (Kaiserslautern). **Subs:** Oliver Bierhoff (Monaco) 74m for Klose; Gerald Asamoah (Schalke 04) 77m for Jeremies; Christian Ziege (Tottenham Hotspur) 84m for Bode
Cautioned: Roque Júnior (Bra) 5m, Klose (Ger) 9m

Without Ballack, Germany had little to offer but sweat and toil. They made sure they sweated and it was Brazil who toiled in the first half. Schneider got round the back of Roberto Carlos twice and got in excellent crosses, while Neuville's movement stretched even these great Brazilian centre-backs, but Klose didn't have the tools at this stage in his career to worry Lúcio. The closest Germany came to a goal was a long-range effort that nearly caught Marcos unawares – to be fair, he probably didn't expect Neuville to shoot from out near the halfway line!

With Hamann and Bode helping shield the defence with great determination, Brazil didn't offer much either, until they woke up a bit after half-time. The shame was that the final swung on an error by Germany's captain and best player. Oliver Kahn had been really superb until now, offering a massive presence behind a defence that played well beyond its level. Rivaldo hit a shot straight at him, probably one of the tamest he hit all tournament, and Kahn covered it easily, only for the ball to wriggle out his grasp and squirt out to Ronaldo, who couldn't miss. Germany only had twenty minutes or so to come back, and with ten minutes left it was a hopeless cause as Ronaldo scored a second from Kléberson's cross, after Rivaldo unselfishly let it run.

Some redemption for Ronaldo, then, after the trauma of the 1998 final. Despite never looking fully fit throughout the tournament – though he did slim down a little during the month – and disappearing from large portion of matches, he managed to finish as top scorer and, more importantly, with a World Cup Winner's medal. How he was judged to have been the tournament's second-best player is anyone's guess. His colleagues worked overtime to compensate for his meagre contribution outside the penalty area. A word of praise here for the coach. Scolari cleverly picked two workhorses in midfield; if you need to carry a big heavy gun to break down the city walls, you need a few elephants.

World Cup Heroes No.32

Oliver Kahn (1969–)

Germany

They don't like Bayern Munich except in Munich; even Germans don't like Bayern Munich. It's like the English with Manchester United in the last twenty years. If you have half a brain and a feel for football, you tend to respect them without actually liking them. The same is true with Bayern; other fans in Germany grudgingly accept they are the country's best team but resent their supremacy.

It's the same with Bayern players. When they play for Germany they have to show they are worth their place much more emphatically than a player from, say, Leverkusen or Schalke 04 would. So for Oliver Kahn to earn the respect of the German fans he had to be *über* good. Kahn was. It took him some time and every tiny mistake was amplified, just as every misplaced pass David Beckham made was seized upon by his detractors in England.

By the time the 2002 World Cup came round Kahn was the best goalkeeper in the world, and that in the face of some stiff competition; Gianluigi Buffon was (is) a superb 'keeper and Iker Casillas a supreme shot-stopper. Kahn's mistake in the final is what everyone remembers – but all these goalkeepers made a mistake or two in the competition. And neither Buffon, nor Casillas, nor Brad Friedel nor any of the others got their team to the final almost on personal effort and willpower alone. Whenever Germany were under pressure, in the game against Paraguay, against the United States especially and against South Korea in the semi-final, Kahn dug them out of it with a crucial save, or gave them belief with a great catch to end a good spell from the opposition.

Kahn signed for Bayern from his home-town club of Karlsruher in 1994 and stayed until he was nearly forty, playing over 500 games. He won eight Bundesliga titles, a UEFA Cup and the Champions League in 2001, when he made three saves during the penalty shoot-out against Valencia. For Germany he played in three World Cups and two European Championships but never played in a winning team; he was the reserve 'keeper behind Andreas Köpke at the 1996 European Championships.

At six foot two Kahn was just normally tall for a goal-keeper, but he was big and heavily muscled, as well as surprisingly quick and presented a formidable obstacle when strikers were one on one. His build made him difficult to challenge on high balls, and he was a noisy, demanding presence behind his defence. If there was a weakness he was perhaps a little less elastic than one or two more classical goalkeepers – Buffon, for example, or Barthez, such a great shot-stopper but not in the same class as Kahn overall.

Kahn played for Germany for another four years – he didn't want to miss the World Cup in his own country, although he was the number two to Jens Lehmann in that tournament. Kahn retired after that competition with eighty-six caps after playing in the third-place match as team captain.

Team of the Tournament, 2002:

Kahn (Germany)

Hong (South Korea)   Lúcio (Brazil)   Ferdinand (England)

Ronaldinho (Brazil)   Tugay (Turkey)   Ballack (Germany)   Rivaldo (Brazil)

Diouf (Senegal)   Ronaldo (Brazil)   Şaş (Turkey)

Subs: Lee (South Korea); Hierro (Spain); Schneider (Germany); Edmilson (Brazil); Vieri (Italy)

Official Team of the Tournament: Rüstü was the second goalie, with **Campbell** at the back not Ferdinand, and **Alpay** and **Roberto Carlos** (oh, please) at the back instead of Lúcio. They included **Yoo** of Korea and **Reyna** of the USA in midfield, not Tugay or Edmilson or Schneider, and had **Klose** instead of Vieri as the fourth striker – he scored three of his goals against Saudi Arabia and was marked out of the semi and the final.

Leading scorers: Ronaldo 7, Klose & Rivaldo 5

Heaven Eleven No.14

Rest of the World (Continental Africa, North & Central America, Asia and Oceania)

Manager:
Bora Milutinovic (he managed most of them)

Goalkeepers:
Brad Friedel (USA): great career, looks like Bruce Willis
Thomas N'Kono (Cameroon): consistent long-serving goalie
Lee Woon-jae (South Korea): stunning at the 2002 World Cup and won over 130 caps

Defenders:

Hong Myung-bo (South Korea): major influence in their success in the 1990s and early 2000s

Rafael Márquez (Mexico): hard man at Barcelona

Mohammed Al-Khilaiwi (Saudi Arabia): attacking right-back in the best side they had

Sami Khuffour (Ghana): held down a place at Bayern for years

Lucas Radebe (South Africa): South Africa's best-ever player

Geremi (Cameroon): left-sided defender or midfielder, tough and had a terrific shot

Marcelo Balboa (USA): great hair, great tackler

Midfield & Wide:

Majed Abdullah (Saudi Arabia): gifted playmaker, was getting on by the time some good colleagues came along

Cha Bum-kun (South Korea): super sharp, but a star before the rest came along, was a regular first teamer at Eintracht Frankfurt and Leverkusen

Ali Parvin (Iran): Iran's best player, an aggressive little Billy Bremner type

Hidetoshi Nakata (Japan): technically gifted and brilliant at set pieces

Yaya Touré (Ivory Coast): awesome athlete, a really big player in every sense

Michael Essien (Ghana): before his injury he was immense – equally at home in defence

Jay-Jay Okocha (Nigeria): the trickster, a complete bag of tricks and set-piece wiz

Forwards:

Enrique Borja (Mexico): Mexico's best in the '60s, a real livewire

Didier Drogba (Ivory Coast): powerful and effective, has an appetite for the big games

Samuel Eto'o (Cameroon): sharp, lethal, ultra-quick

Abedi Pele (Ghana): one of the first African greats, skilful and quick

George Weah (Liberia): great target man, superb in the air and strong as an ox

Omissions: There are other good American goalkeepers, **Kasey Keller** and **Tony Meola** and **Tim Howard**. **Mark Schwarzer** was a candidate and **Mark Bosnich** before his problems. Another Cameroonian, **Jo Jo Bell**, was in the same class as N'Kono. Some good forwards didn't make it; the subtle **Kanu** (Nigeria), and the explosive **Tony Yeboah** (Ghana), America's **Clint Dempsey**, a tough competitor, and the gifted but over-rated **Hugo Sánchez**. **Salif Keita**, the seventies Mali striker who played in France, was a real talent, and was considered, as was the Australian striker **Mark Viduka**.

Likely first XI:

Friedel

Al-Khilaiwi Radebe Hong Geremi

Cha Bum-kun Touré Essien Abdullah

Weah Eto'o

8.2 COACHES

Poor sides don't win stuff even with good coaches, but a good coach can make a huge difference to a decent team. Picking a guy who can do well at international level is very different from picking a guy week in week out at a club. Picking a coach is similar; it isn't necessarily the best club coaches who do the international stuff – often they don't want it. Alex Ferguson had a stint as Scotland manager after the death of Jock Stein and didn't much enjoy it, and Arsène Wenger has always looked quizzical when asked if he would be interested, as if it were a ridiculous question to ask a sane man.

It isn't enough to just use the tactics that brought success in league football to the international stage – ask Graham Taylor, or maybe Giovanni Trappatoni; ten league titles with five clubs in four countries but no trophies on the international stage and was helpless as Italy lost to Korea. International management involves achieving the kind of work ethic and tactical sureness without the luxury of spending four or five days a week drumming your ideas into your players. The international manager has the luxury of choosing the best available players to fit into his scheme, but he must be certain the scheme suits their talents, or be able to spot where a particular player doesn't fit and another man, not so effective at club level, fits the required template better.

An international manager also has to be able to deal with an abundance of big egos within a national squad. The players will all want to be the big cheese they are at their club, and will not want to work hard to learn a slightly different role or adapt their style of play. For years both Sven and Fabio Capello struggled to accommodate Steven Gerrard and Frank Lampard within the same team, but Roy Hodgson has done so. Admittedly he has had help; the system England have played recently has become so widespread that the players have accepted it as a norm and have played within that structure at club level, and that system allows Gerrard to drop a little further back and Lampard to push on, which suits both players. However, for years they both seemed to want to play the same role, yet neither of England's foreign coaches had the courage to either impose their will or to drop one of England's big stars. With proper management of big players, England could/would have gone further than the quarter-finals in 2006.

Old pros would tell you that you need to play the international game to understand it but that's tosh. Luiz Felipe Scolari didn't have international experience, nor did Guus Hiddink, and Argentina's brilliant coach Menotti had a mere two caps. It's no more a prerequisite than having league experience to get on in the Premier League – ask Wenger or Mourinho.

National FAs have two choices. They can go for a homer, a coach of the same nationality as the player. All very well if like Italy you have a strong league full of mostly Italian managers. Not so clever if you are the Ivory Coast, barely have a league at all in which to develop managers and have all your squad playing abroad. So then you opt for the professional coach, preferably one with lots of international experience; there have been a number of very clever specialist international coaches over the years.

Bora Milutinovic, a Serbian coach, was in charge of a different team at every World Cup from 1986 to 2002: Mexico, Costa Rica, United States (for their own tournament, they wanted a guy who would get the best out of them), Nigeria and China. Carlos Alberto Parreira coached Kuwait to the Finals in 1982, the Emirates in 1990, Brazil in 1994 (when they won – but he still got stick for being too defensive), Saudi Arabia in 1998, Brazil again in 2006 and South Africa in 2010, equalling Milo's record.

Frenchman Henri Michel nearly matched them. He was manager of his own country in 1986, Cameroon (French speaking) in 1994, Morocco (also French speaking) in 1998 and Ivory Coast (correctly Cote d'Ivoire, so French speaking) in 2006.

Michel only missed out on joining the other two because he was rather cruelly sacked by (French-speaking) Tunisia after getting them to the 2002 Finals.

Roy Hodgson was one of these peripatetic coaches before settling back in England with Fulham. He managed Switzerland at the 1994 World Cup, and has also managed the Emirates and Finland. Dear old Sven turned up at the 2010 Finals with a new team, Nigeria.

Here are the World Cup-winning coaches:

Year	Winners	Runners-up
1930	Francisco Olazar & Juan José Tramutola (Uruguay)	Alberto Suppici (Argentina)
1934	Vittorio Pozzo (Italy)	Karel Petru (Czecholslovakia)
1938	Vittorio Pozzo (Italy)	Alfred Schaffer (Hungary)
1950	Juan Lopez Fontana (Uruguay)	Flávio Costa (Brazil)
1954	Sepp Herberger (West Germany)	Gusztáv Sebes (Hungary)
1958	Vicente Feola (Brazil)	George Raynor* (England for Sweden)
1962	Aymoré Moreira (Brazil)	Rudolf Vytlacil (Czechoslovakia)
1966	Alf Ramsey (England)	Helmut Schön (West Germany)
1970	Mário Zagallo† (Brazil)	Ferruccio Valcareggi (Italy)
1974	Helmut Schön (West Germany)	Rinus Michels (Holland)
1978	César Luis Menotti (Argentina)	Ernst Happel (Austria for Holland)
1982	Enzi Bearzot (Italy)	Jupp Derwall (West Germany)
1986	Carlos Bilardo (Argentina)	Franz Beckenbauer (West Germany)
1990	Franz Beckenbauer (West Germany)	Carlos Bilardo (Argentina)
1994	Carlos Alberto Parreira (Brazil)	Arrigo Sacchi (Italy)
1998	Aimé Jacquet (France)	Mário Zagallo (Brazil)
2002	Luiz Felipe Scolari (Brazil)	Rudi Völler (Germany)
2006	Marcello Lippi (Italy)	Raymond Domenech (France)
2010	Vicente del Bosque (Spain)	Bert van Marwijk (Holland)

Here are ten great coaches, whose tactics or style had an impact on the World Cup.

* First coach from a different country to manage a team in a World Cup Final
† First man to win the World Cup as both player and coach.

Bora Milutinovic (various)
Showed the way to a number of second-rate teams and became the go-to man if you didn't want to embarrass yourselves in front of the watching world. Got Mexico and Costa Rica through the group matches with only a modicum of talent at his disposal. The first great mercenary.

Egil Olsen (Norway)
We know he was a great coach because he told us so. At a time when direct, long ball football was in vogue he became the arch exponent (sorry, Graham) and his Norway team upset Brazil in a group match in 1998. Thankfully Cesare Maldini's Italy put paid to them in the next round and they slipped back amongst the also-rans.

Carlos Bilardo (Argentina)
Defensive Argentinian coach in 1986 and 1990. He needed a framework for the genius of Maradona so he developed a five-man defence and three-man midfield with Maradona roving behind a target man. It was clever and allowed Maradona to dominate in '86.

Otto Rehhagel (Greece)
Yes, okay, he didn't do much in the World Cup, but his use of limited resources as manager of Greece from 2001–10 created an archetype for many second-tier nations: throw a blanket defence across the field and hope for crumbs. Thanks, mate. In his defence, he did his best with what he had; his teams at Werder Bremen and Kaiserslautern were good attacking sides.

Guus Hiddink (various, esp South Korea)
Another gifted coach who has the ability to lift a team in a very short time in the job. Was tactically astute with South Korea in 2002 with a limited team, and improved Australia in 2006 by insisting that fitness levels be raised as a counter to other sides' superior technique. One of the best judges of the right time and player for a substitution.

Alf Ramsey (England)

Cut his cloth cleverly. Knew he had no wingers so dispensed with them altogether (although it was during the World Cup in 1966 he finally accepted this and the years after he perfected the system). A strict disciplinarian, he insisted players fit in his mould and didn't change his tactics, hence his mistrust of gifted players like Alan Hudson and Frank Worthington.

Sepp Herberger (West Germany)

Masterminded Germany's against-the-odds win over Hungary in 1954, after hoodwinking them by fielding a weakened side in a group match Hungary won 8–3. His teams became the blueprint for German intestinal fortitude.

Telê Santana (Brazil)

Coach of the Brazilians in the 1980s. Realised that to coach a team with that many gifted players you didn't coach them at all, you simply empowered them. It was a philosophy Pep Guardiola adhered to with great success at Barcelona and Joachim Low has adopted with the modern German team.

César Luis Menotti (Argentina)

The cultured, liberal coach who released the inner matador in the 1978 Argentinians and won the World Cup for an obnoxious right-wing military dictatorship that he abhorred. Defiance and collaboration in a weird football paradox.

Rinus Michels (Holland)

Turned football into an art form with Ajax and Holland and Barcelona in the 1970s. The only coach who could handle the one-man revolution that was Johan Cruyff.

8.3 WORLD CUP 2006

Germany seemed an ideal choice as host for 2010 but it was a far from clear-cut decision. Germany's rivals were South Africa and many of the non-European delegates were keen to see a World Cup in Africa, come what may. After Morocco (who seem fated never to get their tournament) and then England were eliminated from the vote, a final round produced a score of 12–11 in Germany's favour, with one abstention, the New Zealand delegate, who ignored the wishes of his federation. Sepp Blatter, obsessed with legacy and sensing an opportunity to open new markets in which podgy FIFA fingers could be dabbled, would no doubt have put his casting vote behind South Africa.

A furore arose when it was revealed that a satirical magazine (a sort of German *Private Eye* or *Onion*) sent messages to various delegates, offering ridiculous bribes like cuckoo clocks in exchange for votes. The demand for a recount was rejected; with the huge sums which investigations have revealed were actually spent eliciting votes from FIFA delegates, a cuckoo clock was hardly likely to be a winning incentive.

Germany ran an efficient tournament and had a dozen excellent stadia ready months before the tournament was due to start. Most of the grounds existed already, apart from the new Allianz Arena in Munich, built to replace the rather tired old Olympiastadion. Germany already had a good transport infrastructure; it was the ideal-sized country, big enough to separate the groups away from one huge urban catchment, but not so big as to present travel issues or time zone changes like the United States or Brazil.

GERMANY

N'LANDS

Hamburg

Hanover

Berlin

Gelsenkirchen

Dortmund

Leipzig

Cologne

Frankfurt

Kaiserslautern

Nuremberg

AUSTRIA

Stuttgart

FRANCE

Munich

**2006
GERMANY**

Germany employed twelve stadia in 2006, three more than in 1974; only one city, Düsseldorf, missed out this time having hosted matches in 1974.

The following stadia were the same as the ones used in 1974, albeit with new sponsors' names.
- **Berlin: Olympiastadion**
- **Hamburg: AOL Arena (Volksparkstadion)**
- **Frankfurt: Commerzbank Arena (Waldstadion)**
- **Dortmund: Signal Iduna Park (Westfalenstadion)**
- **Stuttgart: Gottlieb Daimler Stadion (Neckarstadion)**
- **Gelsenkirchen: Veltins Arena (Parkstadion)**
- **Hanover: AWD Arena (Niedersachsenstadion)**

The five stadia not used in 1974 were:

Munich: Allianz Arena
The new stadium in Munich was completed in time for the 2006 Finals and hosted the semi-final between Portugal and France as well as five other games. The stadium glows red when Bayern play, blue when Munich 1860 are at home, and white when the national team play there – very cool!

Cologne: RheinEnergie Stadion
This is the old Kölner Stadion with a corporate name. The ground dates back to 1923 and enjoyed a significant facelift for the 2006 finals.

Nuremberg: easyCredit Stadion
Would it surprise you to learn that this ground wasn't always called the easy-Credit Stadium? Built in 1928, it was formerly known (and still is to fans of 1.FC Nuremberg) as the Frankenstadion.

Kaiserslautern: Fritz Walter Stadion
A lot of grounds are named after money men or sponsors – it's a prerequisite of them stumping up the cash to build or renovate. This ground in Kaiserslautern is named after a bona fide football legend, the captain of the West Germany side that won the World Cup in 1954.

Leipzig: Zentralstadion
Now the Red Bull Arena earned its place in the line-up as the largest football ground in the old East Germany. The stadium was renovated for the finals, but as yet the home team, newly formed RB Leipzig, is still feeling its way through the lower divisions.

Qualifying

For the first time the holders were not automatically granted a place in the Finals – the new system hasn't yet seen the previous winners not make it, with thirty-two places available. Poor Brazil, they would have to undergo the marathon that is CONMEBOL qualification, eighteen matches all-play-all. One (sensible) change was the ruling whereby teams level on points would initially be separated by the results of the two matches they played against each other – a better measure than goals scored against weak opposition.

They came through the marathon quite comfortably – only two defeats this time, in Ecuador and Argentina, 3–1, following an exceptional first half performance from the hosts. Brazil had won the first game between the two South American big beasts by the same score, with all three goals from the penalty spot, all scored by Ronaldo. That's harder to do than you might think. Brazil won the group on goal difference (which came into play after both sides won 3–1). Ecuador, unbeaten at home where only Peru and Uruguay managed a point, and Paraguay joined them, consigning Uruguay to a second successive play-off against Australia. Home form was especially strong in this series of games – only fifteen away wins in ninety games, with only Argentina managing three, and Uruguay and Bolivia failing to win away – Bolivia actually lost every single away game.

Australia had to go through a ridiculous system. Oceania is a really weak section; most of the teams represent island groups with tiny populations and no competitive professional structure. A mini tournament for the Oceania Federation Cup ended with Australia top of the group and the Solomon Islands second. The islanders celebrated a 2–2 draw with the Aussies as if they had won the World Cup itself. These same two sides then played out a two-leg affair for the Federation Cup, Australia winning 5–1 away and 6–0 at home. However, this was not allowed to count as the final World Cup eliminator so the two sides met again the following autumn, when a 7–0 home win for Australia was followed by a 2–1 away win. Australia had Mark Viduka, Tim Cahill, Harry Kewell, Tony Vidmar, Brett Emerton et al, a whole generation of European based pros, so none of the other Oceania teams could match them, or even come close. In 2001 the Socceroos (silly coinage) set a world record when they beat American Samoa 31–0. Archie Thompson scored thirteen goals that day, and he was only playing because the big European based players didn't bother travelling to play what was little more than a pub team.

After this World Cup Australia joined the Asian qualifying section; it would give them better practice against serious opposition and also meant they avoided this quadrennial play-off against a tough South American team. It was a canny move, and unless they experience a noticeable decline, they will continue to qualify for the Finals as they did in 2010 and already have for 2014.

The two 2006 play-off games against Uruguay could not have been tighter. Both sides won 1–0 at home, Mark Bresciano's goal for the Aussies cancelling Rodríguez's late winner in Montevideo. The European pros kept their nerve in the penalty shoot-out better than the Uruguayans.

It was very much as-you-were in Asia. China had faded after their brief flirtation with the Finals in 2002, so Saudi Arabia, South Korea, Japan and Iran dominated two final groups of four. Bahrain won through to a play-off against a CONCACAF nation. You will be astonished to learn that Mexico and the United States won through easily from the CONCACAF section, with Costa Rica also along for the ride and Trinidad & Tobago earning the right to play Bahrain for that last place.

Trinidad only drew 1–1 at home, but a header from centre-half Denis Lawrence won them the away leg. They had the same mix of islanders and English pros as Jamaica in 1998, and their big star was Dwight Yorke, although he was thirty-five in 2006 and played as a creative midfield player not the predatory striker he was in his heyday at Aston Villa and Manchester United. Trindidad's scorer in the first half was Chris Birchall of Port Vale; a very un-West Indian-looking white guy; Birchall was eligible through his mother, born in Port-of-Spain. The hero of the hour, Denis Lawrence, played for Wrexham, and a move to Swansea after the tournament saw him become an important part of the club's rise under Roberto Martinez; he has subsequently worked with Martinez as a coach at Wigan and now Everton.

African qualification threw up the biggest surprises. Four new nations qualified for the World Cup nations for the first time, while old hands like Algeria, Nigeria and Cameroon missed out. Togo put out Senegal, winning their last match 3–2 away to Congo. Their strike force of Mohamed Kader and the big, quick Monaco forward Emmanuel Adebayor looked a handful. Ghana won their section handsomely; a weak South African side finished only third, which didn't bode well for 2010.

The third group was tough: Egypt were a good side but couldn't match the power up front of Cameroon, who had Samuel Eto'o, or Ivory Coast, who had the powerful combination of Aruna Dindane of Lens and Chelsea's Didier Drogba. Cameroon beat Ivory Coast home and away, but they lost in Egypt, and when they slipped up in the final match, conceding a late equaliser at home to the Egyptians, it was Ivory Coast who sneaked in with a win in Sudan. Drogba and friends would be a threat, but Africa's best team would be missed.

Group Four produced an even bigger shock. Angola beat Nigeria at home in their second game with a late goal from Akwá (born Fabrice Alcebiades). From there on it was nip and tuck between the two, and a defeat in Zimbabwe for Angola handed Nigeria a slight advantage. It was going to be close so Nigeria needed to win the return against Angola. Jay-Jay Okocha gave them an early lead but they couldn't finish it off despite dominating possession, and an equaliser from the veteran Figueireido proved important. Nigeria won their last match easily over Zimbabwe but they were thwarted by that man Akwá, who scored another late winner in Rwanda to send Angola through. They enjoyed the draw for the Finals, too, which pitted them against the Portuguese, their one-time colonial masters.

The North African sides were having a bad time; the top three in each group qualified for the next African Cup of Nations to save another long-winded round of qualifiers, but Algeria couldn't even manage that, finishing way down in fifth in Angola's section.

Tunisia and Morocco did better for the region in the last group, which was marred by crowd trouble at the match between Kenya and Morocco when one person was killed in a stampede at the stadium. Perhaps small beer in the wider scale of suffering on the continent, but Kenya's next game was ordered to be placed behind closed doors. In another tight group the point Morocco dropped at that match in Kenya was crucial, as Tunisia won the silent match and went into their last game needing to draw with Morocco to top the group by a point. They came from behind twice to get the point, defenders Clayton and Chedli scoring the necessary goals.

It was the usual suspects from Europe. Germany were through as hosts. Some pundits thought it just as well; they had the most nondescript side anyone could remember, and may have struggled in one of the better groups. I'm not sure I subscribe to that – the Germans always find a way.

Holland breezed through the first group, with the Czech Republic clinching second and a play-off place. The Czechs scored for fun, with thirty-five goals in twelve matches, nine for the giant six foot seven (and a bit) Jan Koller. Portugal were equally supreme in Group Three, with Pauleta contributing eleven of their thirty-five goals. Slovakia finished second, eliminating an out-of-sorts Russian team.

Italy won Group Five easily, and Norway were an equally comfortable second, five points ahead of Scotland. Italy's only defeat was away to Slovenia, who started well and faded. Scotland were horribly inconsistent. They had a bad start, losing at home to Norway and dropping points at home to Slovenia and in Moldova. A brave away win in Oslo with two first half goals from Kenny Miller was encouraging but a dreadful performance at home to Belarus and a 1–0 defeat the following month was anything but.

England and Poland carved up Group Six between them. England's early win in Chorzów gave them a head start but a slip in Belfast and a 1–0 defeat to Northern Ireland meant they were five points behind the Poles with two games remaining (Poland had only one). A narrow win over Austria at Wembley meant both England and Poland were through – the two second-placed teams with the best record were in the Finals. As it goes England won the group, Frank Lampard's winner giving them a fully deserved 2–1 win over Poland in the last game. Had the goal been scored by a South American pundits would have been in raptures; a controlled volley from a cross dipping over a defender that the Chelsea man had to stretch to reach. Superb technique from a world-class footballer.

The game at Windsor Park was a great night for Northern Ireland and their all-time top scorer David Healy, but it was a smokescreen. They lost at home to Wales, and the only other team either of them beat was Azerbaijan. Northern Ireland finished fourth in the group, Wales fifth. Also rans.

In a group where ten of the twenty serious games (i.e. not involving San Marino) were drawn, Spain drew one more than Serbia, and would have to be content with a play-off place. Belgium were a major disappointment and finished behind Bosnia-Herzegovina in fourth. Serbia conceded only goal in their ten matches, to Raúl in Madrid. Watch this space.

The other second-placed team to go through direct was Sweden. They played really well in their group except against Croatia, who beat them twice, both 1–0, both to a goal around the hour mark from wing-back Darijo Srna. Zlatan Ibrahimovic made a good impression in the group; Bulgaria and Hungary made none, the excellent Dimitar Berbatov apart.

Two groups were much closer. Group Two, one of the big seven-team groups, had four fairly evenly matched sides at the top: Denmark, Greece, Turkey and Ukraine. Compile a mini group of results between the four teams and Ukraine are comfortably on top, with Turkey second. The actual group finished in the same order, although a couple of draws against the weaker sides meant Ukraine were only two points clear. Greece, who had won the European Championship with either a tactical masterclass or stifling negativity, depending on your viewpoint, finished fourth, confirming the view that their victory was a freak one-off.

France drew far too many games, and had to recall some of their veterans to dig them out of trouble. With Henry and Trezeguet never as effective for France as for their clubs, they were struggling to find the net, but they qualified with something to spare in the end. Switzerland, Ireland and Israel were pursuing second place, and a lot of draws meant the issue went right to the last game. Israel were on eighteen points but had finished their schedule, while Switzerland, on seventeen, met Ireland (sixteen) in Dublin; this meant Israel's spot was a false position, as they had a worse goal difference than the Swiss and both their games were drawn. Ireland needed a win and a packed Lansdowne roared them on, but the Swiss were an obdurate, well-organised side and held out for a 0–0 draw.

In the play-offs Spain beat Slovakia 5–1 at home with a hat-trick from Luis García and that was that. The Czechs won home and away against Norway, and looked a good side in doing so. The other tie was a stormy affair. Switzerland won the home leg 2–0 against Turkey, but still had to cope with the seething pit of hate that was Istanbul, one of the most difficult cities to visit as an away team. When Alpay's handball was spotted by the linesman early on, Frei's penalty seemed to settle Swiss nerves and the tie. Not a bit of it. Turkey mounted a thrilling fight-back and headed goals from Tuncay meant they were 2–1 up at half-time. He pinched the second one off Şükür, but given the contrast in their contribution to the game that was fair enough. Emre bought a penalty after Streller foolishly stretched out a leg for him to trip over and Necati converted; now the Swiss only had the slimmest advantage of away goals. Streller's break-away after some careless defending on the left should have finished it but the Swiss weakness on crosses was exposed again as Tuncay grabbed his third from close range.

After the final whistle a massive fight broke out in the tunnel which resulted in six-match bans and fines for Alpay, Emre and Huggel, and a longer exclusion for a couple of Turkish officials, who had been clearly itching to start a fight on the touchline. Alpay should have been banned for longer, he was the principal antagonist. In one night Turkey had undone the good work of 2002.

Finals

The draw was better thought out than last time. Eight top seeds; eight good non-European sides; eight unseeded European sides and seven unseeded non-European sides plus the extra team, Serbia. What you didn't want, as a top seed, was Ivory Coast from Pot B, Holland or Portugal from Pot C, and USA or Serbia as your supposedly weak team.

Germany got it easy, England were okay, although Sweden would be tough, Mexico drew Portugal but also two weak teams while Brazil, France and Spain were all happy enough down at the bottom of the draw. Italy got the USA, which added to a good Czech side and a strong African qualifier in Ghana left a notoriously slows-starting team with work to do.

The press always like to write up a "group of death" and they did so this time with due cause. Serbia had to be in with a non-European top seed, and it happened to be Argentina. The group needed another European side and drew the Dutch, down in the lower pot after their failure to qualify for the 2002 Finals. The non-European side drawn into this group was Ivory Coast. The group had arguably the strongest team in each pot of the draw.

GROUP A

Germany Lahm 6, Klose 17, 61, Frings 87	**(2) 4**	**Costa Rica** Wanchope 12, 73	**(1) 2**	9 June, Munich; 59,416
Poland	**(0) 0**	**Ecuador** C Tenorio 25, Delgado 85	**(1) 2**	9 June, Gelsenkirchen; 48,426
Germany Neuville 90	**(0) 1**	**Poland**	**(0) 0**	14 June, Dortmund; 65,000
Costa Rica	**(0) 0**	**Ecuador** C Tenorio 8, Delgado 54, Kaviedes 90	**(1) 3**	15 June, Hamburg; 50,000
Poland Bosacki 33, 66	**(1) 2**	**Costa Rica** Gómez	**(1) 1**	20 June, Hanover; 43,000
Germany Klose 4, 45, Podolski 57	**(2) 3**	**Ecuador**	**(0) 0**	20 June, Berlin; 72,000

1. **Germany** 9pts (8–2); 2. **Ecuador** 6pts (5–3); 3. **Poland** 3pts (2–4); 4. **Costa Rica** 0 pts (3–9)

Easily the most entertaining opening match the tournament has seen. Germany had been written off. They had a shortage of top-class players and their manager, Jürgen Klinsmann, who had little or no experience and to whom they turned in desperation rather than expectation, commuted from the USA and watched Bundesliga games only on video. To make matters worse their best player, Michael Ballack, was carrying an injury and was left out of the first match. But surely they wouldn't lose to Costa Rica?

No, actually, they wouldn't. Philipp Lahm, the young attacking left-back at Bayern Munich, advanced upfield and curled a delicious right-footed shot into the corner. Six minutes on the clock. Appealing for offside (wrongly) instead of defending is never a good idea, and Paolo Wanchope took advantage a few minutes later, scampering through in that rather unsteady way of his to level. He did the same again in the second half – this time he was offside but the goal stood. Fortunately Klose had scored twice before that, deflecting Schweinsteiger's miscued shot past Porras and then converting a far post cross at the second attempt. Frings added a late fourth with a long-range howitzer to make the scoreline a more accurate reflection of the game; worries about the middle of the defence, but a win, at least. Wanchope scored forty-five goals for Costa Rica, although lots were against Caribbean islands with the population of Leicester; mind you, he probably scored against Leicester while he was at Manchester City. He was fun to watch, beating people without ever seeming to have the ball under control, and he had a dangerous skill of shooting with no back-lift and surprising goalkeepers – they like to see the trigger pulled back. And he always smiled when he scored, which was nice, instead of pumping his first or kissing his badge.

Poland were ineffectual against Ecuador, who scored first, defended well and got a late second through Delgado, now back home after his nightmare spell in England. Ecuador's captain, Iván Hurtado, had a great game; he was thirty-one and playing in Qatar but he had 130 caps and knew his way around a football pitch.

The same two scorers, Carlos Tenorio and Delgado, put paid to Costa Rica, and Kaviedes added a late third. Delgado's finished was hit with astonishing power; had Porras got in the way it might have killed him! Germany beat a defensive Poland, but needed an injury-time goal from Neuville to get the points.

Ecuador decided to rest a few guys against Germany, and Klose got two more goals in a 3–0 win as Germany sought to win the group. There is always a debate when teams do this: there is the benefit of rest for key players, especially those playing with a niggle or in their thirties and struggling with three games in ten days, to be balanced against the risk of meeting the group winners in the next phase. Ecuador probably took a sensible view in this instance; there wasn't much between England and Sweden and these two looked certain to be the second round opponents from the next group.

GROUP B

England	(1) 1	**Paraguay**	(0) 0	10 June, Frankfurt; 43,324
Own goal 3				
Sweden	(0) 0	**Trinidad & Tobago**	(0) 0	10 June, Dortmund;
60,285				
Trinidad & Tobago	(0) 0	**England**	(0) 2	15 June, Nuremberg; 41,000
		Crouch 83, Gerrard 90		
Paraguay	(0) 0	**Sweden**	(0) 1	15 June, Berlin; 72,000
		Ljungberg 89		
Trinidad & Tobago	(0) 0	**Paraguay**	(1) 2	20 June, Kaiserslautern; 46,000
		Own goal 25, Cuevas 88		
England	(1) 2	**Sweden**	(0) 2	20 June, Cologne; 45,000
J Cole 34, Gerrard 85		Allbäck 50, Larsson 90		

1. England 7pts (5–2); 2. Sweden 5pts (3–2); 3. Paraguay 3pts (2–2); 4. Trinidad & Tobago 1pt (0–4)

There really wasn't much between England and Sweden. Neither looked terribly convincing in their opening game. England got an early break against Paraguay when the great Carlos Gamarra deflected Beckham's free-kick past his own goal-keeper, but the game petered out. There were calls in the press for someone with pace to replace Beckham down the right, but he looked fine in this game, rarely giving the ball away and supplying the usual stream of crosses. Sweden made all the running but found veteran goalkeeper Shaka Hislop in unbeatable form. It was a poor effort against a team reduced to ten men just after half-time, but Dwight Yorke was surprisingly effective in a defensive midfield role, showing a bit of unexpected bite in the tackle and using the ball intelligently.

It was more of the same against England and a second point looked possible until Peter Crouch rose to head Beckham's deep cross in under the bar. He owed the team a goal after missing a sitter in the first half (although he wasn't the only one). John Terry spared earlier embarrassment with a terrific hook off the line after a mix up at the back. Steven Gerrard added a second in injury-time with a rising left-footer. Sweden left their winner against Paraguay late as well; Freddie Ljungberg's finish from Allbäck's header back across goal was just enough.

England won the group with a draw against Sweden, but it was another laboured effort that drew fierce criticism from the press. England actually played well in the first half, especially after having to bring on a sub in the second minute when Michael Owen's leg went from under him. He played no further part in the tournament.

Eriksson brought in Owen Hargreaves as the defensive midfielder at the expense of Gerrard. The change was greeted negatively but Gerrard hadn't played well and Hargreaves had a super game, full of good, crisp tackling and energetic runs. Joe Cole looked really lively on the left and he gave England the lead when he chested a clearance and volleyed it back over the goal-keeper's head into the top corner. A special effort. Cole started to confirm his promise in this tournament, but Mourinho clearly didn't fancy him at Chelsea and he stayed there a couple of years too long.

England showed huge fallibility on crosses in the game, both Sweden's goals came from deep crosses and both Allbäck and Mellberg came close from set pieces. Gerrard, on for a fitful Wayne Rooney, who started for the first time since his pre-tournament injury, headed England back in front, but Sweden deserved Larsson's injury-time equaliser.

GROUP C

Argentina Crespo 24, Saviola 38	(2) 2	**Ivory Coast** Drogba 82	(0) 1	10 June, Hamburg; 45,442
Holland Robben 18	(1) 1	**Serbia & Montenegro**	(0) 0	11 June, Leipzig; 37,216
Serbia & Mont	(0) 0	**Argentina** Maxi Rodríguez 6, 41, Cambiasso 31, Crespo 79, Tévez 84, Messi 89	(3) 6	16 June, Gelsenkirchen; 52,000
Ivory Coast B Koné 38	(1) 1	**Holland** van Persie 23, van Nistelrooy 27	(2) 2	16 June, Stuttgart; 52,000
Holland	(0) 0	**Argentina**	(0) 0	21 June, Frankfurt; 48,000
Ivory Coast Dindane 37 (p), 67 B Kalou 85 (p)	(1) 3	**Serbia & Montenegro** Zigic 10, Ilic 21	(2) 2	21 June, Munich; 66,000

1. **Argentina** 7pts (8–1); 2. **Holland** 7pts (3–1); 3. **Ivory Coast** 3pts (5–6); 4. **Serbia & Montenegro** 0pts (2–10)

The group of death was, after all the pre-tournament baloney, a quick death for two of the teams. Drogba's power and pace gave Argentina one or two anxious moments, but they were too skilful and kept the ball too well and Drogba's late goal was mere compensation for a good effort on his part than a serious threat to Argentina.

Argentina's next game was a master class. With Verón gone Juan Román Riquelme had taken over as playmaker. Often dismissed as one-paced, when surrounded by hard-working but neat players like Cambiasso and Mascherano and Sorin, Riquelme was just gorgeous. His orchestration of the annihilation of Serbia was the ultimate puppet-master performance, his awareness of angle and space was magical and he barely misplaced a pass all game, although he seemed to have the ball every thirty seconds. I've been critical of Argentina's attitude throughout the book, and I stand by all of it, but they gave one of the all-time great displays in this match.

On six minutes Juan Pablo Sorín slipped a sweet ball through to Saviola and his cross was met by Maxi Rodríguez who tucked it past Jevric without breaking stride. After eighteen minutes a flick from Riquelme found Saviola, he held off a challenge to move the ball tight to the advancing Cambiasso. To the edge of the box and Cambiasso played it short to Crespo, who ran to his right and then back-heeled the ball into space for Cambiasso, who hadn't stopped. The finish was exact, high and handsome to the right as the goalkeeper dived to the left. One of the great World Cup goals, an absolute joy.

The next was all down to Saviola, who won a tackle on the right and advanced to hit a shot that Jevric half-saved; Maxi Rodríguez was first to the rebound. With Mateja Kezman off the field after a dreadful two-footed challenge, Pekerman sent on the eighteen-year-old prodigy Lionel Messi. Messi's cross from the left was his first contribution, providing an opportunity Hernán Crespo couldn't miss. Saviola had gone before the hour to have a well-deserved rest and leaving to a rapturous reception. Now his replacement, the bull-necked Carlos Tévez, got in on the act, breaking through two weak tackles to score with a curled finish around the unfortunate Jevric, who had done little wrong. A neat passing move played in Messi for his first World Cup goal. There would be tougher challenges ahead than a disappointing Serbia, but the tournament had clear favourites. Holland were also through after Ivory Coast again ceded a two-goal lead before mounting a fight-back.

It was no surprise that neither Argentina nor Holland bared their teeth in the third match, which was entertaining enough but lacking a couple of key players on either side. Holland fielded the speedy left-back de Cler instead of the ponderous but skilful van Bronckhorst and he did well against a nervous Messi, but Tévez looked well up for it (when doesn't he) and came closest to scoring with a rasping drive saved by his future Manchester United colleague Edwin van der Sar.

Ivory Coast, without the suspended Drogba, did really well to come back from two-down to beat Serbia 3–2. They would have caused havoc in any other group.

GROUP D

Angola	**(0) 0**	**Portugal**	**(1) 1**	11 June, Cologne; 45,000
		Pauleta 4		
Iran	**(1) 1**	**Mexico**	**(1) 3**	11 June, Nuremberg; 36,898
Golmohammadi 36		Bravo 28, 76, Zinha 79		
Mexico	**(0) 0**	**Angola**	**(0) 0**	16 June, Hanover; 43,000
Portugal	**(0) 2**	**Iran**	**(0) 0**	17 June, Frankfurt; 48,000
Deco 63, Ronaldo 80 (p)				
Iran	**(0) 1**	**Angola**	**(0) 1**	21 June, Leipzig; 38,000
Bakhtiarizadeh 75		Flávio 65		
Portugal	**(2) 2**	**Mexico**	**(1) 1**	21 June, Gelsenkirchen; 52,000
Maniche 6, Simão 24 (p)		Fonseca 29		

1. Portugal 9pts (5–1); 2. Mexico 4pts (4–3); 3. Angola 2pts (1–2); 4. Iran 1pt (2–6)

This group was over after two rounds. An early goal settled the colonial dispute in Cologne, while the diminutive winger Omar Bravo ran Iran ragged and scored two of his side's goals. In the group's decisive game Maniche's cleverly worked opening goal, set up by a great run from Simão, and Simão's penalty after Marquez's daft handball seemed to hand the group to Portugal, but Mexico came back well. Had Bravo converted a penalty in the second half the end result may have been different, but when Perez was sent off for a dive, the game was done. Neither of the second round opponents represented a kind draw for these two.

GROUP E

Ghana	(0) 0	**Italy**	(1) 2	12 June, Hanover; 43,000
		Pirlo 40, Iaquinta 83		
Czech Rep.	(2) 3	**USA**	(0) 0	12 June, Gelsenkirchen; 48,426
Koller 5, Rosicky 36, 76				
Ghana	(1) 2	**Czech Rep.** (0) 0		17 June, Cologne; 45,000
Gyan 2, Muntari 82				
USA	(1) 1	**Italy**	(1) 1	17 June, Kaiserslautern; 46,000
Own goal 27		Gilardino 22		
Italy	(1) 2	**Czech Rep.** (0) 0		22 June, Hamburg; 50,000
Materazzi 26, Inzaghi 87				
USA	(1) 1	**Ghana**	(2) 2	22 June, Nuremberg; 41,000
Dempsey 43		Draman 22, Appiah 45 (p)		

1. Italy 7pts (5–1); 2. Ghana 6pts (4–3); 3. Czech Republic 3pts (3–4); 4. USA 1pt (2–6)

Italy: competent – indifferent – very good. Czech Republic: good – poor – indifferent. USA: poor – good – indifferent. Ghana: indifferent – very good – good. Thus, a group in which each game was tough to call, never mind the final outcome. Andrea Pirlo played in that deep-lying creative role he enjoys and scored the first goal against Ghana with a superlative thirty-yard strike. He also made a late second for Iaquinta, although Kuffour should have done better than just push the ball into Iaquinta's stride when he tried to intercept. The Czechs dealt easily with the Americans. Milan Baros, like Savo Milosevic before him, so bad for Villa but so good for his country, set up Jan Koller for an early start and then it was the Tomas Rosicky show. The busy little Dortmund player added a second with an absolute snorter that curled away from Keller into the inside side netting. He nearly bettered it with a run from deep and shot that spanked against the crossbar. Another run took him past two defenders, and clear of the defence, and the finish was ice cool, flicked over Keller with the outside of the right boot as the goalkeeper came to challenge.

A goal after two minutes against the Czech Republic reminded Ghana they were a good side, and their midfield looked the equal of the Czechs' talented quartet. The Czechs looked the best team in Euro 2004 until they foundered on the Greek wall in the semi-final, and they had much of the same team. The best of them, Pavel Nedvěd had been injured and this was his last big tournament at thirty-four. Another of the 2004 stars, the rugged

Fiorentina centre-back Tomas Ujfalusi was sent off for a professional foul. Asamoah Gyan missed the penalty, having scored the opening goal, and Ghana had to wait until the eighty-second minute before Sulley Muntari put the game to bed. The Czechs were a huge disappointment. The USA upped their game against Italy, but the match is remembered for three red cards. The goals came early, Gilardino stooping low to head in Pirlo's teasing free-kick, and Christian Zaccardo comically hacking into his own net.

The first card was indisputable, Daniele De Rossi's elbow on McBride was deliberate and brutal and left the American striker with blood pouring from a head wound. The second, for Mastroeni's late tackle on Pirlo, was debatable, it was more of a yellow-and-a-half. Eddie Pope's first card was borderline, but his second for a tackle from behind and brooked no argument. Keller earned his team a point with the save of the tournament from Del Piero, a truly brilliant piece of reflex athleticism.

Czech midfielder Jan Polák did his team no favours in the last match against Italy when he picked up a second yellow for a silly tackle only ten minutes after the first; neither was malicious but both were ill-judged. Italy were already one-up through a fabulous header from Materazzi – Pirlo's delivery, inevitably – and they should have scored more before Inzaghi rounded the 'keeper with no Czech defenders within twenty yards. Materazzi was only on as a replacement for the injured Nesta and it was his first goal for Italy.

The USA were crying foul again after a physical encounter with Ghana, although their problems started when their experienced captain Claudio Reyna was robbed by Dramani, who ran on and finished really well. Clint Dempsey pulverised Beasley's curled cross to equalise, but a soft (like Andrex toilet tissue soft) penalty award restored Ghana's lead. They defended aggressively in the second half, as African sides tend to, but the Americans were short of imagination and created few chances – McBride's header against the post was a brilliant effort rather than a missed chance.

United States Squad 2006:

GK: Tim Howard (Manchester United, 27 years old, 16 caps), Kasey Keller (Borussia Mönchengladbach, 37, 93), Marcus Hahnemann (Reading, 33, 6)

DEF: Chris Albright (LA Galaxy, 23, 20), Gregg Berhalter (Energie Cottbus, 32, 44), Carlos Bocanegra (Fulham, 27, 40), Steve Cherundolo (Hannover 27, 35), Jimmy Conrad (Kansas City Wizards, 29, 15), Oguchi Onyewu (Standard Liège, 24, 14), Eddie Pope (Real Salt Lake, 32, 80)

MID & WIDE: DaMarcus Beasley (PSV Eindhoven, 24, 58), Bobby Convey (Reading, 23, 39), Eddie Johnson (Kansas City Wizards, 22, 18), Eddie Lewis (Leeds United, 32, 69), Pablo Mastroeni (Colorado Rapids, 29, 48), John O'Brien (Chivas USA, 28, 31), Ben Olsen (D.C. United, 29, 34), Claudio Reyna (Cpt, Manchester City, 32, 109)

FWD: Brian Ching (Houston Dynamo, 28, 20), Clint Dempsey (New England Revolution, 23, 21), Landon Donovan (LA Galaxy, 24, 81), Brian McBride (Fulham, 33, 92), Josh Wolff (Kansas City Wizards, 29, 47)

GROUP F

Australia	(0) 3	**Japan**	(1) 1	12 June, Kaiserslautern; 46,000	
Cahill 84, 89, Aloisi 90		Nakamura 26			
Brazil	(1) 1	**Croatia**	(0) 0	13 June, Berlin; 72,000	
		Kaka 44			
Australia	(0) 0	**Brazil**	(0) 2	18 June, Munich; 66,000	
		Adriano 49, Fred 89			
Japan	(0) 0	**Croatia**	(0) 0	18 June, Nuremberg; 41,000	
Croatia	(1) 2	**Australia**	(1) 2	22 June, Stuttgart; 52,000	
Srna 2, N Kovac 56		Moore 38 (p), Kewell 79			
Brazil	(1) 4	**Japan**	(1) 1	22 June, Dortmund; 65,000	
Ronaldo 45, 81,		Tamada 34			
Juninho 53, Gilberto 59					

1. Brazil 9pts (7–1); 2. Australia 4pts (5–5); 3. Croatia 2pts (2–3); 4. Japan 1pt (2–7)

Really easy for Brazil, not so easy for Croatia, who expected to qualify alongside them. Ronaldo, still barrelling along, was back in search of a record, and Ronaldinho was by now regarded as the world's best player. The new stars off the conveyor belt were Kaká, who went to Japan & Korea as a teenager but didn't play, Adriano and Robinho. All three played in Europe; Kaka was the playmaker at Milan, Adriano a brilliant but fitful star at Inter and Robinho, still only twenty-two, was a goalscoring winger with Real Madrid.

Tim Cahill, surprisingly left on the bench by Guus Hiddink, came off it to turn the opening game with two goals. Japan's opener was ill-deserved as Australian goalkeeper Mark Schwarzer was clearly being held as Nakamura scored.

Australia only succumbed to Brazil after half-time; against Croatia, needing only a draw, they gave a gutsy performance to twice come from behind. Hiddink over-thought his selection and left out Schwarzer for a taller goalkeeper, Kalac, who was at fault for the second Croatian goal. The last ten minutes after Harry Kewell's equaliser became tetchy and ended in a flurry of cards. A huge media meal was made out of Graham Poll's failure to send off Josep Simunic after a second yellow card on ninety minutes. Poll compounded the error by issuing said card after the final whistle for Suminic's protests as the teams left the field. What is forgotten is that Poll actually handled a tricky game quite well, spotting a crafty handball for Australia's penalty that no one saw on TV. What goes around comes around and Poll was always a referee who enjoyed the limelight, although this would not have been how he envisioned the attention would fall at this World Cup. What time's the next flight to Tring in Hertfordshire, please?

Ronaldo got his record, passing Gerd Müller's World Cup scoring record. Müller was still better.

GROUP G

France	(0) 0	**Switzerland**	(0) 0	13 June, Stuttgart; 56,000
Togo	(1) 1	**South Korea**	(0) 2	13 June, Frankfurt; 48,000
Kader		Lee Chun-soo 54,		
		Ahn Jung-hwan 72		
South Korea	(0) 1	**France**	(1) 1	18 June, Leipzig; 43,000
Park Ji-sung 81		Henry 9		
Switzerland	(1) 2	**Togo**	(0) 0	19 June, Dortmund; 65,000
Frei 16, Barnetta 88				
South Korea	(0) 0	**Switzerland**	(1) 2	23 June, Hanover; 43,000
		Senderos 23, Frei 77		
Togo	(0) 0	**France**	(0) 2	23 June, Cologne; 45,000
		Vieira 55, Henry 61		

1. Switzerland 7pts (4–0); 2. France 5pts (3–1); 3. South Korea 4pts (3–4); 4. Togo 0pts (1–6)

Had South Korea shown a little more enterprise they might have got out of this group. Their coach, the Dutchman Dick Advocaat, seemed content to play a defensive waiting game and in all three ties he kept Ahn Jung-hwan on the bench and played Choe Jae-jin up front on his own. Ahn had not been on form, but he galvanised the side here, there was a noticeable lift in tempo when he came on.

Togo were in some disarray. Arguments between Adebayor and the coach had led to a change, with the German Pfister brought in, sent away and brought in again. Adebayor's subsequent career suggests belated sympathy is due for the original coach Stephen Keshi, the former Nigerian international. They played well against Korea after all the fuss died down, and deservedly took the lead when the powerful Kader knocked the ball forward of his inhumanly large thigh, surged past the Korean defenders and whacked the ball across Lee – a really decisive finish. Lee, now the Korean captain, tipped over a free-kick to keep his side one-down at the break. The turning point came in the fifty-third minute. Park Ji-sung, the Manchester United midfielder with lungs the size of Kader's thighs, drove through the centre of the Togo defence and was chopped down by Abalo before he could get into the box. Graham Poll sent off Abalo, who had already been booked, and Lee Chun-soo exacted further punishment by curling the free-kick inside the post. Lee Chun-soo was guilty of the tournament's worst coiffure, an achievement of sorts. Ahn won the game with an aggressive run and shot, although a deflection helped loop the ball past Agassa.

France opened with a woeful scoreless draw against Switzerland but were better against South Korea. They would rue a number of missed chances as Park's late goal stole a point. France laboured against Togo for an hour but goals from Vieira and Henry eased their passage, and that of coach Domenech, who must have been dreading a second consecutive humiliating exit at half-time.

Switzerland beat South Korea, but Advocaat made it easy by keeping a single striker formation until far too late in the game. A Philippe Senderos header gave Switzerland the lead and only a couple of long-range shots threatened Zuberbühler's goal until

Ahn's introduction sparked a late rally. The Paraguayan referee spoiled the game, over-ruling an offside flag and allowing Barnetta an easy goal. Senderos had enjoyed a good first full season at Arsenal and played well at the World Cup, but his career went progressively backwards in England when a weakness to the high ball was discovered.

GROUP H

Spain	**(2) 4**	**Ukraine**	**(0) 0**	14 June, Leipzig; 43,000
Alonso 13, Villa 17, 48 (p),				
Torres 81				
Saudi Arabia	**(0) 2**	**Tunisia**	**(1) 2**	14 June, Munich; 66,000
Al-Kahtani 57, Al-Jaber 84		Jaziri 23, Jaïdi 90		
Ukraine	**(2) 4**	**Saudi Arabia**	**(0) 0**	19 June, Hamburg; 50,000
Rusol 4, Rebrov 36,				
Shevchenko 46,				
Kalinichenko 84				
Tunisia	**(1) 1**	**Spain**	**(0) 3**	19 June, Stuttgart; 52,000
Mnari 9		Raúl 71, Torres 76, 90 (p)		
Spain	**(1) 1**	**Saudi Arabia**	**(0) 0**	23 June, Kaiserslautern; 48,000
Juanito 36				
Ukraine	**(0) 1**	**Tunisia**	**(0) 0**	23 June, Berlin; 72,000
Shevchenko 70 (p)				

1. Spain 9pts (8–1); 2. Ukraine 6pts (5–4); 3. Tunisia 1pt (3–6); 4. Saudi Arabia 1pt (2–7)

The two European sides had too much for Saudi Arabia and Tunisia. Spain stunned Ukraine in the opener; the east Europeans appeared tentative in their first Finals appearance, and Spain took full advantage, with the movement of David Villa causing horrendous problems for the Ukrainians. In a highly entertaining game in Munich Tunisia took the lead against Saudi Arabia only for the Saudis to turn the game around and take the lead themselves with a goal from veteran striker Sami Al-Jaber six minutes from the end. A last-minute header from the huge Bolton centre-back Radhi Jaïdi ensured a fair result.

Jaidi marshalled the Tunisian defence expertly against Spain, who only scored their goals in the last fifteen minutes after Mnari surprised them with an early goal, volleying in the rebound after Casillas saved his first shot. Raúl, on for Luis García, who did little in the first half, pounced on a half-stop by the goalkeeper to equalise. The winner was pure Fernando Torres, still with Atlético Madrid, still looking about twelve years old and still with that electrifying burst of speed that his injuries took away. He accelerated away from the defence, went to the 'keeper's left and flicked the ball in with the outside of his right. An injury-time penalty slightly flattered Spain.

Spain's reserves beat Saudi Arabia, while the Ukraine needed a sending off and an iffy penalty to see off Tunisia, who were stubborn and courageous even when clearly outgunned.

SECOND ROUND

Argentina Crespo 10, Maxi Rodriguez 98	(1) (1) 2	**Mexico** Márquez 6	(1) (1) 1	24 June, Leipzig; 43,000		
Germany Podolski 4, 12	(2) 2	**Sweden**	(0) 0	24 June, Munich; 66,000		
England Beckham 60	(0) 1	**Ecuador**	(0) 0	25 June, Stuttgart; 52,000		
Portugal Maniche 23	(1) 1	**Holland**	(0) 0	25 June, Nuremberg; 41,000		
Australia	(0) 0	**Italy** Totti 90 (p)	(0) 1	26 June, Kaiserslautern; 46,000		
Switzerland Ukraine won 3–0 on penalties	(0) (0) 0	**Ukraine**	(0) (0) 0	26 June, Cologne; 45,000		
Brazil Ronaldo 5, Adriano 45, Zé Roberto 84	(2) 3	**Ghana**	(0) 0	27 June, Dortmund; 65,000		

The Argentina match didn't take long to explode into life, but not in the way Pekerman's team would have hoped. Méndez's free-kick travelled too far across the area, Barcelona's Rafael Márquez finished brilliantly for a centre-half. Argentina were level when Crespo and Borgetti challenged for a free-kick; the ball skewed in off Borgetti's head but Crespo was wrongly awarded the goal.

The game was never boring but we had to wait until extra-time for the next goal. Borgetti was a handful – he had the beating of Heinze and Ayala in the air and with more support Mexico might have created more clear chances. Mexico's all-time top scorer, Borgetti plundered stacks of goals in qualifying, and did well here, but he never acclimatised to the Premier League in a disappointing season and a half with Bolton. Messi had a goal questionably ruled offside, but against that Gabriel Heinze was lucky to escape with a yellow card for a blatant professional foul. No

Golden Goal this time around so Argentina had to hold on for a while even after Maxi Rodriguez's wonderful strike from the edge of the area put them ahead.

Germany beat Sweden with some ease in Munich. Early goals help, and they got two, the first when Podolski put away a rebound after Isaksson thwarted Klose, and the second a clean finish from Klose's clever reverse ball. The new German strike force looked Poles apart. Get it? (They were both of Polish origin, Klose and Podolski.) Sweden had a bad day at the office; Lucic was sent off for a second yellow card and Larsson missed a penalty that should never have been given. At least five Germans made sure the referee knew Lucic had already been booked, waving imaginary cards. I hate that, the deliberate effort to see another player punished. We see less of it now after a clampdown, but it was endemic throughout this tournament.

I can't muster the energy to write much about England against Ecuador. Ashley Cole's knee and David Beckham's right foot redeemed another woeful effort. Cole deflected Carlos Tenorio's shot onto the bar after Terry's comically bad header let the striker in on goal, and Beckham's free-kick on the hour cocked a snook at those demanding his omission. He certainly played no worse than Gerrard or Lampard in this competition, despite starting it in a trough of form. The problem England now had was that, having found the right pattern with Rooney up front on his own and two supporting players out wide, they needed the right combination to fill the positions, and Sven couldn't do the jigsaw. And with Neville injured they couldn't find a right-back. Jamie Carragher was a club footballer elevated beyond his ability even at centre-half and was way too slow at right-back, while using Hargreaves there was a waste of England's most in-form midfielder. Conundrums.

Portugal against Holland I covered in *Dirtiest Games*. A disgraceful exhibition from both teams and attempts to blame the referee just added to the shame. Awful. Maniche won the game with a clever individual goal.

Italy beat Australia with a late, late penalty when Fabio Grosso tumbled over Lucas Neill's prone body. Questionable, but Neill was rash to go to ground. Totti kept his nerve to score from the spot past a red-hot goalkeeper; Schwarzer had made three or four good saves in the first half. Australia moaned about the penalty, but Italy were the more accomplished side even after Materazzi was sent off for a two-footed challenge.

Switzerland against Ukraine was hardly a feast of football. Even without Senderos, who was injured, Switzerland looked comfortable against a team in which Shevchenko, supposedly the best striker in Europe, was anonymous. He even missed his penalty in the shoot-out. Fortunately for the Ukraine their next three guys all scored, and the Swiss missed all three of their kicks, the only team to suffer this degree of ignominy in a World Cup penalty shoot-out. They were also the first side to be eliminated without conceding a goal.

Brazil moved up a gear, and Ghana actually played quite well to hold them to three. The first was a result of a poor offside trap. Ronaldo had already been pulled back for an incorrect offside decision and almost immediately sprung the trap again, finishing with minimum fuss as usual. A second goal just before the break when Adriano put in Cafú's inviting cross seemed to end the game. Ghana kept coming, to their credit. Muntari and the captain Stephen Appiah matched Brazil in the centre of midfield, and the forwards peeled off wide to press Cafú and Carlos with some success. But they couldn't find a way past Lúcio in the middle and when Gyan was – correctly – given a second yellow card for diving they were done. Zé Roberto finished cheekily for the third goal, nudging the ball one way past the 'keeper and going around the other side to score.

WORLD CUP CLASSIC No.24
27 June 2006, Hanover, Germany; 43,000

France   (1) 3   Ribéry 41, Vieira 83, Zidane 89
Spain   (1) 1   Villa 28 (p)

Referee: **Roberto Rosetti** (Italy)
Coaches: **Raymond Domenech** (France) & **Luis Aragonés** (Spain)

France (4–2–3–1): Fabien Barthez (Olympique de Marseille); Willy Sagnol (Bayern Munich), Lilian Thuram (Juventus), William Gallas (Chelsea), Éric Abidal (Lyon); Patrick Vieira (Juventus), Claude Makélélé (Chelsea); Franck Ribéry (Olympique de Marseille), Zinedine Zidane (Real Madrid), Florent Malouda (Lyon); Thierry Henry (Arsenal). **Subs:** Sidney Govou (Lyon) 74m for Malouda; Sylvain Wiltord (Lyon) 88m for Henry
Spain (4–3–3): Iker Casillas (Real Madrid); Sergio Ramos (Real Madrid), Pablo Ibáñez

(Atlético Madrid), Carlos Puyol (Barcelona), Mariano Pernia (Getafe); Cesc Fàbregas (Arsenal), Xabi Alonso (Liverpool), Xavi *Hernández* (Barcelona); David Villa (Valencia), Fernando Torres (Atlético Madrid), Raúl *González* (Cpt, Real Madrid). **Subs**: Luis García (Liverpool) 54m for Villa; Joaquin *Sánchez* (Real Betis) 54m for Raúl; Marcos Senna (Villareal) 82m for Xavi
Cautioned: Vieira (Fra) 68m, Puyol (Spa) 82m, Ribéry (Fra) 87m, Zidane (Fra) 90m

The wannabes versus the has-beens. Spain were unbeaten since Luis Aragonés took over as national coach after the 2004 European Championships; France had struggled but improved since recalling some of the legends who had brought them success in the past.

Spain were starting the tiki-taka era, using the patient possession-first game that would provide them with their breakthrough at the next European Championships. France relied on solidity through the middle, Makélélé and Vieira providing an extra barrier in front of Gallas and the veteran Thuram.

Spain knew France could be got at down the flanks and they started well, feeding in Torres and Villa as they moved wide. France looked to get Henry in behind the Spanish central defenders, and Aragonés' team selection was complicit in allowing them to do just that.

Spain struck first; an unnecessary and untypically clumsy challenge from Thuram on the centre-half Ibanez, up for a corner, allowing David Villa to score from the spot. The Valencia striker came into the tournament with only a handful of caps but his movement and passing were a revelation.

France equalised just before half-time and Vieira was at the heart of it, his driving run and pass releasing Ribéry. The young winger had impressed so far with his dribbling at pace and his quick, neat passing, but his finishing had been woeful. Not when it really mattered here, though, he rounded Casillas at speed and tucked the ball past the retreating defenders. Domenech's gamble in leaving out the more experienced Ludovic Giuly was paying off – although one could ask why Giuly was not playing on the other side in place of the wasteful Malouda.

Zidane, with the comfort of good cover behind him, was beginning to find some form and enjoy himself and he put through Malouda with a delicate pass, but the winger couldn't get enough height on his lob to beat Casillas. Aragonés, sensing the tide was turning, brought on Luis García and Joaquin for Raúl and Villa. It changed the game but not in Spain's favour. Torres was forced into the middle, where Gallas consumed him, and Joaquin's runs, while exciting and skilful, ended in the usual blind alleys and poor finishes. A talented player, he disappeared when coaches realised the lack of an end product wasn't going to change – Theo Walcott, take heed.

Zidane took a free-kick about thirty-five yards out with a few minutes remaining. Xabi Alonso just got his head to the ball but it looped invitingly for Vieira to head home at the far post. Spain could muster no response and Zidane scored his side's third, racing clear down the left in injury-time, cutting back too easily inside Puyol and thumping home with his right foot.

Yet again Spain were left holding the bouquet. The fault lay with Aragonés; he failed to match France's power with Senna, his enforcer left on the bench, and his young midfield stars, brilliant as they were, got a pounding from the awesome Vieira. Suddenly France, with Zidane awoken and Ribéry looking a real find, were in contention.

QUARTER-FINALS

Germany Klose 80	(0) (1) 1	**Argentina** Ayala 49	(1) (1) 1	30 June, Berlin; 72,000	
Germany won 4–2 on penalties					
Italy Zambrotta 6, Toni 59, 69	(1) 3	**Ukraine**	(0) 0	30 June, Hamburg; 50,000	
Brazil	(0) 0	**France** Henry 57	(0) 1	1 July, Frankfurt; 48,000	
England	(0) (0) 0	**Portugal**	(0) (0) 0	1 July, Gelsenkirchen; 52,000	
Portugal won 3–1 on penalties					

Germany against Argentina: it was to be hoped the game was better than their last Finals encounter, the drab and dirty 1990 final. It was, but it was no classic. Argentina, after their ebullient showing in the groups, had become more defensive as the tournament wore on. Pekerman left out the clever link player Saviola in favour of the bustling aggression of young Tévez and preferred Lucho González to Cambiasso.

Neither change paid off. González, the Porto midfielder had

played seventeen minutes against Serbia and picked up a knock. He came into the game cold and did very little. Tévez, still learning, played too high and was picked off by Mertesacker and Metzelder – the clever Saviola would have dragged them out of position more and created space.

It was a set play that broke the deadlock, after forty-five minutes in which neither goalkeeper had to make a serious save. Four minutes into the second period Argentina were ahead when Riquelme, who had been nullified by Frings, curled a corner onto the head of Ayala. Germany's equaliser was from a similar direct route, Ballack's free-kick finding Klose unmarked for once. The Werder Bremen centre-forward, top scorer in the *Bundesliga* that year, didn't miss many of those.

Both sides looked tired and scared in extra-time, and neither bust a gut to win the game. Pekerman took off Riquelme for a runner, Cambiasso, and used Julio Cruz for Crespo instead of young Messi for Maxi or González. His third substitution was forced upon him when his goalkeeper picked up an injury. Germany took off Klose, who toiled alone as Podolski helped in midfield, and sent on the willing Neuville. With the best forwards in the match off the field, penalties beckoned and duly arrived.

It was Argentina who died wondering; the Germans were predictably ruthless with their spot-kicks while Ayala and Cambiasso weren't. Pekerman had taken off two of their best dead-ball strikers and didn't use another. Lehmann indulged in a piece of gamesmanship during the shoot-out, appearing to consult notes kept in the back of the goal about each Argentinian kicker. The paper was blank; who knows whether it had any effect, but it was typical of Lehmann, a very smart chap who occasionally veered over into smart-arse.

Argentina inexplicably started a ruckus after the game was over and Cufré, an unused sub, received a red card. Just when we were thinking they'd stopped all that nonsense and were just about the football.

Italy beat Ukraine 3–0. Buffon made a couple of good saves and Ukraine hit the woodwork a couple of times, but one always had a sense Italy were in third gear. None of the close shaves was from Shevchenko, who left with a whimper, and the Ukraine defence couldn't deal with the power of Luca Toni. Italy weren't missing De Rossi; his absence had created an opportunity for Milan's dog of war, Gennaro Gattuso, and his industry and self-lessness alongside Pirlo and behind Totti gave Italy a mightily impressive spine. Played five, conceded one own goal. How very Italian.

France enjoy beating Brazil in the World Cup Finals and have done it more often than anyone else. But never before was it this easy. Forget 1–0, this was a lot more comfortable than Italy's win over the Ukraine. Brazil just didn't show. Gallas pocketed Ronaldo – for a couple of years he was the best man-marking centre-half around – and Ronaldinho and Kaká contributed only in little flashes. Carlos Parreira retreated to the way he instinctively wanted to play – defensively – and his team expired quietly. The two defensive midfielders for Brazil just couldn't cope with the movement of Zidane, Henry and Ribéry, who kept swapping positions, and they were pushed deeper and deeper so the talent ahead of them was cut off from the back six.

France created chance after chance; a header from Malouda, a through ball that Ribéry just lost under his feet, Ribéry's cross flashing across the goal, a header past the post from Vieira.

The goal was from a set play when it came. Zidane took a free-kick out on the left and whipped it right footed over the defence. Henry attacked around the back and smashed the ball past Dida on the half-volley. As the players lined up for the free-kick, Henry's marker decided this was a good time to tie his shoelaces, and had only just finished doing so as Dida picked the ball out of the net. Guess who? The best left-back in the world, according to him. Yes, it was our old friend, Roberto Carlos. Sorry to harp on, folks, but that is unforgivable. That was his last contribution to the World Cup.

England lost to Portugal on penalties for the second major tournament in a row. That's the bare bones of it. England played poorly in the first half (Portugal were only marginally better), lost David Beckham to injury, Wayne Rooney to a red card, and then the match when Jamie Carragher had to retake a penalty, missed it, and watched Cristiano Ronaldo administer the lethal injection to Eriksson's time as England manager.

England were much better after the sending off; not because Rooney, or indeed Beckham were awful – neither were worse than their colleagues up to that point – but because they needed a sense of injustice to fuel the passion Eriksson so singularly failed to tap into. His selection was usually sound, the injury to Owen had forced him into the formation he should have used anyway (shades of Bryan Robson's shoulder in 1990) but he just never seemed to rouse the guys. I don't mean up and at 'em, get it forward, hare-brained gung-ho football, but the instillation of the self-belief required to win these things.

Too much was made of Ronaldo's little wink to his mates. We already knew he was a sneaky little so-and-so, so we shouldn't have been surprised. That referee Elizondo was right to send off Rooney was incontrovertible; he stamped on a player.

England deserve some credit for their rearguard action against a really talented team. And at least they bore their disappointment with some dignity, unlike Argentina. They saw off Figo – his replacement, Postiga came closest to scoring – and neutered Ronaldo, which seems to be easier in World Cup games than club games. I'm still not sure whether that tells us something about him or about Portugal. All the back four defended well, and Hargreaves was immense in the holding role and fully deserved his man of the match award. Hargreaves' injury problems started in earnest the following year after he signed for Manchester United; he has been sorely missed by England.

England Squad 2006:
GK: Paul Robinson (Tottenham Hotspur, 26, 21), David James (Manchester City, 35, 34), Scott Carson (Liverpool, 20, 0)
DEF: Wayne Bridge (Chelsea, 25, 23), Jamie Carragher (Liverpool, 28, 25), Sol Campbell (Arsenal, 31, 68), Ashley Cole (Arsenal, 25, 46), Rio Ferdinand (Manchester United, 27, 47) Gary Neville (Man Utd, 31, 79), John Terry (Chelsea, 25, 24)

MID & WIDE: David Beckham (Cpt, Real Madrid, 31, 89), Michael Carrick (Tottenham, 24, 6), Joe Cole (Chelsea, 24, 32), Stewart Downing (Middlesbrough, 21, 2), Steven Gerrard (Liverpool, 26, 42), Owen Hargreaves (Bayern Munich, 25, 30), Jermaine Jenas (Tottenham, 23, 15), Frank Lampard (Chelsea, 27, 40), Aaron Lennon (Tottenham, 19, 1), Theo Walcott[*] (Arsenal, 20, 1)

FWD: Peter Crouch (Liverpool, 25, 7), Michael Owen (Newcastle United, 26, 77), Wayne Rooney (Man Utd, 20, 29)

SEMI-FINALS

Germany	(0) (0) 0	**Italy**	(0) (0) 2	4 July, Dortmund; 65,000
Grosso 119, Del Piero 120				
France	(1) 1	**Portugal**	(0) 0	5 July, Munich; 66,000
Zidane 33 (p)				

THIRD-PLACE MATCH

Germany	(0) 3	**Portugal**	(0) 1	8 July, Stuttgart; 52,000
Schweinsteiger 56, 78,		Nuno Gomes 88		
own goal 61				

Make that played six, conceded one own goal for Italy. A match that was engrossing rather than exciting for ninety minutes was pulsating in the extra half-hour – a similar pattern to the epic these two countries played out in 1970.

There is a reason extra-time was so exciting and it has every-thing to with history. Germany have never lost a World Cup penalty shoot-out, winning four. Italy were eliminated in 1990, 1994 and 1998 on penalties and it hung over them like a big old hangy thing.

So Marcello Lippi, who in every other circumstance was a typical safety-first Italian manager, did the unthinkable and told his team to throw caution to the wind. Just look at his substitu-tions: Gilardino for Toni was obvious and like for like, he had

[*] Walcott was Sven's "bold selection" as he had played little first team football at Arsenal. I had no problem with the selection, twenty-three is too many in a squad to use, so most are there just as injury cover and it seemed an idea to take the lad for experience. Some critics said it was unfair on Shaun Wright-Phillips but he had done nothing to deserve a berth and was a very similar player to Aaron Lennon.

used it already. Iaquinta for Camoranesi was a goalscorer for a box-to-box wide player, and Del Piero for Perrotta meant he had three out-and-out strikers on the pitch, plus Totti and Pirlo. Unthinkable.

Gilardino hit the post, Zambrotta smacked a twenty-yarder against the bar, Podolski forced a great save out of Buffon – it was all happening at a frantic pace considering nearly two hours had gone and it was hot. Andrea Pirlo, superb throughout, poured one last little pass inside two German defenders and Fabio Grosso slapped it home gleefully from the inside-right position. Two minutes to go in a crucial match and an Italian left-back is in the inside-right slot. The world had gone mad. Grosso did, charging around as if his heart was about to burst from his chest – echoes of Tardelli, I do love a bit of Italian machismo and pride. Two minutes later Gilardino's clever little reverse ball found Del Piero in support and he curled a terrific finish around Lehmann.

Germany had played their part and as always had confounded expectations. Klinsmann was one of the characters of the tournament, kicking every shot, throwing water bottles around and exploding with emotion at every decision, but never inappropriately. They were written off beforehand; we were told they had no world-class players except Ballack. Well Lahm, Klose and Friedrich all looked pretty classy from where I was, and Podolski, Lehmann, Mertesacker and Schneider weren't far behind.

France's win against Portugal was far easier than one goal from the penalty spot suggests. Portugal barely made a chance and seemed more interested in trying to get someone else sent off. Cristiano Ronaldo had a shocker against two full-backs who were France's weak spot.

World Cup Heroes No.33

Miroslav Klose (1978–)

Germany

I feel the same way about Miroslav Klose as I do about Paul Collingwood, the England cricketer. They are sportsmen who amount to so much more than the sum of their natural abilities.

Miroslav Klose is a Polish name. Miroslav moved to Germany to join his father when he was eight years old. He has retained his roots, despite his successful career in Germany, and has a Polish wife and bilingual children.

Klose's football career was a slow burn. He started at Hamburg and signed for Kaiserslautern, a strong but unfashionable club in 1999. He was a steady rather than spectacular goalscorer, and made his debut for Germany in 2001, just in time to make the 2002 World Cup squad. Good in the air but limited on the ground, he was cited as an example of the paucity of talent available to Germany.

A hat-trick against Saudi Arabia made people sit up and notice, but Klose faded in the latter part of the competition against better defenders. It was the 2006 World Cup in his adopted country that made critics realise here was a serious player; his partnership with another Polish-born striker Lukas Podolski, took Germany to the semi-finals when an early demise was predicted. Klose was still great in the air – he really attacks the ball – but his movement had improved enormously and he worked on his touch and his link play.

Klose shows every sign of keeping going until a fourth World Cup where he will probably be used as an impact substitute – a nice option for any manager to have the second highest scorer in World Cup history on the bench. He holds that record equally with his countryman, whose national goalscoring record he equalled in autumn 2013. Klose modestly pointed out it took him twice as many games and Müller was a far better player; he was right but it showed his common sense.

I didn't rate Klose when I saw him first in 2002, I thought him simply a punisher of bad defences, but I admire his hard work, dedication and fitness and he stands as an example that an ordinary player can, in time, become a really rather splendid one. And I think there's something rather heroic about that.

WORLD CUP FINAL No.18
9 July 2006, Olympiastadion, Berlin; 69,000

France	**(1) (1) 1** Zidane 7 (p)
Italy	**(1) (1) 1** Materazzi 19

Shoot-out:

Italy		France	
Pirlo	S 1–0	Wiltord	S 1–1
Materazzi	S 2–1	*Trezeguet*	*M 2–1*
De Rossi	S 3–1	Abidal	S 3–2
Del Piero	S 4–2	Sagnol	S 4–3
Grosso	S 5–3		

Referee: **Hector Elizondo** (Argentina)
Coaches: **Raymond Domenech** (France) & **Marcello Lippi** (Italy)

France (4–2–3–1): Fabien Barthez (Olympique de Marseille); Willy Sagnol (Bayern Munich), Lilian Thuram (Juventus), William Gallas (Chelsea), Éric Abidal (Lyon); Patrick Vieira (Juventus), Claude Makélélé (Chelsea); Franck Ribéry (Olympique de Marseille), Zinedine Zidane (Real Madrid), Florent Malouda (Lyon); Thierry Henry (Arsenal). **Subs:** Alou Diarra (Lens) 56m for Vieira; David Trezeguet (Juventus) 100m for Ribéry; Sylvain Wiltord (Lyon) 107m for Henry
Italy (4–4–1–1): Gianluigi Buffon (Juventus); Gianluca Zambrotta (Juventus), Fabio Cannavaro (Cpt, Juventus), Marco Materazzi (Internazionale), Fabio Grosso (Palermo); Mauro Camoranesi (Juventus), Gennaro Gattuso (AC Milan), Andrea Pirlo (AC Milan); Simone Perrotta (Roma); Francesco Totti (Roma); Luca Toni (Fiorentina). **Subs:** Daniele De Rossi (Roma) 61m for Perrotta; Vincenzo Iaquinta (Udinese) 61m for Totti; Alessandro del Piero (Juventus) 87m for Camoranesi
Cautioned: Zambrotta (Ita) 5m, Sagnol (Fra) 12m, Diarra ((Fra) 76m, Malouda (Fra) 111m
Dismissed: Zidane (Fra) 110m

The game itself was unremarkable. Zidane played well and was an influence on the first half, but Gattuso did enough to stop him running the game, while Vieira got himself in Pirlo's face to stop the Milanese imposing his style on affairs.

The big incidents in the game all involved Marco Materazzi. The big centre-half was not a typical Italian defender, he looked ungainly at times and was reckless in the tackle. So he was when he challenged Florent Malouda after six minutes – clear penalty. Zidane coolly chipped his kick down the middle. Italy were level soon after, Materazzi showing a positive side to his game when he thumped home a header from Pirlo's inviting free-kick. The two goals Materazzi scored in the Finals were his only international goals.

The third incident came with ten minutes to go in extra-time. The game was creeping towards penalties, and both sides seemed to have run out of ideas. Ribéry's runs had dried up and Henry had gone off exhausted; their replacements, Trezeguet and

Wiltord were not of the same calibre. Italy had replaced Totti with the abrasive De Rossi, back from a four-match suspension. It seemed a little wrong that he was able to play in the final after his assault.

With time running out Zidane and Materazzi had a little spat; it all seemed a bit of nothing until Zidane clearly head-butted the Italian defender. The incident has been over-analysed. It does not matter what Materazzi said. Not in the context of the game; if Zidane found it so unspeakable he should have raised the matter afterwards not chinned the man. So Zidane walked. Bizarrely, the next day, he was declared the player of the tournament. Even without the head-butt that decision was wrong. Zidane played well for two matches; Cannavaro was peerless for the entire competition.

France had lost a key penalty taker. The Italians all scored theirs, including Materazzi, who deserves a bit of credit here for keeping his nerve. Grosso, the semi-final match-winner, scored the last kick with his trusty left and the *Azzurri* had won the World Cup.

The win provided a bit of relief for Italian football. The tournament was played while an investigation continued against various *Serie A* clubs (including Juventus and Milan) for match-rigging; none of the World Cup squad were implicated.

World Cup Heroes No.34

Fabio Cannavaro (1973–)

Italy

Fabio Cannavaro was well thought of but not fully appreciated before the 2006 World Cup. He was there in 2002 but picked up a couple of yellow cards and missed the disaster against South Korea – probably a good career move. Four years later, with the great Paolo Maldini retired, the Juventus star was now the lynchpin of the back four alongside Nesta – or Materazzi as it transpired. It is a testimony to his quality that he adapted so comfortably to a change of partner

Cannavaro is only five foot nine, but his timing and jumping are so good it goes unnoticed. Quick, without being a whippet, and solid in the tackle, he is a centre-back you don't notice, because he doesn't do extravagant and he doesn't make conspicuous errors. You just notice that the other sides don't score many goals. Italy conceded two in this World Cup – one hapless own goal and Zidane's penalty in the final.

Cannavaro was born in Naples and started with Napoli before moving to Parma in 1995. After seven years he made his first move to one of the wealthy powerhouse clubs, Inter, and moved on to Juve two years later. Cannavaro won two *Serie A* titles at Juve, but both were scratched off after the bribery scandal which saw them forcibly relegated from *Serie A*. Cannavaro left to join the Galacticos at Real Madrid, where he finally won a league title that he could keep. He retired in 2010 after the World Cup when it became evident he no longer had the pace to compete at the very top, but played one more year in the less demanding Emirates league.

Team of the Tournament, 2006:

Buffon (Italy)
Friedrich (Germany)   Carvalho (Portugal)   Cannavaro (Italy)   Grosso (Italy)
Maxi Rodriguez (Argentina)   Pirlo (Italy)   Zidane (France)   Ribéry (France)
Klose (Germany)   Henry (France)

Subs: Schwarzer (Australia); Lahm (Germany);
Gattuso (Italy); Vieira (France); Saviola (Argentina)

The official team was expanded to a full squad of twenty-three so I haven't bothered with comparisons; it included John Terry and Luis Fifo. 'Nuff said.

Heaven Eleven No.15

Mediterranean Select (Greece, Portugal, Turkey & North Africa)

Coach:
Luiz Felipe "Big Phil" Scolari – okay, he's Brazilian, but he coached Portugal . . .

Goalkeepers:
Ricardo (Portugal): one of the best so far this century
Antonios Nikopolidids (Greece): solid goalie at Euro 2004 and beyond
Alberto da Costa Pereira (Portugal): the first great Portuguese 'keeper after the war

Defenders:
Mário Coluna (Portugal): old-style ball-playing centre-half
Fernando Couto (Portugal): mopsy-haired central defender in the '90s
Noureddine Naybet (Egypt): calm and consistent defender
Salem ben Miloud (Egypt): great full-back in the early years, played fifteen years for Marseille
Hatem Trabelsi (Tunisia): great attacking full-back around the turn of the 2000s
João Pinto (Portugal): great right-back for Porto and Portugal
Giourkos Seitaridis (Greece): neat full-back with the Euro-winning team

Midfield & Wide:
Luis Figo (Portugal): never quite as great as everyone wanted him to be
Lakhdar Belloumi (Algeria): exciting winger in their strong eighties team
António Simões (Portugal): left-winger who supplied bullets for Eusébio
Ali Fergani (Algeria): playmaker in the '70s and '80s; great passer
Jaime Graça (Portugal): creative half-back in the '60s
Mohamed Timoumi (Morocco): exciting attacking midfielder in the '80s World Cup team
Theo Zagorakis (Greece): the go-to guy for Greece for over a decade
Tugay Kerimoglu (Turkey): the creative spark in their greatest side

Forwards:
Cristiano Ronaldo (Portugal): he's very very good, you know
Eusébio (Portugal): oh, I say
Jose Torres (Portugal): towering presence in the '60s
Mimis Papoiannou (Greece): great striker with strong AEK
Athens side in '70s
Lefter Küçükandonyadis (Turkey): first great Turkish player
in the '50s, and I refuse to pick the vastly over-rated Şükür

Likely first XI:

Da Costa

Joao Pinto   Couto   Coluna   Miloud

Zagorakis   Tugay

Belloumi   Ronaldo   Simões

Eusébio

8.4 WORLD CUP 2010

The venue for the 2010 Finals was a cert to be in Africa, in line with a FIFA policy, since revised, of rotating the hosting amongst the continental bodies. The final vote was effectively between South Africa and Morocco, as Egypt polled no votes even though their bid was never officially withdrawn. South Africa had been unlucky in losing out to Germany for the 2006 tournament, but Morocco had bid to hold the tournament on a number of occasions and lost out, so both had a strong case.

FIFA were taking a risk whichever country won. The structure for domestic football and the general transport and support infrastructure in Africa was less well established and less stable than in other parts of the world. South Africa had a handful of ready-made Rugby Union grounds and some residual wealth to fall back on, while Morocco, like most North African nations, had a better-attended domestic competition, and was prepared to invest in new stadia and use the tournament to promote itself as a tourist destination and new economy. South Africa won the final vote by fourteen votes to ten. There were murmurings throughout the preparation that the stadia wouldn't be fit for purpose and the infrastructure would not sustain a tournament of this magnitude. The South Africans bent their backs in the final stretch and delivered a tournament that was no paradigm of efficiency, but equally was not the disaster many predicted.

There were few major surprises amongst the qualifiers; the inclusion of thirty-two teams meant the chances of one of the big nations coming a cropper in qualification were significantly decreased. In Africa four out of the five top-ranked teams made the Finals. Ghana, Ivory Coast and Cameroon won their final qualifying group with something to spare, Nigeria theirs by a squeak. Nigeria were two points adrift of Tunisia with one match to go, and after eighty minutes of the last round the Super Eagles were level at 2–2 with Kenya in Nairobi while Tunisia were at 0–0 in Mozambique. A winner for Nigeria from Obafemi Martins and Dário's goal for Mozambique decided the issue firmly in Nigeria's favour.

Group C of the final round of African qualification was one of the most controversial in World Cup history. Egypt needed to beat their neighbours Algeria by two goals to equal their record in the group; if they won 2–0 the teams would finish with identical points and goal difference and a play-off would be needed.

Algeria arrived in Cairo two days before the game, and their bus was stoned on the way to the hotel; Algeria protested vehemently and the Egyptian press responded with accusations that much of the damage to the bus was caused by the Algerians, who were trying to escalate the significance of the incident. The game went ahead, with FIFA asking the Egyptians to guarantee the safety of the Algerian players and supporters. An early goal gave Egypt momentum, but the second, crucial goal came only after the South African referee allowed over five minutes of injury-time. In the referee's defence Algeria had indulged in some cynical time-wasting so were hoist by their own petard. There were riots in both capitals after the match with many injuries and an awful lot of damage, and nearly 500 Algerians were arrested during disturbances in Marseilles, France.

The play-off took place in Omdurman, Northern Sudan. The neutral venue was requested by Egypt, but despite this the locals favoured Algeria and it was the Egyptian FA's turn to cry foul about the hostility shown towards their team before the match. The game itself was less interesting; a tense affair ended 1–0 in Algeria's favour after Antar Yahia's fortieth-minute goal. Recriminations and disturbances followed after the game, with statements and interventions from President Bouteflika of Algeria and President Mubarak of Egypt. Sixteen months later both Presidents were under pressure after the disturbances of the so-called Arab Spring of 2011; Bouteflika survived and remains

2010
SOUTH AFRICA

After a few traumas (and a couple of strikes) South Africa came up with ten grounds fit for purpose for the 2010 finals.

Johannesburg: First National Bank Stadium & Ellis Park
The FNB in Soweto is the main football stadium in South Africa and hosted ten games in the Finals, including the Final itself. The stadium is often referred to as Soccer City; it holds over 90,000 but the paying capacity for the World Cup was around 85,000.

Ellis Park was primarily a rugby union ground before the 2010 finals, and it hosted the 1995 Rugby World Cup Final won by South Africa in front of President Mandela. It now plays home to the Orlando Pirates as well as regional rugby sides and the Springboks.

Pretoria: Loftus Versfeld Stadium
To the north of Johannesburg lies Pretoria, and the old Blue Bulls rugby stadium, the Loftus Versfeld. The ground hosted six games during the 2010 Finals, but never reached its 50,000 capacity. It is the home ground of the Mamelodi Sundowns.

Go west and you reach **Rustenberg**; in **Phokeng** nearby is the sports stadium run by the local tribal authority, the **Royal Bafokeng** Nation. The stadium hosted six games including England's opener against the USA.

East of Pretoria lies **Nelspruit** and the built-for-purpose **Mbombela Stadium**, used for four group matches. The ground's 40,000 capacity is hardly ever satisfied.

Polokwane is in the north of the country in Limpopo province and the **Peter Mokaba** Stadium is one of five brand new stadia built for 2010. It is now the home to the Black Leopards soccer team, but the 40,000 seater ground is rarely filled.

Bloemfontein is the capital of Free State in the centre of South Africa. **The Free State** Stadium was built for the 1995 Rugby World Cup and witnessed England's humiliating defeat by Germany in the second round.

Another purpose-built stadium, the **Moses Madhiba Stadium**, was located in **Durban** (Kwa-Zulu Natal) over on the east coast of the country. The games in Durban were among the best attended with the ground nearly reaching its 62,000 capacity for all six matches, which included the Spain versus Germany semi-final.

In the far south-west wealthy **Cape Town** built itself a brand new football ground on the site of the old Green Point Stadium. **The Cape Town Stadium** hosted eight matches including one in each knockout stage up to the semi-finals. The city uses the ground for its local team, Ajax Cape Town, and for some huge rock concerts.

Along the coast in Port Elizabeth another new stadium sprung up, the **Nelson Mandela Bay Stadium**, which now houses the Southern Kings super rugby franchise as well as hosting concerts and events.

in office, but Mubarak was forced to stand down and face trial by the administration that replaced his government.

In Asia, North and South Korea managed to play each other twice without triggering a diplomatic incident, and both qualified for the Finals, as, predictably, did Japan and Australia. Saudi Arabia suffered some tough luck; they were pipped in their final group on goal difference by North Korea, and then beaten over two legs by Bahrain for the right to play the Oceania winners, New Zealand. There was only one goal in three hours of football between Bahrain and New Zealand and it came from Plymouth Argyle's Rory Fallon for the Kiwis.

The United States and Mexico qualified in the CONCACAF section, and Costa Rica were set to join them until four minutes into injury-time in their last match in Washington, DC. Jonathon Bornstein's late equaliser for the Americans meant two first-half goals from Bryan Ruiz were in vain and Honduras's win in El Salvador meant they sneaked past Costa Rica on goal difference.

This setback condemned Costa Rica to a play-off against Uruguay, fifth in the South American round robin. A good away win for Uruguay was followed by a 1–1 draw in a foggy Montevideo; Costa Rica protested but the better team qualified.

The battle for the last couple of places in the CONMEBOL section was complicated. From around the midway point (it's a long drawn-out affair in South America, each team play eighteen matches) three teams, Brazil, Chile and Paraguay, pulled away from the rest. Argentina, comfortable at halfway, were in trouble after a humiliating 6–1 defeat away to Bolivia and three consecutive defeats to Ecuador, Brazil and Paraguay. With two games to go qualification was on a knife-edge; Ecuador were a point ahead and Venezuela, Uruguay and Colombia in close attendance. Maradona's selections were becoming increasingly bizarre and paranoid, and he was ridiculed at home and abroad when he selected the thirty-six-year-old Boca Juniors striker Martin Palermo in his squad for the game against Peru. When Peru scored with a minute to go to make the game 1–1 Argentina looked shot, but Palermo's last-gasp winner and defeats for Venezuela, Colombia and Ecuador gave them a reprieve.

Maradona's extraordinary rant to the media seemed to imply that they should trust in his genius and that his decision to pick Palermo was utterly vindicated. Actually they had scraped a win against the bottom team in the group and the decision to select Palermo ahead of Tévez or Agüero was borderline insane. Uruguay had won late as well, Forlán's injury-time penalty giving them a 2–1 win in Quito against Ecuador.

Effectively Uruguay versus Argentina in Montevideo was a showdown for the last qualifying spot. The game was predictably rough, and Argentina needed another late goal from a controversial selection, Mario Bolatti, on loan at Huracán, as well as two red cards for their opponents, also both late in the game. Uruguay survived to fight another day; Argentina qualified despite having no idea who should be in their best eleven, and no idea how to get the most out of the world's best player, Lionel Messi.

In Europe five of the top teams qualified without any fuss. Spain and Holland won every match, Germany and Italy were unbeaten and England lost in the Ukraine but won all their other nine matches, including a very satisfying 4–1 away win in Zagreb over Croatia, the team that denied them a place in the 2008 European Championship Finals. The game saw the emergence of Theo Walcott, who scored a hat-trick, as a potential superstar. Sadly we're still talking about what Walcott could achieve rather than celebrating a superstar. Wayne Rooney, too, was playing like a genuine top-class international striker, and scored nine goals in qualifying.

In two of these strong groups Wales and Scotland barely flickered, winning games only against low-ranked sides and playing no part in the shake-up. Ireland did better, finishing second to Italy without losing a game, but they too had cause for concern, beating only Cyprus and Georgia and failing to score in two matches against Montenegro.

Greece's win at Euro 2004 earned them a seeded place and an absurd group containing only Switzerland as a genuine threat. Switzerland started really badly, surrendering a two-goal lead away to Israel and then losing calamitously at home to Luxembourg. This was only Luxembourg's third-ever win in a

World Cup qualifier, their first for thirty-five years and their first away from home. It was a rotten start for new coach Ottmar Hitzfeld, dual Champions League winner with Borussia Dortmund and Bayern Munich, but he soon whipped them into shape and home and away wins against Greece were enough for them to top the group and send the Greeks to the play-offs.

In Group 1, a tough section, Denmark started well and just about held on. A goal from Jakob Poulsen in a 1–0 win over Sweden in Copenhagen was crucial for the Danes, while a home draw with Albania cost Portugal and meant they would have to try again in the play-offs. Drawing games they ought to have won consigned France to the same fate. They took four points off Serbia but lost in Vienna and drew twice with Romania; the Serbs could afford to lose their last match in Lithuania and still top the group.

The Czech Republic were grouped with their former state-mates Slovakia, Slovenia and Poland, with Northern Ireland and San Marino along for the ride. In the event Northern Ireland did rather well and were in contention until a home defeat to Slovakia. The Czechs and the Poles looked a shadow of earlier teams and it was Slovakia and Slovenia who slugged it out for top spot. Slovenia beat their rivals home and away but their away form was ordinary and a win in Chorzów, Poland in their final game clinched a first Finals spot for Slovakia.

In the play-offs Portugal had the easiest passage, beating Bosnia-Herzegovina 1–0 home and away, while Greece sneaked a win in Ukraine after being held at home. It was a typically obdurate defensive performance and a goal by the Panathinaikos winger Salpingidis was enough.

Russia looked in control of their tie against Slovenia after two goals from Everton's Dimitar Bilyaletdinov gave them a two-goal cushion, but a late goal from Pecnik suddenly made the second tie much trickier. Zlatko Dedic's goal in the second leg put a strong Russian side out and ended Guus Hiddink's run of taking teams to the Finals. It was a disappointing end to his tenure; the Russians looked a gifted side in the 2008 European Championships where they reached the semi-finals.

The most controversial tie was the one between Ireland and France. It was a tough draw for Ireland; France were the strongest of the sides in the play-offs, and when Nicolas Anelka's goal gave them a win in Dublin it looked like the end of the road for Trappatoni's Ireland team. A good Robbie Keane finish (what will they do for goals when he finally quits?) and a stubborn rear-guard performance orchestrated by Richard Dunne took the tie into extra-time in Paris. Ireland looked the likelier winners until a piece of uncharacteristic chicanery from Thierry Henry turned the game. Henry kept a bouncing ball in play on the wing with his hand and ran on to cross to an unmarked William Gallas. It was cruel on Ireland and left a sour taste, and it tarnished Henry's image in the British Isles irreparably, but it wasn't worthy of the yards of print it was afforded in the British and Irish media.

Favourites? Spain, unquestionably, with Holland looking the next best of the European sides. Of the South American qualifiers Argentina had the most talent, but also the indeterminable Maradona factor – would he be an inspiration or a hindrance? Brazil can never be discounted at a World Cup, and some whispered about how strong Ghana and the Ivory Coast looked in qualification.

GROUP A

South Africa Tshabalal 55	(0) 1	**Mexico** Márquez 79	(0) 1	10 FNB, Jo'burg; 84,490
Uruguay	(0) 0	**France**	(0) 0	11 June, Cape Town; 64,100
South Africa	(0) 0	**Uruguay** Forlán 24, 80 (p), A Pereira 90	(1) 3	16 June, Pretoria; 42,658
France	(0) 0	**Mexico** Hernández 64, Blanco 79 (p)	(0) 2	17 June, Polokwane; 35,370
South Africa Khumalo 20, Mphela 37	(2) 2	**France** Malouda 79	(0) 1	22 June, Bloemfontein; 39,415
Mexico	(0) 0	**Uruguay** Suárez 43	(1) 1	22 June Rustenberg, 33,425

1. Uruguay 7pts (4–0); 2. Mexico 4pts (3–2); 3. South Africa 4pts (3–5); 4. France 1pt (1–4)

South Africa were realistic about their chances, they knew they were not a good side, but being drawn with an out-of-sorts French side who were lucky to be there, a Uruguay team that also scraped through qualifying and perennial also-rans Mexico gave some cause for hope.

The first two games were drawn, one a reasonably open game that saw Mexico's captain Marquez cancel out Tshabalala's excellent strike from a lethal South African break. The other match was a dull affair that saw Uruguay comfortably hold an unimaginative French team, despite going down to ten men for the last ten minutes. The games introduced the watching TV audiences to the vuvuzela, a cheap African instrument that produces a sound not dissimilar to a comb and paper, for those old enough to remember granddad's idea of Christmas entertainment. A couple of thousand of these plastic horns produced a migraine-inducing buzz around the stadium. I think I preferred the Mexican wave.

France's next performance was even worse. The game was even, but France lacked any sort of finishing touch, and Mexico scored when Javier Hernández (known by his nickname Chicharito at Manchester United) ran clear of a flat French back line and rounded the 'keeper. Eric Abidal's suicidal tackle gave away a penalty for Mexico's second.

Uruguay, with a tough defence and two effective strikers in the slippery Ajax goalscorer Suárez and the hard-working Diego Forlán, were improving with every game and qualified as group winners after a goal from Suárez saw off Mexico. The reward of a tie against South Korea rather than Argentina was a good incentive.

WORLD CUP SHOCK No.14
22 June 2010, Free State Stadium, Bloemfontein; 39,415

France	(0) 1	Malouda 79
South Africa	(2) 2	Khumalo 20, Mphela 37

Referee: **Oscar Ruiz** (Colombia)
Coaches: **Raymond Domenech** (France) & **Carlos Alberto Parreira** (South Africa)

France (4–3–3): Hugo Lloris (Lyon); Bacary Sagna (Arsenal), William Gallas (Tottenham), Sébastien Squillaci (Arsenal), Gael Clichy (Arsenal); Alou Diarra (Cpt, Bordeaux), Yoann Gourcuff (Lyon), Abou Diaby (Arsenal); André-Pierre Gignac (Marseille), Djibril Cissé (Panathinaikos), Franck Ribéry (Bayern Munich). **Subs:** Florent Malouda (Chelsea) 46m for Gignac; Thierry Henry (Barcelona) 55m for Cissé; Sidney Govou (Lyon) 82m for Diarra
South Africa (4–4–2): Moeneeb Josephs (Orlando Pirates); Anele Ngcongca (Racing Genk), Aaron Mokoena (Cpt, Portsmouth), Bongani Khumalo (Supersport United), Tsepo Masilela

(Maccabi Haifa); Steven Pienaar (Everton), MacBeth Sibaya (Rubin Kazan), Thanduyise Khuboni (Golden Arrows), Siphiwe Tashabalala (Kaizer Chiefs); Katlego Mphela (Mamelodi Sundowns), Bernard Parker (Twente Enschede). **Subs:** Siboniso Gaxa (Mamelodi Sundowns) 55m for Ngcongca; Siyabonga Nomvethe (Moroka Swallows) 68m for Parker; Teko Modise (Orlando Pirates) 78m for Khuboni
Cautions: Diaby (Fra) 71m
Dismissed: Gourcuff (Fra) 25m

The Mexico game had huge repercussions for the French squad. A row between coach Domenech and Nicolas Anelka led to the striker's expulsion from the squad and a player boycott in protest. The boycott was settled but captain Patrice Evra, one of the ringleaders of the protest, was left out of the final game. Domenech also dropped Abidal, Toulalan, Govou and Malouda from his starting line-up, though these omissions were more down to under-performance in the earlier games. French fans looked at the starting eleven and feared the worst. In front of goalkeeper Lloris was the ageing Gallas surrounded by a defence that had collectively failed at Arsenal in the previous twelve months. At the other end was Djibril Cissé, a nomadic trouble-maker of debatable temperament and fitful quality. Only an on-form Franck Ribéry offered any real threat, and the tournament had not seen Ribéry's best so far. South Africa would look to pressure France in midfield, where they had some meaty performers, even without the injured Dikgacoi.

South Africa pressed forward from the start, sensing the discomfort of their opponents, and Tshabalala and Pienaar caused problems down the flanks for the French defence. They deserved their lead, which came from a corner that Hugo Lloris came for and missed, the ball bouncing into the net off Khumalo's shoulder.

A few minutes later France suffered some genuine bad luck when an aerial challenge between Gourcuff and Sibaya resulted in a red card for the Frenchman. Sure, Gourcuff's arm was raised, but there was absolutely no intent to hurt and had the same foul been committed in the other game between Uruguay and Mexico the Colombian referee would not have shown the red card. It got worse for France six minutes later. A quick break from South Africa saw Tshabalala in space down the left side of the French area but he scuffed his shot. Diaby made a dog's dinner of his attempted clearance and Parker was able to put the ball back across goal where Mphela just managed to force it past the scrambling Clichy.

With Uruguay ahead against Mexico, South Africa pressed hard at the start of the second half, knowing another goal or two could see them qualify. Mphela was unlucky twice; his first-time shot from Tshabalala's well-timed through ball clipped the wrong side of the bar, and a powerful drive from outside the area was tipped away athletically by Lloris. As South Africa got over-eager, France began to create the odd chance on the break, and when Henry, who should have played from the start, played in Ribéry, the Bayern winger squared unselfishly for Malouda to tap home. The goal did nothing for France's cause but it made sure South Africa went out too. They became the first home nation to fail to make it out of the group stage, but they went out on a high note after a campaign that exceeded low expectations.

Not so France. The best thing about their campaign was the really cool font used to spell "Lloris" on the goalkeeper's jersey. It was the end of Domenech's damaging and unpopular reign, and former captain Laurent Blanc was brought in to heal the wounds. France have steadied and improved since 2010, but don't look ready to win another international tournament any time soon. They face a play-off even to qualify for the 2014 Finals; South Africa already know they won't be in Brazil.

GROUP B

Argentina	(1) 1	**Nigeria**	(0) 0	12 June, Ellis Park, Jo'burg; 55,686
Heinze 6				
South Korea	(1) 2	**Greece**	(0) 0	12 June, Port Elizabeth; 31,513
Lee Jung-soo 7, Park Ji-sung 52				
Argentina	(2) 4	**South Korea**	(1) 1	17 June, FNB, Jo'burg; 82,174
Own goal 17, Higuaín 33, 76, 80		Lee Chung-yong 45		
Greece	(1) 2	**Nigeria**	(1) 1	17 June, Bloemfontein; 31,593
Salpingidis 44,		Uche 16		
Torosidis 71				
Argentina	(0) 2	**Greece**	(0) 0	22 June, Polokwane; 38,891
Demichelis 77, Palermo 89				
Nigeria	(1) 2	**South Korea**	(1) 2	22 June, Durban; 61,874
Uche 12, Yakubu 69 (p)		Lee Jung-soo 34		
		Park Chu-young 49		

1. **Argentina 9pts (7–1); 2. South Korea 4pts (5–6); 3. Greece 3pts (2–5); 4. Nigeria 1pt (3–5)**

Both Nigeria and Greece were poor and made progress far too easy for Maradona's Argentina and the Koreans. Argentina, brimful of talent and with their best players in the side at last, looked a great attacking side, but no one asked enough questions of their suspect defence – three around the thirty mark and Newcastle's Gutiérrez playing out of position at right-back. Greece had done amazing things at the 2004 European Championships but Rehhagel's stifling tactics were no longer a novelty; two shots on target against a poor defensive unit like South Korea tells its own story.

GROUP C

USA	(1) 1	**England**	(1) 1	12 June, Rustenberg; 38,646	
Dempsey 40		Gerrard 4			
Algeria	(0) 0	**Slovenia**	(0) 1	13 June, Polokwane; 30,325	
		Koren 79			
England	(0) 0	**Algeria**	(0) 0	18 June, Cape Town; 64,100	
Slovenia	(2) 2	**USA**	(0) 2	18 June, Ellis Park, Jo'burg; 45,573	
Birsa 13, Ljubijankic 42		Donovan 49, Bradley 82			
England	(1) 1	**Slovenia**	(0) 0	23 June, Port Elizabeth; 36,893	
Defoe 22					
USA	(0) 1	**Algeria**	(0) 0	23 June, Pretoria; 35,827	
Donovan 90					

1. **United States** 5pts (4–3); 2. **England** 5pts (2–1); 3. **Slovenia** 4pts (3–3); 4. **Algeria** 1pt (0–2)

Numbingly dull. Algeria were even more defensive than Greece, while the other three, including Capello's England side, were sterile and unimaginative. England were the better side for much of the first match against the USA and Gerrard's early goal would probably have been enough but for Rob Green's calamitous error which saw Clint Dempsey's shot slip through his gloves and into the net. A bona fide sleepless night's howler; he made a good save from Altidore in the second half but he was dropped for the next game and seems never to have fully recovered his confidence.

The USA did well to recover from 2–0 down to earn a point against Slovenia, but looked blunt in their last game against Algeria, needing an injury-time goal from Landon Donovan for the win which saw them top the group. England, after a desperate draw against Algeria, needed a win against Slovenia. Jermain

Defoe's twenty-second-minute goal should have settled them, but this was an England shorn of spark and confidence and they stumbled over the line in second place to face the winner of one of the toughest groups.

GROUP D

Germany Podolski 8, Klose 26, Müller 68, Cacau 70	(2) 4	**Australia**	(0) 0	13 June, Durban; 62,660
Ghana Gyan 84 (p)	(0) 1	**Serbia**	(0) 0	13 June, Pretoria; 38,833
Serbia Jovanovic 38	(1) 1	**Germany**	(0) 0	18 June, Port Elizabeth; 38,294
Australia Holman 11	(1) 1	**Ghana** Gyan 25 (p)	(1) 1	19 June, Rustenberg; 34,812
Serbia Pantelic 84	(0) 1	**Australia** Cahill 69, Holman 73	(0) 2	23 June, Nelspruit; 37,836
Ghana	(0) 0	**Germany** Özil 60	(0) 1	23 June, FNB, Jo'burg; 83,391

1. Germany 6pts (5–1); 2. Ghana 4pts (2–2); 3. Australia 4pts (3–6); 4. Serbia 3pts (2–3)

After a scintillating opening performance against Australia (4–0 flattered the losers not the Germans) Germany came down to earth in their second game against Serbia. The referee played a part, sending off Miroslav Klose for two inconsequential challenges and generally ruining what could have been an entertaining game, with Serbia much improved after a listless display in defeat by Ghana. Germany conceded a minute later, still shell-shocked, but recovered well to threaten an equaliser in the second half; an equaliser they would have got had Lukas Podolski put away a penalty after Vidic senselessly handled.

Australia were not as disciplined as in 2006 and were lucky to get both their first point after being outplayed by Ghana, and their first win, in their last match against Serbia. The officials missed a clear handball by Tim Cahill that would have salvaged a point for Serbia and seen them through. Instead Ghana, despite losing their last match, went through along with Germany. They deserve enormous credit; many felt that the loss of Michel Essien, their powerful midfield enforcer would leave them struggling in a strong group. That last match threw up a quirky statistic when German full-back Jérôme Boateng found himself facing his brother Kevin-Prince Boateng, who opted to play for the country of their parents' birth, Ghana.

GROUP E

Holland Own goal 46, Kuyt 85	(0) 2	**Denmark**	(0) 0	14 June, FNB, Jo'burg; 83,465
Cameroon	(0) 0	**Japan** Honda 39	(1) 1	14 June, Bloemfontein; 30,620
Denmark Bendtner 33, Rommedahl 61	(1) 2	**Cameroon** Eto'o 10	(1) 1	19 June, Pretoria; 38,074
Japan	(0) 0	**Holland** Sneijder 53	(0) 1	19 June, Durban; 62,010
Holland Van Persie 36, Huntelaar 83	(1) 2	**Cameroon** Eto'o 65 (p)	(0) 1	24 June, Cape Town; 63,093
Denmark Tomasson 81	(0) 1	**Japan** Honda 17, Endo 30, Okazaki 87	(2) 3	24 June, Rustenburg; 27,967

1. **Holland** 9pts (5–1); 2. **Japan** 6pts (4–2); 3. **Denmark** 3pts (3–6); 4. **Cameroon** 0pts (2–5)

Denmark had not finished their qualifying group in particularly convincing form and they continued that streak here. In their opening game against Holland they conceded a freak own goal when Simon Poulsen's clearing header rebounded into the goal off Daniel Agger's back, and Holland were completely in control thereafter.

In the second round of games, Cameroon, disappointing against Japan, pushed Denmark onto the back foot for the opening half-hour and took a deserved lead, but they were undone by the enduring speed of Danish winger Dennis Rommedahl. First Rommedahl took down a sweet pass from Simon Kjaer, beat his man and laid the ball on a plate for Nicklas Bendtner, then in the second half he left Makoun for dead and fired across Hamidou for the winner.

Alas for Denmark this brief resurgence of form deserted them in the deciding game against Japan – Holland were already through and Cameroon already out. Two superb free-kicks from Honda and Endo left Denmark with a mountain to climb. They were unequal to the task, especially with key man Jan Dahl Tomasson, so excellent in previous major tournaments, seriously out of sorts. His late goal came only after he followed up his own penalty miss, and Japan soon confirmed their superiority by restoring their two-goal cushion. It was Japan's best performance in a World Cup Finals match and they deservedly joined the Dutch in the second phase. It was a sorry end for Tomasson, a selfless team player under-rated outside his own country (and Milan) who retired after 112 matches and fifty-two goals for his country.

The Dutch had put their marker down, without ever hitting top gear.

GROUP F

Italy De Rossi 63	(0) 1	**Paraguay** Alcarez 39	(1) 1	14 June, Cape Town; 62,869
Slovakia Vittek 50	(0) 1	**New Zealand** Reid 90	(0) 1	15 June, Rustenberg 23,871
New Zealand Smeltz 7	(1) 1	**Italy** Iaquinta 29 (p)	(1) 1	20 June, Nelspruit; 38,229
Paraguay Vera 27, Riveros 89	(1) 2	**Slovakia**	(0) 0	20 June, Bloemfontein; 26,643
New Zealand	(0) 0	**Paraguay**	(0) 0	24 June, Polokwane; 34,850
Slovakia Vittek 23, 73, Kopunek 89	(1) 3	**Italy** Di Natale 81, Quagliarella 90	(0) 2	24 June, Ellis Park, Jo'bur;, 53,412

1. **Paraguay 5pts (3–1); 2. Slovakia 4pts (4–5); 3. New Zealand 3pts (2–2); 4. Italy 2pts (4–5)**

Not unusually, a group involving Italy featured four drawn games and few goals until the last match. More unusually it wasn't the Italians who sneaked through without ever playing well.

Italy started unconvincingly with a draw against Paraguay courtesy of a bad error by Villar, the Paraguayan goalkeeper (and captain). The South Americans had taken the lead with a powerful header from Antolin Alcaraz, soon bound for Wigan Athletic from Bruges. Still, no damage was done to Italy as the two weaker looking sides in the group, New Zealand and Slovakia also drew, when Winston Reid salvaged a dramatic injury-time point for New Zealand. It was the Kiwis first point in the World Cup Finals, having lost all three ties in 1974.

That Italy's problems were actually quite acute was shown in their next match against the All Whites of New Zealand. Fabio

Cannavaro no longer looked the massive imperturbable presence of 2006 and when Reid won another set piece the Italian captain could only parry the ball to Shane Smeltz, who gleefully knocked it into the net. Italy huffed and puffed but they couldn't blow the New Zealand house down. They equalised from a debatable penalty and almost conceded a late winner when eighteen-year-old Chris Wood put a late chance just the wrong side of the post. Marcello Lippi, Italy's coach, muttered about possession and chances but that's always a veil, isn't it? Only goals count in football. What was very clear was that Italy missed the injured Andrea Pirlo.

Pirlo still wasn't fit for the deciding game against Slovakia, and nor was first-choice goalkeeper, injured in the opener against Paraguay. Slovakia's playmaker, Marek Hamsik, who played for Napoli in Italy, had been quiet so far, but had his best game against his adopted home. In the first half Hamsik's promptings tested the Italians, who started with their usual caution, and it was no surprise when Slovakia took the lead. De Rossi's woeful pass found Kucka and the midfielder's clever first-time ball found Robert Vittek, a reserve striker at Lille with the lean look of a gangland hit-man. Vittek turned and drove the ball low past Marchetti; a knife between the ribs of Italy's campaign.

Lippi made changes but it was Slovakia who scored a second, Vittek beating Chiellini to Hamsik's cross to convert at the near post. Chiellini and Cannavaro were supposed to be the bedrock of the Italian campaign but they proved something of a liability against mobile forwards – Cannavaro was lucky to stay on the pitch here after a second clumsy tackle on Hamsik went unpunished by the lenient referee. A lesser name would have walked.

Italy went for all out attack, relying on long raking passes from a half-fit Pirlo and it nearly earned them a last-ditch reprieve. Di Natale scored after Mucha saved well from Quagliarella with ten minutes left and Quagliarella put the ball in the net only for a marginal offside decision to thwart the Azzurri. As Italy pressed Slovakia won a throw-in, the centre-backs hesitated one last time and Kopanek ran clear to lob the ball over Marchetti. I can't help feeling Buffon would have anticipated the danger and beaten Kopanek to the ball. Quagliarella scored another with a delicious chip to set up a grand finale and Pepe might have done better with a far-post volley when he cleverly backed off a crammed penalty area, but it wasn't Italy's day. They only started to play when they were all but eliminated, and desperately needed a new striker or two and some pace at the back. Out in the groups, like France in 2002, was not what the holders had anticipated.

GROUP G

Brazil	**(0) 2**	**North Korea**	**(0) 1**	15 June, Ellis Park, Jo'burg; 54,331
Maicon 55, Elano 72		Ji Yun-nam 89		
Portugal	**(0) 0**	**Ivory Coast**	**(0) 0**	15 June, Port Elizabeth; 37,430
Ivory Coast	**(0) 1**	**Brazil**	**(1) 3**	20 June, FNB, Jo'burg; 84,455
Drogba 79		Luis Fabiano 25, 50, Elano 62		
North Korea	**(0) 0**	**Portugal**	**(1) 7**	20 June, Bloemfontein; 26,643
		Raul Meireles 29, Simão 53 Almeida 56, Tiago 60, 89, Liedson 81, Ronaldo 87		
Ivory Coast	**(2) 3**	**North Korea**	**(0) 0**	24 June, Polokwane; 34,850
Y Touré 14, Romaric 20, Kalou 82				
Portugal	**(0)**	**Brazil**	**(0) 0**	24 June, Ellis Park, Jo'burg; 53,412

1. **Brazil 7pts (5–2); 2. Portugal 5pts (7–0); 3. Ivory Coast 4pts (4–3); 4. North Korea 0pts (1–12)**

Ivory Coast were desperately unlucky with the draw in 2006 and it did them no favours again here. North Korea were the lowest ranked team in the competition, but they also faced Brazil and the best team in the fourth pot in the draw, Portugal.

Brazil struggled in their opener. Maicon's fierce drive from an impossible angle gave them a lead and Robinho's pass for Elano to score the second was a blissful. Maicon's goal was hailed in typical hyperbolic press style as a piece of Brazilian magic; it was a bit of hit and hope that beat a badly positioned goalkeeper. The other group opener in Port Elizabeth had been billed from way back by the UK press as Drogba versus Ronaldo, but Drogba's broken arm, suffered just before the tournament, put paid to that.

Under Sven-Göran Eriksson's care the Ivorians were cautious without their talisman, but they kept their shape and the full-back Demel and Tiéné did well to subdue Ronaldo. Drogba, popular across the continent apparently, came on to a huge welcome but was clearly feeling his way.

Drogba returned against Brazil but was well policed by the impressive Lucio – his goal was little more than a consolation. Brazil were better but less than brilliant, Luis Fabiano's cleverly worked opening goal aside. Over in Cape Town Portugal ran riot, putting seven past North Korea – the only surprise was that Ronaldo scored only once, he is a notorious punisher of second-rate defending.

The last two games were uneventful; Ivory Coast were always going to beat North Korea – who knows what opprobrium awaited the hapless outsiders back home – and Portugal and Brazil were always likely to play out a dull draw and ensure they both safely progressed.

GROUP H

Honduras	(0) 0	**Chile**	(1) 1	16 June, Nelspruit; 32,664
		Beausejour 34		
Switzerland	(0) 1	**Spain**	(0) 0	16 June, Durban; 62,453
Gelson Fernandes 52				
Chile	(0) 1	**Switzerland** (0) 0		21 June, Port Elizabeth; 34,872
Gonzalez 75				
Spain	(1) 2	**Honduras**	(0) 0	21 June, Ellis Park, Jo'burg; 54,386
Villa 17, 51				
Chile	(0) 1	**Spain**	(2) 2	25 June, Pretoria; 41,958
Millar 47		Villa 24, Iniesta 37		
Switzerland	(0) 0	**Honduras**	(0) 0	25 June, Bloemfontein; 28,042

1. Spain 6pts (4–2); 2. Chile 6pts (3–2); 3. Switzerland 4pts (1–1); 4. Honduras 1pt (0–3)

The favourites were in the bottom group and started in the worst possible way by losing to Switzerland. Hitzfeld was a canny coach and the Swiss played Spain in the only way it is possible for a disciplined but limited side to play against such an array of talent: defensively, in a disciplined but limited way.

I have never understood why it is considered such poor form for a lesser team to adopt a defensive style against a side with clearly superior firepower. It was the same when Chelsea beat Barcelona in the Champions League in 2012, or when one of the smaller Premiership teams had the audacity to beat Wenger's Arsenal in their pomp. The press (and dear old Arsène) would tell us how bad this was for football and how football should be played the "proper" way. There is no proper way. There is good to watch and boring to watch, but both are legitimate and permissible, and Chelsea and Switzerland weren't Wimbledon, they just chose to cede possession in certain areas of the pitch, fully aware that a significant weakness of both Barcelona and Spain is a tendency to overplay when faced with a massed defence.

In Spain's next two games David Villa exploded into life and provided the rapier tip to go with the fancy bladework. He produced a stunning finish to a fine move for the opener, added a second with a deflected shot and missed out on a hat-trick when he put a penalty wide. Honduras just looked bewildered, they didn't have the tactical nous or the players to counter the Spanish movement and passing.

Villa scored again against Chile, sending a poor clearance by Chile's goalkeeper Bravo back over his head from forty yards. A great team goal from Iniesta gave Spain what seemed a decent cushion, especially when the Mexican referee sent off Chile's Marco Estrada for an innocuous challenge. Chile had matched Spain in the quality of their passing in the first half and they responded bravely and pulled a goal back just after half-time. Chasing the game with ten men against a side so comfortable in possession was tough, and the game petered out in the last twenty minutes.

Switzerland needed a two-goal win against Honduras to ensure their place in the last sixteen, but they were less adept at breaking down stubborn defences than in forming them, and it was Honduras who missed a couple of glorious chances towards the end of a poor match. Both qualifiers would renew old rivalries in the next round, Chile with Brazil and Spain with their neighbours Portugal.

SECOND ROUND

Uruguay	**(1) 2**	**South Korea**	**(0) 1**	26 June, Port Elizabeth; 30,597
Suárez 8, 80		Lee Chung-yong 68		
USA	**(0) (1) 1**	**Ghana**	**(1) (1) 2**	26 June, Rustenberg; 34,976
Donovan 62 (p)		Boateng 5, Gyan 93		
Germany	**(2) 4**	**England**	**(1) 1**	27 June, FNB, Jo'burg; 84,377
Klose 20, Podolski 32,		Upson 37		
Müller 67, 70				
Argentina	**(2) 3**	**Mexico**	**(0) 1**	27 June, Bloemfontein; 40,510
Tévez 26, 52,		Hernández 71		
Higuaín 33				
Holland	**(1) 2**	**Slovakia**	**(0) 1**	28 June, Ellis Park, Jo'burg; 54,096
Robben 18, Sneijder 84		Vittek 90		
Brazil	**(2) 3**	**Chile**	**(0) 0**	28 June, Durban; 61,962
Juan 34, Luís Fabiano 38,				
Robinho 59				
Paraguay	**(0) (0) 0**	**Japan**	**(0) (0) 0**	29 June, Pretoria; 36,742
Paraguay won 5–3 on penalties				
Spain	**(0) 1**	**Portugal**	**(0) 0**	29 June, Cape Town; 62,955
Villa 63				

Every one of the quarter-finals was won by the team expected to win the match, with the possible exception of the USA versus Ghana, where many people expected a vastly over-rated American team to prevail.

Uruguay prevailed against South Korea in the teeming rain through a combination of obdurate defending and a brilliant winning goal from Luis Suárez. After Lee Chung-yong equalised the opener from Suárez, the Koreans had a spell of intense pressure and the Bolton winger missed an easier chance than the one he put away earlier. With then minutes left Suárez seized on a weak clearance from a corner and curled a beauty into the far corner. Even after this Lee Dong-gook should have taken the game into extra-time but his shot was too timid and Uruguay cleared.

Ghana totally dominated the first half of their match against the USA, and should have had more than Boateng's enterprising goal to show for their superiority. The African side seemed flustered by the penalty award that led to the equaliser, and lost control of the game; they were lucky their goalkeeper stayed steady and kept them alive with a couple of crucial saves. Ghana steeled their nerves before extra-time and emerged deserved winners. Asamoah Gyan showed amazing energy and led their line superbly and scored the winner when he took down a long ball, outmuscled two defenders and scored from a tight angle. The Americans were undone by coach Bob Bradley's emphasis on fitness and strength and discipline, and looked a one-dimensional side. It is to be assumed they will show a more imaginative approach in Brazil under Jürgen Klinsmann.

United States Squad 2010:

GK: Tim Howard (Everton, 31 years old, 51 caps), Brad Guzan (Aston Villa, 25, 16), Marcus Hahnemann (Wolverhampton Wanderers, 37, 7)

DEF: Carlos Bocanegra (Rennes, 31, 79), Jonathon Bornstein (Chivas USA, 25, 32), Steve Cherundolo (Hannover, 31, 60), Jay DeMerit (Watford, 30, 19), Clarence Goodson (Start, Norway, 28, 14), Oguchi Onyewu (Milan, 28, 54), Jonathon Spector (West Ham United, 24, 25)

MID & WIDE: DaMarcus Beasley (Glasgow Rangers, 28, 92), Michael Bradley (Borussia Mönchengladbach, 22, 43), Ricardo Clark (Eintracht Frankfurt, 27, 29), Landon Donovan (LA Galaxy, 28, 123), Mauriuce Edu (Rangers, 24, 13), Benny Feilhaber (GF, Denmark, 25, 32), Stuart Holden (Bolton Wanderers, 24, 14), Jose Francisco Torres (Pachuca, 22, 10)

FWD: Jozy Altidore (Hull City, 20, 25), Edson Buddle (LA Galaxy, 29, 3), Clint Dempsey (Fulham, 27, 62), Robbie Findley (Real Salt Lake, 24, 6), Hérculez Gómez (Puebla, 28, 4)

The next day saw two games spoiled by awful refereeing decisions. While Argentina and Germany were the better teams in their matches against Mexico and England respectively, both benefited from some atrocious officiating.

After an evenly contested opening, Argentina took the lead in Johannesburg from a Carlos Tévez header with the striker standing five or six feet offside. The linesman was perfectly well placed, so possibly just oblivious to the rules. That Argentina were the better team thereafter is incontestable, and Tévez's second goal was a spectacular strike, but Mexico were visibly unsettled by the appalling decision for the last twenty minutes of the first half, and lost concentration for Higuaín's goal, Argentina's second.

Earlier in the day an even worse decision had caused controversy in the England versus Germany game. Germany outplayed England for much of the first half, their width and precision too much for a demotivated team playing a pedestrian system. Ironically Germany's opener was straight out of the Charles Hughes textbook, a big punt from goalkeeper Neuer finding Terry and Upson in *"after you, John, no, no, I insist, Matthew"* mode at the heart of the defence. Klose couldn't believe his luck as he ran on to welly the ball past David James, restored to the No.1 shirt after Rob Green's opening display.

More poor defending saw Klose set up Podolski for a second and England were reeling. Then Neuer came for a cross when he shouldn't and was beaten to it by Upson, which gave England some hope, and the game looked wide open again when Frank Lampard feigned to belt the ball from eighteen yards and instead executed a perfect chip over Neuer onto the bar and into the goal. Well, that's what happened, but unfortunately for England the Uruguayan referee didn't see it that way, and was backed up by two equally incompetent assistants. Play on, waved Mr Larrionda, as the watching TV and stadium audience stared in disbelief. The incident did more than any other to bring forward the use of technology to eradicate such controversy

Adding insult to injury another fine Lampard strike hit the bar with Neuer beaten at the start of the second half. Germany made the most of these reprieves, reasserting control and scoring from two beautifully fashioned breakaways. Both goals stemmed from errors by Gareth Barry and both were scored by the exciting Thomas Müller.

Awful as Larrionda's decision was – and not just the English saw it as one of the worst ever seen at this level – England were not good enough in this World Cup. It represented a step backward even from the rather laboured quarter-final appearances of Sven's teams. Capello, a good coach, just never "got" England or English football, and made some poor selections; the use of

Upson in this match instead of Carragher, Dawson or indeed my
mother being one of them.

England Squad 2010:
GK: David James (Portsmouth, 39, 50), Rob Green (West Ham
United, 30, 10), Joe Hart (Birmingham City, 23, 3)
DEF: Jamie Carragher (Liverpool, 32, 36), Ashley Cole (Chelsea,
29, 78), Michael Dawson (Tottenham Hotspur, 26, 0), Glenn
Johnson (Liverpool, 25, 22), Ledley King (Tottenham, 29, 20),
John Terry (Chelsea, 29, 60), Matthew Upson (West Ham, 31,
19), Stephen Warnock (Aston Villa, 28, 1)
MID & WIDE: Gareth Barry (Manchester City, 29, 36),
Michael Carrick (Manchester United, 28, 22), Joe Cole
(Chelsea, 28, 54), Steven Gerrard (Liverpool, 30, 80), Frank
Lampard (Chelsea, 31, 78), Aaron Lennon (Tottenham, 23,
17), James Milner (Villa, 24, 8), Shaun Wright-Phillips (Man
City, 28, 31)
FWD: Peter Crouch (Tottenham, 29, 38), Jermain Defoe
(Tottenham, 27, 39), Emile Heskey (Villa, 32, 58), Wayne Rooney
(Man Utd, 24, 60)

Holland and Brazil saw off Slovakia and Chile with something to spare. Arjen Robben, feeling his way back from injury,
started for the first time in the tournament and scored a terrific
solo goal for the opener, running at the defence and unleash-
ing a quick shot before it was expected. Holland took their
time finishing Slovakia off but never looked in much trouble
and Sneijder's second goal finished the game – there was no
time for the game even to restart after Vittek's injury-time
penalty.

Brazil beat Chile efficiently and scored a terrific team goal
(finished by Luís Fabiano), but they still didn't quite look the
business. Dunga, the coach, was a superb professional but a very
un-Brazilian type of player and this team were moulded more in
his image than some of the crowd-pleasing sides of the past. And
Kaká, supposedly the playmaker, still wasn't firing.

The final two games were a disappointment. Japan and
Paraguay played out a cautious bore-draw before Paraguay

prevailed on penalties, while Spain and Portugal failed to deliver the fireworks the fixture promised. There was plenty of technique and skill on display, but Portugal never really cranked up the pressure on their neighbours and after Villa's goal they subsided without much resistance other than a red card for an off-the-ball incident for Costa. Ronaldo disappeared again; like Lionel Messi he is yet to lighten up the biggest stage of all.

QUARTER-FINALS

Holland	(0) 2	**Brazil**	(0) 1	2 July, Port Elizabeth; 40,186
Sneijder 53, 68		Robinho 10		
Argentina	(0) 0	**Germany**	(1) 4	3 July, Cape Town; 64,100
		Müller 3, Klose 68, 89,		
		Friedrich 74		
Paraguay	(0) 0	**Spain**	(0) 1	3 July, Ellis Park; 55,395
		Villa 83		

The quarter-finals, which pitted South American sides against European or African opposition, provided some better football and more excitement at last. Holland trailed Brazil after ten minutes and had to produce a gritty performance to come back. Holland had to replace Mathijsen with Ooijer just before the kick-off and were still finding their feet when Robinho latched on to Melo's pass to give Brazil the lead; it was the Manchester City striker's last meaningful contribution to the game. Holland were rocking and needed two excellent saves from Stekelenburg to stay in the game at half-time.

The equaliser was a gift from the Brazilian defence. Wesley Sneijder sent in a testing free-kick which was met by Júlio César and his centre-half Juan at the same time; the result was that neither made clean contact and the ball went into the goal. Sneijder was lucky to be credited with the goal as it touched one or both of the Brazilian players on the way in. The defending wasn't too great for the second goal either. Robben's corner was flicked on by Dirk Kuyt and headed in by Sneijder – the oldest routine in the book.

Brazil gave it a go belatedly but Melo's sending-off for an ugly stamp put them at a huge disadvantage, and for the second Finals tournament in a row they went out at the quarter-final stage. Holland were now unbeaten for twenty-four matches and were looking especially determined and obdurate.

The other major South American team, Argentina, fared even worse the next day. They had saved all their defensive frailties for one match and found unforgiving opposition in Germany. The problems started for Maradona's side after three minutes when Schweinsteiger's free-kick was headed down and in by Thomas Müller. Argentina found a measure of control before the interval and enjoyed a good spell after half-time but a shoot-from-anywhere policy, while it kept Neuer busy in the German goal, also meant that a number of shots were taken when colleagues were better placed. Once again Messi was anonymous, forced deep by the excellent Schweinsteiger and powerful holding midfielder Khedira.

Miroslav Klose, on his 100th appearance, should have put Germany two-up in the first half but missed horribly. He made amends after sixty-seven minutes, walking the ball over the line after good work from Podolski. Klose had a terrible season for Bayern Munich but coach Joachim Low kept faith with his top scorer and Klose rose to the World Cup atmosphere, as he had done before. His late second goal put him within one of Ronaldo's all-time record and he has every chance of going to Brazil if fit, where he will make a very useful impact substitute. Full-back Arne Friedrich got forward well to convert Schweinsteiger's cross for the third German goal.

Germany looked the most complete side in the competition at this stage. Good goalkeeper, excellent full-backs, balanced midfield with plenty of goals in it and a knowledgeable and experienced striker; Maradona's confidence and chat was exposed as hollow bombast.

Paraguay were as dull and unadventurous as they were against Japan, losing to a solitary David Villa goal. The game was played at a slow pace with both sides keeping possession for long periods without threatening the opposition goal. Even the purists who fawned at Spain's feet admitted this was a crashing bore.

WORLD CUP CLASSIC No.25
2 July 2010, Soccer City, Johannesburg; 84,017

Ghana   **(1) (1) 1** Muntari 45
Uruguay   **(0) (1) 1** Forlán 55
Uruguay won 4–2 on penalties

Referee: **Olegário Benquerença** (Portugal)
Coaches: **Milovan Rajevac** (Ghana) & **Óscar Tabárez** (Uruguay)

Shoot-out

Uruguay		Ghana	
Forlán	S 1–0	Gyan	S 1–1
Victorino	S 2–1	Appiah	S 2–2
Scotti	S 3–2	*Mensah*	*M 3–2*
Maxi Pereira	*M 3–2*	*Adiyah*	*M 3–2*
Abreu	S 4–2		

Ghana (4–5–1): Richard Kingson (Wigan Athletic); John Paintsil (Fulham), Isaac Vorsah (1899 Hoffenheim), John Mensah (Cpt, Sunderland), Hans Sarpei (Bayer Leverkusen); Samuel Inkoom (Basle), Kwadwo Asamoah (Udinese), Anthony Annan (Rosenborg), Kevin-Prince Boateng (Portsmouth), Sulley Muntari (Internazionale); Asamoah Gyan (Rennes). **Subs:** Stephen Appiah (Bologna) 74m for Inkoom; Dominic Adiyah (Milan) 88m for Muntari
Uruguay (4–4–2): Fernando Muslera (Lazio); Maxi Pereira (Benfica), Diego Lugano (Cpt, Fenerbahçe), Mauricio Victorino (Universidad de Chile), Jorge Fucile (Porto); Álvaro Fernández (Universidad de Chile), Diego Pérez (Monaco), Egidio Arévalo (Peñarol), Edinson Cavani (Palermo); Diego Forlán (Atlético Madrid), Luis Suárez (Ajax). **Subs:** Andres Scotti (Colo Colo) 38m for Lugano; Nicolas Lodeiro (Ajax) 46m for Fernandez; Sebastián Abreu (Botafogo) 76m for Cavani
Cautioned: Fucile (Uru) 20m, Arévalo (Uru) 48m, Paintsil (Gha) 54m, Pérez (Uru) 59m, Sarpei (Gha) 77m, Mensah (Gha) 93m
Dismissed: Suárez (Uru) 120m

While all eyes were on fancied sides like Brazil, Argentina, Germany and Spain, Uruguay and Ghana played out a thriller, the best game of the tournament.

Both sides had grown into the tournament. Ghana had overcome the loss of Essien by packing the midfield and using the willing Asamoah Gyan as a lone striker. Their defensive midfield player Annan looked composed and disciplined, and on the left Muntari had a cultured left foot and a dangerous shot. The defence survived a few shaky moments and were grateful for the form of the unheralded Kingson, who couldn't get a game at Wigan.

Uruguay had a fine defence, with the captain Lugano and the right-back Maxi Pereira outstanding, and Suárez and Forlán looked the most dangerous attacking partnership in the competition. They were a little short of quality in midfield and seemed reluctant to use the gifted but inconsistent Lodeiro, but so far hard work had made up for any shortcomings.

Both sides liked a tackle and the game was feisty from the start without ever teetering over into anarchy. The referee used his cards judiciously and made sure the fiery stuff added to the game rather than detracted from it.

Kingson came to his colleagues' rescue twice in the first half as Ghana struggled to get any rhythm. First he palmed away Mensah's clumsily miscued clearance and then he leaped acrobatically to turn away a short from Suárez, who was turning the Ghanaian centre-halves inside out. Uruguay were hampered by an injury to Diego Lugano, their influential captain, before half-time, but he could have done nothing about Muntari's spectacular opening goal, which bounced evilly as it went past Muslera in first-half injury-time.

The game opened up in the second half, as Uruguay introduced Lodeiro, whose greater range of passing helped stretch the Ghanaians at the back and took the ball out of the areas patrolled by Boateng and Annan. The equaliser came from a free-kick on the left. Kingson positioned himself in the centre and as Forlán hit the ball he moved to his left, expecting the whipped kick into the near corner; instead the ball sailed beyond him and went in just under the bar. Forlán was dragging defenders across the line as players tired, and the space left for Suárez gave the Ajax man two opportunities, but neither was easy and both went narrowly wide. At the other end Gyan was proving a handful for the second string Uruguay centre-backs and twice he nearly barged his way through on goal; the man's stamina was a marvel.

The game became more and more open in extra-time, but the final ball became as tired as the defenders and both goalkeepers remained alert; Muslera saved from Gyan and Kingson tipped away another Forlán effort. Kevin-Prince Boateng came closest with a fierce header from Paintsil's long throw, but the ball fizzed just wide. The tension built to an extraordinary climax. Muslera saved well and Uruguay countered; the attack broke up and some neat Ghanaian passing took the ball back into the Uruguay half and won a free-kick. Muslera missed the chipped cross and the ball fell to Appiah, but his shot was blocked on the line by Luis Suárez. The ball broke to Dominic Adiyah and a goal looked certain until Suárez beat the ball away again, this time with his hands. A red card and a penalty to Ghana was the referee's only option.

The media, prompted by Ghana's Serbian coach, made much of the incident, and questioned Suárez's sportsmanship. In fairness to the player he only did what the vast majority of professional footballers would instinctively have done. What he should not have done was celebrate Gyan's missed penalty quite so gleefully on the touchline, but that is the sort of behaviour we have come to expect of a man who consistently shows no respect for his opponents. Nor should one or two of his team-mates have chosen that moment to taunt the distraught Ghanaian striker. It was really harsh on Gyan, who had a terrific tournament and played with great heart and courage.

The missed penalty was the last kick of the game, and after Forlán tucked away the first penalty of the shoot-out it was a shock to see Gyan walk forward to take Ghana's first kick. He scored one of football's greatest "bottle" penalties, but unfortunately for Ghana, two of his colleagues' nerves failed and Muslera saved twice to send Uruguay into the semi-final. Ghana had come closer than any African country to the last four.

SEMI-FINALS

Uruguay	**(1) 2**	**Holland**	**(1) 3**	6 July, Cape Town; 62,479
Forlán 41, Maxi Pereira 90		Van Bronckhorst 18,		
		Sneijder 70, Robben 73		
Germany	**(0) 0**	**Spain**	**(0) 1**	7 July, Durban; 60,960
		Puyol 74		

THIRD-PLACE MATCH

Uruguay	**(1) 1**	**Germany**	**(1) 3**	10 July, Port Elizabeth; 36,254
Cavani 28, Forlán 51		Müller 19, Jansen 56,		
		Khedira 82		

Holland's win over Uruguay was easier than a 3–2 scoreline suggests. Uruguay showed little ambition in the absence of Suárez (suspended after his red card) – odd, given that they had Cavani and Abreu in their squad, both good-quality forwards. The game was settled in four minutes in the second half when Sneijder scored with a deflected shot, and then Arjen Robben, who had looked the player most likely to win the game, converted Kuyt's cross; the Dutch winger looked as surprised as anyone that he scored the goal with his head.

The game's best moment came in the first-half when Giovanni van Bronckhorst drifted upfield from left-back and unleashed a spectacular shot for the opener; Muslera barely twitched as the ball flew past him. Uruguay's first-half equaliser was another long-distance strike from Forlán but Stekelenburg should have saved it, and Maxi Pereira's second for the South Americans came too late to have any real impact.

The Germany versus Spain game was odd. Germany had looked the best side in the tournament before this game, but seemed to suffer a collective failure of nerve against the side who beat them two years previously in the European Championships.

Neither side created many clear cut chances in a cat and mouse first half where Spain had a predictable amount of possession and probed and pushed, while Germany seemed happy to rely on the counter-attack and the pace of Özil and Podolski.

The second half followed a similar pattern but the German became more and more cautious and allowed Xavi and Xabi Alonso to dominate the centre. Schweinsteiger, so effective in pushing back Argentina, played as a second defensive player alongside Khedira. Klose became increasingly isolated and the Spanish full-backs roamed forward more – Ramos came close to the opener when he got behind Lahm and just missed Alonso's through ball.

The game was settled in the simplest manner, Puyol burying a straightforward header from a corner. Germany were beaten, and didn't create a chance after the goal; Spain should have added a second when Pedro selfishly took the ball on himself when Torres was free for a tap-in. The form of their forwards probably explains why Spain scored so few goals in this tournament. Torres was only just back from an injury that he never fully recovered from, while Pedro just ain't that good. Two years later in the European

Championship Spain played without a recognised striker, preferring Fabregas in an advanced role to an out-of-form centre-
forward. None of the three great midfield players, Xavi, Xabi
Alonso and Iniesta, was a prolific scorer, and without Villa's goals
from out wide Spain would have struggled to win.

Germany won an entertaining third-place match. Thomas
Müller showed how much he was missed against Spain with
another goal, but the winner came from a less familiar source – it
was Sami Khedira's first goal for his country.

WORLD CUP FINAL No.19
11 July 2010, First National Bank Stadium,
Johannesburg; 84,490

Spain	(0) (0) 1	Iniesta 116
Holland	(0) (0) 0	

Referee: **Howard Webb** (England)
Coaches: **Vicente del Bosque** (Spain) & **Bert van Marwijk** (Holland)

Spain (4–2–2–2): Iker Casillas (Real Madrid); Sergio Ramos (Barcelona), Gerard Piqué
(Barcelona), Carles Puyol (Barcelona), Joan Capdevila (Villareal), Sergio Busquets (Barcelona),
Xabi Alonso (Real Madrid); Xavi *Hernández* (Barcelona), Andrés Iniesta (Barcelona); David
Villa (Valencia), Pedro *Rodríguez* (Barcelona). **Subs:** Jesús Navas (Sevilla) 60m for Pedro; Cesc
Fábregas (Arsenal) 87m for Xabi Alonso; Fernando Torres (Liverpool) 106m for Villa
Holland (4–5–1): Maarten Stekelenburg (Ajax); Gregory van der Wiel (Ajax), Johnny Heitinga
(Everton), Joris Mathijsen (Hamburg), Giovanni van Bronckhorst (Feyenoord); Arjen Robben
(Bayern Munich), Mark van Bommel (Bayern Munich), Wesley Sneijder (Internazionale),
Nigel de Jong (Manchester City), Dirk Kuyt (Liverpool); Robin van Persie (Arsenal). **Subs:**
Eljero Elia (Hamburg) 71m for Kuyt; Rafael van der Vaart (Real Madrid) 99m for de Jong;
Edson Braafheid (Celtic) 105m for van Bronckhorst
Cautioned: Van Persie (Hol) 15m, Puyol (Spa) 16m, van Bommel (Hol) 22m, Ramos (Spa)
23m, de Jong (Hol) 28m, van Bronckhorst (Hol) 54m, Heitinga (Hol) 57m, Capdevila (Spa)
67m, Robben (Hol) 84m, van der Wiel (Hol) 111m, Mathijsen (Hol) 117m, Iniesta (Spa)
188m, Xavi (Spa) 120m
Dismissed: Heitinga (Hol) 109m (second yellow card)

The Dutch spoiled the final. It's a simple, bald statement and
it's true. They decided the best way to disrupt Spain was to "get
stuck in" to use old-fashioned parlance and this they duly did.
Howard Webb, the referee, was criticised in some quarters but
when players are clearly putting in crude challenges to hurt and
get a reaction from opponents the referee has little choice but to
shower cards across the pitch with abandon. The Dutch earned
nine yellow cards, two of them to Johnny Heitinga, which
condemned him to an early bath. He should have been taking it

alongside de Jong and van Bommel, both of whom should have seen red – Webb was culpable in missing de Jong's high tackle and was lenient with van Bommel, one of the most unpleasantly macho players of the modern era.

Spain weren't shy of getting a few late numbers in – Sergio Ramos was forgiven one crude lunge after already being booked – and they responded to the provocation with some demeaning gamesmanship.

Football? There was little of it and what there was Spain played. Cesc Fabregas was excellent after coming on for injury-time and it was his intelligent pass that released Andrés Iniesta to score. Iniesta was made Man of the Match but it should have been Piqué for snuffing out the dangerous van Persie. The big disappointment was Robben; faced with Spain's weakness, Capdevila, left-back of borderline international standard, he offered nothing but petulance.

It was a disappointing end to a disappointing tournament. The best team won but didn't play their best football – too much of their possession football had no edge or thrust, or foundered on poor control or decision making from Pedro or the struggling Torres.

Team of the Tournament:

Casillas (Spain)
Maxi Pereira (Uruguay)   Piqué (Spain)   Puyol (Spain)   Lahm (Germany)
Xabi Alonso (Spain)
Schweinsteiger (Germany)   Sneijder (Holland   Müller (Germany)
Forlán (Uruguay)   Villa (Spain)

The official team had the media favourites **Xavi** and **Iniesta** instead of Xabi Alonso and Müller, and **Maicon**'s inclusion continued the ridiculous infatuation with over-rated Brazilian full-backs. **Sergio Ramos** was preferred to Piqué, which is nonsense.

Top scorers: Müller, Sneijder, Villa and Forlán (all scored 5)

Heaven Eleven No.16

Spain

Coach:
Vicente del Bosque – the only man to bring them the World Cup (and it means I can ignore the racist Aragones)

Goalkeepers:
Iker Casillas: captain of the World Cup-winning team and record cap winner
Andoni Zubizarreta: Casillas' great forerunner
Luis Arconada: and the forerunner of Zubi

Defenders:
Fernando Hierro: ball-playing and goalscoring defender, equally good in holding role
Carlos Puyol: cultured defender, distinctive barnet
Jose Pirri: went back from midfield to sweeper and comfortable in both positions
Gerard Piqué: best defensive centre-half Spain have had
Sergio Ramos: attacking right-back in 2010 team.
José Antonio Camacho: redoubtable '80s left-back
Rafa Gordillo: could play either side, often used as a wing-back
Miguel Ángel Nadal: in case we need a beast

Midfield & Wide:
Xavi: the man just doesn't know how to give the ball away
Xabi Alonso: the unheralded one of the three great modern Spanish midfielders
Andres Iniesta: one of the Holy Trinity of the modern Spain midfield
Michel: excellent attacking playmaker in the 1980s
Pep Guardiola: neat, uncomplicated defensive midfielder
Luis Enrique: quality attacking midfielder from the 1990s
Francisco Gento: awesome left-winger in the great Real side of the fifties and sixties
Luis Suárez: talented sixties playmaker, elegant passer and good finisher

Forwards:
Raúl: missed out on the fun in recent years as he ended when they started
David Villa: subtle deep-lying forward or wide man

Emilio Butragueno: the Vulture – Spain's best striker in the 70s and 80s
Alfredo Di Stéfano: not born in Spain, but played his best stuff there so we've let them have him

Likely first XI:

Casillas
Gordillo Puyol Pirri Camacho
Hierro Alonso
Michel Xavi Villa
Di Stéfano

8.5 ENGLAND AT THE WORLD CUP

We do like to gnash and wail and weep and bemoan the disasters that befall our national team. But are we justified?

England's World Cup efforts read thus:

Year	Stage reached	Beaten by
1950	Group stage	USA
1954	Quarter-final	Uruguay
1958	Group stage play-off	USSR
1962	Quarter-final	Brazil
1966	WINNERS	
1970	Quarter-final	West Germany
1974	Did not qualify	
1978	Did not qualify	
1982	Second group phase (quarter-final)	n/a
1986	Quarter-final	Argentina
1990	Semi-final	West Germany (penalties)
1994	Did not qualify	
1998	Last sixteen	Argentina (penalties)
2002	Quarter-final	Brazil
2006	Quarter-final	Portugal (penalties)
2010	Last sixteen	Germany

It doesn't take more than the briefest perusal of this list to work out where our place in the scheme of things lies. England are a quarter-final team, so why do we get so upset when we don't get any further than that, except once in every twenty years or so?

In 1953 Hungary came to Wembley and shattered any perceptions England had that they were among the very best teams in the World. In Budapest the following spring they rubber-stamped that fact with a 7–1 hammering, which remains England's heaviest defeat. Later that year the ease with which Uruguay brushed England aside at the Finals in Switzerland brushed off any final crumbs of delusion.

In the 1950s England were playing catch up. They failed to heed the warning Hungary gave them, remained tactically naïve and over-dependent on skilful wingers (no disrespect to Matthews or Finney, who were sublime footballers).

By 1962 England were a bit more competitive. Jimmy Armfield has gone on record as saying they went to Chile to win the World Cup and were hugely disappointed to lose to the competition's best side. A case could be made for saying England were the second best team at that tournament but were undone by Garrincha's genius and Haynes' inability to translate his own considerable talent to the biggest stage.

Four years later Alf Ramsey synthesised the best English qualities into a team that was the epitome of the mythical bulldog spirit. At its best in adversity, Ramsey's team had enormous self-belief and grit, and, conveniently, three of the best players to wear the shirt playing simultaneously (Banks, Moore, Bobby Charlton) as well as the cometh-the-hour man teams often need to go deep into a World Cup tournament (Hurst). In 1970 the same team came very close and didn't get the breaks they got in 1966; they were the best equipped team to cope with an astonishing Brazilian team and gave a memorable performance against them in the group.

Let us gloss over the dark days of the 1970s. English football once more dug a trench and sat in it; resting on the power of its club football, the FA failed to notice that internationally England had fallen behind the rest of Europe and South America. They made a disastrous appointment in the egotistical Don Revie, who tried to build an England in the same mould of his effective but unlovely Leeds United team. The media clamoured for the appointment of Brian Clough, but Clough too suffered from ego, and was prone to perverse selections simply to prove who was in charge.

Ron Greenwood was a safe choice in the late seventies, but he did nothing to advance England tactically; in 1982 a strong squad stumbled through a World Cup and went out without losing a game because they couldn't / wouldn't / didn't gamble. At the time English clubs were pre-eminent; Bob Paisley's Liverpool team won three consecutive European Cups because they not only injected pace and tempo European sides struggled against, but because they kept hold of the ball. The Liverpool mantra was possession, keep the ball, don't let the opposition play. England singularly failed to translate this to the international stage. Neither Greenwood nor his successor Bobby Robson had a strong enough personality to stamp a style on England, and some good players never coalesced into anything better than a decent side. Also, England didn't have a centre-forward worth the name at international level between Hurst and Lineker. The World Cup campaigns of 1982 and 1986 were as good as we had a right to expect.

In the middle of the 1980s Carlos Bilardo introduced three at the back to Argentina and they won the World Cup. No one adopted the tactic for England until Robson was panicked into using it at the 1990 World Cup (when England went one better than their mean exit point).

The system would have suited England down to the ground if they had adapted in the middle of the decade but there was no move to innovate in a land cut off from world football by the ban imposed after Heysel. Sides such as Watford and Wimbledon were enjoying success with direct, long-ball football that suited the English league but was a nonsense in international competition, as Graham Taylor, the former Watford manager who succeeded Robson would discover.

In the middle nineties the FA let the team down in a massive way. Everybody was aware that Terry Venables' business ventures were not an area where he displayed the soundest judgement, but England let him walk away rather than stand by their man. Given the slack they allowed Sven-Göran Eriksson with his duplicitous private life, their lack of faith in Venables had more to do with cowardice than probity.

Venables' successor Glenn Hoddle was a gifted coach and tactician, and he was also England's best manager at thinking on

his feet and using substitutes – a vital ingredient to success at
international level. Unfortunately he was also a strange man with
strange beliefs and he couldn't keep his trap shut and stick to
football. And his man-management was terrible. Still, the exit to
Argentina in 1998 was glorious in its way. Then came Kevin
Keegan. Keegan was a naïve and loveable comedy turn as a
manager, not an international coach.

And so to Sven, who is retrospectively viewed with such
distaste. He was an appointment to suit the suits, who probably
thought it was good PR and made sound commercial sense. The
FA made a series of appointments around the turn of the century
far more damaging than that of a Swedish manager. Mark Palios?
Pass me that blunderbuss . . .

Eriksson had a good track record and he steered England to
two quarter-finals (three if you include Euro 2004); and that was
the best we could expect. The generation of players we called The
Golden Generation was good, but not as good as we thought, fed
nauseous illusions of Premiership supremacy by a media who, to
adapt a well-worn cliché, knew the cost of a TV deal but not the
value of the game. Eriksson allowed the most talented of them,
Steven Gerrard, to play where he wanted not where he was
needed. All the time we have kicked up about not having a good
holding midfielder, we have had a brilliant player with every tool
needed to do that job. Gerrard, with a better (make that stronger)
manager, could have been England's Pirlo. Capello was supposed
to be the man with the will to resolve those issues, but he never
cared enough. Eriksson and Capello wanted the salary that went
with the job, not the job itself. Which is why they only reached the
quarter-finals.

England are in a holding pattern. Roy Hodgson probably
won't advance them very much, but they won't regress either. His
first tournament, Euro 2012, was a job well done; with really
limited resources and obstinate defending England reached . . .
wait for it . . . the quarter-final. Hodgson is an experienced
manager at international as well as club level and he has the ability to spot a player who can step up. His selection and use of Ross
Barkley in a recent competitive fixture was admirable; the boy
clearly has the right stuff and exposing him early in a game that

was three quarters won was good management. Eriksson or Capello would have used Carrick; Hodgson didn't need to see Carrick and Carrick didn't need half an hour on the pitch to show what he could do. That's international management.

We have made standard excuses for why England consistently "fail".

Excuse No.1: England players play too many games. Is that really true? They play no more than they did in 1966 when England won the World Cup at the end of a long season played on mud bath pitches that were far more draining than the lush surfaces used today. The modern game is much quicker, but conditioning and fitness levels have gone up commensurately. And no one plays every game these days in the era of the twenty-man squad. Aston Villa won the league title in 1980 with the same four midfield players in every game. Couldn't happen today.

Excuse No.2: All the foreigners make it difficult for young English players. That is true, but is used as a smokescreen to hide other faults. English players do emerge, and if a player pushes his way through at one of the bigger clubs it is probably a sign that he has a bit of something about him. The problem isn't getting players to come through; it is the hoovering up of available talent by the big sides (and greedy agents) and then giving those players time on the pitch that is the problem. James Milner and Gareth Barry were both better players at Aston Villa than they are now, and Manchester City have set Scott Sinclair and Jack Rodwell back years. Just as Joleon Lescott belatedly looked like an England player (he was excellent at Euro 2012) City replaced him and did Serbia a favour. Daniel Sturridge was held back at Chelsea – no one realised he was any good until he went on loan to Bolton, and Josh McEachran is going the same way. Quotas aren't the answer and they are illegal – don't let UKIP fool you, EU employment law is vital to commerce as well as human rights and there is no reason why football should be allowed to be an exception, attractive as it may sound purely from the perspective of building an England team.

Excuse No.3: The English game is too frenetic and players don't learn good technique. Well, yes, that is true, but England players have never had basic technique in the way, say, Central European players have, or South American players. England won the World Cup with Nobby Stiles and Jack Charlton in the team – even Sir Geoff wasn't blessed with the sweetest first touch. And it won't change, not with an Academy in every city in the country. There are aspects of football ingrained in a nation's DNA that never change. Things can improve, and probably will, but I very much doubt we will ever produce a generation of ball juggling Brazilian style maestros, just as Brazil will never produce a Frank Lampard. As important as technique is joy. One of the things I most like about Welbeck – and there's a lot to like, his movement and use of space is way ahead of any other contemporary English attacker, Rooney included – is that he smiles a lot when he plays, he conspicuously enjoys playing football. More like him, please, Mr Academy Director.

Greg Dyke, the new FA Chairman, has made the right noises. As a former head of the BBC Dyke understands the need to create a financially sound environment in which creative people can be left to get on with their job and hopefully flourish. He has set a target – winning the World Cup in 2022. Let's hope he and the rest of the international team can live up to it. I'm fed up of being a quarter-final team. Here's to Qatar '22! (I can't believe I just typed that . . .)

8.6 CLUBS

Until the last thirty/forty years, most players who appear for their country played club football in that country. At the 1954 World Cup, for example, there was not a single player in the Finals tournament who played club football outside the country he represented.

These are the percentages of players in the World Cup squads for the Finals that played abroad than in their own country. For this purpose I have not counted Scottish, Irish or Welsh players playing in England as playing overseas, but I have counted English players playing in Scotland, as that has been far less common.

1930   1.21%
1934   0.88%
1938   0.94%
1950   0.35%
1954   0.00%
1958   2.56%
1962   1.70%
1966   1.99%
1970   2.01%
1974   8.24%
1978   6.25%
1982   10.98%
1986   16.80%
1990   22.54%
1994   32.95%

1998   42.19%
2002   44. 57%
2006   53.13%
2010   60.19%

As the competition expanded and featured more African countries and some of the European nations with less wealthy and
prestigious leagues, like the Scandinavians and the former
Yugoslav states, so these percentages increase rapidly.

The first year there was a noticeable increase was in 1974,
when the number of players employed overseas rose from seven
to twenty-nine, including six each from the squads of Argentina,
Sweden and Uruguay. The following tournament saw the last
time that number decreased; there was a steady climb through the
eighties to eighty-five players in 1986, including fifteen of the
Denmark squad, the first time a country had more than half its
members playing abroad. The number topped 100 for the first
time in 1990, as Brazilian and Argentinian players followed other
South Americans off the continent for bigger rewards in Europe.
Four years later, in the United States, Nigeria became the first
country to pick an entire squad of expats.

There are only a tiny handful of countries who rarely have to
call players back from far-flung shores. Inevitably these are the
countries with the big wealthy leagues and high salaries. England,
Germany, Italy and Spain are able to keep most of their best players close to home. Some clubs in Russia and Ukraine have spending power now they are owned by Eastern European oligarch
sugar daddies. In 1994 and 2002 Russia had eleven and nine
players from overseas, but in 2010 Ukraine (Russia didn't qualify) had only three.

The number of players picked for World Cup Finals squad
(not the Home Nations or Ireland) while registered with an
English or Scottish club has risen from twenty in 1994 to ninety-
nine in 2010. Arsenal and Chelsea lead the list overall with thirty-
two (if a player, say Vieira, gets picked for two tournaments, that
counts as two), Liverpool and Manchester United next with
twenty-three. The most overseas players taking part in the Finals
while with one club was twelve Arsenal players in 2006.

The first overseas player was the Chile winger George Robledo, who was at Newcastle in 1950. George was way ahead of his time – we had to wait until 1982 for any player based here to go the Finals as part of an overseas squad: Ossie Ardiles was registered with Tottenham but was actually in France because of the Falklands War, and Francky van der Elst was at West Ham. Four years later Rachid Harkouk was the first UK-based player to represent an African country when he appeared for Algeria. Gradually the numbers increased and the likes of Jamaica and Trinidad and Tobago filling their squad with lower division players has pushed the numbers up.

For Scotland the biggest contributor has been Celtic, closely followed not by Rangers but Aberdeen; ninety-four out of a total of 176 players picked for Scotland were with Scottish clubs, seventy-five were with English clubs and seven played overseas; the first to represent Scotland with a European club was Joe Jordan when he was at Milan in 1982. The first to represent any British side was John Charles of Wales, who was playing for Juventus when he appeared at the 1958 Finals; the first Englishman was Gerry Hitchens, who was at Inter in 1962.

Here are the clubs who have provided players for England squads (again, Bobby Moore in 1962, 1966 and 1970 counts as three for West Ham).

33 players	Manchester United
31	Tottenham Hotspur
24	Liverpool
19	Chelsea
17	Arsenal
14	West Ham United
13	Wolverhampton Wanderers
11	Leeds United
9	Everton
8	Manchester City, West Bromwich Albion
7	Fulham, Newcastle United
6	Aston Villa, Blackpool
5	Blackburn Rovers, Middlesbrough, Nottingham Forest

4   Ipswich Town, Rangers, Sheffield Wednesday,
    Southampton
3   Birmingham City, Bolton Wanderers, Burnley,
    Huddersfield Town, Portsmouth, Preston North
    End, Queens Park Rangers, Sheffield United
2   Bayern Munich, Derby County, Milan, Sunderland
1   Brighton & Hove Albion, Cologne, Internazionale,
    Leicester City, Luton Town, Norwich City,
    Olympique de Marseille, Real Madrid, Stoke City,
    Watford

WHAT THE
FUTURE HOLDS

9.1 WORLD CUP 2014

There has been a lot in the press about Brazil not being ready for the World Cup and about the amount of money spent on the tournament. The same was said of the Olympic Games in Athens and 2004 and the World Cup in 2010 in South Africa. They will be ready, this always happens. And the protesters have a point; there is little indication that any lasting legacy is being created around the World Cup in Brazil. There was the same objection in Britain when the cost of creating the London Olympics started to escalate, but at least there was a legacy and an infrastructure left behind that could serve other purposes in the future. Although I have no doubt much of it will fall into disuse now it no longer represents useful political capital.

Brazil will be fun once it starts and the stadia should be full in a football and country – though that may mean desperate last minute ticket sales at lower prices than the current extortionate rate. It is a long haul for the European fans and ninety-nine per cent of Brazilians can't afford these rates.

And it isn't a bad thing that some of the negative press has reminded us that Brazil isn't all *mardi gras* and samba parties on Copacabana beach. Not that you would think that if you had seen the brilliant 2002 movie *City of God* – changed my view of Rio forever. I shall be watching from the safety of my sofa, coward that I am.

2014
BRAZIL

Twelve cities have been announced as hosts for the 2014 World Cup Finals. The **Maracaña** in **Rio de Janeiro** will again host the Final, as it did in 1950, while five refurbished stadia and six new ones complete the twelve.

The new stadia will be in **Manaus**, capital of the Amazon region, **Cuiabá** in Mato Grosso, **Salvador**, **Recife** and **Natal** along the eastern seaboard and in the country's biggest city, **Sao Paulo**, where the new Corinthians ground will be used.

In the capital **Brasilia** the old **Mané Garrinch**a stadium has been near-demolished and renovated for the World Cup, while existing grounds will be upgraded in **Fortaleza** to the north-east, **Belo Horizonte** north of Rio, as well as **Curitiba** and **Porto Alegre** to the south east.

Progress has been far from smooth, but these things tend to be ready on time, no matter how fraught and eleventh hour, and at the time of writing there is no reason to suppose this will be any different. Sceptics claimed London would fail to deliver the 2012 Olympics on time – they look a bit daft in hindsight.

Qualifying

In Asia two final groups of five yielded Iran, South Korea, Japan and Australia as four direct qualifiers – not even the whisper of a surprise there. Slightly more surprising were the two teams who contested the play-off for the opportunity to clinch an extra place against the fifth placed South American side. Jordan and Uzbekistan drew 1–1 twice, and a penalty shoot-out was finally won by Jordan 9–8, after all ten outfield players on each side had taken a kick. It's a shame Ismailov missed – the two goalkeepers were up next; that would have made a great story. Jordan will probably lose their final eliminator against Uruguay, but any team has a chance over two legs, and Uruguay will need to watch their discipline in the away leg. Jordan are managed by Hossam Hassan, a striker who won 176 caps and scored sixty-eight goals for Egypt.

Argentina qualified easily from the South American section, so too Colombia. Chile came in third in the protracted group and Ecuador just pipped Uruguay on goal difference for the fourth spot. Uruguay's early form was mystifying but they have improved and I suspect their forwards will make them more of a threat in the Finals than either Colombia or Chile.

The big surprise in the CONCACAF section was Mexico. A chronic shortage of goals left them in fourth place behind Costa Rica, the United States and Honduras. Mexico faced a play-off against New Zealand for a place in the Finals. The two-legged tie proved horribly one-sided.

The African zone came down to five final two-leg play-offs which took place in October, after ten groups whittled down the combatants. Burkina Faso, finalists in the last African Cup of Nations, won their last match against Gabon to clinch their place after Congo slipped up against bottom team Niger. Ethiopia did well, beating South Africa to overtake them in their penultimate match and finishing things off with an away win in the Central African Republic. The unluckiest team in the entire qualifying competition has to be Cape Verde Islands, who beat Tunisia 2–0 away to win their group – a mighty effort for a small country – only to have the result reversed because they fielded an ineligible player. Cruel luck, surely he wasn't that good – they didn't sneak Messi in as a ringer or anything . . . hey-ho, rules is rules.

Ghana, Nigeria, Ivory Coast, Cameroon and Algeria (just) were the teams which prevailed.

Nine group winners have made the Finals from the UEFA section: Italy, Holland, Belgium, Spain, Germany and Switzerland (from a really easy group) all made it comfortably. England (phew! Would have killed my sales otherwise) and Russia did well to hold off Ukraine and Portugal respectively, while Bosnia-Herzegovina pipped Greece on goal difference in another lightweight group – deservedly so, they scored thirty goals in ten games compared with Greece's twelve. It's an impressive achievement for a nation of around four million people; they are managed by former Yugoslavia and Paris St Germain star Safet Susic.

FIFA seeded the play-offs between the second-placed teams according to official rankings, so Greece, Portugal, Croatia and Ukraine will avoid each other, as will the four lower-ranked sides, France, Sweden, Romania and, most interestingly, Iceland. Portugal and Ronaldo prevailed over Sweden and Ibrahimovic, while France did well to get by Ukraine after losing 2–0 in Kiev. Greece beat Romania, and Croatia ended Iceland's hopes of a first appearance.

Full 2014 World Cup draw
Group A: Brazil, Croatia, Mexico, Cameroon.
Group B: Spain, Netherlands, Chile, Australia.
Group C: Colombia, Greece, Ivory Coast, Japan.
Group D: Uruguay, Costa Rica, England, Italy.
Group E: Switzerland, Ecuador, France, Honduras.
Group F: Argentina, Bosnia-Herzegovina, Iran, Nigeria.
Group G: Germany, Portugal, Ghana, USA.
Group H: Belgium, Algeria, Russia, South Korea.

Who will be the biggest let-down?
Belgium will struggle to cope with the expectancy and the heat.

Who will be the stars?
Paulinho, Sergio Agüero, Kevin Strootman, Mario Götze & Thomas Müller, Yaya Touré, Leonardo Bonucci, Danny Welbeck, Yevhen Konoplyanka, Gary Medel, Diego Godín. It is to be hoped Messi steps up, and, reluctantly, Suárez will be an influence; shabby as his behaviour has been, he remains a world-class footballer of the highest quality.

How far will England go?
Second round, maybe quarter-finals; after all, England are a quarter-final team.

Who will surprise everybody?
Chile are better than people realise. One of the African countries will revel in the conditions – probably Ivory Coast, if Manchester City don't burn out Yaya Touré, but Nigeria also have a good squad, their best since the 1990s. Both will enjoy the conditions; Nigeria's youngsters, if they play without fear, would be my tip to over-achieve and go deep into the competition.

Who will win?
Everybody assumes Brazil will win at home but the pressure will be huge. I think Argentina will win, hopefully with more grace than they have shown in the past. They have a class squad and aren't managed by a lunatic.

That's all pure conjecture, of course. By the time you read this, the draw will be made with a completely different set of teams and you will be laughing at the silly author. As Fergie once said, in his bluffest Glaswegian. *"Football, eh? Bloody hell!"*

9.2 BEST OF THE BEST

Here is my **Brilliant Players You May Not Realise Were That Good XI**

Borislav Mihailov (Bulgaria)

George Cohen (England)   Marius Trésor (France)

Carlos Gamarra (Paraguay)   Silvio Marzolini (Argentina)

Paul McGrath (Ireland)

Igor Chislenko (USSR)   Téofilo Cubillas (Peru)   Bruno Conti (Italy)

Flórián Albert (Hungary)   Andrzej Szarmach (Poland)

Subs: Lee Woon-jae (South Korea), Albert Shesternev (USSR), Kazimierz Deyna (Poland), Lakhdar Belloumi (Algeria), Enrique Borja (Mexico)

These have been the **Best Ten Matches** in the World Cup to date:

10. **Portugal v North Korea (QF, 1966):** silly goal fest and a remarkable comeback (and the genius of Eusébio).
9. **England v West Germany (1966 & 1970):** these two are almost one match – many of the same players, same managers, and very different results.
8. **Denmark v Brazil (QF, 1998):** goodbye to Denmark and the Laudrups in the best Finals game of the modern era.
7. **Belgium v USSR (last 16, 1986):** amazing technique and stamina from both sides in an unheralded classic.
6. **Brazil v Italy (Final, 1970):** a master class from the masters.

gland (last 16, 1998): tension you could
. loaf with and one of the great backs-to-the-
.ces.

ny v Italy (SF, 1970): some have it at No.1,
ninety minutes was only good – extra-time was
cial.

3. **West Germany (SF 1982):** drama, some unbelievably good play from the French, guts from the Germans
and *that tackle*.

2. **Hungary v Uruguay (SF, 1954):** they blew the final, but
the Hungarians in the semi against a top-notch side were
simply sensational.

1. **Italy v Brazil (2nd phase, 1982):** effectively a semi-final,
and Italy had to win so they couldn't sit and soak. Mind-
boggling skill levels and technique.

These are the **Best Goals** scored in the World Cup to date:

12. Long-range slaps are not normally the sort of goal I include
in these lists as it involves too much chance. But **Bobby
Charlton** made a habit of it, and his bazooka against Mexico
in 1996 was top drawer. Moore nicks in to tackle and squirts
the ball to Charlton who starts off in his own half. The
defence retreat; the Bobster feints as if to switch into his
famous left, then immediately switches the other way to
exploit a tiny gap and belts it with his almost equally famous
right.

11. The Dutch take a quick free-kick against Italy in 1978; you
can see Dino Zoff screaming at his defenders to close **Arie
Haan** down; alas, they ignore him, Haan lets rip and Zoff
can only clutch vainly at thin air as the ball screams past him
into the top corner.

10. A group game between Saudi Arabia and Belgium in 1994
wasn't the most high-profile game in World Cup history. It
was after this goal. Saudi midfielder **Said Al-Owairan** took
the ball from his own half in the sixth minute, ran straight at
the heart of the Belgian defence and just kept going. He took
five defenders out of the game before toe-poking the ball

past the goalkeeper (Michel Preud'homme, one of the best around).

9. In their first group game against Chile in 1974 West Germany are playing a bit of keep ball in the Chilean half, stringing passes together nonchalantly in front of a massed defence. **Paul Breitner**, ostensibly a left-back, pops up on the ball in the middle of the pitch; he is obviously getting a bit bored of the tiki-taki because out of nowhere he unleashes a monster right-footer that the goalkeeper can't quite reach. In here just for nonchalance.

8. **Michael Owen**'s solo effort against Argentina in 1998, taking a pass from David Beckham and giving one of the world's best defences the charge, sprinting away from Chamot, whizzing past Ayala as if he were invisible and thrashing the ball beyond Roa. All at the ripe old age of eighteen.

7. That goal from 1970, when Brazil play pinball and Pelé slides the most exquisitely paced pass into the path of right-back and skipper **Carlos Alberto**, and he sticks it away. Only at seven? The opposition were tired and demoralised.

6. Sweden, 1958, and coach Feola belatedly introduced seventeen-year-old **Pelé** to the starting line-up with predict-ably astonishing results. This goal, in the final, was the best expression of his youthful talent. Didi tosses in a nicely weighted cross; Pelé chests it down past a defender, flips it up and over a second and volleys it low and hard past the 'keeper – all in the blink of an eye. Instinct, yes, but there must be something in great players that allows them to plan goals like that and execute the plan instantaneously. Otherwise it's just luck, and I refuse to believe that.

5. **Esteban Cambiasso.** Who he? He was a hard-working midfield player in the Argentina team that flattered to deceive in the 2006 World Cup Finals. Part of that flattery and deception was a sublime fifteen-pass move that culminated in Cambiasso lifting the ball past Serbian goalkeeper Jevric. All the front play-ers had at last one touch and Crespo's dart to the right to make space and back-heel to return the ball to Cambiasso was a mini masterpiece of attacking play in its own right.

4. Pony-tail flapping he wandered in off the left wing, ball ghosting aside his feet. He swayed one way and turned the other with the merest shift of emphasis at the hip. He appeared to drift a fraction above the ground, Zen-like – and the defenders were entranced, for none so much came as near him as he weaved amongst them. A sudden dash, a spark and a strike and the ball is nestling in the goal. We love you, **Baggio**, we do. Don't think Czechoslovakia were that keen in 1990, mind.

3. **Archie Gemmill.** I can't go through all that emotion again, just read the big piece about Scotland in 1978 if you missed it. A real lump in the throat goal. The artisan turned artist.

2. One potato, two potato, three potato – GOAL! In 1986 **Diego Maradona** beat all the English potatoes and scored. In the next game he beat all the Belgian potatoes and scored again. It was the most devastating exhibition of close control at speed with a football that we had witnessed. The cheating little b******.

1. I'm not a big fan of the tiki-taki. I like a bit of variety. Mix up the possession stuff with a bit of pace and fantasy stuff. My favourite World Cup goal was pure route one, Frank de Boer's unbelievable sixty-yard pass cushioned, flipped and volleyed into the Argentinian goal by **Dennis Bergkamp**. And with a minute to go to win a quarter-final against tricky opposition. After the agony of England's quarter-final defeat it was like a healing balm on a still raw wound. Thank you, Dennis. Please, please, please watch it on YouTube and make sure you have the Dutch commentary. I just watched it four times to make sure I'm right, and confirm that it is, in fact, the greatest goal ever scored. And I'm right.

These are the **Best Ten Attacking Players Never to have Appeared** in a World Cup Finals tournament:

10. **George Weah.** Not really as good as he was made out to be by FIFA, but a real powerhouse and the first global African superstar.

9. **Arsenio Erico.** Paraguayan striker either side of the war who was an inspiration to Di Stéfano. He played his club football and scored over three hundred goals for Independiente in Argentina.

8. **Liam Brady.** Gheorghe Hagi before Gheorghe Hagi was out of short pants. The brilliant Irishman only had foot but it was a cracker. He once scored a sumptuous goal of the month, cutting in off the left flank and curling a shot around the goalkeeper – with the outside of his left foot! He was the first player from the British Isles to be taken seriously in *Serie A*.

7. **Jari Litmanen.** It should be illegal, Ron Atkinson once quipped. Litmanen was a much-travelled playmaker with a variety of European careers – he graced Liverpool late on but Gérard Houllier didn't really know what to do with him. He won four Dutch titles and a European Cup with Ajax. He won nothing with Finland.

6. **Eric Cantona.** King Eric. Nobody really got what made him tick, but at Leeds United and then Manchester United he wielded an enormous influence on the outcome of the English league title, uniquely so for a single player. Finding a manager and a strike partner who could work with him was a challenge, and one that most French managers failed. Cantona was in the French side that failed to qualify so abjectly in 1994. Cantona retired at his peak in 1997; imagine if he had done another year and been welcomed back into the French team; that defence, that Zidane . . . and Cantona. Mmmm.

5. **Bernd Schuster.** Arguably the best midfield player in Europe for a year or two in the eighties but he barely played for West Germany. Why? Because he was arrogant and headstrong. His loss, they did okay without him.

4. **Eduard Streltsov.** Russian playmaker (and playboy) in the late fifties, Streltsov was lost to the game after being imprisoned for rape. No details of the trial were released and it is widely believed Streltsov was removed and taught a lesson for being un-Soviet. He resumed his career but was never the same. The USSR with Streltsov would have been genuine rivals to Brazil in 1962.

3. **Ryan Giggs.** Lovely old Giggsy, still playing at forty. From coruscating winger to crafty playmaker he has won everything he could have won at club level, and nothing at all at international level. Sadly Gareth Bale, Giggs' natural successor, will follow the same path, although his career is still in its infancy so I can't include him here.

2. **Alfredo Di Stéfano.** The masterful deep-lying striker in the Real Madrid side that dominated the early years of the European Cup. He played internationals for Argentina, Colombia and then Spain as an *oriundi*; in 1962 he was declared in Spain's squad for the World Cup but never appeared. Whether injured or out of favour has never fully been established.

1. **George Best.** As per Giggs above, except he was an alcoholic wreck at forty, not still playing in the top division. Best had the lot; pace, aggression, skill, speed, finishing – he could even head the ball as well as most centre-forwards. A true genius, with all the flaws that term normally implies.

These were the **Best Three World Cup** tournaments:

1982
1970
1950

And these were the three worst:

1962
1990
2010

Here is my **All-Time Greatest Squad** to play Mars and all those other aliens in the inter-galactic World Cup. The squad is based on World Cup performance, as this is a World Cup book.

Goalkeepers:
Lev Yashin (USSR), Gordon Banks (England), Oliver Kahn (Germany)

Defenders:
Franz Beckenbauer (Germany), Paul Breitner (Germany), Cafú (Brazil), Paolo Maldini (Italy), Bobby Moore (England), Daniel Passarella (Argentina), Lilian Thuram (France)

Midfield & Wide Players:
József Bozsik (Hungary), Bobby Charlton (England), Didi (Brazil), Garrincha (Brazil), Diego Maradona (Argentina), Pelé (Brazil), Sócrates (Brazil), Marco Tardelli (Italy), Zinedine Zidane (France)

Forwards:
Johan Cruyff (Holland), Eusébio (Portugal), Gerd Müller (Germany), Ronaldo (Brazil)

Likely first XI

Banks

Thuram   Beckenbauer   Moore   Maldini

Bozsik

Garrincha   Pelé   Maradona

Cruyff   Müller

That's an outrageous team. To think Didi, Zidane and Eusébio had to be left on the bench – and Di Stéfano and Best weren't even available.